BERNINA AREA

HUTS

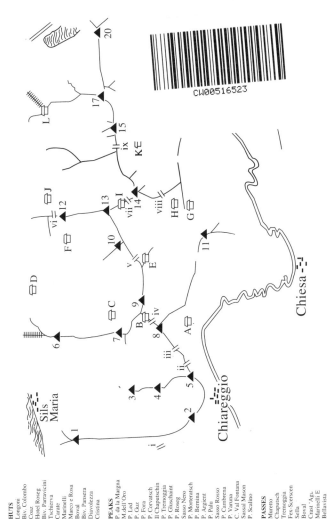

A	Longoni
B	Biv. Colombo
C	Coaz
D	Hotel Roseg
E	Biv. Parravicini
F	Tschierva
G	Carate
H	Marinelli
I	Marco e Rosa
J	Boval
K	Biv. Pansera
L	Diavolezza
M	Cristina

PEAKS

1	P. da la Margna
2	M.dell'Oro
3	P. Led
4	P. Guz
5	P. Fora
6	P. Corvatsch
7	Il Chaputschin
8	P. Tremoggia
9	P. Gluschaint
10	P. Roseg
11	Sasso Nero
12	P. Morteratsch
13	P. Bernina
14	P. Argient
15	P. Palu
16	Sasso Rosso
17	P. Cambrena
18	P. Varuna
19	C. Val Fontana
20	Sassal Mason
21	P. Scalino

PASSES

i	Muretto
ii	Chaputsch
iii	Tremoggia
iv	Fex-Scerscen
v	Sella
vi	Boval
vii	Crast 'Agu
viii	Marinelli E
ix	Bellavista

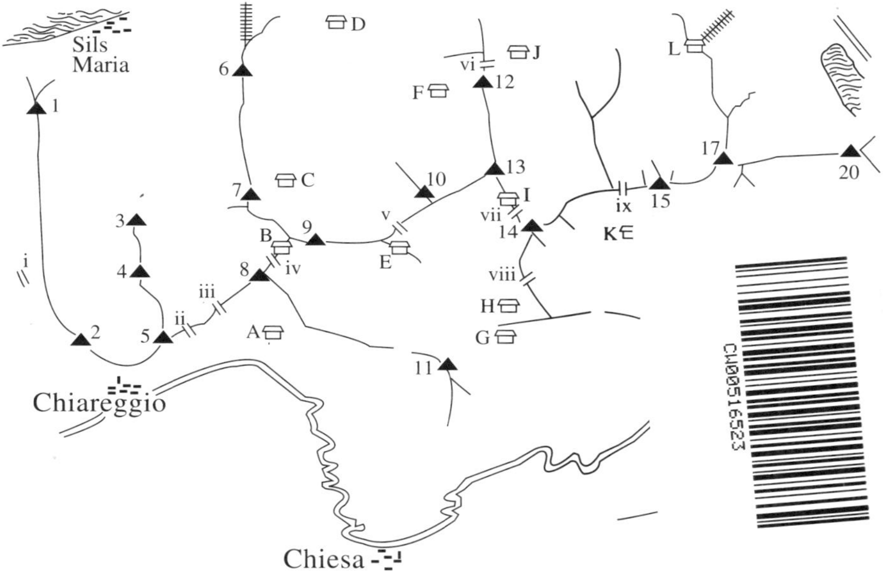

Bernina and Bregaglia *Selected Climbs*
Including Disgrazia and the Albula region

Bernina and Bregaglia

SELECTED CLIMBS
by Lindsay Griffin

General Editor: Les Swindin

ALPINE CLUB . LONDON
1995

Bernina and Bregaglia *Selected Climbs*

First Published in Britain by the
Alpine Club 55/56 Charlotte Road London EC2A 3QT

Produced by the Alpine Club

Topo diagrams drawn by Rod Powis

Cover photographs
Front Peter Hargreaves climbing the penultimate pitch of Route 70 on Pizzo Cengalo (Lindsay Griffin)
Back On the Biancograt of Piz Bernina (Peter Fleming)

Typeset in Plantin from the author's word processor by
Parker Typesetting Service, Leicester
Printed by The Ernest Press, Glasgow

British Library cataloguing in Publication Data. A catalogue record for this book is available from the British Library

ISBN 0-900523-60-3

Contents

Map of Bregaglia region *front end papers*

Map of Bernina region *front end papers*

List of topo diagrams and photographs 6

General editor's preface 11

Author's preface 12

General information
Maps (16): Using huts (16): Using this guide (16):
Equipment (20): Other guide books to the area (20):
Valley bases (21): Comparison of grades (25)

Bregaglia region 27

Huts (Bregaglia region) 28

Huts (Bernina and Disgrazia regions) 228

Disgrazia region 239

Bernina region 258

Albula region 329

Huts (Albula region) 330

General index 349

Index of climbs 353

Topo diagrams and photographs 00

Alpine Club information *back end papers*

Mountain rescue procedures *back end papers*

List of topo diagrams and photographs

Topo diagrams

1 Punta Fiorelli NW face ... 362
2 Punta della Sfinge NW face ... 362
3 Punta della Sfinge NE face ... 363
4 Avancorpo del Porcelizzo E face ... 363
5 Pizzo dell'Oro Meridionale NW ridge ... 364
6 Pizzo Milano SE face ... 364
7 Punta Sant'Anna N pillar ... 364
8 Pizzo Trubinasca N face ... 365
9 Piz Badile NW face – Bramani ... 365
10 Punta Torelli SSE pillar direct ... 366
11 Piz Badile SW face – S pillar ... 366
12 Piz Badile NW face – Ringo Starr ... 366
13 Piz Badile NW face – Fuga dall'Ovest ... 367
14 Piz Badile ENE pillar – The Brothers' route ... 367
15 Piz Badile NW face – Chiara ... 368
16 Piz Badile NE face – Neverland ... 368
17 Piz Badile NE face – White line ... 369
18 Piz Badile NE face – Cassin ... 369
19 Piz Badile ENE pillar ... 370
20 Piz Badile NE face – Another day in Paradise ... 370
21 Piz Badile SE face ... 371
22 Punta Pioda NW ridge ... 371
23 Punta Sertori ENE pillar ... 372
24 Punta Sertori S ridge ... 372
25 Punta Pioda NW ridge ... 372
26 Pizzo Cengalo S ridge – First Tower ... 373
27 Pizzo Cengalo NW pillar ... 373
28 Pizzo Cengalo S ridge direct ... 374
29 Pizzi Gemelli NE wall ... 374
30 Pizzi Gemelli NNW ridge ... 375
31 Sciora Dafora NW ridge ... 375
32 Ago di Sciora SE face ... 376
33 Ago di Sciora N and S faces ... 376
34 Cacciabella N peak NW ridge ... 377
35 Sciora Dadent E face ... 377
36 Piz Frachiccio (N pillar) Sognadoro ... 378
37 Innominata Main summit W ridge ... 378
38 Piz Frachiccio (N pillar) Kaspar pillar ... 379
39 Torre Innominata W ridge ... 379
40 Piz Frachiccio (N pillar) N face ... 380

41 Spazzacaldeira SE face – Leni route 380
42 Roda Val del Neve NW face 381
43 Spazzacaldeira SE face 381
44 Torre Moai E face 382
45 Spazzacaldeira SE face (A and B) 382
46 Cima del Cavalcorte E face 383
47 Cima del Cavalcorte E pillar 383
48 Al Gal/Vergine traverse 384
49 Punta Chiara S ridge 384
50 Punta Bertone SE face 385
51 Punta Moraschini Pillar of the Polar Wind 385
52 Castel W face 386
53 Cima della Bondasca E peak – S spur 386
54 Punta Rasica SW ridge 387
55 Pizzo del Ferro Orientale NW face 387
56 Punta Allievi SW pillar 388
57 Pizzo di Zocca Torrione Est 388
58 Punta Allievi Decadente 389
59 Punta Allievi S ridge 389
60 Punta Allievi E face 390
61 Punta Alleivi Filo Logico 390
62 Scalin W face 391
63 Punta Baroni SE face 391
64 Cima di Castello S face 392
65 Meridiana di Torrone SE pillar 392
66 Picco Luigi Amedeo SE face 393
67 Punta da l'Albigna NW face 393
68 Bio-pillar E face 394
69 Bio-pillar SW face 394
70 Piz Balzet S ridge and 1st Tower 395
71 Torrone Occidentale Punta 2987m 396
72 Torrone Occidentale Punta 2987m 396
73 Le Dimore degli Dei-Kundalini 397
74 Trapezio d'Argento 398
75 Precipizo degli Asteroidi 398
76 Piede dell'Elefante 399
77 Placche dell'Oasi 399
78 Scoglio della Metamorfosi 400
79 Le Dimore degli Dei-Vortice di Fiabe 400
80 Cima Sondrio SSE face 401
81 Torrone Orientale S ridge direct 401

82 Pizzo Ventina SE pillar 402
83 Punta Ferrario S face 402
84 Keschnadel E face 403
85 Piz Sella S face 403

Photographs

86 Piz Ligoncio and Punta della Sfinge N side 404
87 Avancorpo del Porcellizzo E face 404
88 Punta Fiorelli – Cime del Calvo N side 405
89 Trubinasca cirque S side 405
90 Puntas Torelli and Sant'Anna SE side 406
91 Pizzo Trubinasca S side 406
92 Punta Torelli – Piz Badile S side 407
93 Piz Badile and Punta Sertori SE side 408
94 Pizzo Cengalo and Piz Gemelli S side 408
95 Piz Badile SE face 409
96 Pizzo Cengalo SW side 409
97 Punta Moraschini W side 410
98 Pizzo del Ferro Occidentale – Punta Bertone W side 410
99 Cima del Cavalcorte – Punta Bertone E side 411
100 Piz Badile – Trubinasca peaks NE side 411
101 Piz Badile NE face Frank Solari 412
102 Piz Badile NE face 413
103 Piz Badile ENE face Neil McAdie 414
104 Piz Badile NW face Les Swindin 415
105 Pizzo Cengalo N face Les Swindin 416
106 Pizzi Gemelli NW side 417
107 Sciora peaks W side 418
108 Sciora peaks W side 419
109 Dafora – Ago W side Les Swindin 419
110 Cacciabella and Innominata peaks W side 420
111 Spazzacaldeira Fiamma and Dente Peter Fleming 420
112 Frachiccio Pillar N side Paul Nunn 421
113 Piz Frachiccio and Cacciabella peaks E side 422
114 Roda Val della Neve NW face 423
115 Frachiccio Pillar N side Paul Nunn 424
116 Spazzacaldeira SE wall 424
117 Ago di Sciora SE face AC collection 425
118 Spazzacaldeira SE wall 426
119 Pizzo del Ferro Orientale NW face AC collection 427
120 Ferro peaks S side 428

121 Pizzo di Zocca N side Keith Cartwright ... 429
122 Cantun – Castello W side ... 429
123 Ferro peaks and Sciora Dadent – Albigna side ... 430
124 Ferro peaks N side ... 430
125 Piz Bacun S side ... 431
126 Cima dal Cantun N side ... 431
127 Piz Casnil W side ... 432
128 Piz Balzet S side ... 432
129 Punta da l'Albigna NW face ... 433
130 Piz Balzet W face ... 434
131 Punta Allievi SW face ... 435
132 Punta 2987m W face Keith Cartwright ... 436
133 Punta Baroni SE face ... 437
134 Pizzo di Zocca SE side ... 438
135 Punta Rasica S side ... 438
136 Allievi – Baroni – Castello S side ... 439
137 Punta Allievi SE face ... 440
138 Torrone Occidentale S side ... 441
139 Cima di Castello S face ... 442
140 Piz Casnil – Cima dal Largh E side ... 443
141 Piz Casnil and Piz Bacun E faces ... 443
142 Cima di Castello – Forno side Walter Kirstein ... 444
143 Cima di Vazzeda and Monte Sissone E side ... 444
144 Cima di Rosso and Monte Sissone NW side ... 445
145 Torrone – Rasica peaks N side Walter Kirstein ... 445
146 Cima di Rosso and Cima di Vazzeda E side ... 446
147 Monte Rosso W face (Route 321 – skyline ridge) and Kluckerzahn on L ... 446
148 Monte del Forno SE side (L and R skylines are S and E ridges respectively) ... 447
149 Cima di Val Bona (E ridge faces camera) ... 448
150 Torrone peaks S side ... 449
151 Picco Luigi Amedeo SE face ... 449
152 Torrione Moai E face ... 450
153 Punta Rasica S side – Summit block Peter Stokes ... 450
154 Torrone Orientale and Torre Re Alberto SW side ... 451
155 Monte Sissone S side and Cameraccio Ridge ... 451
156 Flat Iron Ridge ... 452
157 Nuova Dimensione Keith Cartwright ... 453
158 Trapezio d'Argento ... 454
159 Precipizo degli Asteroidi ... 455

160	Le Dimore degli Dei	456
161	Monte Pioda N face	457
162	Monte Disgrazia NE side	457
163	Monte Disgrazia NE side	458
164	Pizzo Ventina NE side	459
165	Piz Tremoggia and Sassa d'Entova S side	459
166	Pizzo Cassandra N face	460
167	Monte Disgrazia N face	461
168	Piz Tremoggia and Sassa d'Entova E side	462
169	Piz Gluschaint N side AC collection	462
170	La Sella – Piz Gluschaint N side Walter Kirstein	463
171	Piz Sella S face	463
172	Piz Roseg S side	464
173	Piz Roseg N side Walter Kirstein	465
174	Bernina S side	465
175	Piz Roseg NE face Ian Leslie	466
176	Bernina S side	466
177	Piz Scerscen – Piz Zupo S side	467
178	Bernina – Scerscen – Roseg N sides Walter Kirstein	467
179	Bernina – Scerscen AC collection	468
180	Panorama of Bernina Group N side AC collection	468
181	Bernina – Scerscen N side	469
182	Bernina – Crast'Aguzza S side AC collection	469
183	Piz Morteratsch E face Walter Kirstein	470
184	Bellavista – Zupo – Argent N side	470
185	Piz Zupo E side	471
186	Piz Zupo – Bellavista S side	471
187	Bellavista – Crast'Aguzza N side	472
188	Piz Bernina NE face Walter Kirstein	473
189	Piz Varuna N side	473
190	Piz Scalino N ridge (L) and N face	474
191	Piz Palu N face	475
192	Piz Cambrena – Piz Palu N side	475
193	Piz Kesch E side AC collection	476
194	Diavolezza – Cambrena NW side	476
195	Piz Cambrena N face	477

All unaccredited photographs are by the author.

General Editor's Preface

Traditionally the Alpine Club have published guide books to the Bernese Oberland, the Dolomites, the Ecrins Massif, Mont Blanc and the Pennine Alps so this volume is a new departure as far as the club is concerned. It makes sense that we should produce a guide to the mountain regions covered in this book since together they include peaks and climbs of equal importance in mountaineering terms to those covered in the rest of the Western Alps. The pattern that has been established in the Mont Blanc and Bernese Oberland books is retained here with the inclusion of topo diagrams to supplement text and photographs. In this way we are able to include details of a far greater selection of climbs and so maximise the choice of route available to alpinists than would otherwise be the case. The area covered gives one the opportunity to enjoy the mainly snow, ice and mixed routes of the Bernina Massif as well as the renowned rock climbing that is a feature of the Bregaglia mountains. Sandwiched between these two groups is the magnificent Disgrazia, a mountain worthy of anyone's attention. To the north of the Bernina Massif is the fairly compact range of the Albula Alps. These are peaks of somewhat lower altitude providing either quite interesting easier days out or the opportunity to continue climbing in less settled weather. The consequence is that quite a large number of climbs have been described which we originally intended to produce in two volumes. By the judicious use of thinner paper we hope we have kept this single volume within manageable proportions all be it at a higher price than usual. The author is Lindsay Griffin who somehow finds time to write between his expeditions, during his periods of convalescence and when not busy editing the information section of High magazine. Lindsay is a member of the Alpine Climbing Group and has considerable experience and knowledge of climbing in the Alps. He also has a large number of friends prepared to divulge information and from all of this we benefit. My thanks go to everyone who has helped in any way with the production of this guide book. We always like to hear from users of our guide books when they have useful comments which might aid the accuracy of descriptions used in future editions. We also welcome offers of good quality photographs that might be used in the preparation of photo-diagrams. All comments and offers should be addressed to the General Editor at the Alpine Club.

Les Swindin

Author's preface

The celebrated Bernina and Bregaglia are compact mountain ranges straddling the Italian frontier in the SE corner of Switzerland. This guide, though in no way a definitive record of the climbing in this splendid region, does contain nearly all the worthwhile routes available to the visiting alpinist. In addition, a selection is included from the best outings in the neighbouring Albula range and on the fashionable crags of the Italian Val di Mello.

Historically you will find that several climbs put up before the turn of the century were as hard as any yet discovered in the Alps. They were created by local guides with an impressive pedigree, notably Martin Schocher and Christian Klucker, and were very audacious ascents for the era. The next generation included Walter Risch and Count Aldo Bonacossa, both responsible for a prodigious number of routes, many of which you will undoubtedly aspire to do. In later years the major contributions have come almost entirely from Italians – Miotti, Merizzi, the Rusconi brothers and the 'husband-wife' teams of Giacomelli/Rossi and Brambati/Vitali, to name but a few. All three areas can be accessed quickly and easily from a single base and my preference would be for one in the Val Bregaglia. The villages are quaint in character and have little of the commercialism associated with resorts in the Engadine or Western Alps. The hand of man is less obtrusive, though even here one of the greatest waterfalls in Europe was lost to hydro-electricity. Traditionally the native tongue is Romansch, the fourth official language in Switzerland and a legacy of prolonged Roman influence.

The Albula is primarily a ski-touring venue but offers much to the experienced walker or alpine novice. The selection of climbs has a bias towards those that are more easily accessible to parties based in the Val Bregaglia or Upper Engadine. There are several worthwhile rock climbs and some superb mixed excursions, notably Piz Kesch, but it has to be said that there is little comparison between the rock in the Albula and the solid granites and serpentines found elsewhere in the region.

Also popular with ski and winter mountaineers are the icy peaks of the Bernina, which lie above extensive glaciers: Piz Bernina, at over 4000m, is the highest mountain within a radius of 140km! The valleys are orientated around tourism and St Moritz is possibly the wealthiest resort in Switzerland. Rock quality is variable and although there are some notable, pure rock routes on the Italian flanks, it is the long snow and ice climbs which predominate. The established classics, many of which follow elegant ridges or spurs, are extremely popular. The area tends to attract the middle-grade alpinist and whilst there are some excellent routes in the higher grades and several magnificent and extended high-altitude traverses, many of these are, even today, infrequently trodden.

In contrast, the Bregaglia is a spectacular range of sharp granite peaks and towers that rarely exceed 3300m. A gradual drying-out of the glaciers and snowfields is turning this area distinctly sub-alpine. Yet although the ambience does not compare with that found on high-altitude classics in the Mont Blanc range, the quality of the rock-climbing is as good as, if not better than, any other granite area in the Alps. This is particularly true of the Italian side. Here large white rock-scars, visible on some of the N-facing walls and pillars on the opposite flank of the watershed, are rarely seen and the climbing is as near to perfection as one could wish. Surprisingly, the routes on this side of the range have rarely received international publicity and are still little frequented by other than Italians.

Climbing in this 'Granite Land' is now thoroughly modern in its approach. Rock boots and chalk are 'de rigueur' and well-equipped rappel descents exist for many of the shorter climbs. Popular routes are now those that can be climbed light and fast with little of the commitment associated with more traditional mountaineering. However, this is not to say that committing climbs on big walls do not exist – they do and can be found in several corners of the range.

Although there is a wide variety of quality climbing in all grades, many of the harder routes take steep compact slabs with a rough 'knobbly' texture similar to the best on, for example, the Tuolumne Domes. Bolt-protection is becoming increasingly common, yet local Italian activists have always maintained a strong tradition of 'adventure' and many of the modern climbs involve bold and sometimes serious run-outs.

There are a number of classic ice faces and several demanding gullies, but in recent years these have seldom been in good condition during the summer. However, they are highly recommended to those parties able to visit earlier in the year. Detached to the SW lies a perfectly formed peak of snow and rock – Monte Disgrazia. It is the highest in the group and has a beauty rivalling many of the more famous mountains in the Western Alps.

But these regions are not only for climbers. Huts often lie

towards the heads of overly picturesque valleys and provide very worthwhile goals for walking parties. A ramble through the Val di Mello is undoubtedly one of the most scenically rewarding in the Alps and longer walks/traverses are described in the Huts Sections.

The weather pattern tends to be more settled than in the Western Alps, although even within such a small region weather can be localised and the isolated Monte Disgrazia always seems to attract more cloud. Serious snowfalls are rarely, if ever, a problem in summer but the area, and especially the western Bregaglia, is renowned for its sudden and violent thunderstorms that sweep up from the Lombardy plains. Over the years these have proved fatal to many climbers caught close to the tops of the jagged crests. Perversely, threatening weather in the Bregaglia can often be accompanied by almost cloudless skies over the Bernina and vice versa. More stable conditions tend to occur in late Spring – an ideal time for the ice/mixed climbs – and in Sept/early Oct, when the colours can be brilliant, the atmosphere free from haze and the mountains empty.

The coverage of each area has, to a certain extent, been governed by its popularity and hence there are proportionally more routes on the Badile or in the Albigna valley than, say, the Cameraccio valley or Eastern Torrone peaks.

The author of an Alpine guide cannot hope to have a first-hand knowledge of all the climbs he describes. My thanks, therefore, are extended to friends and correspondents who have helped with route detail: Paul Braithwaite, Gino Buscaini, Keith Cartwright, Al Churcher, Chris Dale, Roger Everett, Peter Fleming, Jan Griffin, Dave Harries, Peter Hargreaves, Luke Hughes, Ian Leslie, Guiseppe Miotti, Neil McAdie, Paul Nunn, Ubaldo Pasqualotto, Tom Prentice, Ian Roper, Peter Stokes, Swiss Alpine Club, Sciora and Albigna Hut guardians, Paolo Vitali and Mike Woolridge. Individual photo credits are noted in the contents pages, but I must thank Bertha Bennet, Paul Kent, Bob Lawford and Frank Solari for the collection or preparation of photo material. Much gratitude also to Rod Powis for his meticulous attention to detail with the art work and to Marian Elmes plus Jeremy Whitehead for painstakingly proof-reading the text. Once again, a very special thanks must go to General Editor Les Swindin who, apart from shouldering the mammoth task of computer typesetting, has provided invaluable support and enthusiasm. The successful completion of this project owes much to his considerable contribution. I hope this guide will stimulate more interest in this delightful area, for it is indeed a region to satisfy the tastes of all mountain lovers – from the alpine wanderer to the dedicated ice specialist or rock athlete. But we must all remember that the mountain environment is a fragile commodity. Please treat it with care.

Lindsay Griffin, North Wales

MAPS

This guide is designed to be used in conjunction with the Swiss (CNS/LK) 1:50000 series and all heights, nomenclature etc. are taken from these maps. For a full coverage of everything described in this guide 6 of these would be needed. However, most parties will be able to operate quite satisfactorily with the 1985 Monte Disgrazia (278) and the 1979 St Moritz/Julierpass (268S, which has the ski routes marked), only requiring Bergun (258) if visiting the northern half of the Albula. Approaches to huts and various peaks/cols are often well-marked, making a comprehensive written description unnecessary.

USING HUTS

Huts allow time to be spent in the range, close to proposed ascents, without the burden of a heavy rucksack. Several routes can be accomplished from a single base before returning to the valley. Although expensive, fees can be substantially reduced on production of a reciprocal rights card (Alpine Club or UIAA/BMC card etc). In Swiss huts it is generally necessary for large groups to pre-book and in some of the more crowded huts of the Bernina it is advisable for individuals to pre-book, in order to guarantee bedspace. Please report to the guardian immediately on arrival and take all your refuse back down to the valley with you.

Most huts offer a restaurant service. In CAI huts there is usually some provision for self-catering, as long as a stove, cooking pots etc are brought. No such facility exists in Swiss huts and here the guardian will cook food that you bring yourself: normally the 'wood tax' covers the cost of this service. Simple food, that can be quickly cooked in a single pan, is preferred. Bivouac huts often have blankets but very little else.

Despite the benefits of hut facilities, during the high season noise and overcrowding have led a number of parties to camp or bivouac a suitable distance away from the hut. The Italians appear to be quite laid-back about this behaviour but the Swiss have a stricter approach. At present, tents appear to be tolerated near to the Sciora hut but are officially banned in the Albigna valley – so be discreet!

USING THIS GUIDE

ROUTE DESCRIPTIONS vary from short explanations to detailed accounts. Many rock routes are described in the form of a TOPO

DIAGRAM and the appropriate reference number appears inside an open rectangle in the margin. A number of modern offerings and indeed several older routes have seen few, or in some cases no, repeat ascents. The information on these climbs should therefore be treated with a certain degree of circumspection. For example, unrepeated routes of Czechoslovakian origin may have technical difficulties substantially higher than quoted! One or two established routes described with short sections of aid may have been climbed completely free. Either details have been unforthcoming, or the aid has been kept to give the climb an overall homogeneity of standard. There are many high quality climbs in the region but those especially recommended are indicated by a star in the index. These routes tend to represent the best of their particular standard and character, in each of the various areas covered by this guide. Certain recommended traverses or route combinations are mentioned in the text and as the selection of climbs described in the Mello valley represents the best on offer, star quality is taken for granted.

The terms L and R or L and R side are always used with reference to the direction of movement of the climber. With mountain features such as glaciers or couloirs etc. the orographical reference to L or R banks is applied when viewed in the direction of flow or looking downwards.

The Alps are in a constant state of flux. Glacial recession or rockfall can significantly alter the character of a route and climbers are urged to assess the current conditions and employ common sense when using this guide book.

FIRST ASCENT details have been included to supplement information on the climb and for this reason first winter ascents have been noted, where known and thought relevant. The UIAA ruling, that the period designated for alpine winter ascents should run from 21 Dec to 20 March inclusive, has been adhered to implicitly. Documentation of this aspect of the sport is far less comprehensive than that for the Western Alps and the omission of a winter ascent does not imply that none has been made. Ski-touring is very popular in the Bernina and winter/spring climbing is practised extensively. Conversely, in the Bregaglia, where access to many of the peaks can be difficult and dangerous (especially on the Italian side), winter ascents are rare.

The first ascent parties are listed in alphabetical order, irrespective of the various roles played by members during the climb. The exception occurs with guided ascents, where tradition dictates that the names of all clients precede those of the guides.

GRADE OF A CLIMB is indicated in the margin. The UIAA system has been used for all rock sections. FREE CLIMBING standards are graded numerically: I, II, III etc. with further refinement possible by the addition of a plus or minus sign. At present this is the system used throughout the region by all nationalities, although only time will tell if French grades are to be universally adopted across the Alps. A table of grading comparisons has been included but should only be used as a general indication, especially at higher levels. AID CLIMBING is graded A0, A1, A2 etc. A0 signifies movement where a nut/sling/peg is simply used as a hold to assist progress. On sections of AI and above climbers will need to stand in slings/étriers.

Shorter rock climbs (generally less than 300m) at lower altitudes, where on the approach and descent snow/ice is rarely encountered and which have a quick, straightforward way-off or a well-equipped rappel descent, are given an overall numerical grading in an attempt to distinguish them from longer undertakings in a more committing situation. This grading is that of the hardest section and the route description or topo will indicate whether the climb is sustained at that level.

Other routes and all mixed or snow/ice climbs are given a FRENCH ADJECTIVAL GRADE. In order of rising difficulty: F Facile (Easy), PD Peu difficile (a little difficult), AD Assez difficile (fairly difficult), D Difficile (difficult), TD Très difficile (very difficult) and ED Extrêmement difficile (extremely difficult). Further refinement is again possible by adding a plus or minus sign to the grades TD and below, but the ED grade is open-ended, eg EDI, ED2 etc.

This overall grading reflects not only the technical difficulty but also the seriousness of the whole enterprise, reflected by the length, altitude and levels of danger and commitment. Hence certain climbs in the AD to TD category, whilst not technically demanding, are very serious and this has been noted in the introduction to the route.

Unless otherwise stated, climbs are graded for a completely free ascent, even though there may be a wealth of in-situ aid available on various pitches. Several ice routes are, generally, only feasible in the winter/spring and their grade reflects the added problems of climbing at this time of year.

With climbs that involve technical difficulties on SNOW AND ICE, the grading is less precise due to the variable conditions throughout the season and from year to year. On routes that involve hanging glaciers, or ice slopes with serac formations, (eg Bernina and Roseg), there are constant changes in the difficulties and objective dangers. Glacial approaches to certain routes in the Bregaglia, notably on the Badile, have become extremely tortuous in recent summers and most ice climbs in this region have lost any appeal after June/early July. Certain ridges to the summits of various peaks in the Bernina are of an easier standard than their approaches.

The average angle of the climb is often quoted in the introduction and the difficulty of certain sections is indicated in the text by angle and, very occasionally, by using the Scottish ice grading of 1 to 5.

An attempt has been made to grade those excursions that are suitable for the walker as opposed to the alpinist. These encompass hut and valley walks, scrambles and several passes. Again, French adjectival grades are used. In order of difficulty these are: P (Piéton) which refers to routes on good footpaths at low or medium altitudes with little or no objective danger. Steep sections will have been made safe and the route will be suitable for any reasonably fit person. PE (Piéton Expérimenté) which refers to routes that are suitable for experienced mountain walkers, who can find their way when paths become indistinct or none existent. Rough ground may have to be traversed and easy snow patches and/or dry glaciers crossed. RE (Randonneur Expérimenté) which refers to routes suitable for experienced scramblers. Easy rock moves in an exposed position may be encountered and steep snow fields, requiring the use of an ice axe for balance and breaking in the event of a slip, may have to be crossed.

PHOTOGRAPHS have route numbers marked and the lines of ascent indicated. If a route is marked on a photograph then the number of that photo appears inside a black rectangle in the margin. A dashed line signifies that this part of the route is not visible. Some routes may be visible on more than one photgraph and where this occurs these additional photo numbers appear at the end of the introduction to the route.

Unless otherwise stated HEIGHTS quoted for the whole climb refer to the vertical interval from the base of the route to its top and not to the amount of climbing involved, which may be much longer. The final TIME gives a good indication for a rope of two, climbing competently at the standard and experiencing no delays due to route finding, other parties, weather etc.

ABBREVIATIONS are used for points of the compass, left, right, hours, minutes, metres and months of the year. Others frequently used are SAC (Swiss Alpine Club), CAI (Italian Alpine Club), c (circa), Pta (Punta) and Pt (spot heights marked on the relevant Swiss map).

EQUIPMENT

On most middle-grade climbs and where long rappels are not anticipated parties tend to use a single 10.5mm or 11mm rope and carry a standard rack. The latter will consist of several slings for spikes/flakes, 4-6 'quick-draws' for the in-situ pegs, several larger hexentrics and a selection of half-a-dozen wires. Cracks in the rough Bregaglia granite can often be shallow and flared, so even on the easier routes a couple of medium-sized Friends will prove very useful. On harder routes and those involving rappel descents, 50m double ropes and a comprehensive rack of wires, hexentrics and Friends will probably be advisable. Steep, compact, 'knobbly' slabs are characteristic of many harder Bregaglia climbs and will often require a bold approach. On less frequented climbs, knifeblades, RPs or even the use of skyhooks for runners should be considered. In the Bernina, where the rock is more shattered, medium-large Hexes and long slings are mostly used. A general indication of the sort of gear required for a particular route is often indicated in the text. A large ski bum-bag is also useful. It is far less awkward to carry than a rucksack, when a small amount of equipment (eg lightweight waterproofs etc) is taken on the route.

OTHER GUIDEBOOKS

There are a number of publications dealing with the separate areas covered in this guide. The SAC Bundner Alpen series has a definitive guide to the Albula published in 1986. In the same series the Bernina-Gruppe, although published in 1990, is basically a reprint of the 1973 edition and therefore rather dated. Similar comments apply to the CAI/TCI Bernina guide by Silvio Saglio (1959). Certain routes in this area are included in the very selective guide Disgrazia-Bernina by Guiseppe Miotti (Ed Melograno: 1984).

The well-known, Rébuffat 'coffee-table' series offers '100 finest routes in the Bergell-Disgrazia-Engadine' which not only covers the Bregaglia, Bernina and southern Albula but also the Silvretta range (Miotti and Alessandro Gogna, Denoel: 1985). This is a 'must' despite the fact that many of the splendid photographs have been printed in reverse!

There is no up-to-date, definitive guide to the Bregaglia. The 1989 SAC 'Sudliche Bergellerberge und Monte Disgrazia' is a comprehensive work to the Swiss side of the range but includes no routes S of the Roma path. The CAI/TCI Masino-Bregaglia-Disgrazia (Aldo Bonacossa/Giovanni Rossi: 2 Vols, 1975 and 1977) gives an excellent coverage of the whole range up till the time of publication. Miotti and Ludovico Mottarella produced a very selective topo guide to the area in 1982 (Sul Granito della Val Masino: Ed Melograno) and a more extensive topo guide by Paolo Vitali is due shortly. The best guide to the Mello valley is by Cristina Zecca and Pietro Corti (Val di Mello: 1989/90: Editrice G Stefanoni – Lecco), although there is '100 best climbs in the Mello' by Luisa Angelici and Antonio Boscacci (Ed Albatross: 1990). There is also a guide to the boulders at Sasso Remenno by Boscacci (Ed Il Gabbiano: 1985) and Al Churcher's 'Italian Rock' (Cicerone Press:1988) will prove useful. On the Swiss side Franco Giacomelli and Renata Rossi have produced a small guide to selected climbs in the Albigna valley and a definitive guide to the Piz Badile (Ed Albatross: 1986 and 1990). Most of these should be available locally.

VALLEY BASES

VAL BREGAGLIA. This deep defile, on the Swiss side of the range, still maintains an atmosphere that is distinctly Italian. Whilst the southern flanks are thickly forested, the northern slopes have open grassy alps and most of the little villages have been carefully preserved. A frequent Post-Bus service, operating with characteristic punctuality, runs through the valley to the border at Castasegna. Most motorists will arrive via the Julier pass, if approaching from the N, or via Milan and Chiavenna if coming from Italy. The téléphérique to the Albigna dam begins from the large carpark at Pranzaira (1195m). During the summer it runs almost continuously from 7am till c4.30pm and is quite cheap (12F return in 1993). Outside of this period times are less frequent but it is possible to ring for service (082 41313, or a direct line from the upper terminus). The ride takes c15min.

Most climbers camp at either Bondo or Vicosoprano. Bondo (823m) is a small village at the entrance to the Val Bondasca, just S of Promontogno. It has a few small pensions and a YHA. The campsite is small, cheap, generally quiet and friendly but with very limited facilities. There is a small supermarket on the main road, which sells most things including gaz, but most people tend to shop in the large supermarkets in Chiavenna (where there are also small climbing shops, a swimming pool etc), which are cheaper. Vico (1067m) has more shops, a bank, dairy, PO etc. The campsite is large and reasonably priced with good facilities. It also appears to be very secure at present. Both sites are quieter and considerably cheaper than those nearer the Bernina. As it is only an hour's drive from Bondo to the Diavolezza téléphérique, the advantages are obvious. Camping 'off-site' in Switzerland is strictly forbidden!

Soglio is a well-known spot for viewing the northern flanks of the Bregaglia and an evening visit is a must (Tombal, 1hr above has even better views!). On rainy days the village of Stampa, with its 'Ciasa Granda' museum, and the hologram display in Castasegna are also worth a visit.

UPPER ENGADINE/VAL BERNINA. These higher and more open valleys hold the popular holiday resorts of St Moritz and Pontresina. Regular Post-buses serve the Engadine, while the narrow-gauge railway, from Sameden to Tirano, is a convenient form of public transport in the Val Bernina. Campsites are expensive, have good facilities but are often very crowded with 'family campers'.

Maloja (1809m) has a tourist office, YHA, bank, PO, supermarkets, etc and the site is situated on the southern shores of the lake, c1km E of the village. There are many short, well-equipped, rock routes on the upper limestone crag overlooking the lake at Sasc da Corn. The campsites at Silvaplana (1815m) and St Moritz (1822m) are more plush, but in St Moritz there is a wealth of Sport and Leisure facilities (including a swimming pool) and plenty of decadent night-clubs. Samaden is home to the main hospital and small local aerodrome. It also has a campsite at Punt Muragl (1730m). Pontresina (1805m) is well-known to continental alpinists. It has a good tourist office and a guides bureau where information and weather forecasts can be easily obtained, plus several useful supermarkets. It is also possible to change money at the railway station. The campsite at Morteratsch (1880m) is quite popular with climbers and is one of the more reasonably priced. Close by, Livigno provides duty-free goods.

For a recorded message of the weather forecast pertaining to the area, dial 038 162 (in French) or just 162 (German/Swiss).

VAL MALENCO. Running N from Sondrio, capital of the industrialised zone of the Valtellina, the upper reaches of this valley are typified by extensive quarrying, mainly devoted to the production of roofing slates. The original roofs in the Val Bregaglia, that give so much character to these quaint villages, were built from Italian stone, carried over the Muretto pass. Chiesa (960m) and the adjacent purpose-built ski resort of Caspoggio are the main centres and are reached by a regular bus service from Sondrio. Chiesa has good supermarkets, several climbing/skiing shops, banks, PO and an excellent tourist office, which posts daily weather forecasts, snow and avalanche conditions etc. However, at present, there are no official campsites in this area.

Here the valley forks, the L branch (Mallero) going to Chiareggio (1612m) and the R (Lanterna) to Franscia (1557m). Chiareggio is a small quaint village with one or two reasonable little supermarkets. There is an infrequent bus service in high summer and the last section of the road, above Ca Rotte, is closed to cars between 10am and 3.30pm. Parking is available, for a nominal fee, on the far side of the village, down by the river. There appears to be no 'official' camping and most people use spots close to the river below Ca Rotte. Tents are also tolerated near the car-parking at Chiareggio, or across the river, at the start of the path to the Porro hut. Further down the valley, San Guiseppe marks the start of the gravel road up to the Scerscen-Entova summer ski station.

The road to Franscia passes through the Lanterna gorge by an impressive piece of engineering. It ends at a bar and large carpark, with the village, small with only one or two hotels, just to the N. Camping is tolerated just S of the carpark, in a secluded site on the far side of the river. A private unmade road, which appears to be used by all and sundry, continues up to the dam at Campo Moro (en route, the Restaurant Longoni stays open most of the year). There is a huge parking area below the Zoia hut and private cars are definitely discouraged from continuing further to the upper dam at Alpe Gela (30min on foot). There is a bus service to Franscia in summer (but only as far as Lanzada outside the season), so if walking from here to the dam take the popular and well-constructed mule track via Alpe Foppa (2hr up and c1hr in descent when carrying light packs).

VAL MASINO. The pleasant holiday village of San Martino (923m) is the usual base and can be approached directly, by local bus, from Ardenno in the Valtellina. Italian railways are cheap and Ardenno lies on the main line from Tirano to Milan. When coming by car there is a scenic alternative that follows a good road from Morbegno, via Dazio and Cevo – highly recommended for its superb views! San Martino has bars, small supermarkets, camping gaz, a mountaineering shop and a climber's cafe with new route book (Bar della Monica). Fiorelli's is an excellent and cheap pizzeria that is heavily used by climbers. Cheap camping is available (poor facilities) c1km up the road towards Bagni – negotiate payment, which goes to the Commune, in Fiorelli's. The main campsite is just before the Gatto Rosso at the entrance to the Mello valley: but beware – it occasionally floods after heavy rain! However, many visitors camp, unofficially, anywhere and everywhere higher up this idyllic but popular valley. The road goes as far as the bar of Gatto Rosso, where there is a large carpark. Unfortunately, unlike Switzerland, many incidents of gear-theft have been reported and the area is becoming notorious for theft (with associated vandalism) from unattended vehicles. About 3km down the valley is Cataeggio – a larger village with shops and bars. The road to the Preda Rossa valley starts just N of here.

The thermal baths at Bagni del Masino (1172m) date from the 13th century and are reputed to be wonderful for rheumatics and skin disease. One can pay for a 20min wallow in a small 'swimming pool' – a marvellous finish to a long trip into the mountains. It is generally open for 2½ months in the summer, at which time it is serviced by the local bus. Using public transport, it is possible to reach a base in the Val Bregaglia in around 4 hours.

GRADING COMPARISONS

UIAA	FRENCH	UK		USA	AUS
IV	4			5.5	12
V−	4+	MS	4a	5.6	13
V	5−	S	4b		
V+	5 5a	VS		5.7	14
	5b		4c	5.8	15
VI−	5+	HVS			
	5c		5a	5.9	16
VI					
					17
	6a				
VI+				5.10a	18
		E1	5b		
VII−				b	19
	6a+			c	20
VII	6b			d	21
		E2			
VII+	6c				
			5c	5.11a	22
				b	
		E3			23
VIII−	7a		6a	c	
VIII	7a+			d	24
		E4			
VIII+	7b		6b	5.12a	25
IX−		E5		b	26
	7b+			c	27
			6c		
IX	7c	E6		d	28
	7c+				29
IX+		E7			30
	8a				

Bregaglia

Brasca Hut 1304m (Capanna Luigi Brasca) CAI. This small yet comfortable hut situated at Alpe Coeder in the Val Codera. Open with a resident warden during the summer but locked the rest of the year. Room for 40

H1
P
From Novate Mezzola, on the main road from Chiavenna to the Como lakes, turn E on a small, tarmacked road and after 1 km, reach the village of Mezzopiana where cars may be left. A waymarked path zigzags steeply up into the beautiful Codera valley, then continues gently in the bed, passing several hamlets and small cafés, to the hut. 3½-4hr

Vaninetti Hut 2577m CAI. This recently constructed shelter stands at the head of the Codera valley, on a small terrace SW of the Pizzo Trubinasca. It lies c100m below the main traverse path used to connect the Trubinasca and Porcellizzo passes. At the time of writing it is surprisingly well-equipped for a bivouac hut, sleeps 9 and always open.

H2
PE
From the Brasca hut follow the path in the main valley to Alpe Sivigia. Take the path through the upper buildings (1939m) towards the Bocchetta della Tegiola. Below Pt 2214m work NE over rough ground towards the Pizzo Trubinasca. Reach a grassy terrace with rock slabs where the 'traverse path' is joined and follow it ESE to the hut. 4hr

H3
PE/RE
From Bondo take the private forestry track W to Ceresc (1288m) where there is a parking place (in order to drive this road it is first necessary to puchase a ticket at Dino's café in the main square at Bondo): 1½hr on foot. There is a good path to Alp Tegiola (1½hr) after which it becomes pretty difficult to follow but leads, in a further 2hr via a steep scree couloir, to the V-shaped notch of the Bocchetta della Tegiola (2490m). Descend the far side until level with Pt 2214m, then follow the previous route, working NE over rough ground, to the hut. c6hr from Bondo

H4
PD–
From the Gianetti hut. This approach will be used by parties returning to the Sasc Fura hut after having climbed the Badile/ Cengalo and descended to the Gianetti hut. From the Gianetti hut the path to the Passo Porcellizzo is signposted and then waymarked. It climbs up through boulder slopes to the NW and reaches the pass via a scree gully (c1hr). The Val Codera side is normally a wide, snow gully and an axe will be useful. It is not particularly steep but

unless the snow is in good condition, it is better to keep on the R side (I/II). Reach the tiny Codera glacier and cross it to the NW. Pick up the waymarked path that traverses almost horizontally to the shoulder below the SW ridge of the Pizzo Trubinasca. The path passes a little above the hut. 2hr from the Gianetti hut

Valli Hut c1900m (Bivacco Carlo Valli) CAI. Situated SE of the Brasca hut above the Val Codera. It is an old shelter, built against the W side of an enormous square boulder, a short distance above the Alpe Arnasca chalets. Room for 9 and always open.

H5
P

From the Brasca hut the path is signposted. It heads SE, crosses the river, and keeping L of the two impressive waterfalls, climbs steeply to old stone dwellings at Spazza. Continue zigzagging up to the Arnasca chalets (1854m). The bivouac lies directly above. 2hr from the hut

Omio Hut 2100m CAI. Situated on a grassy terrace E of the Pizzi dell'Oro in the Valle Ligoncio. It is a popular spot with a warden and restaurant service in summer but locked the rest of the year (though often open at weekends during September/October). Room for 35. When closed it is possible to obtain a key at San Martino, though there is a spacious bivi site under a huge boulder close to the hut. The steep walk from Bagni is through delightful beechwood forests and open grassy pastures, and nowadays forms the first stage of the Roma path.

H6
P

From Bagni del Masino follow an unmade vehicle road NW to open ground, where, on the L, the track to the hut is clearly signposted. It is well-trodden and conspicuously waymarked throughout. Cross the river; zigzag up through woods to Alpe d'Oro; pass several chalets and a good 'gîte' under a large boulder and finally climb open grassy slopes to the hut. 2½hr

Gianetti Hut 2534m CAI. Situated in the upper Porcellizzo valley, immediately S of the Piz Badile. Another very popular hut which continues to maintain a fairly friendly and easy-going atmosphere. With room for 90, it is an important 'staging-post' on the Roma path and is often overcrowded. It is currently being extended (1994). It has a warden and full restaurant service from mid-June to mid-Sept. Outside of that period it is closed but just behind, the Attilio Piacco hut, which has room for 13, remains open as a 'winter refuge'. The approach is delightful yet rather lengthy. Tel: 0342 645161

H7
P
From Bagni del Masino follow an unmade vehicle road NW to open ground. The track to the hut is clearly signposted and well waymarked throughout its length by red paint flashes. After the initial steep zigzags, on a lovely paved surface through beechwood and alongside cascades, several shepherds' huts are passed before the gradient eases to Casera Zoccone (1899m). Cross the river on an excellent bridge and wind up the open grassy hillside to the hut, which is visible from afar. 4hr. Reasonable bivouac sites exist under the big boulders c100m N of the hut. At the time of writing this superb location is spoilt by a profusion of litter and building debris.

The hut can be reached from the Omio hut in 2½-3hr by using the well-marked Roma path. Cables in place for crossing the Barbacan col.

Redaelli Hut c3300m (Bivacco Alfredo Redaelli) CAI. Situated very close to the top of the Piz Badile. This small building, standing just R of the top of the Molteni route and c20m S of the summit ridge, can sleep 4 comfortably. It is bright yellow.

Ronconi Hut 3169m (Bivacco Tita Ronconi). A bright yellow hut belonging to the Gruppo Edelweiss di Morbegno. It stands just below the Passo di Bondo, on the Italian side, and can sleep 4. See Routes 224 and 225 for the approaches from Switzerland and Italy.

Sasc Fura Hut 1904m SAC. Situated at the end of the promontory, coming down from the N ridge of the Badile. There is a warden and restaurant service from 1 July – Sept. Outside of this period the hut is locked (key available in Bondo) but a small 'winter room', with room for 5, is always left open. Room for 50 including beds in the winter room. This is a busy hut though not often full, catering mainly for parties climbing on the Badile. Tel: 082 41252

H8
P
From Bondo it is possible to drive up the private forestry track until it ends just before Laret. To do this it is first necessary to purchase a ticket from Dino Salis's café in the main square at Bondo (8Sfr in 1993 or a hefty fine if caught without). Otherwise take the small signposted track, which starts near the bridge over the Bondasca river at the southern end of the village. This path climbs steeply through the woods to join the forestry track after 30min. Continue along the track to Laret (c1hr). Now follow the signposted path down and across the river on the R. It climbs steeply through the dense larch forest until it emerges dramatically above the tree line, with the hut in full view just above (2hr). c3½hr from Bondo

H9 From the Vaninetti hut. This connection is especially useful to
PD–/PD parties wishing to return to the hut, after having climbed the Badile
91 or Cengalo and descended to the Gianetti hut in Italy. Those with no need to return to either the Sasc Fura or Laret can reach Bondo more directly from the Vaninetti hut, via the Tegiola pass (see Route H3). The descent from the Trubinasca pass is a serious scramble and not recommended to ordinary walkers. See also photograph 100

From the Vaninetti go up c100m to the waymarked traverse path and follow it beneath rock barriers to grass and scree slopes below the V-shaped notch of the Passo della Trubinasca. Climb steeply up through the gully to the pass (2701m: paint flashes, chains etc, 1hr). On the far side carefully descend the couloir and the fairly exposed loose ground below (I/II: early in the season this will be snow-covered and an axe/crampons are useful) to moraine slopes. Go down to the foot of the spur on the R, then head E, passing not far below Pt 2228m to reach the boulder slopes below the Trubinasca glacier. Descend these, crossing small moraine ridges, until a more distinct path leads across towards the northern end of the promontory and finally climbs steeply to the hut. 2hr: 3-3½hr in ascent; 3hr from the Vaninetti hut; c5½hr from the Gianetti hut

Sciora Hut 2118m SAC. Located on grassy moraine slopes in the upper Val Bondasca beneath the Sciora chain. There is a warden and restaurant service from 1 July – 30 Sept. At other times the hut is locked but a small 'winter room' (with room for 10) in the basement is always left open. Just above the hut a profusion of enormous boulders contain several excellent bivouac sites, and both camping and bivouacing seem to be well tolerated in this area. The approach from Bondo is a varied and scenic walk, which becomes rather a grind if transport is not taken to Laret. Room for 42. Tel: 082 41138

H10 From Bondo follow Route H8 to the Laret chalets. The path to the
P hut is clearly signposted and continues parallel to the river, before zigzagging steeply up through the forest to a ruined barn at Naravedar (1843m). Continue up (clearly waymarked), then cross moraine slopes to the hut which is visible from afar. 2½-3hr: 4-4½hr from Bondo

From the Sasc Fura hut. A useful connection via the Colle Vial (2266m). Starting from either hut, sections of this route will be used to gain access to various climbs on the walls of the Badile and Cengalo. Waymarked but only suitable for more experienced walkers.

H11
RE/F
100

Go up the promontory towards the N ridge of the Badile, keeping R of the crest at first. After 30min bear L and reach the E side of the promontory, where a large cairn marks a gap in the crest – the Colle Vial (45 min-1hr). Cautiously go down the far side on a system of ledges, which slant S across the E face of the escarpment. Reach the rubble below and make a slightly descending traverse across it to the crest of a moraine ridge that comes down from Pt 2312m. The track goes down this ridge a little way, then crosses the base of the Cengalo glacier to another moraine ridge coming down from Pt 2087m and the huge N face of the Pizzo Cengalo. Go up this ridge a little way, then traverse across the rubble-strewn Bondasca glacier to the far lateral moraine. Climb up onto the crest and make an almost horizontal traverse NNE to the hut. c3½hr from the Sasc Fura

Albigna Hut 2336m SAC. Situated above the E side of the Albigna lake, beneath the Piz dal Pal. The hut is open from 20 June until the end of Sept with a warden and full restaurant service. Outside of that period it is locked but a winter room in the basement, which can sleep 18, is left open. Easily reached from the téléphérique, it is a popular spot and often very crowded in the height of the season, with 20 places permanently booked for youth groups during August. Officially no camping is allowed in the valley, though tents appear to be tolerated close to the W end of the dam wall. Best be discreet! The approach to the hut runs alongside a waterpipe high above the lake. The tall narrow slab, rising from the lakeside below this point, has two grade V routes which are 5 pitches long (last pitch common to both) and have in-situ protection. They can be reached by rappelling the slab or by a steep grassy descent, which leaves the path some distance N of the slab. In winter short practice icefalls appear below the dam wall. Room for 88. Tel: 082 41405

H12
P

From the téléphérique terminus walk up the track (or take various steeper short cuts) to the observation house at the W side of the dam wall (2165m: 10min). Cross back along the top of the wall and slant up the well-marked path, below the Piz dal Pal, to the hut. 40min from the terminus. In winter this can be avalanche-prone and parties cross the frozen lake to the little bay S of the hut.

The walk down from the dam to Pranzaira or Vicosoprano is a botanist's dream and also allows parties, who have missed the last cabin, to reach civilization in c1½hr. It is clearly waymarked. When near the bottom fork L for Vico or carry on down, crossing the river on a footbridge, to come out on the main road 400m above the téléphérique station. In ascent it would be a steep and sweaty 3½hr

Molteni Hut c2510m (Bivacco Molteni-Valsecchi) CAI. Situated c150m below the Roma path in the Ferro valley and on the S side of a huge flat-topped boulder. It is a small tin hut in rather poor shape and could sleep 9 at a push. Although signposted from the Roma path, it is not easy to find from below and remains largely unfrequented.

H13
PE
120

From San Martino follow the road into the Valle di Mello as far as a yellow signpost showing the start of the path leading up into the Ferro valley. Follow the path, which climbs in steep zigzags to the L of the spectacular waterfalls, past Casera del Ferro (1658m) to reach some deserted shepherds' huts at 1958m (c2½hr). The second building is always open and can be used as an overnight shelter. Above, the path becomes vague and the safest method of locating the hut is to keep up the centre of the valley. The hut is dead in line with the S Spur on the E peak of Ferro Centrale (Route 173). 4hr from San Martino

Allievi Hut 2387m (Rifugio Aldo Bonacossa) CAI. There is room for a total of 140 persons (in two adjacent huts). Situated on an open terrace in the upper part of the Zocca valley, c1km to the SE of the Zocca pass. It has a warden and restaurant service during the normal summer season but outside of this period it is locked (key available in San Martino) and there appears to be no winter room. Situated close to spectacular rock peaks, and forming a major watering hole on the Roma path, it is a popular spot, though overnight accomodation is rarely a problem. For climbers based in Switzerland the quickest approach is via the Pranzaira téléphérique and a traverse of the Zocca Pass (c4hr with fairly light loads: see

Route 340). Otherwise it is a walk of unremitting steepness from the Mello valley! Tel: 0342 614200

H14 P 155 From San Martino follow the road into Mello valley and reach the Gatto Rosso parking place (30min on foot). Continue along the delightful track, passing Cascina Piana (1092m), until a yellow signpost shows the start of the path leading up to the hut. Follow this path which is clearly waymarked and passes through a variety of scenery. Apart from the middle section it is a steep series of zigzags. The stupendous tower of Pizzo di Zocca is seen to full advantage early in the journey but most rock spires only come into full view when close to the hut. 4½hr from San Martino

Manzi Hut c2538m (Bivacco Antonio Manzi) Milan section of the CAAI. Situated on top of a small escarpment, which lies S of the Pta Ferrario, on the eastern side of the upper Torrone valley. Normally left open throughout the year. It can sleep 9 but given the poor state of repair is not used that frequently. Although longer than the walk to the Allievi, the approach is much more amenable and quite picturesque – the Torrone valley holds some of the most spectacular granite walls in the range!

H15 PE 155 From San Martino follow Route H14 and continue along the valley floor to the Casera Rasica settlement. The path now starts to rise through a forest and reaches a bridge at 1298m (2hr). Immediately before the bridge a steep path zigzags up into the Torrone valley to reach Casera Torrone (1996m: a ruined 'gîte' under a large boulder). The path now continues in the same direction towards the head of the valley but is much less distinct. Reach the Roma path coming across from the Passo Val Torrone and follow it E to the hut. 4½-5hr from San Martino

Forno Hut 2574m SAC. Situated c170m above the E side of the Forno glacier below the Sella del Forno. It is a centre for SAC climbing courses. First built in 1889 it now has beds for nearly 100 people, including a winter room which can sleep 24. The hut is open throughout the usual summer period (beginning of July to the end of Sept) and also, on the odd occasion, during winter. It is generally open from 20 March until Whitsun for ski-tourers. At all these times a warden is present and restaurant service (more limited outside of the summer) is available. It is one of the best and most varied hut walks in the range with pine forests, open meadows and an icy glacier. There are few climbs of major difficulty from the hut and the majority of folk are either making a day trip to the hut, crossing passes or climbing easy snow peaks such as the Cima di Rosso etc. Tel: 082 43182

H16
PE

From the first hairpin bend on the road S of Maloja, or from the carpark a few hundred m along the unmade road running S into the valley, follow the signposted track to the Cavloc lake (take the short-cut which zigzags up through forest to the NW tip of this idyllic lake). After passing the buildings at Plan Canin the path becomes progressively more stony and is overlooked by superb granite slabs to the W. Continue onto the R side of the glacier, slightly above its base (paint flashes), then cross diagonally E, normally following markers, poles etc, to the far side. Go up the edge of the glacier until a well-defined path slants up the moraine and, in a wide sweep, reaches the hut. 4hr

Del Grande Hut 2600m (Refugio del Grande-Camerini) CAI. Situated at the foot of the E ridge of the Cima di Vazzeda where there is a superb view of Monte Disgrazia. It does not have a warden but can be locked, in which case the key is available in Chiareggio – check on the way through! There is room for 8 but due to infrequent use it has been allowed to deteriorate. It can be reached from the Forno hut in 2½hr via the Sella del Forno

H17
P/PE
143

From Chiareggio follow the unmade road W towards the Muretto pass then take the L fork and reach the hamlet of Forbisina. Continue along the R side of the Sissone river then follow the well-defined track, which zigzags steeply up through the woods and pastures above to Alpe Sissone (2290m). Now work up to the NW, over rough ground, to the E ridge of the Vazzeda and so reach the hut. 3hr

There are two other routes to the hut from Chiareggio that follow the waymarked track forming part of the Alta Via Della Valmalenco. Both are longer (3½-4hr). From Forbisina continue up the bed of the Valle Sissone to c2000m. The track now cuts up R through rock barriers and slants N across the hillside, passing Pt 2438m, to the hut: Alternatively follow Route 324 as far as the upper chalets at Alpe Vazzeda (2033m), then zigzag steeply W before slanting back S across the open hillside to the hut. Both routes are signposted with the number 3 inside a yellow triangle.

Grandori (Mello) Hut 2992m (Bivacco Odello-Grandori) Milan section of the CAAI. Situated a few m S of the Passo di Mello, at the foot of the NW ridge of M Pioda. A small unlocked hut, with room for 6, in a poor state of repair. It lies c30min above the Roma path and can be reached in 2hr from either the Manzi or Ponti huts

H18 PD From Chiareggio follow route H17 to Forbisina and continue on a good track to Pt 1766m. A vague path now continues up the valley and reaches the lateral moraine on the R side of the Disgrazia glacier. Go up the moraine until it peters out below Pt 2562m. Slant L onto the glacier and head S to the short rock walls below the Passo di Mello. Work up L on steep broken rock then slant back R to the pass. This is quite tricky though there is usually a fixed rope for aid. 6hr+ and serious

H19 PE From San Martino it's a very long haul up the Mello valley! Beyond Casera Pioda (1559m) the path forks. The R fork leads up the centre of the valley to Casera Cameraccio (2233m) and is usually the one taken, as it gives a more direct ascent to the pass. The L fork is well-marked with red paint flashes and goes steeply up the hillside, crosses a terrace and continues up through the forest to a green-roofed building. Another steep ascent leads, via a good bivi boulder at c2000m, to the Alpe Cameraccio ruin where the angle eases (2167m). Head up and across the rough open ground of the wild Cameraccio valley to the pass. 6hr+: 4hr in descent

Walking routes in the area

RE **ROMA PATH**

The popular high-level route on the S side of the Bregaglia. It links most of the huts accessed from the Masino, and parties climbing on this side of the range will, from time to time, use part of this route. It is a clearly waymarked path and quite distinct, except for the section across the head of the Cameraccio valley. Many of the passes have fixed cables and some require an ascent over snow – an axe and crampons are generally needed until at least mid-July.

Today Bagni is the normal starting point, and from here the Omio hut is reached in 2½hr and the Gianetti in a further 3hr. Those requiring a wilder and more interesting approach will walk up the Codera valley, and after a night in the Brasca hut cross the Barbacan pass to the Gianetti. The path continues across the head of the Porcellizzo valley and is nicely sculptured on the ascent to the Passo del Camerozzo (2765m). The far side is tricky at first and has fixed cables, but once in the Ferro valley a good track leads E and crosses the awkward Passo Qualido (2647m: cables) into the remote Qualido valley. Next comes the Passo dell'Averta (c2540m); not too much of a problem unless snow covered. An easy path across the scenic Zocca valley leads to the Allievi hut, c6hr from the Gianetti hut. Still clearly marked the path continues, crossing the Val Torrone pass (2518m, cables down the gully on the far side) and passing below the Pta Ferrario to the snow slopes that lead up to the Cameraccio pass (2898m). Although short, these can be a little nasty later in the season – watch out for stonefall! The far side is easy and leads to the remote upper reaches of the Cameraccio valley. The slopes here are bouldery and the path, although waymarked, is still a bit vague. Crossing below the Passo di Mello the path climbs up to the Bocchetta Roma (2898m, more cables) and descends easily to the Ponti hut (6hr+ from the Allievi hut). Here most parties will descend to Cataeggio but a much finer, though not so convenient, finish is to cross the Corna Rossa pass and descend via the Bosio hut to Chiesa (5hr). Allow 3-4 days, although it has been completed from Novate Mezzola to the Ponti hut in 8hr 24min!

BREGAGLIA CIRCUIT

Serious backpackers will notice the potential for a fine round trip from Bondo via the Tegiola and Porcellizzo passes, the Roma path, a crossing of the Passo Ventina to Chiareggio, then over the Sella del Forno, Casnil and Cacciabella passes to the Bondasca valley.

Punta Fiorelli 2391m

C Savonelli with G Fiorelli, 19 Aug 1901. Winter: D and G Fiorelli, 2 Jan 1954

An elegant slabby pyramid standing just to the S of the Punta Medaccio. It is arguably the most noticeable rock feature on the S side of the Val dei Bagni. The impressive NW face contains a number of difficult routes but unfortunately the older climbs, created by talented alpinists such as Bonatti and Esposito, follow lines of natural weakness which are spoilt by grass and vegetation. A recent addition, however, follows a line of clean compact slabs towards the L side of the face and was only feasible due to the extensive use of bolt-protection.

The sunny S wall is much cleaner and offers a more traditional outing that has still received few ascents.

1 SOUTH-WEST RIDGE

III First ascent party

88

A very worthwhile little route to a spectacular summit, where parties will be rewarded with a heart-stopping view into the depths of the Val dei Bagni. The climbing is continuously interesting and often quite exposed!

From Bagni there are two ways to approach the ridge.
(a) Walk W for a few hundred m and cross the river. Now follow the well-defined path up the L side of the Ligoncio valley, and where it emerges from the trees on to broken stony ground head up L to the peak. Reach a small notch at the base of the ridge via a steep scramble in a rocky couloir (2½hr). This same point can be reached from the Omio hut in c1½hr via the obvious traverse path.
(b) Cross the river directly and take the path that leads up steeply into the Merdarola valley. Follow this as far as the Baite at c1940m and then head W over stony ground to reach the steep grassy couloir leading to the notch at the foot of the ridge. Scramble up this easily to the start of the route. 2½hr On the first half of the climb it is better to follow the crest of the ridge throughout, rather than use easier but vegetated ramps on the L side. Higher, a foresummit is climbed on the L side and a steep slab, followed by a crack, leads back onto the crest. Continue more easily, but in a rather exposed position, to the pointed summit. This is so tiny that you may have to take it in turn to stand on the highest point! 200m: 1½hr

2 SOUTH FACE – MANDELLISI ROUTE

VI: G Capozzo, A Dotti, P Gilardoni and E Molteni, 19-20 July 1969

A0/1

Reported to give reasonably good climbing in a succession of cracks and dièdres. Many old and dubious (?) pegs are still in place but a full rack, including a good selection of small wires and possibly a few knifeblades, should be taken. With a very early start it should be possible to make the round trip from the valley in a day.

Follow Route 1b and reach the centre of the wall, below a steep grassy gully that slants up to the R. The start lies directly below a small roof which is 6m above the ground. Climb over the roof and continue up the crack above (30m: V). Surmount another small roof and follow a grassy dièdre that slants L to a large ledge (III and IV). Climb up for 3m then traverse R to a huge dièdre that leans to the R. Layback up this (IV). At the top, 30m of difficult climbing (V+) leads to the base of a big overhanging chimney. The chimney gives an excellent and exposed pitch (30m: V+). Climb a wide crack on the L and move R, on a detached flake to the base of an awesome-looking dièdre (V). Climb the dièdre (VI and A0/A1). Now make some trying moves up R to overcome an overhanging nose, and climb another prominent dièdre that is capped by a roof (VI: sustained). Climb up and then L to a good ledge (IV) and continue easily for two further pitches to the summit. c260m: 6-8hr

North-West Face

The foot of this steep slabby face is best reached by following Route 1a. The L edge is taken by the Bignami-Bonatti route (V+ and A1: not sustained). This starts by climbing slabs to the L of a large grassy gully and is rather scrappy in the lower half. In the upper section, the climb follows the R side of a prominent rounded spur and appears somewhat cleaner. The compact slabs to the R are taken by the following thoroughly modern route.

3 **SIDDHARTA**

ED2 R Biffa, L Cattaneo, D Corbetta, D Galbiati and O Pazzan, July 1990

88

1

A succession of thin and often memorable slab pitches that are sustained at VI/VI+ with several harder sequences. The climb has been well equipped, and apart from the bolts shown on the topo there are also a number of pegs. This in-situ protection helps to make route finding on some of the featureless slabs a little more straightforward. Most stances sport the usual double bolt-belay and allow the route to be quickly rappelled. A rope of two, capable of climbing reasonably quickly at this standard on the slabs of the Mello valley, should be able to complete the route in a day. Start at a slanting slab beneath an arch 100m to the R of the Bonatti route. 400m

Pizzo della Vendretta 2907m

Quite accessible from the Omio hut yet seldom climbed. The SE face is hidden from most viewpoints and gives a worthwhile little rock climb.

4 **SOUTH-EAST FACE**
IV M Bardelli, E Bozzoli-Parasacchi, V Bramani and S Saglio,
86 16 Sept 1934

Although short, this wall is steep and compact. From a distance it looks impregnable and it is hard to believe that a middle-grade route could breach its defences. The climbing is very varied, on sound granite and in a quiet corner of the range. Mainly III with several harder sections.

From the Omio hut head S along the path before working up and across steep grass and boulders to the foot of the NE ridge of the Pizzo. Go around the base of this ridge and ascend rough ground (snow patches earlier in the season) between the peak and the Pizzi Ratti to the S. Go up towards a scree gully on the R which rises to the NE ridge. To the L is the SE face – steep slabs split by a number a straight crack-lines. Reach the L side of the face and start below the most southerly crack-line (1½-2hr).

Climb the crack to where it peters out below an overhang. Move up R past a block and climb a wide crack. This is a little grassy, so as soon as possible climb out L towards the SSE ridge, then work up R over slabs to where easier ground leads to the summit. 1hr, c3hr from the hut

Descent: The SSE ridge is an easy scramble to the col before the Pizzo Ratti. From here descend steeply N to the valley. Alternatively, climb down the interesting NE ridge (III) and descend the scree gully mentioned above to the foot of the face. 45min-1hr

Cime del Calvo 2967m

Probably F Lurani with A Baroni, 1 Aug 1887

A group of three rock peaks which although fairly accessible from both the Omio and Volta huts are seldom climbed. The reward for doing so is a superb panorama that encompasses the Como lakes, all the main peaks in the Bregaglia/Disgrazia chain and the distant Ortler.

5 **CIMA CENTRALE**
F+
88 *The highest peak of the three. It is most easily reached from the Omio hut via the upper part of the Val Ligoncio. Pass below Pt 2334m and reach*

the small snowfields immediately N of the mountain. From here the most pleasant ascent follows the crest of the NNW ridge, although the broken rocks on the N face are just as easy and lead directly to the summit. I/II: 4hr from the hut

Cima Est (2873m) has an attractive rock wall overlooking the upper Val Ligoncio. The great rounded buttress that forms the N spur gives a climb of c250m, with pitches of IV and V in the lower section (L Puttin and G Scotti, 15 Aug 1934). However, the best route climbs the wall on the L.

6 **EAST-NORTH-EAST FACE**
V P Bernasconi and R Compagnoni, 2 Aug 1959
88

A very varied route with the main difficulties concentrated in the steep lower section. Although it is reported to be well worth doing, there have been relatively few ascents, and in-situ gear is sparse.

Follow the previous route towards the Cima Centrale and work L to the foot of the wall (2hr). The most noticeable feature is a huge ledge system that slants across the face to reach the base of the SE ridge. Start c10m up this ledge system and climb directly up the steep walls above, crossing several small overlaps (3 pitches: IV). Now climb up to and over a small roof (V: the crux!). Continue in the same line, climbing slabs, walls and finally easier ground directly to the summit. c250m: 3-4hr: 5-6hr from the hut

Descent: The best descent lies down the SE ridge. Scramble down the crest for 30min to the point where it becomes horizontal. A short gully leads steeply down the NE face to reach the huge ledge system mentioned above. Follow this down and across the face to the start of the climb. 45min-1hr

Piz Ligoncio 3032m

A Baroni, 1 Aug 1881. Winter: A Calegari with V Fiorelli, 9 March 1940

A large rocky mountain with a distinctive pyramidal appearance when seen from the N. Lying at the junction of three main valleys it is an outstanding viewpoint, but its remote situation makes visits to the summit rare occurences.

7
PD
86

EAST-NORTH-EAST FLANK

F Lurani with A Baroni and G Fiorelli, 8 Aug 1881

The normal route and an interesting scramble. The flank is used to reach the upper part of the NNE ridge, where the climbing is very easy but in a splendid situation.

From the Omio hut follow Route 13 towards the Passo Ligoncio then contour the rough slopes below and E of the Sphinx. Go around the base of a prominent rocky spur falling from a point midway up the NNE ridge of the Ligoncio, and climb scree and easy cracked slabs to the S of this spur. Rock walls above bar access to the upper NNE ridge, so climb up to the R and use a couloir close to the spur to bypass these walls. Climb the broken ground above to the ridge (II: near the top of the couloir the route passes under a huge chockstone that forms a natural arch – rappel in descent). Follow the crest – easy climbing over broken rock – to the summit. 3½hr from the hut

8
AD–
86

NORTH-NORTH-EAST RIDGE

E Strutt with G Pollinger, 2 July 1909 (in descent)

This is a much finer route to the summit than that described previously. It climbs directly up the crest of the ridge from the Sella Ligoncio and has sections of III.

The Sella is the lowest point on the ridge between the Punta della Sfinge and the Piz Ligoncio. The couloir leading directly to the gap from the E is rather nasty and cannot be recommended. Instead there are two slanting couloirs further S. Either can be climbed (rotten rock), though it is probably best to use the one on the R (2½hr from hut to Sella).

Climb up the crest of the NNE ridge in a superb position overlooking the wild Codera valley. The first yellow step has been climbed directly (V) but it is normally turned on the L. Continue mainly on the L flank where there are some interesting pitches, and turn the final tower on the R. 2hr, 4½hr from the Omio hut

North-West Face

The impressive wall overlooking the Codera valley was climbed directly in 1938 by P Riva and A Vinci. At one time it enjoyed the reputation of a fine hard route comparable with some of the best in the range. Unfortunately, since that time major rock falls have occurred. Although the route is still possible (V+ with a section of

A1), certain areas need careful handling and the two pitches through the white rock-scar near the bottom of the face are downright dangerous. A winter ascent was made in 1980, and with considerable icing the loose sections passed unnoticed: the climbers enjoyed a very worthwhile, if somewhat taxing, experience!

Punta della Sfinge (Sphinx) 2802m

M Carli and F Casati-Brioschi with E and G Fiorelli, 17 Aug 1908

The Sphinx lies just to the S of the Passo Ligoncio (2575m) and is clearly visible from San Martino. The E ridge is a huge fin of rock and contains the scooped out slabby NE face, and the slightly higher and steeper SE face. There are numerous short routes of very high quality that can be reached quickly from the Omio hut. Plenty of sunshine and a 'friendly' atmosphere add to the enjoyment. The descent is short and easy, allowing several routes to be completed in the same day.

In contrast the NW face is an impressively smooth wall that has seen at least one major rock-fall. There are several demanding routes but only one so far has gained relative popularity.

The easiest route to the summit follows the SSW ridge from the Sella Ligoncio (II+: 30min). A traverse from the Sphinx to the Piz Ligoncio is highly recommended.

Sphinx North-East Face

This wide slabby face is characterised by numerous cracks, flakes and dièdres, which give the substance to a whole host of interesting routes on excellent granite. A big snow basin usually lies below the wall but in the last few summers has not been present. Most climbs have in-situ protection which makes a standard rack quite sufficient and route finding straightforward. This is a popular spot and climbed on at most times of the year (when conditions allow for a safe approach, winter ascents are not uncommon). The two routes described are perhaps the best middle-grade outings on the face, and lying at either end of the wall can be approached without setting foot on snow.

9 **NORTH-NORTH-EAST RIDGE**
IV+ C Crippa with G Fiorelli, 6 Oct 1954
86
3

Probably the best route on the wall following the exposed crest overlooking the awesome sheer slabs of the NW face. The base of the climb can be reached in 1½hr from the Omio hut by walking up the boulder-strewn ridge above the Passo Ligoncio. Start just left of the crest at a grassy terrace below a huge white slab. The middle section of the route is quite sustained with perhaps the hardest moves occurring where a leftwards traverse is made under the large 'nose'. The 'nose' itself can be climbed direct on the L side of the crest, but the crux pitch is far harder (and more exposed!) than anything below and makes the route rather inhomogeneous (V+ and A0/1). c200m: 2½hr

c60m to the L of the start of the previous climb, a line of cracks and corners gives the 'Fiorelli Route'. 200m: V, 2½hr

Descent: From the summit scramble down the broad E ridge until it narrows at a conspicuous notch. A wire hawser provides an anchor for a 40m rappel down the NE face. A little easy down-climbing leads to a second hawser above the main chimney line, from which a long rappel reaches the ground.

10 **SERENA**
V V Cesarano, L Mottarella and F Sosio, 1978
3

A recommended short route with some excellent climbing. It lies towards the L end of the face and is mainly III and IV.

Approach via the path to the Passo Ligoncio, but a little below the pass work L and scramble up rocks on the L of the snow basin to the foot of the face (1½hr from the Omio hut). A line of huge chimneys (taken by the rappel descent) rises up the wall just to the R of the crest of the E ridge and ends at a prominent notch. Start 30m to the R at some large white detached flakes, and begin the climb with a 10m layback (crux) up the most prominent of these flakes, which lie below and slightly to the L of a R-facing dièdre. c130m to the E ridge: 2hr

Sphinx South-East Face

A slightly higher wall on the 'backside' of the fin and very steep in its upper section. It can be reached in 1½-2hr from the Omio hut by following the path towards the Passo Ligoncio, then contouring below the base of the E ridge and walking up scree to the foot of the face.

11 MORBEGNESI

VI/A1 F Botta, P Bottani, G Dell'Oca, A Passerini and L Romegialli, 20 Aug 1964

The first half of this route takes the conspicuous L-facing dièdre on the R side of the face, that rises directly towards the notch in the E ridge. The dièdre, which gives an excellent route in its own right, ends at a big ledge leading R onto the E ridge. However, the true continuation moves L and climbs the very steep headwall with two short aid sections and more than a little exposure! Magnificent rock, good protection and a sunny aspect have made this a minor classic.

Start slightly to the R of the line of the dièdre and slant L up a crack/corner into the main groove (it is also possible to start on the L and climb slabs into the main dièdre – better but harder – V). Continue up this to reach the large ledge after 3-4 sustained pitches (IV+). Slant up L across easier slabs (III+) to another ledge. There are now two possibilities. Either (a): Make a rising traverse L across a rounded rib, and continue delicately in the same line on slabs above a large slanting roof to an overhang of flakes (V+). Climb through this overhang to a belay at the base of a dièdre (VI and A1); or (b): An easier alternative is to traverse horizontally across the ledge below the slanting roof, and climb the L side of a huge flake which curves back R to the same stance in the dièdre.

Now climb the dièdre (IV+) and follow the steep cracks above (IV/V with a section of aid on bolts) to the E ridge. c250m: 4-5hr. A short descent down the crest leads into the notch and the rappel point. From the large ledge it also seems possible to climb directly to the notch via the huge chimney/dièdre (V+ and A1).

12 NORTH-WEST FACE – PEDER ROUTE

TD/TD+ G Alippi, L Gilardoni, M Lafranconi, R Snider, G Tantardini and
2 R Zucchi, 3-5 Aug 1976. The route has been climbed in winter

This extremely steep slab looks remarkably blank when viewed from the upper Codera valley. It is one of the most compact granite walls in the area and progress is only made by utilising the many thin and sometimes fragile flakes that give parts of the wall a 'scaly' appearance. Nowadays, nearly all the essential pegs are in place, and despite the sustained difficulties the route is rapidly approaching the status of a modern classic. The climbing can be both fingery and delicate and the overall grading will depend on the amount and state of the equipment in place. Take a good selection of small and medium wires plus a dozen quick-draws. Small Friends will also prove rather useful and a very cautious party might consider carrying a few knifeblades.

There are a number of ways to approach the wall. It can be reached directly from the Valli bivouac in 1½hr or from the Omio hut, via the Passo Ligoncio, in 3-3½hr. Both may require crampons until late in the season. The third and most popular method is to start from the Omio hut, but instead of crossing the pass walk up towards the Sfinge until c80m short of the base of the NNE ridge. Here, a scree couloir descends to the R. Scramble down this until it starts to get steep, then make a series of rappels to the base of the wall. The first two pitches of the route climb this line, so many parties only rappel to the grassy ledge at the start of pitch 3 and begin the route from this point.

From the exit onto the NNE ridge one can either finish up the last four pitches of Route 9, or descend in 2-3 rappels to the foot of the ridge. 400m to the summit: 8-10hr

Of the various routes on the big wall to the R, probably the hardest is 'Leggende del Lis' (VIII and A2/3) put up in 1990.

Further R an equally smooth but less steep wall, rising to the base of the N ridge of Pizzo Ligoncio, has two modern routes of Czech and Italian origins.

Passo Ligoncio 2575m

The traditional crossing point between the Codera and Masino valleys but nowadays neglected in favour of the Passo dell'Oro.

13 EAST SIDE

P/PE

From the Omio hut a waymarked path slants up and across grassy slopes to reach the pass (which lies at the foot of the S ridge of the Pizzo dell'Oro Meridionale) via a rocky gully. 1½hr

14 WEST SIDE

PE

From the Valli bivouac go round the base (2064m) of the NW ridge of the Pizzo dell'Oro Meridionale. Now ascend scree and unstable boulders, until a steep couloir leads up R to a prominent shoulder at about half-height on the NW ridge. The path follows a series of narrow ledges that slant across the SW face. Follow these easily but in an exposed position to the pass. 2hr

Pizzi dell'Oro 2703m

These three summits lie on the main ridge to the W of the hut. Although rather modest in stature when seen from the E, there are some notable walls and ridges overlooking the Codera valley. Easily the most inspiring of the three is the S peak, which lies just N of the Passo Ligoncio.

Pizzo dell'Oro Meridionale 2695m

E and P Fasana, 15 Aug 1921

15 **SOUTH-EAST FACE**
II First ascent party

This broken grassy face provides the simplest means of descent. Several lines are possible and none are either interesting or difficult!

From the summit go down to the SE over easy terrain and reach a large grassy area. Scramble down chimneys and broken rock below (I/II) to reach, a few mins below the Passo Ligoncio, the path leading down to the Omio hut. c150m: 30min

16 **SOUTH RIDGE**
IV+ A Calegari with V Fiorelli, 10 Aug 1941

Although not sustained and a little grassy in parts, there are one or two nice slab pitches on this short ridge which rises from the Passo Ligoncio.

Follow the crest as closely as possible taking the first slab direct (crux). Higher, easier climbing on the R flank leads to the summit. 120m: 1½hr

17 **NORTH-WEST RIDGE**
D− E Bozzoli-Parasacchi and V Bramani, 22 July 1934. Winter:
5 B Bottani, P Ciapponi, C Milani and P Volpati, 21 Dec 1970.
Complete ridge: G Bertarelli and L Bongio, 31 July 1960

A traditional middle-grade classic that is still one of the most popular

routes in this corner of the range. Most parties climb the upper half of the ridge, above the narrow ledges that are used to gain access to the Passo Ligoncio from the W. However, highly recommended is the 'integral', which provides one of the longest and most interesting routes of its standard in the region. A standard rack is quite sufficient.

From the Omio hut cross the Passo Ligoncio and slant down the exposed easy ledges to the distinctive shoulder on the ridge (see Routes 13 and 14). The route starts at a large detached flake above a grassy ledge.

To climb the whole ridge, reverse route 14 and reach the base (2064m: this point can be reached in less than 15 mins from the Valli bivouac hut). Start 20m L of the foot of the spur; climb a cracked slab to a huge dièdre/chimney and continue to the shoulder. 600m to the summit: 6hr

18 **NORTH-NORTH-WEST FACE**

III/IV P Grunanger and P Meciani, 16 July 1950, by the route as described

Although infrequently climbed, this is reported to give a worthwhile outing, and might appeal to middle-grade climbers looking for something different away from the more popular venues. Little sunshine reaches this hidden wall and the rock is liable to be lichenous in parts, so allow ample drying time after a period of rain. Standard rack.

Approach from the Valli hut in 1hr; or from the Omio hut, via the Passo Ligoncio, in 2½hr. The lower wall is very steep but is split in the centre by a prominent chimney/crack. Climb this, with the crux – a strenuous pull over a large chockstone – at the top (IV). Now work up L via a dièdre and a succession of flakes to easier slabs in the middle of the wall. Slant L to a small gully and follow it to a prominent line of overhangs near the top of the face. Avoid these on the L and reach a big couloir which leads easily to the NNE ridge c50m below the summit. 300m: 3hr

Passo dell'Oro 2526m

This is the shortest, easiest and most frequently used crossing point between the Codera and Masino valleys. It lies just to the S of the Pta Milano and at the foot of the NE ridge of the N peak of the Pizzi dell'Oro. Steep grassy slopes allow the pass to be reached from the Omio hut in 1-1½hr. From the Brasca hut it is a long haul up grass and scree in the Val dell'Averta to the wide couloir just R of Pta Milano. This often holds snow, which if in good condition will greatly facilitate progress. Otherwise, it is a tedious slog using the rocks on the L side. 3½-4hr from the hut

Punta Milano 2610m

G Bernasconi, P Ferrario and G Silvestri with E and M Fiorelli, 26 July 1910. Winter: V Bramati and G Montrasio with D Fiorelli, 2 March 1952

A spectacular little 'Aiguille' just to the N of the Passo dell'Oro. From a distance it is strongly reminiscent of the more famous Aig Dibona (Ecrins) or the Aig de la Tza (Arolla). At close quarters it is actually quite small and a little vegetated but is nonetheless an elegant and airy summit. The routes described are not too hard and have an atmosphere that is 'sub-alpine'. However, these are popular classics in a more traditional mould and are highly recommended to parties beginning their alpine career, or those simply wishing to have a pleasant day's climbing to a unique summit.

19 **SOUTH-WEST RIDGE**
IV First ascent party
6 *The original route, which though not often ascended as better routes lie close at hand, provides the easiest climb to the summit.*

From the Omio hut follow the Roma path and then go directly up grassy slopes to the base of the peak (c1hr). Walk up to the first small col S of the peak and then follow easy ledges on the W side to a tiny notch at the start of the steep section of the ridge.

The first 20m are indeed quite steep but the correct line is surprisingly only III+. Make a few difficult moves up the L side of the initial buttress to an overhang. Traverse L beneath it for 3m to a dièdre, which gives a tricky bit of climbing to the top of the wall. Now move onto the E side of the ridge and scramble easily up grassy ledges to the large terraces below the summit. On the SE face a delightful friction slab leads to the top (20m: III with one move of IV). c100m: 1hr

Descent: Rappel the friction slab to the terraces and scramble down grassy ledges, keeping fairly close to the crest of the ridge. Rejoin the crest c20m above the base, where there is a rappel anchor. Descend to the notch then follow the easy ledges on the W side of the ridge until it is possible to cross over to the E and go down grassy slopes.

20 **SOUTH-EAST FACE – HO CHI MINH**
IV+ R Guasco and A Parini, 19 July 1936
6

Varied climbing, requiring a wide range of techniques up the obvious chimney/dièdre in the centre of the face. The first pitch meets the easy grassy ramp at mid-height and is avoidable; but a finish still has to be made up the friction slab of the normal route. Standard rack. c120m: 2hr

21 **NORTH-EAST CHIMNEYS**
IV G Barbieri, A and L Pronzati and W Wermelinger, 11 Aug 1924

Good old-fashioned climbing, joining the previous routes at the final slab which gives a contrasting finish to the struggles below. Some parties consider this to be the best route on the peak! Standard rack.

From the foot of the SE face follow the grassy slopes around to the N and go steeply up a short couloir to a col overlooking the Codera valley. At this point the NE face is almost vertical and split by a tall chimney. Climb the chimney in two pitches of 35m (III+ and IV). At half-height a narrowing gives a smooth and rather tight squeeze – ugh! Easier climbing leads to a hole through which it is possible to pass onto the SE face. Finish up the final friction slab. 100m: 1½hr

30m to the L of the previous route, along a grassy ledge, is a dièdre. It has a small roof c10m up, leads to an open gully and forms the line of the 1952 'Bottani Route' (V+).

Cima del Barbacan 2738m

F Lurani with G Fiorelli, 23 Aug 1895 Winter: A Calegari with V Fiorelli, 10 March 1940

A massive pyramid whose huge rock walls, impressive from afar, are disappointingly broken on closer acquaintance. The Roma path crosses the ESE ridge at the Barbacan S pass and from this point it is possible to follow the ridge to the summit. First use the grassy L flank and then the crest itself, which is quite narrow in parts and has some exposed moves over and around large blocks. II+: 1hr

Passo del Barbacan 2598m

This rocky saddle at the foot of the N ridge of the Cima del Barbacan gives the easiest and quickest crossing point between the Brasca and Gianetti huts. On the E side it is probably better to follow the Roma path to near the base of the Cima del Barbacan, and then climb directly up a steep boulder and grass-filled gully to the pass (1½hr).

From the Brasca hut follow the waymarked path up the Val dell'Averta, branching L in the upper reaches to a steep couloir leading up to the saddle. This can often hold snow and in these conditions can be climbed direct. Otherwise, it is best in the upper part to utilise grassy ledges on the L side and so avoid stone-fall in the bed (3½-4hr:PE). Gianetti to Brasca hut 3½-4hr. In reverse c5hr

Pizzo Porcellizzo 3075m

First recorded ascent: J Eschmann, 1835

An easy rock pyramid close to the Gianetti hut. The summit is a wonderful viewpoint and one of the most frequented in the valley.

22 **SOUTH FLANK**
RE/F First ascent party
87

The normal route and no more than a rough walk over steep scree and boulder slopes with a little gentle scrambling in one section. There are various possible lines with little to choose between them.

From the Gianetti hut walk S along the Roma path, then head steeply up grassy slopes to an obvious gap in the lower part of the S ridge. Go through this gap and work up scree (path) alongside the fine rock walls of the S ridge. Towards the top various ramps in the R wall lead up to a huge sloping boulder field. Slog up this to the summit cairn, which overlooks the dizzy drop into the Val Codera. On a clear day it is possible to look W along the whole Alpine chain as it gently curves S to the Ecrins Massif and the isolated Monte Viso. 1½hr

23 **NORTH-NORTH-EAST RIDGE**
IV E Fasana, 5 Sept 1914

This brief but delightful excursion follows the very airy crest above the Passo Porcellizzo. Entertaining climbing makes this a recommended half-day activity, and a quick descent via the normal route gives an effective traverse. IV

From the pass climb the initial steep section on the R side, and when immediately below the first tower make a delicate traverse on rather flaky rock onto the L flank and reach the crest beyond the tower. Keeping L work up the crest, which becomes more crenellated and certainly more exposed! Cross a foresummit and continue along the ridge, now at an easier angle but still a bit tricky, to the top. 100m: 1½hr

Pizzo Porcellizzo South Point – Avancorpo del Porcellizzo

This is the last bastion on the long S ridge of the mountain. The steep wall facing the hut is split by a conspicuous and compelling (?), crack-line that leans to the R.

24 **EAST FACE – ISHERWOOD/KOSTERLITZ ROUTE**
VII R Isherwood and M Kosterlitz, 7 July 1968.
87 First 'free' ascent: G Merizzi and G Miotti, July 1978
4

The crack! Climbed many years before this style of ascent became 'in vogue' and immediately prior to their famous climb on the Badile. Nowadays an almost free ascent gives a fine piece of cragging on a wall that can be reached from the Gianetti hut in less than 20mins. The climbing is steep, sustained and continuously interesting, though a little vegetated in parts due to a certain lack of traffic. Easy scrambling down the SW flank provides the descent. Take a full rack. 130m: 3hr+

Passo Porcellizzo 2962m

This is the quickest and easiest crossing point on the ridge between the Gianetti and Vaninetti huts. It forms an integral part of the journey back to the Sasc Fura hut for those parties who have climbed routes on the N side of the Badile-Cengalo and descended into Italy. Whilst the E side of the pass is a simple ascent over scree and boulders, the W side nearly always holds snow and an axe is recommended. PD−: see Route H4

Punta Torelli 3137m

F Besta, C Bonadei, P Botterini, T de Cambray-Digny, G Cetti and C Gerini, 29 Aug 1875. Winter: A Calegari with V Fiorelli, 6 March 1938

Clearly visible from the Gianetti hut this triangular summit forms the end of the sharp SW ridge of the Pta Santa Anna. From the culminating point the SW faces of the Badile and Cengalo are seen to full advantage and there is a breathtaking view down the length of the Codera valley to the distant Como lakes.

25 **SOUTH-WEST RIDGE**
F+ First ascent party
90

A short and straightforward ascent from the Gianetti hut and usually snow free by mid-summer. See also photograph 92

Walk up grass and boulder slopes to reach the moraine valley lying to the L of the prominent 'tooth' called Torre Vecchia. Follow an intermittent path, which rises steadily to a small yet conspicuous notch at the start of the SW ridge (Bocchetta Torelli: c3040m). Climb the crest of the ridge over large blocks and flakes. Crossing a small gap midway along the ridge provides the only real climbing (II) but a modicum of exposure ensures that one keeps alert all the way to the summit cross. 2hr from the hut

26 **SOUTH-SOUTH-EAST PILLAR DIRECT**
VI C Mauri, G Ferrari and G Fiorelli, 11 July 1955. Winter:
90 R Compagnoni and P Gilardoni, 18 March 1957
10

This splendid eye-catching pillar falls directly from the summit and is an established classic of the region. The climbing is of a similar quality to the Parravicini on the Zocca (what better recommendation) but less sustained. The pillar is short, has easy access and dries quickly after bad weather. The hard pitches have some interesting moves and were traditionally climbed with aid so there are still many pegs in place. See also photograph 92

Approach directly from the hut in c1h of gentle walking. After the initial ramp the climbing becomes quite exposed and the crux pitch provides some strenuous moves on the roof to gain a hanging belay in an airy position. It is best to stop here and avoid rope drag on the pitch above, which looks alarming from below but turns out to be more reasonable than expected. The penultimate pitch is a bold lead up a steep slab of typical knobbly Bregaglia granite. Although technically not that hard it hasn't a glimmer of protection so don't even contemplate falling! 300m: 4-5hr

A more direct start can be pursued up the easy-angled slabs and then the R side of the crest to reach the crux pitch. This is a bit loose and grassy and is rarely climbed (IV).

Torre Vecchia 2913m

This is the dramatic monolith of perfectly clean granite S of the Torelli. Standing at the Gianetti hut who could resist an ascent of its spectacular summit? A certain inaccessibility proves somewhat deceptive. To the N an almost horizontal ridge runs from the boulder slopes of the Torelli and provides an easy scramble to the top. The various faces have several lines with the classic route tracing the SE pillar.

27 **WEST FACE**
VI C Giudici and L Prato, 16 June 1956

The steep crack-line on this short wall. 100m

28 **SOUTH-EAST PILLAR**
V G Fiorelli, 1954
90

An obvious corner slants up R to the crest of the pillar. Above, three pitches of excellent granite on the rounded crest lead to the top. 150m

Punta Sant'Anna 3171m

F Lurani and C Magnaghi with G and G Fiorelli, 26 July 1893. Winter: D Spazzini and G Verri, 29 Dec 1955

Named after the saint's day on which it was climbed. A spectacular spire when seen from the upper Bondasca valley with an impressive pillar rising out of the Trubinasca glacier. It is a popular ascent from the Gianetti hut, and from its summit there are wonderful uninterrupted views down the length of the Codera and Porcellizzo valleys. It offers an interesting array of routes at various standards.

29 **WEST AND NORTH-WEST RIDGES**
PD First ascent party
92

The normal route and a good mountaineering expedition, which although not as long as the standard route on the Cengalo is not dissimilar. Mainly II with a few sections of III–. See also photograph 89

From the Vaninetti hut go up 100m then slant R under the rocks of the SW ridge of the Pizzo Trubinasca. Reach the remains of the Codera glacier lying beneath the Pta Trubinasca, and go up the moraine to the entrance to a couloir that slants up R to the Forcola della Punta – the deep notch between the Ptas Trubinasca and Sant'Anna. When there is good snow in this couloir it is possible to climb the bed throughout, but normally one is forced to take to the smooth yet easy slabs on the R side, only returning to the couloir when near the top (1½hr).

Climb the W ridge, over steep sound and relatively easy granite, to join the top of the N Pillar at the the NW summit (3114m). The continuation – the NW ridge – is rather narrow. Drop down onto the SW side and follow ledges across the W face to mixed ground (can be a snowfield). Continue in the same line until directly below the summit, then climb easy slabs to the top. 1hr, 2½hr from the hut, c4½hr from the Gianetti hut via the Passo Porcellizzo

30 **DESCENT**

90

There is a rappel descent on the SE side for parties returning to the Gianetti hut. It has fixed anchors at 20m intervals and avoids the steep couloir between the Sant'Anna and the Torrone del Badile, which is loose and dangerous in dry conditions.

From the summit go down the SW ridge for a short distance to a collection of slings. Make two rappels to a grassy ledge and follow this N. Climb up 8m to the very exposed crest of a pillar (III/III+) and rappel 20m from pegs into the couloir between this pillar and the E ridge. 2-3 more rappels lead into the base of the main couloir coming down from the gap between the Sant'Anna and the Torrione. When dry, a short icy section on the upper glacier soon gives way to moraine; otherwise it is an easy snow slope. From this point it is less than 1hr to the Gianetti hut.

31 **WEST FACE**

IV A Bonacossa and C Negri, 17 Aug 1934

92

An interesting climb that is only recommended in very dry conditions, when it becomes a feasible alternative to the normal route. Axe and crampons will be needed for the approach.

Reach the foot of the face in 1hr from the Vaninetti hut via some steep snow and ice slopes. On the L side climb a narrow couloir for 3-4 pitches (III when dry) to the mixed ground in the centre of the face. Go up to the steep summit rocks which are cut by a prominent chimney/couloir. Climb this on smooth compact rock (moves of IV), moving out L on to slabs to avoid the last 30m. Easier climbing now leads to the summit. 3hr, 4hr from the hut or 6hr from the Gianetti hut via the Porcellizzo pass

32 SOUTH-WEST RIDGE

AD R Balabio and G Scotti, 11 Aug 1909

90

The classic and nowadays the most popular route to the summit. It is one of the very best ridge traverses of its standard described in this guide and comes highly recommended. From the Torelli a 400m sharp turreted crest leads to the top. The difficulties are not sustained but there is a sobering void on both sides, and if the W face is at all icy sections of the climb can be very time consuming.

From the summit of the Torelli the first big drop in the ridge is thankfully avoided! Slant down scree-covered ledges on the E face for 30m until level with the ridge beyond. Using a horizontal crack, climb round to this (III) and continue more easily along the crest, until a collection of slings forms the anchor for a gripping rappel of 20-25m to a grassy terrace on the E face. Follow the terrace back onto the crest and continue until stopped by the first group of gendarmes. Turn these on the L, climbing along grassy slabs for 30m (III+), until the crest can be regained by pulling over a small overhang (a move of IV+/V−). Continue to a notch and turn the next tower on the L, returning to the crest as soon as possible (III and IV). A short section of scrambling leads to the top of a step. Either climb down or rappel 20m into the gap beyond and continue up the narrow ridge (II), with decreasing difficulty, to the summit. 3-3½hr

33 NORTH PILLAR

TD/TD+ W Bonatti and P Nava, 6-7 Aug 1950. Winter: A and G Giovanoli, Dec 1974

100

7

Undoubtedly one of the most impressive lines in the area and Bonatti's most important contribution to Bregaglia climbing. Unfortunately it has always been overshadowed by the classic routes on its famous neighbour and ascents have been relatively few. It is now a superb free climb, but despite the fair amount of aid used on early ascents there are very few pegs in place. In general the rock is good, although one or two of the easier sections are loose. The hard climbing, sustained difficulties in cracks and dièdres passing the L side of the prominent white rock scar, takes place in the first 300m, after which the angle of the ridge relents and gives pleasant slab climbing in a superb position. Reaching the base of the pillar is a long and tortuous ascent over the Trubinasca glacier and is the main deterrent to attempting this route. 600m: VI−, 2½-3hr for the approach and 10hr for the route

34 NORTH-WEST (KLUCKER) COULOIR

TD/TD+ A von Rydzewsky with A Dandrea and C Klucker, 12 June 1899. Winter: F Giacomelli, R Rossi and P Scherini, 20-22 Dec 1980

The first ascent of this huge L-facing corner splitting the NW face was an outstanding achievement for the era. Over 80 years were to elapse before a second ascent was accomplished! It is desperately exposed to stone-fall during the summer but in winter gives a magnificent ice climb. The main difficulties lie at about one-third height, where the gully bends to the R and becomes a deeply-cut chimney. Two pitches of average angle 60°+, but with two short vertical sections, form the crux. This is a serious undertaking tucked away in the corner of a savage arena, and is graded for a non-summer ascent.

Punta Trubinasca 2998m

M Barbaria and C Klucker, 20 June 1900

A slender pyramid of excellent granite situated at the head of the Codera valley. Seen from the N this spire rises above the L end of a vast precipitious wall that overlooks the Trubinasca glacier. Climbs on the S side are short, most attractive and can be quickly reached from the Vaninetti hut. Little snow should be encountered on the approach after mid-summer. A tremendous outing is the W to E traverse combined with an ascent of the Sant'Anna – a 10hr round trip from the Gianetti hut and 1½-2hr less from the Vaninetti.

The remote situation ensures that alpinists will for the most part have the peak to themselves.

35 EAST RIDGE

PD+/AD− J Heller and G Miescher, 8 Aug 1909

89

This is the shortest route to the summit but is most often followed in descent, when making a traverse of the peak via Route 36. It is continuously steep and quite exposed (especially in the upper section) but is, thankfully, not as difficult as first appearances might suggest.

From the Vaninetti hut follow Route 29 to the Forcola della Punta (1½hr). The initial small step on the ridge is not climbed. Instead, descend a few m to the S and climb up a crack system to the crest, beyond the step (III−). Continue up the ridge, which is split by cracks and chimneys, until close to the summit. The ridge now overhangs alarmingly on the N side, so traverse L below some roofs to a sharp rib on the S face and make a sequence of wonderfully exposed moves (only III+ but seems more!) up onto easy ground leading to the top. 85m: 1½-2hr, 3-3½hr from the hut. Descend by several rather sensational rappels.

36 **NORTH-WEST RIDGE**

IV+ First ascent party

89

A highly recommended outing. Difficulties are limited to the first third of the ridge; thereafter the climbing is straightforward and the whole route can be completed in c6 pitches. The crux is short and sharp but much harder than anything else on the climb: however, it can be overcome by resorting to combined tactics, a pull on the in-situ gear, or even lassoing as on the first ascent. See also photograph 100

From the Vaninetti hut follow Route 29 towards the Forcola della Punta, but long before the couloir work L up boulders and possibly snow to the small notch in the frontier ridge, between the Pizzo and Punta Trubinasca (c2842m: 1hr). Climb cracks just R of the crest of the NW ridge to the first steep section, which takes the form of a large block (III). Turn this by some exposed climbing on the L, rejoining the crest at a horizontal section (III+). The steep bit that follows is climbed slightly on the R to a second higher step. A short traverse onto the Bondasca side leads to a ledge beneath a steep dièdre. Climb the dièdre for 8m (IV+) then regain the ridge. Continue along the sharp and exposed crest, and bypass a short quasi-vertical rise via a steep slab and R-slanting crack on the Codera side (III). The angle now eases and so too the technical difficulties. Follow the ridge, with several short deviations L and R, to the summit (2-2½hr). 160m: 3-3½hr from the hut

37 **WEST FACE**

VI/A1 M Zappa and R Zocchi, 10 July 1966

This short route takes a direct line up the centre of the face and should be attempted late in the season when it is thoroughly dry. It has seldom been

repeated but is reported to be a very worthwhile outing on excellent granite. Most of the aid occurs in the first two pitches, but as the climbing takes place in steep regular cracks, it is suggested that a determined party may convert this route into a high-standard free climb, and it is for this reason that the description is included. There is little in-situ gear so take a comprehensive rack.

Start in the centre of the face, just L of a black water-streaked couloir coming down from a large depression (which can often remain a snow patch until mid-summer).

Climb a crack for 15m, then the dièdre above, and traverse R below a roof for 7m to a stance (80m: VI and A1). Climb up flakes to a vertical wall where a smooth L-slanting dièdre leads up to the depression (IV+ and one or two moves of A0). Climb the obvious flake crack (V) and the short dièdre above (A0: 2 moves), to a good stance on some slabs. Trend R below the headwall and then climb up L to reach a vague rib. Continue up the vertical cracks above until they close. Here it is necessary to make a very exposed traverse L (V and some A0) to reach easier ground. Broken rock leads up to a good ledge from where the summit can be reached more easily (III). c200m: 6hr

38 **WEST RIDGE**
V G Cristofaro, R Minazzi, M Pinardi and C Riva, 7 July 1935
89

This is the most difficult ridge on the peak but a first-rate climb and highly recommended. There are some good honest cracks and chimneys and the climbing is a little more strenuous than normal for routes of this standard elsewhere in the range. Due to its orientation the rock can be a little lichenous in parts and should be allowed ample time to thoroughly dry after bad weather. A standard rack is quite sufficient as there is plenty of in-situ protection.

From the Vaninetti hut go up towards the NW ridge and slant R to the foot of the W ridge, which rises steeply above some lower easy-angled rocks (45min).

Start c20m to the L below a conspicuous triangular roof. Climb a steep dièdre, then the crack through the roof, and move L into a parallel dièdre that leads to a good stance by a jammed block (IV+). Move up to an overhang, then slant R across a wall to rejoin the original dièdre which is climbed to the ridge (V−). This middle section of the ridge is less steep. Small gendarmes are negotiated directly on the crest (III) until the final headwall is reached. Now move onto the L side of the crest and climb a 60m high chimney. The crux is right at the start and involves a strenuous struggle or a wide and elegant bridge over a huge chockstone (V/A0). Thereafter the ground becomes more reasonable (IV+). When possible, move R onto the crest and enjoy the airy situations and pleasant climbing to the top. c200m: 3½hr from the hut

39 **SOUTH-EAST FACE DIRECT**
V+ G Buscaini and S Metzeltin, 8 Aug 1975; to within 30m of the
89 summit

Although short, this steep wall gives sustained climbing up a series of cracks and dièdres in the centre of the face. The start lies half-way up the approach couloir to the Forcola della Punta and can be reached in 1hr from the Vaninetti hut. The route receives plenty of sunshine and is on excellent rock. 140m: 3½hr

Pizzo Trubinasca 2918m

A von Rydzewsky with A Dandrea, C Klucker and M Schocher, 29 June 1896

W of the Punta Trubinasca the ridge rises to an almost horizontal crest. The Pizzo is rather uninspiring from the S, where boulder slopes rise nearly to the highest point. However, a vast and austere N wall overlooks the Trubinasca glacier and has a number of long and demanding routes. Although the summit is quickly and easily reached from the Vaninetti hut, the isolated situation and an overriding feeling of desolation ensure that the peak enjoys a relatively quiet life.

40 **WEST FLANK/NORTH-WEST RIDGE**
F First ascent party
91

This is the normal route. It has little in the way of technical difficulty and provides the quickest and easiest descent from the summit. Far more worthwhile is a complete ascent of the NW ridge, which is only slightly longer and has short pitches of II. See also photograph 89

From the Vaninetti hut follow the main traverse path towards the Trubinasca pass. This path is clearly waymarked and crosses c100m above the hut. After passing below the end of the rock barriers, work up to the R over some very rough ground and reach boulder slopes (snow patches) directly below the horizontal summit ridge. Climb up to the crest (I/II–) a short distance to the L of the highest point (the E extremity of the ridge). 1-1½hr from the hut

41
IV
89

SOUTH-EAST RIDGE

Possibly A and R Calegari with R Balabio, 11 Aug 1909 but more probably A Bonacossa, E Bozzoli-Parasacchi and C Negri, 16 Aug 1934

Although short, this is the recommended route on the S side of the peak combined with a descent of the complete NW ridge. The climbing is very varied with considerable exposure. The views towards the Badile and Cengalo are quite outstanding! See also photograph 100

Reach the gap between the Punta and Pizzo Trubinasca (see Route 36) in 1hr from the Vaninetti hut or 3½hr from the Gianetti hut. This gap is actually composed of a multitude of small rock pinnacles and it is necessary to climb around these to reach a tiny notch below the first tower on the ridge – a very sharply pointed obstacle which gives a tricky ascent (III). Continue along the crest making a 5m rappel into a gap near the foot of a steep step. The step overhangs to the R, so climb up a few m then make a delicate and slightly descending traverse to the L across a big slab (IV), until it is possible to climb directly into another gap on the ridge. Slant up L to reach a ledge, and follow it in an exposed position to a grassy terrace (III). Now regain the ridge and follow the crest, which is broader and less difficult, to the summit. 2-2½hr

Pizzo Trubinasca North Face

There are some very impressive natural lines on this precipitious wall – notably the striking N Pillar. Unfortunately, the rock is often far from the immaculate quality for which the region is famous, and apart from the original 1935 route the climbs are rarely repeated.

The 500m NW face was first climbed in 1956 but is not recommended due to the very poor quality of the rock. The N Pillar (H Burggasser and H Uibrig, 22-23 Aug 1935: V+) is still climbed at irregular intervals and had a winter ascent during the mild spell in early 1989 by A Giovanoli and F Lenatti. Again, parties have not been too favourable in their comments and have found the climbing distinctly scary. Large rock-fall scars are clearly visible in the upper part of the wall, and the traverse pitches just below the top lie beneath giant 'Swords of Damocles'.

A direct route on the L side of the pillar was climbed by a strong Czech team in 1980 (19 pitches: sustained V and VI).

The chimney/crack system, leading up to the gap between the two Trubinasca peaks, was climbed in 1968 (400m: V and A1) but is a poor route. Between this and the N Pillar is a very steep wall with two hard routes. On the R a series of cracks and dièdres was climbed in 1969 with almost 100 points of aid (VI and A2). The line is rather rambling but the rock is reported to be good. On the L some impressive compact slabs have been attacked with a modern approach to give one of the hardest free routes, on a fairly major wall, in the region.

42 **DIXON**
ED2 P Crippa and S Dario, 24-25 June 1989
100
8

Probably still unrepeated at the time of writing, this sustained test-piece involves some very thin and delicate friction work that should appeal to devotees of the bold slab-climbing associated with the Mello valley. The rock is generally quite sound, though the dièdres near the top may contain loose material. 40 pegs and 15 bolts were used and all were left in place: despite this, parties are advised to carry a full rack including RPs, and Friends up to size 3. Fixed anchor points allow the route to be descended by rappel, finishing directly down the overhanging wall below the end of pitch 3. A competent team making an early start will avoid a bivouac.

From the Sasc Fura hut reverse Route 119 and reach the E side of the Trubinasca glacier. Make a tortuous ascent up the heavily crevassed slopes to the foot of the wall. The exact start will depend on the level of the glacier, but lies very close to the 1968 Route which slants up L to the gap between the two Trubinasca peaks. After climbing up to the L end of a large horizontal roof, a traverse R below it leads to a good ledge above the huge overhangs at the base of the wall. Difficult slabs and dièdres follow, taking a line loosely based on a L-facing corner which reaches close to the R side of a conspicuous rock feature, shaped like a nut (fruit-stone). The climb finishes at a prominent flat-topped tower on the SE ridge. 500m: VIII–

Pizzi dei Vanni 2773m: Denc dal Luf 2172m

Further W the peaks of the Cantaccio, Vanni and the 80m needle of the Wolf's Tooth offer short rock climbs that lie waiting for the dedicated explorer. Particularly worthwhile is the scramble over the main summits of the Vanni peaks, beginning at the Tegiola pass. II: 4hr

Torrione del Badile 3148m

A and R Balabio, 19 July 1909. Winter: J Sanseverino, 18 Feb 1965

A sharp tower between the Sant'Anna and Badile. It is situated immediately E of the true Colle del Badile and is nowadays seldom climbed. The W ridge can be followed directly from the col between the Torrione and Sant'Anna (Colle Badiletto 3985m). It is exposed and some of the rock is quite shaky (III–, 45min). Two mind-blowing rappels lead down to the the Colle del Badile and the start of the W ridge of Piz Badile.

43 TD– 104

Colle del Badile 3114m

C Klucker and M Schocher, 6 July 1896, from N to S.
Winter: G Bianchi and E Scarabelli, 18-19 March 1973

A pronounced V-shaped notch at the foot of the W ridge of the Piz Badile. The S side is a short and most unpleasant couloir full of loose blocks. The approach to the W ridge actually climbs the rock 50-60m to the R.

On the N side one of the most fearsome ice couloirs in the range rises from the eastern apex of the Trubinasca glacier. The first ascent was a 'tour de force' – a prolonged epic of step-cutting by the two famous guides. As conditions have worsened over the years, the route has seldom been repeated. The couloir is fairly wide until it forks either side of the Torrione. The narrow L branch leads to the col and in less than perfect conditions will give difficult mixed climbing, with icy sections up to 60°. In common with most other great ice couloirs in the region, this should be climbed 'out of season' when heavy snow cover and a hard frost will minimise the almost constant stone-fall that occurs during the summer. At any time of year crossing the rimaye can often prove a desperate business! 450m: 4-7hr

Piz Badile 3308m

W Coolidge with F and H Devouassoud, 26 July 1867.
Winter: A Calegari with G and V Fiorelli, 16 March 1938

The name 'Badile' is synonymous with that of the Bregaglia. Its international fame is due not so much to the aesthetic appearance of the huge sweeping slabs on the N flanks, but more to certain outstanding routes on the walls and ridges that have written significant chapters in the history of alpinism. The most notable feature is the smooth 800m NE face, which has a 'scooped-out' appearance that explains the derivation of its Italian name – 'The Shovel'. There is a long and almost horizontal summit ridge with the highest point roughly in the middle.

Although by no means the highest peak in the region, it exerts an overwhelming magnetism towards the majority of visiting alpinists. In recent years there has been an extensive development of the open faces, and there are now more than 40 routes from which to chose. Most of these are associated with names that have become identified with the evolution of climbing in the Bregaglia.

Whichever route you choose, remember that the mountain is notorious for sudden storms. There is a serious lightning hazard and escape from the summit ridge in bad weather, even by the normal route on the S face, can prove epic!

44 SOUTH FACE – NORMAL ROUTE

PD First ascent party

95

This is the longest and easiest route on the S side of the peak, and follows a succession of grassy ledges and short gullies that lie in the depression immediately R of the elegant S ridge. Although a popular climb from the Gianetti hut it also provides the quickest and most straightforward means of descent from the summit, and is frequently used by parties completing routes on the N side. This was the first of Coolidge's many contributions to alpine history, when he was a mere 16 years of age!

It is primarily a rock climb, though snow and ice can often linger in the gullies and an axe may be useful early in the season. It is not as serious as the Cengalo but should not be underestimated, especially in descent – as the numerous commemorative plaques will testify (It is currently equipped for 22m rappels). The correct route is no more than III but the line is complex and although cairns mark several of the key points, many parties go astray. The granite is generally good but there is a fair amount of rubble on the ledges, and when making an ascent a wise team will be out in front! See also photographs 90, 92

From the Gianetti hut a vague path, marked by cairns and paint-flashes, leads N over rocky ground to the foot of the S ridge (45min). Start on the W side and reach a couloir that slants up R to the top of the first step. Go up the crest, then follow easy ledges on the R until a more pronounced ledge leads under an overhang to the base of a chimney. Climb the chimney (old fixed rope: III) and exit near to a large metal cross. Follow tracks for 80m up grassy terrain to a prominent ledge, which descends into the huge open couloir on the R (cairn). Climb the couloir, working first up R then back L for 70m, to a ramp slanting up to the S ridge. Climb it (II+) and follow the crest for c40m to another large ledge system leading back into the couloir. Ascend the couloir which is now beginning to open out. After 30m climb one of several possible chimneys on the L to a point on the S ridge immediately below a steep buttress. On the R is a narrow scree couloir. Follow this and the slabs above to broken ground and reach the summit ridge c40m W of the highest point (2-2½hr). 400m: 3hr from the hut

Descent: The route is more difficult to locate in descent and it is all too easy to miss the correct ledge systems that link the main couloir with the S ridge. For example, in the lower section parties often miss the large ledge system that leads back up to the R (facing out). The large cross is a good guide here. Don't be lured into following a false trail down to the top of a steep and nasty gully, where several rappels will be necessary to reach the glacier below. 2hr to the hut. If returning to the Sasc Fura hut over the Passo Porcellizzo, it is not necessary to descend all the way to the Gianetti hut. A traverse W below the Torre Vecchia leads to the path.

45 **SOUTH RIDGE**

AD Above the metal cross on the normal route it is possible to follow the crest of the ridge throughout. This gives very pleasant climbing on sound granite, with difficulties up to V−, but it is possible to escape onto the normal route after almost every pitch.

46 **SOUTH-WEST WALL – SOUTH PILLAR**

D+/ G Fiorelli, E Frisia and R Merendi, 13 Sept 1957. Winter: B, F and

TD− M Bottani, P Ciapponi and V Spreafico, 24 Dec 1974

92

11

This route lies on the shortest and perhaps the least frequented face of the mountain. The face was first climbed in 1904 by an unpleasant couloir towards the L side (The pillar to the R of this was climbed in winter 1992/3 at VI). In the middle is an amphitheatre with a very steep and

conspicuous pillar above. The start of the route can be reached in 1h from the Gianetti hut (crampons useful), and lies c20m to the R of the lowest point on the face. The difficulty of the first pitch will vary according to the height of the glacier. Above, the granite is generally good although care is needed with some of the flakes at the start of the upper pillar. The route is climbed fairly regularly and the hard moves can be well protected, often by in-situ pegs, so a standard rack should be adequate. c300m: VI–, 4-5hr

The WSW ridge used to be considered a classic expedition from the Gianetti hut and was generally combined with a descent of the E ridge to make a traverse of the peak. Nowadays it is rarely climbed. The approach follows a system of loose chimneys, 50-60m to the R of the couloir leading up to the Colle del Badile. The lower section of the ridge has suffered irreparable damage due to rock-fall and can no longer be recommended. The upper section is still quite good (III+) and is used to complete the Bramani route on the NW face.

Piz Badile North-West Face

47 **BRAMANI ROUTE**
TD V Bramani and E Castiglioni, 27-28 July 1937.
104 Winter: E and F Gugiatti and C Pedroni, 22-24 Dec 1974
9

The classic mountaineering route up the great slabs of the NW wall. There is loose rock in some of the chimneys but also fine compact slabs that give delightful friction climbing. Several variations have been established, but if the correct line is followed the difficulties are not too great. Although good in the lower half, the route is increasingly broken by ledges, with the result that overall it is not as worthwhile as other climbs on this side of the mountain. It remains the only route on the wall at an accessible standard, but as there is no descent to the foot of the route all equipment, including ice gear used on the approach, must be carried over the summit. Hence, even today, there is an aura of seriousness and commitment that is less apparent when climbing on the sunnier NE face.

From the Sasc Fura hut reverse Route H9 as far as the Trubinasca glacier, then continue up the E branch below the N ridge of the Badile and reach the entrance to the N couloir of the Colle del Badile. The glacier is very contorted and in dry conditions a labyrinth of crevasses must be negotiated. The rimaye barring access to the couloir can form a vertical unbroken wall. Parties have outflanked it on the rock walls of the Badile (IV/V), or slightly more easily on the Sant'Anna (2 pitches then short rappel into the couloir). The lower section of the wall receives very little sunshine. It is slow to dry and prone to verglas. An early start, necessary to avoid stonefall in the couloir, will result in frozen fingers on the initial pitches! 3-4hr for the approach. 650m: 8-10hr for the climb

48 **RINGO STARR**

ED1 O and T Fazzini and T Gianola, 19 Aug 1985

104 12 *This splendid 'directissima' (dedicated, not to the famous Beatle but to a well-known Italian biscuit!) begins at the base of the couloir, thus avoiding the difficulties and dangers of the final approach to the Bramani route. The correct line is not always obvious from below but there is no mistaking the impressive L-facing dièdre in the steep headwall, which gives four sustained pitches in an outrageous position. Apart from the middle section, which is a little friable and disappointing, the quality is maintained at a high standard throughout. At the time of writing the climb is still an unknown quantity, so take a comprehensive rack and treat the technical grading, shown on the topo, with a certain degree of caution. 650m: 10hr*

49 **GRAND DIEDRE**

ED1 J Benes and L Sulovsky, 21 Aug 1980

104 *The huge bow-shaped corner on the R of the Waterdrop Pillar gives sustained climbing at V/VI on first-class granite. 450m: 15 pitches, VI/VI+ with two short sections of aid, 8-10hr*

Pilastro a Goccia (Waterdrop Pillar)

This is the conspicuous barrel-shaped buttress that terminates on the N ridge c250m below the summit. It now offers four highly technical routes, that are not only sustained but have certain pitches that require a bold approach. Lying below the entrance to the N couloir, the pillar is objectively safe and easier to reach than routes on the true NW face (2½-3hr from the Sasc Fura hut). Although it is more aesthetic to continue to the summit, many parties make a straightforward descent by rappel of the N ridge.

50 **CHIARA**

ED1 F Boffini, G and J Merizzi, G Miotti and G Pirana, 1-2 July and
104 6 Aug 1976. Winter: G Caronti, M Fasano and A Prestini,
15 12-15 Jan 1989

The first route on the pillar and one that required masterly route-finding.

It rapidly became a modern classic. Nowadays it is climbed completly free, though many of the hard sections can still be overcome at A0/A1. Even so, the pitches are by no means overpegged and a good selection of small and medium wires is essential. The prudent party will also carry RPs and possibly a few knifeblades.

In the lower half some of the rock is a little friable and runners behind superficial flakes inspire little confidence. Fortunately, this situation improves considerably as height is gained! After the second pitch it is possible to move L and climb the 'dièdre with flakes' in its entirety, but the rock is poor.

A winter ascent saw many of the slab pitches coated in a thin layer of névé/ice, which required delicate front-pointing and some bold leads! It was a superb achievement and perhaps a pointer towards future winter development in the range? c400m: VI/VI+, 10hr

51 **FUGA DALL'OVEST**
D G and J Merizzi, L Mingotti and C Pinciroli, 6 Aug 1990
104
13 *A slight but rather enjoyable climb starting well L of the Waterdrop Pillar. In this region the face is characterised by two huge arches. The route forces a steep chimney (with a prominent chockstone) through the barrier of overhangs L of the arches onto the slabs above. Thereafter the angle relents, allowing some superb friction climbing up the compact slabs to an exit low down on the N ridge. The rock is excellent and affords good natural protection. Only three pegs were thought necessary and these were left in place. Although the approach up the Trubinasca glacier is still tricky and the face remains in shade for much of the day, this is the only route of an accessible standard on these walls. With an easy descent, it is perhaps worthy of more attention? c350m: V+, 4-5hr*

52 **NORTH RIDGE**
D– A Zurcker with W Risch, 4 Aug 1923. Winter: A Anghileri,
101 C Ferrari and G Negri, 20-21 Feb 1965

There are few rock routes in the Alps that follow such a pure and elegant line. Clearly visible from Bondo it appears smooth, steep and impregnable. In fact it is mainly III with only three harder sections and is undoubtedly one of the finest climbs in the Alps at this standard. Other routes may be more interesting but the audacious position, suspended between the two steep walls of one of Europe's most famous peaks, is without parallel.

The rough slabs are a delight to climb and apart from three pitches, where loose flakes need careful handling, the granite is sound and compact. Despite its length, which should not be underestimated, the ridge is now the most popular route in the Bondasca valley and it is not unusual to find twenty parties on it during the height of summer. Some of these will be slow! Whilst most parties will go down to the Gianetti hut, the ridge is often descended (c20 rappels) by climbers coming off the NE face.

Despite these drawbacks, alpinists of all abilities enthuse over this compelling line. It should not be missed! IV+. See also photographs 92, 100

From the Sasc Fura hut walk up the path to the Colle Vial (Route H11). Continue up the promontory towards the base of the ridge, which from this point appears deceptively foreshortened! The lowest part of the ridge is bypassed via two successive snowfields: crampons are advisable here, although in dry years it is possible to complete the ridge and descend to the Gianetti hut without touching snow (turn the bare glaciated slabs on the L). Reach a small notch at the start of the difficulties (2hr: it is at this point that a descending traverse can be made on the E flank to the climbs on the NE face).

A detailed description of the climb is unnecessary. Apart from two occasions the route keeps to the crest. There are many pegs in place, although some are not always on the correct line! Leaders should avoid the temptation of following alluring ledges, which from time to time lead sideways onto the faces and appear to avoid difficulties on the ridge.

The first difficult pitch – the Risch Slab – occurs one quarter of the way up. It is a huge striated slab capped by a small overhang which is avoided on the R (40m: IV+). Back on the ridge more delightful climbing leads, eventually, to a huge detached block (near the top of the Waterdrop Pillar) and a sort of corridor slanting up to the L. Climb the corridor, then work up the W side of the ridge via slabs and short dièdres, returning to the crest after climbing a small overhang (2 pitches: IV+). Follow the crest, avoiding a steep step by flakes and cracks on the NE face, to an area of pale shattered granite – the scene of an obvious rock-fall. Above, climb a steep smooth slab split by many cracks; continue up a grey dièdre on the R and return to the crest (2 pitches: IV and IV+). This section can be avoided by traversing onto the NE face for 60m then climbing a loose chimney back onto the ridge. The angle and difficulty now relent and the sharp turreted crest is followed for a considerable distance but, in a wonderful position, to the summit. c700m: 5-7hr

When descending it is not always easy to locate the rappel points from above, and prior knowledge of the ridge becomes very useful. Long delays can occur if there are many parties; but with a clear run the average time to the base is 4-5hr

Piz Badile North-East Face

This is one of the traditional 'Six Great North Faces' in the Alps and rises in an unbroken sweep of 800m above the Cengalo glacier. Whilst the original line still attracts the majority of alpinists, there are at the time of writing 14 other routes on the smooth slabs that lie between the N and E ridges.

53 **NEVERLAND**
TD+/ S Brambati, A Carnati and P Vitali, 16 Aug 1986
ED1
102
16

The expanse of sunbaked slabs that lie to the R of the start of the Cassin route terminate on the lower half of the N ridge. They provide thoroughly modern climbing in a high mountain setting, and as yet have had few repetitions. Until 1991 the established routes had been created by 'local' Italians (adept at forcing long bold run-outs on the Mello slabs), and whilst the technical difficulties were sustained they were never extreme.

Although this route appears to be the most reasonable, it is still a serious proposition. Main belays often rely on one poorly-made bolt, and would-be ascensionists should be prepared to climb a long way above their last runner! Climbing on these slabs often utilises thin flakes and the obvious holds tend to be rather brittle.

The climb begins from the highest point on the ledge system that connects the N ridge with the start of the Cassin route. It progresses, more or less directly, over two conspicuous bands of overhangs to the N ridge. From the exit it is a mere 20mins to the base of the ridge. Take a comprehensive rack (Friends and possibly RPs useful). c400m: 6-8hr

Starting at the same point but taking an almost parallel line to the L is 'Diritto d'Autore' put up in 1987 by the same team (c450m: VI+)

54 **ANOTHER DAY IN PARADISE**
TD+ B and K Muller and H Zgraggen, 19-20 July 1991
102
20

This controversial route pursues a very close line to 'Diritto d'Autore' and is of a similar standard, with two harder sections that can both be negotiated at VI and A0. The difference is that whilst 'Diritto' was climbed

with 6 bolts this route sports 120! At the time of writing, twelve months after the ascent, it has already gained considerable popularity, and the climbing is reported to be excellent despite following no obvious line. Although the standard of individual pitches has not been confirmed, the climbing is clearly less serious than that on neighbouring lines. The harder pitches generally have 5-6 bolts and double bolt belays allow a safe and rapid rappel descent. The initial pitches follow a quartz vein to the R of the true start to 'White Line', but can be omitted by beginning the climb from the ledge system used to approach 'Neverland' etc. VII: c700m (for the 'White Line' finish).

55 **THE WHITE LINE**

ED1 I Koller and S Silhan, 22 Aug 1978. Winter: M Clerici,
102 20-23 Dec 1986

17 *This bold piece of climbing by the talented Czech team was the first breach of the steep slabs between the 'Cassin' and the N Ridge. Ahead of its time in concept, it certainly pointed the way towards the opening up of the vast expanses of compact rock on the NE face. Although the difficulties are not excessive, the protection is noticeable by its absence and leaders should have the confidence to make moves of V/VI a long way above their last good runner. Despite this deterrent the route has received a number of ascents and parties report very favourably on the quality of the climbing.*

The initial pitches follow the original start taken by Molteni to the 'Cassin' route. After climbing the latter for three pitches, the route breaks out R alongside the obvious white streak leading to the N ridge. In its entirety it is a lengthy enterprise but most parties will approach from the base of the N ridge and climb the 450m above the 'Cassin', rappelling the N ridge to collect any equipment left on the approach. c700m: VI, 10hr. See also photograph 101

56 **CASSIN ROUTE**

TD R Cassin, G Esposito and V Ratti; M Molteni and G Valsecchi,
102 14-16 July 1937. Winter: P Armando, G Calcagno and A Gogna;
18 C Bournissen, M Darbellay and D Troillet, 21 Dec 1967 – 2 Jan 1968, using siege tactics. D Porta made the first 'alpine style' winter ascent, solo, 18-21 Jan 1981 (third winter ascent)

The huge scalloped depression in the centre of the face is a natural funnel for ice and stone-fall originating from the broken ground below the summit ridge. On the rough-hewn slabs lying wholly to the R lies the most famous route in the entire Central Alps. Details of the first ascent form the scenario of a well-known tragedy, with the two parties starting independently; joining together during the onslaught of a severe and prolonged storm; then arriving exhausted on the summit, only to have Molteni and Valsecchi die from exposure.

Although its reputation has now diminished, this is still a committing undertaking. Rain or snow on the upper face quickly creates a nightmare from which it is difficult to escape, and turns a delightful romp up sunbaked slabs into a major epic – the over-abundance of in-situ pegs/slings a visible testimony! It is not totally immune to stone-fall, though in recent years this appears to have almost disappeared.

The route follows a line of cracks and dièdres which succumb to jamming and laybacking. Surprisingly perhaps, there is little pure friction work. The difficulties, not high by modern standards, are sustained; but they are well-protected and continuously enthralling. Despite the passage of time this is still one of the most desirable rock climbs in the Alps and a lasting tribute to its creator. VI. See also photographs 100, 101

From the Sasc Fura hut follow Route H11 across the Colle Vial and go up the Cengalo glacier to the foot of the route, c100m to the R of the central depression. An obvious ledge system slants up R to a conspicuous 'boss' of rock (125m: II and III, 2hr). There are good bivouac sites on the rognon below the face.

Most parties reach the 'boss' from the base of the N ridge. From the small gap and bivi site (c2090m) at the start of the ridge descend ledges on the E face to the top of a snowfield. Squeeze along the gap behind this and climb up to a good ledge system where it is possible to make a comfortable bivouac. Follow the ledges up L to the top of the 'boss' (2hr+)

All the hard pitches can be climbed on aid; most parties tend to use a little and complete the route at V−/V and A0. When climbed free, the crux is thought to lie in the steep dièdres above the 'snowpatch'. When completely dry (not often!) the upper chimneys give some magnificent pitches and there is a choice of exits. 800m: 6-10hr

57 **EAST-NORTH-EAST PILLAR – THE BROTHERS' ROUTE**
TD+ A and G Rusconi, 14-19 March 1970
102
14

The prominent crack-line in this broad rounded pillar, lying to the L of the central depression, had been an object of attention since 1935. The first ascent was a 'tour de force' but caused much controversy as it involved siege tactics during the winter period, making large amounts of

aid necessary. At first the climbing is not too steep and the difficulties reasonable. The angle then augments and the cracks require a more aggressive approach and some aid. The finish lies in a couloir on the L side of the depression, and is not as sheltered from stone-fall as routes further L.

However it is less demanding than most other routes and has quickly gained classic status (and a lot of pegs!). It is climbed quite regularly, though best attempted in very dry conditions. Unfortunately, an often insuperable problem is the crossing of the huge rimaye at the base of the Cengalo couloir.

The amount of aid climbing is fairly minimal but most parties carry a few pegs and étriers and find large Friends (2½-3½) useful. An all-free ascent is certainly feasible. V+ and A1: c750m, 12-15hr. See also photographs 101, 103

58 ED1 103 19

BRITISH ROUTE

R Isherwood and M Kosterlitz, 8-9 July 1968.
Winter: Z Hofmannova and A Stehlikova, 11-15 Feb 1982

The most prominent feature on the ENE face is the huge crack system which ends in a clean-cut dièdre capped by a roof. In appearance it has similarities to some of the great lines on the walls of the Dru or in Yosemite. As a first ascent it was unintentional; the climbers thought that they were repeating the Corti route. However, it quickly gathered a reputation and has now evolved into the modern classic on the Badile.

As most of the loose material has now disappeared from the bottom section, the rock is generally good throughout. The last 150m below the shoulder are particularly sensational, with the aid moves almost entirely possible with nuts. The cracks are ragged and often wide enough to accept fingers, so there is a common acceptance that, one day, a strong team will make an all-free ascent of this compelling line. As there is remarkably little in-situ protection a comprehensive rack is advised, and most parties will want to carry étriers and a selection of blade pegs. The last few pitches on the NE face can be quite tricky when icy.

It is more convenient to start the route by climbing the lower section of the couloir at night. However, on the occasions when the rimaye has made this impossible, parties have descended from the Colle del Cengalo. V+ and A1/A2: c600m, 14hr. See also photograph 101

59 TD/TD+ 103 19

BATTAGLIA-CORTI ROUTE

F Battaglia and C Corti, 17-18 Aug 1953

The correct line of this enigmatic route remained a source of debate for many years, prompting Corti to make the second ascent in 1975.

Originally, considerable aid was employed (130 pegs) and the traditional 'Badile epic' occurred as the climbers fought their way in the height of a storm to a desperate exit onto the E ridge where Battaglia was killed by lightning. The route is now a high quality free-climb with excellent stances and belays (The two points of aid, in the wet chimney, could be eliminated in very dry conditions). The rock is good and a variety of techniques must be employed to overcome problems on slabs, cracks, dièdres and chimneys. The long rising traverse contains some of the best climbing, but a direct start via the initial pitches of the 'People's' route may well provide the most logical introduction, and is more easily reached from the Colle del Cengalo. VI-and A0: c500m, 8-10hr

60 **PEOPLE'S DIRECT**

ED2 O and T Fazzini and L Gianola, 11 July 1987

103

19

A magnificent crack climb that finishes at the very apex of the ENE face. The first ascent party, responsible for a number of routes on the walls of the Badile, were quick to enthuse on the quality, and considered the climb worthy of modern classic status. A small amount of aid was used in the outrageously exposed upper dièdre, but the remaining pitches succumb to sustained yet well-protected jamming and face moves. The route starts at two-thirds height in the Cengalo couloir and is most easily and safely approached by down-climbing (and rappels) from the Colle. There is no in-situ protection and the individual pitch gradings should be treated with caution. Belay pegs were left in place. VI+ and A1: c500m, 8-10hr

The conspicuous crack-line to the L, approached over the Colle del Cengalo (initially loose rock and scree to gain the L side of the couloir; then 200m of down-climbing and rappels (45°) to a rotten ledge with a peg and sling), was climbed by G Maspes and L Salini, 4 Aug 1991. The route finishes on the East ridge, from where 100m of ascent leads to the summit. The difficulties are sustained at V to VI and on very good compact granite, especially in the upper part. There are 11 pitches with the crux, a wall of VII, near the top of the 10th pitch. The 'Via Tarci Fazzini' is 400m: ED1, 5-7hr

61 **EAST RIDGE**

AD– A von Rydzewsky with C Klucker and E Rey, 19 June 1893

93

A classic outing best combined with an ascent of the Pta Sertori, preferably its S ridge. Although the technical difficulties are moderate, the situations are exhilarating with impressive views across the NE face. If the ledges used to bypass the first section of the ridge still contain snow, then the climb is considerably more tricky. See also photographs 95, 103

From the Gianetti hut follow Route 64 to the wafer-thin saddle between the Pta Sertori and the start of the E ridge (3hr). Bypass the first part of the crest by keeping to ledges on the N side (large blocks with strenuous pull-ups: III), returning to the ridge at the end of this ledge system via an easy dièdre. Almost immediately the ridge is interrupted by a steep smooth slab. Turn this on the S side via a ledge and regain the crest beyond. Follow a long and crenellated section to the summit (1hr). 4hr from the hut

Piz Badile South-East Face

The sunny southern walls are much shorter and more friendly in appearance than their austere northern counterparts. Nevertheless, there are some excellent routes to delight those based on the Italian side of the range. All routes on the wall can generally be climbed from very early in the season till mid-Oct and can be approached, in 1hr from the hut, via Route 64. Technically the most difficult line on this face climbs the small pillar situated at the R extremity. 'La Muchacha de las Bragas de Oro' has 8 pitches of free-climbing with moves of VII. Small and medium wires useful (c300m to the E ridge).

62 **VIA VERA**
TD– C Corti and C Gilardi, 26 Aug 1972. An ascent in winter conditions
95 was made by G Crimella, G Fabbrica, G Rusconi and G Villa,
21 19 Dec 1972

Above the huge block in the centre of the face, a rounded pillar rises almost directly to the summit. Although the technical difficulties are somewhat inhomogeneous, this fine line provides good climbing within easy reach of the Gianetti hut. There are a number of old pegs in place and it is felt that a determined party may well eliminate most of the aid. V+ and A0/A1: c350m, 6-7hr

63 **MOLTENI ROUTE**
D+ M Camporini and M Molteni, 16-17 Aug 1935.
95 Winter: D and G Fiorelli, 14-15 March 1956
21

This is undoubtedly one of the best climbs available from the Gianetti hut. It is at an accessible standard and many parties consider it to be equal, if not superior, to any other route of the same grade on the S side of the Bregaglia. Molteni created a number of worthwhile routes before his demise on the first ascent of the NE face, and this is often considered his finest contribution – linking the weakest points on the face by a splendid piece of route-finding. The climb starts in the middle of the face where two ramps slant up to the L. The crux is a delicate traverse with a fixed rope normally in place. Above, the line follows the crest of the pillar to the R of the normal route and is simply brilliant! V: 350m, 4-6hr. See also photograph 93

Punta Sertori 3195m

G Gugelloni and U Monti with B Sertori, 17 Sept 1900 (W tower). A Bonacossa and C Prochownick, 18 July 1913 (E tower)

A subsidiary peak of the Badile and rather indistinct when viewed from the Bondasca. From the S, however, it appears as a splendid granite tooth overlooking the Colle del Cengalo. The summit is formed by twin rock towers – that to the E being the higher. All the following routes are highly recommended and generally on magnificent rock, making the summit a worthwhile objective in its own right. Despite this accolade parties are strongly urged to continue their ascent to the summit of the Badile via its wonderful E ridge.

64 **SOUTH-WEST FACE**
IV– First ascent party
93

The normal route and a superb climb. The rock is excellent and there is a sensational wafer-thin crest on the saddle between the Punta and the start of the Badile's E ridge.

From the Gianetti hut head up to the W of Pt 2869m and reach the remnants of the tiny glacier that lie between the Badile and Sertori. From the top right-hand corner climb steep slabs to a vertical chimney, 20m high. Climb the chimney (III+/IV–) then zigzag up ledges to reach the razor-sharp crest (125m from the base of the wall). Follow the exposed crest to the foot of the final tower. Climb 3m up the vertical pillar directly in front (huge 'jugs'), then traverse across the SW face on a narrow ledge as far as a vertical chimney. Climb the chimney for 10m (IV–) then finish out L on easier ground to the top of the W Tower.

The highest point is a perpendicular granite tooth and looks most inaccessible! Descend easily to the gap below the tooth then climb down an S-shaped crack on the S face. Now move E to a rib and climb up it to a ledge which leads round onto the E face of the tooth. The last few moves are extremely airy and lead up the steep smooth wall of the E face to the minuscule summit (IV–). 3½hr from the hut

Descent: This is marginally different to the route taken in ascent and is described in detail for parties reaching the summit by either the S ridge or ENE pillar.

From the gap between the two towers go down the S ridge for 10m to a bunch of slings. Make a 20m rappel to a ledge and follow this around to the W. Reach the horizontal crest leading to the E ridge of the Badile, and after climbing along this for a short distance, reverse the normal route, zigzagging down ledges between steep slabs. The upper part of this descent is quite steep and needs care if at all icy. When above the final smooth wall make two 20m rappels to the tiny glacier and go down this to the hut.

65 **EAST-NORTH-EAST PILLAR**

VI G Molinato, M Pinardi and C Riva, 31 July 1932

IV+/A0

101

23

An impressively steep and exposed climb that should only be attempted when the large sloping ledges on the N wall are completely dry. When climbed completely free the roof on pitch 4 is far harder than anything else, but one or two moves of A0 bring the overall standard down to a uniform IV+ and provide some sensational climbing for a route of that standard.

Reach the foot of the pillar easily from the Colle del Cengalo and start on the R where a conspicuous chimney rises to the base of some huge polished slabs. The climb follows a series of cracks and dièdres almost directly to the gap between the two towers. 125m: 2hr

Parties well accustomed to the exposure will be able to make three airy rappels from below the final crack to the foot of the climb.

66 **SOUTH RIDGE**

IV D Contini and P Marimonti 12 Aug 1923. Winter: M Bisaccia,

93 E Peyronel and P Pozzi, 18 March 1956

24

This is undoubtedly one of the best climbs of its standard on the Italian side of the range. It is continuously interesting, the rock is excellent and the difficulties, although not great, are sustained at the grade. What's the catch? Well....this is a popular classic so don't expect to have the route to yourself!

Reach the foot of the ridge in 1hr from the Gianetti hut. The lowest point is a short steep buttress. Start on the R side where a large chimney falls from the grassy terrace at the top of this buttress. 370m:

Punta 2869m (Punta Enrichetta)

This isolated buttress lies to the S of the Badile and when viewed from the E strongly resembles a snail! It can be reached in 30min from the Gianetti hut and provides a number of short climbs that are suitable for a day of dubious weather or simply a relaxing afternoon. The top can easily be reached from the N (1 short rappel in descent). The obvious broad barrel-shaped buttress of the 'S ridge' provides nice slab climbing in the lower half and easier ground above, leading to the final tower. To the R of this the 'S wall' climbs up to the base of a dièdre; moves R to semi-layback a line of flakes, then reaches the huge grassy shoulder. Both routes climb the final tower 20m L of the crest via a dièdre (crux). They are both 200m in height and IV+

Colle del Cengalo c3048m

Probably first reached in 1866 by the first ascent party of the Cengalo. N-S Traverse: A Von Rydzewsky with M Barbaria and C Klucker, 9 July 1892. Winter: P Bernasconi, F Masciadari and V Meroni, 18 March 1957

The broad snowy saddle, rarely corniced, that lies between the Pta Sertori and the Pizzo Cengalo. The majority of parties visiting this col will be engaged in the normal route to the summit of the Cengalo. The S side is easy, but to the N a 400m high ice couloir drops towards the upper Bondasca. Traditionally a fine snow/ice climb, in recent years it has become increasingly difficult and dangerous.

67 **SOUTH SIDE**

RE/F
94 From the Gianetti hut walk along the Roma path for 10min and cross a stream, where a small cairn marks the start of a vague path going N over grass and boulder slopes. Keeping E of Pta Enrichetta (2869m), cross moraine or old snow and climb the rocky couloir to the col, which lies immediately NE of the Punta Sertori. 2hr

68
D–
101

NORTH SIDE

Entry to the couloir is barred by a huge double rimaye which in some years has defeated even the most determined parties. As the climb is serious and exposed to stone-fall, especially near the base, the lower half at least should be completed before dawn – when the first rays of sun strike the upper basin on the NE face of the Badile.

The couloir gives access to some of the great modern climbs on the Badile. Several parties have approached these via the Gianetti hut, down-climbing and rappelling the top section of the couloir. Although longer and more complicated this has definite advantages during high summer. Average angle 44° but steepening to 55° at the top. See also photographs 100, 10

Fr om the Sasc Fura hut cros s the C.olle Vial (Route H11) and reach the Cengalo glacier. This is badly crevassed and the best line of ascent normally keeps close to the walls of the Badile (stone-fall!). Reach the foot of the couloir in 2½hr. This point can also be gained from the Sciora hut in 2hr by using the same approach as that for the NW pillar of the Cengalo. If the glacier to the W of Pt 2087m is too chaotic it may be better to continue along the path towards the Colle Vial and join the approach from the Sasc Fura hut.

Overcome the rimaye – usually least problematical at its L extremity. Now climb the couloir, keeping close to the Cengalo in an attempt to avoid any stone-fall from the summit slopes of the Badile. 400m: 3-4hr with good névé

Pizzo Cengalo 3370m

D Freshfield and C Tucker with F Devouassoud, 25 July 1866. Winter: possibly G Fiorelli and client in 1910

The second highest peak in the Bregaglia and a mountain of massive proportions. The complex N face, over 1200m high, is the biggest in the range. Yet seen from the Upper Bondasca valley it is no match for the smooth and elegant walls of the neighbouring, but distinctly lower, Badile. It is only from the S that the mountain really dominates the scene. Its fine crests and stupendous S ridge are far superior to any other rock structure in the Val Porcellizzo. The view from the summit can be extensive, encompassing the Bernina, Italian plains, Valais and beyond. The many facets of this mountain have been well explored and few secrets remain. There are, however, a variety of established routes, some of which are now accepted to be amongst the very best in the Alps.

69 **WEST RIDGE**
PD First ascent party
96

The normal route and a superb mountaineering expedition that is both longer and more serious than that of the Badile. The summit is normally a huge snow dome, but in dry summers much of this can disappear leaving a vast boulder slope in the upper part of the S face. The route is not altogether obvious in poor visibility, and in common with many standard routes on the 'classic' peaks in the Alps, care should be exercised on several sections where the rock is quite shattered. When enjoying the magnificent view from the summit, spare a thought for the first ascent party who reached this point in an astonishing time of 4hr 40min from Bagni di Masino! See also photographs 93, 94

From the Gianetti hut reach the Colle del Cengalo via Route 67. Follow the ridge above on poor rock, turning the first section of the on the N side, to reach a small col above a couloir on the S face. In very snowy conditions it is possible to climb directly to the W ridge via this couloir but when dry it is rather loose and cannot be recommended. Continue up the ridge over large blocks to a cairn, where it is possible to traverse across the S face on a good ledge system underneath a prominent tower. Reach the gap beyond the tower and continue scrambling up the ridge above. After a short distance work out onto the S flank, ascending easy ground with and only returning to the ridge at the start of the snow dome. The steep boss is usually icy but the angle quickly eases and the crest is followed with no further difficulty to the summit. In very snowy seasons a large cornice can overhang the N face and parties should be well aware of this particular menace. c400m: moves of II, 3½hr from the hut

In descent most parties use the couloir below the small col described above, making a 20m rappel from a bunch of in-situ slings down the last steep step.

70 **SOUTH RIDGE DIRECT – VINCI ROUTE**
TD/ E Bernasconi, P Riva and A Vinci, 16 Aug 1939.)
TD+ Winter: M Bisaccia and P Pozzi, 7 Jan 1956
96
26
28

This brilliant route presents the most obvious challenge at the head of the Porcellizzo valley. It is a narrow fin of granite which is for the most part

of excellent quality. The crux pitches give a succession of precarious moves in a sensational position. Even the easier pitches hold memorable climbing. As a whole the route is technically much harder, though shorter and less committing, than the NW Pillar, and is thought by many to compare favourably with some of the best rock routes found in the Alps.

It is possible to climb the entire ridge from the base – a major undertaking that only a few parties complete. The main difficulties are found above the lower third of the ridge and can be easily reached by a chimney/couloir on the W flank. Hard sections were traditionally climbed with aid and are thus fairly well protected by in-situ pegs. However, flared and shallow cracks mean that a selection of Friends 1½-3 will prove most useful! The lower section makes a good climb in its own right and is described with a separate topo.

Approach as for the Colle del Cengalo, then work up R over moraine debris to reach the R side of the highest boulder-strewn terrace below the W face. Go L to the start of a chimney/couloir that slants up R to the crest (1hr from the hut). 450m to the main summit: VII–, 7½hr

An ascent of the entire ridge, climbed completely free, would require 12-13hr to the summit. 600m: TD+/ED1

Descent: On reaching the S summit (Pta Angela 3215m) there are two possiblities. The most straightforward solution is to continue easily up the W side of the ridge over large blocks to the snow dome (1½hr to main summit). In very dry conditions one can traverse across the boulder field below the dome and reach the W ridge. As this will require parties to carry mountaineering equipment, the preferred method is to descend by rappel. This is complicated and quite serious. From the S summit go down the ridge towards the main peak for 100m and reach a small saddle. Scramble down a slabby depression on the W face for c30m to some pegs. Rappel the slabby couloir below until it drops into a horrendous abyss. Now move L (S) along the central ledge system, which often holds snow, until a short diagonal rappel leads to ledges below the 'Black Dièdre'. Slightly lower down a long and gripping rappel leads to a stance behind a huge flake. Follow ledges S, descending slightly until close to the ridge, then go back N down an easy ramp to some lower ledges. From here two long rappels down steep walls lead to the ground, a little N of the start of the climb. All rappel anchors are in place but allow 3hr for the descent. Very recently a direct rappel line has been equipped alongside the horrendous abyss.

Pizzo Cengalo East Face

Although a number of climbs have been recorded, none have so far gained popularity. This circumstance is no doubt due, in part, to the lack of continuous lines on the face. The best offering comes from the talented Italian team responsible for recent hard free routes on the Badile.

71 INCA TRAIL

VI:A2/3 S Brambati, T Gianola and P Vitali, 13 Sept 1987.
94 Winter: P Crippa and M Rusconi, 3 Jan 1988

This climbs the prominent conical pillar in the upper part of the face. It lies above and to the L of the entrance to the couloir that leads to the gap between the E and main tops. A direct line up slabs and dièdres leads to the foot of the pillar, from where a succession of vertical cracks, lying just R of a huge chimney/dièdre, are climbed to the top. Either make a short rappel down the far side and continue easily to the upper section of the S ridge; or make 8 rappels down the line of ascent (fixed belay points). Sustained free climbing with two short interruptions of A2/3. c300m: 8hr

72 EAST RIDGE

AD– A Bonacossa and C Prochownik, 8 Aug 1920
94

To follow the entire frontier ridge of this peak gives a classic traverse. The best climbing lies in the upper section and can be reached by climbing the disgusting stone-swept couloir on the S face that leads to the gap between the E and main tops. However, it is highly recommended that an approach be made from the Colle dei Gemelli by crossing the E peak. On the easy sections shattered rock abounds and parties should keep as close to the crest as possible to maximise their enjoyment. The difficult pitches occur on sound granite, and this worthwhile expedition is still a popular objective from the Gianetti hut. See also photograph 106

Reach the Colle dei Gemelli in c2hr from the Gianetti hut, then follow the ridge to the top of the E peak (3308m: 1hr). Keep to the crest at first where the rock is sound. When it starts to become more shattered, slant up the S flank (moves of II). Go down 20m to the SE, then follow a series of easy ledges leading W to the col in front of the main peak (30min). The cracked ridge above gives delightful climbing on sound granite to the base of a slab. This is the crux and is overcome using some thin cracks (IV). A smooth and slender gangway slants up to the L. Climb it in an exposed position to easier ground (III+). Reach the ridge on the R and follow the crest, on generally firm rock, to the summit. 5½hr from the hut

Pizzo Cengalo North Face

A complex architecture of pillars and gullies give this enormous face a broken appearance when compared to the graceful walls of the neighbouring Badile. Ascents compare favourably, in both length and seriousness, to almost anything found in the Western Alps. Large areas of loose rock abound and in warm dry conditions stone-fall is a constant danger. After a heavy winter a huge cornice can decorate the upper part of the W ridge and threaten much of the face. There are now a dozen routes from which to choose – 6 by powerful Czech teams. More than half have been put up in winter to minimise objective dangers. Apart from the classic 1897 route and the popular NW Pillar, the others have received little more than a handful of ascents.

73 NORTH FACE DIRECT – KASPER PILLAR

ED1/2 H Kasper and F Koch, 6-7 Aug 1966. Winter: G Kronthaler and E Obojes, 28-29 Dec 1988

A demanding undertaking which forces a direct line up two successive pillars on the L side of the face, joining the Classic route above the ramp. Ideal conditions are rarely found. Plenty of snow and a hard frost will render the mixed climbing safe and enjoyable. Stone-fall from the upper walls will be minimal though a small risk of ice-fall from the cornice is always possible. The pillars are steep, hold little snow and are relatively sheltered from stone-fall; yet their orientation ensures that the cracks will remain icy after a period of bad weather. There are quite a number of old pegs in place. The best, though not the hardest climbing, is found on the lower pillar.

This is a worthy yet serious addition to the great mountaineering routes of the district. Only a fast party finding good conditions will avoid a bivouac.

Reach the foot of the couloir leading up to the Colle dei Gemelli in 1hr from the Sciora hut. Enter the couloir, then traverse R to a scree-covered ledge that leads to the crest of the pillar above its base. Climb the crest to a steep buttress. Avoid it by traversing the L flank until a steep chimney leads back to the crest. Continue up to a smooth section that resembles a steeper version of the famous

'Flat Iron'. The next pitch provides the crux of the first pillar. Starting just R of the L edge, make some thin moves up the wall working R then back L to a series of flakes. Climb these to a stance close to the edge (40m: V+). 15m higher avoid a steep section on the L then return to the crest and climb it directly to the top of the pillar.

Drop down the other side and slant R across a couloir (stone-fall possible) to the base of the second pillar. Climb up and R across a tricky slab to a stance. Reach a crack on the L and follow it for 15m before moving easily R to a dièdre. Climb it for 10m to a stance. Climb up a crack and continue over a small bulge on the R to a ledge. Make a few hard moves L to reach a wide crack and jam it strenuously for 10m. Move into the crack on the L and climb it to a chimney. This is a fight all the way to the capping chockstone where it is possible, and indeed necessary, to move L to another crack. Climb this crack and then make a traverse R across a huge slab to a chimney on the R side of the pillar. The difficulties, which so far have reached a maximum of VI and A0 (but would probably go free), now ease, and above the chimney the ridge is followed up to the L to join the Classic route at the top of the huge ice ramp (7-9hr). 1100m: 12-15hr to the summit

74 CLASSIC ROUTE

TD–/TD 105

Prince S Borghese with C Schnitzler and M Schocher, 29 June 1897. Winter: H Steinkotter and E Stiebritz, 29 Dec 1975 – 1 Jan 1976

Although snow cover was more consistent and more extensive a century ago, the first ascent of this serious mixed route was still an outstanding achievement for the era and one of the most underrated in the Alps. The party had to tunnel an enormous cornice and their timing was perfect; next day they were able to witness the entire 250m long section drop off the summit ridge and devastate the whole route! Subsequent ascents have confirmed this to be the finest mixed route in the Central Alps but opinions vary as to the best conditions needed for an attempt. A heavy covering of well-frozen snow will minimise stone-fall and allow rapid movement up the great ramp. Unfortunately the smooth slabs in the upper section then give hard and somewhat unprotected mixed climbing. Free from their mantle of snow and ice, these slabs are delightful and far from difficult, but dry conditions make the climbing of the lower section much less fine and greatly enhance the risk of stone-fall.

Winter climbing is not practised in this range to the same extent as the Mont Blanc Massif; to embark on this route during those months of

adversity is to accept a challenge as great as many to be found in the Alps. See also photograph 100

From the Sciora hut reverse route H11 towards the Colle Vial, as far as the big moraine that runs up to a steep little buttress, the base of which is marked by Pt 2087m. Using the scree-covered crest or the glacier to the R, reach the top of the moraine where it is possible to bivouac. Go up the snowfield to the L of the buttress and reach the foot of the face, where two huge couloirs separated by a conspicuous pillar split the first part of the wall (1½hr).

Climb up into the L couloir, then slant up R across smooth wet slabs that form a sort of ramp and reach the crest of the pillar after 60m via a short wide crack (IV). Continue traversing R for 70m across flakes and ledges (III+) and enter the parallel couloir. Climb this for 5 pitches to a point where it peters out below overhanging walls. Climb a ramp on the L to the crest of the pillar (poor rock and short sections of IV), arriving at a point where an easy scree-covered ledge runs up L. Follow this to the start of the great snow/ice ramp that splits the middle section of the face.

Climb the ramp for 500m to a shoulder on the N ridge (c2900m). By keeping close to the steep walls on the R, parties can utilize rock belays and convince themselves that they are reasonably sheltered from the stone-fall emanating from hanging gullies above. The angle is sustained at 50° and the climbing generally protectable without resorting to ice-screws. Above the shoulder a huge rounded ridge leads up for almost 500m to the summit. Slant L at first up a vast arena of easy ground to reach the foot of a conspicuous smooth slab split by a single crack. Avoid this on the R by an icy couloir and continue up the ridge, which if dry gives a pleasant succession of slabs with pitches of III and IV. If at all icy it will provide the technical crux of the climb. The final wall is 25m high (IV) and above this, in snowy seasons, a cornice may have to be tunnelled. 1200m; but more than 2000m of climbing: 10-12h

The initial parallel couloirs can be seriously exposed to stone-fall. The dividing pillar has been climbed direct in 6 long pitches (IV and V with a short section of VI) and would provide a safe alternative. This is the later start used by the Rusconi brothers for their 1971 route 'Attilio Piacco' which climbs the R side of the impressive pillar above, in a further 12 pitches (VI and A2/3). It then continues directly up ribs and slabs (IV/V with one pitch of VI and some tricky mixed ground) to reach the top of the NW pillar. 1300m: ED2

75 **RENATA ROSSI ROUTE**
ED3 M Klinovsky and S Silhan, 17-18 Feb 1989
105

An impressive piece of ice-climbing by this very accomplished Czech duo, that at the time of writing is not surprisingly unrepeated. The crux is gaining the hanging couloir, and as suitable conditions for an ascent are rare, the precise moment for making an attempt must be carefully chosen. The first ascent party found the climbing magnificent and whole-heartedly recommend the experience to aficionados of waterfall ice.

Follow the Classic route into the L-hand couloir, but instead of traversing R climb it direct to the ramp (70°-80°). Follow the ramp for 300m to a point where there is a huge white slab on the R with a prominent overhang on the L side. Slant up R and gain some exceptionally steep ice smears which lead, in five demanding pitches (80°-90°), to the base of the long icy funnel in the upper part of the face. A further sixteen pitches (c60°) are required to force an exit onto the W ridge a little short of the summit. 1200m: 15hr+

76 **NORTH-WEST PILLAR**
TD–/TD F Gaiser and B Lehmann, 15 July 1937. Winter: E and F Gugiatti, 23-26 Dec 1972
105
27

Commonly acknowledged to be one of the best climbs in the Bregaglia and rivalling anything of the same length and standard in the Western Alps. Climbed on the same day that Cassin was doing battle with the Badile, it enjoyed an over-inflated reputation for difficulty and has only recently gained the status of a popular classic. Nowadays it is one of the most desirable objectives in the Bondasca valley. Most of the ascent takes place in good jamming cracks and the angle is such that strenuous moves are rare. Due to the lack of an obvious line, especially on the barrel-shaped upper spur, and relatively little in-situ gear, it is not always easy to decide on the best route. Apparently easy options can entice parties rightwards off the pillar to dead ends. The initial climbing takes place on easy but extremely shattered rock. Above, the granite is perfect and the route completely sheltered from stone-fall.

This is a committing route with a wonderful 'high mountain ambience', and as there is no easy descent on this side of the peak all equipment must be carried over the top. One short axe per party and crampons will generally be necessary for the approach and the final snow crest.

Follow Route 74 to the top of the moraine, then work up the glacier W of Pt 2087m to the base of the pillar. Start on the R side, and if possible above the rimaye, at a shattered couloir that slants up to the L (2hr).

It is also possible to start from the Sasc Fura hut, which has the advantage that any equipment left in that vicinity can be collected the next day after returning over the Trubinasca Pass. Follow the path over the Colle Vial towards the Sciora and reach the W edge of the Vadrec dal Cengalo. Go up the glacier to the foot of the pillar (2-2½hr).

The pillar ends on the W ridge well below the summit: in good conditions it is possible to be off the mountain, via the normal route, in 1hr or less. 900m: 6-8hr

Colle dei Gemelli 3101m

First Traverse: A Von Rydzewsky with M Barbaria and C Klucker, 9 June 1892. Winter: R Compagnoni, V Meroni, G Noseda-Pedraglio and E Scarabelli, 12 March 1961

Lies between the Pizzi Gemelli and the Cengalo. The S side is easy but the N couloir is an impressive ice climb that is technically harder and probably more exposed to objective danger than the couloirs of the Badile or Cengalo.

77 **ITALIAN SIDE**

F
96

From the Gianetti hut follow the Roma path until directly below the S ridge of the Cengalo. Now work NE up the stony valley on the R side of this ridge and reach the tiny glacier at its head. Walk up this with absolutely no difficulty to the col. 2hr. See also photograph 94

78 **SWISS SIDE**

D+/TD–
106

Rarely climbed and only recommended very early in the season and after a cold night. The average angle is only 45°, but the exit slopes reach at least 55° and just below half-height there are normally one or two formidable rimayes. Their upper walls can be huge and incredibly steep, providing a crux that is far harder than anything else on the climb. The entrance to the couloir is reached from the Sciora hut by traversing around the foot of the NNW ridge of the Gemelli, then climbing upwards through a complex icefall. c700m: 5-7hr from the hut

Pizzi Gemelli (SE 3262m: NW 3223m)

A von Rydzewsky with M Barbaria and C Klucker, 9 June 1892

Twin summits with an impressive appearance when viewed from the Bondasca valley. Although the highest points are seldom visited these days, the mountain is climbed upon more often than almost any other in the cirque due to the continuing attraction of the magnificent 'Flat Iron' ridge. The smooth walls on the E flank may soon come under scrutiny from the modern 'Sport Climber'!

79 **SOUTH-WEST RIDGE OF SOUTH-EAST SUMMIT**
PD M Porta and Riva with G Fiorelli, 9 Oct 1904
96

The normal route from the Gianetti hut. See also photograph 94

Follow Route 77 towards the Colle dei Gemelli until N of a prominent tower on the SW ridge. Now climb a short snow/scree couloir to a small gap above the tower, and continue up the W side of the ridge (I to II) until it meets the sharp and almost-horizontal summit crest. Turn L and quickly reach the highest point. 3hr

It is also possible to reach the summit crest directly from the Passo di Bondo, by climbing the steep rocks above the apex of the snow/scree slope that lies to the SSE of the main summit. 1hr

The short and exposed traverse between the two summits is IV. The swiftest descent lies down a chimney on the SW face starting from the gap between the two summits.

80 **NORTH-EAST WALL**
TD Z Hofmannova, J Simon and J Skalda, 19-20 Aug 1980
29

A number of routes lie on this very steep white wall overlooking the upper Bondasca glacier. This sustained climb breaches the central section of the face, finishing directly to the SE summit. Compared with most other routes in the valley it is quite remote and defended by a complicated glacier approach. However, for those willing to take up the challenge, for at the time of writing it appears to be unrepeated, the first ascent party promises a worthwhile outing. The rock is generally smooth and sound, though some of the larger flakes may require the 'gentle touch'. In common with a number of routes put up by strong Czech teams during this period, some of the harder pitches may well turn out a trifle undergraded! Allow 2½hr for an approach from the Sciora hut and at least 4hr back from the summit. 400m: 10hr

81 NORTH-NORTH-WEST (FLAT IRON) RIDGE

TD–/V H Frei and J Weiss, 28-29 July 1935. Winter: A and G Giovanoli,
106 30 Dec 1975 – 1 Jan 1976
30

An outstanding creation which produced, at the time, the first grade VI in the Central Alps. The main difficulties lie in the initial 300m – below the conspicuous tower of the 'Flat Iron' (2680m) – and present a compelling challenge when seen from the Sciora. Above, the climbing is much easier and the rock generally rather poor. For this reason few parties these days continue past the Flat Iron, preferring to descend from the end of the difficulties by rappel. 2 bolts and a chain at 45-50m intervals allow a safe and rapid escape.

The lower ridge offers truly magnificent climbing on open slabs: mainly easy laybacking up a succession of flakes, interspersed with short sections of 'padding' on compact granite where the easiest line is not that obvious. Long considered one of the great Alpine classics it is almost as popular as any other route in the Bondasca cirque. In-situ peg protection is adequate so a standard rack should suffice. See also photograph 156

The line of approach to the ridge will depend on the state of the glacier. At present the best route from the Sciora hut follows the path to the Colle Vial (Route H11 in reverse). After crossing the first grassy moraine, contour across the next moraine to the glacier. Go straight up over ice and boulders (cairns), slanting L until level with a large terrace c100m above the toe of the ridge. Traverse 200m R across snow, and climb onto the terrace (II) where crampons etc can be left for the return (1-1½hr). 300m and 3-4hr for the Flat Iron From the terrace at the top of pitch 9 climb leftwards round the wall above, then follow an easy ledge line across the L side of the large tower (2860m) into the gap beyond (poor rock). Climb the ridge for a long way (III with a little IV) to a buttress. Surmount it directly (V–) on shaky rock, then continue over more pleasant ground to the junction with the N ridge at a small col, c50m below the NW summit. Either: Climb a vertical dièdre in the smooth walls above; move R; cross an overhang and reach the crest leading easily to the summit (V and A0). Or: Descend diagonally L for 60m on the NE face to a series of ledges. Follow these to a scree terrace then climb a loose dièdre to the gap between the two summits. From here the main top is IV and the NW summit III (3-4hr). As it is relatively easy to down-climb most of the top section of the ridge, parties completing the whole route will often descend the same way. 900m: 7-8hr

Passo di Bondo 3169m

First recorded visit: H Buxton, D Freshfield and F Tuckett with F Devouassoud, P Michel, J Walther and a porter, 8 July 1865 (W gap) – T Cox and F Gardiner with P Knubel and G Spechtenhauser, 17 Aug 1875 (true E gap): But almost certainly used by smugglers long before this time.

The rocky pass at the foot of the NW ridge of the Pizzo Ferro Occidentale. To the NW and on the far side of a conspicuous tower is the W pass. This is often easier to attain when approaching from the N. The pass provides the traditional link between the Porcellizzo and Bondasca valleys. When coming from the Gianetti hut the exact location is difficult to pin-point and has led to some confusion amongst many parties in the past. Just below the pass, on the Italian side, stands the tiny Ronconi bivouac hut.

At the time of writing the complex state of the Bondasca glacier and a steep loose rock wall on the S side, exposed by glacial recession, have deterred many parties. Nowadays, alpinists forced to descend on the Italian side of the range return to the Swiss side via the Trubinasca Pass.

82 **NORTH SIDE**

PD+

108

In dry years the Bondasca glacier becomes a tortuous maze of crevasses and its ascent can be quite time-consuming without a track to follow.

From the Sciora hut head S over grass and boulder slopes to the moraine on the L side of the glacier. Follow it onto the glacier just below Pt 2374m. Work up the L side then out into the middle. The final rimaye can prove troublesome, and above, the short slope up to the pass will often be icy. 4hr

83 **SOUTH SIDE**

PD–/PD

98

This is, in general, an easier and less serious proposition than the Bondasca side. See also photographs 94, 96

From the Gianetti hut follow the Roma path until beyond the base of the S ridge of the Cengalo. Now head up to the SW ridge of the Gemelli, passing the foot of this spur and slanting up R across a vast scree terrace that finally reaches the base of a vertical rock wall. Traverse R beneath this wall onto the steep icy glacier immediately W of the Ferro Occidentale. Reach the top of the glacier below a loose rock wall. Close to the col, which lies up to the R, stands a conspicuous granite gendarme. Start L of the fall-line and slant up a ledge system below the bivouac hut. Easier rock leads into the gap.

2½-3hr, allow 6hr for crossing the pass from hut to hut in either direction

Colle dell'Albigna 3160m

F Allievi with G and G Fiorelli, 27 Aug 1897, from E to W

The broad snowy saddle betwen the Cima della Bondasca and the Sciora Dadent. On the W side it is reached by a short deviation from Route 82 to the Passo di Bondo (PD+ and 4hr from the Sciora hut: PD and 3-3½hr from the Gianetti hut: F+ and 3½hr from the Molteni hut via the Passo del Ferro), and is often visited by parties climbing the normal route on the Cima della Bondasca, or the S ridge of the Dadent, from Switzerland. The E side is a somewhat different proposition and is rarely climbed.

84 **EAST SIDE**

D/D+

A very worthwhile ice climb with minimal objective danger during winter/spring or early summer. Mid-summer temperatures usually transform it into a disgusting rock wall! The most aesthetic line follows a zigzag couloir, and rock belays should be available for much of the climb. It is possible to avoid the steeper top section of the couloir by climbing the rocks of the Dadent (as on the first ascent). 350m: 3hr, 5½-6hr from the Albigna hut

Sciora Dadent (Dentro) 3275m

T Curtius and R Wiesner with C Klucker, 14 Aug 1888

The highest and most southerly peak in the Sciora chain but becoming increasingly neglected. The great W wall has acres of rock, much of it vertical and compact, but it is broken by huge slabby terraces. There is no continuity of line and no worthwhile free-climbs have so far been recorded. Routes on the E face are far more amenable but there is no easy descent into the Albigna valley.

85 **SOUTH-WEST FLANK**

PD+ First ascent party

108

The normal route from the Sciora hut. In good conditions it provides a commendable general mountaineering route and can offer worthwhile

ski-touring in the spring. However, in recent years the state of the Bondasca glacier has been most discouraging and ascents have become less common.

From the Sciora hut follow Route 82 towards the Passo di Bondo. Immediately R of the W face of the Dadent a snow/ice corridor slants up towards the summit. Climb it and near the top move out L onto the crest of a broken rock buttress. Scramble up this, and bearing L cross a snow slope onto the S ridge. Follow the crest, or easy ground on the W flank, to the summit. 4-5hr

If reaching the corridor looks impractical, continue further up the glacier and climb back up in a wide arc to reach the rocky buttress above the level of the corridor.

86 **SOUTH RIDGE**

PD+ A von Rydzewsky with M Barbaria and C Klucker, 17 July 1891

123

The original route avoids the main difficulties of the crest but still provides a nice climb from the Colle dell'Albigna. It can easily be combined with an ascent of the Cima della Bondasca.

From the Colle dell'Albigna follow the ridge N to the start of the serrated section. Climb down onto the E wall below the first tower and follow a ledge system for c30m to a shoulder. Cross it and take the second (N) of two couloirs that leads back up to the ridge. Now follow the crest (delightful climbing) until it is possible to move onto the W flank, where easy mixed ground leads to the summit. II: 1½hr

87 **SOUTH RIDGE DIRECT**

AD− N Rodio and C Steiner, 24 Sept 1909

A much improved version of the previous route. It climbs the first tower directly up the L side, and continues along the serrated crest where 2-3 rappels will be necessary. The climbing is continuously interesting, on very sound granite and becomes quite entertaining if the crest of the ridge is strictly adhered to all the way to the summit. III+: 2hr

88 **NORTH RIDGE**

AD− G Gugelloni with B Sertori, July 1901

123

A poor route where experience in moving together on loose ground is highly desirable. It is included because it forms an integral part of the classic traverse of the Sciora chain. It also provides a possible descent to the Albigna valley for parties completing one of the routes on the E face, but cannot be recommended.

From the Bocchetta dell'Ago (qv) drop down on the E side and work across ledges to reach the crest of the ridge where it is almost horizontal. This is the lowest point between the Ago and the Dadent (3105m). Follow the crest until it steepens in front of a large tower. Turn the tower on the L, and keeping below the crest on broken ground, follow the ridge all the way to the summit. III–: 2-3hr

In descent it is possible to slant L (looking out) down the walls below the saddle (3105m), and reach the normal approach to the Bocchetta dell'Ago.

89 **NORTH-WEST FACE**

TD H Burggasser, R Leiss and K Noe, 5 Sept 1934. Winter: R Chiappa

109 and G Maresi, 23-24 Dec 1972

An unusual route on this huge rocky wall, in that it can only be recommended when well iced! Late winter and spring will normally provide the best snow/ice conditions and a hard frost will eliminate stone-fall. For this reason it has rarely been climbed, but parties completing winter ascents have commented very favourably on the quality. On the second winter ascent, in 1989, the party found excellent névé and completed the route in 6½hr! Double this time would still be quite respectable, and the route remains a serious proposition. See also photographs 107, 108

From the Sciora hut reach the foot of the couloir that leads up to the lowest point on the ridge between the Ago and the Dadent (1hr). Climb the bed of the couloir to a rather poorly defined fork at about half-height. Climb up into the R fork, which is actually a huge slabby ramp. It must be well covered with good névé as the rock below is very smooth. In the upper section reach a rib on the R and follow it to an overhanging wall. 30m R is the base of a hanging couloir coming down from the summit. Reaching this is the crux of the climb and will involve difficult mixed climbing and possibly a tension traverse. Follow the couloir, which gradually eases in angle, for 200m to the summit. c700m: 12hr

Sciora Dadent East Face

This extensive and complex wall is largely unknown ground. The existing routes are long, of medium difficulty and lie in an unfrequented corner of the Albigna cirque. Approached in c2½hr from the hut they will appeal to those of a more exploratory nature. It is recommended that parties use the normal route (85) as the quickest and easiest means of descent.

90 **EAST PILLAR (NIGG ROUTE)**
D– N Grass and P Nigg, Oct 1967
123
35

Although few parties have repeated this route, all agree that it rivals any of the more established classics of the same length and standard found in the range. The quality of the rock is very good most of the time, but becomes a little friable on the easier ground below the top. The climb is quite varied and continuously interesting but the current enthusiasm for shorter, less committing and more accessible routes will probably maintain its unpopularity.

Start on the L side of the steep initial buttress and climb slabs on the R side of a wide couloir, that slants up to a gap behind a prominent tower on the crest of the pillar (IV+). Climb directly up an overhanging wall behind the gap to a good ledge (IV+). Follow the crest of the pillar on excellent rock for a pitch (IV), then move R along a ledge for 15m. Climb the dièdre above and continue more or less in the same line on the R side of the crest (III). Finally, easier broken ground leads to the summit ridge. 600m: 5-6hr

In 1986 a direct start was added via a series of chimneys and dièdres that begin at the same point as the NE pillar (IV to V+).

91 **NORTH-EAST PILLAR**
AD+/ D Erba, F Giacomelli, G Maresi, R Osio and R Rossi, 15 July 1979
D–
123
35

The R side of the face is more disjointed and has steeper sections separated by areas of broken ground. To the R of the E Pillar is a vague open couloir. The most obvious feature immediately R of this is the NE Pillar. Although it gives some interesting climbing, the line is escapable in several places.

Start at the lowest point on the face, in the prominent gully between the two pillars. As soon as possible reach the ridge on the R and continue more or less on the crest, climbing several towers near the top of the face. Reach the summit ridge c10min to the S of the highest point. 600m: 5hr

Ago di Sciora 3205m

A von Rydzewsky with C Klucker and E Rey, 4 June 1893

One of the most famous peaks in the Bregaglia with a culminating pinnacle – a sensational granite needle – that is the most eye-catching feature of the Sciora skyline. There is a variety of very worthwhile routes of different lengths and standard, but all finish with some impressively exposed climbing. Highly recommended is a N–S traverse; but whatever the route chosen, this beautiful spire should be on the list of every visiting alpinist. It is worth noting that parties based at the Allievi hut can reach the Ago by crossing the Zocca pass. In good snow conditions this is 1hr quicker than an approach from the Albigna dam.

92 **SOUTH FACE**
AD First ascent party
117
33

The normal route and an established classic. It is perhaps done less often these days due to the current preference for more easily accessible climbing. Although a little scrappy below the Bocchetta, the final 100m high pinnacle gives a brilliant climb on excellent granite. The route is steep, and in the upper section outrageously exposed for the grade. Most parties will descend this face and there are well-equipped rappel points. See also photographs 107, 108

From the Albigna hut follow Route 198 towards the Zocca pass, then move out onto the glacier and cross it to below the Pioda. Early in the season it is best to continue along the W side and climb a broad snowy couloir through the centre of the water-worn slabs to the rapidly diminishing Ago glacier. Later, this couloir becomes an unpleasant scree funnel, and it is less tedious to reach the glacier by climbing the crest of the moraine immediately S of Pt 2659m, below the E ridge of the Pioda. Work up the Ago glacier to the top L corner, where an obvious wet or icy gully rises up towards the Dadent (2½-3hr).

Start a little to the R of this gully and slant up R over easy ground for 35m to a short wall (if there is much stonefall in the gully it is possible to start further R and climb directly to the same point). Climb the wall (III) and then work up R to a huge slab. Traverse delicately across it (III), and continue to slant R up a series of ledges, separated by easy chimneys (poor rock), to the Bocchetta dell'Ago (c3100m: 1hr). The final pinnacle lies immediately above, and the route is described by topo (100m: IV–, 1-1½hr). 4½-5½hr from the hut

93 **SOUTH-EAST FACE – SCARABELLI ROUTE**
VI/A1 G Martinelli and E Scarabelli, 14-15 June 1974
117
32

The lower section of this route contains some superb pitches on excellent granite. Only the top half of pitch four still requires aid and all the

necessary pegs are in place. Unfortunately, broken ground in the middle of the route makes the climb somewhat inhomogeneous. It is possible to escape here, either R onto the N face or L onto the normal route, but doing so would involve missing the spectacular finish – a series of tremendous jamming-cracks on the vertical L edge of the N face. The start of the climb lies 20m up the couloir leading to the Forcola di Sciora, where a ledge leads horizontally L into the face. c270m: 6hr, 9hr from the Albigna hut

94
AD
33

NORTH FACE

A Bonacossa and C Prochownik, 18 July 1920

Probably the best route at this standard on the spire. Rising steeply above the Forcola di Sciora, the wall looks quite intimidating with no immediately obvious weakness leading to the summit. Whilst some of the easier climbing takes place on slightly dubious rock, the difficulties are located on excellent granite, suspended above an impressive void! By descending the S face, parties can complete an elegant little traverse; but a rappel descent back to the Forcola is also possible. IV: 120m, 1½hr

95
AD+
108

WEST FLANK

A von Rydzewsky with C Klucker and M Schocher, 9 July 1896

Arguably the easiest route from the Sciora hut, but only recommended when there is good névé in the couloir and on the upper snow-field. Although the technical difficulties are not high, this is a long climb where fitness, route finding experience and the ability to move well over 'classic' alpine mixed terrain will pay dividends. Unless snow conditions are very good, descending this route will be inadvisable and parties should be prepared to walk out via the Albigna valley. See also photograph 107

From the Sciora hut follow Route 100 into the Klucker couloir and climb it to a point where a large scree/snow shelf slants up to the R. Go up this shelf to a shoulder on the NW ridge of the Ago, above the first huge step (c2hr). On the R a narrow ledge leads around onto the W face. Go along this ledge a little way then move up to a steep chimney cutting through the walls above. Climb the chimney (III/III+ when dry; but often not!) to a hanging snowfield, and slant R across it to reach the main ridge at the second gap to the S of the summit. The first gap is the Bocchetta dell'Ago and can be reached directly, but at a much higher standard (2-2½hr). Descend easily on the Albigna side and follow a series of ledges, below a large tower on the ridge, to the Bocchetta. Follow Route 92 to the summit (1-1½hr). 800m: 5-6hr from the hut

96 **NORTH-WEST RIDGE**
AD+/D W Risch, 1 July 1923, avoiding the upper pitches.
109 Winter: D Chiappa, E Scarabelli and R Zocchi, 7-9 March 1971

A long interesting climb and a traditional middle-grade classic. Until fairly recently it enjoyed considerable popularity but is now being increasingly neglected due to the unpleasant nature of the Klucker couloir during most of the summer. The rock is generally good, though a few sections of easy ground will require the 'gentle' touch. This is a far finer route than the W flank, and if the easiest alternatives are taken is only slightly more difficult. See also photograph 107

From the Sciora hut follow Route 95 until above the chimney and then climb back L onto the ridge. Follow the crest in a superb position for 250m to the start of the final pinnacle, where the ridge steepens abruptly (III+; sound rock). Either work up R to reach the large horizontal ledge crossed on Route 92, and continue up this route to the summit. Or, starting on the R of the ridge, climb a vertical crack (30m: V). A little higher slant R up a gangway for 10m; climb another steep crack in a shallow dièdre and continue up the wall above (40m: V) to reach Route 92 just below the summit. 800m: 5-7hr

Direct Variation from the Shoulder: From the shoulder behind the first huge step in the ridge climb directly up the crest for 80m (V and V+). This is great climbing in a tremendous position and avoids the deviation onto the W face.

97 **NORTH-WEST RIDGE DIRECT**
TD H Kasper and F Stussi, 4 July 1969.
107 First winter ascent: F Dellatorre and A Giovanoli, 7-9 Jan 1993

This gives marvellous free climbing on continuously sound granite. The first step is climbed on the L side via a succession of cracks and flakes. Thereafter, all the direct variations to the NW ridge are used to reach the summit.

The beauty of this line is obvious. It has no objective danger and can be attempted at any time during the season, irrespective of the state of the couloir. However some of the cracks on the first step face N and should be allowed ample time to dry after a period of rain. There have been few ascents so parties should not expect to find much in-situ protection.

Reach the foot of the first step in 45min from the Sciora hut. On the

L side, quite close to the entrance to the Klucker couloir, a wide crack slants up to the L. Climb it (III) to a stance on a large block. Move R then climb directly up to a gangway. Follow it R then climb straight up to a large broken terrace (IV to V−).

The upper half of the step is somewhat steeper. Start at the first crack just R of the crest. Jam up it and move L into another crack on the wall L of the crest. Climb this and the smooth walls above, using a succession of cracks and flakes, until a short traverse R leads to the ridge (IV and V with several moves of V+). Two delightful pitches on the crest lead to the shoulder and the junction with Route 95/96 (360m: 5hr). 750m and 9hr to the summit

98 **SCIORA TRAVERSE**

D H Burggasser, H Hunziker, R Leist and K Noe, 18-19 Aug 1934, from Scioretta to Colle dell'Albigna

One of the finest outings of medium difficulty in the region is the traverse from the Dafora to the Ago. Although the technical difficulties are not high, nor indeed sustained, this is a lengthy expedition which should not be underrated. The possibilities of extending the traverse in either direction are obvious, but the meat of the route will be found in this section. Nowadays, relatively few attempts are made on this classic alpine ridge traverse, and although access is much easier and safer from the Albigna side, most parties still seem to start from the Sciora hut.

From the Albigna hut follow the normal route (107) to the summit of the Dafora. Now reverse the Pioda-Dafora traverse, rappelling the steep slabs on the SE face of the Dafora. Descend Route 103 on the Pioda and then climb the N face of the Ago (Route 94), descending the S face (Route 92) to the Albigna glacier. 9hr to the top of the Ago: 12hr round trip from the Albigna hut. From the Sciora hut it is possible to first climb the Scioretta and continue the traverse over the Dadent to the Ronconi bivouac. This will take a long day. D+

The Grand Traverse from the Colle della Scioretta to the summit of the Badile was first completed by D Erba, R Magni and B Rusconi, 28-29 July 1979. TD+

Forcola di Sciora c3080m

A von Rydzewsky with M Barbaria and C Klucker, 11 June 1892, from W to E. Winter: G Balestrini, G Colonna, T Jakel and F Longhi, 8 Jan 1967, from W to E

A deep and dramatic notch between the steep walls of the Ago and the Pioda. The E side is a fairly short snow couloir. Early in the season it is straightforward, but later it may become icy with a slight risk of stone-fall. The W side is one of the longest snow/ice couloirs in the district. Even in good conditions stone-fall is a constant threat and it is strongly recommended that an ascent from this side is completed shortly after dawn. Parties will have to be prepared to move together or solo. By mid-summer the ice has generally disappeared, leaving a thoroughly dangerous and unattractive rubble shoot.

99 **EAST SIDE**

PD A von Rydzewsky with M Barbaria and C Klucker, 19 June 1896

117

This is normally used as a means of access to the Ago and Pioda. It also provides a relatively sure descent.

From the Albigna hut follow Route 92 to the foot of the Ago (3hr). The couloir runs up to the R of the S face of the Ago and is climbed for 150m, finishing over broken ground to the Forcola. 3½-4½hr from the hut. In descent there are rappel slings from time to time alongside the couloir, on the rocks of the Pioda.

100 **WEST SIDE – KLUCKER COULOIR**

AD+

108

A serious proposition that is rarely in condition these days during the main climbing season.

When there is plenty of good névé in the couloir it is possible to make a direct entry. However it is usually better to follow Route 104 and reach the small saddle behind the first step on the NW ridge of the Pioda. From here, traverse easily R into the couloir above its narrow lower section (1-1½hr). Now climb directly up the bed of the couloir; the average angle is 46° but the exit is steeper. 600m: 4hr from the hut

Punta Pioda di Sciora 3238m

A von Rydzewsky with M Barbaria and C Klucker, 12 July 1891. Winter: W Risch and client, 8 March 1929

The most dominant peak in the Sciora chain due to the distinctive summit cowl and falling from it, the huge, smooth NW wall – one of the steepest in the Bregaglia. To the R of this wall are the slender smooth slabs, or 'Piodessa' in the local dialect, of the NW ridge. The continued popularity of this ridge makes the Pioda probably the most frequented of the major Sciora peaks.

101 **SOUTH FACE AND EAST RIDGE**

PD+ First ascent party

123

A very worthwhile normal route which is objectively safe and provides the most straightforward ascent to the summit. However, with sound rappel anchors in place, the S face (Route 103) generally offers the most rapid and convenient descent.

From the Albigna hut follow Route 92 and reach the foot of the couloir leading up to the Forcola di Sciora (3hr). Climb the couloir for a short distance, then make a rising traverse across the SE face of the Pioda on a prominent gangway. This gangway gives easy scrambling and leads to a conspicuous shoulder on the E ridge. On the R side of this ridge is a large sloping scree (snow) basin. Climb up the ridge a short distance, then follow a ledge system 50m above the basin to a projecting block. Climb the smooth wall above, then continue more easily up slabs to a higher shoulder on the E ridge. Work R on broken ground to a succession of steep slabs leading up to the main ridge a little way N of the summit (2½hr). c300m: III (not sustained), 5½hr from the hut

102 **EAST RIDGE DIRECT**

IV R Steinmann and E Vanis, 19 July 1969

Although short this is a particularly fine piece of climbing that follows the crest more or less directly above the shoulder.

From the ledge where the ordinary route traverses R for 50m, climb straight up the steep ridge above on small but positive holds (40m: III+). Now move onto the L side of the crest and weave up this to a stance in a niche (IV). Climb a 50m chimney (III) and slant R on a gangway to the upper shoulder and a junction with the normal route. One last pitch (III−), followed by easy climbing, leads to the summit.

A hard direct start has been added on the 250m 'SE buttress' below the first shoulder.

103 **SOUTH FACE**

AD− A Rydzewsky with M Barbaria and C Klucker, 8 June 1897 but the route described was climbed by R Staub with C Klucker, 16 Aug 1919

More difficult than the normal route and only really ascended when traversing from the Ago. If sound fixed anchors can be easily located and the couloir below the Forcola is in reasonable condition, then this face provides the most rapid descent route from the summit. However, parties who wish to return to the Sciora hut via the Cacciabella pass have to make a lengthy reascent from the Albigna glacier, and for these climbers Route 106 is recommended.

From the Forcola di Sciora make a descending traverse R for 30m and reach the base of a large steep slab. Climb up and across this to a rib of smooth slabby rock. It is possible to climb the crest of this rib to its junction with the E ridge (III+), but it is easier to slant up L just before reaching the rib and climb a series of steep walls. These lead into a scree-couloir. Scramble up the couloir, which slants up to the R and makes an exit onto the upper shoulder of the E ridge. c150m: III, 1½-2hr

104 **NORTH-WEST RIDGE**
D+/ E Bozzoli-Parasacchi and V Bramani, 16 Aug 1935.
TD− Winter: P Maccarinelli and A Valsecchi, 25-26 Jan 1974
109
22

This stupendous line of sweeping slabs has long been considered a great mountaineering classic. However, many parties now feel that its reputation is somewhat overrated. The climbing is not intrinsically that brilliant and the difficulties are neither hard nor sustained. A somewhat disappointing feature of the route occurs at the 'black overhang', where one is forced to traverse into, and then climb, the L edge of the Klucker couloir. Although not difficult, the traverse is often wet and the route will be more enjoyable if left for a very dry spell. On the positive side the route has length, a certain amount of commitment and despite the proximity of the Sciora hut, a splendid feeling of isolation. The best descent, and the one most generally adopted these days, goes down into the Albigna valley so all equipment (including a short axe and possibly crampons) must be carried on the climb. Due to its accessible standard and pleasant well-pegged friction slabs (a standard rack is quite sufficient), this route remains the most popular on the W side of the Sciora chain.

From the Sciora hut walk up to the SE passing close to Pt 2394m. Reach the moraine slopes on the L of the toe of the ridge (2374m). Continue with care up the snow, ice and rubble, moving R over very loose but easy ground to the small gap behind the first step in the NW ridge, c150m above the toe (1-1½hr). Once on the crest the rock is sound and the route-finding straightforward. Belay points marked on the topo are quite close to each other, and it will often be possible with a 50m rope to run two consecutive pitches together. The R-hand finish provides a faster exit. It leads to a small notch on the SW ridge and a rappel descent to the Forcola di Sciora. c700m: 6hr

105 **NORTH-WEST FACE**
ED2 M Belica and J Obuch, 20-21 Aug 1980
108
25

This formidable wall falls in one unbroken sweep of near-vertical granite for 550m. In common with many of the long-standing problems on the major peaks in the range, it finally succumbed to a Czechoslovakian team. The climb starts up a line of chimneys and dièdres on the L side of a vague spur which protrudes from the lower R side of the wall (reached in just over 1hr from the hut). It is probably unrepeated at the time of writing and prospective parties should take a comprehensive rack of aid gear for the sustained and exposed climbing on the lower wall. Above, the obvious ramp beneath the NW ridge has more amenable slabs which can be a little loose in places. 550m: c15hr

Those with vision will note the outstanding possibilities for future super-routes on the walls to the L!

106 **PIODA-DAFORA TRAVERSE**
AD J Heller and G Miescher, 29 July 1909
123

A splendid connecting ridge with considerable exposure, high above the W wall of the Dafora. Traditionally it formed part of the standard descent for parties wishing to return to the Sciora hut. Today, even if the couloir on the W side of the Scioretta is impractical, it still provides the quickest means of reaching the Cacciabella pass (via a descent of the Dafora's normal route and a traverse of the boulder fields below the Innominata ridge). III+

From the summit of the Pioda follow the main ridge N for a short distance until it is possible to climb down to a narrow ledge on the E side. This ledge slants down to the S. Follow it to a second lower ledge system that runs horizontally back N below the summit to the deep notch in front of the Dafora. Now climb the S ridge of the Dafora. Scramble easily at first over a small pyramid-shaped tower, then continue with increasing difficulty up the ridge to a second tower. Turn this on the R and climb the chimney behind it to reach the rocks of the steep SE face above. These give some delightful and exposed climbing on small holds to the foresummit. Follow the main ridge easily to the highest point. 1½-2hr. In the reverse direction the traverse is easier (III–) as it is possible to rappel the difficult pitches on the SE face of the Dafora.

If the summit of the Dafora is to be omitted, then from the deep notch slant down outward-sloping ledges on the E face to reach the E ridge (II+ when dry). Now reverse the normal route (107) to the scree slopes below the Scioretta.

Sciora Dafora (Fuori) 3169m

A von Rydzewsky with M Barbaria and C Klucker, 6 July 1892

The most northerly of the 'Big Four' in the Sciora chain. It has two summits – the N being fractionally higher. It is not a very distinguished peak on the E side, but from the Sciora hut the huge blade of the NW ridge is an impressive sight and one of the most obvious challenges in the upper Bondasca. The climbs on this side of the peak tend to be hard and sometimes frighteningly loose. The net result is that the mountain is being increasingly neglected in favour of the shorter and less committing climbing readily available on neighbouring peaks.

107 **EAST RIDGE**
PD+ H Rutter and A Zuan, 20 Aug 1915, although probably descended
123 in 1907

This is the normal route from the Albigna hut and provides the safest, easiest and arguably the most enjoyable means of reaching the summit. The upper section of the ridge gives some particularly good climbing on sound granite.

From the Albigna hut follow Route 198 towards the Zocca pass until at c2400m and nearly opposite the E ridge of the Dafora. Now cross the glacier and work up the N side of the ridge over scree and, early in the season, snow. Keep to the L of the fall-line of the nasty couloir below the Colle della Scioretta. When almost level with the base of the couloir slant up L over slabby rocks and short walls to the crest of the ridge. Keeping more or less on the crest, follow the ridge, which provides some excellent climbing (III then II), to its junction with the NE ridge. Continue up this (still good climbing) to the summit. 5hr. In the upper section it is possible to traverse up and across the E face to the summit but this is not nearly so pleasant.

The ridge can also be climbed from its base. There are some nice slab pitches of III and IV but the climbing is not sustained and tends to be a little grassy (W Risch and party, 1928).

108 **NORTH-EAST RIDGE FROM SCIORA HUT**
AD First ascent party

This can hardly be recommended these days as it involves an ascent of the W side of the Colle della Scioretta. An easy ledge system leads across from the col to the upper part of the E ridge and from here to the summit is II. Alternatively (and better!), climb directly up the ridge above the col (III+, exposed!). 5hr from the hut

109 **WEST FACE DIRECT**
TD+ H Kasper, G Marini and T Nardella, 28 June – 2 July 1970.
107 Winter: T Fullin and M Indergand, 28 December 1971

This black-streaked vertical wall, rising above a slabby base, has at least three routes. The photograph shows the best attempt so far to create a direct line to the summit. The existing routes all succumbed to massive amounts of aid, and on this particular route all the original bolts and pegs remain in place. After the initial slabs (III) most of the pitches are A2 with only a little difficult free climbing and it should be possible to reach the top in 12hr. This is a climb that will appeal to the traditional 'Big Wall Men' or those with visionary aspirations to create a super free-route! 450m: V+ and A2. See also photograph 109

110 **NORTH-WEST RIDGE – FUORIKANTE**
TD K Simon and W Weippert, 17 Sept 1933. However, the route in its
108 existing form was first climbed by H Kasper, F Koch and G Zryd
31 26 June 1965. Winter: E Neeracher and P Nigg, 8-10 March 1969

Once a great classic and good enough to be one of only four routes in the Bregaglia included in the book 'In Extremen Fels' (the best rock climbs in the Alps). Since 1933 two large rock falls have devastated the upper ridge and it now bears little resemblence to the original route. Although a magnificent line with considerable exposure, it is no longer considered the best that this area has to offer, and with the tendency towards shorter and less committing climbs, where sacs do not have to be carried over the summit, it has become increasingly neglected. VI and A1/2

From the Sciora hut walk up the boulder fields to the SE and reach the remnants of a glacier that lies below the W face. Slant L towards the ridge over easy slabs (II+) and reach a prominent col above the

2nd tower (1½hr). From here, slant L again to reach a huge ramp that cuts up across the face above the direct start.

When climbing the upper ridge it is generally better to avoid the R side where possible, as it is here that the rock is at its worst! 550m: 8½hr from the hut. From the start of the ramp there is a four-pitch direct variation that reaches the top of the huge dièdre climbed on the Direct Start. A tricky traverse up to the R, followed by a compact slab (V+) leads to a magnificent corner. Climb this (IV+) and the easy couloir above to join the Direct Route.

111 **DIRECT START**

VI F Gadola and U Sagesser, 23 July 1969: though climbed as far as the

109 huge dièdre by H Amacher and Sagesser on 10 July 1969

31 *Fairly sustained slabby climbing of excellent quality and on very sound granite. There have been few ascents, and due to its aspect the rock may be a little lichenous in parts. This route could easily be climbed as a separate entity; descent from the pillar-top or from the huge ramp is quite straightforward. Reach the start in 45min-1hr from the hut. 300m: 4hr*

Colle della Scioretta c3000m

A narrow col that is not marked on the map but lies betwen the Dafora and the Scioretta. Unless cold and snowy conditions prevail, both sides are loose, dangerous and exposed to stonefall. Nowadays, it is only used in descent by parties completing routes on the Dafora or Pioda, and wishing to return to the Sciora hut. Even so, more parties are now opting for the longer but safer escape into the Albigna valley. The W side generally retains some snow right through the season and an axe/crampons are probably essential. It is serious for thc grade! Easier alternatives are available for a descent into the Albigna valley, so the E side is not described.

112 **WEST SIDE**

AD A von Rydzewsky with M Barbaria and C Klucker, 6 July 1892

108 From the col go down the main couloir for c150m until it is possible to traverse R across a shoulder and into a subsidiary couloir to the N. Slant down this, taking the broader R fork, and descend steep snow slopes to the scree below. Old rappel anchors occur at regular intervals throughout most of this descent. c350m: 1½hr. See also photograph 109

Scioretta c3046m

H Rutter with A Zuan, 13 Aug 1919

A pleasant little rock peak, though seldom ascended these days.

113 **NORTH RIDGE**
AD First ascent party
109

The ridge can be approached from the Albigna hut via a scree/snow couloir that leads to the main col, S of the Torre Innominata. The slabby crest is now followed to the summit, with the crux occurring on a small tower about half-way up. 4½hr from the hut: III

114 **SOUTH RIDGE**
AD H Frei, M Gabriel, R Honegger and H Rutter, 7 July 1936

This provides a short steep climb on first-rate rock for those arriving at the Colle della Scioretta with the time and inclination to do something else! 40min from the col: III

Innominata Peaks

The jagged crest between the Scioretta and the Cacciabella Pass. On the E side the summits are undistinguished, rising only a short height above the interminable boulder fields that are slowly sliding into the Albigna valley. To the W however, a fine series of pillars offers very worthwhile rock climbs. The main summit is marked on the map as Pt 2930m.

115 **WEST RIDGE OF TORRE INNOMINATA**
IV+ An SAC party guided by U Gantenbein, 8 Aug 1949
110
39

The Torre Innominata (2909m) is not shown on the map but lies just S of the main summit. The W ridge is a brillant little classic on excellent granite and quite popular. An easy start leads to sustained climbing in a fine position on the steep upper half of the pillar.

From the Sciora hut go a short way up the path towards the Cacciabella Pass (blue/white paint flashes), then head E into the boulder-strewn cirque below the Scioretta. Work up L (traces of a path) and reach the foot of the gully on the L side of the ridge (1hr). 300m: 3½hr for the route

Descent: This is the problem! Most parties use the couloir immediately N of the ridge to return to the base of the climb. It is steep, loose and nasty! Most of the snow has disappeared by mid-summer, making the passage quite dangerous, especially when other parties are above. Although longer, it is safer to follow Route 118 across the main summit until it is possible to scramble down to the boulder fields on the Albigna side. Stumble across these to the S Cacciabella Pass and descend to the Sciora.

116 WEST RIDGE OF MAIN SUMMIT – JACQUELINE ROUTE

IV+ J Paul with G Zryd, 26 July 1965

110

37

The main summit 2930m (first ascent: A Bonacossa and R Giacometti, 13 June 1913) is fractionally higher than the N summit, to which it is connected by a sharp and almost horizontal crest. The W ridge is more of a steep wall in its upper section, with an abrupt exit onto the jagged crest at a point somewhat N of the summit. From here a 30m descent over easy slabs leads to the boulder fields on the Albigna side and a walk back over the Cacciabella pass.

This climb is not as fine as the Torre but provides a short and worthwhile alternative when the latter is crowded. The 'raison d'être' is two excellent middle pitches, which look most impressive for their grade when seen on the approach!

From the Sciora hut two approaches are possible. Both will take 1½-2hr.
(a): Follow the path towards the Cacciabella pass. At c2500m leave it and head S, scrambling up to the crest of a broad spur on the R. Go up the middle of the spur over boulders and short rock steps (traces of a path). Near the top slant R on scree ledges to reach a small shoulder below the steep headwall overlooking the W ridge of the Torre.
(b): From the base of the W ridge of the Torre move L and take the uppermost couloir (deep and easy) that leads towards the crest of the ridge on the L. When the couloir becomes steeper, work L (W) on grass and boulder slopes, crossing the heads of other couloirs to reach the ridge. One is now alongside the boulder slopes mentioned in the previous description. Either join this route or, better, continue up the crest of the ridge to the shoulder (I/II).

Once the easy ramp is reached towards the top of the climb, several variations are possible. The most logical climbs steep broken rock on the R, and care must be exercised when handling large blocks and flakes. 200m: 2hr

117 **WEST RIDGE OF NORTH SUMMIT**

III

110

This is a delightful little climb if the crest is adhered to throughout. In common with many routes of this standard, care should be taken with large flakes.

Approach as for the previous route, then slant up L on scree-covered ledges to the base of this well-defined ridge. 4-5 pitches lead to the summit and the rock is best on the crest. It is possible to avoid much of the difficulty by moving onto the R flank, but this is not so pleasant and the rock is loose. 200m: 1½hr

118 **TRAVERSE OF INNOMINATA RIDGE**

III

A useful finish to any of the routes described above. It is highly recommended, quite popular and a good excercise in 'moving together' along an exposed granite crest.

From the small col just N of the Torre slant R up the steep face above (3 pitches; III). Exit onto the Albigna side a little below the summit ridge. Climb up easily to the ridge and continue over the main summit and along the crest (I and II) to the N summit. Descend the ridge for 100m into a notch. This is the False Cacciabella Pass; easily reached from the Albigna side but with a steep, narrow and disgustingly loose couloir to the W. Some people descend this (3 rappels of 20m in the upper section) but it can only be recommended to those parties wishing to simulate full military battle conditions! Instead, continue along the ridge and climb over the apex of a superb tower resembling a house roof. Go down steeply on the far side for 20m to the S Cacciabella Pass. 1½-2hr

Cacciabella Passes – N Pass 2870m: S Pass 2897m

The S Cacciabella pass provides the easiest and most convenient crossing point between the Albigna and Bondasca valleys. It has been used by local hunters for centuries. Perhaps the most popular excursion in this sector of the range is to take the téléphérique to the Albigna dam and walk over the pass to Bondo. This is often lengthened into a two-day expedition by first crossing the Casnil pass having spent a night in the Forno hut. The track is very clearly waymarked on both sides, with cairns and conspicuous blue-on-white paint flashes. The N pass is harder, looser and rarely crossed these days. It is neither waymarked nor described in this book.

119 **EAST SIDE OF SOUTH PASS**

PE

113

From the inspector's house on the W side of the dam the path is signposted. It contours the grassy slopes above the lake and rises gently, crossing a stream and further on passing below the NE pillar of the Frachiccio. It then crosses a deep ravine and finally reaches the grassy slopes below the Cacciabella ridge. Working SW up these slopes, the path arrives at a small saddle in the E ridge of the Piz Eravedar at c2800m. After a short distance on the ridge the path moves on to the S side and climbs steadily up a narrow rocky gully to a small notch – the S pass. 2½-3hr from the dam, 3-3½hr from the Albigna hut

120 **WEST SIDE OF SOUTH PASS**

RE

110

Described in descent as most parties, especially climbers, will be travelling in this direction. By Aug, when all the snow has disappeared, the upper section can become quite serious due to loose blocks inevitably dislodged by parties above.

From the notch follow the path steeply down to the R for a short distance (handrail sometimes in place), then continue more easily in a series of zigzags until it is possible to take to the broad snow or (loose) rock couloir on the L. Follow this down to the lower snowfield and finally the moraine. The well-marked trail continues at first W, then SW down through boulders and scree to reach the grassy slopes above the Sciora hut. 1½hr, 2hr in ascent

Piz Eravedar 2934m

A spiky peaklet between the two Cacciabella passes.

121 **TRAVERSE**

IV– S ridge: F Baumann and H Rutter with C Klucker, 27 June 1925

A short excursion on good granite with far too long an approach to justify doing it on its own!

From the S Cacciabella pass climb straight up the very steep slabs of the S ridge, finishing up cracks to the summit (IV–). Continue down the R side of the N ridge on broken rock (II) to the N pass. 30min

Cacciabella Peaks – N 2980m: S 2969.4m

Almost certainly by hunters, but the first recorded ascents were made by A von Rydzewsky with M Barbaria, A Dandrea and C Klucker, 5 June (S peak) and 28 June (N peak) 1897

The traverse of these two peaks, from N to S, is a highly recommended outing for its length and standard. It can be done with equal ease from either valley, but over the years has become a classic excursion from the Sciora hut. Climbs with short and easy approaches are now very much in vogue, and rising standards in rock climbing have led to these peaks becoming less popular than in the past. The long and tedious approach over boulder slopes could be far more pleasant early in the season, when ample snow cover allows rapid progress. The only disadvantage at this time would be the need to carry an axe and crampons on the climb.

However, do not be deterred! The N peak is one of the best viewpoints in the range, with an extensive panorama over the Val Bregaglia and nearly all the peaks in the Albigna and Bondasca valleys. It is worth climbing for this reason alone.

122 NORMAL ROUTE TO NORTH PEAK

RE+
113

A straightforward though somewhat tedious approach to the Forcola Cacciabella N (2920m), followed by a short and pleasant scramble up the S ridge.

From the Sciora hut walk up the well-marked path towards the Cacciabella Pass. After c20mins it slants L across the hillside and eventually turns uphill, climbing through large boulder fields. This point is just below the base of the (W) ridge coming down from the Innominata Main summit. Leave the path and strike off L, trying not to gain too much height (quite easy!). Work around the L side of a hollow and across grassy slopes. If you are lucky you may stumble across vague paths, but in the end you will have to work up appalling boulder slopes and reach the entrance to the couloir which leads up to the gap between the two peaks. Go up this couloir over blocks and scree. Near the top cross a rounded spur on the L into a narrow subsidiary gully that leads to the L end of the Forcola. This is easier and safer than following the main couloir directly. Turn L and scramble easily up the ridge for 20mins (I+!) to the summit. c3hr

From the Albigna dam follow the path towards the Cacciabella pass, and when directly below the Forcola go straight up a broad and very easy scree couloir to the gap. 2½hr

123
II
110

TRAVERSE OF SOUTH PEAK

From the Forcola the N ridge of the S peak is II. Scramble up the ridge, and at the top either climb the fine slab directly to the summit, or avoid it by taking the easier but more broken ground on the Albigna side (20min). Scramble easily down the S ridge to the Forcola Cacciabella S (2881m: I/II–: 10-15min). Boulder slopes on the Albigna side reach this point and it is merely a matter of a tortuous stumble down to the path. On the Sciora side a broad and much steeper gully must be descended before the boulder slopes are reached. 1½hr to the dam and a little more to the Sciora hut; say 2hr from the Forcola Cacciabella N. See also photograph 113

124
III
110
34

NORTH-WEST RIDGE OF NORTH PEAK

W Risch, 1928

A short and entertaining climb with a fair degree of exposure. The ridge starts above a shoulder, where there is a huge drop to the L and dramatic views of Al Gal and Vicosoprano. The initial section is loose but thereafter the climb is generally on quite good rock. The well-known fourth pitch is a fine sharp crest, that either succumbs to a semi hand-traverse or for the more timid a long and painful 'à cheval'. 250m: 2-3hr for the ridge, 4-5hr to the summit from the Sciora hut

125
IV–
113

NORTH-EAST RIDGE OF NORTH PEAK

A Zurcher with W Risch, 25 Aug 1922. The ridge had been descended two months previously by Rutter and Klucker

An excellent little route that is best combined with an ascent, or traverse, of the Frachiccio. The short couloir leading onto the ridge is rather loose and parties should keep open a watchful eye for stone-fall.

From the Albigna dam follow the path towards the Cacciabella pass until SE of the summit of Piz Frachiccio. Now work up boulder slopes, and climb an easy couloir to the first col S of this summit. Above the col the NE ridge rises in a succession of gendarmes. Climb up the ridge and turn the first gendarme on the L via some steep slabs. Regain the crest and continue to a deep notch. Make a 20m rappel into the gap and climb out the other side, keeping on the crest as far as a prominent gendarme.

Turn it on the L via a wide crack (crux!) and continue easily up to the summit. 100m: 1hr, 3hr from the dam

Piz Frachiccio 2905m

N Rodio and K Steiner, 25 Sept 1909

Routes to the main summit are seldom climbed, but the peak is well-known for its fantastic N pillar which terminates the NE ridge above the Albigna dam. There are now a number of demanding routes, latterly squeezed into the cracks and corners of the sombre NW face. Although these see few repetitions, the classic Kasper route is one of the most popular hard climbs in the range.

126 **SOUTH-WEST RIDGE**
III First ascent party
113

See Route 125. Above the col the ridge is very short but gives a pleasant climb on excellent granite. Unfortunately the approach couloir is rather loose. 20min: 2½hr from the dam

127 **EAST RIDGE**
III A Zurcker with W Risch, 28 July 1923
113

A long, though worthwhile expedition for those wanting a bit of solitude. If time allows, parties are highly recommended to continue to the summit of the Cacciabella via the NE ridge.

Reach the foot of the ridge in 45min from the dam. Move round onto the S side and climb up to the ridge. Follow the crest, which gives a succession of fine pitches over slabs and flakes on generally sound granite (II and III). Higher, the angle eases and whilst the crest becomes a little sharper and more crenellated, it is hardly more than exposed scrambling. 400m: 3-3½hr

128 **SOGNADORO**
VI/A0 F Giacomelli and R Rossi, 11 Oct 1985
113
36 *A much finer finish to a route first climbed in 1980. It starts c130m L of the Kasper route, at smooth slabs below some yellow overhangs. There is some particularly attractive free climbing with considerable exposure above the steep grassy terrace. The latter can also be reached by three unpleasant pitches up a loose and vegetated ramp to the L. The route has seen little traffic, and apart from the lower crux section (VII+ free; originally A1), there is little in-situ gear. 250m: 4-5hr*

129 **KASPER PILLAR**
VII A Cajori, H Kasper, F Koch and G Zryd, 6 Oct 1963.
113 Winter: A Giovanoli and S Negrini 28-29 Feb 1980
38 *Simply a 'must' for climbers operating at this standard as it contains*

some of the best pitches in the Albigna valley. The first ascent heralded a new level of difficulty in the valley, when it was graded ED V+/VI and A2. It has now evolved into a classic free climb and has gained considerable popularity. Plenty of pegs and bolts ensure that the difficulties are very well protected and can be climbed entirely at A0! Take a standard rack and a lot of quick-draws. Only a little aid is needed to bring the standard down to a uniform V+. There is some brilliant and varied climbing, from delicate friction moves to strenuous laybacks and a fine airy crest to finish. The direct start is particularly recommended.

Now for the disadvantages! Some pitches lie on the N side of the pillar, and being a little lichenous can be slow to dry. The climb is not sustained and is broken at one-third height by a big sloping grassy terrace, from which it is possible to escape (or indeed join the route: 111). This does, however, make it a suitable choice when the weather is uncertain. The start is reached in 30min from the dam.

The terraces can also be reached via the start of 'Wasserpulver'. The top section of this route (V−) takes the middle of the slabs above and is not recommended. 250m: 5hr. See also photograph 112

130 **DIEDRO SENSA SOLE**
VII M and S Negrini, 2 Aug 1987
112
40

The sombre N face of the pillar is somewhat shorter. There are a number of prominent lines – all are steep and generally give good crack climbing. This particular climb takes the R wall of the huge arcing dièdre that lies directly below the final exposed pitches of the Kasper route. Although it could be reached via the easy ledge systems followed on Route 131, a direct entry provides the hard technical crux. Start directly below the dièdre at a huge block. c200m: 5hr. See also photograph 115

131 **MAIDEN MAIDEN**
VI+ P Braithwaite and P Nunn, Aug 1981
115
40

Starting above and R of the previous route is a clean cut vertical R-facing corner. The route traverses into the face via an easy ledge system and then reaches the corner from the R. The climbing is very worthwhile, sustained and with good natural protection. In common with other routes on this wall it is a rather sunless outing at most times of the day, yet the rock seems fairly free of lichen. c180m: 3-4hr. See also photograph 115

132 **MAFIA DELLA GLENCOE**
VII P Braithwaite, R Carrington and P Nunn, Aug 1981
112
40

This recommended route weaves an intricate line up the steep slabs to the R of the descent gully. There is a variety of interesting and generally well-protected climbing, with a crux that involves a delicate traverse up and across a hanging slab below the leftward-slanting overlap. Above the fourth pitch the difficulties ease considerably. After reaching the ridge (close to Pt 2624m), climb down the crest for a short distance to reach the top of the descent gully. 160-180m: 3-4hr

Al Gal (Gallo) 2774m

N Rodio and K Steiner, 25 Sept 1909

This sharp rock pyramid is well-seen from the main Bregaglia valley, where the eye is caught by the superb arrow-like line of the NW pillar. It was named at the turn of the century due to the resemblance of its summit crest to that of a cockerel. In Aug 1923 the overhanging 'beak' parted company with its parent mass and the new highpoint, which has survived to this day (!), was ascended by Gyger and Risch the following month. Further rockfalls in the 1970s substantially altered the structure of the classic NW pillar and it can, unfortunately, no longer be recommended.

133 **NORTH-EAST RIDGE**
IV First ascent party
113
48

The classic outing is to traverse the peak, starting with an ascent of this ridge. Highly recommended though short. Combined with a traverse of the Vergine it gives the most entertaining climb of its genre in the valley, is on excellent rock and can be completed in a day from the valley using the téléphérique. The first pitch is the traditional crux, and although a slightly easier and better-protected alternative exists round to the R, most parties climb it! See also photograph 114

From the dam follow the path to the Passo Val della Neve. Continue along the path which keeps close below the E face of the Roda, then go up across scree and boulders (the remnants of the Frachiccio glacier) until directly below the summit (2 large cairns). Scramble up R through steep broken ground (traces of a path) to a shoulder at the foot of the ridge (1½hr).

The summit block, though not quite as tricky as the crux, is a bold effort. By throwing the rope over the upper section of the R edge of the slab some leaders can convince themselves that a certain degree of protection has been arranged! 100m: 1-1½hr

134 **SOUTH RIDGE**
IV– L Bray, E Mann and W Standring with J George, 22 July 1930

Usually taken in descent to complete the classic traverse. Easy scrambling down the crest leads to a steepish slab with rappel slings in place. In ascent it is necessary to move L from the col at the foot of the ridge and climb a dièdre on the W face. Blocks and a chimney lead to the ridge. Follow this to the summit block. c70m: 45min

135 **NORTH-WEST COULOIR**
TD+ M Ballerini, F Castelnuovo and G Rusconi, 30 Dec 1982

For those able to visit the region during the early part of the year, the deep gash to the R of the NW pillar offers one of the most demanding ice-climbs in the area. To successfully overcome the crux – a thin ice smear only 30-40cm wide that forms in the back of a narrow dièdre at half-height (100m: 80°) – a substantial build-up is needed and this favours the months of March to May. In these conditions a good frost should eliminate any stone-fall. The approach over the Passo Val della Neve takes 1½-2hr in summer, but could be hard going and prone to avalanche in heavy snow. A good selection of rock pegs is recommended. 500m: 6-8hr

La Vergine 2708m

A Albertini, L Binaghi and G Brogi, 7 Sept 1913

A squat turretted rock tower which is sandwiched between the Roda and Al Gal. It is a popular summit, very often combined with Al Gal, and easily possible in a day from the main valley using the téléphérique.

136 **TRAVERSE**
IV+
114
48

A classic alpine ridge with a succession of towers and several entertaining rappels. Highly recommended to any party visiting the Albigna valley. Continue over Al Gal to complete a superb mini-expedition on excellent granite.

Approach via the Passo Val della Neve and reach the col between the Roda and the Vergine (1-1½hr from the dam). Early in the season, when the boulder slopes are still covered with snow, the climb will have a nice 'alpine' feel. 2-2½hr for the traverse.

From the final col it is only 30m of scrambling up to the start of the Al Gal ridge. Otherwise, slant down L on a well-defined but loose track to large cairns on the boulder slopes below.

Roda Val della Neve 2626m

Likely to have been climbed before the first recorded ascent of C Prochownik, 29 June 1912

A rather unattractive peak when viewed from the Albigna. A long, broad and rather grassy summit ridge rises only a short height above the boulder slopes. The E walls (at present untouched) could offer some 2-3 pitch climbs on steep granite, but the peak is rarely climbed by the normal routes on this side. In contrast the stupendous NE face falls almost 600m and is a real eye-catcher from Vicosoprano. Viewed from this distance it appears as a huge blank slabby wall on which it is hard to believe that 5 routes have been created, 2 of which are only of moderate difficulty!

137 SOUTH-EAST FACE

II

116

There is little to say about this grassy scramble, except that it offers the easiest route of ascent to, and descent from, the summit. It was probably first climbed by hunters 2 centuries ago.

From the dam follow the good path up the grassy slopes S of the Spazzacaldeira to the Passo Val della Neve (30min). Continue up alongside the E face until directly below the main summit. Walk on for another 5 min until the walls above relent and a small track goes up into an open grassy gully that slants up the face from L to R. Climb this gully, negotiating several rocky steps that appear rather too infrequently amongst the vegetation. Reach a boulder terrace below the summit ridge and scramble steeply up to the highest point (30min). c120m: c1½hr from the dam

138 SOUTH RIDGE

III

A Sommer, 3 Aug 1924

A short ascent from the col at the foot of the Vergine. It is much steeper, more exposed and altogether more interesting than the normal route.

Climb the crest until, at about half-height, it is necessary to traverse out onto the W face via a narrow ledge. Continue in the same direction, and when directly below the summit climb straight up a sort of chimney. At the top slant L up a series of cracks and dièdres to reach the ridge a little short of the summit. c100m: 1hr

139 **NORTH RIDGE**
III– First ascent party
114

Climb almost directly from the Passo Val della Neve. Two short pitches interspersed with grassy ledges give the only difficulty. Thereafter, a long and not unpleasant scramble along the broad ridge leads to the summit. 250m: 2hr

Roda Val della Neve North-West Face

Although quickly reached from the dam by crossing the Passo Val della Neve, this austere wall feels rather remote. Some of the longest climbs in the area are to be found here, and as an alternative venue it provides a complete contrast to the popular short routes in the Albigna valley. The rock is generally compact and firm granite. However, due to its orientation and low altitude, parts of the wall are covered in lichen and climbing should be postponed until the rock has had ample time to dry. The routes described are well-worthwhile for those wishing a little more commitment in a quieter corner of the range. From the Passo the foot of the face can be reached in 30min by descending the steep scree (snow in early season) couloir, keeping to a loose track on the R side.

140 **JACK CANALI ROUTE**
D A Bozzi, J Canali and R Merendi, 26 July 1959
114
42

The classic route, following a ramp/depression leftwards across the face to an exit onto the N ridge. The climbing is surprisingly easy and particularly fine in the upper section. Low down, a steep dièdre provides the crux, and being far harder than anything else makes the route a little unbalanced. Fortunately, it can be easily aided – don't be lured L into what appears to be an easier crack-line! The start of the climb lies roughly at the lowest point on the face and is marked with a spot of red paint. 600m: 5hr

141 **GUFI ROUTE**
D+ F Giacomelli and R Rossi, 15 July 1978
114
42

The start of this route appears to be quite hard, loose and often very

damp. It is best to use the Canali route, breaking out R after pitch 5. Although not a good as the Canali, this is still a fine climb, taking the L side of a prominent pillar in the centre of the face. 600m: 6hr

142 **NIEDERMANN ROUTE**
TD P Frei, U Hurlimann, E Naf and M Niedermann, 26-27 July 1975.
114 Winter: G Alberti and S Negrini, 7-9 Feb 1989
42

The best line on the wall taking the stupendous L-facing corner to the R of the Canali route. The climbing is both sustained and demanding but there are many in-situ pegs although it can be done completely free at VII. Take a full set of wires and 8-10 quick-draws. After reaching the crest of the WNW ridge, 250m of III/IV leads in 2-2½hr to the summit. However, from the end of pitch 7 it is possible to descend by rappel, at first down the upper crack-line and then via the Canali. 600m: 8-9hr

Further R is a similar impressive dièdre taken by the 1978 Czech route (largely A1/2 or VIII−). This is very mossy and generally wet. R again, the front face of the huge pear-shaped buttress is taken by the 1968 Nigg route. The start is marked with red paint: it is climbed less often than the Niedermann and with more resort to aid (VIII−, all free).

Spazzacaldeira 2487m

Possibly L Held, 18 Aug 1876 and probably climbed in winter before the first recorded ascent in Jan 1958

Standing directly above the entrance to the Albigna valley and commanding sensational views over the Val Bregaglia, this lowly mountain mass is well-known to tourists and climbers alike. N of the main summit lies the surreal rock-spire of the 'Fiamma' – a 25m blade that is perhaps the most famous and certainly the most photographed piece of granite in the range. The ascent is a 'must' for any visiting rock climber.

The SE wall, overlooking the téléphérique terminus, remained largely untouched until the late seventies. With the arrival of 'arrampacata sportiva', this steep 300m high wall has been well developed to produce some of the best rock climbing in the range.

143 **SOUTH SIDE**
RE/II−
116

The normal route. It is the easiest way to approach the Fiamma and the usual descent from the main summit.

From the téléphérique terminus (c2100m) reach the observation house on the W side of the dam wall (2165m: 10min). Start walking along the gravel track to the NW but very soon cut up L and follow a path through the boulders above. Pass just L of the largest and most prominent block, close to which it is possible to bivouac. The path is now more clearly defined and zigzags steeply up the grassy spur towards a col just S of the peak. At two-thirds height it enters a grassy gully on the R. Follow this (one or two intrusions of rock merit II−) to a small notch just before the summit. Climb up L over slabs and blocks to the highest point and the best views of the Fiamma. The latter can be reached directly by a careful scramble across broken ledges. c390m: 1½hr, 45min in descent

144 **FIAMMA**
V/V+ H Hurlimann and P Wieland, 8 Aug 1936
111
43

This is displayed on posters and postcards in every village as the 'motif' of the Bregaglia. Despite this publicity the ascent is certainly not an anticlimax. It is an excellent pitch – the epitome of the layman's idea of climbing – and leads to a summit where the apparent instability often gives unnecessary (?) cause for alarm. See also photograph 116

Directly below the Fiamma on the E side is a grassy bay (see Route 153). From here climb the gully above, then work up L and finally back R to reach the small col S of the blade (II/III−). Climb it largely on the E face – a sustained pitch with interesting balance moves and a delicate crux at half-height (above a bolt). Return is made by an awkward diagonal rappel, so it is easier to lower-off and top-rope the second.

145 **DENTE**
VI/VI+ H Rutter and P Wieland, 21 Aug 1944
111
43

The rather more solid and stable(?)-looking structure to the N of the Fiamma. The summit overhangs the NW face of the mountain and is thus more exposed than its neighbour, giving alarming views into the Val Bregaglia and a check as to whether your tent is still standing on the Vicosoprano campsite! The final pitch, an unrelenting thin crack on the E face, is climbed on finger-locks and laybacks. It is very well adorned with pegs and bolts and could be climbed at IV/V and A0. However, a

Friend 2 is useful to 'bridge the gap' at two-thirds height. 70m

Spazzacaldeira South-East Wall

Ease of access, superb quality climbing and an atmosphere akin to a big crag rather than an alpine route, has made this probably the most popular venue in the Bregaglia. It is possible to climb here early in the year, when snow makes the higher peaks impracticable. Huge unbroken sweeps of steep granite are interspersed with grassy areas which the routes avoid. The modern classics provide sustained and varied climbing. Double bolt belays, often with rappel chain, are common, and although the difficult moves are normally well-protected by pegs/bolts, there are still several bold sections. Every party, whatever their ambitions, should aim to complete at least one route on the face and sample the delights of the airy summit pinnacles.

146 **LENI ROUTE – ERWIN KILCHOR START**
VI/VI+ E Frei, E Kilchor and S Negrini, 1981
116
41

This truly modern classic is highly recommended. The last 2 pitches were originally climbed by Jori Bardill and party via the scruffy chimneys to the R. It was left to one of the more prolific climbers in the area to create what is now one of the best and most popular routes on the wall. 6 pitches on splendid granite lead to the top of the 'Plattenturm' where most parties will descend the gully on the far side. There are bolt belays (with chains on the first 3) and good in-situ protection, so only a few Hexes and medium wires are needed. The start, a short blocky chimney, is marked with red paint. The crux, on pitch 2, could be quite hard for short climbers. c140m: 3hr

The steep compact slabs to the R of pitch 4 form the crux of 'Tirami-su', a modern test-piece put up by the indomitable Giacomelli-Rossi partnership (VII+)

147 **NORTH-EAST RIDGE**
IV/IV+ A Sommer, 7 Sept 1928
118
43

The classic route for reaching the summit pinnacles. It is a delightful mountaineering excursion at an accessible standard, making it one of the most popular routes in the valley. Lovers of solitude will either have to climb out of season or simply grit their teeth! The granite is generally excellent, though on some of the easier pitches there are a few hollow flakes.

The foot of the route is a quick 10min dash from the téléphérique terminus. After the initial grassy scramble, the fine arête R of a deep chimney/couloir is climbed to the ridge. Cross back over the top of the chimney on blocks, and pass through a gap in the ridge onto the N side. Slant R on easy ledges below sheer walls for one pitch, then climb a steep crack with plenty of pegs to easier ground. Slant up L to the crest, and keeping as near to it as possible, climb up (particularly fine and exposed) to the tower at the junction with the N ridge. Follow this to the summit. 300m: 3hr, 4½-5hr if the Fiamma and Dente are included

148 NIGG ROUTE

V+/VI− P Nigg and L Proyer, 18 Sept 1967

116

43

The NE ridge can be climbed directly via this 3 pitch variant which is highly recommended. The position on the narrow crest is superb and the difficulties are well-protected by in-situ pegs. A fine variety of techniques are needed before reaching the overhanging crux – the last few moves to rejoin the classic route. 300m: 4hr to the summit

149 FELICI ROUTE

VI H Furrer and R Ruch, 2 Aug 1982

118

43

Another modern classic providing varied and interesting climbing of high quality on the L side of the Pillar. The crux, protected by a single bolt, is a bold friction traverse across a quartz vein. To those with an imaginative mind the large flake on pitch 4 will seem decidedly hollow! Whilst not essential, a couple of large Friends/Hexes will certainly reduce the fall potential on the wider cracks. The start, at the base of an easy ramp, is marked in red paint. From the top of the pillar either rappel the chimney on the L and descend a steep grassy rake to the roofed control point, or carry on . . . 170m: 3-5hr. See also photograph 116

150 SECOND PILLAR

VI+ F Giacomelli, C Pedroni, R Rossi and D Scari, 11 June 1978

118

43

The continuation of the previous route climbs the barrel-shaped buttress above. The crux occurs after slanting L past the small tree and is one hard move over a roof. From the top of the buttress, drop down 10m to the blocks at the top of pitch 4 on the NE ridge. There is a good rappel anchor at this point. 1-1½hr. See also photograph 116

Those who now choose to continue to the summit via the Nigg route will have completed the 'Mosaico' – a combination of routes that gives the longest and most sustained outing on the peak. 350m: 6-8hr

151 **NASI-GORENG**
VI/VI+ R Bosch and H Furrer, 20 June 1982
118
45

A continuously steep and sustained climb, which is considered by several local activists to give the best route on the face. It pursues a direct line up a succession of cracks on the R side of the huge deep dièdre mid-way along the wall. Widely-spaced bolts protect sections of compact granite and encourage some bold run-outs. However, this is essentially a crack climb and can be well protected if large Friends/Hexes are carried for the 20m of fist-jamming on pitch 2. See also photograph 116

The start lies on a small rounded pillar to the R of the line of the huge dièdre. Above pitch 7 either climb round the final buttress on easy ground to the N ridge, or descend the steep grassy bay to the top of the Felici route and rappel the chimneys on the S side (least recommended), or climb the top buttress – the initial slab is thin, poorly protected and can be rather lichenous. 220m: 4-5hr

152 **STEINFRESSER**
VII– T Muller and M Scheel, 9 Aug 1978
118
45

Although not sustained this was the first grade VII to be created on the Swiss side of the range. Wonderful granite gives superb and very varied climbing with little in-situ gear. A Hex 11 will prove useful. See also photograph 116

Start at the R side of the face (red paint mark), below a large pillar with a tree on top. This point can be reached via the concrete road and a path below the cliff in c20min from the téléphérique. From the top, either rappel the route or descend the W side of the N ridge – steep and wonderfully vegetated (30min). 170m: 5hr

The awesome compact walls L of this route have been well bolted to give 4 very sustained pitches (Via da Capo: VIII–).

Spazzacaldeira continued

153 **NORTH RIDGE**
IV
118

Rarely climbed for its own sake but often used, in part, by teams completing routes on the SE wall. There is little actual climbing but this is more than compensated for by the scenery and the superb position.

Follow the concrete road to the base of the NE ridge, then descend to the N and follow a track below the foot of the face. At its end a grassy chimney leads up to the base of the giant bastion that terminates the N ridge. Drop down 10m on the far side and traverse under a huge, smooth and overhanging dièdre. A little further on, climb back up to the crest via a succession of short dièdres – 3 pitches: III and IV (these can actually be avoided further to the W by scree and vegetable ledges).

The crest is now easy walking and scrambling until it meets the NE ridge, where a small tower blocks progress. The tower can be turned on the R, but it is better to climb it and make a 6m rappel on the far side. Traverse along a blocky terrace on the E side of the crest, over a little col and into the grassy bay below the Fiamma. The path continues S to reach the small col on the normal route, just SE of the summit. 300m: 3hr

Cima Scingino 2502m

The most prominent buttress on the SW ridge of the Cima del Cavalcorte. The impressive S pillar overlooking Bagni gives two 400m heavily bolt-protected routes on excellent knobbly compact granite. Both are reached by crossing the ridge S of Alpe Sione and descending SE to the foot of the face (3½hr from Bagni). 'Chisi Ferma é Perdito' (T Fazzani, S Gianola and N Riva, 4 July 1988) has unavoidable moves of VII+/VIII– and 'Delta Minox' (same team, 4 Sept 1988) VIII/VIII+

Cima del Cavalcorte 2763m

F Lurani with G and G Fiorelli, 8 Aug 1882 but possibly before this by local hunters

Although of modest altitude, this superb watchtower is highly conspicuous from the valleys of the southern Bregaglia. The S and E faces are, unquestionably, some of the most dramatic in the range. The peak is regularly visited due to the relative ease with which it can be climbed from the valley and the splendid panorama from the summit. The established classic is the E pillar, but a number of high quality modern routes have been added to the E face.

154 WEST FACE

RE/II First ascent party

97 *The normal route. Very straightforward and not particularly interesting unless the final rib is climbed throughout.*

From Bagni, walk up the Val Porcellizzo on the path that leads to the Gianetti hut. Take the R fork and follow it, via Casera Sione (2015m), to Alpe Sione (2½-3hr). An indistinct track now continues E towards the head of the valley and ends at the foot of a grassy ridge. Go up this ridge and the rocky rib above, until a terrace leads up and R to broken ground. Scramble up this to the summit. 4½hr from Bagni; 2½hr in descent

The rib can be climbed throughout and provides a far more entertaining variant. The last 120m are II

The 400m high S face is reached from the Bocchetto del Cavalcorto (qv) by descending 60m in a gully overlooking the Val di Bagni and traversing up and across a system of grassy ledges (short sections of III to V). An almost direct line up the centre of the face was climbed by Bianchi/Nardella/Robecchi in 1971 (VI and A3 with some dubious rock). Further L is the aptly named 'Mello's Wilderness' (Milani/Panzeri, 1990: VII+ with a little aid).

155 EAST PILLAR

TD– P Bernasconi, M Bignami and V Meroni, 2 Aug 1953

99

47 *A first-class rock climb in the traditional mould. It follows a line of chimneys and cracks on the R flank of the pillar and is steep, strenuous and highly recommended! Most of the original aid remains in place and the difficult sections are short and very well protected (the moves of VI could be bypassed at A0). The approach via the Ferro valley feels wild, and on the route, which generally lies out of sight and sound of the main valley, this sense of isolation is maintained.*

From the Mello valley follow Route H13 towards the Molteni bivouac. After 2hr the deserted shepherds' huts at 1958m are reached. These are always open and the second building can be used as an overnight shelter. Now head SW across stony ground and reach the base of a scree couloir that slants up L to a small col at the foot of the E pillar – the Bocchetto del Cavalcorto (2411m: 4hr from the road). Above, easy grassy slabs (III) lead into the huge chimney/couloir that lies immediately R of the pillar. 350m: 4-5hr

Descent: For all routes on the E face, the most convenient means of descent is to make 6-7 rappels down the huge chimney/couloir (in ascent: L Binaghi and P Tarca, 21 July 1929. D-IV+).

South-East Pillar

The superb prow to the R of the chimney/couloir is as sharp as a ship's bow. It was originally ascended in 1963 by a line of cracks on the L flank which succumbed to a mixture of free and artificial climbing. This route has rarely been repeated and has been superseded by the excellent free climb described below.

156 **MATTINO DOPO**
TD+ E and N Mailander, date unknown
99
46

A fairly sustained route following a series of cracks and slabs on the L side of the pillar. The hard sections are generally traversing movements on compact slabs, and there are c20 in-situ protection points including 3 bolts. Although there are some very fine pitches, the meat of the route is quite short and the top section of the pillar still remains to be climbed. Take a good selection of medium and large Hexes/Friends.

From the Bocchetto del Cavelcorto, climb the initial slabs to the base of the descent couloir. Climb more easy slabs (III) on the R side of the couloir to reach the foot of the very steep pillar, where a fine crack marks the start of the route. 350m: 6hr

157 **EAST FACE – CERCANDO I CEKI**
TD M Colombo and G Riva, 30 June 1985
99
46

This takes the very prominent series of dièdres and cracks to the R of the SE pillar. Individual pitches are quite sustained at the grade and can be well protected if a comprehensive rack is carried; but there is little, if any, in-situ gear. The approach uses the series of grass terraces that slants across the E face from the Bocchetto. The start lies to the L of the enormous detached flake, and the first two pitches climb slabs directly to the R-hand end of another large terrace c80m above. A direct entry can be made via the slabs below the terraces. However, this adds 100m of rather vegetated climbing and cannot really be recommended. 330m: 5-6hr

To the R lies 'Fast Trip', a rather contrived line which moves up to, and then inside, the huge flake. Above, it climbs the difficult slabs and walls alongside the slanting dièdres of the previous route, before finishing up the obvious large steps and cracks on the R (G Camallini, G Manca and M Marzorati, 13 Aug 1988. 330m: ED1, excellent granite).

Monte Sione 2815m

The topographical name applied to two summits – Pta Moraschini (the highest point) and Pta Bertani (2803m), which are separated by the Passo Sione (2686m). The name translates as 'Whirlwind Peak'.

Punta Moraschini

K Abraham with G Fiorelli, 27 July 1907 by the SW flank

A striking summit, with a short but imposing N ridge that has been climbed on the E side (IV) and a conspicuous rounded pillar on the NW face.

158 **PILLAR OF THE POLAR WIND**
TD– F Madonna, G Merizzi and G Miotti, 7 July 1979
97
51

Christened by the first ascent party who, at the height of the summer, found that the peak really did live up to its name! The pillar is impressively smooth when seen from the Gianetti hut, but on closer inspection is much more reasonable than this distant view would suggest. The climbing is not at all strenuous and although it has still received relatively few ascents, this is considered to be one of the better outings in the region. The sun does not strike the walls until the afternoon, and in common with other climbs on N faces at medium altitude, some of the rock can be a little lichenous. Allow ample time for the route to dry thoroughly. All the pitches can be well protected if a full rack, with a predominance of small wires, is taken.

The approach couloir, which is generally scree by mid-summer, can be reached from the Gianetti hut in c2hr. Follow the Roma path and keep traversing below Pt 2301m before ascending steeply to the foot of the pillar. An approach is equally possible from a comfortable bivouac near the shepherds' huts of Casera Zoccone or direct from Bagni in 3½hr. A huge band of yellow overhangs prevents a direct entry and the route traverses in above these from the prominent chimney/couloir on the R. 300m to the top of the pillar: 5hr

Descent: The normal route to the summit is a long and tedious scramble over grassy slopes and vegetated rock on the SW face. It finishes along the upper section of the SE ridge, which it joins some distance below the top. As the peak receives little traffic this line could prove tricky to locate in descent. Alternatively, from the top of the pillar the first ascent party rappelled the couloir on the R (S). This leads, via the ledges on pitch 2, to the base of the climb (slight risk of stone-fall). Prudent parties will carry extra equipment (nuts and slings) to reinforce the in-situ anchors (mostly pegs).

Punta Bertani

G and R Bertolini with E Fiorelli, Aug 1908

Easily reached from the Gianetti hut. The rock on the W face is lichenous and the climbs here are a little disappointing. However, the smooth walls overlooking the Ferro valley have recently been scrutinised and two very worthwhile routes have been discovered.

159 **NORMAL ROUTE**
II First ascent party
97

Unremarkable!

From either the Gianetti hut, or the chalets at 1849m in the Val Porcellizzo, reach the long scree couloir that leads up to the Passo Sione (see Route 158). Just below the pass a short couloir followed by a series of grassy ledges leads up and across the SW face to the summit. 1hr from the pass, 3½hr from the hut

A more sporting alternative is to follow the crest of the S Ridge (III).

160 **NORTH-WEST SPUR**
III E Fasana, 4 Sept 1914
97

A somewhat impressive line when seen from the Gianetti hut. In fact the climbing is quite straightforward and the route appears to see very little traffic. The initial triangular pillar is avoided, and the gap between this and the main face is reached via a gully on the R. 5hr from the hut

161 **NORTH RIDGE**
IV V Bramani and M Castiglioni, 18 Sept 1926
97

This long and almost horizontal ridge runs S from the summit of the Pizzo Camerozzo. Locally it is considered a very worthwhile outing, though nowadays it appears to be attempted less often than in the past. The flanks of the ridge are steep and offer no escape. Some of the climbing is very exposed, especially on the main difficulties which occur during the final rise to the summit. See also photograph 98

From the Gianetti hut follow the Roma path into the scree gully leading up to the Passo Camerozzo. Towards the top move R into a subsidiary gully that leads up to a prominent notch in the N ridge of the Pizzo Camerozzo, about halfway between the pass and the summit. From the notch scramble up the L side of the crest above to the summit of Pizzo Camerozzo (2-2½hr).

(The Camerozzo is a nice little peak in its own right and can be included by parties (with scrambling experience) walking the Roma path).

Continue S down the ridge, and then climb on or near to the crest all the way to the deep gap before the Bertani (mainly III). Just before the gap it is necessary to work across slabs on the R side of the ridge and make a short diagonal rappel on to ledges leading into the gap. The crux follows, an exposed 30m slab climbed from R to L (IV). Above this, the climbing is still quite absorbing until the summit is reached. 6hr from the hut

Punta Bertani South-East Face

This is just one facet of the continuous wall of excellent granite running from the Cavalcorte to the Camerozzo. While it is possible to climb on this face by making an early start from San Martino, it is more convenient to overnight at the shepherds' huts in the Ferro valley (see the approach to Route 155). At the time of writing the walls below the main summit are unclimbed. To the R a narrow chimney/couloir falls from the deep notch in the N ridge. The two climbs described follow lines on the R of this couloir and end on the N ridge, where there is a conspicuous block called 'The Obelisk'. On the first half of the routes slab climbing predominates. Higher, the wall steepens and a series of flakes, dièdres and cracks is used. Throughout, the granite is clean and knobbly but very compact. Both climbs are quite well-equipped, and double bolt belays on each stance allow a rapid rappel descent.

162 **OBELIX**

VI/A1 S Brambati and P Vitali, 4 Aug 1990

99

50

This climbs the huge R-facing dièdre below the Obelisk. Sustained at V to VI with two short sections of aid. Take a full rack and 4-5 pegs. A large Hex or 3½ Friend will also prove useful. c300m: 4-5hr

163 **ASTERIX**
VII– S Brambati and P Vitali, 7 and 8 July 1990
99
50

Probably the better and certainly the harder of the two climbs. As well as the bolts marked on the topo, several pegs were also left in the route. Take a full rack with Friends up to 3½. c300m: 5hr

Ferro Peaks

This chain of attractive summits at the head of the Ferro valley will be a delight to lovers of solitude. The highest point – the Cima della Bondasca – lies towards the W end, and although the western peaks can be climbed easily, some of the others are quite difficult and lengthy undertakings. The icy N walls above the Albigna glacier offer some superb outings to experienced and competent alpinists, but are seldom attempted. To the S the wild upper reaches of the Ferro valley are generally unvisited, except by those walking the Roma path.

Pizzo del Ferro Occidentale 3267.2m

Probably G Gardiner and party, date unknown

The most westerly of the Ferro peaks rises just to the E of the Passo di Bondo and offers no great difficulties.

164 **EAST-NORTH-EAST RIDGE FROM PASSO DEL FERRO**
F+
120

The normal route and a short pleasant scramble up the blocky crest. 30min

165 **NORTH-WEST RIDGE**
PD A Bonacossa with A Baroni and B Sertori, 31 July 1893
98

The attractive sharp crest rising from the Passo di Bondo. See also photograph 96

Avoid the first section of the ridge by following the snow slope on the Bondasca side. Climb back on to the ridge via a difficult crack (III), and follow the crest. Progressively easier climbing leads to a boulder-covered slope and, above, the summit. c100m: 45min

Passo del Ferro c3205m

N-S traverse: R Beachcroft, D Freshfield and J Walker with F Devouassoud, 9 Aug 1864

The broad snow saddle between the W and Central peaks.

166 **SOUTH (ITALIAN) SIDE**

F+

120

A very straightforward ascent over the small glacier that lies to the SW of the Cima della Bondasca.

From the Molteni bivouac hut work up to the NW over vast boulder slopes. Reach the entrance to the glacier that lies on the W side of a long rocky ridge protruding S from the summit of the Cima della Bondasca. Go up the glacier, which steepens towards the top, and reach the pass. 400m of ascent from the hut: 3hr

It is possible to avoid the lower section of the glacier by using a boulder-filled valley on the L. This lies betweeen the S ridge of the Occidentale and a subsidiary buttress to the E. Whether this has any real merit is debatable.

167 **NORTH (SWISS) SIDE**

PD+

This follows Route 82 from the Sciora hut to the Passo di Bondo, but near the head of the glacier works up L to the pass. 800m of ascent from the hut: 4hr

Pizzo del Ferro Centrale (Cima della Bondasca) 3289m

L Held, 1876

A double summit that marks the highest point of the large snow dome at the head of the Bondasca glacier. A small saddle separates the higher E top from the W, and from it a broad snow ridge runs gently N to the Colle dell'Albigna. The dome extends to the E for 300m to a point where the frontier ridge tapers and rises to the E peak – the Cima della Bondasca Orientale.

Ferro Centrale Main Summit

168 **NORTH SIDE – NORMAL ROUTE**

F+/PD+

123

This follows the upper section of the broad ridge that rises gently above the Colle dell Albigna. It can be reached in 4hr from the Sciora hut via the Bondasca glacier or in 3-3½hr from the Molteni bivouac by crossing the Passo del Ferro. It is also less than 30min from the Ronconi bivouac.

The overall difficulty depends on one's starting point for the ridge is no more than a simple walk.

169 **WEST RIDGE**

F+

120

A delightful ascent from the Passo del Ferro.

From the pass either scramble up the easy rocky ridge or the snow to the L to reach the W top. Descend to a snow saddle and reach the main summit by a fine, though shattered, rocky rib. 80m: 30min

170 **SOUTH RIDGE**

AD– L Binaghi, A Bonacossa and U di Vallepiana, 22 Sept 1929

120

Varied climbing on quite good rock once the crest of the ridge has been reached. The difficulties never rise above III. The situation is remote and few ascents have been recorded, so this route should appeal to those parties looking for easier climbing of a more exploratory nature.

The ridge has not been ascended in its entirety; the lower section appears to be very long and rather tedious. Instead, follow Route 166 from the Molteni bivouac towards the Passo del Ferro. From the middle of the glacier plateau (c3040m) cross to the R and climb very rotten rock up onto the ridge, well above the lower section and below the first of two steep steps (2½hr).

Climb up to and then along the sharp crest above, on splendid granite. The steepest section of the ridge is climbed on the L of the crest using a well-protected crack. Now follow a broad ledge R and climb the E flank of the ridge. Finally, return to the crest and follow a succession of wonderful slabs to the summit (1½-2hr). c250m: 4-4½hr from the hut

Ferro Centrale East Peak c3260m

Aureggi, Lurani and Rogorini with A Baroni, 23 Aug 1887

A small rocky point at the eastern end of the large snow dome. The classic traverse of the Ferro peaks is usually terminated at this point; beyond, things start becoming much more serious! Although the rock on this mountain is generally of poor quality, a superb spur of solid granite projects southwards towards the Ferro valley.

171 **NORTH SIDE**

F+/PD+

124

The easiest means of ascent is a simple walk from the Colle dell'Albigna. The difficulties met on this expedition will depend entirely on the choice of approach to the Colle. Together with the main summit this gives a

highly recommended ski-tour during the winter/spring season.

From the broad ridge above the Colle traverse L(E) across the slope and reach the lowest point of the wide and easy frontier ridge. Walk up the ridge to the top (30min). c4hr from the Sciora hut

172
TD–
124

NORTH COULOIR AND EAST RIDGE

E Strutt with P Pollinger, 11 June 1913. Winter: North couloir only, P Bernasconi and V Meroni, 10 March 1977

From the remote SW corner of the Albigna glacier, a fine hidden ice couloir rises to the Bochetta del Torrione (c3170m) – the dramatic notch between the E peak and the Torrione. The rock on the flanks is poor and in the summer months the couloir is constantly bombarded by stone-fall. Understandably ascents have been few, although the E ridge above the gap is crossed from time to time by parties making the complete traverse of the chain. The first ascent was an impressive achievement for the era! This serious route should only be attempted during very cold and snowy conditions, when it will give a superb mixed climb with acute 'high mountain atmosphere'. See also photograph 123

The couloir is 300m high, and splits into two branches, either side of the Torrione. Climb the R branch to the Bochetta (50°, steepening to 60° at the top).

Now climb a crack-line on the Albigna side of the E ridge and reach a small ledge below a slab. Climb steep and exposed slabs to easier ground (45m from the notch: IV+ if dry!). In well-frozen conditions it may well be possible to climb steep mixed ground to the R of this pitch. Move L onto the ridge above the first steep section and climb it easily to a second rise. Turn this on the S side via a shattered ledge and then climb back to the crest over steep slabs and cracks (III/III+: good rock). Generally keeping on the N flank, follow the ridge more easily to the summit. c400m: 8hr

173
TD
120
53

SOUTH SPUR

G Miotti, L Mottarella and M Spini, Sept 1980

A pure gem! It is comparable in difficulty and quality to the Parravicini on the Zocca or the S Pillar of the Torelli. Despite a pleasant sunny aspect the situation is wild, and the solitude gives the whole enterprise a serious air. Ascents are still infrequent so take a comprehensive rack.

As the difficulties are quite short a rappel descent would be perfectly feasible. However, axe and crampons will almost certainly be

needed on the glacier and it is recommended that parties continue along the superb yet straightforward frontier ridge to the Passo del Ferro. From here it is a fast and easy descent back to the bivouac. If a rappel descent is contemplated extra gear should be carried.

From the Molteni bivouac, go up the scree and boulder slopes into the couloir that leads to the Bochetta del Torrione. Cross the rimaye (stonefall!) then slant L to the rocks below the steep walls of the pillar (1hr).

From the good ledge at the end of pitch 10 it is possible to traverse L, and with a bit of luck find some pegs and slings which mark the start of a rappel descent. This will lead to the snowy shoulder on the E side of the small glacier that lies SW of the summit. From here, head W then S down the glacier. At the bottom, follow the L side of a stream bed down to the Roma Path. 260m of sustained climbing on the pillar, 350m to the summit, 6hr

Torrione del Ferro 3234m

H Ellensohn and E Perotti with B Sertori, 29 July 1900

The most inaccessible peak in the Ferro chain. It has rarely been climbed by parties other than those making a complete traverse of the main ridge. The N side is impressively steep, but the S side is more amenable and contains one moderate route that is worth consideration. The complete E ridge, from the Colle Masino via the Ferro Orientale, was climbed by Christian Klucker in 1927 at the age of 74. It was his last new route and was achieved in a round trip of 20hr from the Albigna hut!

174 **SOUTH RIDGE**
AD– O Heid and W Scharer with W Risch, in descent, 26 July 1928
120

Nice climbing with no great difficulty but tremendous 'high mountain ambience'. The situation, well above the upper reaches of the Ferro valley, is truly wild.

From the Molteni bivouac head up towards the Bochetta Ferro-Albigna passing the base of the S ridge (2726m). Work up L over easy ground to reach an enormous scree terrace at the foot of the SE face. Follow this L to a flat shoulder below the steepest part of the S ridge (c2hr).

Start on the R and climb the first obvious chimney leading up to the crest. Climb the crest directly on excellent granite then move round onto the SW face to reach a couloir. Climb this with difficulty (rappel in descent), and finish out R onto the crest above its steep section. Continue more easily until level with the base of the upper slopes on the SE face (these can be snow early in the season). From here it is best to follow the ridge – delightful climbing – all the way to the summit. c300m: 2-2½hr, 4-4½hr from the hut

175 **NORTH COULOIR AND EAST RIDGE**
TD– H Rutter with C Klucker, 28 June 1922
124

Seldom repeated. This climbs the same couloir used by Route 172, but in the upper section takes the L fork to a steep mixed finish onto the E ridge. Easy ground on the S flank now leads to the top. c400m: serious, 60°, 6hr. See also photograph 123

The 500m granite walls on the NE face were climbed in 1989 to give 'Wilderness'. V+/VI and A1

Pizzo del Ferro Orientale 3199m

A and L Bertarelli with G Rigamonti, 28 July 1883

This well-defined double summit marks the eastern end of the main chain. Although rather uninspiring on the Italian side, it has an impressive N face overlooking the head of the Albigna glacier. The W top is the higher by c15m and is 200m distant from the E summit. The E ridge, above the Colle Masino, is an abysmal piece of rubbish and a recent rock-fall in the lower section has done nothing to improve this situation!

176 **SOUTH FLANK**
PD First ascent party

Though an ascent by this route can scarcely be recommended it is still the easiest and quickest way up or down the mountain. It is mainly used by parties completing the traverse of the main ridge or a route on the N face, and is therefore described in descent.

From the E summit scramble along the short horizontal crest to where the E ridge begins to drop towards the Colle Masino. Climb down the shattered E ridge for two rope lengths to a rappel point.

From here, one long rappel leads to the icy slopes at the head of the Qualido valley. Go down these and join the approach to the Colle Masino (Route 184). c2hr to the Allievi hut

From the W summit this route will still provide the best means of descent. The traverse to the E top is normally straightforward and can be completed quickly. However, if a storm makes an instant escape from the ridge mandatory, it is possible to descend directly to the Molteni bivouac. Climb or make two rappels down the S face to reach the snowfield on the SW flank. Descend this, keeping close to the R (W) side where there is a rocky buttress. On reaching a huge boulder-strewn terrace, walk along it to the E until a wide rocky couloir leads down into the Ferro valley. Although unpleasant, the couloir is not difficult, but care is needed with large loose blocks. A rough walk across old moraine leads down to the Roma path. 2hr to the bivouac, but this time could be almost halved early in the season with a good consolidated covering of snow all the way down to the moraine.

Ferro Orientale North-West Face

An unusual mixed face, with two prominent spurs – the 'Ferro Pillars' – descending from the twin summits. As the average angle is not too great, the face can hold snow into the summer months. Local climbers refer to it as their 'mini Grandes Jorasses' and it does bear similar characteristics to that famous N wall in the Western Alps. Apart from the L-hand Pillar, the climbs benefit from a good snow covering and have looked pretty unpleasant in recent summers.

All routes require a certain commitment as there is no easy way down on the same side of the mountain. It is recommended that parties use Route 176 for descent, and via the Roma path return to the Albigna over the Zocca pass. Although the foot of the face is normally reached in 2-2½hr from the Albigna hut, it is worth remembering that it can also be reached in 2hr from the Allievi hut, via the Zocca pass.

177 **LEFT-HAND PILLAR**

D+ G Cesana, P Contini, P Gallotti and F Redaelli, July 1955

124

55

This, the most impressive of the pillars, gives a continuously enjoyable 'mountaineering' route to the E summit. After the first couple of pitches the quality of the granite is good and it offers a varied succession of slabs, cracks and dièdres. There is some wonderful climbing on great fins of rock in the upper section. Summer conditions are ideal as the route should be snow-free and dry. However, in recent years the rimaye has become more open and a fragile snow bridge has made access to the base of the pillar very precarious. 500m: 5½hr. See also photograph 119

178 **ORIGINAL ROUTE**
D
119
E Strutt with G Pollinger, 26 June 1914 (who, in fact, started up the line of the R-hand pillar before making a long leftwards traverse). Winter: P Bernasconi and F Masciadri, 3 March 1957

The first ascent party found perfect névé and completed the climb in a little over 2hr – a very impressive achievement for the era! These days the route is best attempted in spring or very early summer and after a night of hard frost. In these conditions stone-fall will be negligible and alpinists should encounter sustained and enjoyable snow and ice climbing, with short pitches of 60° in the central section of the route. 500m: 3-4hr

179 **CENTRAL COULOIR**
D–/D
119
55
D Erba and O Pivetta, 6 July 1979

When conditions are suitable for an ascent, the most obvious line on the face gives, technically, the easiest climbing. Cold and very snowy conditions are essential to cover the steep entry pitches and minimise stone-fall. Nowadays it is best attempted in winter/spring. The angle is generally 45°-50° but steepens to 60°+ towards the top. 450m: 3-4hr

180 **RIGHT-HAND PILLAR**
D+/TD–
124
55
G Lafranconi and N Nusdeo, 1 July 1964

This is much more broken than the L-hand pillar and the granite is not of the same high quality. Although it was climbed in 'summer' conditions, with a good covering of hard snow it becomes an excellent mixed route, and although probably harder, it is in this form that the climb is recommended. Near the top it is possible to climb up to the L and reach the summit directly. However, it is much more logical to continue over mixed ground, L of the final rocky rib, to reach the W ridge. Sections of rock at grade IV and short icy runnels of 65°-70° will be encountered. c520m: 5-6hr. See also photograph 119

181 **QUAGLIOTTO ROUTE**
D+
119
55
G Bonfanti, P Pivetta and R Quagliotto, 12 July 1987

Perhaps the least attractive line climbs the great ice slope on the R side of the face before joining the top section of the previous route. There are some icy sections of 65° and a little rock at III+. c520m: 4hr

182 TRAVERSE OF MAIN PEAKS

D+
120

Complete traverse, as described, is unknown. W Diehm with W Risch, 2 Sept 1931: from Orientale to Centrale

This is undoubtedly one of the finest high mountain expeditions in the range. The climbing is continuously interesting and requires a variety of techniques on both snow and rock. The situation, high above the Albigna glacier and the sunny yet desolate Ferro valley, is superb.

Many parties only go as far as the E summit of the Centrale (PD). The classic continuation to the Orientale is twice as long and demands a certain amount of commitment. Escape from this section of the ridge, which contains the major difficulties, would not be easy in adverse weather.

Although long mixed traverses are becoming less fashionable, this is an outing that should be given great consideration by any competent alpinist. See also photographs 119, 124

From the Passo di Bondo first traverse the Occidentale via an ascent of the NW and descent of the ENE ridges. Continue over the summit of the Cima della Bondasca and follow the broad snowy ridge to the Eastern peak (4-5hr from the Gianetti hut; 5-6hr from the Sciora hut; 4½hr from the Molteni bivouac). Now scramble down the N flank of the E ridge until it drops steeply into the Bochetta del Torrione. Make 2-3 rappels into this gap.

Climb the short but steep W ridge of the Torrione; a fine ascent even though the main difficulties occur on poor rock. First climb directly up the ridge for one long pitch above the gap (IV: rotten rock). Ascend more easily and move R onto the S face where the granite is good. A delightful slab (easy) leads back to the crest at a good ledge. Traverse immediately onto the N side and climb a narrow couloir between the flank of the ridge and an enormous slab to the L. Continue easily to the summit (1hr).

Go down the E ridge, at first over broken rock on the S flank and then on the N side, using a series of loose but easy ledges. This avoids a collection of sharp rocky 'teeth' on the crest. Make one airy rappel down a short vertical step into the Bochetta Ferro-Albigna (III+ in ascent: 2hr). Escape is possible at this point by descending the steep couloir to the S (stone-fall: III or rappels).

Now climb up the W ridge of the Orientale on good granite. The initial wall is quite steep but only III. Keep more or less to the crest. The rock becomes broken and the climbing easy, but the situation is still very impressive! A scree/snow slope finally leads to the summit (1hr: 5-6hr from the main summit of the Cima della Bondasca).

Descend Route 176 to the Roma path. c13hr round trip from the Molteni Bivouac

Colle Masino 3061m

First traverse (S-N): E and P Fasana and P Mariani, 30 July 1912. The col was first reached in 1893 (see below)

This lies between the Zocca and the Ferro Orientale and is nowadays of little use to alpinists. The N side is a steep and icy glacier slope, whereas the approach from the S is little more than a walk.

183 **NORTH (SWISS) SIDE**
AD A von Rydzewsky with C Klucker, 28 June 1893
124

This rapidly turns into hard ice during the summer and there is some danger of stone-fall from the ridge above. In recent years, the rimaye below the final slopes has become quite tricky. See also photograph 119

From the Albigna hut follow route 198 towards the Zocca Pass. From the end of the moraine walk SW across the glacier, passing below the long rocky ridge with a tower marked Pt 2899m, to reach the snow basin below the col. Cross the first rimaye well to the L and slant up R to the obvious chasm below the final slopes. Overcome this (a rocky outcrop on the L will give a suitable rappel anchor on the descent) and climb directly to the col (40°-45°). In dry conditions the exit may be a loose and unpleasant rock wall. c200m: 4hr from the hut

184 **SOUTH (ITALIAN) SIDE**
F From the Roma path in the Qualido valley stumble up scree and old
134 moraine to the small snow/ice slope below the col. A gentle walk leads to the top. 3hr from the Allievi hut: 30min less from the Molteni bivouac

Torrione di Zocca 3080m

E Bradby and C Wilson, 2 Aug 1911

The large rounded rock tower immediately W of the Bochetta di

Zocca. It can be easily reached from the latter in 20min. A traverse from the Bochetta to the Col Masino, or vice versa, will take c1½hr and is a straightforward scramble (PD). While the N side is a short but steep mixed face that has yet to be climbed, the Italian side is a magnificent wall of impeccable granite.

185 **SOUTH-EAST FACE**

VI P Coste, G Grassi, M Rougier and P Vuarcher, 14 Aug 1982

A superb rock climb directly up the centre of this narrow face. The first ascent party thought it as good as the Parravicini. What better recommendation! A short section of aid (nuts) was needed to overcome a small roof but the rest of the wall gave sustained free climbing. Unrepeated. 300m: 5hr

Punta 2511m

186 **EAST FACE**

VIII– G Merrizi and G Miotti, July 1982

The long rocky crest, running SE from the Passo dell'Averta (c2540m), and separating the Qualido from the Zocca valleys, has many little tops. The E face of this particular point is clearly visible from the path to the Allievi hut. It is an extrememly steep and compact wall with a stupendous R-facing dièdre. Although it is no more than a big crag, the situation feels quite isolated. The dièdre is climbed throughout to a large ledge below the final roofs, where an easy escape is made L via grassy rocks. Scramble down into the Qualido valley and walk back over the Averta pass. This is technically one of the harder climbs in the region and is both sustained and strenuous. The crux is a traverse R under the prominent roof at half-height, using an appalling, rounded, off-width crack. Number 4 Friends essential! 300m: 10hr

Pizzo di Zocca 3174m

G Melzi and A Noseda with G Fiorelli and B Sertori, 2 Aug 1890.
Winter: P Bernasconi, A Bignami, F Masciadri and V Meroni, 10 March 1957

A striking mountain, which when well-endowed with snow is one of the most impressive sights in the Albigna valley. The N side is a large glaciated wall flanked by two long rocky spurs. In recent summers there have been some imposing crevasses near the top of this face, causing problems to not a few parties engaged on the normal route. The S side is a superb and complex formation of ridges and towers, some of which give climbs of neo-classic status. Routes to the summit tend to be relatively lengthy, but the incredible panorama is ample reward. It is worth noting that the Allievi is the closest hut to any route on the mountain.

187 **NORTH-WEST GLACIER**

PD+ A von Rydzewsky with M Barbaria and C Klucker, 15 June 1891.

121 This was also the route taken on the first winter ascent in 1957

The normal route from the Albigna hut, which under good conditions is one of the finest high-mountain expeditions in the valley. In dry summers the upper slopes are icy and large crevasses have proved troublesome. Take one or two ice screws! In this state, Route 188 may prove an easier alternative.

Leave early from the Albigna hut and follow Route 198 to the glacier below the Zocca pass (2½hr). Head SW across the glacier to the foot of the NW slope. Climb more or less directly to the last rimaye. Cross it, possibly up against the rocks on the extreme R, and continue up the ice slope to the gap between the W top and main summit. Scramble up shattered rock on the N side of the crest to the highest point (c500m: 2½hr). 5hr from the Albigna or 4hr from the Allievi hut. Allow 4hr to descend to the Albigna hut

188 **NORTH-WEST RIDGE**

PD+/ 4 members of the SAC guided by W Risch, 1928

AD–

121

A useful alternative to the normal route, when the latter is in poor condition or the rimayes impractical. However, although it is always possible to gain access to the ridge, the rock is bad and the sort of conditions that would normally rule out the normal route, would also make the ridge rather unpleasant. With a covering of frozen snow it becomes a very worthwhile mixed climb in its own right.

The climb begins in the next glacier bay to the R (W) of the normal route. Ascend snow slopes until it is possible to traverse L and climb a couloir on to the ridge, just above a conspicuous tower (Pt 2899m). Climb carefully up the crest on shattered rock to the W top (moves of II/II+). Make an awkward descent of 40m into the gap beyond and continue up the frontier ridge to the main summit. 5½hr from the Albigna hut

189 **WEST-SOUTH-WEST RIDGE**

PD+/ A and R Balabio, A and R Calegari and G Scotti, 6 Aug 1910

AD–

This is the normal route from the Italian side. The climbing is always pleasant and interesting, even though some sections occur on rather shattered rock. The route is long but rarely difficult (several pitches of III) and can be used in descent to complete a fine traverse of the mountain. Early in the season, the approach to the Bocchetta di Zocca (3004m) is quite straightforward. However, in dry conditions stone-fall is a constant threat and it is worth considering the Colle Masino as a starting point. From here the ridge to the Bocchetta is a simple scramble (1½hr), and although long, this alternative gives the safest and most practical route of descent from the mountain, when snow conditions on the N side are poor.

From the Allievi hut follow the Roma path around the foot of the SE ridge of the Zocca. After 30min head up grass and moraine to the tiny Zocca glacier. Above, a narrow couloir leads up to the Bocchetta. When the snow cover is good follow the bed throughout (200m: 35°-40°); otherwise climb loose ground on either side – the L is more sheltered from stonefall but gives harder climbing (2½hr).

The Bocchetta can also be gained from the Albigna glacier via a short steep couloir, but can only be recommended early in the season (Strutt/Pollinger, 1913: AD).

Now follow the WSW ridge, keeping on or very close to the crest. The upper section contains short steps, cols and towers. From the W top descend into the gap beyond (40m: rappel or down-climb awkward slabby rock). Scramble up shattered rock on the L side of the ridge to the summit (2½hr). c400m from base of couloir: 5hr from the hut. Allow 3½-4hr for a descent to the hut

190 **WEST TOP – EAST-SOUTH-EAST (RED ROSE) RIDGE**

TD– K Meldrum, N and J Rogers and I Roper, 10 Aug 1968

A committing rock climb that takes the long sharp crest to the L of Route 191. Although the vertical ascent is not too great, the ridge rises in a series of steps and the amount of climbing is prodigious. Undertakings of this nature are unfashionable at present, but even so, the route has been repeated several times and found to give very fine climbing on excellent granite.

Descending the WSW ridge after completing the route is a lengthy

affair and parties should consider their fitness, as well as technical ability, before setting out on this classic mountaineering expedition. An axe and crampons will generally be necessary on both the approach and descent.

Follow Route 191 into the snow/scree basin below the couloir, then work up L over easy slabs and ledges to reach the foot of the first tower (1½hr). Avoid the initial overhanging section on the R. First climb a grassy ramp, then a chimney (III) and finally slant L up a little gangway to the other side of the crest. Easy ground leads to a point where the ridge steepens. Either climb the crack on the crest (V+), or the one 4m to the R (V) and reach a slab. Climb this and the crack above (30m: V to start), then work up to the R over slabs (IV+) to the foot of a steeper section. Climb it on flaky holds (V) and continue up the easy ground above to the top of the first tower.

Ahead lie three small towers. Turn the first on the R, climb the second directly and turn the third on the L. Go up to the foot of the second tower. Climb easy blocks and a short steep dièdre to a large gently-angled slab on the R flank of the tower. Surmount the steep crack above and the dièdre that follows (V), to reach easy ground. Scramble up to the summit of the tower.

Follow the crest, then a straightforward ledge system low down on the R. Return to the crest and, shortly after, turn a small tower on the L. Now climb up steeper rock (moves of III) until just below and R of the W summit. Reach it by a dynamic pull over the final overhang (1 move of V+). 550m: 6-8hr for the climb

191 EAST-SOUTH-EAST COULOIR
AD– First ascent party

The deep rectilinear snow couloir to the L of the SE ridge is the most obvious line on the Italian side of the mountain. Nowadays it is rarely, if ever, ascended. The prevailing dry conditions make it loose, unpleasant and highly dangerous due to severe stone-fall. Out of season, with a good snow covering and a hard frost, it would allow fast, straightforward cramponning and provide the quickest means of ascent, or descent, on this side of the peak.

From the Allievi hut follow the Roma path around the base of the SE ridge of the Zocca. Go up to the foot of the long deep couloir that lies between this ridge and the 'Red Rose' route on the L. The initial section of the gully is generally straightforward. Higher, climb a little rock step, which could be obliterated under heavy snow and reach the snow basin below the main couloir (1½hr).

Climb the couloir direct (2½hr), and continue up the WSW ridge for another hour to the summit. c500m for the couloir, 580m to the summit: 5hr from the hut

192 **NORTH-EAST RIDGE**
D A Zurcker with W Risch, 30 July 1923. Climbed as far as the N
121 summit by A Castelnuovo with A Fiorelli in 1906

An established classic which gives a long yet very worthwhile mountaineering expedition in a splendid position. In dry conditions it offers continuously interesting rock climbing on sound granite – especially in the upper section. With more snow it becomes a superb mixed route; the difficulty very much dependent on the snow-quality found on the N flank. As the ridge rises gradually and is more than 1km long, the amount of climbing is considerably more than the vertical height would suggest. By descending the WSW ridge, alpinists will enjoy one of the finest traverses over any mountain in the range. See also photograph 134

From the Zocca pass climb the first step in the ridge by a vertical dièdre on the R side of the crest. Rejoin the crest above the first tower, where the climbing becomes easier. Although it is nicer to climb over the two large towers that follow, it is more popular to turn them by using ledges on the S flank. From the prominent gap beyond these towers climb up the ridge for a pitch before moving onto the N side. Regain the crest via a chimney and a succession of slabs, which can be quite tricky if snow covered. Beyond, the ridge is still not easy and, eventually, a series of slabs lead to the N summit.

Climb along the sharp airy ridge and down into the gap before the main top (it is possible to escape from here onto the NW glacier but this is certainly not a straightforward alternative!). Cross the gap and climb a small tower, which is very steep at the start and provides the hardest moves on the route (IV+). The ridge now becomes sharper and even more exposed! It leads to the base of an overhang. Climb on to a narrow ledge and move L to a vertical wall (pegs). Climb the wall and the easier ground above to regain the crest. Follow the ridge for one easy pitch, then climb steeply up an impressive series of smooth slabs. A fine yet scary succession of friction moves leads to the summit. 400m: 6hr

Torrione Est c3010m

This is a subsidiary top on the long SE ridge of the mountain. The most conspicuous feature is an impressive E-facing pillar, whose L edge is taken by one of the finest routes described in this book.

193 **SOUTH-EAST PILLAR – PARRAVICINI ROUTE**
V+ G Cazzaniga, M Dell'Oro and U Tizzoni, 5 Sept 1937.
134 Winter: R Merindi and L Tenderini, 21 Feb 1959
57

One of the very best and most popular of the Val Masino classics. It is an immaculate climb that should be high on the list of any party visiting the Bregaglia. The situations are tremendous, the difficulties are sustained and the rock is perfect! The route follows a line of dièdres linked by short traverses. From the terrace below the last pitch it is possible to climb an easy couloir L of the crest. However, you are strongly advised to finish direct – an outstanding pitch with one move of VI+ if climbed completely free. There is a wealth of in-situ protection so carry a large number of quick-draws.

The route was dedicated to Agostino Parravicini who was killed during an attempt in 1935. 250m and 2½-3hr for the upper pillar.

It is possible to climb the lower two-thirds of the ridge by keeping slightly R of the crest, using a chimney/groove system interspersed with grassy ledges (c350m: sections of III and IV: 2hr). It is also possible to start on the R side of the face. Follow an easy traverse line into the centre, where a large grassy gully leads up (steps of III and IV–) to the huge terrace below the upper part of the pillar (c300m: 1½hr). Most parties, however, avoid these approaches as follows:

From the Allievi hut walk up towards the Zocca pass and take the large scree couloir that comes down from the E face of the Pizzo di Zocca. On the L is the NE ridge of the Torrione Est. Near the top of the gully slant L on easy ground to reach a large open couloir/dièdre on the ridge. 120m above is a saddle on the conspicuous shoulder that lies below the steep, upper section of the pillar. Climb the couloir (II and III) and when below the shoulder turn it on the L to reach a huge terrace system. These terraces cut across the whole of the SE face below the steep upper part of the pillar (1hr or less from the hut: equipment left at the base of the couloir/dièdre can be recovered on the descent).

Descent: From the summit of the Torrione it is possible to continue along the SE ridge to the summit of the Zocca. This is not uninteresting (IV), although several sections are rather loose.

Gendarmes are generally turned on the E side (2½hr). Starting with a complete ascent of the SE pillar, parties can arrive at the summit of the Zocca via one of the longest rock routes on this side of the range (TD–/TD: 800m, c7hr). Unfortunately the lack of homogeneity in the difficulties, combined with the scrappy nature of the lower pillar, make the proposition of this ascent rather unattractive.

Instead: From the top of the pillar scramble down to the NE, where a slabby couloir slants down the face on the R. Descend this on appalling rock and make two rappels towards the bottom to reach the scree couloir used on the approach. Quite unpleasant but only 1½-2hr to the hut!

194 **NORTH-EAST (BONATTI) PILLAR**
VI R Bignami and W Bonatti, 21 June 1953
134
57

Although overshadowed by its more prestigious neighbour, this has seen many ascents over the years. The difficulties are concentrated above the conspicuous dièdre and there is some excellent exposed climbing. The granite is generally sound, but in one or two places large loose flakes look rather worrying. Although not as sustained nor as long as the Parravicini, it is technically a little harder and has far less in-situ protection. Take a full rack. 200m (upper section): c3hr

Pizzo di Zocca North Summit

195 **ICE A GO-GO**
D M Caslini and G Colombo, 22 July 1984
121

A delightful middle-grade mixed route up the NNE face. Nowadays it is only feasible very early in the season. Mainly ice-climbing at 40°-60°, with a little rock (IV). 450m

196 **NORTH-WEST RIDGE**
AD/D A Zurcker with W Risch, 28 Aug 1922

This beautiful and compelling line flanking the NW glacier has only moderate rock difficulties. Now for the bad news – the granite is absolutely diabolical! However, under a heavy covering of well-frozen snow the ridge will provide excellent mixed climbing. The crux will almost certainly be the traverse from the N to the main summit, and the whole expedition will take 8-10hr. The route is graded for these conditions. c500m

Passo di Zocca 2749m

This lies to the E of the Pizzo di Zocca and is one of the most important crossing points in the range. The S side is an easy scree slope, but an ascent from the N involves crossing the upper reaches of the Albigna glacier and climbing a short snow/ice slope where crampons can often be useful. Despite this, the pass has been used for centuries and was quite popular with smugglers, who had no qualms about making the crossing unroped. Using the Albigna téléphérique, a traverse of the pass provides the quickest approach to the Allievi hut for parties based in Switzerland. This may be preferable to those car owners worried about the increased theft and vandalism in the Mello valley.

197 **ITALIAN SIDE**

PE

134 *A short and straightforward walk over boulder slopes.*

From the Allievi hut follow the path NW into the obvious moraine valley, and walk up the scree and boulder-filled couloir to the frontier ridge. The pass lies just L of a conspicuous pinnacle. 45min-1hr (30min or less in descent). The fine 80m rock spike passed on the ascent is called the 'Petit Capucin'. It can be climbed via the SW face (V, A0).

198 **SWISS SIDE**

F

121 *Early in the season the ascent is quite straightforward, although one or two hidden crevasses may be lurking. Later, bare rubble and ice can make the crossing rather unpleasant.*

From the Albigna hut follow the path S to the Cantun stream. Cross it (no bridge at present) and continue above the lake. The path has been beautifully sculptured into the cliffs at the foot of the Punta da l'Albigna. Finally it descends to the moraine near the head of the lake (45min). Continue up the moraine; pass beneath the Castel and reach the upper section of the glacier. There may be a rimaye, in which case it is best crossed on the R (but watch out for stone-fall from the flanks of the Pizzo di Zocca!). An easy-angled slope leads up to the pass. 3hr from the hut: allow c4hr from the téléphérique terminus

Punta Vittoria 3012m

This small peak, insignificant when seen from the Albigna, stands on the frontier ridge between the Punta Allievi and the Zocca pass. It has a number of rock routes on the Italian side that are not often ascended.

199 **WEST-SOUTH-WEST PILLAR**
IV+ P Gallotti and P Maffioli, 5 July 1953

Possibly the best route on the peak. Varied climbing on sound granite. Mainly IV with two pitches of IV+. The difficulties terminate at two-thirds height and thereafter only scrambling remains to the summit. Go down the N flank of the E ridge and return easily via Route 211 to the foot of the peak. 350m: 3hr

Punta Allievi 3121m

This superb example of rock architecture stands directly above the Allievi hut. On the Swiss side it is yet another minor 'bump' on the long ridge running S from the Castello to the Zocca pass. The Italian side is a complete contrast. Stunning ridges and pillars intermingle with smooth sweeping slabs and form one of the finest climbing arenas in the region. Nearly a dozen routes now force their way up these impressive walls. All are worthwhile and on impeccable granite: indeed, the S ridge has long been considered one of the most desirable rock-routes in the range.

200 **NORMAL ROUTE**
F+
136 *The summit is only a few mins above Route 211 to the Castello. In descent, any snow can usually be avoided by scrambling down the R flank of the W ridge to the saddle before Pt 3012m. 2½hr from the Allievi hut, c1hr in descent*

201 **SOUTH-WEST PILLAR – ENGLISH ROUTE**
V/V+ K Meldrum, J and N Rogers, 30 Aug 1967
131
56 *A short steep climb that has become quite popular. The approach from the Allievi hut, via Route 211, is quick (45min) and straightforward. The granite is good except for the first chimney, but this can easily be avoided on the R. Above, there is some fine climbing, especially on the long crux pitch which, incidentally, is as hard as anything on the S Ridge. The route finishes on the frontier ridge about 200m W of the summit and a fast descent can be made by reversing the normal route. c300m: 3hr. See also photograph 136*

202 **SOUTH RIDGE – GERVASUTTI ROUTE**
D+/ TD– 131 59 58
G Gervasutti and C Negri, 16 Sept 1934. A Bonacossa soloed the SW couloir to join the party above the second tower and roped with them for the upper section. Winter: G Gugiatti and C Pedroni, 21-22 Dec 1971

Surprisingly, Gervasutti was involved in very few first ascents in the Bregaglia, but with this he established one of its best and most famous classics. The climbing is very varied – strenuous work in cracks and chimneys alternates with delicate friction moves on open knobbly slabs. The upper section is in a splendid situation! The difficulties are sustained at III to IV+ with two or three harder pitches. On the latter, there are now so many pegs in place that it is easy to reduce the standard by making a few moves at A0. Escape is possible at two points: After the 'Prima Dito', by making 4 rappels down the W face or after the 'Secondo Dito' by reversing the easy SW couloir. c500m: V+, 5½hr. See also photographs 136, 137

203 **DECADENTE**
VII– 137 58
J Merizzi, U Pasqualotto, M Preti and E Tessera, 24 Aug 1990

This six-pitch climb to the top of the 'Primo Dita' is a fine example of the several short rock routes, of excellent quality, that lie close to the Allievi hut. The climb runs alongside the crest of the ridge, L of the dièdre taken by the initial part of the Gervasutti route and has fairly sustained pitches on superb granite. Rappel descent to the W.

The walls to the R of the ridge have been climbed by several routes that cross the 'Basin' at mid-height. One of the best of the older climbs is the 'Boga Route' (M Dell'Oro and U Tizzoni, 18 Aug 1937), which takes the rightward slanting crack-line, that starts 100m R of the foot of the S ridge at a smooth bulbous slab. Above the basin the big chimney/crack system on the L side of the E Pillar is followed to the top (c450m: TD, VI, 6-8hr)

To the R the most prominent feature is the golden E Pillar, rising above the large ledges that cut across the middle of the E face. Its defences were first breached in 1967 by the 'Via dei Camosci'. This gives some nice free-climbing on the L flank of the crest, but reaching this, via the huge grey dièdre on the walls below, requires some extensive aid-climbing. The upper section is described, as it could provide an easier (though not as good!) finish to Filo Logico; a better finish to the Boga; or even a route in its own right by approaching along the central ledges.

204 **CAMOSCI ROUTE – UPPER SECTION**
TD– T Nardella, A Parolo, P Piasini and T Speckenhauser,
137 30-31 July 1967

Steep and exposed climbing in chimneys and dièdres, close to the crest of the pillar. See also photograph 136

At the L end of the central ledges there is a small saddle below the crest of the pillar. Cross this saddle and descend L towards the 'Basin' for 40m to reach the base of a chimney/dièdre that slants up to the R. Climb it (40m: IV) then traverse 4m L and climb a dièdre to the crest of the pillar (VI–). Traverse L for 6m then climb directly up slabs and cracks to a small terrace (V+). Above lies a series of vertical cracks. Climb these for two pitches (VI), then slant more easily up L to the foot of a chimney. Climb this for 30m then move down to a terrace at the foot of the final part of the pillar (IV). Climb a crack that slants up to the R for 15m, then follow the dièdre above for 8m before traversing L for 6m using a horizontal crack (V+: very delicate), to a stance. One more pitch (IV) leads to the top of the pillar. c220m: 3-4hr

205 **FILO LOGICO**
TD+/ S Brambati and P Vitali, 14 July 1990.
ED1 First winter ascent: D Fiorelli and C Perlini, Feb 1993
137
61

This brilliant route, on splendid red granite, reaches the foot of the pillar directly and then climbs the quasi-vertical front face via a succession of wildly exposed cracks and flakes. Although most of the route is sustained at V+/VI–, the crux pitch has one or two moves of VII– that are poorly protected. An easy escape can be made from below this pitch by following the central ledges rightwards to join the approach to Route 206.

There are some bolts and pegs in place, but a full rack, with Friends up to 3½ and slings for spike belays, is essential. If there is any snow remaining in the 'Basin' the first two pitches will be very wet. For this reason it is recommended that the route is not attempted early in the season.

Start directly below the upper pillar, at the base of the most obvious and widest black crack on the E face. This point can be reached in under an hour from the Allievi hut. c400m: 6-8hr

206 **EAST FACE – ERBA ROUTE**
TD– A Erba and A Fumagalli, 28 July 1973
137
60

The modern classic of the Allievi which rapidly became the second most popular route after the S ridge. It is a very attractive chimney/crack system

that begins from the central ledges, which at this point are more than 100m above the base of the wall. A direct start can be made by climbing the first 4 pitches of the 1980 Czech route, but as this is rather out of keeping with the rest of the climb, parties traverse onto the ledges from the easy couloir to the R of the face (reached in 1hr from the hut: stone-fall possible). The climbing is excellent – seldom using the chimneys but weaving a tenuous line up the open walls to either side. Just when things begin to look desperate, easy options miraculously appear and allow the climb to continue at a reasonable standard. There is plenty of in-situ protection as the two hard sections were originally pegged to bring the overall standard down to a consistent V/V+. c240m from the ledges, VI: 380m with the direct start, 5-6hr from the base of the couloir

Punta Baroni 3225m

This rocky summit lies between the Cima di Castello and Punta Allievi. It rises but a few m above the S Castel glacier and can be reached in less than 5mins from the approach to the Castello (Route 211). In dry years it is possible to keep to broken rocky ground below the Punta Allievi and so reach the summit from the Allievi hut without having to set foot on snow. From the upper Zocca valley the peak appears almost pyramidal in shape and the SE face is a wonderful smooth granite wall.

Punta Baroni South-East Face

207 **SONDRIO CITY**
TD/ P Ghetti, F Gugiatti, C Pedroni and T Speckenhauser,
TD+ 10-11 Aug 1969
133
63

Technically, this is a very demanding route and has seldom been repeated. The crux occurs at mid-height where, on the first ascent, some hard aid-climbing was needed to overcome an extremely steep and somewhat featureless wall. The route was subsequently climbed completely free by G Miotti, who was forced to make some thin and strenuous moves on tiny rugosities protected only by the original in-situ gear (poor pegs and two bolts, all in a very bad state). Re-equipping this pitch would turn the route into a classic test-piece for modern climbers, but at the moment it will still require a very bold lead (ED1/2: VII+). A comprehensive rack with a few knife-blades, RPs and perhaps a skyhook should be taken. The foot of the face can be reached in 1½hr from the Allievi hut, and most of the route has been equipped for a rappel descent. It is possible to escape from the route three pitches below the top by following the big ledge to the R. c350m: VI and A2/3, 8hr. See also photograph 135

208 **SENZA SOLE**

TD– K Meldrum, N Rodgers amd I Roper, 6 Aug 1968

133

63

Another very good route that, in common with Sondrio City, has received little attention. It follows a prominent line of chimneys that slant R from near the centre of the wall to finish on a small col well N of the summit. The technical difficulties are generally quite reasonable but the crux pitch will prove rather demanding if climbed completely free! c350m: V1, 5-6hr. See also photograph 136

Cima di Castello 3388m

D Freshfield and F Tuckett with F Devouassoud and A Flury, 31 July 1866. Winter: N Zaquini with E Fiorelli, Jan 1903

If one considers the Disgrazia massif as separate from the main range, the Castello becomes the highest peak in the Bregaglia. From the summit, which overlooks the Zocca, Albigna and Forno valleys, there is the most remarkable panorama encompassing almost every major mountain from the Bernina to the Badile. The normal routes – one from each of the three surrounding valleys – all involve long and gentle glacier expeditions. Whilst an ascent by one of these routes may not give the most interesting of climbs, the rewards on reaching the summit are ample compensation and the mountain is very popular. It is especially recommended to alpine novices, given a reasonable standard of fitness.

209 **NORMAL ROUTE FROM ALBIGNA VALLEY**

PD–

122

The easiest route to the summit and also the most frequented (though generally not overcrowded to the same extent as the most popular Bernina peaks). In high summer it is usually a matter of 'trench warfare' – jockeying for position on a well-beaten track!

From the Albigna hut follow Route 219 towards the Passo dal Cantun. Once on the upper plateau below the pass at a little over 3000m, turn S and reach the Bocchetta dal Castel (3106m). Go through this onto the S Castel glacier. Work up alongside the ridge on the L until it is possible to climb up on to it above the rocky section. Follow the crest easily to the summit. 1200m: 5hr from the hut.

In spring, ski ascents are made by following the S Castel glacier in its entirety, starting from below the Zocca pass.

210 NORTH RIDGE

PD/PD+

122

The normal route from the Forno hut. The final ridge is a popular alternative when coming from the Albigna in order to make a traverse of the mountain. Steepish mixed climbing in a fine position, with surprisingly good rock! See also photograph 142

From the Passo dal Cantun (Route 220), it is possible to traverse the horizontal rocky ridge in its entirety to reach a small col below the final step. Although this is quite interesting, it is both quicker and more straightforward to reach the col directly. From the Forno side climb a short snow couloir or, in dry conditions, relatively sound rock on the R side. When coming from the Albigna hut it is simply a matter of ascending a moderately steep snow slope from the upper plateau.

Now climb directly up the ridge (sections of II+) to reach a snow crest leading to the foresummit. The latter is a snowy dome and the true summit – a rocky top – lies 200m to the S. 5hr from either hut

211 NORMAL ROUTE FROM ITALY

PD–

136

Possibly the least monotonous of the standard routes and marginally quicker, as it gains height more rapidly in the initial stages. Early in the season, when it is feasible to glissade snow patches on the lower part of the route, it can give a very swift descent. See also photographs 122, 131, 155

From the Allievi hut head N up stony ground to reach the valley between the Pta Allievi and the SE ridge of Pta Vittoria (3012m). Go up it to a rocky barrier and starting on the L, slant up R to reach the higher continuation valley. Work up the L side of this, and towards the top scramble up R then back L to a chimney/couloir. Climb this to the lowest point in the frontier ridge (2-2½hr: I/II, all this section has a rough track and is cairned from time to time).

Now go onto the S Castel glacier. There are few crevasses and it is a gentle walk up to join Route 209 at the point where it climbs onto the snowy crest of the W ridge just before the summit. 4½hr from the hut

Cima di Castello South Face

Although only 350m high, this rock wall is one of the most impressive in the area. It rises out of the couloir leading to the Colle del Castello and is characterised by two stupendous pillars separated by a steep hanging gully. Perhaps the most attractive feature is the huge orange slab, bounded on the R by the precipitous crest of the S Pillar. Of the seven existing routes, several are unrepeated and only one has received more than a handful of ascents. The best lines have sections of demanding aid-climbing and require a certain commitment that is somewhat unfashionable at present. Both the central couloir and areas to the L of the main climbs disgorge large amounts of rock and water, so it is recommended that parties attempt routes late in the season, when the catchment areas high on the face have thoroughly dried.

The approach from the Allievi hut will take c2hr. Follow Route 217 into the couloir leading up to the Colle del Castello. The S Pillar starts just below the entrance to the couloir, while for the R-hand Pillar one must climb up for c100m before traversing L to the foot of the wall.

212 **LEFT-HAND COULOIR**
VI– O Seifer and R Valisek, 19 Aug 1980
136
64

Rising up below the huge orange slab is a chimney-couloir which receives a lot of drainage. The rock is quite good on the lower section but deteriorates badly in the easier upper section, which is threatened by stone-fall from the couloirs to the R. The first ascent party reported fine climbing in cracks and chimneys, with sustained difficulties of IV to V. Just L is a similar couloir first climbed in Sept 1926. It is looser, wetter and more exposed to stone-fall! c250m of climbing: 4-5hr. See also photograph 139

213 **CZECH DIRECT**
ED2 O Seifer and R Valisek, 30-31 Aug 1980
139
64

The only attempt, so far, to force a line up the steep golden slab required a considerable amount of hard aid-climbing. The first ascent party used 40 pegs and 4 bolts and the route is probably unrepeated. However, the main difficulties are actually quite short. In the future it may be possible for a party, capable of climbing the hard slabs in the Mello valley, to turn this line into a superb high-standard free-climb. 350m: 12-16hr

214 **SOUTH PILLAR**
ED1/2 N Rogers and I Roper, 8-9 Aug 1969
139
64 *A direct start to the pillar is somewhat threatened by stone-fall from the hanging couloir, and also involves the distinct prospect of failing to breach the formidable initial overhangs! The few parties to repeat the route have confirmed the quality and sustained nature of the climb, the steepness of the rock and the great difficulty in retreating were this to prove necessary. The first pitch is common to the previous two climbs and starts L of a large fallen block at the foot of the face. There is little in-situ gear so take a full rack and a selection of 8-10 pegs. There are several comfortable bivouac sites in the upper half of the route. 350m: 12-15hr*

215 **RIGHT-HAND PILLAR**
TD F Anghileri, G Castagna, D Missaglia and G Stefanon, 28 Aug 1966
139
64 *The first ascent of this pillar was made in 1954 by B Corti and R Osio, who climbed the huge chimney system, which is clearly visible in the centre of the wall and leads directly to the summit. Unfortunately, many of the pitches were quite loose. On the second ascent a major variation was established, following the line of cracks and chimneys to the L. Subsequent parties have continued to take this line. The climbing is reported to be quite good and a little harder than the original route, but the rock still leaves much to be desired! 350m: 6-7hr*

A recent addition starts 100m below the Colle and takes a fairly direct line to the summit (R Assi and P Danielle, 25 June 1986. 350m: TD+, VI+). The R side of the face is characterised by a huge prow which forms the base of a hanging pillar. From the end of the first pitch of Route 215, 'Via Jacuba' moves R from the enormous flake and climbs a very steep series of rightward slanting cracks up the pale-coloured granite beneath the arch. It then follows an easier crackline just R of the hanging pillar to the summit. There is some hard and strenuous climbing but the route is escapable. Although the rock is very good on the first 3 pitches, it is only moderately so above. Only nuts/Friends were used for protection on the first ascent (J Merizzi and U Pasqualotto, 15 Aug 1989. c300m: 8-9 pitches, VII but not sustained). Parties based in Switzerland should note that, in good conditions only, all climbs on the R side of the face could be reached by a short descent from the Colle del Castello. The face is bounded by the ESE ridge which, although a fine line, is a rather scrappy route (III/IV with a short section of V−: 2hr from the Colle)

Colle del Castello 3215m

Traverse (S-N): C Klucker and a porter, 2 Sept 1889.
Winter: A Bonacossa, A and L Bonzi and R Kuster, 15 March 1926

Often referred to in Italy as the Passo Lurani after an early pioneer of the Masino group. This is an important col as it offers the easiest passage between the Forno and Zocca valleys. Early in the season the S side is a pleasant snow couloir of moderate angle. As this dries out it becomes loose and badly exposed to stone-fall.

216 **NORTH (SWISS) SIDE**
PD– F Allievi with A Baroni, 15 Aug 1896
142

A lengthy but not uninteresting glacier walk. Parts of the journey can be badly crevassed and often test one's route-finding ability.

From the Forno hut the approach is identical to that used to reach the Passo del Canton (Route 220). From the last glacier terrace below the walls of the Castello move S and reach the col via a short snow/ice slope. 3hr

217 **SOUTH (ITALIAN) SIDE**
PD
136

Should be completed very early in the day to minimise the stone-fall, that not only originates from the flanks of the couloir but also from the gullies on the S face of the Castello. See also photographs 131, 155

From the Allievi hut follow the Roma path for a few minutes to the first stream. Now go up the stony ground on the R of the stream, skirting the base of the S Pillar of the Allievi (Pt 2580m), to reach the remnants of W Rasica glacier. Go up over moraine and snow-patches to the foot of the couloir leading to the Colle. In good frozen conditions climb the bed throughout to the top. When this is impractical, it is probably best to climb out R on loose ground and follow a vague rib that leads up to the frontier ridge a little above the col. 2½hr

Castel 2924m

U Canziani and C Prochownik, July 1912

The conspicuous 'corner-stone' at the end of the Castello's W ridge. These days it appears to be rarely climbed despite a very worthwhile, yet largely unknown, route on the W face.

218 **WEST FACE**
TD– G and G Steiger, 25 July 1963
122
52

Sustained climbing in a series of cracks and dièdres. A direct line was thwarted at two-thirds height by a barrier of very steep walls, yet despite the long traverse the route has been highly recommended by several parties. The rock is generally sound, though in common with the Punta da l'Albigna it can be a little lichenous in parts. It is possible that the relatively long approach and descent, when compared to other rock routes in this largely 'cragging' area, has proved an effective deterrent. However, it may provide solace to certain alpinists visiting this increasingly popular valley.

From the Albigna hut follow Route 198 towards the Zocca pass. The path passes directly below the Castel. Go up scree to the L side of the face and start at the lowest point, where an easy slabby groove c100m high slants up to the R (1½hr). The difficulties are confined to the first 300m; thereafter only scrambling remains to the summit. 550m: 4-5hr

Descent: From the summit reverse the ridge to the second small notch (c150m W of the top). Go down to the S in a steep chimney which leads to slabs and more broken ground. Descend to the moraine and follow it down to the Albigna glacier. By mid-summer it should be possible to return to the start of the route without having to set foot on snow.

Passo dal Cantun c3260m

A von Rydzewsky with A Dandrea and C Klucker, 16 July 1895 (E to W)

The broad snow saddle on the ridge connecting the Castello to the Cantun lies 100m N of Pt 3265m. It gives a fairly simple glacier crossing between the Forno and Albigna valleys but is seldom used in this manner. It is a long yet varied expedition and is frequently reached by parties making ascents of the two great peaks mentioned above.

219 **WEST SIDE**
PD–
122

From the Albigna hut follow Route 198 towards the Zocca pass. After the path descends to moraine near the head of the lake, continue S for a short distance and then follow a track E into a side valley. Reach the crest of the moraine on the R and follow it to the top (bivouac sites: c2hr). Step on to the N Castel glacier and walk up it keeping to the L. Steeper slopes lead up to a plateau. Cross the plateau and reach the pass directly via a short snow slope. 4hr

220 EAST SIDE

PD–/PD

142

From the Forno hut go up the centre of the glacier and then work across to the R side below a rock barrier. This barrier forms the end of the ridge coming down from Pt 3312m on the NE ridge of the Cantun. Early in the season work up through the rock and moraine debris onto the glacier above, and walk up it to the SW. Near the top come back R and climb a short steep snow slope to the pass (4hr). It is often easier, especially later in the season, to continue along the Forno glacier towards the Rasica, before slanting back R (NW) below the Castello to reach the snow slope that leads to the pass.

Cima dal Cantun 3354m

A von Rydzewsky with M Barbaria and C Klucker, 18 June 1891. Winter: A Bonacossa and E Bontadini, 22 Dec 1924

Many alpinists consider this to be the most attractive summit in the Albigna. It is predominately a snow peak and offers a fine variety of ascents. Pride of place goes to the beautiful N face, which although neither high nor difficult is one of the finest ice climbs in the region.

221 SOUTH-WEST FLANK

PD–

122

First ascent party

The normal route and a very worthwhile expedition. It is the shortest and easiest route from the Albigna hut and is understandably popular. Novice alpinists will find this an excellent introduction to glacier peaks and in high summer will have little difficulty in following the well-beaten piste. Incidentally, it is also high on the list for ski-tourers.

From the Albigna hut follow Route 219 towards the Passo dal Cantun and reach the upper plateau of the N Castel glacier. Now turn NE and head straight for the summit. Finally climb a short slope of snow and broken rock to reach the NW ridge a few minutes below the top. 4-4½hr: 2½-3hr in descent

222 **SOUTH RIDGE**
PD N Rodio and R Trumpler, 2 Sept 1908
122

This is the easiest route from the Forno hut, though in fact it is more often climbed from the Albigna valley. It provides a good scramble along the crest from the Passo dal Cantun and is often combined with an ascent of the Castello. Highly recommended as an introduction to general mountaineering for those with a certain degree of fitness – otherwise it becomes a hard slog! See also photograph 142

From the Passo dal Cantun follow the snow ridge to the almost horizontal rocky crest beyond. Scramble along this, turning a tower on the R, to the summit (moves of II/II+). 30min

223 **NORTH-EAST RIDGE**
AD– A von Rydzewsky with M Barbaria and C Klucker, 28 June 1892
126

This highly recommended excursion follows the serrated crest above the Furcela dal Scalin. The latter can be reached directly from the Forno hut via a traverse of the Scalin. A complete traverse from the col immediately N of the Scalin is a minor classic (AD) and will take 3½-4hr. Although easier later in the season when it is largely rocky, the route becomes a finer outing in more mixed conditions.

Above the Furcela the first part of the ridge is rather narrow, and is generally climbed on the L side to the top of the first step (moves of III). Continue more easily along the snowy crest and reach the foresummit. The final rocky section gives superb climbing in a splendid position. Various small towers are turned on the R before a delightful snow crest leads to the summit. 2hr

224 **NORTH FACE**
AD+ C Godet and H Rutter, 18 Aug 1912
126

The middle-grade classic of Bregaglia ice-climbing. Very popular in the past, though these days it is rarely in good condition after early July and becomes a sheet of black ice by Aug. Ironically, in recent years the long serac barrier that used to block the L side of the face has totally disappeared. In good conditions the ascent is now far more straightforward and objectively safe. The average angle is 50° with the steepest part usually just above the rimaye.

From the Albigna hut follow Route 228 past the base of the Bio pillar and walk onto the Cantun glacier. Cross it to the S and negotiate a zone of crevasses shortly before the rimaye (2½hr).

Cross the rimaye, which normally presents little problem, and climb up the face to the L of an isolated rock buttress. Exit onto the NE ridge or slant up R and reach the summit directly. 300m: 3hr, 5½hr from the hut

Punta 3312m

The foresummit of the Cantun, situated just over halfway along the NE ridge, has two excellent ice routes on its NW face. From the top the easiest descent is to continue over the Cantun and down the normal route.

225 **NORTH-WEST FACE ORIGINAL ROUTE**
AD+ F Giacomelli and R Rossi, 8 July 1979
126

A pleasant route which climbs the ice slope and steep mixed ground above to the summit. Recommended in snowy conditions and after a good frost. c400: 2½hr to the foresummit

226 **MATCHSTICK COULOIR**
D+ D Bianchi, F Castelnuovo, F Giacomelli, N Riva, R Rossi and
126 G Rusconi, 6 July 1980

One of the few modern 'gullies' in the range and perhaps one of the finest. It is an aesthetic line; beautifully direct, narrow and contained between solid granite walls – the feeling is distinctly 'Scottish'. The difficulties are not high (Scottish 3), and early in the season with a hard frost, stone-fall is nil. The harder sections are adequately protected with nuts and pegs so 2 or 3 ice-screws will be quite sufficient.

From the Albigna hut follow Route 228, cross the Cantun glacier and work L to the foot of the couloir (2½hr). 2 pitches of 50° lead to the first narrows. One long steep pitch (70°-75°) leads to a good stance on the R. 2 more pitches lead to the second narrows which is climbed on the L (70°). Climb up for 2 pitches (60°), then overcome a short rocky section on the L to reach the final ice slope. Go up this (60° then 55°) to the summit ridge. c400m: 4hr, 6½hr from the hut

Furcela dal Scalin 3100m

This gives access to, or escape from, the NE ridge of the Cantun. The Albigna side is quite difficult, somewhat dangerous, and most unpleasant – it is not described!

227 **EAST SIDE**

PD A von Rydzewsky with M Barbaria and C Klucker, 28 June 1892

From the Forno hut cross the glacier and walk up to Pt 2556m, which lies just S of the opening to a scree-covered valley. Go up the valley and reach the small glacier and rubble slopes that lie to the NE of the Scalin. Curve up the glacier to the S, and when at c2800m traverse horizontally to the E ridge of the Scalin. Cross it at a small yet obvious notch just above a pinnacle and descend to the glacier on the far side. Go up this easily to the pass (2hr). The E ridge of the Scalin, above the notch, gives a pleasant rock climb with moves of III–.

Scalin 3164m

U Canziani and C Prochownik, early July 1912

The twin summits of this rock tower lie on the ridge which continues N from the Cantun towards the Casnil Pass. They are rarely an outright goal for most alpinists, yet are often traversed on route to the Cantun when climbing the latter's NE ridge from the Caciadur pass – a highly recommended expedition! The S peak forms the highest point.

228 **NORTH RIDGE**

PD+/ First ascent party

AD–

A nice little climb with expansive views over the Forno and Albigna cirques. Although fairly straightforward, parts of the ridge are really quite exposed!

Follow the path due E from the Albigna hut, contouring the steep grassy hillside above the moraines on the L side of the lower Cantun glacier. The path rises and crosses a large boulder field below the Bio pillar (2843m). Reach the moraine on the R and follow a path on the crest. At the end of the moraine slither down onto the glacier and walk up it to a short couloir. This leads directly to a col on the ridge between the Scalin and a hump to the N called the Caciadur (3040m: 2½-3hr).

Start up the crest of the ridge but almost immediately go on to the Forno side. Work up a series of ledges just below the crest to the base of a tower. Climb this directly by a crack (III–), then continue more easily along the ridge to the foresummit. Easy climbing, again on the Forno side, leads to the highest point. 1hr, 3½-4hr from the hut

229 **SOUTH-WEST RIDGE**

PD+ First ascent party (in descent)

Usually taken in descent as part of the traverse to the Cantun. It is short and steep with moves that are III– in ascent.

From the summit move onto the Forno side and climb down a chimney/couloir to the Furcela dal Scalin (30min). The first rocky section across the Furcela is extremely narrow and can be either semi hand-traversed or crossed 'à cheval'.

230 **NORTH SUMMIT – WEST FACE**

VI/A1 M Hunziker and M Pasini, 5 Oct 1985

62

Recommended by the first ascent party as it offers varied and continuously interesting climbing on good rock. The steep walls above the Cantun glacier feel surprisingly remote and although the route is not of the same superb quality as those on the Bio pillar, it should appeal to lovers of solitude looking for a suitable alternative to the more popular venues. A small amount of aid was used on the first ascent but all the essential pegs were left in place. The route was not rigged for a rappel descent (although this could be easily arranged – the wall is not that high) so parties must descend the N ridge, which means carrying ice gear etc on the mountain.

Follow Route 224 onto the upper Cantun glacier and walk up to the foot of the wall (c2hr). The start lies directly below the N summit. On the L, the wall features a series of arches that curve to the R. Directly above is a huge stepped corner that also leans to the R and has for its R wall a vast steep slab. The route begins by climbing up to a niche at the base of the corner. It then moves L and follows the ramps and overlaps that overlook the corner (quite sustained at V and A0) to finish up steep cracks and corners just R of the summit fall-line. 230m: 4-5hr

Caciadur 3040m

This is the hump of scree and broken rock to the S of the pass with the same name. The N ridge is an easy scramble but the S is quite a nice little rock climb (III)

Pass di Caciadur 2938m

A von Rydzewsky with C Klucker, 9 July 1891 (E to W)

An easy crossing point on the watershed between the Forno and Albigna valleys. It is rarely used due to the proximity of the Casnil passes (qv) RE/F in either direction

Casnil Passes – Pass da Casnil N (2975m) and S (2941m)

Used for centuries by hunters, traders etc.

These two passes form the easiest and most practical linkage between the Forno and Albigna valleys. Traditionally the N pass was preferred as it is far more direct. However, in recent years the dry summers have left bare ice on the Albigna side and a steep loose rock couloir on the Forno side of this pass. Nowadays, the S pass is invariably used. It is quite straightforward (no need for crampons) and also very popular with spring skiers. Crossing this pass during the summer months is one of the most frequented excursions in the Bregaglia.

231 **WEST SIDE**

RE/F

127

Just beyond the Albigna hut a large boulder with a painted signpost marks the start of a well-beaten track to the pass. This path at first heads E, and then turns more to the N as it zigzags up a grassy spur towards two small lakes lying just E of the Piz dal Pal. Not far below the lakes take a R fork, which crosses the stream and continues up the grassy hillside to a broad rocky ridge. Walk E along the crest of the ridge – a fine place to admire the whole Albigna valley – until directly below Pt 3039m (the rocky hump on the main divide, separating the N and S passes).

To reach the S pass; cross the boulder slope on the R without gaining too much height and contour around the S flank of Pt 3039m. 2½hr

To reach the N pass; from below Pt 3039m, make a rising traverse across a snow slope on the L to a deep-blue glacial lake just below the col. If this slope is icy, a quick, easy and safe alternative is to scramble up loose ground to the top of Pt 3039m and descend a track along the crest to the col.

232 **EAST SIDE**

RE/F

141

From the Forno hut cross the glacier to the broad scree slopes below the pass. The path starts on the R close to Pt 2453m, and zigzags steeply upwards to reach the snow. Continue up the R side at first then slant L across the gentle slopes of the glacier (rope unnecessary) to the S pass (2½-3hr).

To reach the N pass it is easiest to start on the L of a direct line to the col. Leave the glacier below the walls of Pt 3039m. Slant up R on a vague track to reach the upper section of the steep scree couloir leading directly to the pass. Scramble carefully up loose ground on the L to the top.

Parties should allow 5hr from one hut to the other when crossing the S pass. Usually by mid-summer, parties will only cross via the N col if they wish to climb Piz Casnil on route.

Punta da l'Albigna 2824m

J Cottinelli and P Schucan, 22 Aug 1910

This shapely yet rather austere rock pyramid terminates the long NW ridge of the Cantun. The 500m high NW face stands in full view from the Albigna hut and provides an excellent introduction to the longer middle-grade routes of the region. Despite its lowly altitude, climbing on this face has a 'high mountain' atmosphere and plenty of exposure on the upper wall. Rapid access to the foot of the face, combined with a straightforward descent, have made this one of the most popular goals in the area, and the peak is often climbed in a day from Vicosoprano using the téléphérique.

233 **NORTH FLANK**

PD

123

The normal route reaches the summit via the Bocchetta della Punta da l'Albigna – a notch in the long narrow saddle that lies below the ESE ridge. These days it is used almost exclusively as the descent route by parties completing the NW face. Early in the season there will be snow below the Bocchetta and an axe could prove useful, but normally it is possible to descend to the hut without setting foot on snow.

From the highest point of the mountain, at the E end of the sharp summit ridge, a few airy moves lead to the top of a chimney facing SE. Descend this easily (II), and at the bottom slant down R on a narrow earthy ledge to an obvious flake that is well adorned with slings. Make a 20m rappel down the vertical wall below to a large grassy terrace, and follow a track E along the ridge to the Bocchetta (in ascent follow the grassy terrace below the steep summit walls all the way to the W ridge. Go through a notch and climb a 5m chimney (III) on the L side of the ridge to the summit).

Descend N on scree or snow patches, keeping fairly close to the rocks on the L. Finally work round L below these rocks to reach the crest of the moraine and, lower down, the approach path to Route 236

Punta da l' Albigna: North-West Face

The traditional classic on this side of the peak takes the short but aesthetic NW ridge. It is reached via a traverse across the giant basin lying above and to the L of the lower walls. However, it also provides the most logical finish to any route on these popular lower walls. Due largely to a sunless aspect, parties should delay attempting routes immediately after bad weather in order to allow the rock to thoroughly dry.

234 **MEULI ROUTE**
AD+ K Freund, H Gschwend and C Mueli, 16 Sept 1961
129
67

The most famous route on the mountain is now, deservedly, a medium-grade classic. It is inevitably very popular and variations abound. In fact there are pegs and, more recently, bolts all over this part of the face (Modern Times, 1990, V−). The direct finish, though quite popular, has a rather loose chimney to start. A standard rack will be more than sufficient. The overall grading applies to an ascent to the summit.

From the Albigna hut follow the path S down grassy slopes and along by the old water-pipe to cross the Cantun stream (no bridge anywhere over this river at the time of writing). Cross the scree and boulder slopes, descending slightly to the foot of the route. The start is marked on the rock at the base of a steep L-facing dièdre, which lies to the L of the huge couloir splitting the middle of the face (30min). 300m and 3hr for the route: 500m and 5-5½hr to the summit

235 STEIGER ROUTE

D+ G and G Steiger, 26 July 1962

129

67

A somewhat harder and more sustained proposition than the Mueli. For this reason it is climbed far less frequently – take a full rack! The easier lower section contains some loose rock, but higher the route offers excellent crack climbing on exposed slabs. The approach is almost the same as the Mueli. Continue traversing at a lower level across the boulder slopes below the base of the large central couloir (stone-fall!). 80-100m to the R is a prominent spur and the climb starts at its lowest point. As with the Mueli route, the overall grading is applicable for an ascent to the summit. 350m and 4hr for the route: 500m and 6hr to the summit

236 NORTH-WEST RIDGE

AD K Mersiovky and H Perret, 15 July 1943

129

67

This superb little route, with fine exposure, provides a worthwhile finale to routes on the lower wall. However, the foot of the ridge can also be reached by an easy traverse from the L. The rock is basically sound, although many of the flakes that are ubiquitous in the upper section appear a trifle hollow! A standard rack with a number of long slings should be more than sufficient. See also photograph 123

Follow the approach to Route 234 but after crossing the river stumble up a discontinuous track in the side of the moraine (cairns) towards the foot of the NNE ridge. This ridge lies above the huge snow/boulder filled basin that slants R above the lower walls. On the crest of the moraine a large cairn marks the start of the traverse across to this basin, via a series of grassy ledges and smooth slabs (sections of II). Walk up the R side of this basin, and via a loose gully reach the shoulder at the foot of the NW ridge (1½-2hr). It is nicer but time consuming to climb along the crest of the ridge on the R side of the basin. There are some impressive views down the NW face and the climbing is a good deal harder than first appearances would suggest!

From the shoulder walk round to the R for 30m and reach the foot of a gully on the W face that slants up L to the crest of the ridge. The first pitch climbs the black slabs on the R and is sparsely protected. The key to the second pitch is to step round onto the W face quite low down, below the big corner. Harder variants exist to the L closer to the crest. c150m: 2hr to the summit

Bio-Pillar 2843m

This glorious pillar of golden granite symbolizes the best of the modern rock-climbing available in the valley. At present there are seven routes, all of which give high quality climbing. Access is straightforward; the routes, though short, are generally steep and sustained with plenty of exposure; there are superb views across the glacier to the N face of the Cantun and the descent is quick and easy. For the rock athlete this is a big crag in a mountain setting – what more could one ask for?

The start of each route is marked in red paint (Q1, Q2 etc) as follows:

Q1 Bio-Pillar Original Route V+
Q2 Arabella Mainly IV/V+ with one move of VI
Q3 Snoopy VI+
Q4 Miki V+
Q5 La Rosa Rossa VI+

The crest of the pillar R of Q1 is taken by Moby Dick (VI), and a series of dièdres which lie between Q4 and Q5 gives the line of Berg Sea (VII/VII+, not sustained). Approach the foot of the pillar in 1hr from the Albigna hut by following Route 228. 3hr would seem to be the average time for an ascent of most routes. Three are described below.

237 **ORIGINAL ROUTE**
V+ L Blattler and K Heuitschi, 28 July 1971
69

The classic route, taking an impressive line directly up the front face of the pillar. The orientation is SSW so the lower half of the route does not receive the sun until late morning. Although not sustained at the grade, there is some outstanding climbing and the hard pitches involve quite strenuous but eminently protectable cracks. As there are a number of in-situ pegs a standard rack should be sufficient – with the emphasis on a good selection of medium-sized wires. 200m

238 **MIKI ROUTE**
V+ F Giacomelli and R Rossi, 13 July 1980
68

After the highly desirable Original Route this is probably the most popular climb on the pillar. It follows a series of cracks and dièdres on the sunny SE face and most of the pitches succumb to good layback technique. It is a harder proposition than the Original Route, being more sustained and having surprisingly little in-situ gear except at the belay points. Take a full rack. 180m

239 **LA ROSA ROSSA**
VI+ F Giacomelli and R Rossi, 19 Aug 1985
68

Steep crack climbing in a series of dièdres on the R side of the SE face. The crux, a short overhanging crack through the roofs above the second belay, is much harder than anything else on the climb. A comprehensive rack should be carried as there is little in-situ gear. 140m

Descent: From the summit go down the ridge to the N for a few m to a small col. Follow a path down the couloir on the R, over steep slabs and loose rock, to reach the foot of the SE face in c20min.

Piz Casnil 3189m

J Caviezel and H Lavater-Wegmann, 24 Aug 1880

A very popular summit with a panorama that encompasses most peaks in the range. It is frequently climbed by parties crossing between the Forno and Albigna huts. Routes are short, fairly accessible and the ridges especially are well established classics.

240 **SOUTH RIDGE**
II
127

The normal route which although somewhat imposing from many angles is much easier and less exposed than it looks. Highly recommended.

From the N Casnil pass, reached from the Albigna or Forno huts by routes 231 or 232, go up large blocks on the L side of the ridge for 100m. Slant R to the crest and follow it directly to the summit. The rock is generally sound, although as on many climbs of this standard, the prudent alpinist will not pull too hard on any of the large blocks or flakes. The correct route is no more than II (sustained) but many parties appear to find 'unavoidable' sections of III. 200m: 1-1½hr

241 **SOUTH-WEST FLANK**
II
127

When descending this side of the mountain, most parties will use this route.

From the summit go down the W ridge for a short distance, as far as the top of a wide rocky couloir splitting the SW face. Descend the steep buttress on the R (W) of the couloir via blocks and flakes (100m, II with a possible short rappel at the end). This leads to the boulder field 50m to the W of the S ridge. Scramble down this over large blocks to the Casnil pass. 1hr

242 **NORTH RIDGE**

II–/II

141

A nice climb which is longer than the S ridge but offers easy scrambling with the odd move of II. Often used in descent to make a highly recommended traverse of the peak. See also photograph 127

From the Forcola dal Riciol scramble up the ridge to the first step and bypass it on either flank (N is generally easier). Return to the ridge after c100m and continue up a series of ledges on the L flank, climbing back to the crest via a short chimney at the beginning of a horizontal section. Follow the crest, which is rather airy at first, to the summit. 1hr

243 **EAST RIDGE**

IV

W Risch, 1922

141

A Bregaglia classic and a most impressive solo ascent for the era. The climb is varied and has a succession of excellent pitches in cracks or on compact slabs, regularly interpersed with good stances. Although the fastest approach begins at the Forno hut, the route can be conveniently climbed from the Albigna by crossing the Casnil pass (allow 1hr extra).

From the Forno hut follow Route 232 towards the Casnil pass until reaching the small glacier at c2750m. Traverse R across scree and follow a vague track up a steep couloir to a small gap in the base of the ridge, just above the lower tower. It is possible to climb directly up the crest from here over two towers, but most parties take to the stony couloir on the R of the ridge, and only rejoin it above its pinnacled crest at a small saddle (2½hr).

The ridge now becomes steeper and more continuous. Climb up easily to the base of a large slab. A fine pitch of 40m (IV) is followed by easier climbing to a prominent yellow step (III). Climb up delicately rightwards to the crest and follow a crack to a stance (IV). Continue up the steep crest on excellent 'juggy' granite (III+) to a small notch where you may be lucky to find a route book concealed in a cairn (6 pitches from the start of the difficulties). The angle eases and three further pitches up the blocky crest lead to the summit. c300m: 5½hr from the hut

On the S flanks of the E ridge are several superb pillars of orange granite. Two of these have yielded very worthwhile climbs.

244 **FORNOKANTE**
IV+ M Mehli, 3 Sept 1977
141

Parallel to the S ridge is a deep rocky couloir and R of this is a fine crest of excellent granite. Although the approach is rather unpleasant, the climb itself is sustained and considered well worth the effort!

From the Forno hut follow Route 232 towards the E ridge, but instead of traversing R from the foot of the glacier, slant up L below the walls of the ridge and climb loose unsavoury ground to the foot of the pillar (2½hr). Turn the first steep wall by climbing up the rocky couloir on the L. Return to the crest as soon as possible and climb steeply upwards, negotiating small overhangs and slabs, to an easier central section. Above lies a fine golden slab with a roof at its base. Climb this via a succession of cracks and reach a small notch behind a prominent gendarme. A superb slab leads to easier ground. Reach the E ridge and follow it without further difficulty to the summit. c200m: 3-4hr

245 **SOUTH-EAST PILLAR**
V+ M Mehli and A Rogantini, 15 July 1973
141

This steep pillar lies towards the R side of the face and c20m to the left of a wide and very prominent couloir. The route takes a crack system on the crest of the pillar to a difficult compact slab (crux). Above, there is another hard pitch round an overhang before easier climbing in dièdres and chimneys leads to the top. The granite is excellent, the stances good and the difficulties well protected. Although it is possible from the top of the pillar to descend the E ridge without too much problem, it is recommended that parties continue via its fine upper section to the summit. c200m: 4-5hr, 6-7hr from the Forno hut

Forcola dal Riciol 3044m

The col between the Piz Casnil and Bacun. In previous years it could be reached from the Forno glacier via snow slopes in a gully bed. Nowadays this approach has been transformed into a hard and tedious scramble over steep scree slopes and smooth slabs. It is no longer recommended and the col is reached exclusively from the Albigna valley, on route to climbs on the adjoining peaks.

246 **WEST SIDE**
RE
125

From the Albigna hut follow the path towards the Pass da Casnil. On reaching the twin lakes below the Piz dal Pal, continue N on a path that soon bears E into a narrow valley. Reach a small group of lakes at Pt 2652m, then slant up L over stony ground (vague track) to reach the crest of the moraine under the walls of Piz Bacun. Follow the track along the crest (slight danger of stone-fall from some of the loose rock couloirs above) and continue up easy snow slopes. A short gully leads to the col. 2½hr

The track leading to the moraine is not obvious; in the early part of the season the ground above the last lakes is generally snow covered and parties keep in the wide depression that leads directly up to the col.

Piz Bacun 3244m

L Bernus and T Curtius with J Eggenberger and C Klucker, 27 Aug 1883

An impressive rocky pyramid that was a source of inspiration for the great Engadine guide – Christian Klucker. From afar its complex ridges entice, but on closer inspection fail to live up to expectation. Although it is, even today, a relatively popular excursion from either the Forno or, more likely, the Albigna hut, special care must be taken with loose rock. On the crests this takes the form of unstable blocks but on the flanks large areas of shattered granite are common. However, there are one or two exceptions. . . .

247 **SOUTH CHIMNEYS**
III
Used in descent by the first ascent party
125

This is the normal route from the Albigna hut and provides the easiest access to, and descent from, the summit. There are some sections of enjoyable climbing on quite compact rock, but there is also a fair amount of rotten terrain. Watch out for stone-fall from parties above!

From the Albigna hut follow Route 246 to the Forcola dal Riciol but not far below the col slant up L to the foot of a broad couloir on the SW face. Climb this carefully over loose rock until it is possible to move R and follow a ramp, that slants across the face to the top of a poorly defined pillar (friable rock). Reach a cairn at the foot of a deep chimney. The chimney is hardest near the bottom (III) but soon relents and leads to an exit on to the SW ridge, not far from the summit. 4hr from the hut

248 **EAST RIDGE**
III– First ascent party
125

This is the easiest route from the Forno hut. From below the Forcola dal Bacun a rotten rock rib on the NE face leads up to the ridge, not far from the summit. Roughly the same point on the ridge can also be reached from the Albigna hut. Cross the Forcola dal Riciol and traverse horizontally to a steep earthy rake that slants up R to the crest. Nasty! The crest gives good climbing all the way to the summit. 5hr from either hut. See also photograph 141

249 **NORTH RIDGE**
III T Curtius with C Klucker, 27 Aug 1885

Following the crest of the ridge throughout from the Forcola dal Bacun is highly recommended. The climbing, over large blocks and delightful slabs, is on sound 'juggy' granite. Some of the difficulties can be avoided by taking to the shattered rocks of the E flank. This route gives the most logical connection between the Bacun and the Largh, and both summits can be climbed on the same day. 1½hr from the Forcola

250 **SOUTH RIDGE**
IV N Finzi with J Biner and A Schaller, 29 Aug 1921
125

The ridge rises in a series of steps above the Forcola dal Riciol and does not appear to see much traffic these days. There are some fine pitches in cracks and dièdres, but these are interrupted by sections of easy broken ground. 200m: 5hr from the Albigna hut. See also photograph 141

251 **SOUTH-WEST RIDGE**
AD+ A Bonacossa and R Botsford, 9 July 1912. Winter: D Erba,
125 G Maresi, D Stramboni and M Valsecchi, 20-21 March 1973

Thought to be the best ridge on the mountain. It is a long climb on very good granite over several large towers. The lower section of the ridge, first climbed in 1910, is rather monotonous and is usually omitted. The upper section feels surprisingly remote, and more often than not parties will be able to enjoy fine views and exposed positions uninterrupted by the proximity of other parties. IV

From the Albigna hut follow Route 246 towards the Forcola dal Riciol. Go along the moraine until directly below a saddle on the

SW ridge. Climb up short tricky walls and steps to this saddle, which lies immediately below the point where the ridge steepens and sports a series of pinnacles. Climb the first step directly and continue along the crest via some excellent pitches. Higher, turn a huge block on the L and return to the crest via a chimney. Now climb up to and over the SW summit; descend 20m into a large gap beyond, and work up the L side of the ridge where the rock is, unfortunately, a little poorer. Reach a col which marks the top of the couloir used on the normal route. Above is a blocky wall leading to a double gendarme. Climb it and turn the gendarme on the S side to reach easy ground leading up to the summit. 400m: 6-8hr from the hut

252 **SOUTH PILLAR**

V+ D Maida, R Merendi, P Pellegrini and L Tenderini, 11 Sept 1959

The flanks of the SW ridge have areas of stupendous golden granite that will undoubtedly provide a venue for many 3-4 pitch routes in the future. One existing climb takes the L side of the red pillar below the SW summit. This top is the first main tower on the SW ridge above its steeper section. The initial pitches follow a chimney on the L side of the lower step, are entirely on rotten rock and are most unpleasant. Thereafter the climbing is superb! There are some pegs in place but a full set of wires is recommended.

The route starts above the end of the moraine on the path up to the Forcola dal Riciol (1½hr from the hut). Scramble up to, and climb, 3 pitches in the loose chimney (III/IV) to the crest of the pillar. Climb a dièdre on the L then move up and L across a compact slab (crux) well L of the crest, finishing up a well-pegged dièdre to a good stance. Above, 3 pitches up cracks and dièdres (IV and V) lead to a terrace below the summit block. It is now possible to go R onto the ridge. c250m: 3-4hr

Descent: Either use this route as a start to the SW ridge and continue to the main summit, or climb down the ridge until just beyond the huge block, from where it is possible to rappel down the S face and reach the moraine.

Forcola dal Bacun 3107m

T Curtius with C Klucker, 27 Aug 1885 (E side only). A Sommer, 29 July 1924 from NW to E

A broad depression on the ridge N of Piz Bacun and used exclusively as an access point for both this and the Cima dal Largh. The NW side is a horrendous slog up the Valun dal Bacun and is reserved for masochists. The Forcola is normally approached from the Forno hut, though by crossing the E ridge of the Bacun it can be reached from the Albigna.

253 **EAST SIDE**

RE/F

A direct ascent from the Forno glacier is extremely tedious and exposed to stone-fall. Instead, the lower section is avoided by a traverse below the E ridge of the Bacun.

From the Forno hut cross the glacier and reach the foot of the large scree-covered valley between the E ridges of Casnil and Bacun. Work up L over slabby rock, and then back R above the barrier in the centre of the lower section of this valley. A cairned path now slants up and R through a zone of grassy slabs below the impressive terminal pillar of Piz Bacun's E ridge. It enters the valley leading up to the Forcola dal Bacun, becomes more vague, and basically zigzags up to the col (snow early in the season). 2½hr

254 **FROM ALBIGNA HUT**

F+

141

From the Forcola dal Riciol make a descending traverse across steep scree slopes under the walls of the Bacun's E ridge, until below a short scree couloir leading to a saddle on the ridge. This is lower than the point reached on Route 248 when climbing the E ridge. Scramble carefully up the couloir and go down, only a short distance, on the far side. Now traverse across the flanks of the Bacun (sometimes icy and exposed to stone-fall) to reach the scree-covered valley not far below the Forcola dal Bacun. 4-4½hr from the hut

Cima dal Largh 3188m

M Barbaria and C Klucker, 29 June 1891. The two other summits had already been climbed by Curtius and Klucker in 1887.

A curious group of three towers with impressive, quasi-vertical walls of excellent granite. The SE point is the highest and appears as a distinctive 'thumb' on the ridge N of the Bacun. Once a popular and celebrated ascent, it is now considered to have a fairly long approach for what amounts to a few good pitches of climbing. It is best climbed in conjuction with the Bacun, though it seems that a decreasing number of parties are making the effort these days.

255 **EAST WALL**
III First ascent party

The normal route and approached from the Forcola dal Bacun. Although short, it is an exposed and delightful climb on excellent rock.

Follow the ridge N from the Forcola and turn two pinnacles on the R side. Towards the end the crest becomes quite narrow and finally reaches the steep walls of the E Summit. Climb a crack in a slab on the R side of the crest and reach a large ledge. Now move slightly R and climb up a short pillar, before working up and L across another slab to the crest. Move up and traverse L along a ledge onto the S face. A short chimney, followed by a slab, leads directly to the summit. c80m: 1½hr. Rappel descent.

256 **TRAVERSE**
IV R Biehler and H Hossli, 18 Aug 1909 (E to W)

The traverse of all three summits is best done from W to E (although it is easier in the reverse direction). Start the route by slanting down and across the upper part of the Bacun glacier below the Forcola, to reach the W ridge of the W summit. The climb follows the crest throughout and is sustained at III, with the hardest section (IV) on the ascent of the W ridge of the E summit. Although a magnificent little excursion with sobering exposure, it is infrequently climbed. 4-5hr round trip from the Forcola dal Bacun

257 **MOTTA FAGA RIDGE**
D/D+ A Carjori and W Hartman, 11 August 1965

Included to stimulate the interest of adventurous alpinists! Standing high above the upper Val Bregaglia and clearly visible in profile from Vicosoprano is an elegant slender rock pillar. Its continuation leads up to the W summit, although escape is possible onto the Bacun glacier. The easiest way off is via the Forcola dal Bacun and down to the Forno hut. However the most logical (?) continuation from the W top is over all three summits and back to the Albigna hut, via a traverse of the Bacun. This way you will have been on the go for 12-15hr but will have the satisfaction of completing an enterprise of a length rarely equalled anywhere in the range (TD−).

Start from the hamlet of Roivan on the main road and walk up the Valun dal Largh. At about 1600m leave the valley and climb up the steep forested hillside on the R to reach the top of Motta Faga (1931.6m: 3hr). This is a good bivouac spot which sometimes has a few pools of water. As few people do this route, getting this far will probably require a few 'bushwacking' skills!

Climb the obvious rounded pillar above in 6 long pitches (sustained IV with the last pitch V). The ridge now becomes easier, though the summit is still a depressingly long way off. Continue up the crest (quite sharp in places) and, higher, climb over or around several towers (some moves of IV). Near the top drop down into the narrow gorge of the Valun da lan Purteia on the R, and climb up it to reach the NW ridge of the Largh via a few easy pitches. Go up this ridge to the W summit. c1050m from the foot of the pillar. 5hr

Peaks on the ridge N of the Cima dal Largh give nice scrambles and some inspiring viewpoints, but are very rarely ascended.

Piz Balzet 2869m

H Rutter and A Zuan, 11 Aug 1919

A very popular peak at the end of the long SW ridge of Piz Bacun. The name is derived from a curious oasis of vegetation at the base of the stupendous W wall. The latter lies close to the dam and overlooks the téléphérique. There is a fine variety of rock routes on both the W and S faces, which due to their accessibility and sound granite can be recommended on a first visit to the Albigna valley.

258 **EAST RIDGE**
II+ First ascent party
128

The normal route and a popular goal from the Albigna hut. The final ridge is particularly nice and quite airy, but climbing round the N side of the first tower requires experience in handling loose material.

From the Albigna hut follow Route 246 towards the Forcola dal Riciol. Where it turns E into the narrow valley, head straight up boulder slopes to reach the foot of a broad scree couloir on the R of the 1st (E) tower. Follow a path up the couloir and, higher, a sort of chimney system (moves of II) leading to the col. Scramble a little way across the N face (poor rock) to a dièdre that slants up R through the steep but broken walls above. Climb it (large flakes, II+). At the top move back L in an open couloir and scramble over large blocks to the gap between the E tower and the main summit. Move onto the S side and climb a steep groove via a series of flakes (II) to the horizontal section of the ridge. Follow this easily for one rope length to the summit. 3hr from the hut

Descent: Either (a) Reverse the above; or (b) On reaching the gap before the 1st Tower, traverse easily across blocks on its N face and, at the end, climb down steeply for 10m to a good terrace. One airy rappel off a bolt leads to the col on the normal route; or (c) On reaching the gap before the 1st Tower follow an obvious path S down some grassy ledges on the L side (looking out) of a couloir. When it starts to get steep, make two rappels down the wall into the bottom of the couloir and scramble down to the boulder slopes.

259 **SOUTH RIDGE**
IV W Risch, 1922
128
70

This is one of the finest climbs of its standard in the area and a good introductory rock route for parties making their first visit to the valley. Access is quick (45min from the hut) and the climbing is varied, relatively exposed and on magnificent granite. The difficulties are sustained at III but there is a pitch of IV on the Tower. Another vintage solo first ascent by one of the region's most famous guides. c250m: 2-3hr

Piz Balzet – First Tower

260 **SOUTH RIDGE**
V A Schelbert, 29 July 1966
128
70

A short steep climb of medium difficulty. With the current vogue for this type of route in the Albigna valley, it has become quite popular. The approach and descent are quick. The climb is interesting, on good granite, and gets the sun for most of the day. 130m: 1½hr

261 **SOUTH FACE**
VI/A2 H Kaspar, 27 Sept 1969
128
70

The obvious line of old bolts up a yellow slab in the centre of the face marks the start of this aid route. The main obstacle is a roof at the beginning of the second pitch. Sections of this climb have now been done without aid but the whole route awaits transformation to a super-desperate free climb and a 'test-piece' for the future. Best effort so far; VII+ and A1. 130m

Piz Balzet – West Face

This huge wall drops more than 1000m into the great gorge carved by the Albigna river. There are two prominent features; The huge central gully -The 35 Gully – that splits the face, and towards the R side of the face near the base, the Albigna Ghost – a fine visage naturally sculptured in the granite, which scowls menacingly at passengers in the téléphérique cabins!

262 D 130

SOUTH-WEST RIDGE

H Battig and G Zryd, 1960

This route, which is often referred to as the 'Albigna Ghost', provides enjoyable though not sustained climbing on good rock, with several sections of IV. A certain amount of lichen and vegetation will be encountered, so it is wise to allow the route to dry throughly after bad weather. Apparently this is the only climb on the face that is still regularly ascended!

The start is no more than 20min from the téléphérique station. Climb the dièdre, finishing over a little roof, to a grass ledge and move L into the huge scree bowl. As all this is often wet, an alternative is to slant up L from the base of the dièdre and climb the smooth L side of the slab – but this is harder (V). Now slant up L above the 'Ghost' via cracked slabs onto the ridge. Climb c10m R of the crest to reach a big overhang. Turn it on the L (often wet) and climb a dièdre back onto the crest. Follow the crest, with diminishing difficulty, all the way to the forepeak. Climb over this and continue along the exposed and entertaining ridge to the summit. 750m: 6hr

When 100m below the forepeak, escape is possible by slanting R on ledges that lead to a gap in the ridge just before the main summit.

263 VI+/ A2+ 130

FACE TO FACE

G Alberti and P Luthi, 24 Sept 1983

A demanding climb up the front face of the 'Ghost' to reach the SW ridge after 7 pitches. Although the third pitch is rather friable, the rest of the route is on sound and very compact granite with shallow or blind cracks. The party climbed directly up to the R side of the 'lips', then traversed across them before working up the L 'nostril' and finishing directly between the two 'eyes'. Copperheads were left on the fifth pitch and all the belays were equipped. Knifeblades, rurps and large Friends will prove very useful. It has been repeated and the aid pitches are at the top end of their grade! 150m: 6-7hr

264 **35 GULLY**
ED1 D Bianchi, F Castelnuovo, N Riva and B Rusconi, 2 May 1981.
130 Winter: D Porta, 2 Feb 1987

A sensational line which at present takes pride of place as the hardest ice couloir in the district. It is at its best in spring, after which it is generally transformed into a stone-chute. Good conditions are not easily found and are essential for crossing the avalanche-prone shelf at the foot of the face. There are many sections of 70° ice and at least one short vertical step, separated by easier climbing. The name celebrates the thirty-fifth anniversary of the 'Ragni Section' of the Lecco CAI. 800m: 6-10hr

The gully to the R was climbed by Bianchi and Castelnuovo on the 11 April 1982. 750m: 10½hr, V and 85° ice, TD+/ED1

265 **WEST PILLAR**
TD− R Giovanoli and P Wieland, 2 Sept 1945
130

Although once thought to be a good climb, this is now almost totally neglected. It is a very long route with considerably more climbing than the vertical interval would suggest. The middle section has interesting climbing on sound granite (V−), but reaching it is somewhat exposed to stone-fall. Also the upper pinnacled section of the ridge is rather loose, and in common with all the routes on this face parts of the climb can be lichenous. 800m: 6-8hr

Piz dal Pal 2618m

This little climbing ground stands immediately N of the hut. There are several ridges that give pleasant outings (II/III), and some harder slabs on the W flank (VI). Best of all are the 2-3 pitch routes on the excellent granite walls of the prominent tower (IV+ to VII).

Punta Rasica 3306m

A von Rydzewsky with M Barbaria and C Klucker, 27 June 1892

The bold outline of this rocky pyramid, whose name derives from the word meaning 'saw tooth', impresses most when viewed from the Zocca valley. There is a wide variety of worthwhile routes on all sides of the peak but it is the fine ridges that have become the established classics. It is fitting that the crux of any of these lies at the top, where the summit of the mountain is formed by a spectacular blade of granite c10m high. Incidentally the summit is not at the intersection of the main ridges but a little way along the northern crest. Most routes are lengthy undertakings and have a 'high mountain' feel, so this is definitely a peak for alpinists rather than the pure rock athlete.

266 **SOUTH-EAST RIDGE**

AD First ascent party

142

This is the normal route for parties based in Switzerland. The ridge is gained via the N side of the Colle Rasica, which in recent years has been a bare ice slope and subject to moderate stone-fall from the poor rock on the flanks. In these conditions the ascent is fairly serious and will be hard for the grade. Once on the ridge it is highly recommended that parties keep to the crest. This is quite sharp and gives exposed climbing on sound granite – much more enjoyable than working across the easier but loose ground on the S flank. See also photographs 145, 153

From the Forno hut follow Route 272 to the Colle Rasica (3hr). Starting on the L climb up to the crest and follow it on firm rock to a steep buttress. This can either be climbed using the L edge followed by the chimney in the middle, or bypassed on the S side. Continue up the crest, or on ledges that lie slightly L of the ridge, to the foresummit where the three main ridges join. Up to this point the difficulties never exceed III. Move across to the foot of the summit fin, which is not only impressively steep but undercut at its base. Make a long stride onto the SE edge and boldly layback it (V−). The difficulties ease after a few moves and the highest point and 'log book' lie just up to the R (1½hr). 4½hr from the hut. Aspiring cowboys can (sometimes) protect (or even aid) this pitch by lassoing a high projection, and then straddling the arête – bucking bronco style!

267 **NORTH RIDGE**

AD+ G Polvara and V Ponti, 30 July 1922

142

An established classic which gives entertaining climbing along a wonderfully sharp and serrated crest. It is highly recommended in either direction – in descent it provides a safer route back to the Forno glacier than reversing the N side of the Colle Rasica. It is, however, a lengthy expedition rising slowly above the Rasica glacier, and despite its quality is being ignored by today's alpinists.

The approach from the Forno hut is straightforward. When coming from the Allievi it is possible to climb a rocky rib on the R of the couloir leading to the Colle del Castello – see Route 217. See also photograph 153

From the Colle del Castello follow the crest of the ridge, making short deviations onto the L side from time to time to avoid the difficulties. Pass over two rocky humps and reach a knife-edge, which gives some delightful climbing to the foot of the first steep buttress. This buttress is generally referred to as the N peak. Ignore a tempting chimney on the R, and instead climb the crest directly on good holds to the top (c3261m). Go down easily into a gap and avoid the next tower on the R side. Continue along the sharp exposed crest; climb over a second tower and then make a rappel into the gap beyond. This gap is the lowest point between the N and main summits.

Go up to an overhanging buttress and climb it on the R flank via a slab and dièdre. Continue along the crest to the N side of the summit towers. So far the rock difficulties have been II to III with one or two sections of IV. Climb down a few m on the E side of the ridge and follow a crack across to the base of the 'fin'. Layback this (V–: see Route 266) to the summit. 4-4½hr: 7-8hr from either hut. When descending the ridge the rappel pitch can be climbed just R of the crest on superb granite (20m: IV+).

268 SOUTH-WEST RIDGE – BRAMANI ROUTE

D A Bonacossa, E Bozzoli-Parasacchi, V Bramani and C Negri,
135 14 July 1935. Winter: G Miotti and C Pedroni, 1976
54

This is a magnificent classic and one of the longest ascents on the Italian side of the range. The amount of climbing is considerably more than the vertical interval would suggest. It is often likened in length and difficulty to the Badile's N ridge. Here the comparison must end – the Rasica is a much finer and more varied climb! Cracks and chimneys alternate with compact friction slabs – all on perfect granite. A direct start has been added to the slabs below the ridge (IV+). This is usually wet and has failed to become popular. A standard rack is sufficient but an axe and probably crampons will be needed for the descent. See also photograph 153

Reach the foot of the rounded buttress (Pt 2737m), which lies to the L of the base of the ridge, in 1hr15min from the Allievi hut. On the R a couloir slants up to the crest of this step. Climb up easily until just below the top of the buttress, then slant R over ledges to an open dièdre at the base of the ridge. Climb the dièdre and the S-shaped couloir above. Higher, take the R fork of the couloir to the crest of the ridge and follow it, making two deviations onto the SE face to avoid major difficulties on the crest, to the summit. 600m: 6-8hr from the hut

Descent: The easiest route on the Italian side is the WNW face (Castelnuovo/Fiorelli, 1906). Nowadays it provides the most popular descent for parties returning to the Allievi hut. Axe and crampons are advised.

From the summit rappel the fin and go down the SW ridge for c60m to a notch. Slant R down the W face for c20m and reach a vague rib where the first rappel anchor is located. The wall below is only 120m and is descended in several rappels (II/III in ascent), the last over a gigantic rimaye. Go down the steep snow/ice slope and then head towards the Castello, until it is possible to descend a glacial valley that flows from the Colle del Castello towards the Roma path. 2½hr to the hut

269 **NORTH SUMMIT – EAST PILLAR**

VI/A2 C Baudenbacher and R Hellstern, 15-17 Aug 1971

142

A hard route that takes a huge dièdre on the L side of the white triangular face rising vertically from the Forno glacier. The dièdre is approached from the R via a ramp (V+) and the first two pitches are partially overhanging (VI and A2: several bolts). Above, four pitches of IV and V lead to the summit. The route has seen few ascents but the granite is excellent and most of the original aid was left in place. Dispensing with this aid is an obvious project for a team of strong crack climbers! 200m: 6-8hr

Colle Rasica 3195m

First traverse (S to N): A von Rydzewsky with A Dandrea and C Klucker, 16 July 1895. The col had been previously reached by Klucker and party, from the Forno glacier, on 26 July 1891

The lowest point on the frontier ridge between Pta Rasica and Pizzo

Torrone Occidentale. Reaching this col forms part of the normal routes to the peaks mentioned above. The N side is a short but relatively steep ice slope and is climbed quite frequently (see Route 272). The S side is a nasty couloir which has generally degenerated into a rubbish-chute by summer. In these conditions it is quite dangerous and not recommended.

Torrone Occidentale 3351m

E Albertario and F Lurani with A Baroni, 12 Aug 1882

The highest of the Torrone peaks. Although rarely climbed from the N, the S side has some first-rate routes on the crests or flanks of the long granite ridges. Situated close to the Allievi hut, these have become quite popular.

270 **SOUTH FACE AND SOUTH RIDGE**
PD+ First ascent party
138

The simplest means of reaching the summit from the Allievi hut and undoubtedly the best descent. It appears to be quite safe from stone-fall and gives interesting climbing on reasonable rock.

Follow the Roma path E from the Allievi hut until it begins to rise to the Passo Val Torrone. Now head up to the NE over rough ground and reach the slabby S face of the mountain (c1hr). The L side of the face is split by a prominent chimney that slants up to the R. Starting on the L climb up easy slabs into the chimney and follow it to the top. The rock is solid and quite smooth in parts and gives some entertaining climbing. Near the top it can be wet and a narrow section provides the crux (III: rappel in descent). Work up R on the scree (snow) slope to reach the junction of the SW and S ridges.

Scramble easily up the S ridge until it is possible to move R onto the slope overlooking the Val Torrone, and climb across this to the E ridge. Reach the crest via a loose couloir and follow it to the summit (3-3½hr). 4-5hr from the hut

If the slopes are icy then it is better to continue up the S ridge, which gives some very pleasant climbing at II/III. Keep slightly L near the top and reach the summit via a very steep chimney and some cracked slabs.

271 **SOUTH RIDGE**
AD+ A Bonacossa and C Negri, 12 Sept 1935
138

An excellent little route which is a traditional classic and still a popular outing from the Allievi hut. The initial crest is only c150m high, has three steep sharp steps, and offers several quite superb pitches on perfect rock. Above this it is possible to traverse the boulder/snow slope to the W and descend Route 270. Purists, however, will continue up the S ridge, which although much easier, provides continuously varied climbing all the way to the main summit.

Follow Route 270 to the foot of the S face, then slant up R over slabs to a dièdre below a col at the foot of the ridge. Climb the dièdre (IV/IV+) to the narrow crest (1½-2hr). The first step is the easiest and gives a fine pitch on 'juggy' rock directly up the crest (40m: IV−). The second is sharper and more exposed. Climb it either on the crest, or slightly to the L via compact slabs to an airy stance (50m: V−). The third step is shorter, less steep, but even more exposed! Climb it, moving slightly R of the crest near the top (20m: IV+, a superb pitch) and continue up the much easier ridge to the summit (II/III). 500m: 4hr, 5½-6hr from the hut

272 **NORTH-WEST RIDGE**
AD−/ C Branch, E Garwood, E Kingscote with A Rauch and M Schocher,
AD 30 Aug 1891
138

This is the normal route from the Forno hut. The ridge starts from the Colle Rasica and an approach to this gap from the Italian side involves climbing a nasty loose couloir which is exposed to stone-fall. The N side has been a bare ice slope in recent years (see introduction to Route 266) but when well covered with snow can be fairly straightforward, though there is still risk of stone-fall later in the day from the loose walls of the Rasica. The ridge itself gives very pleasant climbing and is altogether less serious than the approach. The position is splendid and the rock mainly sound (pitches of III). See also photograph 145

From the Forno hut walk up the E side of the glacier. In the upper reaches work around to the SW (more crevassed!) and reach the snow slope below the Colle Rasica. The rimaye can prove troublesome but the average angle of the slope above is not too great. Easy broken rock leads to the col (3hr).

Go up the steep crest on shattered rock towards a notch c40m deep. Just before reaching this notch climb down a crack on the S face and follow a system of ledges into the couloir. Reach the gap and climb out the far side on the crest – a fine pitch on good rock. Continue along the ridge, which can give entertaining mixed climbing early in the season, to the final tower. This overhangs alarmingly to the N so climb onto the S side via a splendid crack. Move round to the E face and climb up, with some trepidation, to the top (3hr). 6hr from the hut

273 EAST RIDGE

AD+ A Corti, P Foianini and O Lenatti, 12 Aug 1934

138

This route, approached via the N side of the Breccia del Torrone Occidentale (c3236m.), gives a similar climb to the normal route (291) on the Torrone Centrale. The ridge is easy, although the rock requires careful handling and the approach is only recommended in good snow conditions. With an early start it is possible to complete an interesting traverse of the mountain by descending the previous route. See also photograph 145

The highest rocky point on the ridge between the Centrale and Occidentale is called the Pta Alessandra (3269m). Reach the foot of the snow/ice slope directly below this in 2hr from the Forno hut. Cross the rimaye (difficult) on the L and climb up the slope for 150m to below the steep walls of the Alessandra. Work up R, passing through a bottleneck to the slope below the Breccia. Either climb directly to this col or move R to a prominent ice rib (which can be reached directly from the glacier via the slopes below the Occidentale) and climb it, finishing on mixed ground to the ridge (2½hr). Follow the crest, which gives easy scrambling to the top (1hr). c450m: 5½hr from the hut

274 TRAVERSE FROM TORRONE CENTRALE

D

138

A highly recommended, though seldom completed, crossing of the frontier ridge. It is best attempted from the Italian side by first climbing the normal route to the Centrale then descending Route 270 at the end of the afternoon. Very fit parties, wishing to prolong an already energetic day, could continue over the Pta Rasica. See also photograph 150

From the Manzi hut follow Route 289 or 290 to the summit of the Centrale and descend the W ridge (Route 291) to the Colle del Torrone Occidentale. Go easily along the E ridge of the Pta Alessandra, turning a huge monolith on the L, to reach the summit block. Turn it on the L to gain the W ridge (III) and climb back up this to the top (1hr from the col). Reverse the ridge and continue along the crest to the Breccia del Torrone Occidentale (III; good rock; 1hr). The easy crest of the E ridge leads up to the summit of the Occidentale (1hr). Descend Route 270. 12hr round trip from the Manzi hut

Escape from the ridge is possible at the Colle del Torrone Occidentale by descending the couloir on the S face (short, steep, loose and exposed to stone-fall!). A better alternative is to go down a system of ledges on the S face of the Alessandra, starting from the Breccia. These lead into the bottom of the couloir mentioned above (II/III).

Torrone Occidentale: South-East Face

A number of routes have been climbed on the walls overlooking the Val Torrone. Highly conspicuous are the twin rounded pillars – the Siamese Pillars – that lie below the upper scree/snow slope. These give two thoroughly modern climbs of excellent quality that can be reached in c1hr from the Manzi hut (crampons usually necessary). The final pitches receive drainage from the slopes above, and for this reason the routes are best attempted late in the season, preferably in Sept when the snow has long since departed. The L pillar gives 350m of climbing at VI+, with a few short sections of easy aid that could probably be free-climbed. This route – 'Il Tempo del Broncio' – takes a fairly direct line up the L side of the pillar in 9 pitches (sustained at V and VI: bolt belays) and was climbed on 17 July 1988. On the R-hand pillar 'Scacciapensieri', climbed on 16-17 Sept 1989, weaves its way up the centre of the face and has longer sections of aid (A1 and A2) with free-climbing up to VI+ (12 pitches and 500m of climbing: 26 bolts and 7 pegs left in place). Both routes were put up by S Brambati, A Carnati and P Vitali, give well-protected climbing in cracks and dièdres, and are well-equipped for rappel descents.

Punta 2987m

This forms the base of the long SW ridge of the Occidentale. Its beautiful granite walls are immediately obvious from the Allievi hut and can be reached in 30-45min. The low altitude, sunny aspect and quick straightforward descent have made this a popular playground.

From the top it is possible to continue up the main ridge to the summit of the Occidentale, but most parties will traverse grassy ledges and scree on the S face to reach the top of the chimney on the normal route.

275 **SOUTH PILLAR**
V J Merrizi and G Miotti, June 1975
132
72

Yet another fine discovery from this prolific pair. It rapidly became a modern classic and is nowadays one of the most popular ascents from the Allievi hut. It is similar in style to the Gervasutti route on the Pta Allievi but is both shorter and less taxing. The climb begins on the W face, 40m from the base of the pillar, where a lichenous dièdre leads up to the crest. From the end of pitch 13 a rappel descent has been established down a couloir on the E face and allows a quick return to the base of the pillar. The climbing is extremely varied with a succession of cracks, chimneys, slabs, overhangs and sharp edges, all well-protected and on good granite. Take a standard rack with plenty of quick-draws. c320m: 4-5hr

276 **SOUTH-WEST PILLAR**
VI+/A2 E and F Gugiatti, 13 July 1974
132
72

Several notable climbers consider this to be one of the better rock routes in the region, but due to the high technical difficulties it has not gained the popularity of the S Pillar. The climbing is generally quite slabby, and although several overlaps have to be negotiated, it seems unlikely that the few aid moves shown on the topo have not been eliminated. All the necessary pegs for protection and aid are in place, but the prudent climber will carry a wide selection of wires and Friends. c300m: 6-8hr. See also photograph 138

277 **PARRUFFONE**
VI+ J Merizzi and U Pasqualotto, 11 Aug 1990
132
71

Another worthwhile route at an accessible standard that starts below the second chimney system to the L of the SW Pillar. The bottom section offers some really great crack climbing on excellent granite. Higher, the route breaks out L on a 'hidden' buttress and some of the rock can be a little lichenous. The crux roof on the second pitch is considerably harder than anything else if climbed completely free but an aid move at this point would reduce the grade of the climb to a fairly homogeneous V+. Take a standard rack with a few larger Hexes/Friends. The first ascent party left 6 pegs in place. c300m: 4-5hr

278 **MELONIMASPES CRACK**
V+/VI G Maspes and O Meloni, 12 July 1990
132

This slanting crack system, towards the L side of the wall, gives superb climbing. The first ascent party feels that the route has all the qualities needed for an instant modern classic. The granite is impeccable, the climbing is sustained at an accessible standard (V to V+) and the protection is excellent. The approach is short (c1hr from the Allievi hut) and each stance has been equipped with a rappel anchor, usually two pegs. The move of VI, fairly low down on pitch 2, can easily be bypassed at A0. The climb starts at a stance (with a fixed nut and peg), which generally lies 5-10m above the snow. A leisurely start is recommended as the sun does not strike the wall until late-morning. Take a reasonably full rack with a good selection of small and medium wires. c280m: 3-4hr

Picco Luigi Amedeo c2800m

G Silvestri with two soldiers in 1919

This dramatic spire of golden granite is often referred to as the 'Grand Capucin' of the Bregaglia. It lies immediately N of the Passo Val Torrone, and although it appears rather incidental when seen from the W, the SE wall, topped by a conspicuous cowl, rises vertically for almost 400m above the stony slopes of the Torrone valley. Climbs on this wall have the length and commitment equal to most routes in the range, but the total absence of a snowy landscape does not give an atmosphere associated with higher mountains.

279 **NORTH-NORTH-EAST RIDGE**
III+/IV− First ascent party

The easiest route to the summit and a short but quite interesting ascent.

From the Allievi hut follow the Roma path towards the Passo Val Torrone, and go up boulder slopes to the foot of an obvious couloir that slants R to the ridge, well N of the summit (1hr). The base of the 'couloir' takes the form of a ramp with beautiful slabs. Climb this ramp and the short narrow gully above onto the ridge. Scramble easily along the W side of the ridge and climb a short dièdre to the gap between a tiny foresummit and the N top. Slabs lead to the highest point (1hr: 2hr from the hut). To reach the S and slightly lower summit, climb down steeply into the gap and pad up the gently inclined slab to the top. See Route 281 for a rappel descent.

280 SOUTH-SOUTH-WEST RIDGE

V/A1 R Bignami and W Bonatti, 7 June 1953

138

A short route, which savours a little of the exposure found on the SE wall without the commitment or technical difficulty of the climbing. The line is a little devious, only reaching the crest of the ridge at about two-thirds height and avoiding the huge summit block on the W face. Some of the climbing is very good but lower down it is a bit grassy. The standard is mainly IV with only a few harder sections and one short horizontal traverse on aid. Ascents are infrequent so expect to find little in-situ gear. See also photograph 151

From the Passo Val Torrone walk up easy ground to reach the L side of the ridge. Start in a steep rocky couloir and climb it for 60m, via some slabs and vegetated rock, to a system of dièdres. Climb these dièdres which eventually slant R to the crest. Climb two successive steps separated by a sharp horizontal crest to the foot of the final pillar, where Route 281 comes in from the R. This pillar looks completely blank, so traverse L on easy ground, climb a few m down a couloir, then slant up L in a dièdre to reach the easy-angled ground. Go up to the gap between the N and S summits. c200m: 4hr

281 SOUTH-EAST FACE

TD+/ N Nusdeo and V Taldo, 1-2 June 1959

ED1

151

66

The most noticable feature on this sensational wall is the huge central crack-line. Although more recent climbs have been added to either side, including the ferocious 'Electroshock' (Fazzini, Gianola and Riva, 1989: VIII/VIII+ and A0), which takes the walls to the L in 12 bolt-protected pitches via a conspicuous R-slanting crack that forms the L side of a huge flake, the original route – a milestone in Bregaglia climbing – remains one of the very best in the range. Pitch after pitch of sustained, strenuous and well-protected cracks lead into some improbable terrain below the frightening summit cowl. Retreat, though not impossible, would be quite problematical above the cave pitch. A fast party should just avoid a bivouac but, if in doubt, pick a warm night or adopt 'Big Wall' tactics! The foot of the face can be reached in 1hr15min from the Allievi hut or 30min from the Manzi bivouac. Once the SSW ridge is joined at the final pillar, follow it L and either continue to the summit, or make about 3 long rappels, from well-equipped anchors, down the SW face. A very comprehensive rack with a few large Friends (3 and 3½) is recommended. 370m: VII –, 12hr

Meridiana di Torrone 2493m

Twin summits on the ridge S of the Passo Val Torrone and close to Pt 2384m. On the E side a narrow and exposed grassy rake cuts up from R to L and ends on a sort of shoulder to the S of the summits. From this shoulder a sheer wall of golden granite drops into the Val Torrone. This face quickly comes into view after leaving the Mello valley on route to the Manzi bivouac, and is unquestionably one of the most spectacular 'Big Walls' in the Bregaglia.

At the time of writing the two routes described below have not been repeated.

282 **EAST-SOUTH-EAST FACE – OUTLANDOS D'AMOUR**
ED2 O Meloni, R Tassoni and U Villotta, 3-4 Sept 1988 (after considerable preparation)

Apart from the recent routes on Monte Qualido, this presents one of the greatest attractions to 'Big Wall' climbers in the region. It follows an improbable line up the centre of the wall, bypassing the huge roof at two-thirds height on the L. The route could well become popular in the future as it is not overlong, nor are the difficulties extreme (strenuous free-climbing where many of the hard moves could be aided, interspersed by pitches of moderate artificial climbing). However, retreat would not be easy above mid-height and the exposure in the upper section must be outrageous! Carry two sets of Friends and wires, plus c20 pegs (mainly blades, half-a-dozen angles and a rurp). There are no real bivouac sites in the upper section and it is recommended that hammocks are carried. All bolts and main belay pegs were left in place.

Follow Route H15 towards the Casera Torrone and on reaching two giant boulders, c15min above the point where the valley begins to open out, head L to the foot of the wall. The climb starts R of a huge yellow dièdre (the most obvious on the wall) and directly below the awesome roof, high on the face. Climb up steep and grassy walls to the foot of the dièdre.

Climb a grassy crack a few m R of the dièdre to a ledge (20m: IV with a section of V+). Continue up the thin 7-shaped crack above (25m: A2). Traverse R and climb a dièdre to a big roof (25m: VI with moves of VII−). Go up, then L round the roof (15m: A1). Traverse L on an almost-horizontal crack (40m: hard A2). Go up onto the prominent grassy ledges and follow these L to a tree (the only tree on the face; at the time of writing a fixed rope was still hanging in this vicinity). This is an excellent bivouac site and the only comfortable one on the route!

Climb a crack on the L then traverse R for 3m and go up to a huge detached flake. Chimney up behind this to a stance on the L (40m: VI−, then A1 and V+). Climb a short wall directly above the stance, then move R and reach the top of a small pillar (25m: VI and A0 to start, then IV). Climb the dièdre above to a stance at the base of a crack, L of the main corner (25m: VI then IV). Leave the dièdre and climb this overhanging crack. It gets mighty thin higher up, so as soon as possible move out L and climb a dièdre in its entirety to reach a stance (45m: V+ to VII−: watch out for serious rope-drag!). This point is below and to the L of the awesome roof at two-thirds height on the face. Climb up and traverse L, passing a grassy corner to reach an overhanging crack that slants up to the R. Climb it and exit L onto a stance (40m: hard A2 and a little VI). Traverse R a few m to a vertical crack and climb it to a small terrace on the L (30m: VI then A1). Climb a ramp on the R and the crack that follows (overhanging at the start), to an exit L onto the SE Pillar. (30m: VI+/VII and A1). Go up slabs on the L to a grassy crack. Climb the crack and continue up vegetated rock to the bottom of a fine slab (50m: IV+, then easy). The fifteenth and last pitch climbs up the L side of the slab to a grassy ledge. Now slant up L on easy ground to the summit (40m: VI at the start). c500m: allow 2½ days

Descent: Scramble easily down grassy rock on the W face to reach the path in the Zocca valley.

283 **SOUTH-EAST PILLAR**
ED2 S Brambati, A Carnati and P Vitali, Completed on 15 July 1989
65 after several days work

Another addition to the wall by well-known local activists takes the rounded pillar that flanks the L side of the face. It is reported to give 'a splendid and continuously interesting climb in a fantastic position'. Although this is undoubtedly true, after c250m the route runs quite close to broken vegetated ground and it appears that escape might be possible at several points. However, it is a high standard free-climb with very little aid (a few moves at A0) and a competent party, able to climb the hard pitches reasonably quickly, should complete it in a day. Double bolt belays at each stance allow a safe and efficient rappel descent. Apart from the bolts shown on the topo, there are c8 pegs in place. However, it is recommended that several more, plus a complete set of nuts and Friends, are carried. 550m

Punta Chiara 2951m

A pyramid of excellent granite situated near the head of the Val Torrone and a little way N of the Roma path. The S ridge, which rises in a series of steps, is an established classic and is conveniently located to the NW of the Manzi bivouac.

284 **NORTH RIDGE**

PD–

150 *An easy scramble which is generally descended by parties completing the S ridge. See also photograph 138*

From the summit scramble down the blocky ridge to the Torrone glacier (10min: II). Descend the glacier under the W face of the peak, and passing close to the base of the S ridge, go down moraine and scree slopes to the Manzi hut (45min-1hr).

285 **SOUTH RIDGE**

D– C Mauri and G Ratti, 21 June 1953.

150 First winter ascent: C Gianetti and G Maspes, 1992

49 *This is an excellent route of medium difficulty and highly recommended to climbers operating at this standard. The foot of the ridge can be reached in 20min from the Manzi bivouac, or c1½hr from the Allievi hut via the Roma path. Although the initial step can be climbed, most parties start around to the W, where an 80m chimney-couloir slants up R to the crest. Higher up the ridge, more direct lines are possible on the crest at VI. c350m: V, 4-5hr*

Punta Ferrario 3258m

L Binaghi and A Malinverno, 8 Sept 1930

Yet another stupendous granite pillar in this valley of impressive rock walls. It forms the final bastion of the ridge that runs S from the W summit of Torrone Centrale (Pta Melzi: 3275m). The peak is rarely ascended; the easiest route is a long and complicated affair that starts at the Colle del Torrone Occidentale and traverses the W flanks of the Pta Melzi to reach the N ridge. The showpiece, which rivals the SE face of the Luigi Amedeo, is the S face – a huge barrel-shaped buttress with an obvious barrier of roofs at three-quarters height.

Punta Ferrario: South Face

286 **ORIGINAL ROUTE**
TD E Frisia, V Taldo and C Zamboni, 4 Oct 1959
150
81

The only route on the wall to have received several ascents. This is no doubt due to the small amount of aid required and the quality of the climbing, which is reported to be both varied and interesting. Towards the L side of the face the angle eases and the huge slabs are well broken by cracks and dièdres. After climbing these slabs, the route is forced to move R at the barrier of overhangs, where a central break, climbed in one hard pitch, allows access to the summit slabs. Much of the climbing is very good and sustained at a reasonable grade (III/V), but the difficulty of the crux pitch makes the route somewhat non-uniform. There is usually a small snow patch at the foot of the face, and from here the route is reached by climbing up the easy slabs on the L for 100m (1hr from the Manzi hut). c350m: 6hr

287 **DIRECT ROUTE**
ED1 B Ciernik, J Hyzny, M Marek and F Piacek, 18 Aug 1980
150
81

The most recent route on the face (from a strong Czech team) takes the huge central dièdre. Whilst it is open to conjecture as to whether this provides the best climbing on the wall, it certainly takes the best line, and uses far less aid than the 1963 route further R. It joins the original route 4 pitches below the summit at the yellow overhangs. Large easy-angled slabs in the vicinity of these roofs hold snow after the spring, and it may be prudent to attempt this route later, rather than earlier, in the season. Prospective parties should also be aware when viewing the accompanying topo, that the Czechs have a certain reputation for undergrading! 430m: 10hr

The pillar situated between the two previous routes was climbed in July 1990. It gave a completely free climb at VI, with two short sections of VI+

288 **WEST FACE – DESCENT**

A number of rappel descents have been made of the W face. A few m to the S of the summit a dièdre-chimney goes down the face to a large smooth slab. It is possible to climb down this dièdre for 10m and then make a 40m rappel to the bottom of the slab. Below, three long rappels down a huge steep chimney with an enormous chockstone near the top, lead to the glacier. From here the easiest descent is down the glacier and round the W side of Pta Chiara to the Roma path. Allow 2-2½hr

Torrone Centrale 3290m

A von Rydzewsky with M Barbaria and C Klucker, 8 July 1891

A complex mountain and the least climbed of all the Torrone peaks. There are two summits separated by the the snowy saddle of the Colle del Torrone Centrale (c3250m). The W (lower) peak is often referred to as Pta Melzi (3275m) and has a long S ridge which terminates in the impressive buttress of the Pta Ferrario. Routes to the summit are fundamentally mixed climbs and a good covering of snow is highly desirable. The traverse along the frontier ridge to the Occidentale is a particularly rewarding expedition.

289 **SOUTH COULOIR**
PD+/ A von Rydzewsky with M Barbaria and C Klucker,
AD– 24 June 1900 in descent
150

This is the normal route on the Italian side and early in the season, when snow conditions are still good, it is the easiest and quickest of any route to the summit. The 'Great Couloir' is exposed to stone-fall and is best completed shortly after dawn.

From the Manzi bivouac walk up the Roma path to the small glacier that lies between the Torrone Orientale and the Ferrario. Go up it to the NW This is generally quite straightforward as there are few crevasses (2hr). At its head lies the large snow/ice couloir leading directly to the Colle del Torrone Centrale. Climb it for c250m to the col (40°: 1-1½hr), and follow the W ridge via a short snow crest and broken rocks to the summit (30min). 3½-4hr from the hut

290 **SOUTH-EAST FACE**
AD– L Binaghi, F Maccagno and A Malinverno, Aug 1932
150

This useful variation to the normal route is worth knowing when the S couloir is in poor condition. It provides the safest way off the mountain after mid-morning (or earlier!) and will be used habitually by parties attempting the peak from this side in mid-summer.

From the base of the S couloir slant up R on a conspicuous ledge system to reach a small scree slope. Work up L over a series of easy walls to a dièdre, then climb up its R wall (III) on sound rock to the SE ridge. Turn L and scramble easily over large blocks to the summit. 4-4½hr from the hut

291 **WEST RIDGE FROM FORNO GLACIER**
AD+ First ascent party
145

The normal route from the Swiss side but relatively serious. It is a fine snow and ice route when in condition, but is unlikely to be so after the beginning of July. A very early start is necessary if the party intends to return the same way. See also photograph 150

From the Forno hut go up the L side of the glacier. Near the top work across to the foot of the N face (2hr). A glacier shelf rises from L to R and reaches the rocks of the NW spur. Cross these rocks at their narrowest point and traverse the slope on the R to reach the crest of a snow/ice rib on the NW face. Climb this steeply to the Colle del Torrone Occidentale (2-2½hr). Reach a small notch a little further up the W ridge via the snow slopes on the N face. Now climb the sharp crest of the ridge, at first on ice, then rock to the top of Pta Melzi. Descend into the snowy saddle of the Colle del Torrone Centrale and scramble up easy broken rocks to the summit (30min-1hr). 400m: 4½-5½hr from the hut.

It is obviously possible to leave the snow/ice rib at any stage and reach the Colle del Torrone Centrale directly.

292 **NORTH-WEST SPUR**
D– Unknown but descended by J Deiters, J and M Jolles with L Baer
145 and W Risch during the night of 27-28 Aug 1930

Early in the season this gives an excellent mixed climb with rock pitches of IV. Unfortunately, in a drier state some of the rock appears to be rather friable and the quality of climbing diminishes. However, in these conditions the normal route will be bare ice and exposed to stone-fall, so this route could offer a very practical alternative. After leaving the normal route the spur is climbed directly on the crest for 250m to the summit, and though continuously interesting has received very few ascents. 400m: 5hr from the Forno hut

Colle del Torrone c3180m

K Schulz with A Burgener and C Perren, 27 July 1883 (N to S)

The lowest point on the ridge between the Torrone Centrale and Orientale. Just to the E stands the spectacular finger of the Ago del Torrone. The approach towards this col from the Italian side is described in Route 296. The N side is a steep ice slope of less than 200m, followed by a short section of mixed ground. It is a serious little climb which is exposed to stone-fall and is rarely attempted these days (AD+: 50°-55°, 2-3hr).

293
IV+
150

Ago del Torrone 3233m

N Finzi with F Biner and R Lagger, 4 Aug 1923

An amazing 40m granite monolith, which in the past was often referred to as 'Cleopatra's Needle'. It simply cries out to be climbed, yet the length and seriousness of the approach have deterred most parties and few ascents have been recorded. The first was a real 'tour de force'; the tower eventually succumbed after several attempts, and then only to combined tactics. Nowadays it is a pleasant exposed pitch of medium difficulty and on excellent rock.

From the Colle del Torrone traverse the N side of the ridge to the Ago. Starting on the L side of the N face climb up a steep wall and move R to a rib. Go up this via a dièdre on the L; move down L along ledges and climb steep slabs, finishing up the W face to the summit. 30min: rappel descent

Torrone Orientale 3333m

R Paulke and A Rzewuski with J Eggengerger and C Klucker, 29 July 1882

This slim granite pyramid is possibly the most attractive summit at the head of the Forno glacier and was Klucker's first new route. For parties based at the Forno hut it is the most reasonable of all the Torrone peaks. There are two summits connected by a short and exposed rocky crest, with the S top being the higher. From it falls a sharp ridge with a profile clearly visible from the vicinity of San Martino. This gives one of the more remote 'classics' in the Bregaglia. Superb views, especially of the Disgrazia, make this summit a worthwhile objective and one that is unlikely to be shared with other parties.

294 **NORTH-EAST FLANK**
AD– First ascent party
145

The normal route from Switzerland and a highly recommended mixed expedition. It is probably the easiest route to the summit and safer than any of the Italian approaches. In common with many other routes of this nature it is best attempted early in the season, before crevasses become too much of a problem.

From the Forno hut walk easily yet tediously up the L side of the glacier (continuously up and down over ridges/troughs) and reach the foot of a well-defined glacial spur that comes down from the summit rocks. Climb the glacier slope on the L of this spur, moving R at the top to reach the rocks of the NE face (4hr). The slope usually has few crevasses but one or two of these can be enormous. If this is the case it is better to climb the spur (steep bulges and smaller crevasses) throughout.

On the NE face climb a slabby rib followed by two successive chimneys (III–) which lead to the summit ridge (1hr). 5hr from the hut

It is also possible to continue up the snow slopes to the saddle (c3200m) on the frontier ridge. From here climb the ENE ridge to the top. This is a delightful little rock climb on sound granite but is more difficult than the normal way (III/III+ at the start: 1hr).

295 **NORTH-WEST SPUR**
AD G Donni, H Frei and R Honegger, 1936
145

An elegant little line which is reasonably straightforward in dry conditions where the rock-climbing standard never exceeds III. In perfect mixed conditions it becomes harder (AD+) but even more worthwhile.

Start directly below the summit. Cross the rimaye (difficult in recent summers) and climb the 45° ice slope to the base of the spur. Continue more or less on the crest, which offers very varied climbing, until c50m from the top. From here the easiest finish is to slant R onto the W ridge and follow it to the N summit. c300m: 6hr from the Forno hut

296 **WEST RIDGE**
AD+ K Schulz with A Burgener and C Perren, 3 Aug 1883
150

This ridge, approached via the S side of the Colle del Torrone, provides the most practical route to the summit from the Italian side. However, ascents are still a rare occurrence! The Torrone glacier is generally easy

but by mid-summer the rimaye below the couloir can be extremely difficult to cross. Dry conditions will produce severe stone-fall and an ascent can only be recommended early in the season, when good snow cover and a night-time frost should provide a safe passage.

From the Manzi hut follow the Roma path towards the Passo Cameraccio, but continue up the glacier to the SW of the Torrone. Between the smooth face of the Torrone and the walls supporting the Ago lies a steep and narrow couloir. Climb this to a shoulder on the L, then continue working up to the L over easy ground to reach the upper snow/ice slope below the Ago.

The Colle del Torrone actually lies to the W of the Ago and it is not necessary to reach it. Instead, scramble up broken rock to the R of the Ago and gain the start of the W ridge (3hr). The ridge itself is rather poorly defined. After c15min of easy scrambling a tricky slab leads to a scree terrace. Above is another slab 20m high. Climb it and the smooth strenuous chimney that follows, to a slightly impending wall. Pull over onto ledges below the N summit (III+). From here it is best to turn this summit on the L and follow the crest SE to the highest point (1½hr). 4½hr from the hut

See Route 297 for an alternative descent.

297 **SOUTH RIDGE DIRECT**

TD J Canali and R Osio, 18 July 1956. Winter: G Della Torre and

154 E Majoli, 23-24 Dec 1970

83 *This superb edge – reminiscent of the Cengalo S. ridge – is one of the great traditional classics on the Italian side of the range. The climb more or less follows the crest throughout, and some of the pitches are mighty exposed! The situation is wild and remote; the approach lacks the comforts of a decent hut and there is no really easy or convenient descent from the summit to the foot of the route. With these deterrents it is not hard to see why such a splendid climb sees relatively few ascents compared with those in the Allievi cirque. So far there does not seem to have been a completely free ascent, and as the difficult pitches have many pegs in place, it is possible to climb the route at V and A0/1. A good selection of wires and plenty of quick-draws will prove useful, and if the usual descent is taken, ice gear will have to be carried. 380m: 6-8hr. See also photographs 150, 155*

The climb starts immediately above the Passo Cameraccio, which is reached in 1hr from the Manzi hut (crampons often useful early in the season).

Descent: The usual descent is to go down the N ridge to a small notch between the two summits. Immediately below, a steep chimney-couloir descends the W face to the upper snowfields. Rappel this chimney (anchors in place; III+ in ascent and loose) then reverse Route 296 to the glacier. In a dry summer the couloir will be free of snow and it might be possible to reach the top of this by keeping to the rocks on the E flank of the upper snowfield.

It is also possible, in a dry year, to descend the ENE ridge to the saddle at c3200m without having to negotiate too much snow. From here, zigzag down ledges and short walls on the S face to where it drops away in a steep cliff, quite close to the bottom. Almost directly in line with the saddle try to locate the top of a chimney and make two rappels (pegs in place: IV in ascent) to the slopes at the head of the Cameraccio valley. Walk back to the pass. Allow at least 3hr

One of the finest expeditions in the range, which by late summer will be almost entirely on rock, is the complete traverse from the Rasica to the Orientale. It was first completed by H Frei and E Schillinger, 13 Aug 1933, in 14hr. A traverse from Monte Sissone to the Rasica (19hr) has also been recorded.

Cameraccio Ridge

This long spiky crest runs S from the Torrone Orientale and is studded with small towers and summits. The steep slabby faces overlooking the Val Torrone, and the more precipitious walls above the wild Cameraccio valley, are relatively remote and do not offer any easy lines. For these reasons the summits are rarely visited; many of the harder climbs have received only one or two ascents and several are unrepeated. A number of routes are briefly outlined below but at present this is still an area where the adventurous climber, who likes to explore rock walls far removed from the popular venues, will be truly in his element.

Punta Cameraccio 3024m

O Bignami and L Binaghi, 18 Aug 1923

A very rarely visited summit that lies only 200m S of the Passo Cameraccio. Although there are easier ways of reaching the top, eg the S ridge via the Cameraccio valley, the N ridge is the best – short, airy and interesting.

298 **NORTH RIDGE**
V A Bonacossa, N Pietrasanta and H Steiger, 31 Aug 1932
154

From the pass climb the E side of the ridge, then the crest, to the base of a superb tower. Climb this on the W flank by a steep and exposed pitch which gives the crux of the climb. Continue more easily along the airy crest for a short distance to the summit. 75m: 1hr

Descent: From the top of the tower a 20m rappel leads to a ledge on the E face. Follow this back onto the ridge and so down to the pass.

299 Torre Re Alberto 2832m

D/D+
154

A Bonacossa and G Gervasutti, 6 Oct 1933

Although no more than a huge monolithic block on the crest of the Cameraccio ridge, seen from the upper Val Torrone it appears as a distinct and imposing tower. The first ascent was of historical importance as to reach the summit involved climbing the first pitch in the range at a true grade of VI or above, and was probably Gervasutti's hardest lead. A relatively long approach, combined with the difficulty of the final 20m, unprotected slab, has meant that few ascents have been recorded.

Follow Route H15 towards the Manzi bivouac, but before reaching the Roma path traverse E across the valley to the base of the first prominent couloir S of the Torre. This couloir comes down from a point on the ridge just N of a small tower that lies mid-way betweeen the Torre and the Pta Meridionale (4-4½hr from Gatto Rosso). Climb the couloir, which has one or two sections of IV, to the top (c2700m: 1½hr). From here, a sharp ridge leads N towards the Torre. Go along grassy ledges on the Cameraccio side, then climb a 30m chimney back onto the crest, not far below a 4m high monolithic block that precedes the final tower. Climb along the ridge and over the block (very exposed) to a small gap. Move up L onto the smooth slab just below the summit and climb it to a point where it steepens. A difficult 3m traverse (V1+, and some distance above the last runner) leads R to a crack. Climb it to a shoulder and finish up short easy slabs to the top (1½hr). 7-7½hr from the road or 3½hr from the Manzi hut

On 4 Nov 1966, M Zappa and R Zocchi climbed directly up the W face towards the summit block. This slabby face has a prominent dièdre on the L side and the party climbed more or less up it to below the overhangs near the top. From here they slanted R along the obvious ramp-line to reach the S ridge in the vicinity of the monolithic block. 300m: D/D+, IV+ to the ridge

Torrione Moai

E Frosi and I Guerini, 3 Sept 1973

The most obvious feature on the E side of the Cameraccio crest. It is a remarkable golden granite tower which resembles an Easter Island statue. Although rising barely 50m above the surrounding flanks, the E face falls c250m into the middle reaches of the Cameraccio valley. Whilst undoubtedly a compelling objective, the easiest route to the summit involves a very long approach over broken ground, with only a little climbing to finish.

300 **NORMAL ROUTE**

IV

152

From Alpe Cameraccio an enormous ramp/gully cuts up R through the rock walls on the flanks of the Cameraccio ridge and eventually reaches the crest. It is the only obvious means of access to the crest on this side. Follow it as far as a huge scree-covered shoulder/terrace behind the Torrione (2-2½hr). Climb easy rock on the W side of the tower and then traverse R to reach a belay in a narrow gully. Climb the gully and continue up flakes to the crest (III). Follow the crest to a overhanging section; avoid it on the R via a ledge, and climb a short dièdre (IV) to the summit (30min). c50m

Torrione Moai: East Face

The smooth steep grey wall below the Torrione is split by a single crack. The foot of this can be reached in 3½-4hr from Gatto Rosso via Alpe Cameraccio. On both routes described below the rock is excellent.

301 **ORIGINAL ROUTE**

VII P Masa, J Merizzi and G Miotti, 1978

152

The crack! Some thin slab climbing is needed to reach the foot of the crack, after which a succession of sustained pitches leads to the final

tower of beautiful red granite (escape L possible onto normal route). Climb this tower via a series of exposed cracks and corners. 250m: 6-8hr

302 **BANDEIRAS**

VII– G Maspes and M Vannuccini, 13 May 1990.

152

44

The wall to the L of the previous route gives vary varied climbing that is often quite strenuous. The route begins about 50m to the R of the conspicuous long black chimney (often dripping) that lies well L of the summit fall-line. At this point a series of poorly defined dièdres slant slightly R up the wall, and there is a peg and sling 15m above the ground. The climbing is very sustained at V to VI with several harder sections, and although the crux can be aided there is an unavoidable move of VI+. 7 pegs, which include 3 belay points, plus a bolt remain in the route so it is advisable to carry a small selection, plus a full rack of wires, Hexes and Friends (up to 3½hr). c200m: 6-7hr to summit

Punta Meridionale del Cameraccio 2743m

A Bonacossa and G Gervasutti, 5 Oct 1933; via the NNE and descent of the SW ridges

Often referred to by local climbers as 'La Botte'. This final rocky bastion on the Cameraccio crest dominates the upper Val di Mello. The W face, overlooking the Val Torrone, is slabby and quite vegetated, but the 'hidden' E side has vertical monolithic granite walls with an atmosphere distinctly 'Yosemite'! The S pillar rises in two clear-cut steps; the top of the lower step is considered a separate summit – the Torre Darwin.

303 **EAST FACE – TYRANNOSAURUS REX**

ED2 O Meloni and U Villota, completed on 22-23 Sept 1989

A great route for the 'Big Wall' aficionado – unrepeated and having lengthy sections of aid climbing. Although a spectacular climb with an easy approach, the situation feels surprisingly remote and the route is unlikely to gain major popularity due to the preponderance of artificial work. Retreat from the upper section would be quite problematical. Take 2 full sets of Friends and wires, 2 rurps, 7 blades and knifeblades plus 5 angles. The hangers were removed from all the bolts.

Follow Route H19 into the Cameraccio valley and go up to the foot of the walls on the E side of the Darwin-Meridionale summits. A large grassy ledge slants up through the base of these walls. Follow this ledge right to the end, below the most prominent chimney-couloir in the centre of the face (c3hr).

Climb up easily for 45m to the base of the chimney. Follow it (grassy), finishing via a slanting crack onto a good terrace (125m: IV and V). Climb the overhanging cracks above and traverse L at the top to a huge grass ledge half-way up the wall (90m: VI+ and A1, with a short section of A2+). From the R-hand end of this ledge (excellent bivouac site) climb up flakes and smooth walls to a bolt, then pendulum R to a fine terrace (55m: A1 to A2+). Climb a dièdre, a ramp and a succession of dièdres above, that lead out R to the base of an overhanging chimney (135m: A1/2 with some V+). Climb the chimney and huge dièdre above to a good ledge, and finally some cracks on the R to the crest of the ridge (70m: A1 and V/V+). Scramble up the crest to the summit. c600m of actual climbing, 2-3 days

The first ascent party rappelled the route but would emphatically dissuade others from doing the same! They felt that it would have been very difficult without a fixed rope in place on the traverse and recommend trying the NNE ridge.

304 **SOUTH PILLAR**
VII+ I Guerini, G Merrizi and B Villa, 19 Aug 1978
155

This impressively steep and narrow pillar rises from the shoulder formed by the summit of the Torre Darwin. It is clearly visible from the upper Mello valley and is most easily reached via the grassy slabs on the W side (see the route below). It is probably unrepeated and there is little information available on the nature of the climbing. 300m: 7hr

Torre Darwin 2442m

A number of hard mixed free and aid routes have been done on the vertical E wall, below and to the L of the Meridionale. The prominent pillar that forms the L edge of this face and is clearly seen in profile from the Mello valley, gives a route at a more accessible standard.

305 **SOUTH PILLAR**
V+/ I Guerini and M Villa, 23 July 1974
A1/2
155

The first 150m of climbing, up to the prominent shoulder at just below half-height, is on pleasant though rather grassy slabs. Above, the rock is

steep, clean and rather more difficult. The half-dozen aid moves on the first ascent could be done on nuts/Friends and would probably go free to a powerful crack climber.

Follow Route H19 as far as Alpe Cameraccio (2167m: 2-2½hr). From here the pillar is seen in profile and is reached in 30min via a steep overgrown gully. Move onto the SW side overlooking the Val di Mello, and start at the base of the grey slabs, half-way between the top of the gully and a huge chimney-couloir on the L side of the face. Work up these slabs to the shoulder (moves of IV). Now climb the second crack/dièdre system L of the crest to a terrace (30m: V). Move slightly to the R and continue up the system, avoiding two small roofs, to a poor stance (35m: V+). Climb a crack which slants up to the R and finish over a large flake onto a sloping terrace (25m: IV+ with 3 points of aid). A long pitch, still on the L of the crest, leads via a narrow chimney, slabs and flakes to a grassy ledge on the R (V with 3 aid moves -A1/2). Climb a gully on the R, then move up and across slabs on the R (IV+) to a ledge. Another two pitches (slabs IV+, then an easy ridge) lead to the top. c300m: 6hr

Descent: Go down the N ridge to the col below the Pta Meridionale (III and IV), then climb down the easy vegetated slabs on the SW flank and work back round below the pillar to the top of the steep overgrown gully used on the approach.

Passo di Mello 2992m

First recorded crossing (E to W): H Buxton, D Freshfield and F Tuckett with F Devouassoud, P Michel and J Walther, 7 July 1865

A broad saddle forming the lowest point of the ridge between the Cima di Chiareggio and Monte Pioda. The Odello-Grandori bivouac hut stands a few m S of the pass. See Routes H18 and H19 for the various (lengthy) approaches.

Monte Sissone 3330m

R Beachcroft, D Freshfield and J Walker with F Devouassoud and a porter, 10 Aug 1864. Winter: F Muller with C Klucker, 1903

MONTE SISSONE

An easy snow peak on the frontier ridge, with splendid views of the Disgrazia massif. It is a popular summit, especially with spring skiers, and is often combined with an ascent of the Cima di Rosso. The traverse of the mountain gives, perhaps surprisingly, the shortest, quickest and easiest crossing between the Forno and Mello valleys.

306 **NORTH RIDGE**
F+ First ascent party in descent
144

A straightforward medium-length glacier expedition and a very worthwhile outing for the alpine novice. In high summer there will usually be a good piste leading to the summit. See also photograph 143

From the Forno hut go back down the path, taking the L fork to the Forno glacier. Walk up the L side (rather tedious – a succession of ridges and troughs) until past the rocks at the base of the W flank of the Cima di Rosso. Work up to the E into the huge glacier basin coming down from the Passo Sissone (3157m). The initial slopes are relatively steep and usually icy but any crevasses are clearly visible. Reach the pass and walk S along the broad snow ridge and over a few blocks to the summit. 4hr and 900m of ascent from the hut

307 **SOUTH FLANK**
F First ascent party
154

A rather tedious ascent over boulder-slopes. However, early in the season old snow will make this route considerably more pleasant. See also photograph 155

From a point on the Roma path almost due S of the mountain, slog up the boulder-filled valley between the S and SE ridges. On reaching the final bastion, head up L for 60m over steep yet quite straightforward rocky terrain and reach a notch in the W ridge. 50m of easy scrambling along the crest leads to the summit (1½-2hr). 2½-3hr from the Grandori (Mello) hut: 3-3½hr from the Manzi hut

The SE ridge, climbed from the Chiareggio pass, gives a pleasant alternative. It is mainly scrambling with sections of II. The first step is avoided on the L. (45min)

Early in the season, when the snow conditions are good, another possibility is to climb the prominent easy couloir to the L of the S ridge. This is a more interesting variation to the normal route and reaches the W ridge c200m from the summit. The couloir will be subject to stone-fall unless well-frozen, and should be completed shortly after dawn (PD).

308 **WEST RIDGE**

AD J Heller, A Michel, G Miescher and P Schucan, 1 Aug 1909

144

The long (1km) and almost-horizontal crest between the Torrone Orientale and the Sissone provides a continuously interesting and varied mixed climb. It is a minor classic, and although not so popular these days can still be highly recommended. After descending the ENE ridge of the Torrone to the saddle at c3200m, continue along the crest, turning the first big buttress on the S side, to the Sissone (pitches of III–). Despite the ridge rising only a short distance above the slopes to either side, a 'high mountain' ambience is maintained throughout the traverse. 5hr from summit to summit. See also photograph 154

Cima di Rosso 3366m

W Coolidge with F and H Devouassoud, 30 July 1867.
Winter: E Main with C Schnitzler and M Schocher, 16 Feb 1896

One of the highest summits in the range and considered by many to be the most beautiful peak in the Forno valley. Not surprisingly it is a popular mountain offering a variety of commendable routes, though the classic lines on the N face have suffered badly in the 'droughts' of recent years. The summit offers outstanding panoramic views with the eye irresistibly drawn to Monte Disgrazia, which from this angle is seen at its best. When starting from the Forno hut it is easily possible to 'bag' Monte Sissone in the same outing.

309 **SOUTH-WEST FLANK**

F+/PD– First ascent party

144

A very straightforward glacier ascent. It is ideal for the alpine novice and one of the most popular excursions from the Forno hut in all seasons. Indeed, during spring it is a classic goal for ski-mountaineers and probably climbed as much as any summit in the range. In high summer there will normally be a well-trodden piste.

From the Forno hut follow Route 306. Once above the initial steep slopes bear L and reach the foot of a short steep snow slope that leads to the upper section of the W ridge. Climb the slope and follow the crest of the ridge easily to the top. c940m and 3½hr from the hut. The ridge running S to the Sissone is fairly broad throughout its length and usually presents no difficulty. It can be crossed in 1-1½hr

310 **EAST-SOUTH-EAST RIDGE INTEGRAL**
D– M Galeazzi and C Negri, 11 Aug 1942
146

Remotely situated, seldom climbed, but probably the best rock route in the cirque overlooking the Sissone valley and Chiareggio. There is no convenient base – the nearest hut is the Del Grande but this is poorly sited for the route, which is best approached directly from Alpe Sissone. The rock is generally very good and the climbing fairly sustained at II to III– with several harder pitches.

This is a route for those with the spirit of adventure required to make a lengthy approach into a rarely visited arena.

From Alpe Sissone follow the vague track SW. Cross the base of the long SE ridge of the Vazzeda, and then work up the moraine to reach the base of the ESE ridge (1½-2hr). This point can also be reached in a shorter time from the Del Grande hut, by slanting down and across some fairly unpleasant ground, and passing through a notch in the SE ridge of the Vazzeda.

The first step is climbed by an obvious chimney/crack system on the crest and has several pitches of IV. Descend to a gap (which can also be reached from the glacier to the R of the ridge – Bonacossa and Orio, 1925) and continue up the ridge. Higher, there is an exposed narrow section, and the final step is best turned on the R (shattered rock). By keeping to the crest as much as possible the difficulties on the entire ridge above the gap are never more than III. c500m: 3-4hr for the ridge

Descent: This is the difficult bit. There is no easy way down on this side of the mountain! The only possible solution is to descend the E side of the Passo Sissone to the Sissone glacier. A short but rather steep rock wall below the pass may well require a couple of rappels.

311 **NORTH-EAST RIDGE VIA CIMA DI VAZZEDA**
AD+ A von Rydzewsky with M Barbaria and C Klucker, 29 June 1892,
146 via an unpleasant ascent of the NE face of the Vazzeda. The N ridge of the Vazzeda was first climbed by E Gretschmann and W Kirschten, 14 Aug 1925

A well-established classic, which early in the season offers a varied and

continuously interesting traverse over rock, mixed terrain and snow/ice ridges. In recent years parties climbing in Aug have found several long sections of poor rock, and recommend attempting the route quite early in the season when it will be far more enjoyable, albeit at a higher standard. As this is a long expedition in an impressive position, a certain level of commitment as well as fitness is needed. See also photograph 144

From the Forno hut follow Route 306 past the rocks of Monte Rosso and then turn E up the first side glacier. Keeping towards the L it is a straightforward trudge up to the Passo Vazzeda (2967m: 2-2½hr). This lies 400m S of the Cima di Val Bona and should not be confused with the Passo di Val Bona to the N!

The first section of the N ridge is quite easy and leads to a steep step. Climb this step via a dièdre and crack to the top. There is usually a fixed rope in place on this 35m section – otherwise it is IV. Continue carefully along the crest on fairly dubious rock to the final buttress (III). Climb it on the R side via an exposed crack with a small roof (IV–); or avoid it altogether by traversing L over easy but loose rock to the E ridge. Either way leads to the main summit of the Vazzeda (II). 2½hr. Go down the S ridge via a short couloir on the Forno side to a gap. Climb easily over the S summit and descend steeply to the next col – the Forcola di Rossa (c3200m). Climb over the narrow crest of the following tower on loose shattered rock and reach a small col at the foot of the NE ridge of the Rosso (short sections of III). This ridge usually gives delightful climbing over snow and blocks (good belays) to the summit. 3hr

Descending the normal route will take 2-2½hr, making the round trip from the Forno hut a 10hr expedition.

312 NORTH FACE

AD+/ W Amstutz and A Bonacossa, 15 June 1930.
D– Winter: P Bernasconi and F Masciadi, 15 March 1959
144

The 'pièce de résistance' of this mountain is one of the more famous alpine ice classics described in this guide. Early in the season, when conditions are good, it presents the most compelling face climb in the Forno cirque and ascents are fairly frequent. Although the route is longer, and in drier conditions more exposed to stone-fall than the N face of the Cantun, the difficulties are very similar.

It is best to start and then keep quite well L of the Central spur, from which the main stone-fall emanates. Although it is possible to finish direct, the rock is fairly poor and most parties top out onto the NE ridge. The face is steepest (55°+) at the base and crossing the rimaye will usually provide the crux. Thereafter the angle gradually eases, but deteriorating snow conditions have forced a number of parties to take the easy option of traversing onto the Central spur at three-quarters height. 2hr are needed for the approach from the Forno hut via Route 311 (towards the Vazzeda) and thereafter, 4½hr is the average time required for an ascent. 400m

313 **CENTRAL SPUR**
D–/D J Cleare and M Springett, 22 July 1969
144

Although rarely climbed in its entirety, the upper section above the great tower is often used as an escape by parties experiencing poor snow conditions on the N face. There are several quite nice pitches on sound granite, but much of the route is steep and loose and the climbing rather unsatisfactory. Under a heavy covering of well-frozen snow this could prove a very rewarding mixed climb and the overall difficulty probably a grade higher.

The lower section of the rib is rather ice-polished and inhospitable – a direct entry has, so far, been avoided. Climb onto the crest from either flank (usually the L but both have a certain exposure to objective danger) and follow it to the base of the 'Great Tower' at three-quarters height. So far the climb has been on broken ground of moderate difficulty (III) but includes two good crack pitches of IV and IV+.

Now slant up the R flank of the tower on despicable rock (IV–) and return to the crest immediately above it (III). Continue more easily to the summit over huge granite blocks (II). 400m: 6hr

314 **NORTH FACE – RIGHT HAND ROUTE**
D+/ H and O Heinzle and W Rinderer, May 1964. Winter: E Gutensohn
TD– and F Ruf, 20 March 1966
144

Seldom in condition after early summer as a plentiful snow cover on the initial rocky barrier is needed to gain entry to the upper couloir. The climbing is intrinsically very good and no harder than the N face, but it is blatantly obvious that objective dangers are high. If you are not exposed to ice fall from the séracs to the R, you are in the firing line of stone-fall from the L! Not surprisingly few ascents have been recorded. Good snow and a night of hard frost are necessary to render this route an attractive proposition to most mortals. 400m: 5hr

315 **NORTH-WEST FACE**
AD A von Rydzewsky with C Klucker and E Rey, 8 June 1893
144

A classic glacier climb in a splendid position and traditionally a popular

outing from the Forno hut. Nowadays it is rarely ascended during the summer months; considerable recession has left a very steep ice bulge above an unaccomodating rocky barrier at the base of the route. In good snowy conditions it is highly recommended, and can be almost a grade easier.

From the Forno hut follow Route 311 towards the Vazzeda and reach the foot of the face in c1½hr. Choice of route on the first steep section will be largly subjective! Above trend L on easier ground and cross a large and sometimes troublesome rimaye near the top of the face. Now slant up a steep snow/ice slope to the W ridge and follow it easily to the summit. c550m: 5h from the hut

Cima di Vazzeda 3301m

A von Rydzewsky with M Barbaria and C Klucker, 29 June 1892. Winter: D Cerini, O Vigano and P Vignati, 16-17 March 1948

A rather impressive jagged crest lying immediately N of the Cima di Rosso. Unfortunately, closer inspection reveals that the rock is not the usual roughly-hewn granite but a sort of shattered limestone. Geologists find this the most interesting peak in the Bregaglia! Heavy stone-fall puts the flanks of the mountain out of bounds during the summer months but the ridges hold a certain attraction. The classic excursion is the N-S traverse, finishing on the Cima di Rosso. It has already been described in that section.

316 **EAST RIDGE**
AD A Corti, G Foianini and A Lucchetti Albertini, 25 Aug 1929,
146 although it had been descended by Bonacossa and Polvara in 1921

Interesting climbing on comparatively solid rock (although loose material will always be encountered from time to time) makes this the best route on the mountain and a more attractive proposition than the E ridge of the Rosso. It is rather too remote to be attempted from the Forno hut (3hr for the approach), but for parties operating from the Italian valleys the Del Grande hut is conveniently situated at the foot of the ridge. Although long, the climb is not sustained at the grade. III+. See also photograph 143

From the Del Grande hut go up scree slopes to the foot of the tiny glacier that lies NE of the peak. Slant up L to reach the crest of the ridge at c2800m (30min). Follow the crest throughout – easy at first, then becoming more tricky with the crux occurring where a steep buttress forms at the junction of the E and SE ridges. Climb this buttress on the L flank via a dièdre and some slabs. The top of the buttress can also be reached at a slightly lower standard by following the SE ridge: start from a small notch just N of Pt 2840m. This ridge is well defined with many steps of excellent red rock and is highly recommended. Above the buttress the gradient eases. The crest becomes turreted and leads, without undue difficulty, to the summit (from where the most convenient descent will involve reversing the same route). 500m: 3hr

On the NW face a route has been climbed on the steep ground to the L of the central couloir (poor rock and serious stone-fall). However, very early in the season, or during the winter/spring months, a hard frost would transform the couloir into a steep ice gully and allow it to be climbed direct (c400m, TD, 85°: T Heyman, 5 May 1993)

Cima di Val Bona 3033m

An easy peak that is probably climbed in spring, by ski-mountaineers, more often than at any other time of year. The unfrequented Italian side holds a little gem – one of Gervasutti's (surprisingly) few contributions to the range.

317 **NORMAL ROUTE**
F

After a gentle ascent of the glacier bay to the W (see Route 311), a short and easy scramble up broken rocks leads directly to the summit. 2½-3hr from the Forno hut

318 **EAST RIDGE**
AD+ R Chabod, A Corti and G Gervasutti, 15 June 1933
149

This highly recommended outing gives some interesting climbing on first-class granite. Although access is relatively easy, the ridge is situated in one of the less frequented corners of the range and should appeal to those parties who wish to 'get off the beaten track'. See also photograph 143

The foot of the ridge can be reached in 1hr from the Del Grande hut. It is almost as easy to approach from the Forno hut by crossing the Sella del Forno and descending to c2600m, before contouring the head of the valley to the foot of the ridge (1½hr).

The toe of the ridge is generally avoided by climbing directly to the small notch beyond it. This is most easily done from Pt 2538m to the S. Above, the first part of the ridge is quite steep and forms the L side of a triangular face. Climb up steps and a short dièdre on the crest, before moving onto the R side, where a fine slab provides a difficult pitch. Continue more or less on the crest – fairly sustained and continuously interesting – to the foresummit. The angle now relents and the difficulties ease. Follow the crest, turning any problems on the L, to the main summit. IV+: c450m, 4-5hr

If returning to the Del Grande hut or the foot of the ridge, scramble down the easy broken rocks of the normal route to the glacier, and work across it below the S ridge to the Passo Vazzeda (2967m). From here, there is a straightforward descent on the Italian side. 2-2½hr down to Chiareggio

Passo di Val Bona 2956m

An easy glacier pass between the Cima di Val Bona and Monte Rosso. The walk from the Forno hut (see Route 311) is quite straightforward and has few crevasses to worry about (2-2½hr). On the Italian side a rough walk S from the upper Val Bona (see Route 324), followed by a short icy slope, leads to the col (4hr from Chiareggio: F).

Monte Rosso 3088m

L Norman Neruda with C Klucker, 16 Aug 1889

Although hardly one of the most impressive peaks in the Forno valley, it does offer some moderately worthwhile climbing and is quite popular due to its proximity to the hut.

319 WEST FLANK

PD– *This is the normal route. It is mainly steep scrambling and has little to recommend it. It is most often used as a quick descent to the Forno hut after completing one of the better routes on the peak.*

From the hut the shortest approach is to go down the path for 5 mins and then head SE across moraine and rubble. Passing below remnants of the tiny glacier coming down from the Sella del Forno, reach the foot of the NW ridge at c2600m. Climb up via an obvious line of weakness (vague track in the scree), to the base of a conspicuous rock buttress on the crest. Now move R onto the W flank and scramble over snow patches and easy rock to the summit. 450m: 2hr

The NW ridge can be climbed directly along the crest to where it joins the NE ridge. This is very pleasant and has pitches of III on sound granite. However, escape onto the W flank is always close at hand.

320 **SOUTH-EAST RIDGE**

PD A and R Balabio, A Calegari and G Scotti, 25 Sept 1908

A blocky crest which gives a delightful scramble from the Passo di Val Bona. 30-45min from the pass: moves of II

321 **NORTH-EAST RIDGE**

AD–/AD First ascent party

147 *Undoubtedly the best climb on the mountain and a popular classic. It was an impressive performance on the part of our indomitable duo, who had the audacity to attempt a virgin peak by perhaps the least likely line! The imposing narrow section beyond Pt 2991m will appear doubly impressive early in the season, when snow on the E flank covers the appalling scree slopes and gives the climb a true 'high mountain' ambience.*

From the Sella del Forno it is usually better to traverse the broken boulder slopes below ice fields on the W flank of the ridge and work up under the Kluckerzahn. Now scramble up loose ground to a small col, which marks the base of the ridge leading up to Pt 2991m. Early in the season, when approaching from the Forno hut, there is no need to reach the Sella. It is normally possible to slant up R on easy snow slopes and reach the small col directly.

Scramble directly up the crest, where steep pull-ups over large granite blocks lead to the exposed summit of Pt 2991m (I and II). The ridge now becomes narrow and serrated and things look more serious. Climb along this entertaining airy section to the base of a prominent buttress (III). Climb directly up the front face of the buttress – the crux is a steep slab split by a thin crack (III+) – finishing up a crack on the L. The ridge above is more broken yet still quite interesting and leads easily to the summit (3hr). 4h from the Forno hut

The buttress can be avoided completely by traversing unpleasant ground on the E flank – steep scree slopes and loose rock.

Kluckerzahn c2860m

Situated near the base of the NE ridge of Monte Rosso, this tower has a spectacular appearance when seen from above the Forno hut. The imposing prow has been climbed by a mixture of free and artificial work, which used 25 bolts in the upper section (160m: VI and A2). Fortunately for aspiring conquistadors the E side is short and far more amenable.

322 **EAST RIDGE**

III+

147

An entertaining little morsel that is easily combined with an ascent of the NE ridge on Monte Rosso.

Climb the R side of the ridge via a series of flakes for 15m to a large sloping platform. Get onto the block and pull up very steeply on huge 'jugs' to an abrupt finish on the small flat and rather exposed summit. 30m: 15min

Sella del Forno 2768m

An old and established smugglers' pass. It provides the easiest and most popular crossing point between the Forno and Italian valleys – as the large amounts of litter on the col will testify!

323 **WEST SIDE**

RE

From the Forno hut follow the waymarked path (red on white paint flashes) alongside a waterpipe to reach the remains of the tiny glacier that comes down from the Sella. Go up the L side over scree and boulders, finally slanting R over a short stretch of bare ice to reach the boulder slope leading to the pass. 1hr

324 **EAST SIDE**

RE

From Chiareggio start up the road that leads towards the Muretto pass but soon leave it to follow a well-marked path to Alpe Vazzeda. This crosses the river and after reaching the lower chalets (1832m)

climbs above a gorge to the upper chalets at 2033m. The path now slants NW across the hillside to Alpe Monterosso (2220m). Red paint marks now indicate the way up the R side of the Val Bona where, higher, rough walking over moraine and scree finally leads to the col. 3½-4hr

Monte del Forno 3214.2m

L Held, Aug 1876

A very popular ascent from the Forno hut and a superb viewpoint. It is climbed regularly in winter/spring by parties reaching the Sella del Forno on ski. The rock on the mountain is not the usual rugged Bregaglia granite but a sort of shale referred to as 'Anfibolite' which is far from solid. The ridge N to the Pizzi dei Rossi (3026.5m) gives a worthwhile scramble – either come back the same way or descend to the Muretto pass over loose rock, a small glacier and steep scree. The lower flanks of the mountain hold several granite slabs/walls, which provide a number of 4-5 pitch routes up to grade VII (details at hut).

325 **SOUTH RIDGE**
PD– First ascent party
148

Early in the season, when the ridge lies under a healthy covering of frozen snow, this route will provide a splendid introduction to Alpine mountaineering for the less experienced climber. By Aug only a few snow patches remain and the bulk of the ascent lies over steep boulder and scree slopes. The reward is an excellent panorama of the Disgrazia and western Bernina.

From the Sella del Forno go up the ridge past a huge cairn to Pt 2944m, where there is a marker pole (paint flashes). At this point do not be misled by the sight of rough granite boulders – the rock soon takes a significant change for the worse! Slant up across the W flank, following traces of a path to a conspicuous rock wall that seems to encircle the mountain. L of the crest a track leads into a narrow chimney/couloir that slants up to the L. It is 60m high, has a number of loose blocks, and can become quite dangerous when several parties are doing battle simultaneously. Climb it to the summit scree slopes (II). It can be avoided by moving c40m L and climbing a rightward slanting quartz ramp (II+: sound rock and a recommended alternative, but can be difficult to locate in descent). Zigzag up the steep scree slopes to the summit cairn, a route book, and those excellent views! 2½-3hr from the hut

326 **EAST RIDGE**
F A and R Balabio, A Calegari and U Franci, 19 Aug 1910
148

Although the mountain is seldom climbed from the Italian side, this ridge gives the quickest ascent from the Muretto pass and Maloja. It is suggested to those parties who, having reached the summit from the Forno hut, would like to descend via new ground.

From the summit go SE for a few m, then climb down a steep wall on the L to the top of the E ridge. Descend this to c2800m. The rock on the flanks is atrocious so it is worth keeping as near to the crest as possible, although on the narrow middle section, which is quite exposed, one might be excused for taking to the N flank. Low down the ridge broadens and succumbs to easy walking/scrambling. If lucky you will see ibex, which tend to frequent this quiet corner of the range: if luckier you will pick up a vague track (waymarked with red on white paint flashes) that traverses steep loose scree and boulder slopes to the N, before slanting down the grassy hillside to the Muretto pass. 650m: 1½hr (2½hr in ascent)

Passo del Muretto (Muretto Pass) 2562m

An old and very well established pass that separates the Bregaglia from the Bernina range. It provides the easiest crossing point between Switzerland and the upper Italian valleys and was used by traders for centuries.

327 **FROM MALOJA**
PE Follow Route H16 towards the Forno hut. Just before Plancanin the first stone building is encountered on the R, and shortly after a signpost indicating the path to the pass. Follow this path which descends to a small bridge over the Orlegna river and then makes a fairly steep ascent up the L side of the valley. Higher, it crosses scree and boulder slopes and is a little vague in parts. It finally leads to the L-hand of two cols, just N of the rounded hump of Pt 2627.7m. 2½h-3hr from the road

328 **FROM CHIAREGGIO**
P A well signposted and unmistakable jeep track makes a fairly gradual ascent all the way to the large uninhabited border control point c 5min below the pass. 2½hr

329 **FROM FORNO HUT**
RE
148 *This is a very useful connection that is now well waymarked with red on white paint flashes. It traverses the rough ground on the Italian slopes of Monte del Forno.*

From the marker pole on the S ridge of Monte del Forno (see Route 325) slant gently down to the NE and traverse scree slopes (possible snow patches). Cross the lower section of the E ridge and continue in much the same line to the W col of the Muretto pass (2586m). 2½hr

Mello Valley

This extravagantly beautiful valley, with an abundance of colourful flowers, compact glaciated granite and spectacular waterfalls, has often been likened to California's famous Yosemite. In the last decade it has become a favourite haunt for many European climbers. The atmosphere is certainly cosmopolitan and the ambience unmistakably Italian – sunny, friendly and relatively inexpensive.

The rock architecture is impressive: many of the routes follow big features and have more than 300m of climbing. Linking routes on adjacent crags gives a number of classic outings that are more than double this length. The climbs follow cracks, slabs or a mixture of the two, and the granite is rarely less than perfect. Nearly all the routes are of a very high quality and tend to dry quickly after rain. Climbing is often possible from the beginning of April to the middle of Nov. It can get pretty hot in Aug!

So far, routes in the valley have been subject to a fairly rigorous bolting ethic. Protection on the thin smooth open slab pitches is frequently minimal and occasionally non-existent. Falls with 'death-potential' are rare but you could easily lose a lot of skin!

Whilst there is little in the valley to attract the climber operating below grade VI (what easy climbing there is tends to be serious), the nearby Sasso Remenno has a wealth of routes at all standards. This is not only the largest boulder in the Alps but also the only one with its own guidebook! It lies beside the road, 2km S of San Martino, and has routes up to 60m in length. The easiest are generally found on the S and W faces. For a rainy day there is always the old bolt route over the 6m roof on the N wall. Other bouldering possiblities are endless!

The routes descibed below, although only a small selection of those available, provide some of the best climbing in the region. Unlike the rock walls of the Bregaglia mountains, heights given in the introduction to each route indicate the total length of the climb.

In winter the waterfalls on the S side of the valley freeze easily. A reasonable introduction is to climb the gully near to the start of the path up to the pastures of Arcanzolo. The ice can be thin but rock protection is good. Much harder sport can be found on the falls at the base of the Mezzola and Romilla valleys. However, these are longer climbs and can be quite serious. The S facing Ferro waterfall and the gorge L of the Dimore Degli Dei can also give good medium grade routes when in condition.

330 **MIXOMICETO**
VI+ A Gogna, I Guerini, G Merizzi and G Miotti, 1977

Climbs on the steep slabs that flank the Cascata del Ferro are truly atmospheric. This route follows an obvious leftwards traverse line on the walls R of the fall, and can be reasonably well-protected by small wires and Friends. 80m

Climb up a large block onto the slab above and traverse diagonally L under the flake (VI+ to start then V+). Climb a small groove to a belay (IV+ then III). Work up L on the upper slab to a tree belay (III+). Descend to the R down easy slabs.

If you thought that was easy, try Lo Scivolo (The Slide!) which takes a direct line up the slabs L of the waterfall. Above a small roof near the base, the route is protected by 5 bolts with the crux at about 20m. 30m: VII+

Precipizio degli Asteroidi

This is the motif of the Val di Mello – the 'El Capitan' of the region. This hugh bastion stands proud above the lower valley, overlooking the Gatto Rosso. There was great competition for the first ascent of the upper wall, with Boscacci and Merizzi being just pipped to the post. The route described below has become an established classic and is one of the finest 'expeditions' in the valley. It starts from the half-way terrace and reaching this is no mean undertaking! Over to the R, the awesome E face of Monte Qualido is the home to several 900m+ 'Big-Wall' routes.

331 **OCEANO IRRAZIONALE**
VII I Guerini and M Villa, 1977
159
74

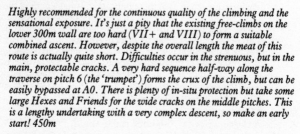

Highly recommended for the continuous quality of the climbing and the sensational exposure. It's just a pity that the existing free-climbs on the lower 300m wall are too hard (VII+ and VIII) to form a suitable combined ascent. However, despite the overall length the meat of this route is actually quite short. Difficulties occur in the strenuous, but in the main, protectable cracks. A very hard sequence half-way along the traverse on pitch 6 (the 'trumpet') forms the crux of the climb, but can be easily bypassed at A0. There is plenty of in-situ protection but take some large Hexes and Friends for the wide cracks on the middle pitches. This is a lengthy undertaking with a very complex descent, so make an early start! 450m

Approach: from Gatto Rosso (Panscer, 1061m) go up towards the wall, following a path in the bed of a river that comes down from a narrow valley on the L (Val Livincina). After 30min a waterfall is reached. Go up L to a vertical wall with a chimney-dièdre, the base of which is concealed by a large tree. Climb the chimney (20m: IV/V) and continue up a wooded slope, crossing a short wall with the aid of a hugh iron spike/fixed rope. Reach the top of a promontory overlooking a gorge and follow a fixed rope horizontally into the stream bed. Scramble up the rocks on the far side to a ledge and continue up a narrow path to the start of the wooded terrace that leads out into the middle of the face (2hr).

200m along the wooded half-way terrace is a huge rounded vertical pillar taken by the excellent 'Anche Per Oggi Non Si Vola' (VII+ and A1; VIII+ free). The R side of this is defined by a long series of cracks. Start about 30m to the R of this line of cracks at a large flake chimney.

Descent: lengthy, complicated and notoriously difficult to follow! Detailed descriptions only appear to baffle, so the following, combined with some old-fashioned route-finding, might(?) do the trick.

From the top of the Precipizio, go W down steep grassy slopes keeping close to the rocks. Where these drop abruptly into the narrow gorge of the Val Livincina, make a rappel off an isolated tree. Reach and scramble down a buttress between the bed of the gorge and the wall to the L (E) until it is necessary to make another long rappel from a tree. Keep working down the L side of the gorge, and where the ground levels off above a very steep drop, a 'track' goes L (E) over some bushy steps and descends through trees to the start of the half-way terrace. 3hr

Trapezio d'Argento

Opposite the bridge leading to the houses of Ca'di Carna, a small water-striped slab rises out of the woods. This is the Trapezio. Above, and separated from it by a wooded terrace, is the Tempio, characterised by its enormous slanting roof. When coming from Gatto Rosso, leave the valley path just before the bridge and strike up L on a track (red paint marks) leading to the base of the slab. 15min

332 **STOMACO PELOSO/L'ALBA DEL NIRVANA**
V+ P Gossemberg and I Guerini, 1976
158
73

This combination gives very varied and enjoyable climbing. It is eminently protectable once past the first pitch! The latter, Stomaca Peloso, climbs the big bald slab on the L side of the Trapezio, and the first runner only appears after 20m. The original start to L'Alba lies L of the wooded gully and climbs a narrow chimney on the L side of a large flake. (The awesome pair of overhanging cracks through the large roof above the stance on pitch 4 give some of the hardest technical climbing in the valley – IX and IX+!) Take a good selection of nuts and Friends. 160m

Descent: From the last stance it is possible to climb the overhanging chimney on the R (VII) and reach the top of the crag by a slanting crack (V+). Most parties, however, rappel to the wooded terrace and either go down this, making a rappel over the steep section at the bottom (or down Stomaco Peloso); or go up this, then L over the top of the crag on grassy ledges to where a good path comes down from the Val Qualido.

333 **BITTER LEMON**
VII
158
73

This follows a tenuous line up the slab between the two big black water stripes. Quality slab climbing but oh so bold! (the hard moves are generally made to reach the protection bolts). Small wires and RPs may help. 55m, but just possible in one run-out!

Climb the middle of the slab direct. Some parties have split the pitch by making a thin traverse R to the belay on Nuova Dimensione. Climb up R to the black stripe (bolt) then slant up L (crux and second bolt) to the top of the L-hand stripe. Rappel route 332

334 **NUOVA DIMENSIONE**
VII– A Boscacci and J Merizzi, 1977
158
73

One of the valley's most notable offerings and a popular target for those trying to break through into the harder grades. It has great historical significance as the first grade VII to be created in Italy. Nowadays the crux moves are considered to 'just' make the grade. However, the climb has lost nothing of its boldness, and with two long traverses requires competence in both second and leader alike. Small wires are useful. 135m. See also photograph 157

Le Dimore degli Dei (Dinosaur)

Reached in 20-25min from Gatto Rosso via the main valley path. Immediately before Cascina Piana a stream intersects the path. Cross it, then head up L on a track to the base of a large buttress. The most obvious feature is a huge R-facing arch high up on the crag.

335 **IL RISVEGLIO DI KUNDALINI**
VI/A0 I Guerini and M Villa, 1976
160
75

This magnificent and very varied route is one of the best known in the valley, and is often combined with another on the Metamorfosi (qv). The climbing is quite sustained and reasonably well-protected, if a good selection of nuts and Friends are taken. However, as a number of pitches involve long traverses, both leader and second should be of equal ability. Avoid the route after heavy rain as the traverse under the arch is slow to dry. The one move of A0 can be climbed free at VI+/VII–. 400m

Start by scrambling up a grassy ramp to a ledge, that lies directly below the L-hand end of the huge arch. The first pitch traverses horizontally R using a crack below a long roof.

Descent: From the top of the route walk L(W) through the beech wood to a well-made path (the approach to the Scoglio della Metamorfosi). Follow this down to the valley. 30min

Le Dimore degli Dei: Right Side

336 **VERDE GEMMA**
VII− Hassan and Morlacchi, 1986

Starts from a nice grassy meadow below the slabs immediately to the right of the Kundalini buttress. Reach it by leaving the main path just after Cascina Piana and head up a steep wooded slope. The three routes here follow lines of bolts, yet the climbing is still quite bold and there is a definite need to maintain upward momentum when committed to the thin friction moves. 100m

There is a large block buttress towards the L end of the slabs. Climb up onto the R side, then slant up L on top of it, before moving up to a belay point below the main slab (40m: III to IV+). The first bolt is up to the R. Above it, climb straight up (crux) to a grassy rake (30m). Climb up to a bolt, move L (VI) then work back R (V+) to the top (30m). Rappel the route.

The line of bolts on the R, reached from the top of the first pitch, gives Dolce Psicodramma (VII−). Climbs on the continuation slabs above are either desperate or require some aid.

337 **VORTICE DI FIABE**
VI+ I Guerini, M Mazzucchi and V Neri, 1977

77

An excellent introduction to routes of this standard in the valley. The climbing is very 'British' in style and is eminently protectable. The hard section under the arch has a number of in-situ pegs and could easily be negotiated at A0. 110m

From the grassy meadow at the base of the R side of the Dimore degli Dei (see Route 336), move L then slant up to the R in a grassy depression/rake that runs above the top of Verde Gemma etc. Go through a small beech wood then traverse R, crossing a stream, to reach a forested terrace below an area of steep slabs known as the 'Stella Marina' (45min from Cascina Piana). High up on the L side is a prominent curving arch. The climb starts below this at a flake.

From the final tree belay 3 rappels (directly down the line of 'Ricordando Una Stella', a bold VII−) lead to the ground.

338 **PATABANG**
V F Madonna, G and P Masa and J Merizzi, 1979

A superb yet uniquely serious undertaking that takes the slabs above Stella Marina. This is an 'Adventure' route which epitomises much of the spirit of bold free-climbing in the valley. For those operating very comfortably at this standard it is an experience not to be missed! 200m

Follow the same approach used to reach Stella Marina (see route 337). On reaching the beech wood continue up R in the grassy gully, passing the top of Vortice and a prominent arch on the slabs to the L, to a large fir tree. 1hr from Cascina Piana

A few m after the big fir, a smaller tree allows you to gain access to the slab above. Now traverse L along a prominent white vein and towards the end (but still R of a black water stripe) climb up to the R side of an arch, where there is a good stance and nut belay. This pitch is more than 70m long and without a glimmer of protection! Fortunately it is mainly III/III+ with only a few moves of IV/IV+ half-way up the slab.

The next pitch is the one to lead! Climb up (V) to the start of a white vein and traverse horizontally R along it (III and IV; no protection) to a vertical black stripe. Go up this, passing a flake, to a belay. A miscalculation by the second on the initial moves of this pitch would result in a pendulum rivalling any yet witnessed in the valley!

Continue up the stripe to a tree belay (40m; V then IV+; adequate protection). Work up L on the easy slab to a tree at the top (40m; III).

Descent: Go up into the grassy gully where there is a path next to an old stone wall. Follow this path down to the base of the Metamorfosi.

Scoglio della Metamorfosi

Situated high above the valley floor and containing the best rock to be found in the Mello, this buttress offers two magnificent classics of international fame. The approach is both signposted and waymarked. Follow the main path in the valley as far as an obvious beautiful swimming pool in the river. A well-defined track now zigzags up to the L via a dense wood and a moraine, to cross the stream below a waterfall. Continue up the far side (well-made rock steps where it becomes steep) to the L end of a beech wood that lies above the Dinosaur. Go up L then into a wet gully that leads to a higher wood below the Metamorfosi. Walk up to the R side of the crag where there is a cave-like depression. 1hr from Gatto Rosso

339 **LUNA NASCENTE**
VI+ A Boscacci, M Ghezzi and G Milani, 1978
160
76

Probably Boscacci's finest creation and thought by many to give the best route in the valley at any grade. Linked with Kundalini it provides nearly 800m of continuous climbing, with only a short walk in the middle. This combination could truly claim to be the best granite outing of its standard in Europe. There are two moves of A1 on the first pitch. 340m

A well-beaten track leads to the start of the route, which lies towards the R side of the cave. The first pitch is 15m and climbs easily up to and then over a desperate overhang (2 aid moves on in-situ wires). Above, it moves L into a chimney and then basically follows a series of cracks on the R side of the buttress. These can be very well protected given a wide selection of nuts and Friends.

Free climbing the first pitch is at least VII+ and nearly all parties use aid. An easier alternative, rumoured to lie somewhere to the L, remains a bit of an enigma. Care should be taken to avoid a serious rope-jam around the overhang at the end of the second pitch.

Descent: This lies to the E of the crag. Go up through the trees to a grassy area where an old stone wall and two conspicuous vertical stones indicate an old path. Go down this path into a gully. After a short descent the path traverses E over easy rock and around a spur to reach a second gully. The path descends steeply alongside the stream and eventually traverses back W, through the beech woods, to the foot of the route. Some parties have also rappelled the steep wooded gully immediately R(E) of the crag.

340 **POLIMAGO**
VII P Masa and J Merizzi, 1979
76

Another brilliant route which certain climbers consider to be even better than Luna! After a common start (2 moves of A1) it follows a curving

line on the upper slabs to join Luna at the top of the sixth pitch (possible rappel descent down Luna and into the wooded gully on the R). It is more varied, probably a grade harder and certainly less well protected than the latter. 360m

Placche Dell'Oasi

This highly popular area offers the best easy climb in the valley. It can be reached in a little over an hour from Gatto Rosso and is situated a few mins above the valley path, just past the bridge over the Torrone stream (Pt 1298m).

341 **UOMINI E TOPI**
IV G Miotti, 1977
79

A classic outing and undoubtedly the most worthwhile route of its standard in the valley. As usual, protection is sparse but most of the climbing is fairly easy padding up friction slabs. Beware straying L on the initial big bald slab. It's much harder (V/V+) and totally devoid of runners. 350m

Start just up to the R of the base of the 'Sperone' and climb up on to the slab passing the bulge on the R. From the top of the crag walk E through the trees above some slabs, then fight your way down through the forest to reach the path descending from the Val Cameraccio.

342 **LA CHIUSA**
V–/V

This lies in a secluded hollow directly below the Oasi and a little above the banks of the Mello river. 105m

The middle of the wall is steep, hard and well protected by bolts (VII?). On the L side is an easy slab. Climb this (IV then III) to a steepening, where undercut flakes lead out L (V–/V: Friends) to the upper slab. Follow this more easily to trees (IV– then II). Go up to the R and slant L up the wall beneath a flake (25m: IV+). Pad gently up the final slab to the top (40m: I/II). Traverse L through the trees to the main path.

Piede dell'Elefante

This tremendous W-facing friction slab lies below San Martino and not in the Mello valley itself. It is situated at the bottom of the hillside opposite the Sasso Remenno and can be reached in 15min from the main road – crossing the river can be fun! Highly conspicuous are a number of quartz veins that slant across the bulbous slab, and also a small stone building at the top L.

343 **CRAZY HORSE**
VI G Miotti and L Mottarella, 1978.
78 *Superb delicate climbing but, yet again, a bold run-out with little in the way of protection. Fortunately, the crux moves occur at the start of the first main pitch. A few small wires are useful. Descend to the R. 100m*

Disgrazia and Bernina Groups

Ponti Hut 2559m CAI. Room for 85. Tel: 0342 611455. Located N of the prominent lateral moraine in the upper Preda Rossa valley. Open during the summer with a warden and restaurant service. At other times the hut is locked (key fom San Martino) but a small winter room, with room for 6, is always left open. It is one of the main overnight halts for parties walking the Roma Path and also serves as a base for ascents of Monte Disgrazia. These reasons, combined with an easy walk from the road-head, often produce overcrowding. At the time of writing the approach to this hut has been lengthened by a rock-fall on to the valley approach road. A new road is being built but is unlikely to be opened before 1995.

H1 P From Cataeggio in the Val Masino drive up the road to a carpark at Preda Rossa (1935m: c2½hr on foot). The path ahead is clearly sign-posted and waymarked. It makes a gentle ascent along the bed of the valley before rising L through rocky terrain to the hut. 2hr

Desio Hut c2830m CAI. Room for 20. Situated just below the Passo di Corna Rossa on the E side. It has no warden and is always left open.

H2 PE From the Ponti hut follow the good waymarked path up onto the lateral moraine then descend onto the glacier. Cross it (usually dry with no crevasses) and follow a path up scree and broken ground to the pass. 1-1½hr

H3 P From the Bosio hut walk up the beautiful Valle Airale. From Pt 2569m the path takes to a rib leading N and then works up over scree to the hut. 3hr

Rauzi Hut c3640m (Bivacco Alberto Rauzi) Room for 9 Associazione Amici di Chiareggio. Situated c100m from the summit trig point of Monte Disgrazia in the direction of the NNE ridge.

Porro Hut 1965m CAI. Room for 50. Tel: 0342 451404. Situated on the Alpe Ventina half way between Chiareggio and the Ventina glacier. 5 min further, at 1970m, stands the Refugio Ventina, a private hut of about the same size. There is a warden and a healthy restaurant service during the usual summer period but outside of the season it is locked (key available in Chiareggio), though a small annexe, with bunks for 3, remains open all year round. Easy access has made this a popular daytime venue.

H4
P

From Chiareggio cross the river to the S and follow the unmistakable mule track up to the hut. 1hr

It is possible to reach the hut from Maloja in c5½hr by crossing the Muretto pass. When descending to Chiareggio the track enters a clearing with some chalets before making a big bend to the R. At this point it is possible to make a short cut by leaving the track and dropping down the hillside to reach the Forbisina path. Shortly before reaching this hamlet head SE and cross a footbridge over the Sissone river, then follow a path to join the mule track leading up to the hut.

Taveggia Hut c2850m (Bivacco Angelo Taveggia). Milan section of the CAAI. Situated c30m above the Ventina glacier and a little below the shoulder at the foot of the E ridge of Pta Kennedy. This shoulder lies 350m to the SW of Pt 2882m (Sentinella della Vergine). It is a small and moderately well-equipped hut that is never locked. However, with only room for 4 it can quickly become crowded. The approach via the Ventina glacier is lengthy but relatively gentle and objectively safe. Crevasses on the latter part of the journey seldom cause problems. Parties based in Switzerland have reached the hut via the Muretto pass. This is a very hard day and unless a light sac is carried, at least 9hr should be allowed.

H5
F+/PD–
164

From the Porro hut follow the well-marked path along the moraine to reach the Ventina glacier c400m above the snout. It is worth making a short detour here to look at the markers showing the extent of recent glacial recession. Walk up the middle of the glacier to c2800m, then work N across a glacial shelf to below the shoulder at the foot of the E ridge of Pta Kennedy. An easy fault-line in the rock slants up R to the hut. 3hr

Oggioni Hut 3151m (Bivacco Andrea Oggioni). Room for 12. Constructed by the CAI to commemorate one of the fatalities of the epic retreat in 1961 from the Central Pillar of Freney on Mont Blanc. Situated in a splendid position on the Colletto del Disgrazia and is clearly visible from 100m or more, when approaching via the Canalone della Vergine. It is very well equipped and always open. Due to the difficulty in returning to this hut after a route on Disgrazia and the close proximity of the Taveggia bivouac, it is not that popular – though a night spent here, overlooking the N face, is magic!

H6
PD
163

Scramble up behind the Taveggia hut to gain the glacier of the Canalone della Vergine. Make a more or less horizontal traverse W and cross an obvious neck in the NNE ridge of the Pta Kennedy, above the base. A fairly steep but straightforward ascent now leads to a more crevassed area. Work through this to the upper basin and so reach the hut. 1-1½hr: 300m of ascent. See also photographs 162 and 164

Bosio Hut 2086m CAI Room for 60 Tel: 0342 451655. Situated in the beautiful Airale valley on the opposite side of the river to the chalets of Alpe Airale. Open with a warden and restaurant service from 1 July – 15 Sept but locked outside this period.

H7
P

From Chiesa or from Torre di S Maria there are excellent waymarked paths via Alpes Lago or Acquabianca to Alpe Serra (1927m) and thence to the hut. 3hr or 3½hr respectively. It can also be reached from the Porro hut via the Passo Cassandra in 5½hr (PD).

Colombo Hut c3170m CAI. Room for 8. This is a small bivouac shelter, which appears to be seldom used. Situated on the rocks to the N of the Fuorcla Fex-Scerscen. It is not in particularly good shape. It is reached from Sils Maria in 4-5hr and from the Marinelli hut in 3hr (F/PD-: see Routes 51 and 52).

Longoni Hut 2459m CAI Room for 37 Tel: 0342 451120. Situated on a shoulder at the base of the SW ridge of the Sassa d'Entova. It provides a popular overnight stop for parties engaged on the Alta Via della Valmalenco and would be a convenient base for those tackling the southern approaches to the Tremoggia chain. Generally open, with a resident warden, from mid-July to mid-Sept. It is reached by walking less than 30min from a point on the well-maintained, unmade road that leads up towards the Scerscen-Entova Hotel.

H8
P
165

For those without transport it is best reached directly from Chiareggio. Just E of the village, the Alta Via (signposted '4' inside a yellow triangle) leaves the main road and climbs up through the forest to reach the quarry workings and various buildings of Alpe Fora. These lie at the end of a wide unmade road that leaves the access road to the Scerscen Ski Station 1 km W of Alpe Entova. Now follow the Alta Via to the N and after crossing a stream, take the R fork. Follow this E and finally SE, above extensive rocky cliffs, to a shoulder on a promontory, which lies at the base of the long SW ridge coming down from the Sassa d'Entova. The hut is slightly to the SE (2½-3hr). From Alpe Fora it is just as convenient to walk the dirt roads and reach the hut from the E.

A longer but very beautiful walk, which will appeal to the more adventurous, starts from a bar on the main road 1k E of Chiareggio. A steep and somewhat overgrown path climbs up through the forest to the marvellously-sited chalets at Alpe Senevedo Sup and from there, NW to the quarries at Alpe Fora.

Scerscen-Entova Hotel 3001m Room for 120 Tel: 0342 451198 or 451681. Privately owned summer ski-station situated on the S bank of the Lower Scerscen glacier. Part of the building operates as a refuge and overnight accommodation is available, although the tariff is, understandably, higher than at CAI huts. It is an excellent starting point for many of the climbs in the Tremoggia – Sella group and even the Bernina. A clearly signposted road leaves the main highway at S Guiseppe and runs, via Alpe Entova, to the end of a service téléphérique (luggage only) at 2672m. Although unsurfaced it is quite suitable for private cars up to c2350m after which a taxi service operates the remaining distance. A steep track now zigzags up the rocky ramparts above, allowing the Hotel to be reached in a mere 45min walk (P). Open 15 June till 15 Sept

Palu Hut 1947m Room for 30. Privately owned. Situated above the shores of Lago Palu and below the hamlet of Alpe Roggione. It is a popular watering-hole on the Alta Via and is easily reached from the téléphérique terminus at Alpe Palu. Generally open during much of the Spring, at various times in the Autumn and fully operational from the beginning of July to Mid-Sept.

H9 Take the road out of S Guiseppe towards the Scerscen-Entova Hotel
P and after a km or so, branch R on a dirt road and follow it up to the 'Rifugio Barchi' (c1740m). Private cars can be left here (large carpark: 40min on foot from Scerscen road). A well signposted and unmistakable mule path leads up through the forest to the hut. (1-1½hr)

Longer but far more picturesque is to continue further along the Scerscen road until above Prati della Costa. Now take the 'Botanical Path' W through Il Barchetto (trees and shrubs identified with their Latin names etc) and continue up through the forest on a well marked track, not shown on the map, which reaches the NW tip of the lake.

Carate Hut 2636m (Carate Brianza hut) CAI. Room for 22. Tel: 0342 452560. Situated on the Bochetta delle Forbici. Passed en route to the Marinelli hut from Alp Musella and clearly visible from the latter. Open, with a resident warden, from July to Sept. 3½hr from Franscia: 2hr from Campo Moro

Marinelli Hut 2813m CAI. Bed spaces for c250. Tel: 0342 451494. Situated on a rocky promontory, N of the tiny Caspoggio glacier and below the base of the SW ridge of Piz Argient. It is the largest hut in the region and has grown out of necessity, providing the most convenient base for the majority of routes on the Italian side of the range. It is open, with a resident warden, during Easter, Whitsun and from the beginning of July to the end of Sept. Full restaurant service is available for most of that time. At other times the hut is locked.

H10
P/PE

The quickest route to the hut starts from the dam wall of Campo Moro (lower lake). From the 'carpark' on the road, immediately below the Zoia hut, walk across the dam and follow the old quarry road down the valley to the W. The R fork (signposted) leads steeply up and across the hillside, before contouring around the lower slopes of the Sasso Moro to join the old path from Alp Musella at c2240m (1hr). The track now zigzags wearily up the stony valley, reaching the Carate hut on the Bocchetta di Forbici and providing superb views of the great glaciers S of the main peaks (1hr). Head N under the rocky walls of the Musella, cross a saddle in the ridge beyond and walk across the base of the tiny Caspoggio glacier. Reach the hut from the E. 1hr: 3hr from Campo Moro

H11
PE
172

A popular alternative starts from the end of the private road below the upper dam wall of the Lago di Gela (Alpe Gela, c2020m). Walk up to the top of the dam wall and cross it to the W side of the lake. A good path, signposted to the Bignami hut, slants N across the hillside. Reach this hut in c1hr from the roadhead. A well-marked path (paint flashes, etc) now heads NW, crossing two small streams and finally climbing scree and a short snow slope to the Bocchetta di Caspoggio (2983m). From here there is usually a well trodden piste down the snow on the R side of the tame Caspoggio glacier. The hut is clearly visible and is reached after a short ascent. 2½hr: 3½hr from Alpe Gela

H12 A longer approach leaves the road at the village of Franscia. From
P/PE the carpark at the end of the tarmacked road follow the minor road NW towards the village and just before the bridge, take a path on the R. This quickly develops into a well-constructed mule track and zigzags up through steep forested terrain on the S side of the rocky knoll (1857m). Reach the delightfully situated Alpe Foppa in 1½hr. Bear W and continue to Alpe Musella (2076m: 30min). From here continue to the hut via route H10. 4-4½hr from Franscia car-park

Longer still and less used, is an approach from the roadhead by the quarries at the SW end of the village. Follow the path N, past the Refugio Scerscen, to Alpe Campascio and finally Alpe Musella. 2½hr

H13 It is also possible to reach the hut, from the start of the service
RE téléphérique to the Scerscen-Entova hotel, by crossing the Forcella
168 d'Entova (2831m). This is quite rough going and if partially snow covered can be delicate, especially when sun-softened later in the day. Allow at least 2hr to the hut.

In winter a careful assessment of the snow conditions is necessary as all routes are prone to avalanche. However, parties generally feel that Route H11 gives the safest passage.

Bignami Hut 2382m CAI. Room for 90. Tel: 0342 451178. Situated on the approach to the Marinelli hut at the base of the long rocky NE ridge of Sasso Moro. Resident warden and normal facilities during the spring and summer seasons. A small winter refuge lies just below the main hut. It can be reached from Alpe Gela in c1hr (See Route H11).

Parravicini Hut 3183m (Bivacco Agostino Parravicini) CAI. Room for 6. Situated c800m SE of the Fuorcla da la Sella, at the top of the rocky escarpment rising out of the Lower Scerscen glacier. Rather spartan, but always open!

From the Marinelli hut the bivouac can be reached in c2hr via Route 73 to the Sella Pass (F). It is also possible to approach directly from the Lower Scerscen glacier via the wide snowy couloir that splits the rocky escarpment just W of the hut (PD–). When coming from Piz Sella it is not necessary to reach the head of the couloir, as an easy ramp slants down from the W to meet the couloir at about two-thirds height. Parties based at the Scerscen Ski-station can use the well-signposted 'Sentiero dei Camosci' which leads across the lower section of Piz Sella's S face to reach the upper Scerscen glacier direct. c2hr: see Route 69

Marco E Rosa Hut 3597m CAI. Overnight accommodation for 45. Tel: 0342 212370. This fairly small metal hut is the highest in the range. Situated c300m W of the Fuorcla Crast'Aguzza at the base of the Spalla ridge of Piz Bernina. There is a resident warden during the summer months. Restaurant service is often very basic and the hut is quite expensive. However, it has proved a life-saver to many parties caught in bad weather on the Bernina, and when these conditions prevail can often become very crowded. When the warden is absent the hut is usually locked but the old wooden building remains open as a winter refuge.

H14 PD– 187 Swiss side: At the time of writing the only approach used during the summer months is via the Fortezza ridge and the Bellavista terrace. Short cuts to the terrace, commonly referred to as the 'Fuora' or, further to the W, the 'Buuch' have become both complex and dangerous, although they are sometimes skied during the winter.

From the Diavolezza follow Route 118a to the start of the Bellavista terrace, which cuts across the upper slopes of the mountain above the highest icefalls of the Morteratsch glacier. Cross it to the SW, then descend into the head of the cirque below the Crast' Aguzza. Continue W to the Fuorcla Crast' Aguzza and so reach the hut (4hr). Due to the popularity of this approach, parties will normally be following a well defined piste. However, without this aid the exact location of the hut can be quite tricky to ascertain in bad visibility. See also photograph 184

H15 F+/PD– 182 Italian side: From the Marinelli hut follow the path NE across the scree. It rises gradually alongside the rocky spur coming down from the Passo Marinelli Occidentale and reaches the glacier. On the L is the W pass and up to the R is the E. Go through the W pass (45min). Continue N across the almost-horizontal, Upper Scerscen glacier, passing quite close to the rocks at the foot of the long spur coming down from the Crast'Aguzza (Pt 3131m). Slant up a steepening snow slope, below the entrance to a wide couloir leading up to the Fuorcla Crast' Aguzza and reach the base of the rock buttress to the NW. Go round this on the L and climb up the rocks above, slanting R to the crest. This leads to a snow-shoulder with the hut situated just up to the L.

The buttress is almost 200m high and equipped throughout with metal cables, making the ascent quite straightforward. However the lower section is not immune from stone-fall, especially during the heat of the day (3-3½hr from the Marinelli hut: 2hr in descent). Early in the season the wide snow couloir can often provide a swift and uncomplicated ascent. It is seldom used during the summer months, as by this time it has generally become a stone swept icy funnel.

In winter the hut is normally reached on skis, by crossing the Fuorcla Bellavista to join the Swiss approach.

Pansera Hut 3546m (Sasso Rosso bivouac) CAI. Room for 4. Situated 350m S of the Pass of the same name. It sits atop a rocky knoll at the end of the NW ridge of the Sasso Rosso and lies at the 'gateway' to the Altipiano. Although a convenient base for routes on the S slopes of the Zupo – Palu chain, it is infrequently used and has been allowed to fall into a state of considerable neglect. Always open.

H16 PD– 174 From the Marinelli hut follow Route H15 as far as the glacier, then turn R and cross the snowy shoulder that forms the E Marinelli Pass. Contour across the Felleria glacier, passing close to the base of the S ridge of Piz Argent. The gradient of the slope now gradually increases all the way to the pass and is cut by numerous crevasses. The easiest line varies. In certain years it is best to keep in the centre; whilst in others, the most straightforward approach lies close to the rocks of Piz Zupo, though here one can sometimes be threatened by falling ice. From the pass the hut is reached in a few minutes. 2½-3hr. See also photographs 172, 177, 186

Zoia Hut 2021m CAI. Room for 40. Tel: 0342 451405. Situated a couple of mins walk above the road at Campo Moro. As the road is often ploughed throughout the winter months to provide access to the dam, this hut can be open for much of the year.

Cristina Hut 2287m. Room for 20. One of the several privately owned and modest dwellings S of Alpe Prabello and close to the flanks of Piz Scalino. A major overnight halt for walkers engaged on the Alta Via della Valmalenco.

H17 P The easiest approach starts at the Zoia hut, where a well-marked path winds its way up and around the flanks of Monte Spondasca to Alpe Campagneda. Now head S across flat and often marshy ground to Alpe Prabello (1-1½hr to the hut). If walking from Franscia leave the road at the top of the big hairpin bends, where a signposted path leads up through the forest to the hut.

Coaz Hut 2610m SAC. Room for 80. Tel 082 66278. A 16 sided edifice situated on the W side of the lower reaches of the Roseg glacier. Named after Johann Coaz, the well known topographer who made the first ascent of Piz Bernina, it is a very popular establishment, especially with day trippers. It has a resident warden at Easter, Whitsun and from mid-June till mid/end Sept. At other times of the year the winter room remains open.

H18 From the railway station at Pontresina a private unmade road runs
P up the R side of the Roseg valley. For those wishing to travel in style, horse-drawn carriages can be taken from the railway station as far as the Hotel Roseg. Alternatively a pleasant, though busy, footpath follows the L side of the river. Either way is a 1½hr walk to the hotel. The well-marked path now slants gently up the grassy hillside to the small Alp Ota restaurant (2257m). Continue along the Murtel terrace and contour round to the hut (4½hr from Pontresina).

H19 From the middle station (2699m) on the Corvatschbahn, take the
P well-trodden path to the Fuorcla Surlej (2755m: 20-30min) where
170 there is a privately owned restaurant with overnight accommodation for 60 (more expensive than SAC rates). The views to the S from this point are quite dramatic, especially early in the morning. An easy path now slants down the hillside to join the previous route on the terrace. 2½hr from téléphérique station to the hut

In winter the safest route lies along the bottom of the Roseg valley but in good snow conditions, a popular alternative is to approach from the top station of the Corvatschbahn and ski across the flanks of Piz Corvatsch.

Tschierva Hut 2583m SAC. Room for 100. Tel: 082 66391. Situated on the R(E) bank of the Tschierva glacier. There is a resident warden from the beginning of April to mid-May and from mid-June till mid-Oct. At other times of the year the winter room remains open. It is a popular base and often quite crowded, but during quieter periods it is not unusual to see herds of chamois moving across the neighbouring slopes.

H20 P From the railway station at Pontresina follow Route H18 as far as the Hotel Roseg. Just before reaching the hotel, where the path crosses the river, the track to the Tschierva hut forks L and climbs up into the ablation valley, alongside the lateral moraine on the L side of the glacier. Later it reaches the crest where the views are more dramatic (3½hr to the hut from Pontresina). In descent, and especially when there is still snow in the bed, it is much quicker to follow the ablation valley throughout.

The hut can also be reached from the Fuorcla Surlej in 2½-3hr via a good footpath down to the Roseg Hotel.

It is also possible to reach the Tschierva hut from the Coaz hut. From the latter descend the path to the glacier lake in the main valley (Pt 2159m). Reach the lateral moraine on the L bank of the Tschierva glacier and follow a small track up the ablation valley to c2500m, where it is possible to cross the flat dry section of the glacier directly to the hut. 2½hr

In winter, either use the same approach or, keeping more to the centre of the valley, go up the glacier until level with the hut.

Boval Hut 2459m SAC. Room for 100. Tel: 082 66403. Situated above the L bank of the Morteratsch glacier. It is one of the busiest huts in the Swiss alps and often rather overcrowded. It is well frequented by day trippers who, after a delightful walk, can take a well deserved lunch on the terrace and enjoy the magnificent scenery. There is a resident warden from Easter to Mid-Oct and at other times of the year a winter room is left open.

H21 P From the small railway station at Morteratsch the path is well signposted and unmistakable. Wide at first, it quickly leaves open ground and zigzags up through woods to Chunetta. A scenic walk along the pretty ablation valley and finally on the moraine itself leads to the hut. 2½hr

The hut can be reached from the Diavolezza in c3hr via the Isla Persa (See Route 118). During the summer guided parties leave the Diavolezza each day at 11.45am to cross to the Isla Persa and from there descend directly down the glacier to Morteratsch (4hr and 15 Francs!). It is worth going to look at the markers below the snout which show the extent of glacial recession over the years.

In winter, approach directly up the Morteratsch glacier reaching the moraine to the S of the hut.

Diavolezza 2973m. Accommodation for around 180. Tel: 082 66205. This is a plush, privately-owned hotel and restaurant at the terminus of the téléphérique. It provides convenient access to most of the routes on the Swiss side, in the Eastern part of the range. It is an inspiring viewpoint with a splendid panorama across the Pers glacier to the majestic snowy peaks of the Palu, Bellavista and Bernina. Accommodation is expensive and should be reserved in advance. A small section is run more on the lines of an alpine hut where bed space, though still pricy, is somewhat cheaper than the main establishment – however, you must buy a meal! It is open all year round except from mid-Oct to mid-Nov and sometimes during May.

It can be reached in 8min from the Bernina Suot Station by a fairly expensive ride in the cable car; or in 2½-3hr on foot via the unmistakable path.

ALTA VIA DELLA VALMALENCO

PE/RE The high-level walk of this region is clearly waymarked by paint flashes and, at various points, yellow triangular signposts. It is a little contrived and a more direct version is now described.

Starting at Chiesa cross the Passo Ventina to Chiareggio and walk up to the Longoni hut. Traverse directly to the Marinelli via the Forcola d'Entova or make a long detour via Lago Palu, Rif Scerscen and Alpe Musella. Reach the Val Poschiavina via the Bignami hut and cross the Campagneda pass to the Cristina hut. Traverse the N flanks of the Scalino range to finish at Caspoggio.

Disgrazia Group

Geologists consider this to be a separate range, isolated from the main Bregaglia chain but with the line of demarcation passing through the Sella di Pioda. To the N and W lie the granites, while to the S and E the rock is serpentine. As Monte Pioda is generally considered a subsidary peak of Disgrazia, it has for geographical convenience been included in this section.

Cima d'Arcanza 2714m

1 **NORMAL ROUTE**
PE F Lurani with A Baroni, 16 Aug 1881

A minor summit above San Martino but a magnificent viewpoint – one of the best in the region! The path begins from the big bend in the river to the N of San Martino and just past the point where it bifurcates. Although vague at first, it slants up R towards the watercourse and then becomes well-constructed, often waymarked with a red letter A. Two particular 'belvederes', overlooking the Mello valley, are outstanding. Above Arcanzolo climb up to the last building and locate a path that tenuously traverses S around the wooded hillside to reach twin huts and limited open pastures. Above, paths become most elusive, any resemblance to the map is largely illusionary, and a machete might be useful! Reach the NW ridge leading to the foresummit, turn the latter on the L and follow the rocky SW ridge to the main summit (c7hr for successful bushwackers).

Monte Pioda 3431m

L Stephen with M Anderegg, 20 Aug 1862

Seen from several directions as an attractive rocky pyramid, this peak is in reality no more than a shoulder on the long NW ridge of Monte Disgrazia. Despite being a splendid viewpoint, and reached by a number of straightforward routes, the summit is rarely visited.

2 **EAST RIDGE**
PD– The usual route. An easy 20min scramble on rotten rock following
161 the crest of the ridge from the Sella di Pioda. Splendid views but uninteresting climbing. I/II

3 **SOUTH-WEST RIDGE**
PD+ L Binaghi, C Feloy and G Guggeri, 5 July 1931

Fairly interesting climbing on reasonable rock.

The ridge begins well above the Roma traverse path. Avoid the first step by walking up the glacier on the R (towards the Passo Cecilia). Move L on to the ridge via a broad scree terrace and reach a prominent shoulder (2½hr from the Ponti hut). Starting with a steep juggy wall (III), follow the crest to join the NW ridge c50m below the summit (2½hr). 350m: III, 5hr from hut

4 **NORTH-WEST RIDGE**
PD+ First ascent party
161

Perched high above the contorted Disgrazia glacier, this route has a savage ambience. There are frightening views across the great ice routes on the N face of Monte Disgrazia. The climbing itself is pleasant and fairly exposed, but the lower horizontal portion could be quite delicate if snow covered.

Immediately above the Passo di Mello the ridge is impressively crenellated. Avoid this first section by snow slopes to the SW and climb back to the crest on sound rock. Follow the ridge more or less directly, turning several gendarmes. It eventually joins the SW ridge c50m below the summit. 450m: III, 3hr from the Passo di Mello

Monte Pioda North Side

An isolated corner of the range with a less than straightforward approach. There are two faces separated by a prominent spur. On the R the NNW face is an attractive triangle – mainly snow with a finish on mixed ground. The NE face is much steeper and seamed by rocky ribs. The rock is poor and in dry conditions stone-fall is common place. Ascents have been few but with a heavy covering of well-frozen snow, these routes are clearly worth a visit.

5 **NORTH-NORTH-WEST FACE**
AD+/D O Lenatti and C Sicola; F Longoni and L Tagliabue. 9 Aug 1937
161

A direct line up the middle of the steep triangular snow face, finishing on mixed ground. In less than perfect conditions the upper section will be quite tricky. Approach from Chiareggio or the Grandori bivouac. 400m: 4hr

6 **NORTH SPUR**
AD/ AD+ 161 G Bava and A Corti, 9 July 1928.

Although easier and safer than the face routes, the same conditions apply. The ridge is gained from the W above its base. The line is now unmistakable and the crest becomes even sharper before the junction with the NW ridge c50m from the summit. 450m: 4hr

7 **NORTH-EAST FACE**
D+/ TD− 161 O Lenatti, F Longini and L Tagliabue, early Sept 1936

Characterised by a series of rocky ribs separated by steep icy couloirs. The obvious line follows the central couloir, taking the R fork at half-height. Finish close to the top of the N spur. Due to the aspect of this face, parties are less likely to find suitable conditions for a safe ascent. 450m: 5-6hr

Monte Disgrazia 3678m

E Kennedy, L Stephen and T Cox with M Anderegg , 24 Aug 1862. Winter: E Main with M Schocher and C Schnitzler, 16 Feb 1896 (from the Forno hut!)

Higher than any peak in the Bregaglia by nearly 300m, this icy pyramid is considered by many to be one of the most beautiful summits in the Alps. It is an isolated mountain of classic proportions and rises abruptly from the deep Italian valleys. Nowadays, the name is commonly thought to originate not from some great 'disaster' but from a corruption of 'Desglascia' or 'Disghiacca', which most probably refers to continuous ice fall from the northern flanks.

The summit, spoilt only by a huge metallic trig point, offers unparalleled views over the southern flanks of the Bregaglia and Bernina. With good visibility, some of the major peaks in the Valais, Oberland, Austrian Alps and Dolomites can be clearly identified.

The N side offers a selection of magnificent routes on snow/ice or over mixed ground, but ascents from this direction are sporadic. A reputation for sudden storms (the peak appears to 'suck' cloud from the Italian plains) and a long and complex approach, deter all but the more adventurous. With no easy way off, a winter ascent on the great N face will present one of the most committing challenges described in this book.

8 **NORTH-WEST RIDGE**
PD+ First ascent party
167

It would be disappointing if this majestic mountain could be climbed by a straightforward and somewhat monotonous 'Voie Normale' as is the case with many of the great Alpine peaks. Here we have an exposed and continuously interesting mixed climb and although not the easiest way to the summit, it is the most popular. Under normal conditions the ridge is straightforward but the difficulties increase considerably after heavy snowfall. On this climb an aura of commitment is more apparent than any inherent technical problems and the route can feel serious despite the presence of other parties. See also photograph 162

From the Ponti hut follow a good waymarked path above the moraine on the W bank of the Preda Rossa glacier. Higher it becomes less distinct. At c2900m cross the upper end of the moraine and walk up the glacier to a saddle at its head – the Sella di Pioda (3387m: 2½hr). Above lies the NW ridge. The first section is steep and can be climbed direct or turned more easily on the R, returning to the crest above a gendarme. Mixed climbing (which could be predominately rocky by mid-summer) leads to the foresummit (3650m). A classic snow ridge, on which large cornices can develop, now leads to the main summit. It is interrupted by a large block – the 'Bronze Horse'. Climb over this (II/III) and follow the steepening ridge for 100m to the trig point. 1000m of ascent: 5hr from the hut

9 **FROM FORNO HUT**
AD

Very fit parties can climb the mountain from Switzerland. This is now recognised as a long, classic and celebrated ski-tour which can be achieved in a round trip of 15hr. Not surprisingly, it is seldom attempted during the summer, even though it provides one of the finest excursions of its standard in the region.

Make an early start from the Forno hut and climb Monte Sissone, descending to the Roma path (see Routes 306 and 307 in Bregaglia section). Follow this path SE and reach the base of the tiny glacier that lies below the Cecilia Pass. Walk up the glacier and climb the broad snow slope which rises to the gap on the Preda Rossa/Mello watershed (c3230m). Slant onto the Preda Rossa glacier, climb up to the Sella di Pioda and follow the NW ridge to the summit. 30km round trip from the hut! 10hr

10
PD

SOUTH-WEST (BARONI) RIDGE

F Lurani with A Baroni, 23 July 1878

Not a popular ascent. The broad crest is reached via steep rocks from below the final slopes leading to the Sella di Pioda. It gives tedious scrambling over loose ground (stone-fall). However, as an alternative means of descent it does provide the shortest route from the foresummit to the Preda Rossa glacier, and is entirely on rock of moderate difficulty (II). 4½hr

Monte Disgrazia South-East Ridge

This can be followed integrally from the Passo Cassandra or joined at the E summit by climbing the NE spur. The former is relatively safe and straightforward while the latter is far more interesting! Both can become considerably harder after heavy snowfall.

11
AD–
162

FROM PASSO CASSANDRA

A Bonacossa and P Torti, 23 July 1913 Winter: L and P Tagliabue with O Lenatti and G Schenatti (As far as the E summit), 5 Jan 1937

From the Passo Cassandra (see Route 21) follow the crest of the ridge, occasionally making small deviations onto the rocks of the S flank. There is little difficulty in good conditions and it should be possible to reach the E summit (3648m) in 2½hr. The connecting ridge between E and Central summits is only tricky if large cornices are present. Generally it can be crossed in 45 minutes and gives enjoyable scrambling on sound rock. Between the Central and Main summits the ridge is more serrated. It is better to climb over all the towers as there the rock is at its best (II/III), though sometimes it may be necessary to move briefly onto the N flank to circumnavigate difficulties. 6hr, c4hr in descent. See also photograph 164

12
AD+
162

VIA NORTH-EAST SPUR OF EAST SUMMIT

F Pratt Barlow and S Still with J Anderegg and P Taugwald, 29 Aug 1874

The approach to the foot of the spur is threatened by ice fall from the massive sérac barrier on the E face. At the time of writing this sérac appears to be relatively stable. A true assessment of the dangers can only be made from close at hand as the route on the glacier at this point is invisible from below. Once on the spur, alpinists will enjoy excellent, and objectively safe, mixed climbing amidst some of the finest scenery in the area.

From the Taveggia bivouac walk back along the snow terrace below the icefall of the Ventina glacier, until approaching the foot of the Passo Cassandra. A large glacial ramp runs NW between the icefall and the flanks of the SE ridge. It is crevassed and although normally straightforward it has, on occasions, proved quite time-consuming. Near the top move L and climb up onto the NE spur via the snow slopes on its E flank. Follow the crest in a fine position to the summit rocks. These are solid and present little difficulty (II/III+) when free from snow. Continue to the main summit via Route 11. 6hr

It is also possible to reach the foot of the spur from the Oggioni bivouac. Although this rather circuitous route adds more time to the whole expedition, it is free from objective danger. Cross Col Kennedy to the uncomplicated slopes of the upper Ventina glacier. Traverse horizontally across these and reach the crest of the spur from the W side.

Monte Disgrazia continued

13 **COULOIR DELL'INSUBORDINATO**
D/D+ R Casarotto, G Federico, A Gogna, L Mario, C Mauri and E Molin,
163 7 Sept 1979

The great ice couloir falling from the gap between the E and Central summits is of fairly uniform angle, with a maximum of 65° near the base of the climb. The rimaye can be avoided by climbing the rock c40m to the R. In good conditions stone-fall is negligible. 300m: 4hr

The thin ice couloir on the NNE face of the E summit was climbed by B Balatti and M Ranaglia, 1 Sept 1989, to give 'Hypergoulette' – a 300m ED1 with crux sections of 95°.

14 **NORTH-NORTH-EAST RIDGE – CORDA MOLLA**
AD+ B de Ferrari with I dell'Andrino (upper section only), Aug 1914
167 Complete ridge: A Bonola, A and P Corti, 2 Aug 1928.
Winter: F and G Grandori, 26 Dec 1940

A brilliant mixed route of a quality equal to any other of its standard in the Alps. Following the crest from the Oggioni hut gives even difficulty on both rock and ice. The position is outstanding, with spectacular views across the N face and a wide panorama of the Bernina. A long and awkward approach still deters many parties and the ascent will generally feel very wild and remote. In good conditions the technical standard is not high, making the route a classic undertaking for the middle-grade mountaineer.

In well-frozen conditions it is only 1hr from the Taveggia to the

Oggioni, and many parties overnight at the former hut leaving their bivi gear to be picked up on the descent. However, it can easily get crowded! See also photographs 162, 163

From the Oggioni bivouac climb slopes L of the ridge to the top of Pt 3295m. In recent years these slopes have been very icy and the alternative, along the crest of the ridge, has presented an awkward step.

Continue without undue difficulty, mainly rock with a few short snow crests, until stopped by a large buttress. Climb this by a couloir/chimney on the R side (30m: good rock). The ridge becomes narrower with some delightful pitches on rough red rock which are usually climbed on the E flank. After 2hr a point is reached where it is possible to escape quite easily onto the Ventina glacier. The ridge now begins to rise towards the summit and the fine snow crest that follows gives the route its name. At first the ascent is gradual, but at mid-height the ridge merges into a 45° slope. This is often icy and screws can be useful. About 100m below the summit rocks move L and climb steep 'juggy' serpentine (III) to reach the SE ridge, and Rauzi Bivouac hut, just below the summit. c500m: 3½-4hr from the hut

Descent: The most convenient descent on this side of the mountain follows the rock rib immediately S of the upper slope.

Climb down or rappel the rocky section below the bivouac hut, branching slightly R to reach a rocky rib that drops towards the Ventina glacier. Descend this rib (rappels) to reach the snow below and cross an awkward rimaye onto the glacier. Either: Walk across the glacial cirque below the NNE ridge, crossing Col Kennedy to reach the Oggioni hut (safest) or: traverse E to the rounded snow-ridge that forms the base of the NE spur of the E summit. Cross this and reverse Route 12. There is only a small deviation needed to visit the Taveggia bivouac before continuing down the glacier to the Porro hut.

In good conditions a long but safe alternative for those returning directly to the Porro hut is to go down the SE ridge to Passo Cassandra. This completes a fine traverse of the mountain.

Monte Disgrazia North Face

Remotely sited above the crevasse-strewn Disgrazia glacier, this mighty ice wall now boasts a variety of excellent routes that are seldom attempted. Conditions have rarely been suitable for an ascent during recent summers, and unless the rock is well snowed-up stone-fall can create a constant threat. A large and complex crevassed zone bars access to the upper plateau of the glacier and a direct approach from Chiareggio (or the Passo di Mello) is not normally feasible. Instead, parties descend to this plateau after a night in the Oggioni hut.

The face is bounded on the R by a prominent snowy spur, commonly referred to as the 'Spigolo Inglesi', and on the L by the 'Corda Molla'. The original route on the true N face climbed the ice slope immediately R of the rocky spur, that itself lies below and to the R of the ghastly central sérac. The spur was crossed at two-thirds height to gain the top of the sérac and a direct line pursued up the mixed ground above to the summit (Direct Route: TD 8hr). Today's alpinists normally follow a combination of several variants to this route, which gives the safest and most logical line on the face. Although a prestigious ascent and generally thought to represent the hardest of the pure ice faces in the region, the difficulties, together with those of the Spigolo, are not high in good conditions. Both have now suffered the ignominy of ski descents!

15 **NORTH COULOIR**

D+/ TD− A Borghetti and M Valsecchi, 1980. Winter: R Assi, F Tessari and G Villa, Jan 1983

167

The wide rectilinear couloir leading to the Corda Molla ridge is nearly always icy, but objectively safe in well-frozen conditions. The average angle is 60°. 300m

16 **SUPERDIRECT**

ED1 R Alde, B Ferrario, C. Mauri and D Piazza, 28 Aug 1960.

167 Winter: directly over the sérac barrier by N Riva and M Della Santa, 13 Jan 1983

Climbs the steep couloir below and to the L of the central sérac, finishing with a difficult ice pitch out R onto the very lip of the barrier (at the time of writing this would be very hard), then continues directly to the summit. Definitely not for those of a nervous disposition! Periodically the sérac has appeared relatively stable (?), attracting the more adventurous exponents of 'Piolet Traction'. It was climbed directly in 1983 (twice) and again in 1985. Serious! 70°-90°: 650m

17 **CLASSIC ROUTE**
TD– First ascent of the line described is unknown but the original route
167 was climbed by A Lucchetti Albertini and G Schenatti, 10 July 1934. Winter: E Colonaci and R Merendi, E Lazzarini and V Taldo, 6 March 1960

Highly recommended after a night of hard frost with the face well covered in névé. These conditions should allow rapid progress on the initial slopes and eliminate the risk of stone-fall from the upper rocks. The average angle is 55° but the 'narrows' has a section of 60°+. The approach from the Oggioni hut is short but not straightforward, and a very early start is advisable.

Go down steep rocks immediately to the W of the Oggioni hut and reach an icy couloir leading to the Disgrazia glacier. An alternative descent starts a little way up the Corda Molla ridge at a point where it is possible to slant L (facing out) down the steep snow slopes on the W side, crossing a rocky rib before reaching the glacier. Either way is not easy (AD territory) and the rimaye is often enormous. Rappels may be desirable and a thorough inspection should be made the previous evening.

Now cross the gently-angled but crevassed glacier and reach the foot of the large ice slope, well R of the central sérac (allow 2hr). Climb the slope, passing through the steeper 'narrows' (usually icy) to an exit onto the NW ridge at a small saddle. Immediately above is the steep section of the ridge below the foresummit. The main summit can be reached in less than 45min. 550m to ridge: 5-6hr from the rimaye

18 **SPIGOLO INGLESI**
D/D+ W Ling and H Raeburn, 8 Aug 1910. Winter: L Cattaneo and
167 A Molteni, 8 Jan 1978

An unfortunate misnomer as the first ascent was made by two of Scotland's foremost ice-climbers. Although not as difficult as the NE face of Piz Roseg, it was a very advanced achievement for the period. Despite its classic status, and the fact that it is so obviously easier and less serious than the N face, relatively few ascents have been made. The climb is entirely on snow and ice and at an average angle of 52° (55° towards the top). Large cornices, that can sometimes form in a spectacular manner on the NW ridge, may threaten the ascent. Otherwise, the route is generally safe from objective dangers and offers a less committing option to those parties finding the sight of the N face routes too frightening!

Follow Route 17 to the foot of the face. Climb the snow/ice slope on the R to reach the crest of the spur above the rocky section. If the rocks are dry the crest can be followed throughout (short sections of III). Now climb the pure snow crest above. It merges into a plain slope which steepens to an exit onto the NW ridge. From here the summit can be reached in 1hr. c500m: 5hr from the rimaye

19 **SUPERCOULOIR**

ED1 N Riva and M Della Santa, 12 Jan 1983

167

These days nearly every major peak appears to have a 'supercouloir' and the Disgrazia is no exception! This open shallow couloir rarely, if ever, forms outside of the winter/spring season. The first ascent party approached from the Oggioni hut and found crossing the glacier both difficult and dangerous. In good snow conditions access from the Passo di Mello would be reasonably straightforward. The climb is not sustained but has some steep sections (70°-80°) above half-height. The party descended the Spigolo Inglesi and the next day climbed the central sérac of the N face direct to complete an impressive outing! 600m: c6hr

The 'Masa-Tessera' route climbs the rib immediately to the R of the Supercouloir and has pitches of IV on surprisingly sound rock.

Punta 3483m

This is the minor top crossed on the SE ridge, mid-way between Pt 3312m and the E summit. The SW pillar has a recent rock route which is reported to be very good. On the icy NE face two routes were created in 1985. The first (B Balatti, G Lafranconi, F de Marcellis and R Riva, 15 June) pursues a fairly direct line to the summit. TD: 700m. The second (B Balatti, R Riva and G Rompani, 30 June) gives easier climbing on the face to the L. D−: 700m: 3hr

20 **SULLA STRADA DELLA FOLLIA**

TD− D Brambusi and L Maciani, Sept 1988

This is a ten-pitch rock climb on excellent serpentine. It is bounded on the L by a couloir and on the R by a snow slope. It is also the most easterly pillar on the S face of Disgrazia. The route starts directly below the summit and is sustained at IV/V+, with the hardest pitches (one of VI+) just below the top.

G Sertoli with A Scilironi, Aug 1883. Winter: A Bonacossa and C Prochownik, 21 March 1920

A beautiful little peak near the head of the Ventina glacier. It is undoubtedly the most frequented summit in the Disgrazia range and the normal route is popular with ski-mountaineers in the spring. In early summer the N face offers a number of classic snow/ice routes.

21 **SOUTH-WEST RIDGE**

PD–/PD Descended by A Balabio and A Calegari, 10 July 1910

166

Although perhaps not the easiest route to the summit, this is by far the most popular. Parties must first reach the Passo Cassandra. The nearest base is the Taveggia bivouac, but with an early start reasonably fit alpinists could make the ascent from Chiareggio. The Ventina glacier is usually straightforward, with no serious crevasse problem even late in the season. The approach is long but quite gentle and the final ridge very easy. A superb mountain ambience makes this a splendid introduction to alpine snow peaks. See also photograph 164

From the Porro hut follow Route H5 up the Ventina glacier and reach the base of the short steep snow slope leading to the Passo Cassandra. The rimaye can be difficult but the slope above generally remains snowy, allowing a straightforward passage even late in the season. At the time of writing there is one rather tricky crevasse just before the angle eases below the col. Once on the ridge the climbing is easy and will be mainly a scree walk by August. A snow calotte can more or less be avoided on the S side. 30min from pass to summit. 2½hr from the Taveggia bivouac and 6hr from Chiareggio.

The Pass can also be reached from the S. 3½hr from the Bosio hut via the W branch of the dry Cassandra glacier or 3hr from the Ponti hut via the Passo di Corna Rossa. The final couloir is an easy but tedious ascent over scree and rotten rock.

22 **NORTH FACE**

AD A and R Calegari and G Scotti, 28 July 1914

166

This established classic takes a direct line up the face to the L of the prominent central spur. It is a popular climb early in the season, when snow conditions are usually good and the rotten rock outcrops are well-cemented. There are several possible variations; those to the L, which finish on the NE ridge, are more straightforward.

From the Porro hut, follow Route H5 towards the Taveggia bivouac and reach the foot of the face in c3hr. From the bivouac hut it is simply a matter of retracing the path along the flat snow terrace. This can take up to 1hr.

Climb the broad snow slope L of the rocky outcrops until directly below the summit. Now work back R up the middle of the face and finish via the final section of the NNW spur. The average angle is 45°. 450m: 4hr from the rimaye

23 **NORTH-NORTH-WEST (CENTRAL) SPUR**
AD De Pazzi Geri, G Mattai Del Moro, F Pennati with
166 I Dell'Andrino, 4 or 5 Aug 1914

A fine mixed climb leading directly to the summit. However, it can only be recommended in cold and snowy conditions. 450m: 4½hr

24 **WEST-NORTH-WEST FACE**
AD A Corti and A Lucchetti Albertini, 10 Aug 1930, although this face
166 had been descended as early as 1910. Winter: F Grandori and B Perotti, 2 Jan 1942

To the R of the Central Spur several lines have been climbed. The most obvious follows an open couloir immediately next to the spur, but the mixed face to the R is equally possible. c350m: 3½hr

Pizzo Rachele 2998m

E Bertarelli and S Bonacossa with G Confortola and M Schenatti, 28 Aug 1887. Winter: F Grandori, C and P Odello and B Perotti, 3 Jan 1944

A rocky pyramid that is easily reached by a short scramble from the Passo Ventina. Local opinion suggests that the E Pillar is one of the best middle-grade rock routes in the Disgrazia massif.

25 **EAST PILLAR**
IV F and G Grandori and B Perotti, 25 Aug 1943. Direct start: G Rossi and F Villa, July 1952

The E face is composed of a number of red spurs separated by deep broken couloirs. This pillar forms the demarcation between the SE and ENE walls. It is poorly defined at first but becomes distinctly impressive in the upper section. The climbing is sustained and on good sound serpentine.

Reach the foot of the face from the Porro hut by crossing the Passo Ventina (2½-3hr). Alternatively, it is 1hr from a comfortable bivouac in the vicinity of the Larghetti di Sassersa. Reach the latter by a good waymarked path from Primolo in 3hr or directly from Chiesa in 3½hr. A vast scree slope leads to the base of the pillar.

Start slightly on the R of the fall-line and slant up L over a series of slabs to reach a small shoulder (IV). This point can be reached more easily from the L by slanting up fairly steep and grassy rock for 80m (the start for this lies immediately L of a very steep little wall). Above the shoulder climb a gully and short wall (IV), then move R to a second shoulder on the crest of the pillar. Climb the pillar for two fine pitches (III and IV) to a large ledge. Move R and climb a smooth wall to a niche. Reach a diagonal crack up to the R and follow it back L above the niche. Traverse L above an overhanging block and climb up to a stance (20m from the large ledge: IV). Slant R on a superb slab (III), then climb directly upwards for 6m (IV−), before moving back L to the foot of a crack. Either climb this crack or a similar one to the R (III+), and reach a stance below twin dièdres with prominent overhangs. Avoid these on the R, where two pitches of easier climbing lead to the summit. 300m: 4hr

Descent: Easily down the NNE ridge to the Passo Ventina in 1hr (F); or go down the S ridge, using a gully on the E flank, to the head of a large scree couloir that leads down under the E face. Although steeper and looser than the NNE ridge, this gives a much shorter return to the base of the route.

26 **CASSANDRA-RACHELE TRAVERSE**
AD A and P Corti, 2 Aug 1919
166

A long and splendid traverse which keeps to the crest throughout. The rock is generally good except for the final crossing of Pizzo Rachele. It is especially recommended early in the season, when snow crests alternate with longer sections of rock and make the crossing all the more rewarding. Although the difficulties are not high (the most entertaining section occurs on the descent from the Cima Sassersa: II+), fitness and stamina are very important. Parties generally start from the Taveggia bivouac and take c6hr from the Passo Cassandra to the Passo Ventina. 12hr round trip from the Porro hut.

Corni Bruciati 3114m

F Lurini with A Baroni and P Scetti, 27 Aug 1881.
Winter: G Pizzi and G Tavelli, 2 Feb 1921

It would be rare indeed to find this peak included on a list of aspirations of foreign parties visiting the region. It is, however, highly recommended to experienced scramblers, who have just completed the Roma Path. The summit is a splendid viewpoint and attention is unashamedly directed towards the mighty Disgrazia. There are three summits of reddish rock, the Central being the highest.

27 **SOUTH-WEST RIDGE OF CENTRAL SUMMIT**
RE/F– First ascent party

A straightforward ascent in a fine position. Early in the season snow in the approach couloir will make the climb more agreeable, and an axe (and sometimes crampons) will prove useful.

From the Ponti hut cross the moraine below the Preda Rossa glacier. Contour the rough ground to the S and reach a small snowfield (just S of Pt 2409m) below the Central and SW summits. Go up the snowfield and the couloir above (snow/scree and rotten rock at the finish) to the Bochetta di Preda Rossa (2851m: 2hr) Now scramble up the final pyramid by a nice blocky ridge – easy but with obvious loose sections (1hr). Parties can conveniently complete this route from the main valley – parking the car by the Preda Rossa chalets at 1955m. 4hr for the ascent

Punta Kennedy 3283m

A and R Balabio and A Calegari, 2 Aug 1910. Winter: A Bonacossa, G Brioschi and P Orio, 20 March 1927

Not marked on the map but situated c200m to the E of Pt 3295m (Corda Molla ridge). It is separated from the latter by the snowy saddle of Colle Kennedy (c3250m). The mountain is best known for its classic E ridge.

28 **NORTH-NORTH-EAST RIDGE**
PD First ascent party
163

A long glacier approach leads to a short but delightful snow ridge.

Follow Route H6 from the Taveggia bivouac towards the Oggioni hut. On reaching the upper part of the Canalone della Vergine strike up L and reach the elegant snow crest. Follow it directly to the summit. 2hr from the bivouac, 30-40 min from the Oggioni hut. It is easier but slightly longer to climb the slopes to Colle Kennedy and follow the W ridge to the summit.

29 **EAST RIDGE**
AD A Corti with G dell'Andrino, 21 July 1920.
163 Winter: E and G Lenatti, 7 Feb 1957

Many alpinists consider this to be the most beautiful and interesting rock climb of its standard in the Disgrazia range. Here the ambience is more akin to the Western Alps and the superb red rough serpentine allows safe and positive footwork.

By carrying all their equipment on the route, parties have been able to descend to the Oggioni hut and complete the ascent of the Corda Molla ridge the following day. However, when conditions remain good well into the afternoon, fast parties have been able to accomplish this magnificent combination in one day. Axe and crampons will normally be needed on the approach and descent. The difficulties are well-protected by in-situ gear and a standard rack is quite sufficient.

Although it is possible to climb this route from the Porro hut or even Chiareggio, the approach is long and a night spent in the Taveggia bivouac, prior to the ascent, is recommended.

Immediately above the hut scramble easily up to the broad saddle on the E ridge. Follow the ridge to the first gendarme which is turned on the R. Most parties avoid this initial uninteresting section by walking up the snow slopes to the R and climbing back up to a notch in the ridge via an icy couloir. This couloir lies between the gendarme and a rocky spur to the W.

Reach the foot of a wonderful smooth slab – the crux! Climb it (40m: IV), then make a direct assault on the vertical step above, reaching the crest of the ridge at the base of an easy-angled slab (IV). Climb this slab for 80m and continue on the L side of the crest to a group of gendarmes. Turn these on the L via an exposed ledge that runs across the precipitous S face. The ledge ends at a smooth buttress. Climb over a small overhang (6m: IV) back onto the crest. Continue up the ridge more easily to another steep step. Avoid this on the L and cross a short slab (IV–) to regain the ridge. Follow the crest to a small gap, then take a series of very fine dièdres on the L flank to the summit. c420m: 3hr

Pizzo Ventina 3261m

A and R Balabio and A Calegari, 2 Aug 1910.
Winter: L Binaghi and A and E Bonacossa, 19 March 1931

This rugged summit lies a short distance N of the Oggioni hut and has two long rocky ridges facing Chiareggio. It is rare to find good rock-climbing in the Disgrazia mountains but it is on this peak that notable exceptions occur. Several well-defined red pillars, that rise from the Canalone della Vergine to the crest of the ENE ridge, offer very worthwhile routes. However, as most parties visiting this area will concentrate on the classic snow and ice climbs, this peak remains largely unfrequented, and the climbs described will appeal to those of a more exploratory nature.

30 **SOUTH COULOIR**
PD First ascent party

The easiest route to the summit.

From the Oggioni hut cross the upper glacier to the foot of a short snowy couloir, that leads up to the E ridge just below the summit. The gully is steep but quite straightforward in good conditions – otherwise climb easy broken rock on the R side. 1hr from the Oggioni hut; 1½-2hr from the Taveggia bivouac.

The short SSW ridge is a pleasant little rock climb with several pitches of III.

31 **NORTH RIDGE**
PD+/ R Bassi, E Frassi and G Mattai del Moro, 20 Aug 1914.
AD– Winter: P Paredi and clients, Dec 1972
162

Climbed integrally along the crest from Alp Zocca, this becomes a lengthy expedition. It can be shortened by joining the ridge at various points from the E. The situation is most appealing – high above the chaotic Disgrazia glacier with ever widening views across the upper Val Malenco to the Bernina range. Although mainly scrambling, the route has several interesting sections of II and III on sound rock. 6hr from the Porro hut. See also photograph 164

32 **EAST-NORTH-EAST RIDGE**
AD+ A Corti with I Dell'Andrino, 27 Aug 1917
164

This long sinuous ridge is rather less sustained than the famous E ridge of Punta Kennedy, and although not quite in the same class is still a very worthwhile undertaking. The main difficulties are to be found on the two prominent steps in the ridge, which are themselves studded with numerous towers. From the base of the first step there is a vertical interval of nearly 500m to the summit. However, the actual amount of climbing is substantially greater, and parties will need to move together on much of the easier ground. The upper part of the ridge provides a very fitting conclusion to routes on the SE face.

From the Porro hut cross the main river and reach the moraine on the R side of the valley. Follow this S towards the Canalone della Vergine. A loose rocky couloir goes up to the crest of the ENE ridge at a point where it steepens abruptly to form the first step. An easy scramble up the couloir leads to a notch in the ridge at c2700m (2hr). The notch can also be reached from the snow slopes to the W of the ridge but this approach is at least an hour longer.

The first step has three successive triangular towers. Climb it, keeping more or less to the crest where the rock is at its best. The ridge now changes direction, and after a short horizontal section rears dramatically upwards to form the second and much larger step. This is subdivided into several towers and is again best climbed near the crest, with several excursions onto the N flank to avoid major difficulties (c4hr III and IV). The ridge now makes a short descent before rising gently, and without further difficulty, to the summit (1hr). 7hr from the hut

33 JACK CANALI ROUTE

D/D+ V Duroni, P Paredi and F Pozzoli, 8-9 July 1972.
Winter: L Cattaneo and A Molteni, 25 Dec 1977

This route climbs the most prominent pillar on the E face and joins the ENE ridge close to the top of the first step. Nobody is sure who actually first climbed the pillar but the 1972 route has been repeated on a number of occasions and several variations established. The pillar is steep, sustained and quite exposed, with rough red serpentine of the best quality. Old pegs in place should assist route finding, especially on the first part of the climb. The route was dedicated to the great Italian guide who took part in the first ascent of the 'Cassin' ridge on Mt McKinley.

From the Porro hut follow Route 32 past the entrance to the rocky couloir, and reach the base of the Canalone della Vergine. The climb starts L of the lowest point of the pillar, just above a snow bowl (1½hr). Climb the bottom slabs for two easy pitches (III) to a good ledge. Now slant L to a vertical dièdre and climb it (IV and V). Slant up R for two pitches to a good ledge (IV), then climb directly above it for three more pitches to another good ledge (IV and V). Reach the sharp and exposed crest above and climb it for two pitches (IV). Now slant L on slabs then come back R to rejoin the crest, which is followed directly to the junction with the ENE ridge (several pitches of III/IV: 6hr).

It is now possible to reverse the ENE ridge to the approach couloir and scramble down this to the moraine. Otherwise continue up the ridge for a further 2½-3hr to the summit (III/IV). c500m for the pillar, 800m to the summit

34 **SOUTH-EAST (TRANQUILLITY) PILLAR**
TD– G Merizzi and G Miotti, 29 June 1979
80

This splendid climb, on excellent rough red rock, deserves to become a modern classic of the region. The main difficulties are confined to the first half of the pillar and there are one or two problematical moves if a completely free ascent is to be achieved. Above, the climbing is much easier but perhaps even more magnificent!

From the Porro hut follow Route 33 to the Canalone della Vergine. The climb starts at the same height as the rocky outcrop that divides the glacier into two, and is well above the base of the pillar taken by the 'Jack Canali' route. An axe and crampons will be necessary for this approach (2hr). The pillar is 300m and will take 5-6hr

Descent: The pointed top of the pillar forms a detached tower, not far below the crest of the ENE ridge. It is possible to descend to the L and climb nice red slabs to the ridge at c3050m. From here the summit could be reached in less than 2hr. However, a quick escape can be made down the gully alongside the pillar. This lies c40m L of the pillar and is an easy scramble down scree until above a short steep buttress. Rappel 10m down this buttress and reach the start of a ledge, which slants up in a westerly direction to gain the upper plateau of the Canalone. Scramble easily across this ledge to the glacier.

Torrione Porro 2357m

Directly above, and to the NE of the Porro hut, a slabby rock face is clearly visible. There are a number of short rock routes which can be easily climbed in the morning from Chiareggio, and are thus ideal when the weather is uncertain.

35 **WEST FACE – PEPPO PEREGO ROUTE**
IV– G Marini and G Praolini, 27 Aug 1948

The best route on the face. The start can be reached in 20-30min up the steep scree slope behind the hut.

Half-way up the R side of the face is a prominent area of reddish slabs which are bounded on the R by a deep gully. Below the slabs some steeper walls fall to a vegetated terrace that runs leftwards across the bottom of the face. Start on this terrace at the base of a dièdre that slants up to the L. Climb the dièdre (20m: II), then traverse R and ascend a chimney to reach a stance on the slabs near to their L-hand side (III+). Slant up the superb slabs, working L to reach a small tree (50m: II/III). Another fine pitch above leads to the crest of the spur, which forms the L edge of the slabs in their upper part (IV–/IV). Continue up the line of the spur, which leads directly to the summit (2 pitches: moves of II/III). 200m: 2-2½hr

Descent: Walk easily down to the S, then back round on scree to the foot of the route (20min).

Punta 2648m

36 **NORMAL ROUTE**
PE First recorded ascent by A Balabio and friend, 3 Oct 1913 but probably visited by hunters many years previously.

This minor summit lies on the ridge N of the Punta Rosalba and is separated from it by the Bochel del Cane (2551m). It overlooks the reservoir of Lago Pirola. It is an outstanding viewpoint; the best in the area that can be reached by non-climbers. It is an easy 2hr walk from the Porro hut and makes a very pleasant day-outing from Chiareggio.

Piz de la Margna 3158m

First recorded ascent: J Caviezel, Krattli, Robbi and Zuan, June 1857

Although of little interest to the hardened alpinist this is a very popular day-ascent from either Maloja or Sils Maria. The merit of this summit, especially to those new to the area, lies in the extensive panoramic view over all three ranges – Albula, Bernina and Bregaglia. The famous granite spires to the SW contrast boldly with the glaciated peaks to the E. Near at hand, the wild upper reaches of the Fedoz valley are a far cry from the multitude of colourful sail boards, on the deep blue lakes of the upper Engadine.

37 NORTH-EAST RIDGE – NORMAL ROUTE

PE/RE

A good path followed by easy grass and scree slopes. Early in the season an axe is often very useful. The route and the extent of snow cover can be easily viewed from the main road.

From the entrance to the campsite at Maloja take the partially made-up road to the chalets at Ca d'Starnam. When coming from Sils it is usually possible to park the car at Vauglia. The walk from here is about 30min shorter than that from Maloja. Follow the well-trodden path into the small cwm between the SE and NE ridges of the Margna and strike up R to reach the latter at a conspicuous shoulder. The crest is either snow or scree and presents no difficulty to the summit. 4hr from Maloja: 2-2½hr in descent

38 NORTH SIDE

RE/F–

A shorter but more strenuous ascent. It is a good deal more pleasant under conditions of firm snow and if the central couloir is climbed directly to the summit, crampons will be necessary and the ascent will feel quite 'alpine' (PD).

From the Col de Maloja follow the footpath through the Palza wood to the terrace with Pt 2005m. Contour into the Murtairac valley and go up it to the headwall. On the R is the Central couloir which is reasonably steep in its middle section. The normal route slants L up a scree/snow couloir to the conspicuous shoulder on the NE ridge, where the previous route is joined. 3½hr to the summit

39 **SOUTH-EAST RIDGE**
AD– H Frick with C Zippert and H Casper, 14 Aug 1918

This offers considerably more technical interest but the difficulties are very short when compared to the lengthy approach and descent. It will still appeal more to the mountaineer than the rock climber, though the crux, climbed free, probably warrants V. The route can be extended by a fine traverse of the Crasta da Fedoz – the sharp jagged ridge lying S of the Fuorcla da la Margna. V

From Maloja or Sils follow the path used to reach the foot of the NE ridge and continue across scree slopes to the Fuorcla da la Margna (2886m; 3hr). It is also possible to reach this point from the Plancanin huts in the Forno valley by an appalling ascent of the obvious scree couloir.

Climb the first part of the ridge from R to L then struggle up a deep and narrow chimney to reach the sharp crest. Climb along this (exposed) to an almost vertical buttress. Getting up this provides the crux but there are usually plenty of pegs in place for protection and often aid! Excellent climbing on sound rock leads to a shoulder and from here it is simply a matter of walking over snow or scree for 30min to the summit. c250m: 3½hr, 6½hr from Maloja

Piz Fora 3363m

E Burckhardt with B Cadonau, 24 Aug 1875

An attractive snowy pyramid in a wild and remote situation on the frontier ridge. There is no readily available accommodation close at hand so whilst it is quite feasible to make the round trip in a day from valley bases, a bivouac high on the Swiss or Italian approaches will provide an unforgettable experience and allow a more leisurely ascent.

Apart from the routes described, the SW ridge, approached from Chiareggio via the Bocchetta di Fora (3293m), gives the most direct ascent from Italy (5½hr).

40 **NORTH-NORTH-WEST RIDGE**
F

The normal route on the Swiss side. The ascent is quite straightforward and the final ridge can be approached from either the Fex or Fedoz valleys, although the former is preferred.

From Sils, there is a road up the Fex valley to Crasta where, in the grounds of the white church, lies the grave of Christian Klucker. The road continues as far as the hotel at Curtins. Cars, however, are normally allowed only as far as Vauglia, after which you must walk to the roadhead (c45 min) or take a horse-drawn carriage. Cross the bridge to a track which slants across the hillside, passing two small tarns (2301m: possible bivouac) and finally reaching the small Guz glacier. Although crevassed, this generally presents little difficulty and is ascended to the snowy saddle of the Fuorcla Fex-Fedoz (3114m). A long and pleasant snowy ridge, interrupted now and again by rocky outcrops, leads to the summit. 5-6hr from Vauglia

41 **EAST-NORTH-EAST RIDGE**

F

Useful for making a traverse of the mountain. The ridge rises gently from the Fuorcla dal Chaputsch (See Routes 43 and 44). When approaching from the N it is not necessary to reach the col, as the ridge can be gained directly above its first rocky section and continued on snow all the way to the summit. However, this misses a nice piece of climbing and it is recommended that parties include the initial scramble – especially the small tower (the Chaputsch; 2937m) at the foot of the ridge. 430m: 1½hr

42 **DESCENT BY NORTH-NORTH-WEST RIDGE INTEGRAL**

PD

The ridge can be climbed in its entirety over the summits of Piz Salatschina, Led and Guz. However, it is best taken in descent having reached the summit via another route from the Swiss side eg the ENE ridge. This expedition gives one of the most enjoyable traverses of its standard in the range. The crossing from the Fuorcla Fex-Fedoz to Piz Salatschina takes 3hr and gives an excellent scramble on sound rock if the crest is adhered to throughout. It is then recommended that the ridge is followed all the way to Sils, though it is possible to slither easily down scree slopes into the Fex valley whenever one desires. c7hr from Piz Fora to the road at Vauglia.

Fuorcla dal Chaputsch 2929m

This is the lowest point in the ridge connecting Piz Fora with Piz Tremoggia. It has been well known to hunters and smugglers for centuries and is both a shorter and more direct link between Chiareggio and Sils-Maria than the Tremoggia pass further E.

However, crevasses on the Fex glacier can often prove more troublesome than those encountered on the Tremoggia.

43 **SWISS SIDE**

F+

From the roadhead at Curtins follow a good path up the Fex valley to the foot of the glacier (1½hr). Continue up the centre of the glacier to the col. 4hr from Vauglia

44 **ITALIAN SIDE**

PE/RE

165

From Chiareggio follow Route H8 to Alpe Fora (c 1½hr). Continue N on the Alta Via as far as the R fork mentioned in the description to the Longoni hut. The L fork is poorly defined. It climbs up scree slopes and finally a wide easy couloir to the pass. 2-2½hr from Alp Fora and a similar time from the Longoni hut

Pass dal Tremoggia 3014m

After the Muretto pass this is probably the easiest crossing point between the Val Malenco and the upper Engadine. It has been used by smugglers for many years and is still fairly popular today. It lies at the foot of the SW ridge of Piz Tremoggia and can be reached from the Fuorcla dal Chaputsch, along the scree covered ridge, in 30min.

45 **SWISS SIDE**

PD−

There are a number of ways to reach the Tremoggia glacier from Plaun Vadret and the upper Fex valley. Traditionally, the route climbed up through the Curunellas – the steep rocky walls below the glacier – and then moved R at the top (see Route 51). The pass is but a short distance across the easy glacier. 4-5hr from Vauglia

Otherwise, follow the winter ski route which avoids the Curunellas completely on the R side. The best line follows the lower remnants of the Fex glacier, then steep moraine on the R bank until it is possible to work back L, up little gullies and slabs, to reach the Tremoggia glacier almost directly below the pass.

A more roundabout way is to use the alternative route on the steep flanks of the Chaputschin to the Fuorcla Fex-Scerscen and cross below Piz Tremoggia to the Pass.

46 **ITALIAN SIDE**

PE/RE
165

The approach is the same as for the Fuorcla dal Chaputsch until the path divides. Take the R fork, towards the Longoni hut, but then branch L, following one of the main streams that comes down from the vicinity of the large cwm below Piz Tremoggia. Above, the path turns sharp L towards the pass, and a little higher becomes rather vague (this point can be reached directly from the Longoni hut). An obvious large couloir/depression is climbed directly to the pass. 3hr from Alp Fora: c30min less from the Longoni hut

Piz Tremoggia 3441m

J Weilenmann, 1859

Remotely situated at the head of the tranquil Fex valley, this dome-like snowy peak will appeal to lovers of solitude. It can be climbed in a long day from Sils, if an early start is made but romantics will prefer to overnight at a bivouac somewhere in the vicinity of Plaun Vadret or even at the Colombo hut. On the Italian side however, the mountain is quickly reached from the Scerscen ski-station. Although infrequently climbed, the SW ridge is a nice little rock route.

47 **NORTH-EAST RIDGE**

F+

The ridge can be climbed throughout from the Fuorcla Fex-Scerscen. The recent dry summers have produced a steep ice fall at the start. Above, easy scree slopes lead all the way to the summit. It is actually easier to use the slopes on the Italian side, working up towards the saddle between the peak and Piz Malenco to the SE. 1hr (though the approach from Sils probably warrants PD)

48 **SOUTH-EAST RIDGE**

PD–/PD
168

The long ridge above the upper slopes of the Scerscen glacier rises over two lovely snowy peaks – the Sassa d'Entova (3329m) and Piz Malenco (3438m) – before reaching the gentle slopes below the summit of Piz Tremoggia. The traverse of this ridge from the Scerscen ski-station is a delightful expedition with magnificent views N over the Sella peaks and S across the Italian valleys to Disgrazia. See also photograph 165

Go onto the glacier and walk up alongside the ridge, reaching the crest shortly before the summit of the Sassa d'Entova. The ridge leading to the Piz Malenco has a steeper rocky section with a couple of interesting chimney pitches. Less aesthetic, but somewhat easier, is to avoid this section altogether by slanting down to the N below the rocks and then reach the summit via snow slopes on the NE flank. Continue to the top of Piz Tremoggia without further difficulty. 2½hr

49 **SOUTH-WEST RIDGE**
AD C Klucker and I Ziegler, 28 Oct 1879
165

A minor classic but one on which other parties will seldom be encountered. The difficulties are entirely on rock; black slate in the lower section turning to yellow limestone higher up. On much of the easier climbing, especially low down on the ridge, loose rock abounds but the difficult pitches are generally quite solid. The ridge contains a number of steps and towers which can often be avoided by ledges on the S side. This would miss the whole point of the climb. Its 'raison d'être' is the steep climbing on the crest, not the unrewarding broken ground on the flanks! IV

From the Pass dal Tremoggia the ridge is easy at first to a small overhanging section. Turn this on the R to reach an imposing tower. On the L is a conspicuous narrow crack and on the R side, another similar crack. Climb the one on the R and continue up slabs to the top of the tower (1V). Beyond a broadish saddle is another steep section, which gives superb climbing on the crest. The rock now changes to limestone and is climbed just below the crest on the L flank. The ridge finally becomes snowy and is followed pleasantly to the summit. 400m: 2½hr

Piz Malenco 3438m

E Burckhardt with H Grass and C Jossi, 3 Oct 1878

The snowy peak to the SE of Piz Tremoggia. It rises only a short distance above the upper slopes of the Scerscen glacier and can be easily reached directly or from the Fuorcla Fex-Scerscen (F+). Best combined with an ascent of the Tremoggia (see Route 48).

Sassa d'Entova 3329m

F Besta with G Schenatti, Sept 1884

In common with the neighbouring Tremoggia and Malenco, the summit is an excellent viewpoint which is quickly and easily reached from the Scerscen Ski-station (see Route 48).

50 **SOUTH-WEST RIDGE**
F+ A Balabio and F Barbieri, 20 July 1910
165

A long and easy-angled scramble that rises directly behind the Longoni hut. It is a worthwhile outing that can be easily achieved in a day from the valley by driving up the Scerscen road to reach the hut. The W flank is more gentle and if approaching from Alpe Fora the ridge can be gained at a number of different points. The upper section of the ridge can also be approached from the E, by contouring boulder slopes above the steep zig-zags on the Scerscen access road. Early in the season, snow slopes on the upper part of the ridge give the route more of an 'Alpine feel'. c800m

Fuorcla Fex-Scerscen 3122m

First recorded crossing: F Grove and J Wedgewood with P Jenny and A Flury, 29 Aug 1861

A major glacier pass between Sils-Maria and the Marinelli hut and a popular spot with spring skiers. It is a broad snowy saddle between the Piz Tremoggia and the Sella group with the tiny Colombo bivouac hut at its northern end. Neither side is difficult but the approach from Switzerland is long and quite complicated.

51 **SWISS SIDE**
PD– J Weilenmann, 1859

A long and gentle walk along the unfrequented yet picturesque valley of the Fex, followed by a steep ascent to the Tremoggia glacier. The traditional route climbs the rocky walls of the Curunellas below the glacier but appears to have seen few ascents in recent years. A long but straightforward and safe alternative is to follow the line of the winter ski route (See Route 45) to the S of the Curunellas. Once on the upper glacier, walk up it to the NE. Cross the snow ridge S of Pt 3043m and so reach the pass.

A third alternative uses the steep slopes close to the Chaputschin. This route is also a useful means of descent from the pass, especially early in the season, but after heavy snowfall certain sections become very susceptible to avalanche.

Follow Route 40 into the Fex valley and reach Plaun Vadret (2122m; 3hr from Sils). The path now becomes vague and reaches the walls of the Curunellas, slighty L of centre, where there is a rocky spur on the R of a very deep couloir. Go up the spur then cross a gully on the R to a grassy plateau. Now work up R, over scree and easy rocky ridges, to the glacier and slant L across it to the Fuorcla. 4-5hr from Vauglia

One can also leave the main valley at Plaun Vadret, zig-zagging up very steep slopes of grass and scree to the rocky escarpments of the Chaputschin – tedious! Continue below these to the L side of the Tremoggia glacier and go up it, close to the flanks of La Muongia, to reach the pass. In good conditions it is possible to descend to Vauglia in less than 2½hr by this route.

52 **ITALIAN SIDE**

F

176

This is an easy 1hr walk across the glacier from the Scerscen Ski-station.

From the Marinelli hut take a good path to the N. After a short distance it bears round to the L and traverses up and down over a series of moraine ridges (well marked with paint flashes) finally descending onto the N side of the Scerscen (inferior) glacier. Walk up this, below the impressive red walls and pillars of the Sella – Gluschaint group, to the pass. 3hr

Sasso Nero 2917m

Although of little interest to the climber, this extensive rocky summit is noted for its truly wonderful view of the Italian side of the Bernina group and almost equally inspiring panorama of the Disgrazia Massif. The N side of the Scalino is also seen to full advantage. Whilst the summit is easily reached at any time of the day, parties are recommended to make the ascent very early in the morning when the visibility is at its best, and to carry plenty of camera film.

53 **SOUTH-EAST RIDGE**

PE

176

The summit is normally reached from Lago Palu by following the Alta Via track as far as the Bocchel de Torno (2203m). Now make a

straightforward ascent of the broad ridge, crossing ribs and hollows, to the flat-topped knoll of Pt 2917m, which is generally considered to be the highest point. 2-2½hr

As a prelude, the traverse of the fine, sharp arête of Monte Roggione (2361m) from the Passo Campolungo (2167m) will enhance the expedition.

The summit can also be reached easily along the NW ridge from the Forcella d'Entova (see approaches to the Marinelli hut) in 1hr, turning any difficulties on the R flank.

Monte Motta 2336m

The ski-lift terminates just below the summit of this minor peak, which overlooks Chiesa. A little to the E at c2236m stands the 'Rifugio Motta' – a centre for mountain activities (Room for 20, Tel: 0342 451406). The serpentine crags in this area have recently been developed and give a range of well-equipped rock climbs from III to VII+. Topos can be seen in the Rifugio or at the tourist office in Chiesa.

Piz Corvatsch 3451m

First recorded ascent: J Coaz and party in 1850

In the days when alpinists began their season with training walks from the valley, this was one of their favourite destinations. Today it is even more popular, in both summer and winter, due to the proximity of the upper terminus of the Corvatschbahn – a two-stage téléphérique system. Nonetheless, it is still a worthwhile goal and one of the best viewpoints in the area.

54 **NORTH – SOUTH TRAVERSE**
F

From the upper terminus of the Téléphérique, a broad snow ridge leads easily over Piz Murtel (3433m) to the summit (30min or 3½-4hr from the road at Surlej via the Fuorcla Surlej). Snow can linger on the S ridge early in the season but normally there is enjoyable walking/scrambling on good rock. Some parts are quite narrow. 1½hr should be adequate time to make the descent to the Fuorcla dal Lej Sgrischus (c 3238m), where an easy escape can be made into either the Fex or Roseg valleys. The descent to Silvaplana will take a further 2½hr. It is also possible to prolong this fine day by continuing over the Crasta dal Lej Sgrischus (3303m) to the Fuorcla Fex-Roseg (3068m; 1½-2hr). Here, traces of a path, on either side of the ridge, lead down into the respective valleys.

The W or Furtschellas ridge is also a worthwhile outing of no particular difficulty.

Il Chaputschin 3386m

J Coaz and party, 23 July 1850

An attractive pyramid culminating in a rocky summit. It is one of the most popular ascents from the Coaz hut for both summer alpinists and spring skiers. It can be approached from either the Fex or Roseg valleys, though the majority of climbers use the latter. However, when the snow on the Chaputschin glacier is reasonably consolidated, fit walkers can complete an interesting traverse of the peak in the day from Silvaplana, by using the Corvatschbahn.

55 **NORTH RIDGE**

F First ascent party (from the Fuorcla Fex-Roseg)

169 *The normal route and a short and straightforward glacier plod from the Coaz hut.*

From the hut follow the path NW to the first moraine and go up it onto the glacier. Ascend the glacier to the snowy saddle on the N ridge and follow the crest, at first on snow and then rock, to the huge cairn on the summit (2hr). A more direct ascent from the hut is also possible. However, there is an easier though slightly longer alternative, generally followed when the Chaputschin glacier is badly crevassed. Continue northwards along the path, then strike up the hillside to reach the snow fields E of Piz dal Lej Alv. Walk up to the saddle S of this peak and continue over Pt 3172m to join the previous route.

The summit can be reached in around 4hr from the Fuorcla Surlej, by leaving the path to the Coaz hut just below Pt 2743m.

From Sils a good path leads to the Sgrischus lake at 2618m (2½hr). A less well defined path now crosses the stony plateau to Lej Alv and climbs steeply up scree, past Pt 2928m, to a tongue of ice coming down from the main ridge, just S of Pt 3172m. Climb this tongue to the crest, where the previous route is joined. 5-6hr: 3-4hr in descent

56
PD
170

SOUTH-WEST RIDGE

This pleasant rocky ridge, reached via the Fuorcla dal Chaputschin, can be used to effect a traverse of the mountain. In some years the glacier approach can be quite complicated.

It is generally best to head SW from the hut and reach the glacier via a terrace in the vicinity of Pt 2821m. Go up the glacier. This may involve a large detour to the L in order to avoid a notable zone of crevasses. Reach the col (3221m) and follow the rocky crest of the SW ridge all the way to the summit (3hr). The crest can be easily reached, at several points, from the gentle upper slopes of the glacier. This avoids going all the way to the col and will save c30min. Half-way along the ridge is the Chaputschin Pitschen (3328m), a small peak that can be included en route, via a nice, short scramble up the W ridge.

The complete traverse from Piz Corvatsch to Il Chaputschin or vice versa can be completed in 4-5hr.

Fuorcla dal Gluschaint 3369m

First recorded traverse: E Burckhardt with P Jenny, 28 July 1874

The lowest point in the ridge between La Muongia and Piz Gluschaint. The small 'bump' of the Piz da la Fuorcla (3398m) lies about 200m to the S. Although rarely used for this purpose, it provides the shortest and easiest link between the Coaz hut and the Colombo bivouac or Scerscen Ski-station. This opens up several possibilities of multiple ascents from one base. The S side is a fairly steep snow/ice couloir almost 200m high. It is reached from the Fuorcla Fex-Scerscen in a few min. In good firm névé the ascent can be swift and straightforward but by mid-summer it is usually quite icy, and in these conditions it is best to climb the relatively sound rock on the L side of the couloir (1-2hr: PD). The N side is a crevassed glacier walk (see Route 60).

Piz Gluschaint 3593.7m

The 'Shining Mountain' is not only the highest but also the most attractive peak of the Sella group. It is a popular ascent from the Coaz hut and in summer there will nearly always be a good track to follow on the normal route. Some of the ridges are established classics and offer climbing as good as any to be found of a similar standard, elsewhere in the range. Despite the difficulties being only moderate in good conditions, most of the routes are not suitable for the inexperienced. However, middle-grade alpinists are spoilt for choice!

57
PD
169

NORTH-EAST FACE – NORMAL ROUTE

Descended, for the most part, by E Burckhardt and H Grass, 7 Aug 1875

A lengthy expedition that winds its weary way up the tortured Roseg glacier. Large crevasses are frequently encountered and without a good 'piste' to follow, finding the correct line can often be time consuming. Prudent parties will make an early start, which should allow them adequate time to descend the steep upper slope before it becomes too sloppy. See also photograph 170

From the Coaz hut, follow the path onto the glacier and go up it to the S. At about 2800m it is necessary to sweep around to the L, in order to avoid a steep and badly contorted section. Now head up towards the N ridge, finally passing between two seriously crevassed zones to reach its foot. Work L into the depression between Piz Gluschaint and Cima Sondrio – the W peak of La Sella. Cross the rimaye, which can often be a substantial obstacle, and climb the steep slope above. Either reach the E ridge directly and follow its rocky crest to the summit; or better, near the top of the slope break out R onto the upper section of the N ridge, where the angle is gentle, and continue with no further difficulty to the top. 4hr: less than 2hr in descent

Occasionally, when the lower section of the glacier has proved too horrendous, parties have descended from the hut and reached the foot of the central rock rognon (designated by Pt 2587m), then climbed this onto the glacier.

58 **NORTH RIDGE**

AD+ M von Kuffner with A Burgener and C Perren, 22 July 1883

109

Beautifully sculptured, this seductive crest sweeps upward in a gentle arc to the summit. It is probably the finest mixed route available from the Coaz hut. Although objectively quite safe, the lengthy approach and splendid position above the complex Roseg glacier give this climb considerable 'high mountain ambience' and make it ideal preparation for those parties who aspire to the hardest 'Grandes Courses' in the Alps. Maximum angle 45°.

It normally takes c2½hr to reach the foot of the ridge from the Coaz hut, via the Normal route to the NE face. Cross the rimaye, which can often be quite difficult late in the season, and climb the broad rounded snow ridge, which gradually becomes steeper and narrower, to a sort of shoulder. Above, the crest becomes progressively more rocky and is followed without undue difficulty to the summit. Dramatic views down the precipitous S face to the Scerscen glacier and beyond to the Italian valleys. 400m: 3hr

59 **NORTH-WEST FACE**

AD+/D– E Burckhardt with H Grass, 7 Aug 1875

169

This steep mixed face is characterised by shallow couloirs separating parallel rocky ribs. It is this icy face, so clearly seen from the Engadine, that prompted local admirers to give the peak its name.

Surprisingly, the first recorded ascent of the mountain was achieved via this flank, the party discovering a cairn on the summit. The origins of their sudden disappointment have continued to remain a mystery! There is an obvious line leading directly to the summit, though a number of similar alternatives are possible, all having an average angle of 50°-55°. The face is not often in condition and ascents are relatively scarce but early in the season, under a good covering of well frozen snow, it is highly recommended. The crux will generally occur towards the top, where steep icy rocks must be negotiated before reaching the summit ridge. 300m: 3hr

60 **SOUTH-WEST RIDGE**

AD– T Curtius with C Klucker and J Eggenberger, 29 Aug 1883

170

This short, but elegant, rocky ridge begins from the Fuorcl'Ota (c3365m), the slight depression in the ridge E of the Piz da la Fuorcla (3398m). It is a highly recommended outing and quite popular with alpinists based on both the Swiss and Italian sides of the Massif. A

descent of the NE face completes the classic traverse of the peak. The difficulties are not sustained but the climb is one of the most enjoyable of its standard in the region and on good rock throughout.

From the Coaz hut follow the normal route as far as the two seriously crevassed zones below the N ridge. Continue up the glacier to the SW, where the angle eases and reach the Fuorcl'Ota by a short snow slope (3-3½hr). It is sometimes better to pass between the two zones and reach the foot of the N ridge, then head SW above the crevasses to the upper glacier.

The Fuorcl'Ota lies immediately above the Colombo bivouac. It can either be reached directly, up steep broken rock, as on the first ascent (c1hr); or, perhaps more easily, via the Fuorcla dal Gluschaint (c1½hr).

A large rounded snow crest leads up to the first steep buttress. This can either be turned on the L on snowy rock (III) or taken direct (IV with a few moves of IV+). Continue up the crest to the foresummit – the Pitschen – and climb it via a chimney on the R (several short pitches of III). Go easily down the other side to a col and follow the ridge above, in a splendid position, to the summit (230m: 1½hr). Parties based on the Italian side of the range will often descend by this route, making short rappels down the difficult pitches.

Sella Group

These summits provide easy glacier excursions from the N but the Italian side has rock walls c500m high. The quality of the rock, in some parts, is at least as good as anything found in the range. Steep faces and prominent ribs or spurs are separated by loose couloirs, where stone-fall is an ever present threat. With the opening of the Scerscen Ski-station a number of modern routes have been worked out on these walls.

Cima Sondrio 3542m

This lies between the Gluschaint and the twin peaks of La Sella and is easily reached from the upper slopes of Route 57. The S side is a rock wall some 500m high.

61 **SOUTH-EAST RIB**
AD A Corti with N Dell'Andrino, 12 Aug 1920

This rib of reasonably sound crystalline rock rises from the base of the prominent couloir separating the two main Sella peaks and can be reached from the Ski-Station in c30min. 2½hr from the Marinelli hut, III/III+

Climb a short distance up the prominent couloir, then take a ramp that slants up to the L and reach the narrow gully that leads to the Forcola Sondrio (the notch to the E of the summit). Climb the L side of the gully until it is possible to get out onto the rib. Up till now, stone-fall has been a constant possibility and this section should be completed very early in the day. Above, enjoyable climbing on the crest, in a fine position, leads to the summit ridge. 500m: 3-4hr. A traverse from here to the Gluschaint can be completed in 45min.

Cima Sondrio: South-South-East Face

The S face is bounded on the L by a snowy couloir that falls from the gap between the Cima Sondrio and Piz Gluschaint. The wall immediately to the R of this couloir has two prominent spurs, that rise out of a conspicuous ramp cutting across the lower third of the face.

62 **CONJUNCTIO SPIGOLORUM**
D+ G Miotti and D Scari, 15 July 1985

82 *A very pleasant climb that takes the crest of the first (R Hand) spur until, at about half-height, a traverse is made up and L to the crest of the second spur. The rock is good, except for the initial pitches on the ramp and a short section of loose blocks just above the crux.*

From the Scerscen Ski-station cross the glacier to the NNW and reach the foot of the face in 1hr. An obvious ramp slants up L from the glacier. The ramp can either be followed throughout (II and III), or joined at mid-height by climbing directly up a chimney/gully (2 pitches of III/III+). There follows some enjoyable climbing on the crest of the spurs and the crux occurs on the final wall, where the obvious hard section is turned on the L. 500m: 4-5hr for the face

La Sella 3584m and 3564m

E Buxton, W Digby and A Johnston with A Flury, 22 July 1863.
First Traverse (E to W): E Burckhardt with P Egger, 27 July 1874

These twin black rocky horns on the frontier ridge are separated by a deep gap, which gives the mountain its name. Both peaks are usually climbed from this gap but the traverse over the summits is also worthwhile. The E peak has a particularly fine rock climb on its S face.

63 PD 170

NORMAL ROUTE

A complex glacial approach to the saddle, then a short and easy ascent to either peak.

There are a number of possible routes to the saddle, depending on the state of the glacier. Follow route 71 towards the Fuorcla da la Sella. The most common approach appears to use the slopes to the W of the rocky rognon Pt 3057m but it is sometimes better to pass below this Pt and climb slopes well to the E. Occasionally a more direct line can be taken to the foot of the N ridge of the E peak: only local knowledge of the prevailing conditions, or the existence of a track, will allow parties to make the correct decision at the Coaz hut. The two peaks are only 200m apart and each can be reached from the gap in 10-15min. 4hr from the Coaz hut

64 PD+

TRAVERSE

Usually taken from E to W and provides a slightly more sporting excursion than the normal routes.

When below the E summit, on the normal approach to the saddle, easy slopes lead up to the crest of the frontier ridge at the base of the peak (c4hr). Climb snow and easy rocks on the N flank of the E ridge to the summit and descend the W ridge to the saddle (30min). Climb the W peak by following easy snow slopes on the N flank to reach the crest of the N ridge. Climb this ridge on good rock, with little difficulty, to the summit (15min). Come back down the ridge for c30m then slant back L down the W face to steep snow slopes N of the frontier ridge. The rock on the W face is rather poor and care should be exercised. Descend the steep snow/ice to a gently angled plateau and cross this to the tracks of the normal route on Piz Gluschaint. 45min: 7½hr round trip from the Coaz hut

65 **SOUTH COULOIR**
AD+ A Bonacossa and C Prochownik, 15 Aug 1910

Badly exposed to stone-fall during the summer months: however earlier in the year, when the nights are cold and there is a good covering of snow, this provides a very worthwhile ice route to the saddle. Together with many of the icy couloirs that seam the extensive S face of the Sella group, this is a good winter/spring objective with easy access from the ski-station just across the glacier. The couloir is fairly broad at first, narrowing at half-height to a steeper icy runnel. Rarely climbed. c500m: 4hr

66 **SOUTH FACE OF EAST PEAK**
D+/ F Bergoni and C Nana, 30 June 1976
TD−

A fine, difficult, though rather inhomogenous climb on the obvious pillar of sound red rock. Pegs will be found in place on the more difficult pitches.

Start in the couloir leading up to the gap between the two summits. After crossing the rimaye move R onto easy rock and climb up this for 200m to the base of a prominent chimney (II/III). It is also possible to climb the couloir throughout, moving R onto the rock when level with the base of the chimney, but this is rather exposed to stonefall. Climb the dièdre in the back of the chimney (V and A0/A1, with half a dozen points of aid: VII free) to a jammed block. Struggle strenuously over this (V) to a good belay. Climb an easier pitch in the dièdre, moving L to reach a small terrace above a roof (IV then III). Now move up to a sort of rib, slightly on the R, and climb it to the base of another dièdre (III+). Slant L across a tricky wall and climb up on quartzy knobbles to reach the foot of a pillar (V/V+ or A0, then IV). Climb the pillar to where the angle eases (III). 3-4 pitches (I/II) lead to the summit. 500m: 4-5hr

Ils Dschimels 3508m and 3479m

E Burckhardt with H Grass, 27 July 1874.

These rather indistinct 'Twins' hardly rise above the frontier ridge E of La Sella. Their summits can be reached easily in 1½hr from the Fuorcla da la Sella, using the gentle snow slopes on the N flank of the ridge. On the S side a steep icy couloir curves up to the gap between the two summits. On either side of this couloir lie two beautiful pillars of rough red rock. Low down they are characterised by compact slabs and walls but higher they narrow to a serrated crest. The prominent snow couloirs that lead to the gaps E and W of the summits are quite easy in good conditions (PD: 1½-2hr). The peaks are rarely climbed by parties other than those making a complete traverse of the Sella group.

67 **SOUTH FACE OF EAST PEAK**

D/TD L Giana and S Mella, 5 July 1952 and 12 Aug 1953

Two parallel lines running directly to the summit but on each side of the crest of the pillar, were climbed by the same party in consecutive years. Both gave fine climbing on sound slabby rock with difficulties of IV/V. c450m: 4-6hr

Directly up the centre of the pillar is 'Dirretta della Bollicine' an excellent TD route, with sustained climbing of V/VI on the first buttress.

Piz Sella 3517m

An undistinguished snow dome at the eastern end of the chain. It is quite a popular ascent from the Marinelli hut and can be reached in 45min from the Fuorcla da la Sella via the NE flank – a gentle snow plod. The S face contains some of the best rock in the group and one or two of the climbs are as good as any in the range. Having completed one of these routes, climbers will descend via the Parravicini bivouac (see Huts Section).

68 **SOUTH-WEST SPUR**

AD+ A Bonola, A Corti and V Schiavio, 7 Aug 1928

171

The most obvious feature on the SW face is a narrow couloir that rises directly from the glacier to a point just E of the true summit. L of this is a striking red pillar whose base has been striated and polished by the glacier. The climb in question reaches the crest of the pillar above the lower section and is an established classic. Despite the moderate difficulties, many alpinists still consider it to be the finest rock climb in the Sella group. On the spur the rock is excellent and the climbing eminently protectable with a standard rack. IV/IV+

Reach the foot of the spur from the ski-station in 1hr or from the Marinelli hut in 1½hr. Well L of the base, easy ground (often a snow slope) leads to the foot of a prominent rocky couloir that slants up R towards the crest of the spur, above the lower glacier-polished slabs. Climb the couloir for three pitches (III), then leave it and work up towards the crest of the spur over short walls separated by easier ground. In this section various lines are possible and parties should attempt to follow the most logical route! Once the spur is reached it is best to climb L of the crest, over short walls and one memorable narrow chimney (IV), to a small gap below a tower. It is possible to turn this tower on the L but much better to climb it direct on compact rock (30m: IV/IV+). Continue on the L side of the crest, which gives most enjoyable climbing, to the final snow slope (III/III+). One pitch up this leads to the summit. c530m: 4hr

Piz Sella: South Face of East Summit

To the R of the great Central Couloir rise two well-defined spurs, both very steep in their lower sections but easing towards the top. The SW spur is the most impressive and rises in several steps. It is broad at the base and takes the form of a huge red triangular wall – the 'Triangolo Rosso'. To the R lies the S (actually SSW) spur, which almost merges with the main SW spur c130m below the summit.

The foot of the face is reached in 1hr from the Scerscen Ski-station. From near the base of the Central Couloir, climb up a snow slope on the R to a huge scree-ledge that lies below the Triangolo Rosso.

69 **SOUTH SPUR**
TD– G Miotti and D Scari, 12 July 1985
171
85

This is a fine climb, not high in the grade, on good rock. The major difficulties occur on two consecutive pitches low down on the initial pillar. From the end of the difficulties, where it is easy to climb up L to the crest of the SW spur, the first ascent party escaped to the R and descended Route 70, making two rappels directly down the walls at the bottom of the face.

The huge scree-covered ledge below the Triangolo continues R to a sign that marks the start of the 'Sentiero dei Camosci', a sort of 'Via Ferrata' equipped with chains that leads across the S face to the Upper Scerscen glacier and the Parravicini bivouac. Go along this 'path' until below the couloir that separates the two spurs, then climb up the R side of the couloir for c60m (III/IV) until it begins to narrow. From here climb easily up to the R and reach the base of the spur, close to its L edge. 500m: 5-6hr to the summit of E peak

A direct line up the Triangolo was climbed by Miotti and Pozzi in 1986. 250m: V/VI

70 **SOUTH-EAST FACE**

AD–/ A Bonacossa and A Corti, 6 Aug 1909

AD

171

85

The original route on this side of the mountain avoids the challange of the lower part of the S spur, by climbing easy ground to the R. It is a pleasant climb with only moderate difficulties (II/III). The rock is reasonably sound, though the easy ground tends to be a bit loose.

Immediately R of the S face a wide snow couloir runs up alongside the flanks of the spur. It terminates abruptly after 200m, the continuation provided by a steep and narrow gutter through the rock walls above. Reach the base of this couloir, using the 'Sentiero' mentioned in the previous description, in c1hr from the ski-station, or directly from the Marinelli hut in 1¼hr. Climb the couloir for c150m then break out L on a narrow ledge-system, that leads into another slimmer couloir above its steep lower section. Cross a vague rib, then go straight up over easy ground, finally moving L to join the crest of the S spur above the point where the angle relents. Either continue up the S spur or climb up L to the crest of the SW spur and follow it to the summit of the E peak, several hundred m from the main summit. c600m and 3-3½hr to the main summit

Fuorcla da la Sella (Sella Pass) 3269m

J Coaz and party, 20 Aug 1850 (Swiss side). First traverse: G Saraz with P Jenny and J Reudi, 12 Aug 1859

This pass lies at the foot of the SW ridge of Piz Roseg and is one of the most frequented in the Bernina Alps. The Italian side is very straightforward and generally used as an approach to the Roseg or Piz Sella. However, it does not allow a fast descent. Height is only lost gradually and crossing mushy snow on the Scerscen glacier-plateau in the afternoon can tax all but the fittest.

The Swiss side is one of the most crevassed glaciers in the

range and when approaching from the Coaz hut, a significant part of the route runs in line with these crevasses. In summer there is normally a well-beaten track but, even so, it's a long plod with a vertical interval of over 800m. Fortunately, in descent height can be lost quite rapidly.

71 **FROM COAZ HUT**

PD

173

Follow the path on to the glacier and go up it to the S. At about 2800m traverse E, almost horizontally across the Roseg glacier, on a sort of shelf. Pass below Pt 3067m and reach the Sella glacier. Go up it, taking the line of least resistance, to the gentle snow slopes that lead to the pass. 3-4hr in good conditions: 2hr in descent. See also photograph 170

72 **FROM TSCHIERVA HUT**

PD

173

Not as popular, though part of this route is often used in descent by parties reaching the summit of the Roseg from the N side. See also photograph 178

Cross the Tschierva glacier to the SW and reach the crest of the moraine on the far side. Climb the slopes of the Aguagliouls to reach a broad saddle at the foot of its NW ridge, a little to the S of Pt 2770m (1¼hr). Make a slightly descending traverse S to the moraine on the L side of the Sella glacier and go up it until forced onto the glacier itself. It is generally best to keep to the L at first, before working out into the centre and following crevassed slopes, at a gradually diminishing angle, all the way to the pass. c4hr from the hut in good conditions, 3hr in descent

73 **FROM MARINELLI HUT**

F

171

Follow Route H15 towards the Marco e Rosa hut. When near the rocks of the Crast Aguzza (Pt 3131m) bear L and cross the plateau of the Upper Scerscen glacier in a wide arc to the W. The slope steepens gradually to the broad saddle forming the pass. 450m: 2½hr, c1½hr in descent. See also photograph 176

74 **SELLA – GLUSCHAINT TRAVERSE**

AD+

173

This tremendous journey along the frontier is perhaps the best ridge traverse of its standard in the range. The quality of this expedition is second only to the Roseg – Scerscen – Bernina traverse but the difficulties and level of commitment are much less. It is a lengthy undertaking which will test the fitness of the party and is infrequently attempted, so tracks are unlikely to be found between Piz Sella and Piz Gluschaint. The best starting point is the Coaz hut, to the N, as an escape from the ridge and descent in that direction is always possible. It can also be done as a round trip from the Marinelli hut, by descending the SW ridge of Piz Gluschaint and returning over the Fuorcla Fex-Scerscen. Round trip from either hut 8-10hr.

Superstars requiring a fuller experience will continue the traverse over the Muongia to the Chaputschin. This is still technically straightforward but will require a total time of 12hr to reach the Coaz hut and is worthy of D–

Piz Aguagliouls 3118m

The continuation of the NW ridge of Piz Roseg terminates in this small peak. It forms the cornerstone at the junction of the Tschierva and Roseg glaciers. There is little here to interest the summer mountaineer, though during the winter months it is considered a worthy goal by ski-tourers. It is said that the view is always most spectacular from the lesser summits and this is certainly true of the Aguagliouls. Close at hand lie the giants of the Bernina group and to the W the chaotic glaciers of the Sella and Roseg are seen to full advantage. All the ridges are easy and the summit can be reached in about 2hr from the Tschierva hut (F). The N to S traverse offers an alternative approach to Piz Roseg's NW ridge and could prove useful when the glacier is badly crevassed.

Piz Roseg 3937m

A Moore and H Walker with J Anderegg, 28 June 1865; though the N summit (Schneekuppe) had been reached by F Bircham with P Jenny and A Flury, 31 Aug 1863.
Winter: A Swaine with C Klucker, 28 Dec 1892

When seen from the NW, this peak, one of the most prestigious in the Bernina Alps, appears as a slender snowy spire. The long summit crest, that contains three separate 'tops', is hidden from view and the vast walls of rock or ice, that form the flanks of this mountain, are seen only in profile. Although it lacks the sheer beauty of the Palu, to some it is the finest summit in the range.

Perhaps it is fitting that, unlike most of the other great peaks in this region, there is no easy chink in the armour; no 'Normal route' that could be declared a 'walk'. The S face is an impressive precipice of decomposing rock and is best left well alone. Conversely the NE face, crossed almost entirely by a large sérac barrier at half-height, is well known to Alpine ice climbers. Indeed, it is one of the most famous throughout the European Alps.

Any route to the summit is a lengthy undertaking and can be tricky and/or dangerous in bad conditions. Despite this, the mountain exerts a certain allure and will continue to remain a popular goal for those with the necessary experience to take up the challenge.

75
AD–
175

WEST FACE AND NORTH-WEST RIDGE

J Weilenmann with F Poll used this route as far as the Schneekuppe on 21 July 1864

Generally considered the easiest route to the summit and climbed frequently from both the Coaz and Marinelli huts. When conditions are favourable, winter and spring ascents are not uncommon, although many parties stop at the Schneekuppe. The Italian approach is longer but more straightforward and will take about the same length of time as that from the Coaz hut. However, the descent of the Sella glacier is quite fast, whereas a return trip to the Marinelli hut involves climbing back up to the Sella pass and a slow crossing of the Scerscen glacier in the middle of the day.

From the Coaz hut follow Route 71 to the upper part of the Sella glacier, then cross it to reach the foot of a huge couloir on the W face of the Roseg. This couloir rises to a conspicuous shoulder on the NW ridge just S of Pt 3598m. From the Marinelli hut Route 73 is used to reach the Fuorcla da la Sella from where a 20min descent leads to the foot of the couloir.

In dry conditions, the base of the couloir becomes a broken rocky barrier split by a number of narrow icy gullies, and the entry pitches can be fairly steep. Start at the R-hand extremity and slant up into the wide couloir (stone-fall possible). Climb this for c300m to a steep and often icy exit onto the shoulder. In bad conditions it is feasible to use the broken rocks on either bank. Climb the easy snow slopes on the L side of the NW ridge to a huge rimaye, above which a much steeper slope leads to the Schneekuppe (3920m). Keeping on the L side throughout, descend the long and sharp snow crest into the gap and climb up to the main summit via a narrow and predominantly rocky ridge. In dry conditions this gives an exposed but fairly straightforward traverse but after fresh snow the climbing can be quite delicate and a time of 1½-2hr is not unusual for this crossing. 700m from the glacier: 6-7hr from either hut

76 NORTH-NORTH-EAST RIDGE – ESELGRAT

AD
178

H Cordier and T Middlemore with J Jaun and K Maurer, 18 Aug 1876

Sometimes referred to as 'La Crasta'. Although slightly more difficult than the normal route from the Coaz hut, this gives a fine varied expedition in a splendid position and is considerably more sheltered from objective danger. It is a classic mixed climb over typical high mountain terrain and many parties regard it as one of the best middle-grade ridges in the region. The Tschierva glacier is complex and badly crevassed but normally a well-beaten track will show the way. As it is safer than the W face, especially later in the day, most parties descend the same way. See also photographs 173, 175, 179

There are two methods of reaching the upper level of the Tschierva glacier depending on the year in question. A good track runs SE from the Tschierva hut down to and then along the moraine. After 15min it crosses a small river flowing out of the Vadrettin da Tschierva. Normally it is best to descend to the main glacier and cross the flat plateau to the crest of the medial moraine, keeping well away from the ice cliffs alongside Pt 2907m. Climb this moraine to the foot of the rocky crest forming the NW ridge of Piz Umur. Keeping alongside this ridge, to avoid a badly crevassed zone, go up the glacier on the R and reach the upper plateau. Cross this in a wide arc to the W and climb easy slopes to a snow shoulder on the lower part of the NNE ridge (3hr). On the latter part of this glacier crossing, only the most unimaginative will fail to notice the huge sérac barriers on the R side of Piz Roseg's N face. A huge icefall from this quarter would certainly sweep the approach but the time spent in the danger area is, thankfully, minimal.

After descending to the main glacier below the Vedrettin da Tschierva, it has proved easier in some years to continue up the L side to the foot of the icefall. It is sometimes possible to keep on the glacier until past the icefall, but if not, climb the rocks on the L and follow broken ledge systems below Piz Morteratsch, until it is possible to return to the glacier above the icefall. Make a slightly descending traverse across the plateau and turn the base of Piz Umur to join the previous route.

The lower part of the NNE ridge is rounded and straightforward. Cross two easy gendarmes on excellent rock and reach the foot of a prominent buttress. Although better to climb this direct (III+ with one or two moves of IV), it is easier to turn it on the L flank (III−). Now follow the rocky crest to the next steepening and turn it on the R, regaining the ridge above via an icy gully. Easier ground now leads over Pt 3598m to the snowy shoulder where Route 75 is joined (c2hr). Continue over the Schneekuppe to the main summit. 700m from the upper Tschierva glacier. 7-8hr from the hut

77 NORTH-NORTH-WEST RIDGE INTEGRAL

AD+ J and R Wainewright with C Grass and M Schocher, 10 Sept 1889

173

Below Pt 3598m the NW ridge descends in two steep steps to the Fuorcla dals Aguagliouls. A direct ascent from this pass can only be recommended in very dry conditions as the line follows the N side of the ridge, where conditions are normally icy. It does however allow an objectively safe climb of the Roseg and avoids crossing any serious glacier terrain. Despite these advantages the route is a lengthy expedition from the Tschierva hut and is less interesting than the NNE ridge. It sees relatively few ascents.

From the Tschierva hut traverse the Aguagliouls and reach the Fuorcla (3148m). The first steep step is climbed on the L side via slabby rock and a prominent dièdre (III/IV). The second larger step, also climbed on the L, is somewhat easier (II/III) but is quite slabby and can be tricky if not completely snow free. The rock is reasonable though, inevitably, one or two loose sections must be negotiated. The upper section can be bypassed by snow slopes on the L. Continue up the normal route to the summit. 800m: 8-9hr

78 SOUTH-WEST RIDGE

D/D+ C and G Stuart with A Simond and F Summermatter, 30 June 1909

172

Rising directly above the Fuorcla da la Sella, this well defined frontier ridge, simply bristling with small pointed gendarmes, provides one of the best and longest 'mountain' rock climbs in the whole of the Bernina. The rock is generally sound, and the difficulties are quite sustained at the grade. The climbing is always interesting although, on occasions, short sections of broken ground interrupt the continuity. Were the situation more accessible, the route would enjoy considerable popularity. As it is, the lengthy approach and the amount of climbing on the ridge, which is far greater than the vertical interval would suggest, combined with the fact that there is no quick and easy descent from the summit, gives this route a degree of commitment and seriousness that deters most alpinists.

Fitness and technical competence are of equal importance, as the round-trip from one of the main huts will take c14hr. Prospective parties should seriously consider starting from a bivouac on the lower rocks or the neighbouring Parravicini Hut.

From the Sella pass, traverse below the lowest rocks on the Italian side and reach the crest via a snowy couloir. Continue up the crest, where the rock is sound and the difficulties are sustained at III/IV, to the foot of a huge tower. Climb the obvious big crack on the L side then slant up R, over a series of ledges, to the crest of the ridge above the tower (III). Follow the ridge over a second tower to a broad saddle and continue over four successive gendarmes to the foot of a very steep buttress about 50m high. Slant up the L side, where a succession of difficult moves (IV) lead to the top. The angle now eases but the ridge becomes very sharp and serrated. The crest can be followed throughout, although many of the crenellations can be avoided by some exposed climbing on the S side (III/IV). The final step is taken direct and is thankfully quite straightforward. Pull onto the exposed summit ridge with some relief and a well deserved view into the spectacular depths of the Morteratsch – Bernina cirque. c600m: 6-7hr

79 **EAST-NORTH-EAST RIDGE**

AD+ C Branch and E Garwood with M Schocher and C Zippert,

172 15 Aug 1892

This sharp crest of rock and ice rises from the Porta da Roseg to the E summit – the Roseg Pitschen. It is rarely climbed but is described here in descent, as it forms an integral part of the wonderful Roseg-Scerscen-Bernina traverse. The rock in the lower section is quite loose and care should be exercised even if the descent is made by rappel. This is a serious undertaking which is probably easier and certainly safer in cold icy conditions. See also photograph 173

From the main summit follow the fine snow crest E down to a saddle, then climb a steep snow/ice slope and broken rocks above, to the top of the Pitschen. Climb down the ridge ahead, over interesting mixed ground and relatively solid rock, to the top of the huge steep buttress that overlooks the Porta da Roseg (the last section can be quite tricky and it is usual to climb on the rocks forming the S flank of the ridge – a short rappel is often necessary). From the top of the buttress descend a steep couloir of poor rock on the S face (IV in ascent) then traverse across slabs of rotten rock (snow patches) to the Porta. 400m: 3-4hr

Piz Roseg: North-East Face

Although not intrinsically as difficult, nor as steep, as several other well-known European classics, climbs on this face continue to remain very high on the list for connoisseurs of pure alpine ice. In appearance the wall is both formidable yet strangely beautiful and not dissimilar to the Lyskamm. At approximately one-third height, an alarming barrier of séracs interrupts the entire face. Fortunately, these often unstable ice cliffs can be breached at a few weak points. The original route takes the widest and most obvious break just R of centre, then slants L above the barrier to finish close to the main summit. Together with the N face of the Lyskamm, this remains Christian Klucker's greatest masterpiece and was climbed without the benefit of crampons in a mere 5½hr of step cutting. 34 years were to elapse before a second ascent! Since that time a considerable number of routes and associated variations have been added to the wall and some of the more notable are mentioned below.

80 **ORIGINAL ROUTE**
D+ L Norman-Neruda with C Klucker, 16 July 1890.
175 First winter ascent: W Gross and U Sievers, 1959

The shortest route, which generally follows the line of least resistance to the saddle between the two summits. In common with the other routes on this face, difficulties are greatly augmented in drier conditions when increasing amounts of steep and loose rock must be negotiated. The easiest approach to the central break slants up from the L and is threatened by icefall from the sérac above. Thereafter the route is objectively safe in snowy conditions. Average angle 52°

From the Tschierva hut follow Route 76 towards the NNE ridge and reach the foot of the face in c3hr. Start L of the lowest rocks, where the rimaye rarely presents a problem, and slant up R over snow at 40°-45° to the central break in the sérac barrier. Cross the rock band on the R at its lowest point (60°), then climb the slope above and slant L through the rocky outcrops to finish up an icy couloir (55°-60°). Continue directly up on 50° snow/ice slopes to the saddle, or slant L to the main summit. c600m: 6-8hr from the rimaye

81 **DIRECT ROUTE TO SCHNEEKUPPE**
TD– H Huss, R Muller and W Gut, 13 June 1943.
175 Direct start: K Diemberger and K Schonthaler, early July 1958

This is probably the safest and most logical line on the face, especially if the direct start (possible in very snowy conditions) is taken. The upper slopes reach an angle of more than 60° and are normally icy. c650m: 7-9hr

82 **SCHMID ROUTE**
TD G Haider and J Schmid, 26 August 1962
175

This follows the obvious steep couloir on the R side of the face. Apart from the finish, which is slightly steeper, the difficulties are similar to the Direct. Stone and ice fall can be funnelled into the couloir and the climb is best attempted under snowy conditions and during a very hard frost. c650m: 8hr

The slim icy gully that splits the large rocky buttress to the R of this route was climbed by P Gabarrou and H Bouvard on the 14 June 1985. 70° ice in the gully led to the steep upper wall which gave several short vertical sections. A direct line was pursued to the Schneekuppe. 600m: TD, 8-10hr

83 **DIRECTISSIMA**
TD+/ED1 K Diemberger and K Schonthaler, 14 July 1958
175

The hardest and objectively the most dangerous route on the wall, which should only be attempted during very cold and snowy conditions and after prior inspection of the stability of the central sérac barrier. A direct line through the lower rocks gives some difficult mixed climbing and leads to a ramp line that cuts up R through the ice cliffs. Thereafter, straightforward 55° slopes lead directly to the main summit. 650m: 10-12hr

84 **NORTH FACE OF ROSEG PITSCHEN**
TD G Bertone and P Resinelli, 16 July 1964
175

Although sheltered from ice fall, originating from the L end of the huge sérac, the central section of this narrow face is composed of steep and very rotten rock. It gives a good and relatively safe mixed climb (pitches of 70°) when well endowed with hard névé but has seen few ascents. 500m: 7-8hr

Porta da Roseg 3522m

First traverse: P Gussfeldt with C Capat, H Grass and P Jenny, 13 Sept 1872

This deep gap, separating the Scerscen from Piz Roseg, lies in the very heart of the Bernina range. The N side rises only a little distance above the Upper Tschierva glacier, yet for many years remained one of the most popular ambitions amongst accomplished ice-climbers visiting the area. Nowadays it is seldom climbed and most parties attempting the SW ridge of the Scerscen reach the col from the Italian side.

85 **NORTH COULOIR**
AD+ First ascent party
175

In good conditions this is reasonably straightforward by modern standards. The approach from the Tschierva hut via Route 76 takes 3hr and a further 2hr should be allowed for the couloir. The rimaye always provides the crux and is best attempted early in the season when there is still considerable snow cover. Thereafter the slopes are 60° gradually easing to 50° at the top, where there can sometimes be a cornice. Good rock belays are possible on the R but the climbing is always steeper near the edge of the couloir. 220m. See also photographs 173, 181

86 **SOUTH COULOIR**
AD–/AD H Cordier with P Jenny and Wieland, 8 Sept 1875
172

Early in the season this is a broad and straightforward snow couloir, but in drier conditions it is better to climb the rocks on the flanks. Stone-fall can present a serious problem later in the day so the ascent is best attempted around dawn. c300m: 45°

From the Marinelli hut follow Route 73 towards the Sella Pass and reach the foot of the couloir in c2hr. If conditions are good, climb the bed directly to the gap in 1-1½hr. Otherwise take to the rocky spur on the R side of the couloir. At about two-thirds height this becomes a little more tricky and it is easier to cross the couloir and climb the broken rocks on the L to the top (1½-2hr).

Piz Scerscen 3971m

P Gussfeldt with C Capat and H Grass, 13 Sept 1877

The third highest peak in the range, like the Roseg, has no

straightforward route to its summit. Technically the easiest lines lie on the Italian side but the rock on this 600m rusty-red wall is very poor, and stone-fall is a constant threat in less than perfect conditions. The Swiss side is glaciated and the most obvious feature, a pronounced spur, gives one of the finest lower-grade ice routes in the Alps. With no easy descent, parties sometime continue to the summit of the Bernina and so complete one of the most highly recommended expeditions described in this book.

87 **NORTH-WEST SPUR – EISNASE**
AD+ First ascent party
181

One of the finest and most famous of all the classic ice routes in the range. Although an ascent of the ice nose can often be more difficult than anything found on the NNE ridge of the Roseg, it is generally considered an easier proposition. It provides the normal route to the summit from Switzerland and if the snow is reasonably consolidated and the ascent has been completed in good time, it can be descended without undue problem. The overall grade reflects the difficulties encountered on the ice nose. At the time of writing these are fairly straightforward and the route is objectively safe throughout. This is a popular excursion and in high summer a well-trodden piste is often clearly visible from as far away as the Julier Pass! See also photographs 178, 179

Leave the Tschierva hut early and follow Route 76 to the upper plateau of the Tschierva glacier, from where it is possible to crampon easily up to the saddle of the Fuorcla da L'Umur (3273m, 2½hr). This same point can be gained from the E. Scramble up the ridge – a mixed spur of ice and rough rock, which steepens to below the huge prow that gives the route its name. Climb this 'nose' on the L, R or even direct depending on conditions. Two pitches are normally sufficient to complete the difficulties and the angle is rarely more than 55°-60°. Above, the rounded slopes of the spur lie back at a modest angle of 30° and few crevasses are encountered before the final rimayes. A short 40° slope (often icy) leads to the summit ridge. 700m: 3-4hr, 5½-7hr from the hut

The icy ramp in the middle of the NE face was first climbed in 1898 to exit on to the rounded spur above the ice nose. Similarly, the R side of the NW face was climbed in 1890. One can either slant L at two-thirds height to reach the NW spur, or keep R to finish on the summit ridge, just above Pt 3875m (the Schneehaube). Both routes are AD+/D and have failed to become popular. The NE face is the more serious of the two and is exposed to sérac-fall in the initial stages.

88 SOUTH-WEST RIDGE

PD+/ AD– 177

P Gussfeldt with J Aymonod and E Rey, 22 Sept 1887

Rising above the Porta da Roseg this ridge offers, in dry conditions, a pure rock climb as far as the Schneehaube. The situations are superb and although the rock is broken, the difficulties are not high and generally less than those encountered reaching the Porta. These days it is usually climbed from the S, giving perhaps the safest ascent to the summit from the Italian huts. In very snowy conditions the climbing can become quite delicate and, in this case, an ascent of the SW couloir is preferable. The ridge forms an important part of the finest traverse in the range, from the Roseg to the Bernina. See also photographs 172, 181

Above the Porta, follow the crest without undue difficulty to the foot of the huge rock tower. About half-way up to this point a steep step can be climbed direct, but is more easily turned on the R. Traverse across the S side of the Great Tower, over slabs and sometimes mixed ground, to a prominent rib. On the far side of this, a steep couloir (III/III+ when dry) leads back to the crest above the tower. Continue easily to the snowy summit of the Schneehaube (3875m). A long snow crest now snakes up to the main summit. It is usually quite straightforward but can often form large cornices. A short shattered rock ridge leads to the highest point. 450m: 3-4hr

89 SOUTH-WEST COULOIR

PD/PD+ 177

P Gussfeldt with H Grass, 15 Sept 1879 (as far as the Schneehaube). Winter: Unknown but climbed solo by W Risch on 29 March 1938

The easiest route on this side of the mountain. Early in the season, when well endowed with snow, it provides the normal route from the Marinelli hut. As conditions become drier the couloir is increasingly bombarded by stone-fall and should only be attempted after a very cold night. During the recent dry summers it could hardly be recommended! See also photographs 172, 174

From the base of the couloir leading to the Porta da Roseg (2hr from the Marinelli hut) slant up R to the start of a snowy couloir/ramp that rises diagonally up to the summit ridge, just E of the Schneehaube. The lower section is divided by a rocky outcrop. Take the R branch, which is, incidentally, less exposed to stone-fall and follow it throughout to the ridge, a few mins from the Schneehaube. The main summit can be reached from here in 1hr. 550m: 5-7hr from the hut

90 **NORTH COULOIR**
D–/D R Pavesi and E Tessera, 7 Aug 1988

This takes the obvious slender ice gully rising out of the SE corner of the Tschierva glacier and arrives on the horizontal section of the summit ridge at c3920m, just to the R of the rocky E top (3954m). There is a certain danger from falling ice in the lower section and the route is serious for the grade. c350m: 4hr

Piz Umur 3252m

This rocky crest, at the foot of the Scerscen, often provides a consolation prize for parties confronted with dubious weather conditions. Situated in the heart of the tormented Tschierva glacier and surrounded by the greatest peaks in the range, the summit offers a most inspiring panorama. The best excursion is a traverse from N to S finishing at the Fuorcla da l'Umur. This gives enjoyable scrambling on broken rock and was first climbed by J Frohmann with N Kohler and C Zippert, 25 July 1909. 4-5hr round trip from the Tschierva hut: PD

Piz Bernina 4049m

J Coaz with J and L Ragut Tscharner, 13 Sept 1850.
Winter: C Watson and party, 4 Feb 1880

The most easterly 4000m summit in the Alps; the undisputed queen of the Bernina range and the highest peak described in this guide. The first ascent party, who attempted the climb ostensibly for survey purposes, named their mountain after the pass that demarcates the massif to the E. Heavily glaciated on all sides, the highest point of this magnificent peak lies entirely in Switzerland and 400m N of a shoulder on the frontier ridge called La Spalla (4020m). The flanks provide a gamut of routes from long but straightforward glacier expeditions to technically difficult ice and mixed climbs with a certain degree of objective danger. Pride of place, however, is afforded to the classic 'Biancograt' -one of the most famous snow crests in Europe.

91 SOUTH-EAST RIDGE – SPALLAGRAT

PD F Brown and F Tuckett with C Almer and F Andermatten,
182 23 June 1866

This is the normal route and used by parties on both the Swiss and Italian sides to make the safest and easiest ascent. Both approaches lead to the Marco e Rosa hut and are described in the Huts Section. Most parties start their climb from either the Diavolezza or Marinelli huts, returning the same day. However, the route is long and tiring and a night spent in the Marco e Rosa hut, whilst rather taxing on one's pocket, allows the ascent to be completed in a more leisurely two days. Above the hut, the ridge is mainly snow with one or two sections of easy broken rock. Over 1000m of ascent from either hut. See also photograph 187

At most times of the year, a well-battered piste leads N from the Marco e Rosa hut across gentle snow slopes. Climb these slopes to their apex, from where a broken rocky ridge, with several fixed ropes, leads to the Italian summit – La Spalla (1½hr). A beautiful snow crest, quite sharp in places, is followed to the N with a final section on broken rock just below the highest point. 2hr from the hut: 6hr from the Diavolezza, 7-8hr from the Boval, 6-7hr from the Marinelli

When approaching from the Marinelli hut a huge couloir is clearly seen splitting the S face of La Spalla. It is normally subject to stone-fall from the atrocious rock on its flanks but when these are snow covered and well cemented in place by a severe frost, it offers a direct ascent to the SW ridge, a little below the Italian summit. First Ascent: L Held and party, 15 Sept 1875: AD+: 45°-50°: 5hr from the hut

92 EAST RIDGE

PD/PD+ First ascent party
188

This ridge, reached from above the chaotic 'Labyrinth' of the upper Morteratsch glacier, was the line followed by the successful survey party in 1850. Nowadays a much safer and shorter approach is made to the upper ridge via the Marco e Rosa hut. It is a classic excursion which, when combined with a descent of the Spallagrat, offers a delightful traverse of the peak.

From the Marco e Rosa hut follow the normal route N across the snow slopes, then traverse R to cross a shoulder on the E ridge of La

Spalla, well above Pt 3664m. Make a rising traverse across the bowl in front and climb onto the E ridge of the main summit, just below the point where the crest begins to steepen. Climb the rocky ridge, with no particular difficulties, to a snow crest shortly before the summit. 2-2½hr

93 **NORTH-EAST FACE**

D+ First ascent of the route described: L Norman Neruda with

188 C Klucker, finished via the Berninascharte to Piz Bianco (Alv), 18 June 1890. A direct finish to the main summit was achieved in 1911

Together with the N face of the Cengalo this is the highest in the Central Alps and rivals many of those found in the W. Access to the gentle, middle section is via a steep couloir splitting the huge rock bastion of the Saas dal Pos. The length of this couloir is not far short of many of the major ice routes found in the range but is considerably less than half the height of this expansive glaciated face! Although first climbed over 100 years ago, the face still commands great respect and is infrequently ascended. Good training, fitness and stamina are more important here than modern front-pointing technique. The upper slopes are fully exposed to the rising sun, making an early start essential in order to complete the climb before conditions become hazardous. Indeed, the couloir is exposed to stone-fall and this section should be climbed before the sun's rays reach the top of the Saas dal Pos. Aesthetically, however, the face has one major flaw. Parties need never fear total commitment as, in the upper section, escape is possible onto the E ridge or even across the flanks to the Marco e Rosa hut. Conversely this makes it feasible to climb the upper part of the route early in the morning via the approach to Route 92. This gives a pleasant little mixed climb of c300m (AD/AD+)

Leave the Boval hut and follow the good track S along the crest of the moraine and finally down onto the glacier. Go up the R side to the base of the Saas dal Pos (c1hr). Enter the obvious long deep L-slanting couloir to the E of Pt 2713m. Climb this couloir, finishing on the E side of the final rocks via mixed ground (450m: c5°: 3-4hr) Continue up the ridge over more mixed terrain, which in some conditions can prove quite tricky, to the snowy dome of the Saas dal Pos (3256.9m: 30min-1hr). The angle is now fairly gentle and a broad rounded ridge is followed to the upper face. The slope steepens; a final rimaye can sometimes prove difficult, after which increasingly steeper ice leads to the summit rocks. When snowy and well frozen, these provide a safe and direct finish, over interesting mixed ground, to the top. Otherwise, it is perhaps more logical to slant R above the rimaye and climb snow/ice all the way to a steep exit (50°-60°) onto the Berninascharte, between the main top and Piz Bianco. Finish easily from here up the final rocky section of Route 95. 1300m: 4½-6hr, 9-12hr from the hut

94 NORTH-EAST FACE DIRECT

TD

188

The lower section of the NE face was first climbed by J Ludwig with H Grass and A Arduser, 5 Oct 1879. They started above and to the R of the rocks forming the base of the Saas dal Pos, following a narrow couloir that slants up to the L alongside these rocks and beneath the walls of the huge sérac barrier. The party then reached the summit by way of the E ridge. On the 21 June 1931, K Schneider and F Singer climbed through the E side of the icefall to the R and finished directly to the summit of the Bernina. Finally, during the night of the 28-29 June 1969, H Danler, H Gasser, H Hochfilzer and A Schlick climbed through the R side of the icefall and finished directly to the summit of the Piz Bianco. Difficulties in the icefall will vary enormously from year to year and have sometimes been relatively moderate but the obvious and considerable danger from sérac avalanche has always made these routes very serious undertakings. At the time of writing the entire barrier appears absolutely hideous and could only be recommended to those with strong suicidal tendencies! For these reasons, the routes are very rarely repeated and the direct lines warrant an overall grading of at least TD.

95 NORTH RIDGE – BIANCOGRAT

AD

181

First complete ascent: P Gussfeldt with H Grass and J Gross, 12 Aug 1878. Winter: C Colmus with C and U Grass, 15 March 1929

So much praise has already been bestowed upon this magnificent arcing snow ridge that little new can be said. It is perhaps the most beautiful and most coveted climb in the range, due mainly to its wonderfully compelling line – 'the ladder into the sky' – and stupendous position. It is certainly one of the most famous in Europe. As such it has unfortunately formed the arena for a number of accidents, generally to parties of limited experience attracted by the enormous status attached to the ascent. Although the difficulty and seriousness of this undertaking should not be underestimated, in good conditions, when the crest is well consolidated and the upper rocks warm and free of snow, the climbing can be reasonably straightforward. An early start is recommended, in order to complete the snow crest before conditions deteriorate. Fast competent parties sometimes choose to retrace their steps from the summit but most will opt for the far longer yet less demanding descent of the normal route to the Boval hut. Short rock sections of IV–. See also photographs 178, 188

The first part of the approach to the Fuorcla Prievlusa is a little tedious and can also be confusing in the dark. As parties often lose precious time locating the correct line, it is not a bad idea to make a thorough inspection the previous evening. From the Tschierva hut, contour SE to the crest of the moraine on the L side of the glacier, then continue in the same direction using the stony ground between the moraine and the glacier. A poorly defined path slants up L over boulders and scree to a rocky couloir. Slant steeply up this to the base of an enormous boulder, from where a very well-marked path leads gradually up and across a series of narrow terraces below the rocks of Piz Morteratsch. It finally crosses a scree slope to reach the glacier at c3000m. In favourable conditions the edge of the glacier can be followed all the way. Work up L on an increasingly steep snow slope, which splits into two separate bays near the top. The one on the R leads to the base of a couloir below the deep gash of the Fuorcla. Climb the steep ice couloir directly, for 130m, to the col (3430m: 3-4hr).

At first, the ridge is rocky and it is best to climb on the R side for c50m before returning to the crest. Now continue on the crest to the start of the snow ridge (1hr). The way ahead is wonderfully clear and follows the elegant line between light and shade. The angle is not too great and the ridge only begins to really narrow higher up, fully concentrating the mind on perfect crampon technique! The summit of Piz Bianco is reached in c2h. Go along the nearly horizontal crest (good rock) until forced to make a short and awkward descent L (IV–, or rappel) into the gap – the 'Berninascharte'. If many parties are on the ridge then this can be a bottleneck, resulting in a long delay. Fortunately, the way to the main summit is now easier than it looks! Go along the ridge and either climb over the large gendarme or turn it on the R to a second gap beyond (III/III+). Climb steeply up the crest, on sound rock, until the angle eases and the difficulties rapidly decrease. Although quite pleasant when dry, the climbing on this section can become far more demanding when the rocks are snow-covered (1-2hr). 600m from the start of the ridge: 7-9hr from hut to summit

96
D+
178

WEST FACE

T Graham Brown with A Graven, J Knubel and A Zurcher, 18 Aug 1930

Of all the great ice faces in the range, this is probably the most mysterious. A reputation for objective danger and a long and complex approach to this wild and unfamiliar corner have deterred all but the most ardent connoisseurs of such climbs. Although the average angle of the face is not that steep and the technical difficulties not high if an exit is forced onto the Berninascharte, the route will always be a serious proposition for its grade. Several ominous sérac barriers are usually in evidence, and L of the slope a large expanse of loose rock covers the flanks of the Biancograt, subjecting the route to stone-fall. Careless parties on the upper section of the Biancograt can substantially add to this threat. This is a route that is best attempted outside the summer season, when well frozen and snowy conditions will curtail stone-fall and the mountain can be enjoyed in the solitude that it deserves. See also photograph 179

From the Tschierva hut follow Route 76 to the foot of the NW ridge of Piz Umur, then go up the crevassed glacier on the L, keeping close to the ridge, until past the Fuorcla da L'Umur. Work out into the centre of the glacier and go up to the foot of the face (c3½hr). Start on the L close to the rocks and climb directly towards the summit. Although it is often possible to keep L of all the sérac walls, the lower part of the route may still lie within range of a hefty ice fall! If a direct line is pursued in the upper section, the last three pitches give steep mixed climbing and raise the overall grade to TD−. The rock on this section is poor and is best climbed when well cemented in place by an armour of ice. Otherwise climb steeply L on snow or ice to the Berninascharte and follow the ridge to the summit (4-5½hr). 550m: 7½-9hr from the hut

To the L, the W buttress, leading to the summit of the Piz Bianco, has received few ascents. It is reported to give a very interesting climb, with pitches of IV on reasonable rock. J Burton-Alexander with M Schocher and S Platz, 28 July 1899. c500m: D

In 1993 the right-hand edge of this spur was climbed by P Gabarrou and T Heymann (VI); sound rock).

97 **GRAND TRAVERSE OF ROSEG-SCERSCEN-BERNINA**
TD–/ U Campell with K Freimann, 19 Sept 1929.
TD Winter: A Forni, F Gugiatti and C Pedroni, 25-28 Dec 1969
177

This is, perhaps, the least known of the major alpine traverses. Although, in good conditions, the technical difficulties are not great, the route covers a magnificent variety of terrain with equal involvement on rock, snow and mixed ground. The crux will invariably be the serious descent of the ENE ridge of the Roseg. The easiest combination, via the normal route to the Roseg and a descent from the Bernina to the Marco e Rosa hut, will still take a very full day. For a round trip from the Tschierva hut, descending by the Biancograt (Amstutz and Risch 1932), add another 5hr. More often, parties just make the crossing from the Scerscen after an ascent of the Eisnase, returning to the Tschierva hut via the Biancograt. This is a classic expedition at D/D+ (12-14hr). The complete ridge has only one point of escape – at the Porta da Roseg – and this can hardly be recommended once the day warms up. Thus, the length and commitment of this traverse make the overall grading higher than the sum of its individual parts and it is still rarely completed. A winter ascent will provide an atmosphere equivalent to a major Himalayan traverse and undoubtedly gives one of the greatest adventures in the range. See also photograph 182

For the normal route on the Roseg start at the Coaz or Marinelli huts. In very snowy conditions, parties have left the ridge at the Porta da Roseg and climbed to the summit of the Scerscen via its SW couloir. However, this is hardly aesthetic when compared to a crossing of the frontier ridge! From the summit of the Scerscen, continue down the NE ridge, using the rocks on the S side, to reach a snowy saddle. Go along the sharp rocky crest, negotiating numerous gendarmes, to the E summit (3954m) where there is an alarming drop! Climb or rappel the S side and rejoin the ridge at a snowy saddle. Continue along the ridge to a rocky tower. Climb over it or turn it on the R, to reach the Fuorcla Scerscen-Bernina (the lowest point on the connecting ridge). The climbing throughout all this sector is intricate and impressively exposed. Several airy rappels are generally made to avoid short tricky pitches of down-climbing. A narrow icy crest leads up to the rocks of La Spalla. Unfortunately these are none too solid and can either be climbed direct (III/III+), or avoided more easily by a traverse across the S flank to a wide couloir leading back to the ridge above. Continue wearily to the main summit and after returning to La

Spalla, one last effort is needed to descend the normal route to the Marco e Rosa hut. 5km and 1700m of ascent: 14-18hr

Fuorcla Prievlusa 3430m

First traverse: C Robarts with P Jenny and A Flury, 15 Aug 1868

This deep notch S of the Piz Prievlusa lies at the foot of the Biancograt (see Route 95). The approach from the Boval hut is rarely, if ever, climbed these days. It is not easy and is also exposed to rock and ice fall.

Piz Prievlusa 3610m

B Wainewright and J Pennington-Leigh with H and C Grass, 19 July 1882

This is more of a shoulder on the sharp rugged SSE ridge of Piz Morteratsch, rather than a distinctive summit in its own right. It is rocky on all sides and has only one easy route to the top. Even this gets few ascents!

98 **NORTH RIDGE VIA WEST FLANK**
PD First ascent party
183

Usually straightforward but probably best climbed in snowy conditions to minimise stone-fall in the couloir. See also photograph 188

Follow Route 95 from the Tschierva hut but instead of going R towards the Fuorcla Prievlusa, enter the snow bay on the L. A heavily crevassed area is usually avoided by keeping close to the rocks of Piz Morteratsch. At the head of the bay a loose rock wall rises to the lowest point on the connecting ridge between Piz Prievlusa and the Morteratsch (Pt 3531m). On the R a prominent couloir slants up R to the crest. Climb this (II/III when dry) and continue S for 15min, up the easy snow ridge, to the summit. c4hr from the hut

The short yet impressive S ridge, rising only 180m above the Fuorcla Prievlusa, appears to be very rarely climbed and remains something of an enigma. It rises in two steep steps. The first is comprised of appalling rock and the main overhanging section must be turned on the L (III/IV). Higher, the second steep section is climbed by a smooth slab slightly to the R, regaining the crest after 35m (delicate climbing on sound and rather compact rock: V−). The obvious continuation is the SSE ridge of the Morteratsch.

Piz Morteratsch 3751m

C Brugger and P Gensler with K Emmermann and A Klaingutti, 11 Sept 1858

Together with the Piz Palu and the mighty Bernina, this is the most frequented summit in the range. It is a stupendous viewpoint – the best in the Massif, and indeed rivals any to be found in the Central Alps. The walk to the Boval hut, an ascent of the normal route and descent to the Tschierva hut will give one of the best expeditions of its class anywhere in the Alps. Varied scenery on both the approach and descent, combined with equal interest on both snow and rock, make this an ideal introduction to the higher Alpine peaks.

99 **NORTH RIDGE**
PD− First ascent party
183

The normal route. A delightful snow climb, which due to its overwhelming popularity can simply result in following a well-defined 'trench'. The overall difficulty depends on the approach to the Fuorcla Da Boval (Routes 101 and 102) and the grading given refers only to the ridge.

From the Fuorcla drop down on to the Tschierva glacier and walk along it below the jagged rocky crest, until it is possible to slant up a steeper slope to a small, snow saddle. Climb the broad and easy crest above, until it steepens below a large snow/ice boss leading to Pt 3611m. Turn this boss by traversing slopes on the L into a sort of valley. Make a long rising traverse up steeper slopes and rejoin the ridge, S of Pt 3611m. Easy slopes now lead to the final rocky top (1½hr). After heavy snowfall, the slopes on the normal route can become avalanche prone and climbing the boss becomes the only practical means of ascent. It is often icy and gives 4 pitches at a maximum angle of 50°. PD+ and quite popular.

100 NORTH-EAST RIDGE – CREST OF HOPE

AD+/ D– 183

First complete ascent: A Pfister and P Schucan, 10 Oct 1908

An established classic which, after the N ridge, is considered to give the best route on the mountain. In common with all rock climbing on the N side of the range, experience is needed in handling loose material. The technical difficulties are not high but the route is very long and simply exudes 'high mountain ambience' in the splendidly positioned, upper section! It will be necessary to climb a large proportion of the route unroped in order to complete it in a reasonable time and snowy conditions higher up will greatly augment the standard. Locating the easiest line is not that straightforward, especially in the lower section. Despite its status there is often a good chance of having this climb to yourself. III/III+

From the Boval hut go S down the path but instead of following it onto the moraine, continue along the ablation valley. Work up alongside the main stream, issuing from a tongue of snow that protrudes from the lower Boval Dadains glacier (white arrow on large boulder). After a few hundred m bear L onto the moraine crest and follow it to a slabby rock barrier where a cairned track slants up to the L along a grassy rake. Continue in the same direction, crossing a large scree slope, until below a second and steeper rock barrier. Towards the L end, a cairn marks the entrance to a gully. Climb this gully into a wide couloir with a steep buttress above and to the R. It is possible to follow the couloir throughout but this is unpleasant and it is better to make excursions onto the L flank where the rock is sounder (short steps of II+). Higher up regain the couloir, where it becomes a slabby ramp slanting up to the L. Follow it to the crest of the ridge and a huge blocky shoulder with a large cairn (3083m: c3hr).

The broken rounded buttress above has a friendly line of weakness up the L side of the crest. This gives pleasant scrambling (I/II) to a horizontal section of ridge. Go along the crest at first, then take the easy snow slopes on the R to below a second and sharper horizontal section, where the ridge bends to the R. Climb a steep slabby pitch, on the R side of the initial step, to the crest (III/III+), then continue in a splendid position, on generally quite sound rock, to a tower. An easy gully on the S side (rappel slings in place) leads down to the col at the foot of the final ridge (II+). It would be possible to avoid this second horizontal section by following the glacier to the R, returning to the ridge at the col via a steep ascent of a broad icy couloir. Apart from the potential danger from stone-fall, this would undoubtedly miss the best climbing of the day and is not recommended.

The ridge above is steep but well broken and care is needed with loose blocks and flakes. Climbing on the crest is less hazardous but harder and more exposed. Generally parties will climb on the N flank, where the maximum difficulties encountered will be III–/III. Eventually easy ground leads to the summit snow dome. This is quite steep and could be climbed direct. However, at this stage you will be excused for slanting up L, on the edge of the rock, to reach the haven of the S ridge. A broad easy snow crest leads back R to the summit. c900m of climbing: 8hr from the hut

Other ridges on the mountain are poorly rated and appear to be rarely repeated. The SW ridge is reached from the 'Terrassa' (see Route 102) by traversing the Vadrettin da Tschierva, then slanting up a conspicuous scree terrace to the crest. After turning an initial buttress on the L, the ridge is followed directly. Much of the rock is poor but the maximum difficulty is III. c500m: AD, 6hr from the hut

The SSE ridge, reached by a S to N traverse of the Piz Prievlusa, is a difficult rock climb. If the crenellated crest is followed throughout, the rock is, for the most part, fairly reasonable. However, this involves overcoming some formidable difficulties, which have generally been avoided by climbing easier but much looser ground on the exposed flanks of the ridge (3½-4hr: 6-7hr from the Fuorcla Prievlusa: D+ IV/V). The complete traverse from the Morteratsch to the Bernina was first done by A Gunther and H Melchior, 2 Sept 1932 in 19hr.

Fuorcla da Boval 3347m

First recorded crossing: E Burckhardt with C Grass and C Jossi, 6 Oct 1878. However, the col was most certainly reached by chamois hunters before this date

The lowest point in the jagged rocky crest between Piz Boval and the Morteratsch. Whilst rather steep on the W side, from the E the gentle slopes of the Vadrettin da Tschierva rise benignly to the col. As a crossing, it is one of the most popular in the range and the 'High Point' of the classic traverse from the Morteratsch to Roseg valleys.

101 WEST SIDE

PD–/PD

Serious and exposed scrambling in the upper section.

From the Boval hut the path is depressingly obvious as it snakes steeply up the grassy spur to a conspicuous knoll. Continue up steep slopes of boulders and scree, slanting L near the top into a small valley. Follow the bed (stream/snow patches) then work up L to the rounded crest of a broad moraine ridge. From this point the correct route to the col is extremely well marked with red paint flashes. The path zigzags up the moraine to the base of a vast and broken rock wall. Ascend a few short steps on the R then slant up L to the base of a chimney. Climb this (II/II+), then zigzag up to the R over quite steep, slabby walls of excellent granite, split by a succession of ledges (I/II). Near the top, a long ledge system leads back L to the col. 850m from the hut: 2½-3hr. Early in the season and with good snow cover, some parties climb the steep couloir slightly S of the col. Although this avoids the intricacies of the rock wall, it is not a popular alternative.

102 EAST SIDE

F+

An easy glacier walk where crevasses are almost non-existent.

From the Tschierva hut follow the track NE up scree slopes to a rocky barrier. The path works up the R side of this, zig-zagging through short walls and grassy ledges, to a huge scree terrace called, surprisingly, the 'Terrassa' (3120m). Follow this round to the Vadrettin da Tschierva. Walk up the glacier, keeping towards the L side. Gentle slopes lead all the way to the col. 800m from the hut: 2-2½hr

Piz Tschierva 3545.9m

J Coaz and party, 18 Aug 1850

No more than a gentle walk from the upper Vadrettin da Tschierva but a popular ascent that can be easily included on the return from a climb of Piz Morteratsch. Regularly ascended on skis during the winter months.

103 EAST RIDGE

F

The normal route. A very broad and easy angled snow and scree ridge, on which it would be difficult to come to any harm. The greatest danger is probably sunstroke on the glacier.

From the upper plateau of the glacier reach the Fuorcla Misaun (3336m but not named on map) via easy slopes of snow and scree. Walk up the ridge for c1km to the summit cairn. 200m: 30min

Piz Boval 3353m

A viable alternative when all else fails! The crest N of the Fuorcla da Boval contains a number of small sharp rocky peaklets, generally grouped under the name of the Crasta da Boval (highest point 3401.4m). This almost horizontal crest is long and hard in places, though various spires give short climbs on sound rock from the snow slopes to the W. Piz Boval lies at the northern end of this chain and can be combined with an ascent of one of the neighbouring mountains, or simply 'bagged' as a short and pleasant excursion from the Boval hut.

104 NORTH-WEST RIDGE

F/PD

This ridge rises steeply but with no particular difficulty from the deep notch at Pt 3208m. This col can be reached in 3-3½hr from the Boval hut via the Fuorclas da Boval and Misaun. It can also be reached via the Boval Dadour glacier in 3hr but the couloir on this side, leading up to the col, is quite steep. The easiest ascent to the summit climbs fairly directly up broken rock from the upper Misaun glacier.

105 VIA EAST RIDGE OF CORN BOVAL

PD

This gives a surprisingly fine, yet not too difficult scramble. The Corn Boval (c3081m) lies above the Boval hut, just E of a small col marked 3080m.

Walk up the track towards the Fuorcla da Boval and after 30min work up R to the bottom of the E ridge. A broad crest, with a fine succession of easy angled slabs, leads delightfully to the top of the Corn (2hr from the Boval hut: this is a nice ascent in its own right and an escape is perfectly straightforward from this point). Easy climbing up the broad E ridge of the Piz Boval leads to the summit (1½hr). c500m: 3½hr from the hut

Piz Misaun 3248.6m

Although frequented by spring skiers, little interest is shown in this minor peak during the summer months. It can be reached directly from the Boval hut, via the lower reaches of the Boval Dadour glacier and the NE ridge, in 3hr (F); or from the Fuorcla da Boval via the col (3208m) to the NW of Piz Boval, and the broad stony SSE ridge (1½hr: F). Peaks further N, eg the Chalchagn, can be climbed directly from Morteratsch but they are long and tedious outings over rough ground.

Fuorcla Crast'Aguzza 3601m

First recorded ascent from the N side by J Hardy and E Kennedy with A Flury and P and F Jenny, 23 July 1861.
First traverse: F Tuckett and E Buxton with F Biner, P Jenny and C Michel, 28 July 1864

One of the most important 'breaks' in the middle of the range. Together with the Fuorcla Bellavista, it provides the easiest crossing point of the frontier ridge in the heart of the Massif. In fact it is very rarely traversed. The pass provides the 'gateway' to the normal route on Piz Bernina and is thus reached almost continually during the summer months (and quite regularly the rest of the year!), from one side or the other. Standing 300m to the W is the Marco e Rosa hut and approaches to the col (F+/PD−) are described under the huts section.

Crast'Aguzza 3854m

J Specht and J Wellenmann with J Pfitschner and F Poll, 17 July 1865. Winter: E Main with M Schocher and C Schnitzler, 6 Feb 1896

When approaching along the Bellavista terrace, this well-known peak appears as a rocky 'Aiguille' on the skyline. It is this aspect that has made it a small 'motif' of the Bernina range and it is often found on postcards from the area. It is in fact a fairly narrow fin, with a 600m S face and a short, but steep, icy wall to the N. There are tempting views of the surrounding greater peaks yet their very presence makes the overall panorama somewhat limited. Apart from the classic E and W ridges, the rock on the mountain is poor and other routes are almost never climbed. The S face is AD (III). When the temperatures are low and conditions icy, the N face provides an interesting mixed climb. Several lines are possible between the rocky ribs but an obvious rightward-slanting gully reaches the summit directly (c200m: D) The proximity of the Marco e Rosa hut means that a short climb on this peak can easily be followed by an ascent of, for example, the Bernina on the next day.

106 WEST RIDGE

PD First ascent party

187

The normal route and clearly visible from the Marco e Rosa hut. Unless very dry, the climbing tends to be mixed on the lower half of the ridge. Although not especially interesting, the ascent is short and usually quite straightforward. Short sections of II.

From the hut curve around the head of the Fuorcla Crast' Aguzza, then slant up the glacier to reach a terrace on the W ridge, just below the first short steep step. This can be climbed just L of the crest (III) but it is normally turned on the R via a system of ledges. Above, mixed climbing on the ridge leads to a snowy shoulder. Broken rocks are now followed, turning any obstacles on the L, along the gently rising crest that leads to the summit. c200m: 2hr from the hut

107 EAST RIDGE

AD– E Burckhardt with P Egger and H Grass; early Aug 1874

187

The E to W traverse of the peak is a classic, with the ascent providing a highly recommended little rock route. The ridge in question falls to the N of the Fuorcla da l'Argient and forms the L boundary of the icy N face.

Just short of the Fuorcla da l'Argient, reached in 40 min from the Marco e Rosa hut, cross the rimaye and climb a steep ice slope to below the E face. Start just R of centre and climb up for two pitches to reach the L end of a large scree/snow terrace, slanting down from the E ridge. Scramble up R to the crest of the ridge. So far the rock has been a little dubious but it now improves and the crest is climbed directly, in a splendid position, until a small shoulder is reached (III/IV–). Above lies a bulging nose of rock. Turn this on the S side by following an obvious ledge for 20m, until a slabby line of weakness leads back onto the crest above the steep section. An exposed and knife-edged rocky crest leads up to the summit. c180m: 2hr, 3½hr back to the Marco e Rosa hut

Fuorcla da l'Argient 3705m

L Bombardieri with C Folatti and P Mitta, 25 July 1933

Lying between the Crast'Aguzza and Piz Argient, this col is easily reached, via relatively steep snow slopes, from the 'piste' leading to the Marco e Rosa hut. The Italian side is an impressive, rectilinear snow/ice couloir.

108 **SOUTH COULOIR**
D–/D
182

Climbed during the first traverse of the col but rarely attempted since. Early in the season a good coating of névé should extend to within 100-150m from the top. Thereafter the couloir steepens and will undoubtedly be icy. It should, however, present little serious problem to competent parties. 400m

Piz Argient 3945m

Seiler and Seldeneck with C Grass, J Walther and a chamois hunter, 1869. Climbed in winter: Jan 1905

Although the fourth highest in the range, it is not as popular a goal as many of the surrounding peaks. The Swiss side presents a gentle aspect, with beautiful sweeping snowy curves leading to a shimmering summit dome. The S side is a huge precipice of red rock – one of the biggest in the range. The mountain is best traversed in conjunction with the Zupo to give a magnificent, yet entirely straightforward, high-altitude expedition.

109 **NORTH-NORTH-WEST RIDGE**
PD–
184

Most parties will make a traverse of the peak and the preferred direction is from the Fuorcla da l'Argient to the Fuorcla dal Zupo. The ascent of the NNW ridge is a straightforward snow climb.

Reach the Fuorcla da l'Argient in c40min from the Marco e Rosa hut or 4hr from the Diavolezza. A broad crevassed slope leads up to a sort of saddle, which lies to the S of the snow boss marked 3825m. The ridge narrows and is sometimes corniced but generally leads, without further difficulty, to the summit. There is an impressive view, over the wide expanses of the Scerscen glacier far below, to the Disgrazia Massif. c250m: 1-1½hr from the Marco e Rosa hut

110 **NORTH-EAST RIDGE**
F+ First ascent party
184

This broad and gentle snow crest, rising from the Fuorcla dal Zupo (3851m), gives the easiest route to the summit. It can be descended in c10min. c100m: 15-20 min, 1½hr from Marco e Rosa hut. See also photograph 177

111 **SOUTH RIDGE**
TD–
177

In common with most of the great walls on the Italian side of the frontier ridge, the imposing S face of this peak, on closer inspection, is composed of rather dubious rock. The sole exception appears to be the crest of the long S ridge, whose base, just above the Fellaria glacier, is marked by Pt 3213m. The original route (Bonacossa and Rossi 1909) reached the upper part of the ridge via unpleasant climbing on the SE flanks and cannot be recommended. A direct ascent, which follows the crest more or less throughout, was made on the 11th August 1944 (Negri and partner. First winter ascent: A Marini and G Maspes, Feb 1993). This route has been repeated from time to time and found to be very worthwhile, with good rock and interesting climbing (moves of IV+ to V+ in the upper half of the route). The start can be reached in 1½hr from the Marinelli hut. Unfortunately, a detailed description is lacking, making this a suitable and recommended goal for more adventurous alpinists. 700m: 6-9hr

Piz Zupo 3995m

L Enderlin and Serardi with Badrutt, a chamois hunter, 9 July 1863. Winter: E Main with M Schocher and C Schnitzler, 19 Feb 1896

The second highest summit in the Massif and for many years considered one of the Alpine ‘four thousanders’. The name is Romansche and means ‘Hidden Peak’. On the Swiss side it is a most beautiful sight, even though it rises but a short distance above the glacial slopes to the N. A traverse of the frontier crest is irresistible and can be accomplished in either direction but is best taken from W to E, preferably in conjunction with the Piz Argient. The icy W face can be climbed directly to the summit (150m: PD/PD+, 1-1½hr) but is not considered as worthwhile as an ascent by one of the ridges.

112 **SOUTH-WEST RIDGE**
F+ First ascent party
184

This is the easiest route from the Swiss side. A delightful little climb which, though perfectly straightforward, can sometimes be corniced in the lower section. See also photographs 177, 186

The ascent to the Fuorcla is easy and takes c1hr from the Marco e Rosa hut or 4hr from the Diavolezza via the Bellavista terrace. The ridge above has a sobering drop on the Italian side but can be climbed slightly L of the crest, between snow and rock, for most of its length. c150m from the col: 30min

113 **NORTH-NORTH-WEST RIDGE**
PD−
185 D Freshfield with H Devouassoud, 14 Aug 1871

*This rises as a narrow and mainly rocky crest from the Pass dal Zupo. It provides the normal route from the Italian side.
See also photograph 184*

From the Pass dal Zupo the rocky crest finally gives way to a sharp and exposed snow ridge leading to the summit. c150m: 45min-1hr, 30-40min in descent

The complete Argient – Zupo traverse will take 2-2½hr from Fuorcla da l'Argient to Pass dal Zupo or vice versa (PD). In the event of the northern slopes below the Pass dal Zupo being in bad condition, it may be wise to make the easy descent to the Altipiano di Fellaria and return over the Fuorcla Bellavista.

114 **SOUTH-EAST RIDGE**
PD+ D Marinelli with H Grass and B Pedranzini, 4 Aug 1880
185

*A very worthwhile rock climb on the largely unfrequented Italian side of the peak. It can, however, be approached with equal ease from either the Diavolezza or Marinelli hut. The nearest shelter is the Pansera bivouac hut, 20-30 min from the start of the climb.
See also photograph 177*

From the Marinelli hut follow Route 116 towards the Pass dal Zupo, bearing L in an arc to reach the foot of the ridge at 3600m (3hr). This same point can be reached from the Diavolezza by crossing the Fuorcla Bellavista and traversing the head of the Altipiano (3½hr in good conditions). Climb up on to the ridge via a steep ice slope, 50-60m high. The crest above gives enjoyable climbing with pitches of II/III–. This section ends at a snowy shoulder above which the ridge becomes more broken and leads without further difficulty to the summit. 400m: 2½hr

Pass dal Zupo 3840m

First traverse: F Tuckett and E Buxton with F Biner, P Jenny and C Michel, 28 July 1864

Not to be confused with the Fuorcla of the same name, this col is the lowest point on the frontier ridge between Piz Zupo and the Bellavista. Although an easy ascent on the Italian side, to the N a steep slope of rock and ice falls more than 120m to the glacier. The pass is normally reached by parties traversing the Bellavista or Zupo.

115 **SWISS SIDE**

PD/PD+ From the Diavolezza follow Route H14 towards the Marco e Rosa hut. When past the western end of the Bellavista terrace, head up to the rimaye directly below the col. Crossing this chasm can sometimes be quite awkward and the slope above, climbed just L of a loose rocky rib, is at least 40°. c4½hr

116 **ITALIAN SIDE**

F+

185 From the Marinelli hut follow Route H16 as far as the Passo di Sasso Rosso, then curve round to the L and head NW up the gentle slopes of the Altipiano. Finally, a short but steep snow/ice slope leads to the col. 3½-4hr. See also photographs 177, 186

Bellavista 3922m

E Burckhardt with H Grass, 10 Sept 1868

The name refers to an almost horizontal snow crest connecting four separate tops, with the highest point located at the western end. Fairly gentle snow slopes drop less than 200m to a huge terrace on the N side – a plateau that gives easy access to the peaks close to the Marco e Rosa hut. To the S a broken rock wall, steeper but of similar height, falls to the vast expanse of the Altipiano di Fellaria.

The mountain is usually traversed from E to W and offers a panoramic view that certainly lives up to its name.

117 **TRAVERSE**

PD– First ascent party

184

An excellent and popular introduction to high-altitude mountaineering. It is a straightforward, though lengthy, expedition culminating in an easy walk along a broad ridge. Highly recommended to fit parties with some experience of glacier crossings, who are otherwise relatively new to the game. Although equally feasible from Switzerland or Italy, few parties appear to use the southern approach. See also photographs 186, 187

From the Fuorcla Bellavista, climb the large triangular snow face to the first summit (3804m) and continue over the snowy tops of 3888m and 3892m to the final rocky point. Descend the crest easily in 15 min, on sound rock, to the Pass dal Zupo, then go down the S flank and walk back along the top of the Altipiano to the Fuorcla Bellavista. Parties often continue the traverse over the Zupo, which is generally easier than descending the steep slopes to the N of the Pass. 2hr for the traverse

Fuorcla Bellavista 3688m

First traverse: E Cooke, Hartman and S Hoole with P Jenny, A and J Walther, 15 July 1864

This broad glacier-pass, between the Bellavista and the W peak of Piz Palu, provides the easiest crossing point on the frontier ridge in this part of the range. Although the southern approaches are not so popular, there is normally, throughout the summer months, a well defined trench on the Swiss side.

118a **SWISS SIDE VIA FORTEZZA RIDGE**

PD–

187

At the time of writing this is the only route used during the summer months and is normally reached from the Diavolezza hotel. There are a number of possible approaches to the ridge, depending on the state of the Pers glacier. In theory, the quickest involves following the path from the hotel, taking the first fork on the L down to the glacier. Cross the glacier to the SW and climb the snow slope, just L of the rocks of the Rifugi dals Chamuotschs, to the crest of the ridge. Alternatively, it is possible to keep lower down when crossing the glacier and climb the slopes on the R of these rocks. Both these approaches run into problems if the L(W) bank of the glacier is badly crevassed.

Recently this has been the case and little, if any, time has been gained over a more straightforward ascent from the Isla Persa. See also photographs 192, 194

Descend the main path to the glacier (ignoring the first L fork) and cross it to the Isla Persa, where there is water and covered bivouac sites amongst the rocks. Now climb the easy slopes and the broad snow ridge above to the rock buttress of the Fortezza. Climb this on the R flank, via a short steep nose of rock (II) and more broken ground (with another little section of I/II), to join the ridge just below the top. Continue S up the rounded snowy ridge to the start of the Bellavista Terrace. Cross a slope on the L to the pass. c3hr from the Diavolezza: 2-2½hr in reverse

118b
PD– *The approach from the Boval hut is well marked, but longer and not often used. However, some parties choose to descend by this route and continue the walk down to Morteratsch, as this avoids a tiring re-ascent to the Diavolezza at the end of the day.*

From the hut, follow the path S along the crest of the moraine. After about 30min it descends on to the glacier. Cross the dry glacier in a wide arc to the L and reach the moraine on the far side. Follow it N for a short distance to where it splits around a fine lake in the ablation valley. Either path can be taken as they unite beyond the lake and zigzag up alongside a small stream, first E, then SE to the crest of the Isla Persa (c2hr) Halfway up the slope, a fine stone 'house' under a rock wall on the L could provide a comfortable bivouac. Join the previous route and continue over the Fortezza to the Fuorcla (c4hr from the hut: 2½hr in descent). 'Short cuts' to the Bellavista terrace, via the Foura in the upper part of the Morteratsch glacier, have become both complex and dangerous.

119 ITALIAN SIDE

F+/PD–
174

From the Marinelli hut follow Route H16 as far as the Passo di Sasso Rosso (3hr). To the N lies the white expanse of the Altipiano, almost reminiscent of an Arctic ice cap. Cross it, rising gently at the end, to the col. 4-4½hr from the hut: 3hr in descent

Piz Varuna 3453m

A large, glaciated outlier to the SE of the Altipiano and well-seen from the Palu-Bellavista crest. The summit is an outstanding viewpoint but, being a little off the beaten track, is seldom visited.

120 **WEST RIDGE**
PD–
189

This rises gently from the Passo di Gembre (c3236m) and is usually climbed via the slopes on the N flank, in 1hr. The lower W summit can either be climbed or avoided as desired. The pass is easily reached from the Passo di Sasso Rosso, by heading E down the glacier until a broad snow ridge, leading SE along the frontier, descends to the foot of the W ridge (30-40min). This same point can be reached more directly from the Bignami hut in less than 3hr, via the Fellaria Orientale glacier. The icefall must be circumvented on the extreme R up against the flanks of the Cima Val Fontana, and can sometimes be complicated and not a little dangerous. At present it is straightforward and the gradient not too steep.

Cima Val Fontana 3070m

An easy peak to the NE of the Bignami hut. It can be reached from the Passo Confinale (2628m) via the E ridge in 1hr; or from the W, via an ascent of the Felleria Orientale glacier to c2700m (below the icefall), then a climb up the flanks of the mountain to reach the ridge N of the summit (F+). 2hr from the hut

Sasso Rosso 3481m and 3546m

This is hardly a summit but more of a long rocky crest descending from the pass of the same name. The highest point carries the Pansera bivouac shelter and is less than 10 min from the pass. Pt 3481m is easily reached along the rocky ridge or from the snow slopes to the N. The SW ridge, above Pt 3014m, is a steep and very fine scramble. It is easily reached from the Bignami hut and clears quickly after bad weather, providing suitable compensation for those parties thwarted by poor conditions on the higher peaks. c500m: PD, 4-5hr from the hut

Cima Quinto Alpin 3333m

This is the name given locally to the rocky point above the Passo Marinelli W. The S face was climbed by N Battista and N Celso on 16 Aug 1980 to produce an accessible little climb. 200m: III/IV, 2½hr

Punta Marinelli 3182m

First recorded ascent: E Strutt with J Pollinger, June 1909

A very popular little peak just E of the hut. It is normally traversed but the quickest way off from the summit is to descend an easy couloir on the E face.

121 **TRAVERSE**

PD

174

This is best taken from S to N. The S ridge, which begins from the snowy saddle to the N of the Cima Felleria (3080m), is rather jagged and gives interesting climbing with moves of II/II+. The descent of the N ridge is an easy scramble (2½hr round trip from the hut). The traverse of the Cima Felleria from the Bocchetta di Caspoggio can also be included – it is an easy scramble which adds less than an hour to the overall expedition.

122 **SOUTH-WEST FACE**

II/III A Bonacossa and C Prochownik, 26 Aug 1910

This short but enjoyable outing takes a direct line to the summit, with the best climbing occurring in the upper section. c200m: 1hr

Punta 2940m

Lying to the NW of the Bignami hut and approached across grassy slopes, the SSW pillar of this small peak gives a recommended route of 200m. Not sustained, V+/VI

Cime di Musella

The jagged, rocky crest S of the Marinelli hut contains 4 distinct summits that can be climbed separately or linked together to form a fine traverse. The walls and ridges now contain a whole host of short rock routes generally on sound gneiss. The low altitude allows climbing to take place when the conditions are poor or the weather too uncertain for an attempt on one of the major peaks. For this reason the summits are very popular and routes on the S faces are often climbed well outside the summer season. Several routes are now briefly mentioned, and further details are available at the hut:-

Cima di Caspoggio 3136m: The NNE ridge from the Bocchetta is reasonably easy and highly recommended (45min). The NW couloir gives a nice little snow and ice route, early in the season, after a night of hard frost (1hr). The easiest descent is down the E flank via a couloir.

Musella Orientale 3079m: The NW wall, climbed in 1942, gives a worthwhile outing (IV/V), but especially recommended is the obvious 'Red Dièdre' on the N face, climbed in 1980 (150m: IV/V). On the S face, 'Marino 40' (200m: V+) and the 'Nana 1983 variant' (VI/A2 or VII free) are particularly good.

Musella Centrale 3088m: This, the highest of the summits, is usually reached via a straightforward ascent of the E ridge (1½hr from the hut). The NNE ridge gives a good route, first climbed in 1911 (III: 1hr).

Musella Occidentale 3094m: the complete W ridge, starting from the gap with Pt 2744m gives an interesting route (II/III–: 2-2½hr from the hut). The S wall has a number of hard routes dating from 1940.

The first complete traverse, from W to E, was made in 1903 (5-8hr round trip, III/IV not sustained).

Sasso Moro 3108m

This massive rocky pyramid, which can look very impressive when viewed from certain directions, lies N of the huge reservoirs at Campo Moro. It is most easily climbed from the Bignami hut via the slopes to the R of the NE ridge, finishing directly on snow. It is even more straightforward from the Forcella di Fellaria (2819m), walking up the corridor to the L of the NNE ridge and finishing up gentle snowslopes (F+: 1-1½hr). This summit offers one of the finest panoramic views in the area and is well worth a visit.

Piz Scalino 3323m

A team of surveyors working on a Lombardy map project, 1830

This isolated high-point lies well to the S of the main chain and, although there is a hut close at hand, it can be easily climbed in a day from Campo Moro. The summit is a most attractive triangular rock pyramid, well-seen from the main resorts of Chiesa and Caspoggio. The N face is impressive, has rarely been climbed and would give a hard mixed route in the right conditions. The NE face above the Scalino glacier gives a nice little mixed climb and similar comments apply to the well-defined N ridge to the R. All the other ascents are quite straightforward. In winter/spring the peak becomes a classic goal for the ski-mountaineer, with a long and superb run back to the road. As an early season training climb or for alpinists new to the game, this is an ideal choice. As a viewpoint for the neighbouring mountain ranges, especially the Disgrazia, it is quite unique.

123 NORMAL ROUTE VIA NORTHERN GLACIER

F+/PD−

190

From the parking spot at the Campo Moro dam reach the Zoia hut in a couple of min and follow Route H17 to the chalets of Alpe Campagneda (2145m). Follow the main path E to the lakes (Pt 2276m). Now head SE to where tracks in the steep scree slopes lead up to a small depression in the N ridge, below the steep upper section, and S of a rocky hummock called 'Il Cornetto' (2848m). This point can also be reached directly from the Cristina hut by crossing marshy ground below the N face. The depression gives instant access to the magnificent Scalino glacier. Follow it S, at a gentle gradient, to the crest of the SE ridge and scramble up this, over broken rock, to the summit cross. 1300m of ascent and 4½-5½hr from Campo Moro. From the lakes mentioned above it is possible to continue on the path, which is in fact part of the Alte Via, all the way to the Passo Campagneda, and climb up the Scalino glacier from its base. Although longer, this avoids the arduous toil up the steep scree.

Peaks further W in this chain offer pleasant walking in summer and some good N-facing mixed lines in winter/spring.

Piz Palu 3905m

First ascent of E peak: probably M and P Flury and O Heer with G Colani and J Madutz, 12 Aug 1835. W and Central peaks: K Digby with P Jenny and a porter, 1866. Winter: (E peak) W Bulpett and R Wainewright, 24 Feb 1890. (Central peak) W Bulpett and E Main with M Schocher and M Weibel, 20 Feb 1891

Parties arriving at the Diavolezza are rewarded by some truly memorable views. The centre piece is undoubtedly the Palu. Seen from this angle, its graceful architecture is considered by many to be amongst the most beautiful sights in the Alps and the famous profile, of three almost perfectly aligned pillars, has featured prominently in several well-known cinematic productions. There are three summits – the W (3823m) and Central (highest) peaks lie on the frontier, while the E peak (3882m) stands entirely in Switzerland. It is the most frequented mountain in the Bernina range and on a fine Sunday during August can receive more than 150 ascents. The reasons for this are simple. Access via the téléphérique obviates the need to make a long and tiring hut walk. The ascent presents little technical difficulty and generally involves following a well-defined trench. Finally, to reach these attractive summits requires crossing sweeping snow crests, which provide a fine example of classic Alpine terrain.

124 **EAST RIDGE**
PD Part of the route described was followed by the first ascent party of
191 the E peak

This is the most popular route and a superb introduction to high-altitude climbing for parties who have gained some experience with axe and crampons. Depending on the weather during the previous winter, the summit ridge can sport some magnificent cornices which, in the past, have caught out the unwary. See also photograph 192

Follow Route 136 towards the Fuorcla Pers-Palu until the glacier levels out at c3200m. The main trench now continues up the long slopes above, eventually working R to reach a small col at the base of the E ridge of the mountain above Pt 3731m. Two steep rope-lengths on the crest lead to a point where the gradient eases. The crest becomes narrower and may well be corniced, so if in doubt keep to the L! A broad dome of snow, with a few rocks to the S and a superb view across the Altipiano, marks the E top (4-4½hr).

Go down the easy slope in front to a wide saddle then climb the ridge, which becomes much narrower and leads to the highest point (30min). 900m of ascent from the Diavolezza

It is wise to reflect, at this point, on the fate of 9 climbers who posed for a group photograph on the summit cornice. . . .

125 **WEST RIDGE**
PD First ascent party of main summit
192

Sometimes climbed up and down by parties returning from the Marco e Rosa hut but generally used to effect the classic traverse of the three peaks. See also photographs 184, 186

From the Fuorcla Bellavista walk up to the base of the ridge and climb the rocky crest, which gives delightful easy scrambling on sound rock. The W peak (Piz Spinas) is gained in 30min. Continue down the ridge, which is rocky at first, to reach the narrow snow crest between the two peaks. Climb easily up the broadening snow ridge to the main summit (30min, 1hr from the Fuorcla). Cornices are usually far less of a threat on this section.

126 **TRAVERSE**
PD Georg, Wachtler and Wallner with C and H Grass, 22 July 1868

A magnificent expedition in either direction. As it is generally attempted from the Diavolezza, parties seem to be divided into two schools of thought. Most favour an E to W traverse. This has the advantage of less height gain and allows the snow bridges of the normal route to be crossed while still frozen. It also has the easiest way off (down the Fortezza ridge) at the end of the day. Others feel that in snowy conditions the crossing of the Pers glacier in the afternoon is hard work and the steep re-ascent to the Diavolezza extremely tedious. Of course, those with no need to return to their starting point can continue straight down the Isla Persa to the Morteratsch glacier. An ascent of the Fortezza ridge is certainly longer, and in recent summers the Pers glacier has remained 'dry' up to c3000m, making the question of an afternoon crossing largely academic. 8hr round trip from the Diavolezza

Though rarely done this way, the traverse can also be completed from the Marinelli hut by reaching the Fuorcla Pers-Palu. 11hr round trip

127 **GREATER TRAVERSE**
AD+/D− *The E to W traverse can be continued over the Bellavista by fitter and more ambitious alpinists. This adds about 3hr to the expedition. The most popular scenario is for parties to finish the day by walking across to the Marco e Rosa hut (c8½hr from the Diavolezza) from where, the following morning, they can attempt the Bernina. The complete traverse*

of the Frontier ridge as far as the Crast' Aguzza and descent to the Marco e Rosa hut, was first done before the turn of the century. This sort of excursion highlights the very best that the range has to offer and will take 13-15hr. Due to its length the high overall grade seems appropriate.

128 **SOUTH BUTTRESS**
PD First descended by E Heinzelmann, E Imhof and A Ludwig,
174 10 Aug 1897

Although infreqently climbed, it does give the shortest route from the Marinelli hut to the main summit. As the face gets a lot of sun the slopes can often be bare and icy. However, it is worth knowing that in reasonable snow conditions, a party surprised by bad weather could descend to the shelter of the Pansera bivouac hut in 1hr.

The buttress protrudes into the upper part of the Altipiano and is well defined. In its lower section it forms a broad snowy ridge with a rocky toe. Work up the glacier to the L of this toe then climb the 40° snow/ice slope onto the broad crest. The steep shattered rock above is easy but needs careful handling (1½-2½hr from the Pansera hut; 4½hr from Marinelli). A spur which is longer, but of similar character and difficulty, descends from the main ridge about 200m E of the E summit, at a point where the gradient changes. c250m: 5½hr from Marinelli hut to E Peak

129 **NORTH-NORTH-EAST FACE OF EAST PEAK**
D–/D A Bedetti, R Soresini and M Zappa, 29 Sept 1963
191

A convoluted ice face L of the N Spur. The risk of ice fall from the central sérac barrier is obvious and, together with the difficulties met in overcoming this obstacle, will vary from year to year. The slope above is quite steep and can sometimes have a tricky corniced exit directly onto the summit. c550m: 3-5hr

130 **NORTH SPUR OF EAST PEAK**
AD+/ M Von Kuffner with A Burgener and M Schocher, 22 Aug 1899.
D– Winter: R Coatti, R Soresini, M Zappa and R Zocchi, 26 Jan 1964
191

The easiest of the three great pillars yet aesthetically the most appealing. Although the difficulties are not great, they are fairly sustained at III/III+ on the rock buttress. Above, the perfectly defined 'snow' ridge can be relatively straightforward in good névé, but quite time-consuming and more serious if icy. On the very crest of the buttress the rock is basically sound and there are some enjoyable pitches over huge rough blocks and flakes. However, on the flanks it can range from poor to downright abysmal! For this reason the quality of the climbing fails to match the sheer magnificence of the line. The average angle is surprisingly low and height is gained slowly, making the route feel far longer than its vertical interval would suggest. Once committed there is no escape and the exposed position, high above the Pers glacier, provides a sober atmosphere. However, for those parties competent at the standard it offers a superb introduction to alpine 'Grandes Courses'.

Although the spur can be climbed from its foot, the approach can be dangerous and the climbing loose and unpleasant. It is rarely done, nor indeed is it recommended. Instead, follow the normal route to above the icefall, and where the gradient eases, traverse SW along a glacial shelf above the rocky rognon that contains Pt 3146m. The last section might be threatened by a large sérac fall from high on the L but the risk seems slight and the danger area can be crossed in a minute or two. Avoiding what appear to be easier possibilities to the L, climb directly up the steep loose rock to the crest of the ridge. It is recommended that parties now try to climb as close to the crest as possible and not be seduced by 'promising' excursions along the flanks. At half-height, a steep tower blocks progress and it is necessary to follow the obvious yellow break on the L side of the ridge. After a rope-length the angle eases and a return should be made to the crest. In the upper section, most parties will be forced to climb the E flank until a few pitches of easy broken ground eventually merge with the ice crest. This is 6 full rope-lengths, 40°, and in a splendid position guaranteed to concentrate the mind. The top can sometimes be corniced and has, on rare occasions, provided the technical crux. With relief, pull abruptly onto the flat summit. c580m: 5-6hr for the climb, 7½-8½hr from the Diavolezza

131 **NORTH COULOIR**
TD– W Dobiasch and O Feutl, 15 May 1931. Winter: A Bedetti,
191 G Noseda-Pedraglio, V Meroni and M Zappa, 18 March 1962

A steep contorted hanging glacier sandwiched between the E and Central spurs. Understandably it has had relatively few ascents though parties, having found the route in a safe and stable condition, comment on the continuously interesting and varied climbing when weaving a line through and around the huge labyrinth of ice walls. Difficulties are normally not great but the hazardous nature of the enterprise is reflected in the overall grading. At present, an ascent will be exposed to the threat of snow and ice avalanches from the numerous séracs, and also rock fall from the flanks of the spurs. It is best attempted very early in the season when heavy snow will blanket crevasses and short ice walls. The climb should start very early – during a night of hard frost. Prior inspection is essential to determine whether the route is justifiable – the choice is yours! 700m: Generally 50°-55°: 5-6hr

132 **NORTH SPUR OF CENTRAL PEAK – BUMILLERGRAT**
TD H Bumiller with J Gross, C Schnitzler and M Schocher, 1 Sept
192 1887. Winter: P Nava, A Pizzocolo and V Taldo, 26 Jan 1964

Technically, this is perhaps the most difficult of the three pillars though, conversely, it is the least sustained throughout its length. The lower buttress is avoided by easier, though potentially dangerous snow slopes to the R but above, a 350m section of steep rock topped by a huge ice cliff provides a formidable barrier! The first ascent party avoided this by climbing delicate mixed ground on the L flank and, finding perfect conditions, completed the route in 6hr – a sensational achievement for that period. Nowadays, this central section is climbed direct making the route the finest mixed climb in the whole Bernina range. Fairly dry conditions are recommended as the rock will be free from ice and the upper snow slopes well consolidated. Once on the spur, the climb is objectively safe but the approach should be completed shortly after dawn, and the previous night should be cold. Ascents are quite regular and the rock is well pegged, so take only a small selection of nuts and several ice-screws for the sérac-wall. If the easier variations are taken the grade is reduced to D/TD–. See also photograph 191

Leave the Diavolezza and descend the path to the Pers glacier (possible bivouac sites), taking the first fork to the L after 100m. Cross the glacier, and keeping well out from the foot of the spur (below Pt 3168m), reach the couloir on the R (1½hr). Climb over rimayes and up steep slopes for 250m until it is possible to slant L up an easier-angled snowfield to the ridge. Most of this section is exposed to serious ice avalanches from the various sérac barriers that threaten the whole length of the couloir. The ridge is gained above the lower rock buttress at a prominent snow crest, that rises gently to the base of the second steep rock step (1½-2hr).

Go up easily to the base of this step. The next five pitches provide the crux and although the rock is not perfect, it is certainly very good. Keeping just slightly L of the crest, climb a grey slab (35m: IV+), then a succession of flakes for two pitches (IV) to a conspicuous overhang. Climb this and the dièdre above (IV+) to a small hole perforating the crest of the ridge. Traverse L and climb a yellow corner back onto the crest (V–). Continue up the crest for five pitches (III, becoming more mixed) to the ice bulge. From the base of the grey slab it is possible to traverse L across the E flank on an obvious break, and climb mixed ground and icy runnels back onto the ridge, 2-3 pitches below the ice bulge. This is much easier but the rock is poor and protection hard to arrange. The ice wall can usually be bypassed by an exposed, two-pitch traverse across the E flank but in dry conditions bare rock slabs make this quite tricky. At the time of writing a direct ascent is quite feasible (c30m: maximum angle 75°). The slopes above seem almost flat by comparison but concentration should be maintained, as the route is not quite over yet! In good conditions the summit can be reached in 30min. c750m: 7½-9½hr from the Diavolezza

133 **NORTH-EAST FACE OF WEST PEAK**

TD–/ I Dell'Avo and P Corti, 2 Aug 1939

TD

191

The tumbling hanging glacier that lies wholly to the R of the Central spur displays, not far below the exit, a most impressive and almost totally unbroken, sérac wall. In 1930, F Devantay with J Gotte and S Rahmi took a similar start to that used in Route 132 then continued R on moderate slopes to reach the R-hand end of the sérac barrier, not far from Piz Spinas. Turning the barrier, they reached the easy-angled terrace above and followed it L to the Central summit. This is an illogical line which, not surprisingly, has seen few repetitions. Nine years later the R side of the hanging glacier – a narrow couloir between the lower séracs and the rocky triangle on the L flank of the W Spur – was climbed to reach the plain snow slopes, leading directly to the summit of Piz Spinas. With a good covering of consolidated névé a safer line may be found over the rocks further R and several variations have been recorded. Otherwise, the first half of the climb is seriously exposed to ice fall and there can be one or two mixed pitches and narrow icy runnels up to 60°-65° before reaching the upper slopes. A hard frost is clearly desirable, making this route an obvious target for a winter/spring ascent. c650m: 5-7hr

134 **NORTH SPUR OF WEST PEAK**

TD– J Burton-Alexander with F Grass and C Zippert, 31 July 1899.

191 Winter: R Coatti, M Curnis, V Quarenghi, R Soresini and M Zappa, 5 Jan 1964

This graceful, rectilinear crest completes the great trilogy. It is climbed a good deal less than the other two, though in perfect conditions it is easier than the Central Spur. It is primarily a classic snow and ice climb with a

little mixed ground in the central section. A good covering of well-frozen névé is desirable, though strangely, this happens infrequently. Often, when excellent conditions are found low down, the upper crest can present a layer of powder snow overlaying ice. The rock, in general, is rather poor and in dry conditions the climb not only becomes unsafe and poorly protected but also considerably harder than anything else on the mountain. Although snow conditions are known to have been better at the turn of the century than they are today, this was still a most impressive ascent for the era. The best descent is down the W ridge but in snowy conditions this can be quite time-consuming. Instead, parties have followed the E ridge almost down to the lowest point between the W and Central summits, from where a short steep snow slope leads quickly down to the Altipiano. It is an easy walk from here back across the Fuorcla Bellavista.

Starting from the Diavolezza, follow Route 132 down to the Pers glacier and reach the foot of the spur in 1½hr. An obvious long and narrow snow couloir splits the lower section. Climb it in its entirety and reach the steep rocky section of the ridge above, at about half height on the spur. The next section, although short, is somewhat steeper. Climb straight up on broken rock and cracked slabs, keeping more or less on the crest (III; mixed), to the base of the sharp snow ridge. This is 300m high and gradually steepens all the way to the summit. 650m: 6-9hr, 7½-10½hr from the Diavolezza

135 **NORTH-WEST FACE OF WEST PEAK**
D+ I Dell'Avo, N and P Corti, 31 July 1939
191

Direct access to the ice face R of the W spur is barred by an enormous sérac. Above and slightly to the R is a second sérac, which at the time of writing looks quite menacing. The route in question turns the first barrier on the R and quickly comes back above it to climb the final, plain and objectively safe, ice slope to a logical exit on to the W ridge. The climbing is clearly more straightforward than either the spur or the NE face and although the start is threatened by ice fall the time spent in the danger area is short and, overall, the route is less dangerous than the NE face. The safest line of ascent would be to climb the initial couloir of the W Spur and after 150-200m slant R into the middle of the face, above the first sérac barrier. Whichever start is chosen, this is a route of classic status, medium difficulty and very much in the traditional mould. 550m: 5hr. See also photograph 192

Fuorcla Pers-Palu 3457m

First recorded traverse: E Strutt with J Pollinger, 1 July 1908

The lowest point on the watershed between Piz Cambrena and Piz Palu. It can be reached from the Marinelli hut in c5hr by crossing the Altipiano and climbing a short snow couloir to the col. However, this is very rarely done and the pass is commonly reached from the N by parties en route to the Cambrena. Most of the approach is identical to the normal route on Piz Palu and there is usually a well defined 'trench', obviating any need to exercise route-finding ability!

136 **WEST SIDE**

PD– First ascent party

192

From the Diavolezza walk SE along the crest of the ridge, finally descending a short rocky step to a col just W of Saas Queder (or use the snow slope above the short ski-tows on the L flank of the ridge). The path crosses scree and boulders to reach another col between Saas Queder and Piz Trovat. Just down to the E are flat, though uncovered, bivouac sites, which provide alternative accommodation to the expensive hotel. Water can normally be found lower down in a hollow.

The path continues up and around the NE flank of Piz Trovat, crossing a projecting spur to reach the Fuorcla Trovat at 3019m. Descend a steep path to the R and reach the glacier. Most parties aim to arrive here by dawn and will take about 1hr to cover this stretch in the dark. Walk across the flat Pers glacier and descend into a shallow hollow to reach the start of the cirque coming down from the Fuorcla Pers-Palu. The track normally keeps out from the rocks of the Cambrena and slants R up steep slopes. Go through a complicated icefall, where there can be some monstrous crevasses and weird snow bridges though, in general, negligible threat from falling debris. At c3200m the glacier bay becomes almost level. Plod up the long slopes above, leaving the main track which heads off R towards the Palu, and slant up L to the large rimaye below the col. Cross the rimaye and climb a short steep snow slope (sometimes hard bare ice) directly to the Fuorcla. 3½hr from the Diavolezza. See also photographs 191, 194

Piz Cambrena 3604m

Probably Cruzemann with G Colani, 5 Aug 1863

The last major peak on the main watershed. Situated entirely in Switzerland at the SE corner of the Pers glacier, the double summit is formed by a conspicuous rounded 'calotte' perched above a steep rocky N wall. The eastern snow dome is the highest point. The mountain is a popular ascent from the Diavolezza either by the classic E to W traverse or via the famous 'Eisnase'. In recent summers all the various ice/mixed routes on the N side have dried out and look most unattractive. Due to their ease of access (by téléphérique) they are obvious targets for winter and spring ascents.

137 **SOUTH-SOUTH-WEST RIDGE**
PD– H Cordier and F Delaborde with K Maurer, 2 Sept 1876
192

The easiest route to the summit but normally used in descent to complete a fine traverse of the mountain. A short ascent from the Fuorcla Pers-Palu. See also photograph 194

From the Diavolezza reach the Fuorcla by Route 136. Walk along the easy rounded snow ridge to the steeper broken rocks below the summit calotte. Scramble up these to the gentle snow slopes above. Keeping slightly on the W side, walk up a short distance to the highest point. 30min: 4hr from the Diavolezza

138 **BY TRAVERSE OF PIZ D'ARLAS – NORTH RIDGE**
PD+
194 Possibly Cruzemann and Colani but generally attributed to E Burckhardt with H Grass, 13 Sept 1868

The rocky twin-summits of the Piz d'Arlas are seldom climbed for their own sake. As a means of ascent to the Cambrena, this classic traverse provides a delightfully varied expedition, once the initial scree-slog has been mastered, and can easily be continued to the summit of the Palu. It is the most popular route to the Cambrena and for those with a little experience of non-technical Alpine peaks, it provides an ideal introduction to the next stage in their careers. At first the rock is poor and the ascent rather tedious, but persevere – once past the N summit things improve dramatically! Difficulties are the same in either direction so this is a favourite means of descent for parties completing routes on the N face. See also photographs 192, 195

From the Diavolezza follow Route 136 to the Fuorcla Trovat. It is possible to continue SE along the crest to the foot of the NW ridge of Piz d'Arlas but normally, parties descend on to the Pers glacier and walk up the L side to the same point. A huge buttress marks the start of the ridge and is turned on the R. Easy rock leads back on to the crest some way above the top of the buttress. Now toil up steep scree slopes (traces of a path) or, early in the season, snow. Reach a final rocky section. Climb it (loose but with no particular difficulty) to the N summit (3357m). The ridge turns S and rises gently to the S summit. It is broad and easy at first but then narrows and has lots of entertaining sharp bits and small gendarmes. The rock is good and difficulties can be climbed or turned at will. Towards the end a prominent tower is turned on the L and easy ground leads to the S summit (3467m). Descend easy rocks to a snow saddle and follow the broad ridge to the top of Piz Cambrena. c600m: 4-5hr from the Diavolezza

139 **NORTH-NORTH-WEST SPUR – EISNASE**
AD H Frick with H Kasper and C Zippert, 23 July 1916.
195 Winter: before 1965

Although not quite as famous as the Scerscen ice nose, this is still a coveted ascent for alpinists with ambitions to climb the classic ice routes of the range. In earlier years it enjoyed a certain reputation for difficulty, but this is no longer the case. The climb is now considered relatively straightforward and is unquestionably easier than the Scerscen. In recent dry summers the line has appeared most unattractive with long sections of shattered rock. Go early in the season to enjoy this fine mixed climb with a short steep ice pitch and all the atmosphere of an ascent at high altitude. See also photograph 194

From the Diavolezza follow Route 136 over the Fuorcla Trovat to the Pers glacier and cross it towards the foot of the spur (Pt 3031m). Slant up the slope L of the base of the spur and reach the rimaye (1½hr). Climb the snow/ice slope to reach the crest of the ridge a little above the initial buttress. In certain years it can be easier to reach this point via the slopes to the R of the spur. Follow the ridge, normally a nice mixture of rock and ice, to where it steepens through a final rock barrier below the 'nose'. Climb the rock and the steep ice pitch above (generally 30-45m and 55°-60°) to reach the broad and easy snow slopes where the difficulties cease. The nose can often be turned by easier slopes on the L. Reach the summit in a further 30min. c500m: 3½-5½hr, 5-7hr from the Diavolezza

Piz Cambrena: North-West Face – Central Couloir

This excellent ice/mixed route, perhaps the most striking line on the mountain, had to wait a surprisingly long time before receiving its first true ascent. With the advent of modern ice techniques an attempt was made in 1974 but the party traversed R at two-thirds height onto the rock wall and climbed steep mixed ground, on solid rock (V), to the summit. The first direct ascent took place in winter – the party following the narrow couloir R of the true finish. Finally in 1985 the ubiquitous Gabarrou, finding perfect conditions, romped up the main continuation line of the couloir in a mere 2hr. Although winter conditions are not really necessary, this is a route to be done very early in the season and after a cold night. By mid-summer the couloir has turned into a repulsive stone-swept chute.

140 GABARROU ROUTE

TD– P Gabarrou, 19 June 1985

195

In the upper section the true line of the couloir needs a good covering of firm névé over the slabby mixed ground. The difficulties are shorter and less sustained than the Swiss route.

Reach the foot of the Central couloir in 1½hr from the Diavolezza. Gabarrou, in fact, climbed the slopes on the L of the couloir but it is more logical to climb the main couloir itself, which is relatively straightforward and about eight pitches long. At two-thirds height a rocky section bars access to the upper slopes. Climb a narrow gully (70°-75°) then slant L up a snowy ramp. A steep ice wall leads to more open icy slopes and finally a short runnel through the upper rock band. Tough ice on the plain 65° slope of the sérac leads onto the calotte from where the summit is easily reached. 500m: 5-7hr

141 SWISS ROUTE

TD–/TD L Denber, G Deplajes and N Joos, 5 Dec 1979

195

The R-hand finish takes the obvious narrow gully and is more sustained than the previous route. It starts with a steep ice pitch (c75°) and ends with a little mixed climbing (IV). Rock protection should be available for much of its length. 500m: 5-7hr.

Piz Caral 3421m

K Heumann and E Novarese with L Giacomelli, 8 Aug 1880

A subsidiary summit on the E ridge of the Piz Cambrena. Early in the season it is an attractive little snowy pyramid.

142 **NORTH-EAST RIDGE**
F+/PD– A and E de Rethy (King and Queen of Belgium) with M Schocher and B Supersaxo, 1 July 1907

A lengthy and delightful rock/mixed scramble above the Forcula dal Caral. The route can easily be climbed in a day from the road starting near the Bernina pass.

When approaching the Bernina Pass from the N, a small unmade road forks R off the main highway, crosses the railway and goes alongside the dam-wall to the far side of Lago Bianco. From the end of this road cross the alluvial plain and slant up scree and finally a steeper glacial slope (few crevasses) to the broad snow saddle of the Forcula (1½hr)

Follow the crest of the ridge above, at first on reasonably sound 'juggy' rock then snow, to the summit. c600m: 2hr, 3½hr from the roadhead

143 **NORTH FACE**
PD A Bonacossa, 18 July 1912

Early in the season this will give a straightforward snow climb reached after a long plod up the Cambrena glacier. 40°-45°: 4-5hr from the Bernina Pass

Sassalmasson 3031m

First recorded ascent: W Rey with G Colani, 17 Sept 1846

This popular little summit above the Bernina Pass is the most easterly peak in the Cambrena chain. Routes to the top generally require little more than basic skills and provide a suitable transition into 'Alpinism' for the hardened hillwalker. It is a classic ski ascent, and as the Pass is open throughout the year, the summit is probably reached as much in winter as during the summer months. In the distance can be seen the Ortler range and close at hand there are dramatic views of the N side of Piz Varuna.

144 **WEST RIDGE VIA SASSALMASSON GLACIER**

F

All routes to the summit are easy and this is perhaps the best. Take axe and crampons but normally a rope is unnecessary.

From the end of the unmade road mentioned in the approach to Route 142, slant across the hillside above the lake and reach a stony valley below the mountain. Go up this valley and at the top move R on to the remains of the Sassalmasson glacier. Slant up to the W ridge, reaching it at a small shallow col before the final steeper section. Any crevasses are usually obvious. Follow the rocky crest (I!) to the summit. 730m from the Bernina Pass: 2½hr

The W ridge can be can be followed in its entirety from the Forcula dal Caral. This is just as easy and probably no longer in time.

145 **DESCENT BY SOUTH-SOUTH-EAST RIDGE**

RE/F– Parties can complete a pleasant traverse of the peak by scrambling down the SSE ridge to a prominent shoulder, then heading down the N flank towards the Lake.

Piz Trovat 3146m

This superb viewpoint, SE of the Diavolezza, is easily reached from the latter in 30min (see Route 136). The SW wall above the Pers glacier gives a fine little practice rock climb of over 200m, taking an almost direct line to the summit (First ascent: A and H von Borsig, 6 Aug 1925).

Munt Pers 3207m

This splendid and extremely popular viewpoint/picnic spot can be reached in just over an hour from the Diavolezza, by following the well-defined track NW along the crest of the ridge.

Piz Languard 3261.9m

Geographically this peak lies outside the boundaries of the main Bernina range. However, for parties based in the Engadine, it provides one of the most popular training walks and the chance to see not only a superb panorama of the great snow-capped peaks to the S but also flocks of ibex, still grazing the slopes of the mountain in fairly large numbers. In high summer hundreds of people make the ascent, generally via the chair-lift to Alp Languard and a steady climb up the stony hillside to the Berghaus Languard (3200m). This has a restaurant and twenty beds available for those wishing to overnight – usually an impossibility unless booked well in advance! (2½-3hr). Far better is to take the cable railway up to Muottas Muragl and following the well signposted track, cross the Val Muragl and climb up to the Sengatini Restaurant (2731m). The views up the length of the Roseg valley are simply superb! The path continues above the avalanche barriers to join the previous route (c3½hr to the summit). If variety is required on the descent, it is also possible to traverse SE and cross the Fuorcla Pischa (2874m) into the head of the wilder Val dal Vain and descend this in 2-2½hr to the Bernina Suot railway station.

Piz Muragl (3157m) is also popular but a 'quiet' approach can be made via the steep and narrow valley of Champagna. Start behind the aerodrome at Samedan. The path is good at first but becomes a little vague towards the head of the valley. Cross the Fuorcla Val Champagna (2803m) and reach the summit from the N. 4-4½hr

Albula Alps

Huts

Chamanna Jenatsch 2652m SAC. Tel: 082 32929. Situated in the upper Val Bever. Room for 60. Open at Easter, Whitsun and July-Aug, but generally meals can only be provided if booked in advance. For those based in the Engadine, the hut is most easily reached from the Julier pass by crossing the Fuorcla d'Agnel in 3½hr. It can also be reached from the téléphérique terminus on the summit of Piz Nair in 3hr or from Spinas station in 3½hr.

Chamona d'Ela 2252m SAC. Situated in the Val Spadlatscha. Room for 28 in the new and 12 in the old hut. Well-signposted paths can be followed from Filisur in 3½hr or Bergun in 2½-3hr to the hut. No telephone.

Chamanna d'Es-cha 2594m SAC. Tel: 082 71755. This nice hut lies to the S of Piz Kesch in the Val d'Es-cha. Room for 50. Open in Spring and from the end of June to the start of Oct. A well-marked, almost horizontal track leads from the Albula pass in 1½hr. (The Kesch hut, SAC Tel: 081 731134, with room for 85 (40 in the winter room), lies to the N of Piz Kesch and can be reached from Bergun in 2½-3hr. Open in Spring and from July till the end of Sept).

Chamanna da Grialetsch 2542m SAC. Tel: 081 463436. Situated just S of the Fuorcla da Grialetsch. Room for 75. Open in Spring and from July to the end of Sept. A number of well-marked paths leave the vicinity of the Fluela Pass. The lowest follows the main valley. Another starts higher up the road at a carpark, about 2 km below the Pass and skirts the base of the Piz Radont. Times are much the same, 2-2½hr. The quickest route starts from Durrboden, reached via a 13km drive up a narrow paved road from Davos. The 4 km trail is poor at first but then improves, to reach the hut in 1½hr.

Piz Duan 3130.8m

146 PE/RE Although not strictly in the Albula, this peak gives simply magnificent views of the main chain S of the Val Bregaglia. Starting from Casaccia a nice steady walk up the Val Moraz leads to the Lago da la Duana (at Maroz Dent a classic walking excursion leaves the main valley to reach and then descend the Val da Cam – 6hr from Casaccia to Soglio via Plan Vest). A straightforward ascent up the remains of the Duan glacier leads to the summit. 6hr

Piz Lunghin 2780m

147 PE

Another easily-reached walkers' peak with excellent views. It is approached from Maloja via the well-marked path to the Lagh dal Lunghin – the source of the river Inn. The track rises through open slopes of grass and boulders, reaching the lake in 2hr. A further 30min is needed to gain the Lunghin pass, where a signpost indicates the route to the summit. 3hr from Maloja. From Pass Lunghin, an alternative descent heads W to the Septimer pass then follows the valley S to Casaccia. 3hr

Piz Grevasalvas 2932m

148 IV

A broad rugged summit of crystalline granite rising above the Lagh dal Lunghin. The most enjoyable climbing is found on the SE ridge. Starting at a small col above the base, the crest is climbed throughout. The lower section of the ridge has a large tower (III/IV) with relatively sound rock but the upper section is more straightforward. 3-4hr from the lake. The E flank of the mountain gives a quick and easy descent. Alternatively parties can complete a fine traverse by descending the SW ridge to the Pass Lunghin. (1½hr in ascent; an easy scramble).

Piz Lagrev 3164.5m

M Arpagaus and R Held, 9 Oct 1875

The highest peak S of the Julier pass and an easy walk from Alp Guglia (3½hr). Excellent panoramic views. The ridges above Sils give interesting excursions on crystalline granite.

149a **SOUTH-WEST RIDGE**

III

The Fuorcla Grevasalvas can be reached from Plaun da Lej, via the delightfully named Crap Mellen, in 2½hr. The SW ridge looks impressive but is only III and somewhat broken. Turn the first small towers on the L, then continue on the crest to the summit. 2½-3hr from the col

149b **SOUTH-EAST RIDGE**

IV

The SE ridge of the S Summit (Pt 3080m) is somewhat better. The start is reached by a long traverse across scree from Crap Mellen.

Climb the steep crest throughout. Parties will encounter poor rock from time to time but also enjoy some entertaining climbing (III/IV: pegs in place). Either descend easily to the SE and come back round to the foot of the ridge; or continue along the S ridge, not without interest, to the main summit. 5-5½hr from Plaun da Lej

The best descent on this side of the mountain is to follow the NE ridge a short distance, then go down scree slopes to the S. Come round below the SE ridge and return via Crap Mellen.

Piz da las Coluonnas 2960m

150 IV The prominent N pillar of this peak can be reached in less than 30min from the Julier pass. It offers fairly sustained slab climbing on relatively sound rock. The crest is poorly defined until a scree terrace is gained at about half-height. Now climb steep walls somewhat L of the crest (pegs in place) and reach Pt 2786m (c350m: III/IV; 3-4hr). Continue easily up the ridge to Pt 2808m where it is possible to go down a large scree couloir to the S and return via the Grevasalvas lake to the Pass. From Pt 2786m, a further hour of scrambling along the ridge leads to the main summit. From here descend the S ridge to the first major col and head down to the Grevasalvas lake.

Piz Polaschin 3013m

This fine-looking pyramid forms the most easterly summit of the Lagrev group.

151 III The foot of the N ridge is quickly reached from the Chamanna dal Stradin (2161m) and gives a very worthwhile climb on reasonably sound rock. The first very steep step is by-passed on the R side. Start the second step slightly on the L and slant up R on steep slabs to reach a notch behind a small tower. Now climb the crest and scree slopes above to the final steep buttress where an easy escape L is possible. Reach the crest via a broken chimney on the L and continue with increasing ease to the summit. c600m: 4-5hr. Descend the SE ridge until it is possible to cut down L onto rough ground and follow this to the road.

Corn Alv 2992m

This is dolomitic in character, with some impressive walls rising out of massive scree slopes. It lies due N of the Julier Pass and can be conveniently reached from there in a couple of hours.

152 **WEST RIDGE**
IV P Binkert, Aug 1979

This is a very good outing on sound rock and a modern climb of medium difficulty.

From the S summit (2980m) the main ridge falls SW to a gap before a prominent tower (Pt 2927m), where it turns to the S. The climb ascends the W ridge of this tower. Walk up the Val D'Agnal as far as Pt 2568m, then toil up scree to the foot of the W face. Two 'ribs' protrude on either side of the face. Start at the lowest point of the L-hand rib where there is a ringbolt! Climb straight up for a pitch then follow the crest up to the L. Reach the foot of a red wall which is just R of a conspicuous water-worn chimney on the L side of the tower. Climb up 8m then traverse L to the chimney. Up the chimney for 6m then climb a very smooth wall on the R (IV). Continue up the L flank of the ridge above, then the crest itself, which gives some delightful moves (III) in a splendid position, to the top of the tower. 4-4½hr from the Julier Pass

Descend into the gap and either go down rocky steps and scree to the S, returning direct to the Julier Pass: or follow the main ridge easily to the summit and go down the NE ridge to Col 2865m. Turn W to regain the foot of the climb or E for a direct descent to the road in 1½hr.

Piz Guglia 3380m

One of the highest peaks in the Albula and although conveniently situated close to the road and main tourist resorts, it retains a feeling of splendid isolation. Despite a straightforward ascent from the E and a magnificent panorama of the Bregaglia/Bernina, this showpiece of the upper Engadine is not quite as popular as one might imagine. There are several steep granite walls and on the N side a very impressive pillar. However, the overall quality of the climbing is marred by very indifferent rock.

153 EAST RIDGE
I/II

The Fuorcla Albana (2870m) can be gained from the Chamanna 2161m (Alp Guglia) via the Munteratsch valley or by the well-trodden path from Pt 2311m in the Suvretta valley. The way up the ridge is usually very obvious and turns the foresummit on the S flank before reaching the highest point. 5hr: 2½-3hr in descent.

154 SOUTH RIDGE
II/III

This joins the E ridge at the foresummit and is a much finer alternative to the normal route, albeit at a slightly higher standard.

From the Fuorcla Albana go up the E ridge for only 10min to where a large scree terrace crosses the S flank. Follow the terrace to the rocky walls just S of the lowest notch in the S ridge. Climb these walls and near the top slant R into the gap. Avoid the first steep section of the ridge by some nice 'juggy' slabs to the L. Continue more or less on the crest to the foresummit, from where the highest point is easily reached. 2½hr from the Fuorcla

155 NORTH PILLAR
IV+

First impressions suggest this superb pillar to be an all-time classic of the region. Unfortunately closer inspection reveals that much of the rock is fairly mediocre and few ascents have been recorded. Go expecting a compelling line and an atmosphere that is wonderfully wild and remote. In these respects you will not be disappointed!

First reach the Fuorcla Guglia (2891m). This is a delightful walk up the picturesque Guglia valley – rich in many species of flowers and wild animals but often used for military practice by the Swiss army! 2hr from Alp Guglia

Climb up the ridge turning a fine finger of rock, that is well visible from below, on the W flank (III). The ridge becomes quite sharp and leads to the top of the first step – Piz Gugliet. Descend into the gap beyond. This initial section is fairly long and can be avoided by approaching the gap via a steep scree couloir on the W side. Above, the ridge takes on a more formidable appearance. Climb up the L side, returning to the crest by some tricky smooth slabs below yellow overhangs. Traverse L across slabs (IV+) to a smooth dièdre/depression in the face. Climb a steep rib on the L, working back R over a further series of slabs to rejoin the dièdre (IV). Follow it to a steep terrace (III+) which leads R to the crest of the pillar above the impressive section. Thankfully the difficulties now ease and the ridge is followed directly to the summit. c450m: 4hr

Piz Gritsch 3098.2m

An attractive three-summited granite mountain and a highly recommended viewpoint.

156 **SOUTH-WEST RIDGE**
III– H Cornelius, 30 June 1913

The base of the ridge can be approached in one of three ways, largely depending on one's pocket! Either from Champfer via the Pass Suvretta in 2½-3hr: or from Corviglia Station via the Fuorcla Schlattain (2873m) in 1½hr: or from the téléphérique station on the summit of Piz Nair in 20-30min. The ridge is quite long but not sustained and various steep steps and towers can generally be turned on the N side. Much of the climbing is good but there are, not surprisingly, a number of sections of broken and somewhat loose ground. The final crest over the three summits is relatively straightforward. 2½hr

The best descent is to follow the NE ridge to the first saddle, then traverse back below the southern slopes of the peak on easy but tiresome scree slopes.

Las Trais Fluors 2910m

157 First traverse: J Ludwig and A Sadler with B Cadonau,
III– 19 Sept 1878.

The traverse of all three of these dolomitic towers gives a highly recommended and popular outing. It is usually taken from W to E and several variations are possible. The climbing is entertaining, often steep but with good holds and on reasonably solid limestone. The foot of the towers can be reached from Corviglia via the Chamanna Saluver (2632m) in 1½hr, or from Celerina via Marguns in 3hr. 1½hr for the traverse

Piz Ot 3246.4m

This superb granite pyramid is one of the more notable peaks in the Albula and still holds a small glacier on the NW face. It is a superb viewpoint and a very popular ascent from Samedan. A well-marked path, the Ot-Weg, leads W via the Valletta da Bever and provides a straightforward slog all the way to the summit (3½-4hr).

158 **SOUTH RIDGE**
III– H Cornelius, 18 Aug 1913

This is considered to give the best route to the summit. It can either be climbed integrally from the Fuorcla Valletta or joined above Pt 3092m via a steep scree slope. If the crest is followed throughout, the difficulties are no more than III– but even these can generally be avoided on the flanks of the ridge. 5-6hr from Samedan

Crasta Spinas 3044m

159 Sharp granite crests and a distinctive summit block characterise this
III– satellite peak of Piz Ot. Highly recommended is the W to E traverse, beginning at the saddle (2957m) and descending to the Valletta. The climb follows the crest of the ridge more or less throughout, with difficulties up to III– on continuously good rock. From the ridge below the summit block, move R into the middle of the W face before ascending to the highest point. 3½hr to the saddle from Samedan: 1½-2hr for the traverse

The N ridge is also recommended. The standard is the same but the rock is not quite as sound (1hr).

Piz d'Err 3378m

160 J Ammann, A Rzewuski, C Schroter and Stebler with P Mettier,
PD– 23 Aug 1890

This elegant pyramid lies towards the northern end of a small chain of 3000m glaciated peaks that are generally accessed from the Jenatsch hut. The summit offers impressive views, especially to the W where long arid slopes rise from the banks of the Marmorera reservoir. The normal route follows the Err glacier to the SE of the peak and gains the broad saddle just E of Pt 3308m. Now traverse across to the rocky crest that forms the summit and reach the highest point via the SE ridge. 2-2½hr from the Jenatsch hut

Piz Jenatsch 3250m

The traverse of this long rocky crest is a recommended expedition which can be combined with an ascent of the Err. The rock is a form of crystalline granite and the difficult pitches are on reasonably sound rock.

161 **SOUTH-EAST RIDGE**

III From the hut, contour E initially before climbing steeply to below Pt 3073m. Reach the ridge, which is almost horizontal at first and follow the crest, up and over various towers, to the end of the narrow section. Easy slopes of scree and snow lead to the summit (3hr). Some of the difficulties can be avoided but by keeping more or less to the crest, there are some entertaining pitches of II/III.

Descend the W ridge to the first broad scree couloir on the L and go down it to the large rubble-strewn terrace below the S face of the mountain (c1hr to the hut). Alternatively, those requiring a more energetic day will continue along the W ridge to Piz d'Err. In the latter section more climbing at a similar standard (II/III) occurs on the traverse of the Corn Jenatsch.

Piz Calderas 3397m

E Burckhardt with H Grass and C Jossi, 28 Sept 1878

Lying just S of the Err, this is the highest and arguably the most beautiful peak of the group. It is higher in fact than anything in the Bregaglia and its summit is a popular and highly acclaimed viewpoint.

The normal route is a delightful glacier expedition; straightforward but not long enough to become tedious (F). A wide arc is usually made to the S in order to avoid the steepest section of the glacier. 2½hr from the hut

162 **NORTH RIDGE**

PD+ C Diener, 13 July 1887

This rather indistinct feature allows the Err and Calderas to be combined in a fine traverse. An initial snowy section above the col leads to some pleasant climbing on relatively sound rock. III–

A 350m couloir on the NW face holds snow and ice, at an angle of 45°, for most of the year. Unfortunately it requires a long and tedious approach up the slopes above Alp Flix. (PD+)

163 **EAST RIDGE**
III

This sharp rocky ridge provides the best climbing on the mountain. Although the two large towers in the upper section can be avoided, for maximum enjoyment it is strongly recommended that the crest is followed throughout.

Go up the moraine on the N side of the Calderas glacier and reach the base of the ridge at a point where, on the L, a couloir slants up through the lower rocky barrier. Climb this couloir from R to L finishing up the rib on the L side. Cross the large scree terrace to the upper ridge and follow the crest to the highest point. This gives some nice climbing on sound rock over the various towers. 3½hr from the hut

Piz d'Agnel 3205m

This rocky pyramid stands at the head of the Agnel valley. It can be climbed easily from the Jenatsch hut in 1½-2hr via a simple walk up the Agnel glacier to the Fuorcla da Flix (3065m) and the broad stony NW ridge (F). However it is equally possible to climb it from the Julier Pass by crossing the Fuorcla d'Agnel (3½hr).

164 **EAST RIDGE**
III

This can be followed integrally from the Fuorcla d'Agnel and gives over 1km of climbing. Some sections are quite sharp and provide interesting moves across smooth slabs. At other times the ridge is rather broken and when traversing the E and Middle summits offers no more than simple scree walking. 3-3½hr

Many parties just climb the final ridge. The saddle between the Main and the Middle summits can be approached from the S via a steep scree slope; or from the Agnel glacier to the N via a short but steep snow slope. Follow the scree covered ridge, interrupted at half-height by a short sharp rocky crest, to the summit rock barrier. Slant R over a steep slab to a crack and climb it to a small pedestal. Above, a short vertical crack and some loose blocks lead to the highest point.

Piz Suvretta 3114m

The prominent steep-sided peak standing just NW of the Suvretta Pass. From the summit there is an excellent panorama of the Err group.

165 **NORTH RIDGE**
V+ A Florineth and P Keller, 17 June 1974

A short climb over three steep steps. The second can be avoided on the L but if climbed direct gives one of the hardest pitches recorded on the high peaks of the Albula.

From the Suvretta Pass reach the col (2976m) at the foot of the ridge in 2hr. The first step is climbed in two pitches (III). A sharp and exposed crest leads to the second step. Climb this direct for two pitches (III+ then V+, moving R in the upper part). Continue easily up the crest to the summit. 1½-2hr

Scramble down the S ridge to the Fuorcla Suvretta (2968m) and return to the Pass (c1hr).

Ela Group

Lying well N of the Err group, these dolomitic peaks are less accessible to those based in the Val Bregaglia or Upper Engadine. Parties generally overnight at the Ela hut, though some routes can be climbed in a long day from the road.

Piz Mitgel 3158.8m

D Freshfield with F and H Devouassoud, 1 Aug 1867

Less popular than the other main peaks in the group. There are some steep walls broken by giant scree couloirs and terraces. The ridges are sharp and provide the best means of ascent.

166 **SOUTH-EAST RIDGE**
III A Pfister and P Schucan, 5 July 1908

This is by far the most interesting route on the mountain, following the narrow crest that connects the Mitgel with the Corn da Tinizong.

The ridge can be reached from the Chamona d'Ela by crossing the Fuorcla da Gravaratschas (N of the Tinizong); or via the Pass digls

Orgels (2699m) crossing the scree slopes S of the Tinizong (2½hr). This same point can also be reached from the road at Tinizong in 4-4½hr. Climb onto the ridge, close to its lowest point, via an easy scree couloir. The climbing is pleasant at first, increasing in difficulty towards the top. All of the steep steps can be taken direct but it is more usual to turn some of them on the S side. 4-5hr

Descent: Go down the N ridge – mainly scrambling – and return over the Fuorcla da Gravaratschas. Early in the season it is possible to use the large couloir/depression on the E face to effect a quick descent.

Corn da Tinizong (Tinzenhorn) 3172m

D Freshfield, F Devouassoud and E Hauser with P Jenny and A Flury, 7 Aug 1866

The 'Matterhorn' of the Albula and a popular goal from the Ela hut. Its massive striated walls appear impregnable from a distance and the S face in particular is impressively steep. Closer inspection reveals these faces to be rather more broken and like other peaks in this group, once off the ridges loose rock abounds.

167 NORTH-EAST FACE – NORMAL ROUTE

II

R of the main bulk of the NE face, a broad rocky rib runs N towards the upper section of the NNE ridge. A little below a depression in this ridge, slant up L on scree terraces. The route now more or less follows the line of the ridge, bypassing steep buttresses on the E flank. The rock throughout the upper section is quite good and there is a fair degree of exposure. Mainly scrambling with short walls of II. 3-4hr from the Ela hut. A longer but more interesting variant is to climb the NNE ridge from its base.

168 WEST RIDGE

III

The sharp ridge falling towards the Mitgel is not as hard as it appears. It was first descended by Freshfield and party after their ascent of the NE face, though nowadays a traverse of the peak in the reverse direction is the most logical outing.

Begin at the same point as the Mitgel route and follow the ridge easily E. As it steepens, it is usual to climb just L of the crest.

Route-finding expertise becomes important higher up where it is sometimes better to return to the crest. The rock is quite good, the situations exciting and the climbing most enjoyable. The correct route is no more than III. c400m: 2½-3hr, 5-5½hr from the hut

Pass d'Ela 2724m

This is an important pass on the ridge between Piz Ela and the Corn da Tinizong. Excellent way-marked paths lead from Naz/Preda (below the Albula pass) in 4-4½hr or from the Ela hut in 1½hr.

Piz Ela 3338.7m

A Flury, P and G Jenny, 17 July 1865

The highest peak in the group is a truly massive dome whose summit provides a magnificent panoramic view. There are a number of highly desirable routes on this peak but all are lengthy expeditions despite the proximity of the hut.

169 **WEST RIDGE**
PD W Grobli with P Mettier, 8 July 1880

The normal route from the Ela hut.

Walk up the path towards the Pass d'Ela until at an altitude of c2600m. Traverse E over grass and scree on the flanks of the ridge and reach the col at the start of the steeper section rising up to the W summit. The wall above is c450m high. It is easier to start 100m L of the crest and zigzag up rocky steps to join the ridge in the vicinity of a huge slab. Now continue more or less on the crest, avoiding major difficulties by deviations onto the L flank. The ridge connecting the W and Main tops is crossed entirely on the S flank. II+/III−: 4-5hr

170 **SOUTH-EAST RIDGE**
AD A Pfister and P Schucan, 8 Sept 1907

A recommended route of medium difficulty following the crest throughout in a splendid situation. For the most part the rock is very good and the climbing, over towers and along sharp crests, is always interesting.

Reach the Fuorcla da Tschitta (2831m) in 2½-3hr from the Ela hut by first crossing the Pass d'Ela. However the Fuorcla can also be reached in much the same time from Naz/Preda in the valley, so making the ascent possible in a day from the road. Avoid the first tower on the E side and reach the foot of Pt 3180m. Start well to the R in order to avoid an initial steep section, then climb easily back to the ridge via a steep couloir (some loose ground). Above Pt 3080m the crest of the ridge is followed throughout (II/III) with the crux occurring on the second steep step a short distance from the summit. 500m: III+, 4-5hr from the Fuorcla

171 **SOUTH-WEST PILLAR**

AD+ P Ettinger, W Weckerdt and Mr amd Mrs Wensel, 12 July 1931

On the vast S face a well-defined pillar lies to the R of the huge deep couloir that falls from the gap between the W and Main summits. The main difficulties are on fairly good rock, although on a few sections loose material needs careful handling. The upper section of the pillar is very exposed and provides some fine pitches.

Start well R of the foot of the pillar and go up scree to a terrace, which lies below the steep walls in line with the main summit. From the L end of this scree terrace slant L up an obvious slabby ramp-line. This leads to the crest of the pillar at about half-height (II/III). Just before the crest climb a steep corner on the R of a rounded buttress (IV) to a terrace on the crest. The next section is climbed more on the L flank (IV) and the last buttress directly up the crest (IV then III+). Continue more easily to the top. c550m: 5hr

Piz Kesch 3417.7m

J Coaz and J Rascher with C Casper and J Tscharner, 7 Sept 1846

It is fitting that the highest point in the Albula range should also be one of its finest peaks. Centrally situated, the view from the summit is magnificent. With a clear atmosphere it is possible to see the whole Alpine chain from the Ortler to the Oberland. Heavily glaciated to the N, it feels like a major Alpine mountain and one or two of the routes provide the best climbing in the range. Although the Albula is generally considered lesser fare than the main ranges to the S, middle grade mountaineers or those new to alpinism are strongly recommended to include the Kesch on their list of alpine classics.

The mountain is understandably popular but the majority of ascents start at the Kesch hut to the N. For those based in the Engadine it is far more convenient to use the Chamanna d'Es-cha.

172 EAST FACE – NORMAL ROUTE

PD–
193

A straightforward ascent of a glacial cirque with a rocky scramble to finish.

From the Es-cha hut to the S of the peak, the route is very well-marked to the Porta Es-cha (3008m) at the foot of the NE ridge of the Keschnadel (not named on map). The path follows the moraine to the Vadret Es-cha and reaches the Porta via 20m of fixed chain. Go on to the Porchabella glacier to the N of the peak (1hr). Walk up the length of this glacier terrace to the final rocky bastion. A short snow/ice slope on the R leads onto the NE ridge. Follow the L side of the ridge to the summit. At about half-height parties will often follow a series of ledges right across the E face and finish up the broken rocks of the 'Keschgrat' (1½-2hr). About 3hr from the hut

173 KESCHGRAT VIA NORTH-EAST RIDGE OF KESCHNADEL

AD+
193

P and M Schucan, 29 July 1906 (Keschnadel NE ridge): P Gussfeld with H Grass, 28 Sept 1877 (Keschgrat)

This is undoubtedly one of the finest and most interesting climbs in the range. The Keschnadel (3386m) is the massive rocky aiguille standing proudly to the SW of the Porta d'Es-cha and connected to the main summit by a long and almost horizontal ridge – the Keschgrat. The climb follows a succession of ridges, chimneys and slabs and is very varied. The main difficulties are concentrated in two short pitches, on eminently solid gneiss with a profusion of positive holds.

From the Porta d'Es-cha go up the Porchabella glacier a short distance and reach the snowy saddle at the base of the ridge (1½hr from the hut). This point can also be reached more directly from the S via a steep scree gully. Climb an easy crack which leads onto the N flank and continue up straightforward ground to the ridge. Fine climbing on the crest leads to the large shoulder, where the main difficulties begin.

The first buttress can be climbed direct (IV) or turned on the R to reach the lower of two terraces on the N flank. Traverse up R to a couloir/chimney and climb it, making an exit L across a smooth wall to reach the second terrace (III+). Traverse R again and climb up to a small notch in the ridge. A smooth slab gives a hard pitch (IV), after which a move R and a thin crack lead back on to the crest (III+/IV−). The top of the Keschnadel is only a short distance away (2hr).

Now head N at first, then back S, finally descending a scree couloir to the main ridge leading to Piz Kesch. Follow this with little difficulty to Pt 3405m. The next section has some fine climbing and leads, via the E flank, down to the deepest depression in the ridge. Follow the crest to a large gendarme before the summit. Climb it, at first on the crest and then via a ledge on the E side, finally making a 10m rappel into the notch on the far side of the gendarme. Easy and more broken ground leads to the summit (1½-2hr). 350m: IV, 5-5½hr from the hut

174 **KESCHNADEL EAST FACE**
TD− H Naef and O Wenk, 30 June 1965
84

One of the hardest of the recommended rock climbs created on the major peaks of the Albula. Although the face is not high, the difficulties are sustained and on good quality gneiss. Pegs are in place but, like the other hard climbs in the range, this route is far from popular so a comprehensive rack is advisable. To reach the start it is necessary to first gain the large shoulder on the NE ridge, then slant down L over scree to the middle of the face and reach a conspicuous niche below an overhanging chimney. c230m: V+ and A2, 5-6hr

Schwarzhorn 3146.4m

Clearly visible to the SW of the Fluela pass, this jagged pyramid marks the eastern end of the Albula chain. The rock on the peaks W of the pass is metamorphic and far from solid in places. This is emphasized by the huge black scree slopes crossed on the approach. Due to its attractive shape, easy access and well-defined path to the summit, this is one of the most frequented mountains in the region.

175 **NORTH RIDGE**
III O Schuster with J Engi, 28 June 1892

The most interesting route to the summit and with better rock than other ridges on the peak. Although the difficulties are not high, the climb is long, often exposed and commands a certain respect. Early in the season an axe may prove useful but it should be possible to make this decision from the road.

From the Fluela Pass walk along the N bank of the Schottensee to reach the path that slants SE up the huge scree slope. Reach the remains of a small glacier, then go up another scree slope to a large saddle (between the main peak and the Klein Schwarzhorn – Pt 2968m) on the N ridge (1½hr). Follow the crest of the ridge, either over or around (E flank) small gendarmes, to reach two grotesque 'teeth' which are clearly visible from low on the ridge. Turn these on the W side and continue along the crest, crossing various depressions, to the base of the final buttress. Climb slabs on the crest to the last steep step, then move round onto the L side, where the difficulties ease and broken ground leads to the summit. 300m: 3½-4hr

Walk down the broad S ridge to the saddle (2883m), from where a very well-worn path (the Schwarzhornweg) leads E to the road c15 min below the Hospice.

Piz Radont 3065m

O Schuster with J Engi, 28 May 1892

The traverse of this peak, just N of the Grialetsch hut, makes an agreeable outing. It can, however, be comfortably climbed from the road via the upper path to the hut.

176 **TRAVERSE WEST-EAST**
III O Schuster with J Engi, 28 June 1892

The col at the foot of the ridge can be gained from the S via a scree couloir. The first steep step can be climbed direct or more easily on the L side. Start the second step slightly on the R in a crack and continue on very good rock to a gendarme. The next part of the ridge is usually taken on the L side, coming back to the crest via a slanting crack. Continue up the blocky ridge to the summit. 1½hr and sustained at the grade.

Go down the E ridge a short distance then descend the SE spur on the R to a prominent shoulder. Below the shoulder the climbing is straightforward but rather loose and leads to scree slopes on the S side of the peak (1½-2hr to the hut). It is easier if the upper section of the spur is avoided by using a huge couloir on the L (E), returning to the crest at the shoulder.

The S face is a slabby wall with prominent crack lines. The direct line in the middle of the face, finishing some 30m to the W of the summit, gives a good route (III/IV: 1½hr).

Piz Vadret 3229m

Fitch and Hartmann with P Jenny and Stiffler, 1 July 1867

The highest and most interesting peak of the small Grialetsch group at the E end of the main chain. The remnants of three small glaciers below the crenellated summit ridge give the peak its name and provide a 'high mountain atmosphere'. The rock is gneiss and not always of the best quality.

177 **NORTH-WEST RIDGE**
III+ W Greg with J Engi, 16 Sept 1896

A classic of the region and although not the easiest, it is nowadays the most popular route to the summit. The traverse of this heavily serrated ridge is relatively short but continuously interesting with superb views of the surrounding ranges. An axe and crampons will be needed on the approach.

From the Grialetsch hut follow a good path, which slants up to the crest of a steep moraine well visible to the S. Follow this path, which continues around the base of the NE ridge of Piz Grialetsch to the glacier of the same name. Walk up the gentle slopes to the gap between the Grialetsch and Vadret at the foot of the latter's NW ridge (Fuorcla Vallorgia 2969m: 2hr).

Climb the first steep buttress on the ridge or avoid it completely on the L. Continue along the ridge, initially on the L but then more or less on the crest, climbing over many pinnacles. Higher, parties will want to avoid some of the difficulties, especially two pointed gendarmes which must be turned on the R. 250m: 2hr to the summit

Descent: It is easiest to go down the huge couloir on the W face but in dry conditions stone-fall could prove problematical. It is also possible to go down the SE ridge a short distance, then descend a loose couloir on the R but this requires a long walk back over the

Fuorcla Barlas-ch. Parties will often return by the route of ascent, having left their ice equipment at the Fuorcla Vallorgia.

Fluela Weisshorn 3085m

Although geographically outside the Albula, this popular peak provides an enjoyable half-day outing from the Fluela pass and is worthy of inclusion in this section.

178 **SOUTH RIDGE**

III

This rocky ridge, almost 1 km in length, begins a short distance above the Hospice. It is not sustained and consists mainly of walking/scrambling, interrupted by short pitches of II/III on generally sound rock.

Walk up the grassy slopes to the E, passing a small dam, and turn the initial bastion of the ridge on the L side. Now follow the crest of the ridge throughout. At first it runs NE, then NW, finally reaching a prominent saddle above which the ridge rises more steeply to the S summit (3060m). An easy crest leads quickly to the highest point. 3-4hr from the road

Descent: Either walk down the easy NW ridge and follow a well-worn path back to the road, just N of the Pass; or go back down the S ridge to the prominent saddle then descend scree to the W and return to the road via grassy slopes.

Two low-level walks on the southern slopes of the region are highly recommended:

SENTIERO PANORAMICO

P A delightful and very popular 5hr tramp from Casaccia to Soglio via the hamlets of Roticcio and Durbegia. A gentle descent of 1hr will take you to the border-post of Castasegna.

VIA ENGADINA

P A classic 19km excursion from St Moritz to Maloja. Parties generally start from the top station of the Signal téléphérique above St Moritz Bad. It is possible to buy a special ticket, which will allow you to not only make this journey but also to ride back from Maloja on the Post Bus. It is an easy waymarked path via Alp Suvretta, the Julier Pass road and Grevasalvas. Allow 6-7hr

General index

Agnel, Piz d' 338
Aguagliouls, Piz 279
Al Gal (Gallo) 114
Albigna
  Colle dell' 91
  hut 32
  Punta da l' 163
Allievi
  hut 33
  Punta 147
Alta via della Valmalenco 238
Alv, Corn 333
Arcanza, Cima d' 239
Argient
  Piz 304
  Fuorcla da l' 304

Bacun
  Forcola dal 172
  Piz 170
Badile
  Piz 64
  Torrione del 63
Balzet, Piz 175
Barbacan
  Cima del 50
  Passo del 51
Baroni, Punta 150
Bellavista 307
  Fuorcla 308
Bernina, Piz 289
Bertani, Punta 129
Bignami hut 233
Bio-pillar 166
Bondasca, Cima della 130
Bondo, Passo di 90
Bosio hut 230
Boval
  Fuorcla da 300
  hut 237
  Piz 301
Brasca hut 28
Bregaglia circuit 37
Bruciati, Corni 252

Cacciabella
  passes 108
  peaks 110
Caciadur 162
Caciadur, Pass di 162
Calderas, Piz 337
Calvo, Cime del 40
Cambrena, Piz 322
Cameraccio
  Punta 198
  Punta Meridionale del 201
  ridge 198
Cantun
  Cima dal 157
  Passo dal 156
Caral, Piz 325
Carate hut 232
Casnil
  passes 162
  Piz 167
Castel 155
Castello
  Cima di 151
  Colle del 155
Cavalcorte, Cima del 123
Cengalo
  Colle del 78
  Pizzo 79
Chaputsch
  Fuorcla dal 260
Chiara, Punta 191
Coaz hut 236
Colombo hut 230
Coluonnas, Piz da las 332
Corvatsch, Piz 266
Crast'Aguzza 302
Crast'Aguzza, Fuorcla 302
Cristina hut 235

Darwin Torre 202
Del Grande hut 35
Desio hut 228
Diavolezza hotel 237
Disgrazia, Monte 241
Duan, Piz 330

Ela
  Chamona d' 330
  Pass d' 341
  Piz 341
Entova, Sassa d' 264
Eravedar, Piz 109
Es-cha, Chamanna d' 330

Ferrario, Punta 191
Ferro
  Centrale, Pizzo del (Cima della Bondasca) 130

- Occidentale, Pizzo del 129
- Orientale, Pizzo del 134
- Passo del 130
- peaks 129
- Torrione del 133

Fex-Scerscen, Fuorcla 264
Fiorelli, Punta 37
Fluela Weisshorn 347
Fora, Piz 259
Forno hut 34
Forno
- Monte del 214
- Sella del 213

Frachiccio, Piz 112

Gemelli
- Colle dei 87
- Pizzi 88

Gianetti hut 29
Gluschaint
- Fuorcla dal 268
- Piz 269

Grandori (Mello) hut 36
Grevasalvas, Piz 331
Grialetsch, Chamanna da 330
Grisch, Piz 335
Guglia, Piz 333

Il Chaputschin 267
Ils Dschimels 274
Innominata
- peaks 106
- Torre 106

Jenatsch
- Chamanna 330
- Piz 337

Kennedy, Punta 252
Kesch, Piz 342
Kluckerzahn 213

La Sella 273
Languard, Piz 326
Lagrev, Piz 331
Largh, Cima dal 173
Le Dimore degli Dei (Dinosaur) 220
Ligoncio
- Passo 46
- Piz 41

Longoni hut 230
Luigi Amedeo, Picco 187
Lunghin, Piz 331
Malenco, Piz 263
Manzi hut 34
Marco e Rosa hut 234
Margna, Piz da la 258
Marinelli
- hut 232
- Punta 311

Masino, Colle 138
Mello
- Passo del 203
- Valley 216

Milano, Punta 49
Misaun, Piz 302
Mitgel, Piz 339
Molteni hut 33
Motta, Monte 266
Moraschini, Punta 126
Moro, Sasso 312
Morteratsch, Piz 297
Munt Pers 326
Muretto, Passo del 215
Musella, Cime di 311

Nero, Sasso 265

Oggioni hut 229
Omio hut 29
Oro
- Meridionale, Pizzo dell' 47
- Passo dell' 48
- Pizzi dell' 47

Ot, Piz 336

Pal, Piz dal 178
Palu
- hut 231
- Piz 314

Pansera hut 235
Parravicini hut 233
Pers-Palu, Fuorcla 321
Piede dell' Elefante 225
Pioda, Monte 239
Placche dell'Oasi 224
Polaschin, Piz 332
Ponti hut 228
Porcellizzo
- Avancorpo del 52
- Passo 52
- Pizzo 51

Porro
  hut 228
  Torrione 256
Precipizo degli Asteroidi 217
Prievlusa
  Fuorcla 296
  Piz 296
Punta 2511m 139
Punta 2648m 257
Punta 2869m (Punta Enrichetta) 78
Punta 2940m 311
Punta 2987m 185
Punta 3312m 159
Punta 3483m 248

Quinto Alpin, Cima 311

Rachele, Pizzo 250
Radont, Piz 345
Rascia
  Colle 181
  Punta 178
Rauzi hut 228
Re Alberto Torre 199
Redaelli hut 30
Riciol, Forcola dal 169
Roma path 36
Ronconi hut 30
Roseg,
  Piz 279
  Porta da 286
Rosso
  Cima di 205
  Monte 211
  Sasso 310

Sant'Anna, Punta 54
Sasc Fura hut 30
Sassalmasson 325
Scalin 160
  Furcela dal 160
Scalino, Piz 313
Scerscen, Piz 286
Scerscen-Entova hotel 231
Schwarzhorn 344
Scingino, Cima 123
Sciora
  Ago di 94
  Dadent (Dentro) 91
  Dafora (Fuori) 103
  Forcola di 98
  hut 31
  Punta Pioda di 99
Scioretta 106
Scioretta Colle della 105
Scoglio della Metamorfosi 222
Sella
  Fuorcla de la 277
  Piz 275
Sentiero Panoramico 347
Sertori, Punta 76
Sfinge, Punta della (Sphinx) 43
Sione, Monte 126
Sissone, Monte 203
Sondrio, Cima 271
Spazzacaldeira 118
Suvretta, Piz 339

Taveggia hut 229
Tinizong, Corn da (Tinzenhorn) 340
Torelli, Punta 53
Torrione
  Est 144
  Moai 200
Torrone
  Ago del 195
  Centrale 193
  Colle del 195
  Meridiana di 189
  Occidentale 182
  Orientale 195
Trapezio d'Argento 219
Trais Fluors, Las 335
Tremoggia
  Pass dal 261
  Piz 262
Trovat, Piz 326
Trubinasca
  Pizzo 60
  Punta 57
Tschierva
  hut 236
  Piz 300

Umur, Piz 289

Vadret, Piz 346
Val Bona
  Cima di 210
  Passo di 211
Val della Neve, Roda 116
Val Fontana, Cima 310

Valli hut 29
Vaninetti hut 28
Vanni, Pizzi dei: Denc dal Luf 62
Varuna, Piz 310
Vazzeda, Cima di 209
Vecchia, Torre 54
Vendretta, Pizzo della 39
Ventina, Pizzo 254
Vergine, La 115
Via Engadina 347
Vittoria, Punta 146

Zocca
  Passo di 146
  Pizzo di 139
  Torrione di 138
Zoia hut 235
Zupo
  Pass dal 307
  Piz 305

Index of Climbs

Bregaglia Group			
Huts			
H1	Brasca hut	P	28
H2-4	Vaninetti hut	PE/PD−	
H5	Valli hut	P	29
H6	Omio hut	P	
H7	Gianetti hut	P	
	Redaelli hut		30
	Ronconi hut	PD−/PD+	
H8-9	Sasc Fura hut	P, PD−/PD	
H10-11	Sciora hut	P, RE/F	31
H12	Albigna hut	P	32
H13	Molteni hut	PE	33
H14	Allievi hut	P	
H15	Manzi hut	PE	34
H16	Forno hut	PE	
H17	Del Grande hut	P/PE	35
H18-19	Grandori (Mello) hut	PE/PD	36
	Roma path	RE	
Bregaglia circuit			37
Punta Fiorelli			
1	SW ridge	III	38
2	S face – Mandellisi route	VI:A0/1	
	NW face		39
3	Siddharta	ED2	
Pizzo della Vendretta			
4	SE face	IV	40
Cime del Calvo			
5	Cima Centrale	F+	
6	Cima Est (ENE face)	V	41
Piz Ligoncio			
7	ENE flank	PD	42
*8	NNE ridge	AD−	
	NW face		
Punta della Sfinge (Sphinx)			43
	NE face		
*9	NNE ridge	IV+	44
	Descent		
*10	Serena	V	
	SE face		
*11	Morbegnesi	VI/A1	45
*12	NW face – Peder route	TD/TD+	
Passo Ligoncio			46
13	E side	P/PE	
14	W side	PE	
Pizzi dell'Oro			47
Pizzo dell'Oro Meridionale			
15	SE face	II	
16	S ridge	IV+	
*17	NW ridge	D−	
18	NNW face	III/IV	
Passo dell'Oro			48
Punta Milano			49
19	SW ridge	IV	
*20	SE face – Ho Chi Minh	IV+	50
21	NE chimneys	IV	
	Cima del Barbacan	II+	
	Passo del Barbacan	PE	51
Pizzo Porcellizzo			
22	S flank	F−	
23	NNE ridge	IV	
S point – Avancorpo del Porcellizzo			52
24	E face – Isherwood/ Kosterlitz route	VII	
Passo Porcellizzo		F	
Punta Torelli			53
25	SW ridge	F+	
*26	SSE pillar direct	VI	
Torre Vecchia			54
	W face	VI	
*28	SE pillar	V	
Punta Sant'Anna			
29	W and NW ridges	PD	
30	Descent		55
31	W face	IV	
*32	SW ridge	AD	56
*33	N pillar	TD/TD+	
34	NW (Klucker) couloir	TD/TD+	57
Punta Trubinasca			
35	E ridge	PD+/AD−	
*36	NW ridge	IV+	58
37	W face	VI/A1	
*38	W ridge	V	59
39	SE face direct	V+	60
Pizzo Trubinasca			
40	W flank/NW ridge	F+	
*41	SE ridge	IV	61
	N face		
42	Dixon	ED2	62
Pizzi dei Vanni: Denc dal Luf			
	Torrione del Badile	III−	63
43	Colle del Badile	TD−	
Piz Badile			64
*44	S face – Normal route	PD	
45	S ridge	AD	65
*46	SW wall – S pillar	D+/TD	
	NW face		66
47	Bramini route	TD	
*48	Ringo Starr	ED1	67
49	Grand Diedre	ED1	

	Pilastro a Goccia (Waterdrop Pillar)		
*50	Chiara	ED1	
51	Fuga dall'Ovest	D	68
*52	N ridge	D−	
	NE face		70
53	Neverland	TD+/ED1	
*54	Another day in Paradise	TD+	
*55	White Line	ED1	71
*56	Cassin route	TD	
*57	ENE pillar (Brothers' route)	TD+	72
*58	British route	ED1	73
59	Battaglia-Corti route	TD/TD+	
*60	Peoples direct	ED2	74
*61	E ridge	AD−	
	SE face		75
62	Via Vera	TD−	
*63	Molteni route	D+	
	Punta Sertori		76
64	SW face	IV−	
	Descent		
65	ENE pillar	VI	77
*66	S ridge	IV	
	Punta 2869m (Punta Enrichetta)		78
	Colle del Cengalo		
67	S side	RE/F	
68	N side	D−	79
	Pizzo Cengalo		
*69	W ridge	PD	80
*70	S ridge direct (Vinci route)	TD/TD+	
	E face		82
71	Inca trail	VI:A2/3	
72	E ridge	AD−	
	N face		83
73	N face direct (Kasper pillar)	ED1/2	
*74	Classic route	TD−/TD	84
75	Renata Rossi route	ED3	86
*76	NW pillar	TD−/TD	
	Colle dei Gemelli		87
77	Italian side	F	
78	Swiss side	D/TD−	
	Pizzi Gemelli		85
79	SW ridge of SE summit	PD	
80	NE wall	TD	
*81	NNW (Flat Iron) ridge	V	89
	Passo di Bondo		90
82	N side	PD+	
83	S side	PD−/PD	
	Colle dell'Albigna		91
84	E side	D/D+	
	Sciora Dadent (Dentro)		
85	SW flank	PD+	
86	S ridge	PD+	92
87	S ridge direct	AD−	
88	N ridge	AD−	
*89	NW face	TD	93
	E face		
*90	E pillar (Nigg route)	D−	94
91	NE pillar	AD+/D−	
	Ago di Sciora		
*92	S face	AD	95
93	SE face (Scarabelli Route)	VI/A1	
*94	N face	AD	96
95	W flank	AD+	
96	NW ridge	AD+/D−	
97	NW ridge direct	TD	97
*98	Sciora traverse	D	98
	Forcola di Sciora		
99	E side	PD	99
100	W side (Klucker couloir)	AD+	
	Punta Pioda di Sciora		
*101	S face and E ridge	PD+	100
102	E ridge direct	IV	
103	S face	AD−	
104	NW ridge	D+/TD−	101
105	NW face	ED2	102
*106	Pioda-Dafora traverse	AD	
	Sciora Dafora (Fuori)		103
107	E ridge	PD+	
108	NE ridge from Sciora hut	AD	104
109	W face direct	TD+	
110	NW ridge (Fuorikante)	TD	
111	Direct start	VI	105
	Colle della Scioretta		
112	W side	AD	
	Scioretta		106
113	N ridge	AD	
114	S ridge	AD	
	Innominata peaks		
	Torre Innominata		
*115	W ridge	IV+	
	Main summit		107
116	W ridge (Jacqueline route)	IV+	108
117	W ridge of N summit	III	
*118	Traverse of Innominata ridge	III	
	Cacciabella passes		
	S pass		
119	E side	PE	109

120 W side	RE	
Piz Eravedar		
121 Traverse	IV−	
Cacciabella peaks		110
122 Normal route to N peak	RE/II−	
123 Traverse of S peak	II	111
124 NW ridge of N peak	III	
125 NE ridge of N peak	IV−	
Piz Frachiccio		112
126 SW ridge	II	
127 E ridge	III	
128 Sognadoro	VI/A0	
*129 Kasper pillar	VII	
130 Diedro Sensa Sola	VII	113
131 Maiden Maiden	VI+	
132 Mafia della Glencoe	VII	114
Al Gal (Gallo)		
*133 NE ridge	IV	
134 S ridge	IV−	115
135 NW couloir	TD+	
La Vergine		
*136 Traverse	IV+	
Roda Val della Neve		116
137 SE face	II	
138 S ridge	III	
139 N ridge	III−	117
NW face		
*140 Jack Canali route	D	
141 Gufi route	D+	
*142 Niedermann route	TD	118
Spazzacaldeira		
143 S side	RE/II−	119
*144 Fiamma	V/V+	
*145 Dente	VI/VI+	
SE wall		
*146 Leni route (Erwin Kilchor start)	VI/VI+	120
*147 NE ridge	IV/IV+	
*148 Nigg route	V+/VI−	121
*149 Felici route	VI	
150 Second pillar	VI+	
*151 Nasi-Goreng	VI/VI+	122
152 Steinfrasser	VII−	
153 N ridge	IV	
Cima Scingino		123
Cima del Cavalcorte		
154 W face	RE/II	124
*155 E pillar	TD−	
N top – SE pillar		
156 Mattino Dopo	TD+	125
157 E face – Cercando i Ceki	TD	
Monte Sione		
Punta Moraschini		126
*158 Pillar of the Polar Wind	TD−	
Punta Bertone		127
159 Normal route	II	
160 NW spur	III	
*161 N ridge	IV	
SE face		128
162 Obelix	VI/A1	
*163 Asterix	VII−	129
Ferro peaks		
Pizzo del Ferro occidentale		
164 ENE ridge from Passo del Ferro	F+	
165 NW ridge	PD	
Passo del Ferro		130
166 S (Italian) side	F+	
167 N (Swiss) side	PD+	
Pizzo del Ferro centrale (Cima della Bondasca)		
Cima della Bondasca – main summit		
168 N side – Normal route	F+/PD+	
169 W ridge	F+	131
170 S ridge	AD−	
E peak		
171 N side	F+/PD+	
172 N couloir and E ridge	TD−	132
*173 S spur	TD	
Torrione del Ferro		133
174 S ridge	AD−	
175 N couloir and E ridge	TD−	134
Pizzo del Ferro Orientale		
176 S flank	PD	
NW face		135
*177 Left-hand pillar	D+	
178 Original route	D	136
179 Central couloir	D−/D	
180 Right-hand pillar	D+/TD−	
181 Quagliotto route	D+	
*182 Traverse of main peaks	D+	137
Colle Masino		138
183 N (Swiss) side	AD	
184 S (Italian) side	F	
Torrione di Zocca		
185 SE face	VI	139
186 Punta 2511m- E face	VIII−	
Pizzo di Zocca		
*187 NW glacier	PD+	140
188 NW ridge	PD+/AD−	
189 WSW ridge	PD+/AD−	
		141

190 W top – ESE (Red Rose) ridge TD–
191 ESE couloir AD– 142
*192 NE ridge D 143
Torrione Est 144
*193 SE pillar (Parravicini route) V+
194 NE (Bonatti) pillar VI 145
N summit
195 Ice a Go-Go D
196 NW ridge AD/D
Passo di Zocca 146
197 Italian side PE
198 Swiss side F
Punta Vittoria
199 WSW pillar IV+ 147
Punta Allievi
200 Normal route F+
201 SW pillar V/V+
*202 S ridge (Gervasutti route) D+/TD– 148
203 Decadente VII–
204 Camosci route (upper section) TD– 149
*205 Filo Logico TD+/ED1
*206 E face – Erba route TD–
Punta Baroni 150
SE face
*207 Sondrio City TD/TD+
208 Sensa sole TD– 151
Cima di Castello
209 Normal route from Albigna valley PD–
*210 N ridge PD/PD+ 152
*211 Normal route from Italy PD–
S face
212 Left-hand couloir VI– 153
213 Czech Direct ED2
*214 S pillar ED1/2 154
215 Right-hand pillar TD
Colle del Castello 155
216 N (Swiss) side PD–
217 S (Italian) side PD
Castel
218 W face TD– 156
Passo dal Cantun
219 W side PD–
220 E side PD– 157
Cima dal Cantun
*221 SW flank PD–
222 S ridge PD 158
*223 NE ridge AD–
*224 N face AD+
Punta 3312m 159
225 NW face Original route AD+
*226 Matchstick couloir D+
Furcela dal Scalin 160
227 E side PD
Scalin
*228 N ridge PD+/AD–
229 SW ridge PD+ 161
230 N summit – W face VI/A1
Caciadur 162
Pass di Caciadur RE/F
Casnil passes
231 W side RE/F
232 E side RE/F 163
Punta da L'Albigna
233 N flank PD
NW face
*234 Meuli route AD+ 164
235 Steiger route D+ 165
*236 NW ridge AD
Bio-pillar 166
*237 Original route V+
*238 Miki route V+
239 La Rosa Rossa VI+ 167
Piz Casnil
*240 S ridge II
241 SW flank II
242 N ridge II–/II 168
*243 E ridge IV
244 Fornokante IV+ 169
245 SE pillar V+
Forcola dal Riciol
246 W side RE 170
Piz Bacun
247 S chimneys III
248 E ridge III– 171
*249 N ridge III
250 S ridge IV
*251 SW ridge AD+
252 S pillar V+ 172
Forcola dal Bacun
253 E side RE/F 173
254 From Albigna hut F+
Cima dal Largh
*255 E wall III 174
*256 Traverse IV
257 Motta Faga ridge D/D+
Piz Balzet 175
258 E ridge II+
Descent

*259	S ridge	IV	176
	First tower		
260	S ridge	V	
261	S face	VI/A2	
	W face		177
262	SW ridge	D	
263	Face to Face	VI+/A2+	
264	35 Gully	ED1	178
265	W pillar	TD−	
	Piz dal Pal		
	Punta Rasica		
266	SE ridge	AD	179
*267	N ridge	AD+	
*268	SW ridge (Bramani route)	D	180
269	N summit – E pillar	VI/A2	181
	Colle Rasica		
	Torrone Occidentale		182
270	S face and S ridge	PD+	
*271	S ridge	AD+	183
272	NW ridge	AD−/AD	
273	E ridge	AD+	184
*274	Traverse from Torrone centrale	D	
	SE face		185
	Punta 2987m		
*275	S pillar	V	186
*276	SW pillar	VI+/A2	
277	Parruffone	VI+	
278	Melonimaspes crack	V+/VI	187
	Picco Luigi Amedeo		
279	NNE ridge	III+/IV−	
280	SSW ridge	V/A1	188
*281	SE face	TD+/ED1	
	Meridiana di Torrone		189
*282	ESE face – Outlandos D'Amour	ED2	
283	SE pillar	ED2	190
	Punta Chiara		191
284	N ridge	PD−	
*285	S ridge	D−	
	Punta Ferrario		
	S face		
286	Original route	TD	192
287	Direct route	ED1	
288	W face – Descent		
	Torrone Centrale		193
289	S couloir	PD+/AD−	
290	SE face	AD−	
291	W ridge from Forno glacier	AD+	194
292	NW spur	D−	
	Colle del Torrone	AD+	195
293	Ago del Torrone	IV+	
	Torrone Orientale		
*294	NE flank	AD−	196
295	NW spur	AD	
296	W ridge	AD+	
*297	S ridge direct	TD	197
	Cameraccio ridge		198
	Punta Cameraccio		
298	N ridge	V	199
299	Torre Re Alberto	D/D+	
	Torrione Moai		200
300	Normal route	IV	
301	E face	VII	
302	Bandeiras	VII−	201
	Punta Meridionale del Cameraccio		
303	E face – Tyrannosaurus Rex	ED2	
304	S pillar	VII+	202
	Torre Darwin		
305	S pillar	V+/A1/2	
	Passo del Mello		203
	Monte Sissone		
*306	N ridge	F+	204
307	S flank	F	
*308	W ridge	AD	205
	Cima di Rosso		
*309	SW flank	F+/AD−	
310	ESE ridge integral	D−	206
*311	NE ridge via Cima di Vazzeda	AD+	
*312	N face	AD+/D−	207
313	Central spur	D−/D	208
314	N face – Right-hand route	D+/TD−	
315	NW face	AD	209
	Cima di Vazzeda		
*316	E ridge	AD	
	Cima di Val Bona		210
317	Normal route	F	
*318	E ridge	AD+	
	Passo di Val Bona		211
	Monte Rosso		
319	W flank	PD−	
320	SE ridge	PD	212
321	NE ridge	AD−/AD	
	Kluckerzahn		213
322	E ridge	III+	
	Sella del Forno		
323	W side	RE	
324	E side	RE	
	Monte del Forno		214
325	S ridge	PD−	
326	E ridge	F	215

Passo del Muretto		
327 From Maloja	PE	
328 From Chiareggio	P	216
329 From Forno hut	RE	

Mello Valley

330 Mixomiceto	VI+	217
Precipizo degli Asteroidi		
331 Oceano Irrazionale	VII	218
Trapezio d'Argento		219
332 Stomaco Peloso/L'Alba del Nirvana	V+	
333 Bitter Lemon	VII	220
334 Nuova Dimensione	VII−	
Le Dimore degli Dei (Dinosaur)		
335 Li Risveglio di Kundalini	VI/A0	
336 Verde Gamma	VII−	221
337 Vortice di Fiabe	VI+	
338 Patabang	V	222
Scoglio della Metamorfosi		
339 Luna Nascente	VI+/A1	223
340 Polimago	VII/A1	
Placche dell'Oasi		224
341 Uomini e Topi	IV	
342 La Chiusa	V	
Piede dell' Elefante		225
343 Crazy Horse	VI	

Huts (Disgrazia/Bernina) 228

H1	Ponti hut	P	
H2-3	Desio hut	P	
	Rauzi hut		
H4	Porro hut	P	
H5	Taveggia hut	F+/PD−	229
H6	Oggioni hut	PD	
H7	Bosio hut	P	230
	Colombo hut	F/PD−	
H8	Longoni hut	P	
	Scerscen-Entova hotel	P	231
H9	Palu hut	P	
	Carate hut	P	232
H10-13	Marinelli hut	P	
	Bignami hut	P	233
	Parravicini hut	F	
H14/15	Marco e Rosa hut	F+/PD−	234
H16	Pansera hut	PD−	235
	Zoia hut	P	
H17	Cristina hut	P	
H18/19	Coaz hut	P	236
H20	Tschierva hut	P	
H21	Boval hut	P	237
	Diavolezza hotel		

Alta via della Valmalenco PE/RE 238

Disgrazia Group 239

	Cima d'Arcanza		
1	Normal route	PE	
	Monte Pioda		
2	E ridge	PD−	
3	SW ridge	PD+	240
4	NW ridge	PD+	
	N side		
5	NNW face	AD+/D	
6	N spur	AD/AD+	241
7	NE face	D+/TD−	
	Monte Disgrazia		
*8	NW ridge	PD+	242
9	From Forno hut	AD	
	South West (Baroni) ridge		
10	SE ridge	PD	243
*11	From Passo Cassandra	AD−	
*12	Via NE spur of E summit	AD+	
13	Couloir dell'Insubordinato	D/D+	244
*14	NNE ridge (Corda Molla)	AD+	
	North face		245
15	N couloir	D+/TD−	246
16	Superdirect	ED1	
*17	Classic route	TD−	247
*18	Spigolo Inglesi	D/D+	
19	Supercouloir	ED1	248
	Punta 3483m		
20	Sulla Strada della Follia	TD−	
	Pizzo Cassandra		249
*21	SW ridge	PD−/PD	
*22	N face	AD	
23	NNW (Central) spur	AD	250
*24	WNW face	AD	
	Pizzo Rachele		
*25	E pillar	IV	
26	Cassandra-Rachele traverse	AD	251
	Corni Bruciati		252
27	SW ridge of Central summit	RE/F−	
	Punta Kennedy		
*28	NNE ridge	PD	
*29	E ridge	AD	253
	Pizzo Ventina		254
30	S couloir	PD	

31 N ridge PD+/AD−
*32 ENE ridge AD+
33 Jack Canali route D/D+ 255
*34 SE (Tranquility) pillar TD− 256
Torrione Porro
35 W face – Peppo Perego route IV− 257
Punta 2648m
36 Normal route PE

Bernina Group 258

Piz da la Margna
*37 NE ridge PE/RE
*38 N side RE/F−
39 SE ridge AD− 259
Piz Fora
40 NNW ridge F
*41 ENE ridge F 260
*42 Descent by NNW ridge PD
Fuorcla dal Chaputsch
43 Swiss side F+ 261
44 Italian side PE/RE
Pass dal Tremoggia
45 Swiss side PD−
46 Italian side PE/RE 262
Piz Tremoggia
*47 NE ridge F+
48 SE ridge PD−/PD
49 SW ridge AD 263
Piz Malenco F+
Sassa d'Entova 264
50 SW ridge F+
Fuorcla Fex-Scerscen
51 Swiss side PD−
52 Italian side F 265
Sasso Nero
*53 SE ridge PE
Monte Motta 266
Piz Corvatsch
54 N-S traverse F
Il Chaputschin 267
55 N ridge F
56 SW ridge PD 268
Fuorcla dal Gluschaint
Piz Gluschaint 269
57 NNE face PD
*58 N ridge AD+ 270
59 NW face AD+/D−
*60 SW ridge AD−
Cima Sondrio 271
61 SE rib AD 272
SSE face
62 Conjunctio Spigolorum D+
La Sella 273
63 Normal route PD
64 Traverse PD+
65 S couloir AD+ 274
66 S face of E peak D+/TD−
Ils Dschimels
67 S face of E peak D/TD 275
Piz Sella
*68 SW spur AD+
E summit – S face 276
*69 S spur TD−
70 SE face AD−/AD 277
Fuorcla de la Sella
71 From Coaz hut PD 278
72 From Tschierva hut PD
73 From Marinelli hut F
*74 Sella-Gluschaint traverse AD+
Piz Aguagliouls 279
Piz Roseg
*75 W face and NW ridge AD− 280
*76 NNE ridge (Eselgrat) AD 281
77 NNW ridge Integral AD+ 282
*78 SW ridge D/D+
79 ENE ridge AD+ 283
North East face
*80 Original route D+ 284
*81 Direct route to Schneekuppe TD− 285
82 Schmid route TD
83 Directissima TD+/ED1
84 N face of Roseg Pitschen TD
Porta da Roseg 286
85 N couloir AD+
86 S couloir AD−/AD
Piz Scerscen
*87 NW spur (Eisnase) AD+ 287
88 SW ridge PD+/AD−
288
89 SW couloir PD/PD+
90 N couloir D−/D 289
Piz Umur PD
Piz Bernina
*91 SE ridge (Spallagrat) PD 290
92 E ridge PD/PD+
*93 NE face D+ 291
94 NE face direct TD 292
*95 N ridge – Biancograt AD
96 W face D+ 294
*97 Grand traverse
(Roseg-Scerscen-Bernina) TD−/TD 295

Fuorcla Prievlusa		296
Piz Prievlusa		
98 N ridge via W flank	PD	
Piz Morteratsch		297
*99 N ridge	PD−	
*100 NE ridge (Crest of Hope)	AD+/D−	298
Fuorcla da Boval		299
101 W side	PD−/PD	300
102 E side	F+	
Piz Tschierva		
103 E ridge	F	301
Piz Boval		
104 NW ridge	F/PD	
105 Via E ridge of Corn Boval	PD	
Piz Misaun	F	302
Fuorcla Crast'Aguzza	F+/PD	
Crast'Aguzza		
106 W ridge	PD	303
*107 E ridge	AD−	
Fuorcla da L'Argient		304
108 S couloir	D−/D	
Piz Argient		
*109 NNW ridge	PD−	
*110 NE ridge	F+	305
*111 S ridge	TD−	
Piz Zupo		
*112 SW ridge	F+	306
*113 NNW ridge	PD−	
114 SE ridge	PD+	
Pass dal Zupo		307
115 Swiss side	PD/PD+	
116 Italian side	F+	
Bellavista		
*117 Traverse	PD−	308
Fuorcla Bellavista		
118 Swiss side via Fortezza ridge	PD−	
119 Italian side	PD−	309
Piz Varuna		310
120 W ridge	PD−	
Cima val Fontana	F+	
Sasso Rosso	PD	
Cima Quinto Alpin (S face)	IV	311
Punta Marinelli		
121 Traverse	II+	
122 SW face	III	
Punta 2940m (SSW Pillar)	V+/VI	
Cime di Musella (various routes)		
Sasso Moro	F+	312
Piz Scalino		313
*123 Normal route via Northern glacier	F+/PD−	
Piz Palu		314
124 E ridge	PD	
125 W ridge	PD	315
*126 Traverse	PD	
127 Greater traverse	AD+/D−	
128 S buttress	PD	316
129 NNE face of E peak	D−/D	
*130 N spur of E peak	AD+/D−	
131 N couloir	TD−	317
*132 N spur of Central peak (Bumillergrat)	TD	318
*133 NE face of W peak	TD−/TD	319
*134 N spur of W peak	TD−	
*135 NW face of W peak	D+	320
Fuorcla Pers-Palu		321
136 West Side	PD−	
Piz Cambrena		322
137 SSW ridge	PD−	
*138 By traverse of Piz d'Arlas (N ridge)	PD+	
*139 NNW spur (Eisnase)	AD	323
NW face – Central couloir		324
*140 Gabarrou route	TD−	
*141 Swiss route	TD−/TD	
Piz Caral		325
142 NE ridge	F/PD−	
143 N face	PD	
Sassalmasson		
*144 W ridge via Sassalmasson glacier	F	326
145 Descent by SSE ridge	RE/F−	
Piz Trovat		
Munt Pers	F	
*Piz Languard	F	

Albula Group

Huts

Chamanna Jenatsch		330
Chamona d'Ela		
Chamanna d'Es-cha		
Chamanna da Grialetsch		
146 Piz Duan	PE/RE	
*147 Piz Lunghin	PE	331
148 Piz Grevasalavas	IV	
149 Piz Lagrev	aIII, bIV	
150 Piz da las Coluonnas	IV	332
151 Piz Polaschin	III	
Corn Alv		333
*152 W ridge	IV	

Piz Guglia		
153 E ridge	I/II	334
154 S ridge	II/III	
155 N pillar	IV+	
Piz Grisch		335
156 SW ridge	III–	
*157 Las Trais Fluors	III–	
Piz Ot		336
158 S ridge	III–	
*159 Crasta Spinas	III–	
160 Piz d'Err	PD–	
Piz Jenatsch		337
161 SE ridge	III	
Piz Calderas	F	
162 N ridge	PD+	
*163 E ridge	III	338
Piz Agnel	F	
164 E ridge	III	
Piz Suvretta		339
165 N ridge	V+	
Piz Mitgel		
166 SE ridge	III	
Corn da Tinizong (Tinzenhorn)		340

167 NE face (Normal route)	II	
168 W ridge	III	
Pass d'Ela		341
Piz Ela		
169 W ridge	PD	
170 SE ridge	AD	
171 SW pillar	AD+	342
Piz Kesch		
*172 Normal route (E face)	PD–	343
*173 Keschgrat via NE ridge of Keschnadel	AD+	
*174 Keschnadel E face	TD–	344
Schwarzhorn		
*175 N ridge	III	
Piz Radont		345
176 W-E traverse	III	
Piz Vadret		346
*177 NW ridge	III+	
Fluela Weisshorn		347
*178 S ridge	III	
Sentiero Panoramico	P	
Via Engadina	P	

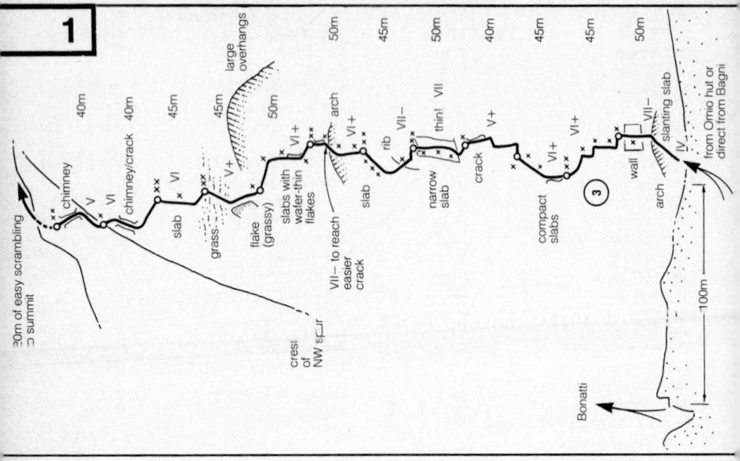
1
from Omio hut or direct from Bagni
Bonatti
100m
50m
IV
slanting slab
VII–
arch
wall
45m
VI+
3
VI+
45m
compact slabs
40m
V+
crack
50m
VII
thin!
narrow slab
VII–
rib
45m
slab
VI+
arch
VII– to reach easier crack
50m
VI+
slabs with wafer-thin flakes
crest of NW spur
large overhangs
50m
flake (grassy)
45m
V+
grass
45m
VI
slab
40m
chimney/crack
VI
V
40m
chimney
20m of easy scrambling to summit

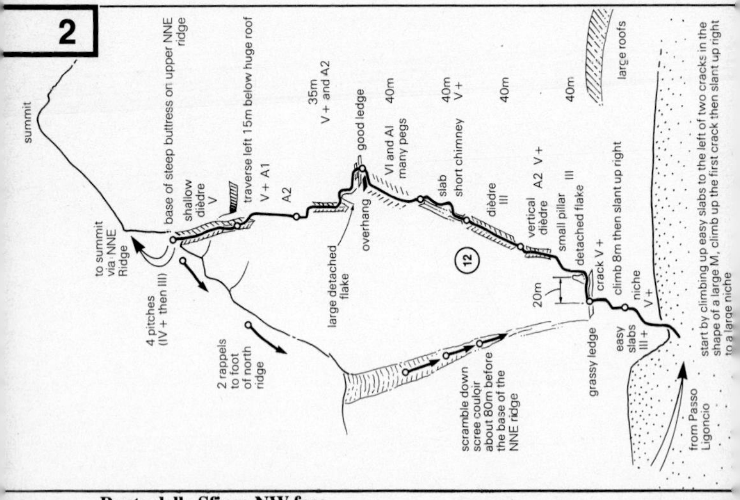
2
from Passo Ligoncio
start by climbing up easy slabs to the left of two cracks in the shape of a large M, climb up the first crack then slant up right to a large niche
large roofs
easy slabs III+
grassy ledge
niche V+
climb 8m then slant up right
crack V+
20m
40m
detached flake III
small pillar
vertical dièdre
A2 V+
dièdre III
40m
short chimney
slab
40m V+
12
VI and AI many pegs
40m
good ledge
overhang
large detached flake
35m V+ and A2
A2
V+ A1
traverse left 15m below huge roof
shallow dièdre V
base of steep buttress on upper NNE ridge
to summit via NNE Ridge
4 pitches (IV+ then III)
2 rappels to foot of north ridge
scramble down scree couloir about 80m before the base of the NNE ridge
summit

Punta della Sfinge NE face

3

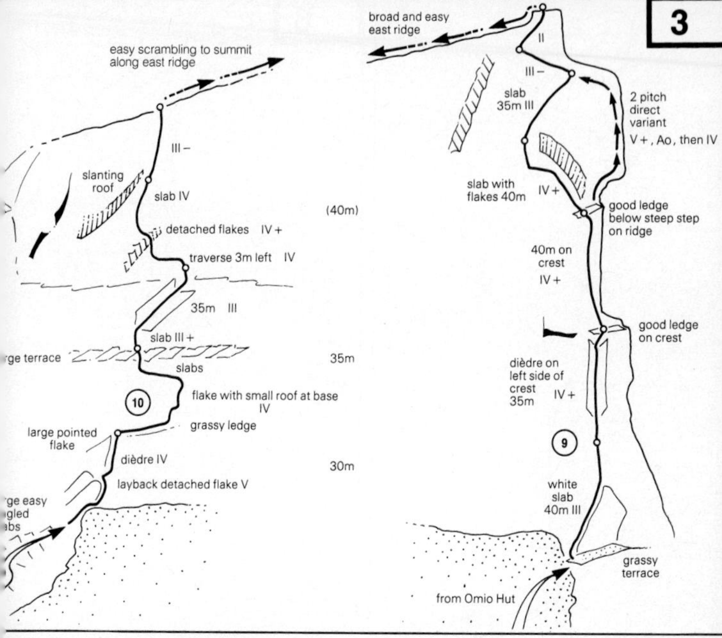
easy scrambling to summit along east ridge
III –
slanting roof
slab IV
detached flakes IV +
traverse 3m left IV
35m III
slab III +
slabs
(40m)
35m
10
flake with small roof at base IV
grassy ledge
large pointed flake
dièdre IV
30m
layback detached flake V
broad and easy east ridge
II
III –
slab 35m III
2 pitch direct variant
V + , Ao, then IV
slab with flakes 40m
IV +
good ledge below steep step on ridge
40m on crest
IV +
good ledge on crest
dièdre on left side of crest
35m
IV +
9
white slab 40m III
grassy terrace
from Omio Hut

4

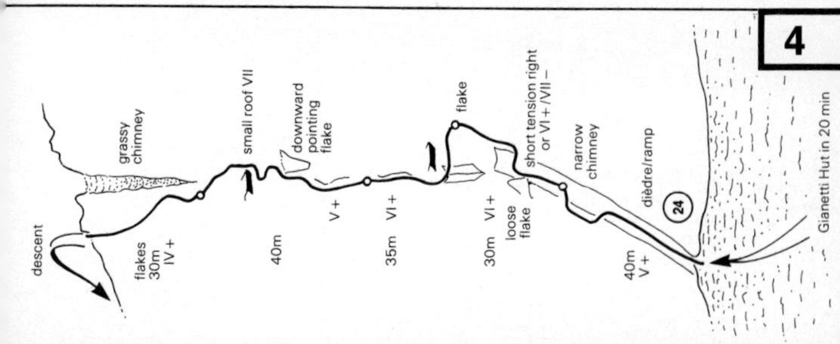
descent
grassy chimney
flakes 30m IV +
small roof VII
40m
downward pointing flake
V +
VI +
35m
flake
VI +
30m
loose flake
short tension right or VI + /VII –
narrow chimney
dièdre/ramp
24
40m V +
Gianetti Hut in 20 min

Avancorpo del Porcellizzo E face

Pizzo dell'Oro Meridionale NW Ridge

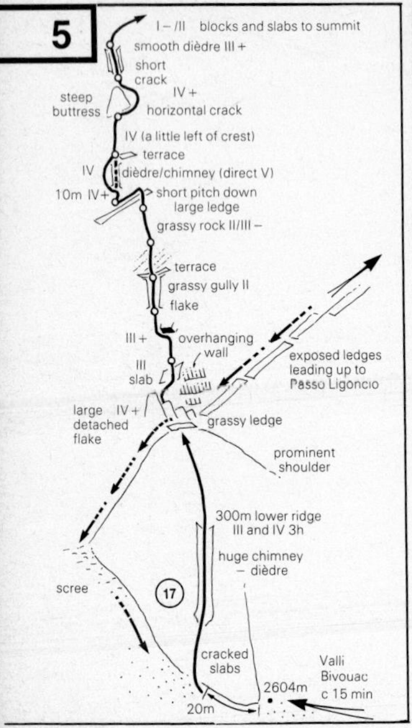
5
I – /II blocks and slabs to summit
smooth dièdre III +
short crack
steep buttress
IV +
horizontal crack
IV (a little left of crest)
terrace
IV
dièdre/chimney (direct V)
10m IV +
short pitch down
large ledge
grassy rock II/III –
terrace
grassy gully II
flake
III +
overhanging wall
III slab
exposed ledges leading up to Passo Ligoncio
large IV + detached flake
grassy ledge
prominent shoulder
300m lower ridge III and IV 3h
huge chimney – dièdre
scree
17
cracked slabs
Valli Bivouac c 15 min
2604m
20m

Punta Milano SE face

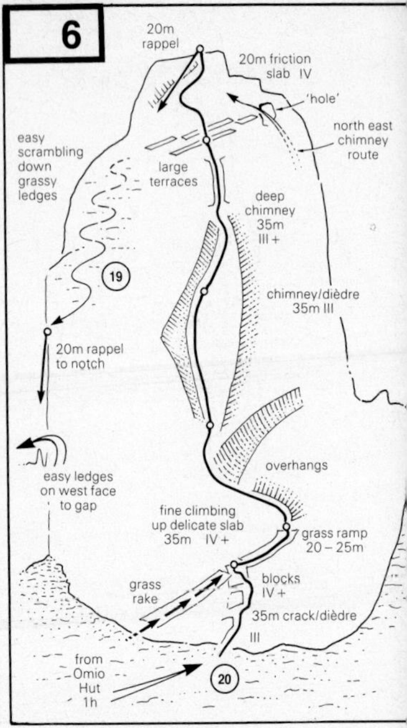
6
20m rappel
20m friction slab IV
'hole'
north east chimney route
easy scrambling down grassy ledges
large terraces
deep chimney 35m III +
19
chimney/dièdre 35m III
20m rappel to notch
overhangs
easy ledges on west face to gap
fine climbing up delicate slab 35m IV +
grass ramp 20 – 25m
grass rake
blocks IV +
35m crack/dièdre
III
from Omio Hut 1h
20

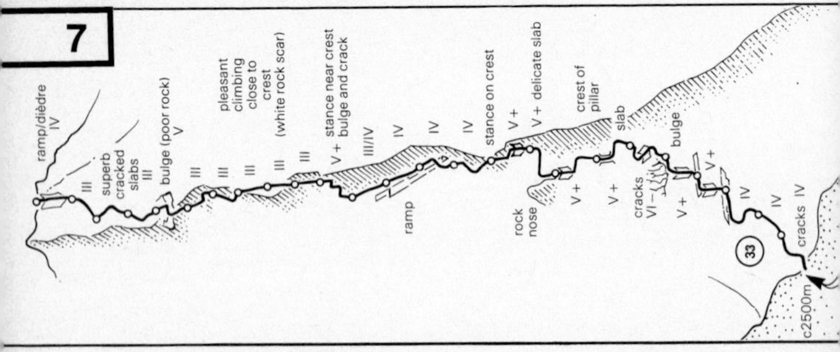
7
ramp/dièdre IV
III
superb cracked slabs III
bulge (poor rock) V
III
III
III
III
pleasant climbing close to crest (white rock scar)
III
V +
stance near crest bulge and crack
III/IV
IV
ramp
IV
IV
stance on crest
V +
V + delicate slab
rock nose
V +
crest of pillar
V +
slab
cracks VI –
bulge
V +
V +
IV
IV
cracks IV
33
c2500m

 Punta Sant'Anna N Pillar

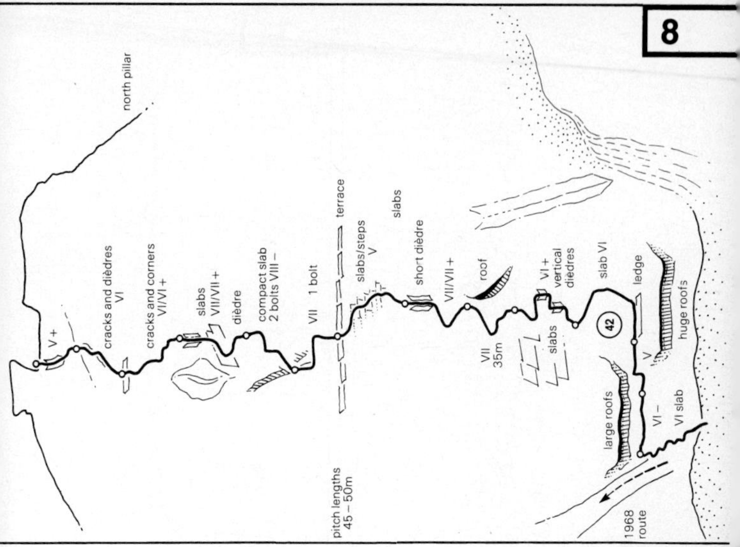
8
north pillar
V+
cracks and dièdres VI
cracks and corners VI/VI+
slabs VII/VII+
dièdre
compact slab 2 bolts VIII−
VII 1 bolt
terrace
slabs/steps V
slabs
short dièdre
VII/VII+
roof
VI+ vertical dièdres
slab VI
ledge
huge roofs
42
VII 35m
slabs
V
large roofs
VI−
VI slab
pitch lengths 45 – 50m
1968 route

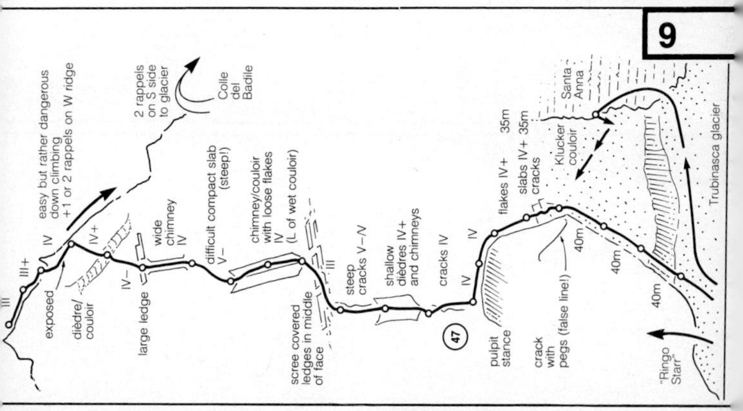
9
III
III+
IV
easy but rather dangerous down climbing +1 or 2 rappels on W ridge
2 rappels on S side to glacier
Colle del Badile
IV+
exposed
dièdre/couloir
IV−
large ledge
wide chimney IV
difficult compact slab V− (steep!)
chimney/couloir with loose flakes IV (L of wet couloir)
III
scree covered ledges in middle of face
steep cracks V−/V
shallow dièdres IV+ and chimneys
cracks IV
IV
IV
47
pulpit stance
flakes IV+ 35m
slabs IV+ 35m cracks
Klucker couloir
Santa Anna
crack with pegs (false line!)
40m
40m
40m
Trubinasca glacier
"Ringo Starr"

Punta Torelli
SSE pillar direct

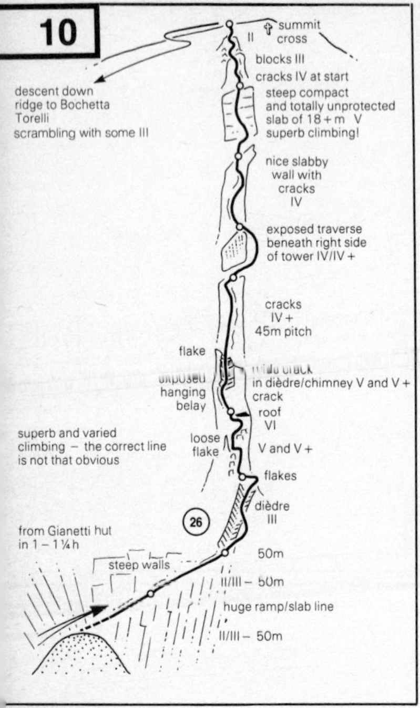
10
summit cross
II
blocks III
cracks IV at start
descent down ridge to Bochetta Torelli scrambling with some III
steep compact and totally unprotected slab of 18 + m V superb climbing!
nice slabby wall with cracks IV
exposed traverse beneath right side of tower IV/IV +
cracks IV + 45m pitch
flake
in dièdre/chimney V and V + crack
hanging belay
roof VI
superb and varied climbing – the correct line is not that obvious
loose flake
V and V +
flakes
dièdre III
26
from Gianetti hut in 1 – 1¼ h
50m
steep walls
II/III – 50m
huge ramp/slab line
II/III – 50m

Piz Badile
SW face – S pillar

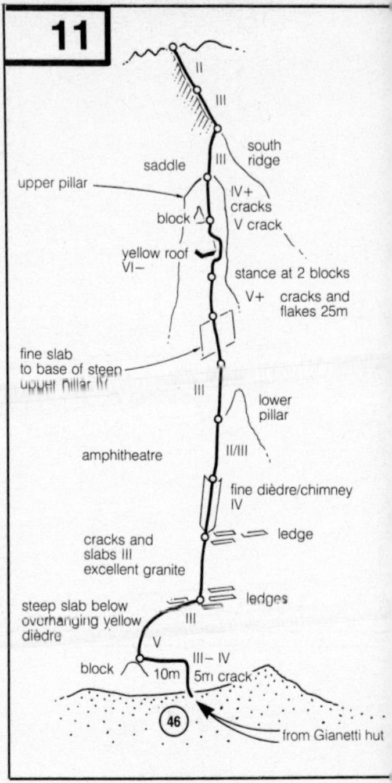
11
II
III
south ridge
III
saddle
upper pillar
IV+ cracks
block
V crack
yellow roof VI–
stance at 2 blocks
V+ cracks and flakes 25m
fine slab to base of steep
III
lower pillar
amphitheatre
II/III
fine dièdre/chimney IV
ledge
cracks and slabs III excellent granite
ledges
steep slab below overhanging yellow dièdre
III
V
block
III– IV
10m
5m crack
46
from Gianetti hut

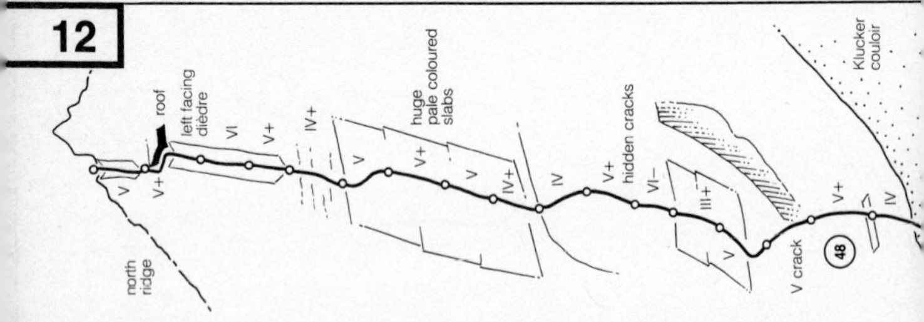
12
roof
left facing dièdre
VI
V+
IV+
huge pale coloured slabs
hidden cracks
Klucker couloir
V
V+
V
V+
V
IV+
IV
V+
VI–
III+
V
V crack
48
V+
IV
north ridge

Piz Badile NW face – Ringo Starr

13

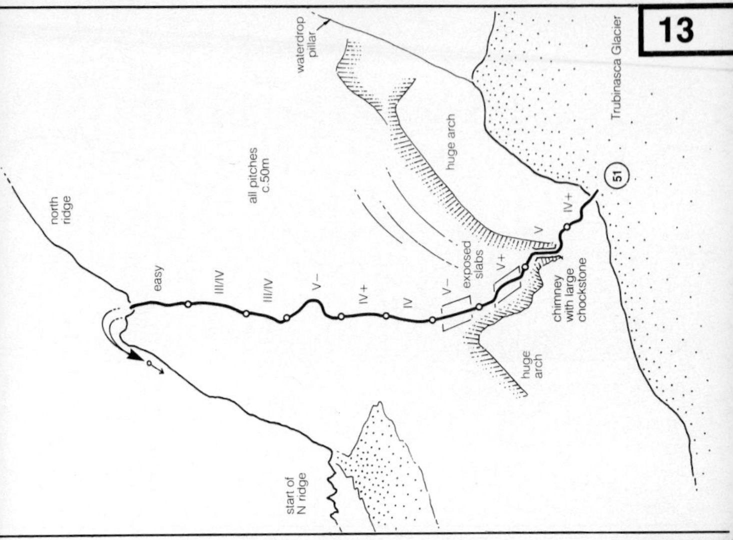
north ridge
easy
III/IV
III/IV
V–
IV+
IV
V–
exposed slabs
V+
V
IV+
all pitches c.50m
huge arch
waterdrop pillar
Trubinasca Glacier
51
chimney with large chockstone
huge arch
start of N ridge

14

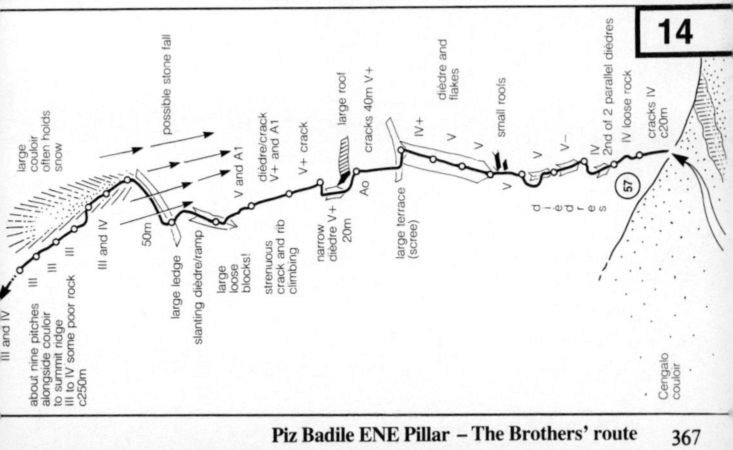
III and IV
about nine pitches alongside couloir to summit ridge III to IV some poor rock c250m
III
III
III
III and IV
large couloir often holds snow
50m
large ledge
slanting dièdre/ramp
possible stone fall
large loose blocks!
V and A1
strenuous crack and rib climbing
dièdre/crack V+ and A1
V+ crack
narrow dièdre V+ 20m
large roof
Ao
cracks 40m V+
large terrace (scree)
IV+
V
V
dièdre and flakes
small roofs
V
V
dièdres
V–
IV
2nd of 2 parallel dièdres
IV loose rock
cracks IV c20m
57
Cengalo couloir

15

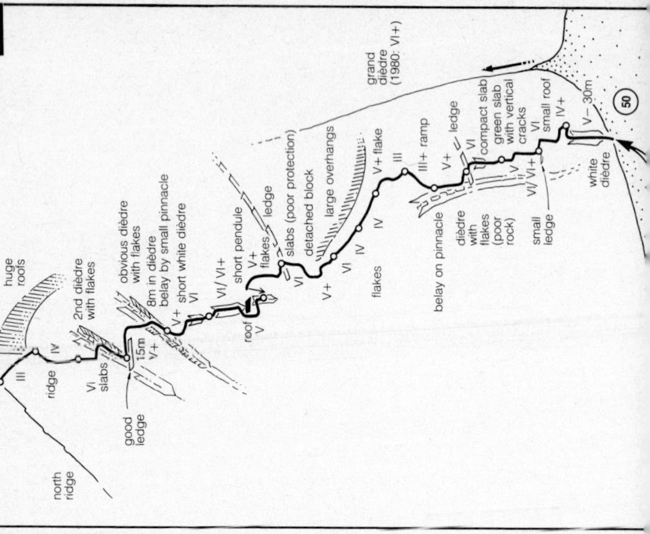
huge roofs
2nd dièdre with flakes
obvious dièdre with flakes
8m in dièdre
belay by small pinnacle
short white dièdre
short pendule
ledge
flakes
slabs (poor protection)
detached block
large overhangs
V+ flake
III+ ramp
ledge
compact slab
green slab with vertical cracks
small roof
V– 30m
50
grand dièdre (1980: VI+)
white dièdre
small ledge
dièdre with flakes (poor rock)
belay on pinnacle
flakes
roof V
15m V+
good ledge
VI slabs
ridge
north ridge
III
IV
V+
VI
VI/VI+
VI/ VI+

16

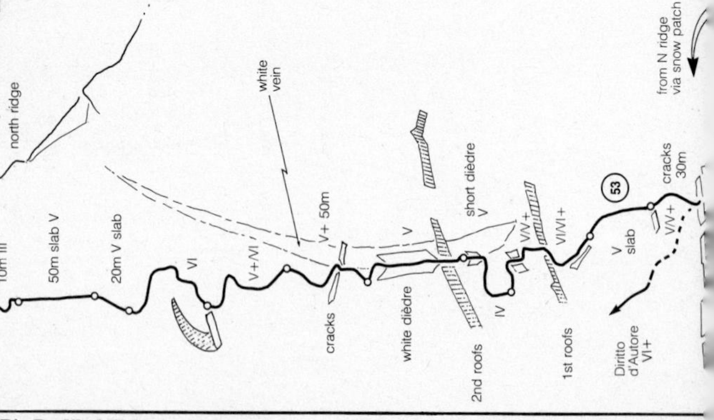
north ridge
10m III
50m slab V
20m V slab
VI
V+/VI
white vein
V+ 50m
V
short dièdre V
V/V+
VI/VI+
53
cracks 30m
from N ridge via snow patch
V slab
V/V+
IV
cracks
white dièdre
2nd roofs
1st roofs
Diritto d'Autore VI+

17

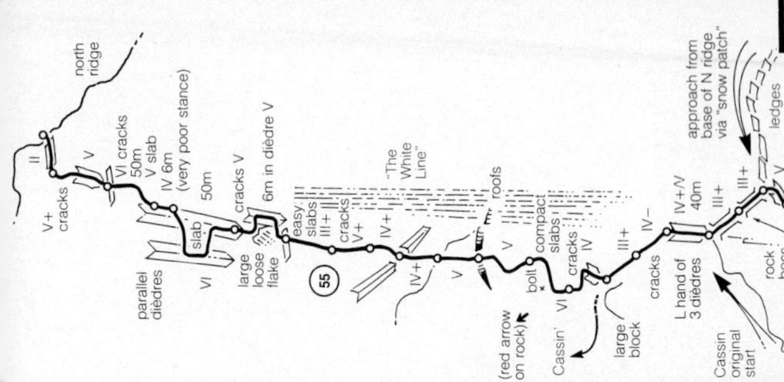
north ridge
II
V+ cracks
V
VI cracks 50m V slab
IV 6m (very poor stance)
50m
cracks V
6m in dièdre V
slab
parallel dièdres
VI
large loose flake
easy slabs III+
cracks V+
IV+
"The White Line"
55
IV+
V
roofs
V
compact slabs
cracks IV
bolt
VI
(red arrow on rock)
Cassin
large block
III+
IV–
cracks
IV+/V 40m
L hand of 3 dièdres
III+
III+
V
Cassin original start
rock boss
approach from base of N ridge via "snow patch"
ledges
cracked slabs V+
IV
chimneys
IV
slab V

18

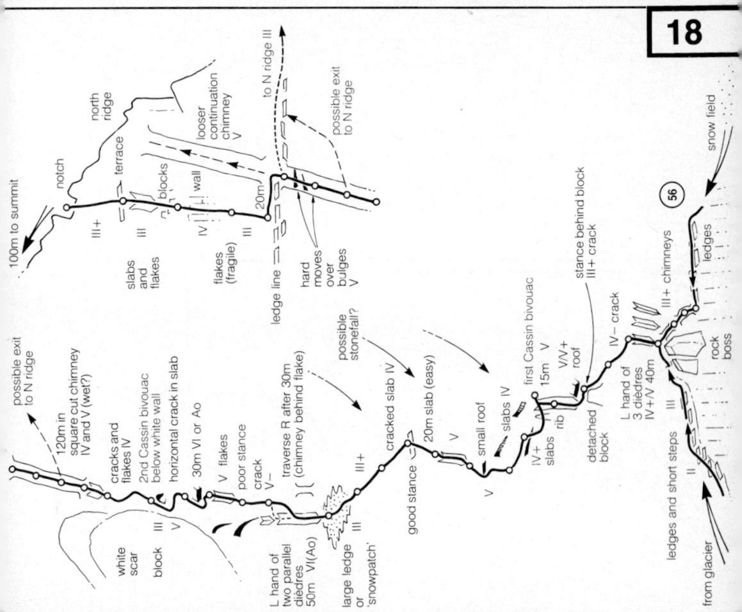
100m to summit
notch
III+
terrace
north ridge
III
blocks
slabs and flakes
wall
IV
looser continuation chimney V
III
flakes (fragile)
20m
to N ridge III
possible exit to N ridge
ledge line
hard moves over bulges V
possible exit to N ridge
120m in square cut chimney IV and V (wet?)
cracks and flakes IV
2nd Cassin bivouac below white wall
horizontal crack in slab
30m VI or Ao
V flakes
poor stance
crack V–
traverse R after 30m (chimney behind flake)
white scar
III
block
V
L hand of two parallel dièdres 50m VI(Ao)
large ledge or 'snowpatch'
III
III+
possible stonefall?
cracked slab IV
good stance
20m slab (easy)
V
small roof
V
slabs IV
rib
IV+ slabs
first Cassin bivouac
15m V
V/V+ roof
detached block
stance behind block III+ crack
IV– crack
L hand of 3 dièdres IV+/V 40m
III
III+ chimneys
rock boss
II
ledges and short steps
from glacier
56
ledges
snow field

Piz Badile ENE pillar

19

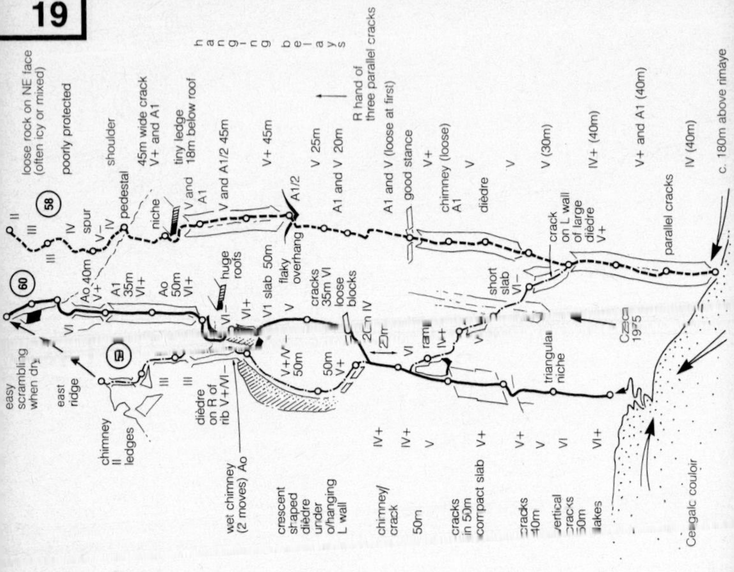

20

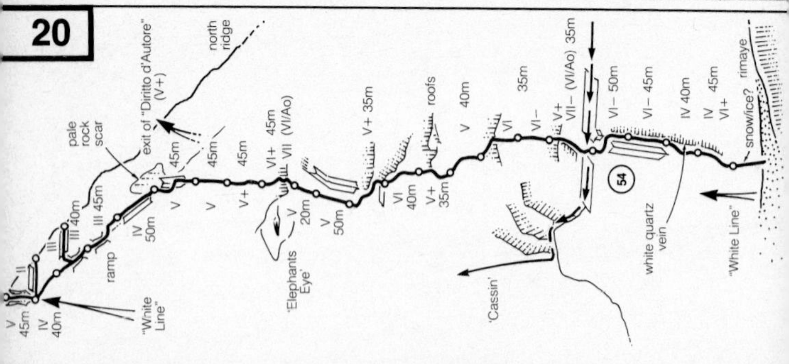

Piz Badile NE face – Another day in Paradise

Punta Pioda NW ridge

22

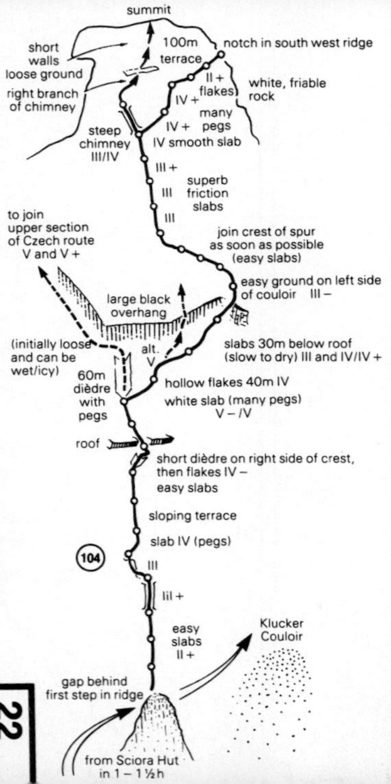
summit
short walls
loose ground
right branch of chimney
100m terrace
notch in south west ridge
II +
flakes
white, friable rock
IV +
many pegs
IV +
steep chimney III/IV
IV smooth slab
III +
III
superb friction slabs
III
to join upper section of Czech route V and V +
join crest of spur as soon as possible (easy slabs)
easy ground on left side of couloir III –
large black overhang
(initially loose and can be wet/icy)
alt. V
slabs 30m below roof (slow to dry) III and IV/IV +
60m dièdre with pegs
hollow flakes 40m IV
white slab (many pegs) V – /IV
roof
short dièdre on right side of crest, then flakes IV –
easy slabs
sloping terrace
slab IV (pegs)
104
III
III +
easy slabs II +
Klucker Couloir
gap behind first step in ridge
from Sciora Hut in 1 – 1½h

Piz Badile SE face

21

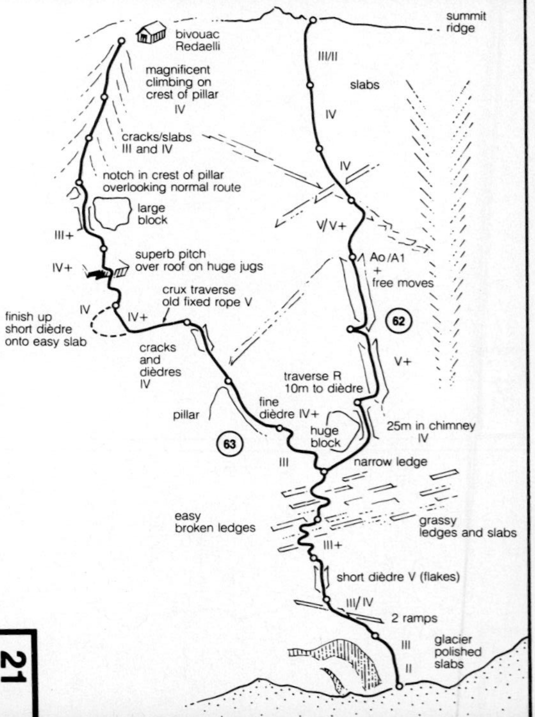
summit ridge
bivouac Redaelli
III/II
magnificent climbing on crest of pillar IV
slabs
IV
cracks/slabs III and IV
IV
notch in crest of pillar overlooking normal route
large block
V/V+
III+
superb pitch over roof on huge jugs
IV+
Ao/A1 + free moves
crux traverse old fixed rope V
IV
IV+
finish up short dièdre onto easy slab
62
cracks and dièdres IV
V+
traverse R 10m to dièdre
pillar
fine dièdre IV+
huge block
25m in chimney IV
63
III
narrow ledge
easy broken ledges
grassy ledges and slabs
III+
short dièdre V (flakes)
III/ IV
2 ramps
III
glacier polished slabs
II

Punta Sertori ENE pillar

23

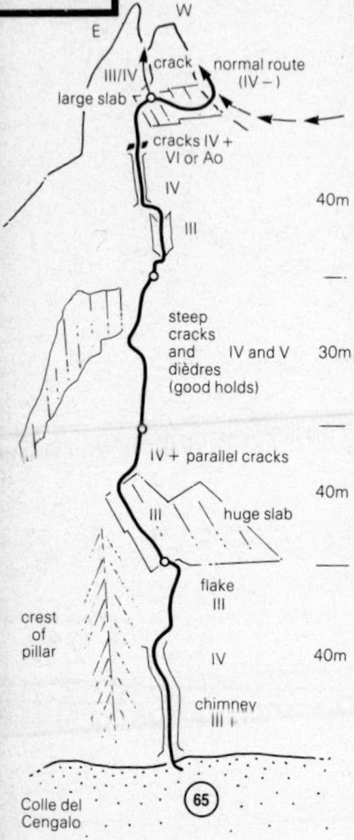

Punta Sertori S ridge

24

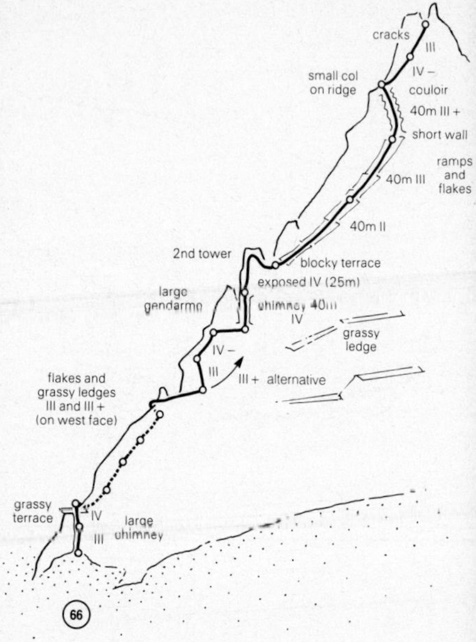

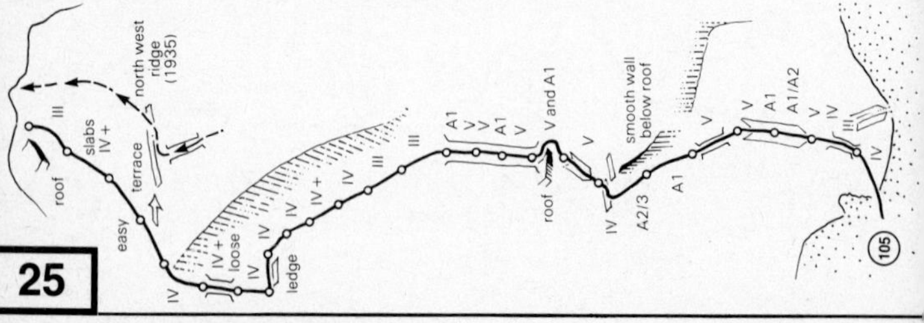

25

Punta Pioda NW face

26

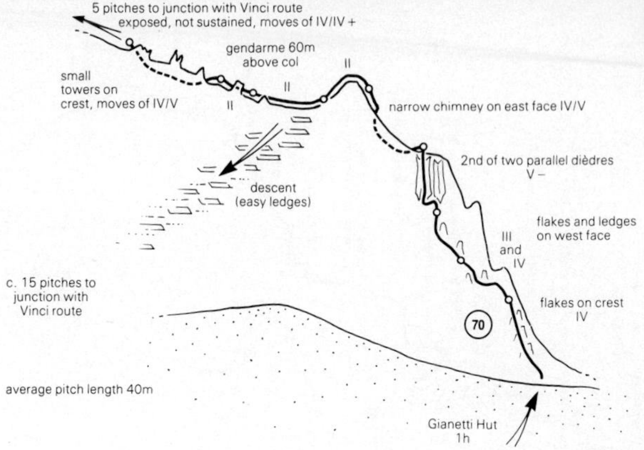
5 pitches to junction with Vinci route
exposed, not sustained, moves of IV/IV +
gendarme 60m
above col
small
towers on
crest, moves of IV/V
II
II
II
narrow chimney on east face IV/V
2nd of two parallel dièdres
V –
descent
(easy ledges)
flakes and ledges
on west face
III
and
IV
c. 15 pitches to
junction with
Vinci route
flakes on crest
IV
70
average pitch length 40m
Gianetti Hut
1h

27

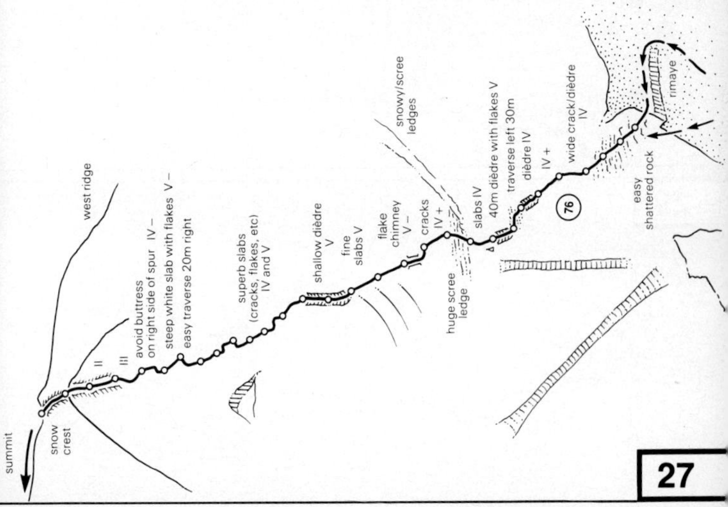
summit
snow
crest
west ridge
II
III
avoid buttress
on right side of spur IV –
steep white slab with flakes V –
easy traverse 20m right
superb slabs
(cracks, flakes, etc)
IV and V
shallow dièdre
V
fine
slabs V
flake
chimney
V –
cracks
IV +
snowy/scree
ledges
huge scree
ledge
slabs IV
40m dièdre with flakes V
traverse left 30m
dièdre IV
IV +
wide crack/dièdre
IV
76
easy
shattered rock
rimaye

28

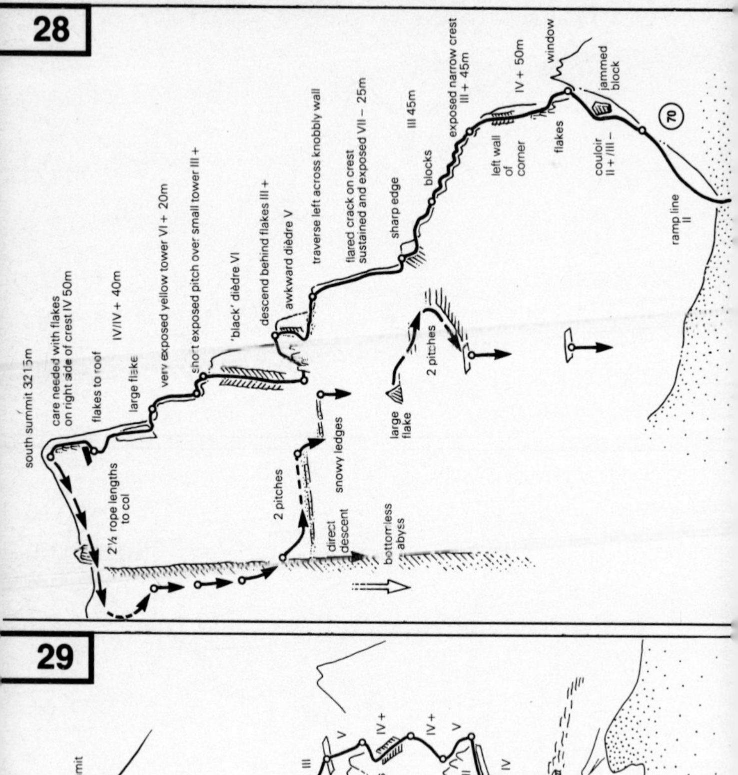
south summit 3215m
care needed with flakes on right side of crest IV 50m
flakes to roof
IV/IV + 40m
large flake
very exposed yellow tower VI + 20m
shot exposed pitch over small tower III +
'black' dièdre VI
descend behind flakes III +
awkward dièdre V
traverse left across knobbly wall
flared crack on crest sustained and exposed VII – 25m
sharp edge
III 45m
blocks
exposed narrow crest III + 45m
left wall of corner
IV + 50m
flakes
window
jammed block
couloir II + /III –
70
ramp line II
2½ rope lengths to col
2 pitches
snowy ledges
direct descent
bottomless abyss
large flake
2 pitches

29

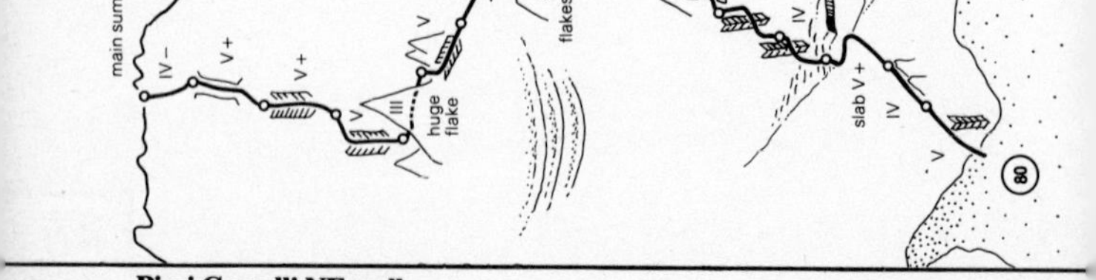
main summit
IV –
V +
V +
V
III
huge flake
V
III
V
flakes
IV +
IV +
V
II
IV
IV
slab V +
IV
V
80

Pizzi Gemelli NNW ridge

30

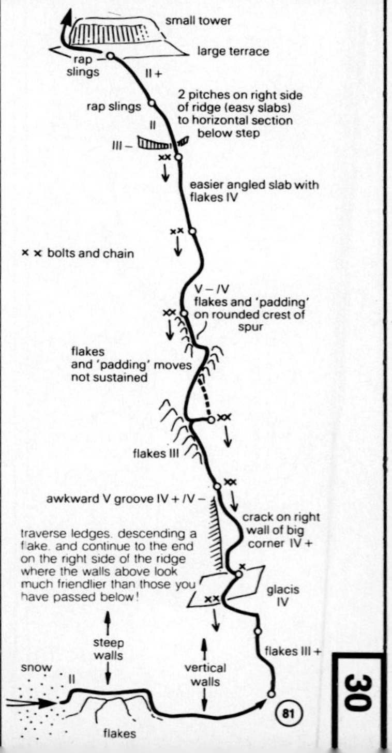

31

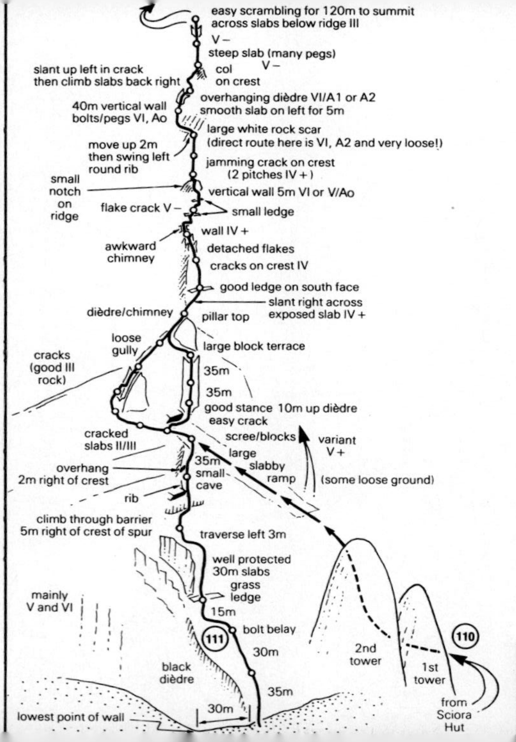

Sciora Dafora NW ridge

32

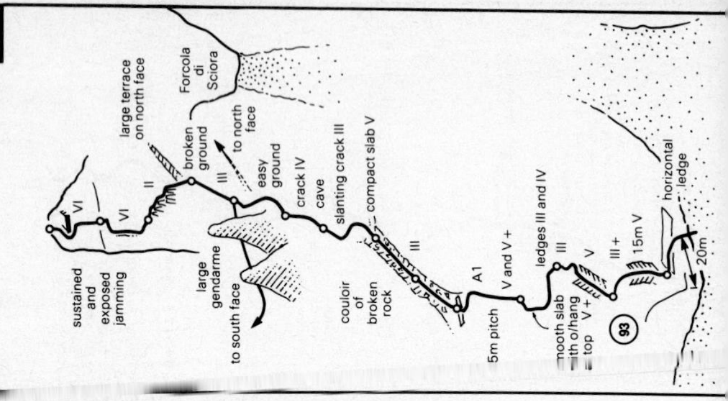
Forcola di Sciora
large terrace on north face
broken ground
to north face
VI
VI
II
III
sustained and exposed jamming
large gendarme
to south face
easy ground
crack IV
cave
slanting crack III
compact slab V
III
couloir of broken rock
A1
5m pitch
V and V +
ledges III and IV
III
V
V +
III +
15m V
20m
horizontal ledge
93

33

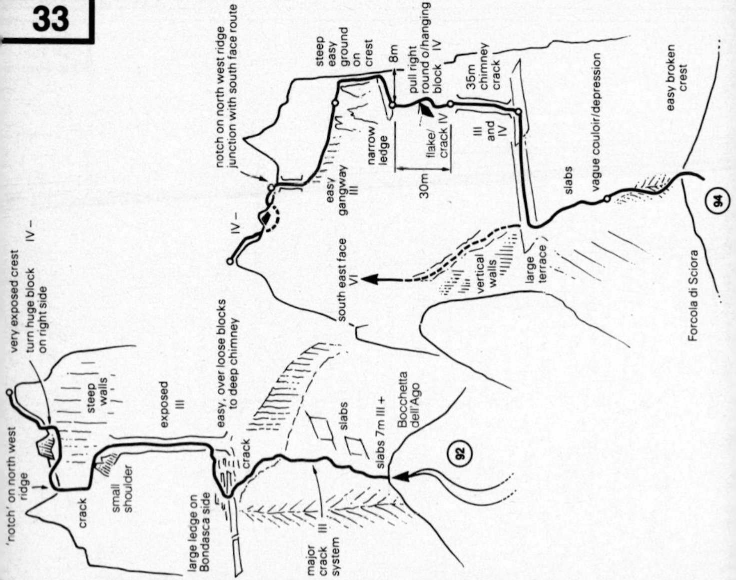
very exposed crest IV –
turn huge block on right side
'notch' on north west ridge
crack
small shoulder
steep walls
exposed III
easy, over loose blocks to deep chimney
large ledge on Bondasca side
crack
major crack system III
slabs
slabs 7m III +
Bocchetta dell'Ago
92
notch on north west ridge junction with south face route
IV –
south east face VI
easy gangway III
narrow ledge
30m
flake/ crack IV
steep easy ground on crest
8m
pull right round o/hanging block IV
35m chimney crack
III and IV
vertical walls
large terrace
slabs
vague couloir/depression
easy broken crest
Forcola di Sciora
94

34

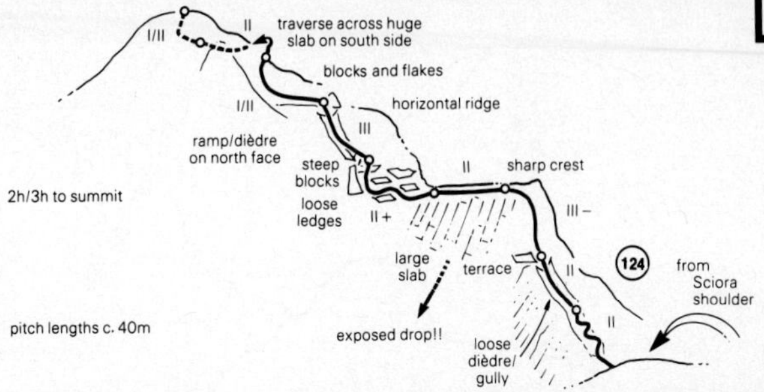
I/II
II
traverse across huge slab on south side
blocks and flakes
I/II
horizontal ridge
III
ramp/dièdre on north face
steep blocks
II
sharp crest
2h/3h to summit
loose ledges
II +
III –
large slab
terrace
II
124
from Sciora shoulder
II
pitch lengths c. 40m
exposed drop!!
loose dièdre/ gully

35

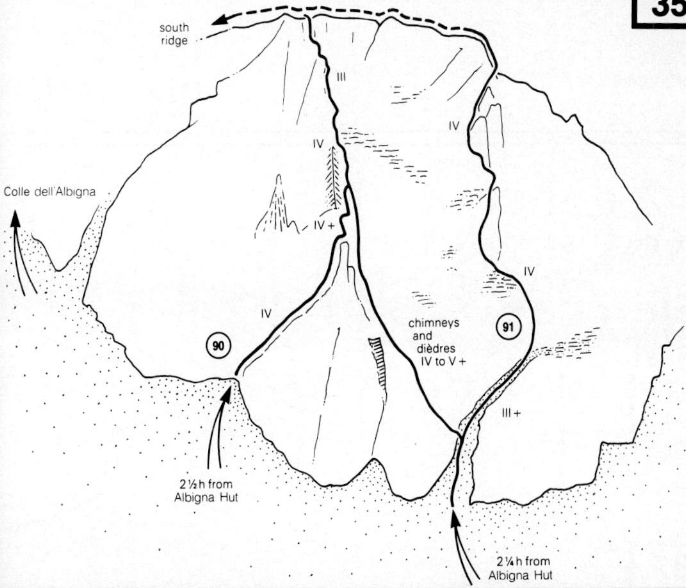
south ridge
I
III
IV
IV
Colle dell'Albigna
IV +
IV
IV
chimneys and dièdres IV to V +
91
90
III +
2½h from Albigna Hut
2¼h from Albigna Hut

Piz Frachiccio (N pillar) Sognadoro

36

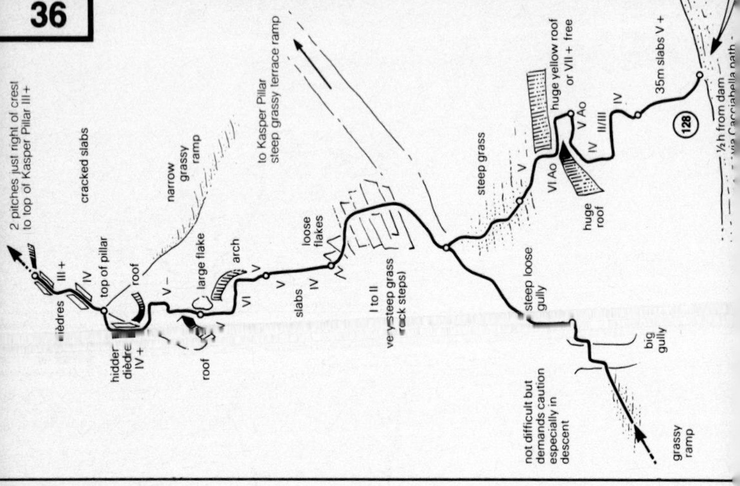

2 pitches just right of crest to top of Kasper Pillar III+
cracked slabs
narrow grassy ramp
to Kasper Pillar steep grassy terrace ramp
III +
IV
top of pillar
roof
V –
large flake
arch
V
V
VI
slabs
IV
loose flakes
IV +
roof
I to II
steep grass
V
VI Ao
huge yellow roof or VII + free
V Ao
IV
II/III
IV
35m slabs V +
huge roof
steep loose gully
big gully
not difficult but demands caution especially in descent
grassy ramp
128
½h from dam

37

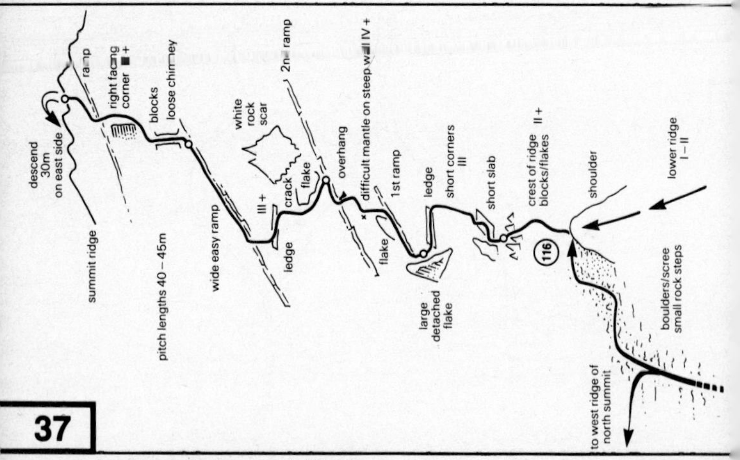

descend 30m on east side
summit ridge
ramp
blocks
loose chimney
pitch lengths 40 – 45m
wide easy ramp
white rock scar
III +
crack
flake
overhang
ledge
1st ramp
flake
large detached flake
ledge
short corners III
short slab
crest of ridge blocks/flakes II +
116
shoulder
lower ridge I – II
boulders/scree small rock steps
to west ridge of north summit

Inominata Main summit W ridge

38

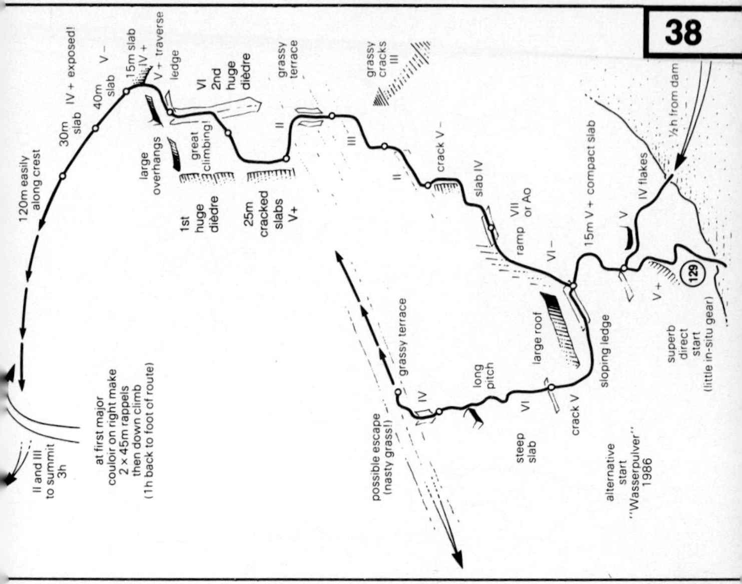
120m easily along crest
30m slab
40m slab
IV + exposed!
15m slab
IV +
V –
V + traverse
ledge
large overhangs
great climbing!
VI
2nd huge dièdre
1st huge dièdre
25m cracked slabs V+
II
grassy terrace
grassy cracks III
III
crack V –
II
slab IV
VII or AO
ramp
VI –
15m V + compact slab
IV flakes
V
½ h from dam
V +
129
large roof
sloping ledge
superb direct start (little in-situ gear)
grassy terrace
IV
long pitch
VI
crack V
steep slab
possible escape (nasty grass!)
alternative start "Wasserpulver" 1986
II and III to summit 3h
at first major couloir on right make 2 × 45m rappels then down climb (1h back to foot of route)

39

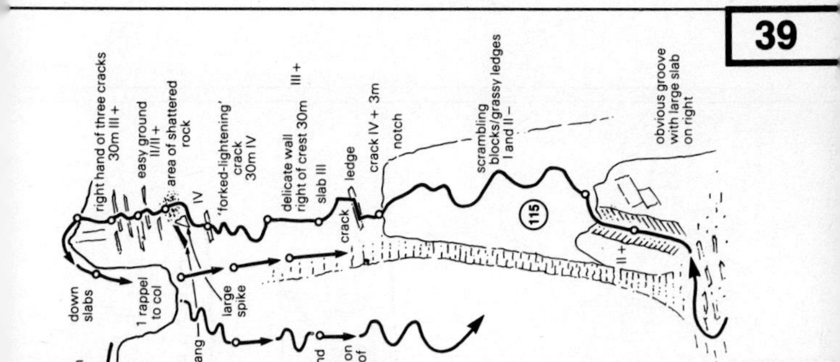
to main peak
down slabs
1 rappel to col
overhang
large spike
loose and nasty ground on the left of couloir
right hand of three cracks 30m III +
easy ground II/II +
area of shattered rock
IV
'forked-lightening' crack 30m IV
delicate wall right of crest 30m
III +
slab III
crack
ledge
crack IV + 3m
notch
scrambling blocks/grassy ledges I and II –
115
II +
obvious groove with large slab on right

40

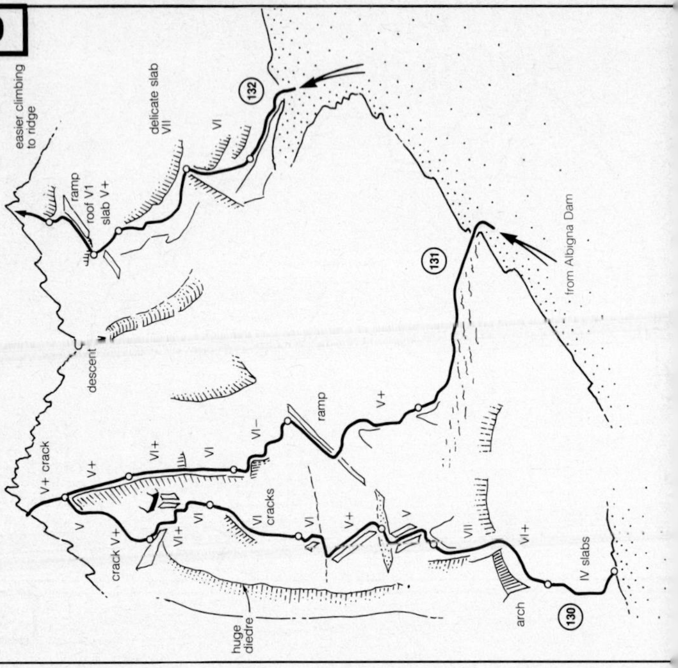
easier climbing to ridge
delicate slab VII
VI
132
ramp
roof V1
slab V+
descent
V+ crack
V+
VI+
VI
VI–
ramp
V+
131
from Albigna Dam
V
crack V+
VI+
VI
VI cracks
VI
V+
V
VII
VI+
IV slabs
arch
130
huge diedre

41

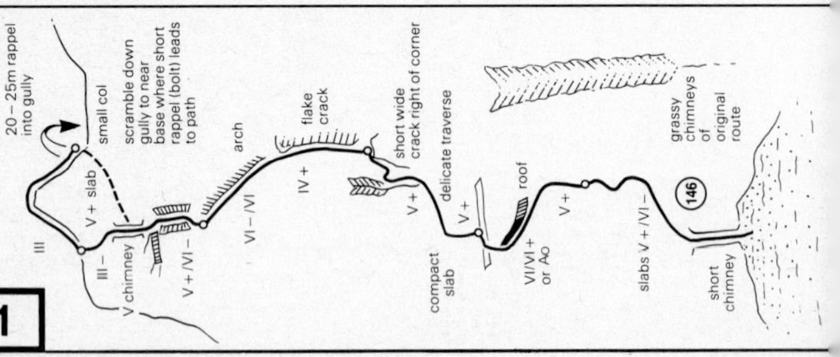
20 – 25m rappel into gully
small col
scramble down gully to near base where short rappel (bolt) leads to path
III
V + slab
III –
V chimney
V + /VI –
arch
VI – /VI
flake crack
IV +
short wide crack right of corner
V +
delicate traverse
V +
compact slab
roof
VI/VI + or Ao
V +
slabs V + /VI –
146
grassy chimneys of original route
short chimney

42

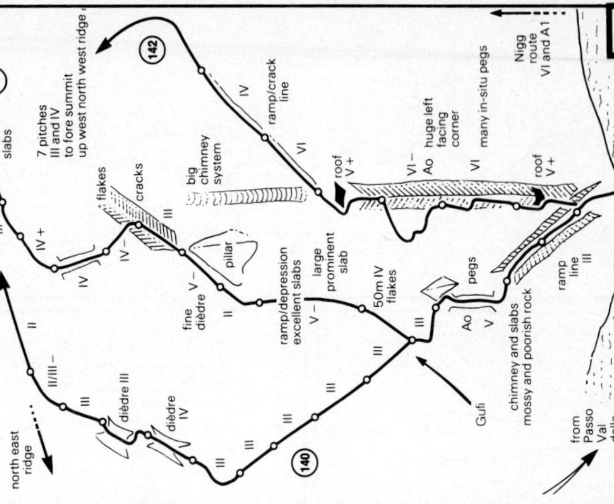
to summit/broken rock
141
slabs
II
III
IV +
IV
7 pitches III and IV to fore summit up west north west ridge
142
IV
ramp/crack line
VI
big chimney system
roof V+
VI –
Ao
huge left facing corner
VI
many in-situ pegs
roof V+
Nigg route VI and A1
flakes
cracks
III
IV –
pillar
V –
fine dièdre
II
ramp/depression excellent slabs
V –
large prominent slab
50m IV flakes
III
pegs
Ao
V
ramp line III
chimney and slabs mossy and poorish rock
Gufi
to summit on north east ridge
II
II/III –
III
dièdre III
dièdre IV
north east ridge
III
III
III
III
140
from Passo Val della Neve

43

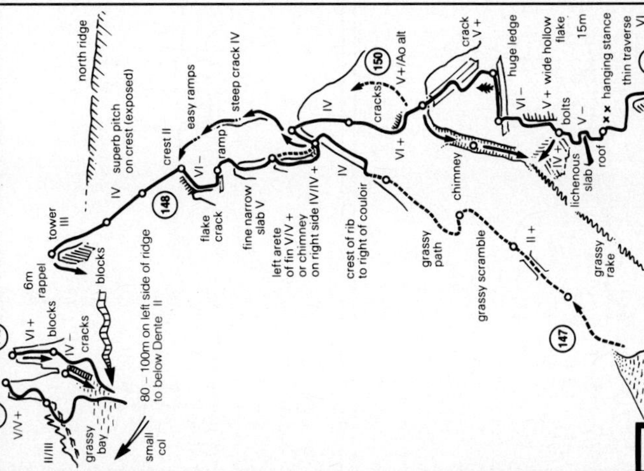
144
V/V+
II/III
grassy bay
small col
145
VI +
blocks
IV –
cracks
6m rappel
blocks
80 – 100m on left side of ridge to below Dente II
tower III
IV
superb pitch on crest (exposed)
north ridge
148
crest II
easy ramps
VI –
ramp
flake crack
steep crack IV
fine narrow slab V
left arete of fin V/V+ or chimney on right side IV/IV +
IV
crest of rib to right of couloir
150
V+/Ao alt
cracks
IV
VI +
grassy path
chimney
crack V +
huge ledge
VI –
V + wide hollow flake
15m
bolts
V –
IV +
hanging stance
thin traverse VI
roof
lichenous slab
grassy scramble
II +
149
slab IV + /V –
bolt
easy ramp
wide flake crack V
grassy rake
147

44

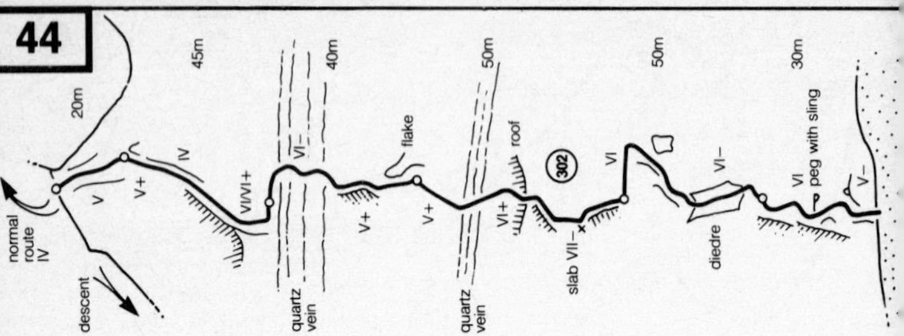
20m
45m
40m
50m
50m
30m
normal route IV
descent
V
V+
IV
VI/VI+
VI–
quartz vein
V+
flake
V+
quartz vein
VI+
roof
302
slab VII–
VI
VI–
diedre
VI
peg with sling
V–

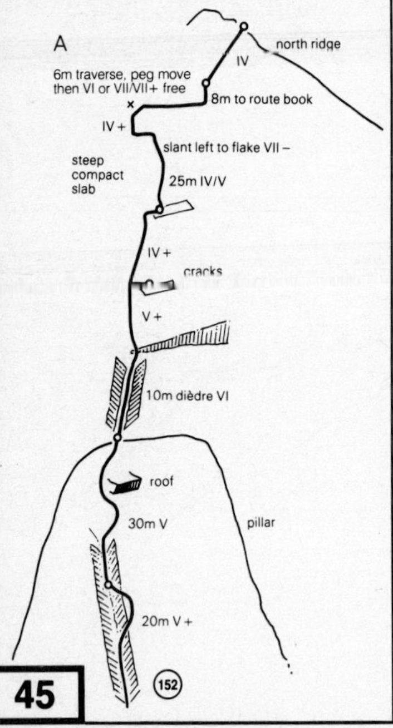
A
north ridge
IV
6m traverse, peg move then VI or VII/VII+ free
8m to route book
IV +
slant left to flake VII –
steep compact slab
25m IV/V
IV +
cracks
V +
10m dièdre VI
roof
30m V
pillar
20m V +
152

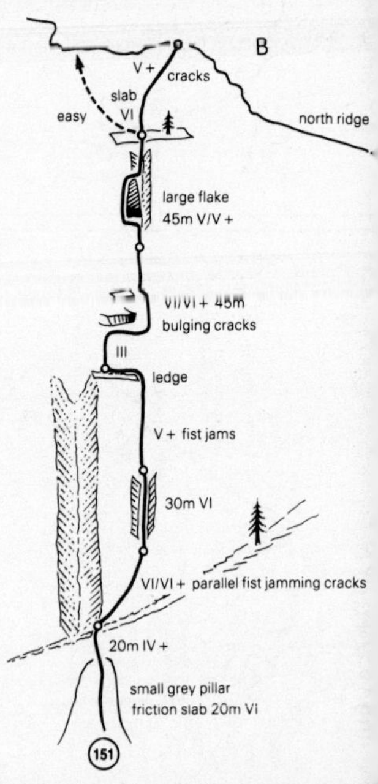
B
V +
cracks
slab
easy
VI
north ridge
large flake
45m V/V +
VI/VI + 45m
bulging cracks
III
ledge
V + fist jams
30m VI
VI/VI + parallel fist jamming cracks
20m IV +
small grey pillar
friction slab 20m VI
151

45

 Spazzacaldeira SE face

46

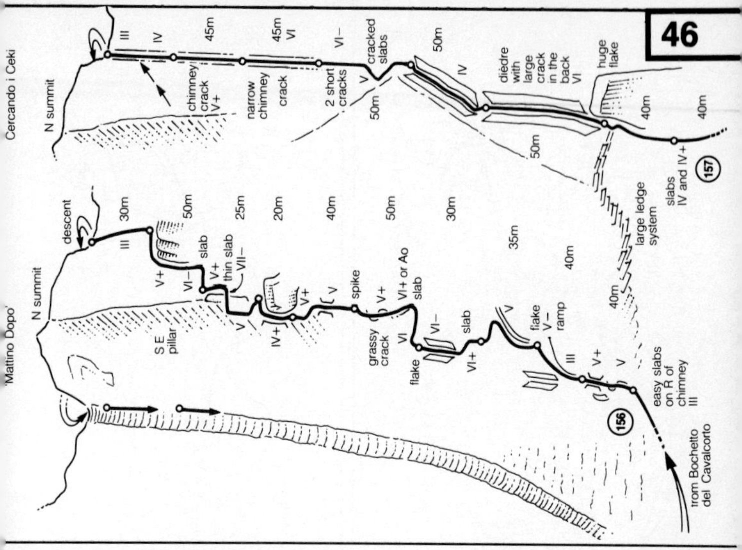
Cercando i Ceki
N summit
III
IV
45m
45m
VI
VI–
chimney/
crack
V+
narrow
chimney
crack
2 short
cracks
V
50m
cracked
slabs
50m
IV
dièdre
with
large
crack
in the
back
VI
huge
flake
40m
40m
50m
slabs
IV and IV+
157
'Mattino Dopo'
N summit
descent
30m
III
50m
V+
VI–
slab
V+
thin slab
VII–
25m
20m
40m
V+
V
IV+
S E
pillar
spike
V+
grassy
crack
VI
VI+ or Ao
slab
50m
VI–
flake
slab
VI+
30m
35m
V
flake
V–
ramp
40m
III
V+
V
large ledge
system
40m
easy slabs
on R of
chimney
III
156
from Bochetto
del Cavalcorto

47

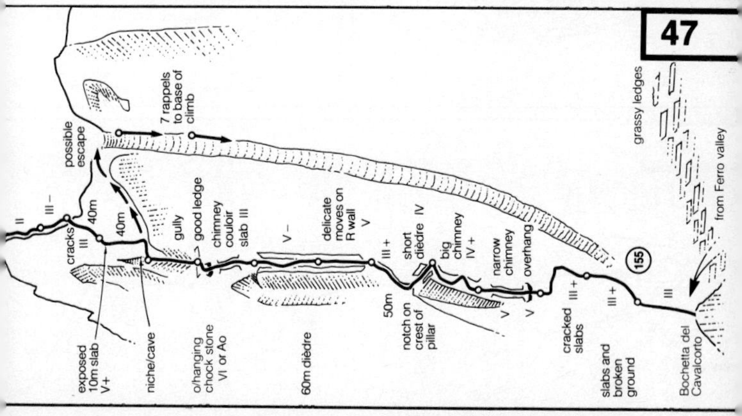
II
III–
cracks
III
40m
40m
possible
escape
7 rappels
to base of
climb
exposed
10m slab
V+
niche/cave
gully
good ledge
chimney
couloir
slab III
o/hanging
chock stone
VI or Ao
V–
60m dièdre
delicate
moves on
R wall
V
III+
50m
notch on
crest of
pillar
short
dièdre IV
big
chimney
IV+
narrow
chimney
overhang
V
V
cracked
slabs
III+
III+
slabs and
broken
ground
155
III
Bochetta del
Cavalcorto
grassy ledges
from Ferro valley

48

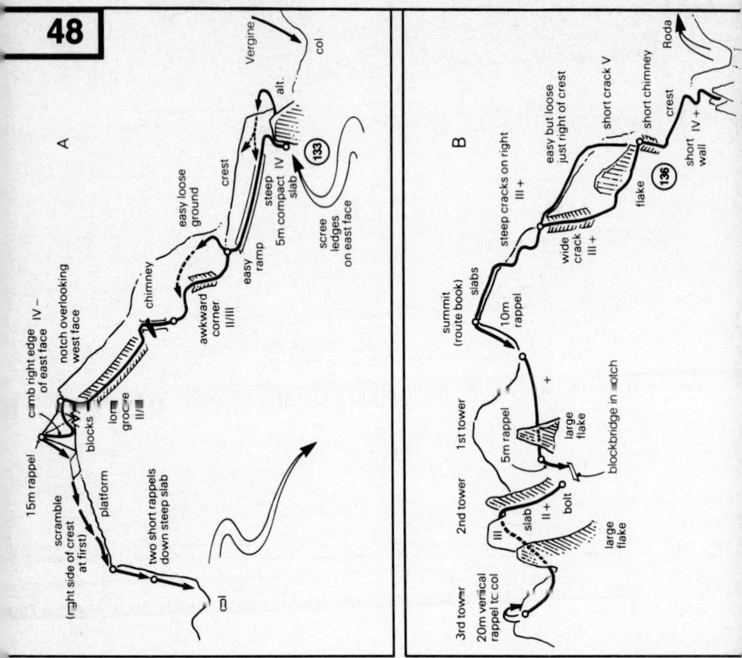
A
Vergine
col
alt.
133
IV
steep
5m compact
slab
scree
ledges
on east face
crest
easy loose
ground
easy
ramp
chimney
awkward
corner
II/III
notch overlooking
west face
IV –
climb right edge
of east face
blocks
15m rappel
scramble
(right side of crest
at first)
platform
two short rappels
down steep slab
col
B
Roda
short crack V
short chimney
crest
IV +
short
wall
136
easy but loose
just right of crest
flake
steep cracks on right
III +
wide
crack
III +
slabs
summit
(route book)
10m
rappel
+
1st tower
5m rappel
large
flake
blockbridge in notch
2nd tower
slab
II +
bolt
III
large
flake
3rd tower
20m vertical
rappel to col

49

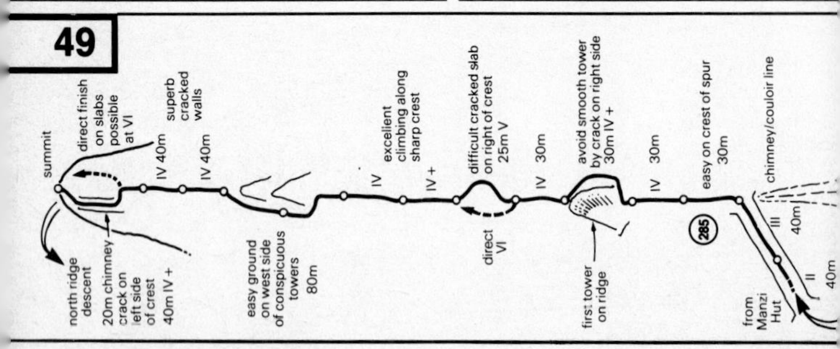
summit
north ridge
descent
direct finish
on slabs
possible
at VI
20m chimney
crack on
left side
of crest
40m IV +
IV 40m
IV 40m
superb
cracked
walls
easy ground
on west side
of conspicuous
towers
80m
IV
excellent
climbing along
sharp crest
IV +
difficult cracked slab
on right of crest
25m V
direct
VI
IV
30m
avoid smooth tower
by crack on right side
30m IV +
first tower
on ridge
IV
30m
easy on crest of spur
30m
285
chimney/couloir line
III
40m
II
40m
from
Manzi
Hut

Punta Bertone SE face

50

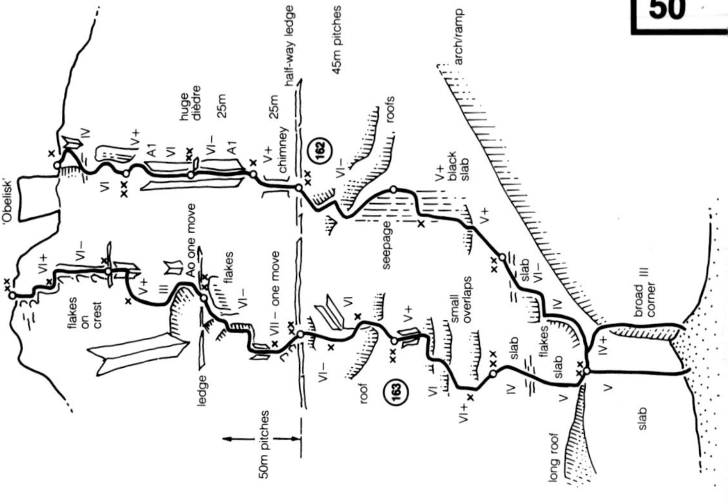
'Obelisk'
half-way ledge
45m pitches
arch/ramp
huge dièdre
25m
chimney
162
roofs
black slab
seepage
small overlaps
slab
flakes
broad corner
long roof
163
roof
50m pitches
VII – one move
Ao one move
flakes on crest
ledge

51

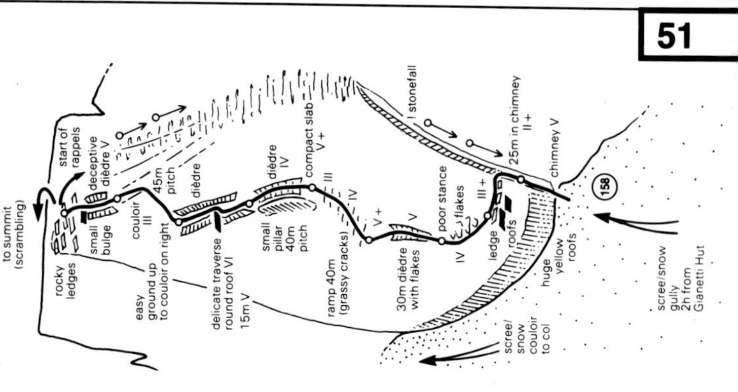
to summit (scrambling)
start of rappels
deceptive dièdre V
rocky ledges
small bulge
couloir III
45m pitch
easy ground up to couloir on right
dièdre
delicate traverse round roof VI
15m V
small pillar 40m pitch
dièdre IV
compact slab V+
ramp 40m (grassy cracks)
30m dièdre with flakes
poor stance flakes
stonefall
25m in chimney II+
chimney V
158
ledge
roofs
huge yellow roofs
scree/snow couloir to col
scree/snow gully 2h from Gianetti Hut

Punta Moraschini Pillar of the Polar Wind

52

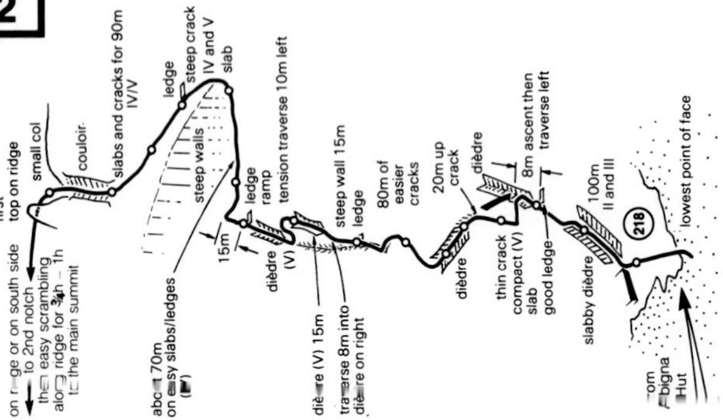
first top on ridge
small col
couloir
slabs and cracks for 90m IV/V
ledge
steep crack IV and V
slab
steep walls
ledge
ramp
tension traverse 10m left
15m
dièdre (V)
steep wall 15m
ledge
80m of easier cracks
20m up crack
dièdre
8m ascent then traverse left
100m II and III
218
lowest point of face
dièdre
thin crack compact (V) slab
good ledge
slabby dièdre
dièdre (V) 15m
Hut

53

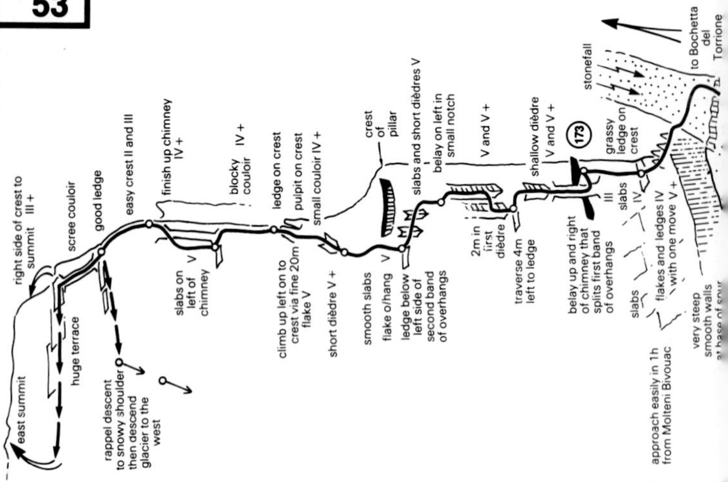
right side of crest to summit III +
scree couloir
good ledge
easy crest II and III
finish up chimney IV +
blocky couloir IV +
ledge on crest
pulpit on crest
small couloir IV +
crest of pillar
slabs and short dièdres V
belay on left in small notch
V and V +
shallow dièdre V and V +
173
stonefall
to Bochetta del Torrione
grassy ledge on crest
III
slabs IV
slabs on left of chimney
V
climb up left on to crest via fine 20m flake V
short dièdre V +
smooth slabs
flake o/hang
V
ledge below left side of second band of overhangs
2m in first dièdre
traverse 4m left to ledge
belay up and right of chimney that splits first band of overhangs
slabs
flakes and ledges IV with one move V +
very steep smooth walls
approach easily in 1h from Molteni Bivouac
east summit
huge terrace
rappel descent to snowy shoulder then descend glacier to the west

Punta Rasica SW ridge

54

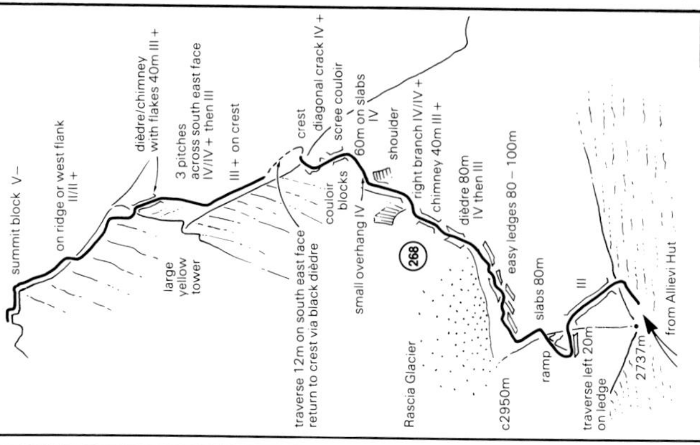

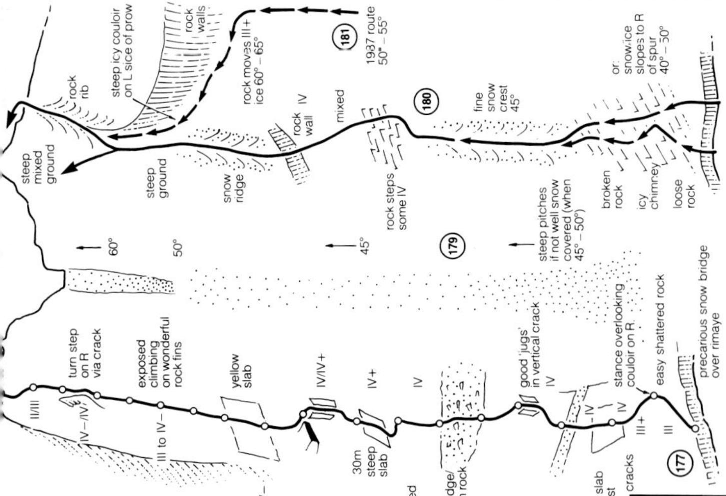

55

Pizzo del Ferro Orientale NW face

56

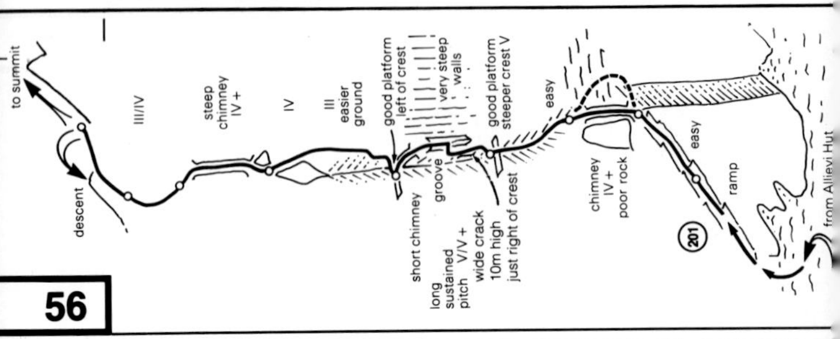
to summit
descent
III/IV
steep chimney IV+
IV
III easier ground
good platform left of crest
very steep walls
good platform steeper crest V
easy
short chimney
groove
long sustained pitch V/V+
wide crack 10m high just right of crest
chimney IV+ poor rock
easy
ramp
201
from Allievi Hut

57

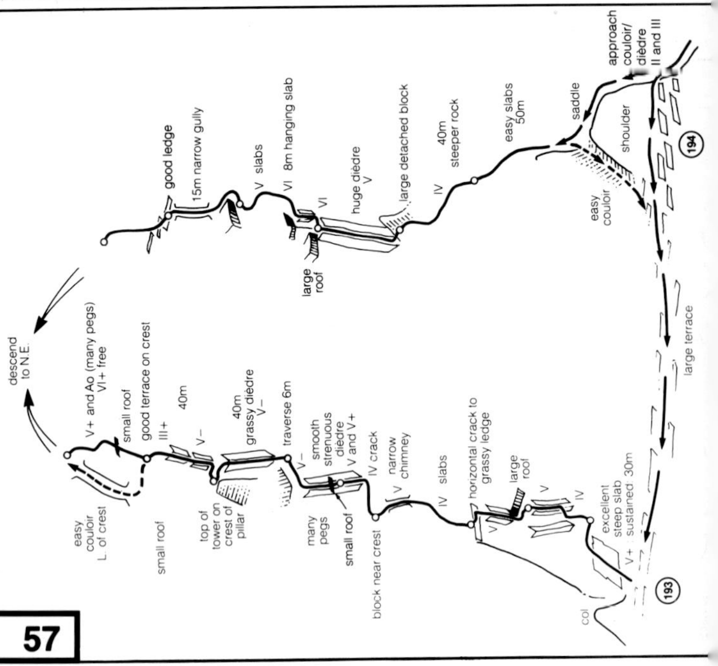
descend to N.E.
V+ and Ao (many pegs) VI+ free
small roof
good terrace on crest
III+
40m
V–
40m grassy dièdre V–
traverse 6m
V–
smooth strenuous dièdre V and V+
IV crack
V narrow chimney
IV slabs
horizontal crack to grassy ledge
large roof
V
IV
excellent steep slab V+ sustained 30m
easy couloir L. of crest
small roof
top of tower on crest of pillar
many pegs
small roof
block near crest
V
col
193
large terrace
good ledge
15m narrow gully
V slabs
VI 8m hanging slab
VI
huge dièdre V
large detached block
large roof
IV
40m steeper rock
easy slabs 50m
saddle
approach couloir/dièdre II and III
shoulder
194
easy couloir

Pizzo di Zocca Torrione Est

58

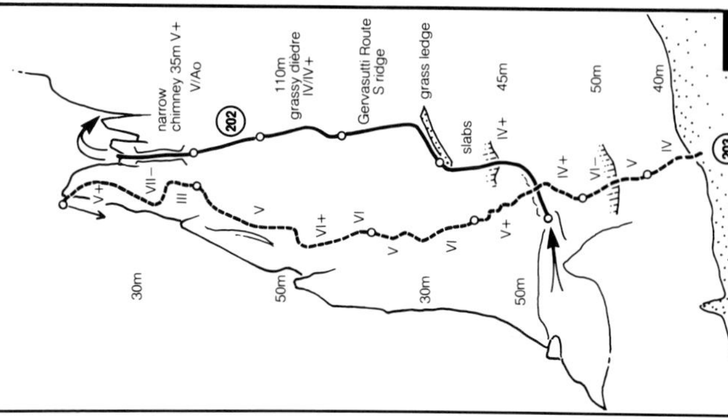

narrow chimney 35m V+ V/Ao
202
110m grassy dièdre IV/IV+
Gervasutti Route S ridge
grass ledge
45m
slabs
IV+
50m
40m
IV
203
V
VI–
IV+
VII–
V+
III
V
VI+
VI
V
VI
V+
30m
50m
30m
50m

59

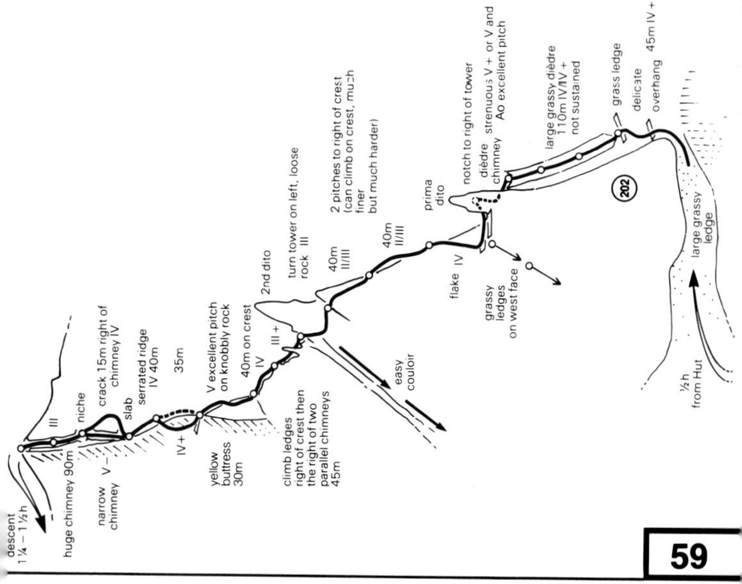

descent 1¼ – 1½ h
huge chimney 90m
narrow chimney V–
III
niche
crack 15m right of chimney IV
slab
serrated ridge IV 40m
35m
IV+
yellow buttress 30m
V excellent pitch on knobbly rock
40m on crest IV
III+
climb ledges right of crest then the right of two parallel chimneys 45m
easy couloir
2nd dito
turn tower on left, loose rock III
40m II/III
40m II/III
2 pitches to right of crest (can climb on crest, much finer but much harder)
flake IV
prima dito
grassy ledges on west face
notch to right of tower
dièdre chimney
strenuous V + or V and Ao excellent pitch
202
large grassy dièdre 110m IV/IV + not sustained
grass ledge
delicate overhang
45m IV +
large grassy ledge
½ h from Hut

Punta Allievi E face

60

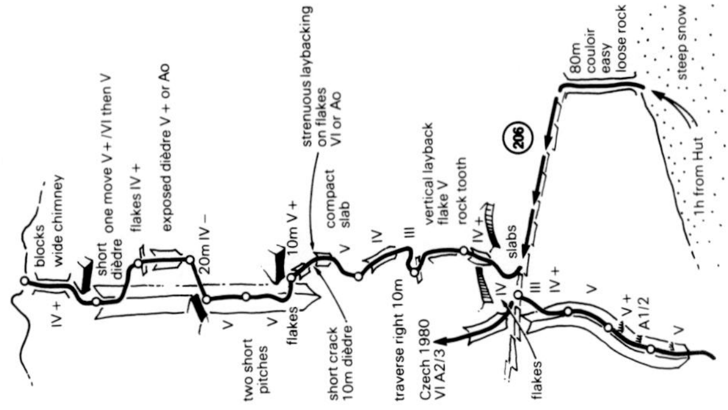

61

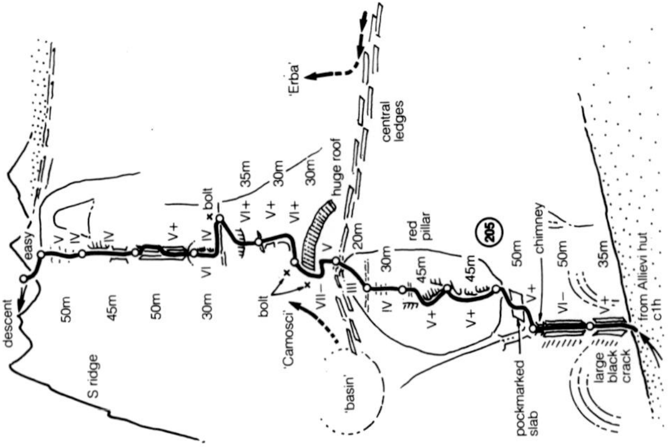

 Punta Allievi Filo Logico

62

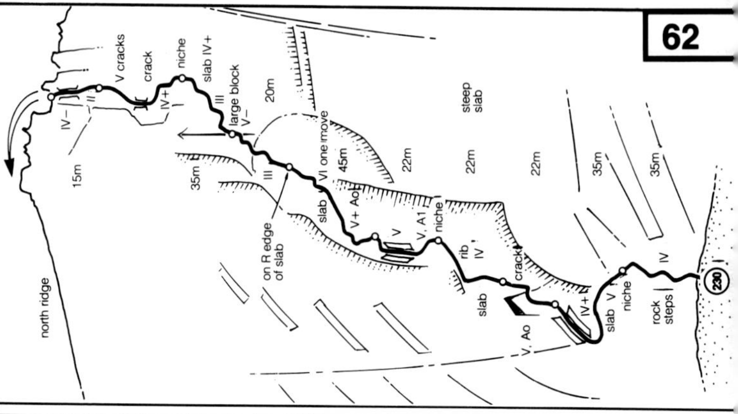
north ridge
15m
IV–
II
V cracks
crack
IV+
niche
slab IV+
III
large block
V–
20m
35m
III
VI one move
45m
22m
steep
slab
22m
22m
35m
35m
on R edge
of slab
slab
V+ Ao
V
V, A1
niche
rib
IV
crack
slab
V, Ao
IV+
slab V
niche
IV
rock
steps
230

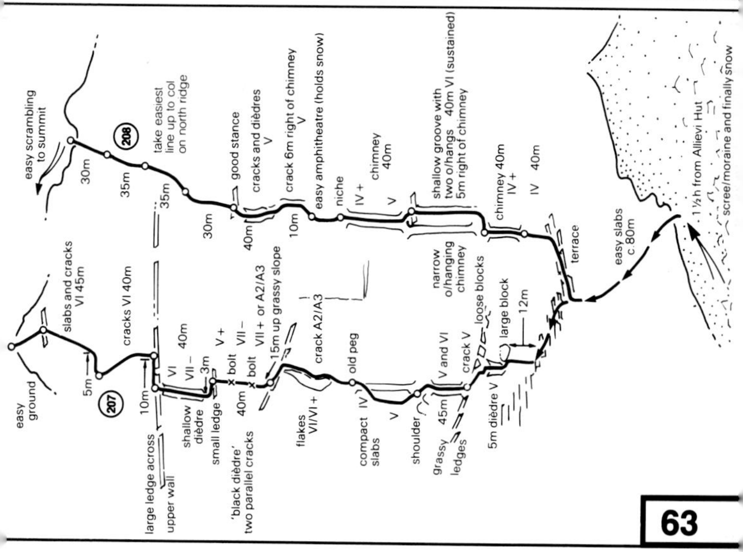
easy scrambling
to summit
30m
35m
208
take easiest
line up to col
on north ridge
35m
30m
good stance
cracks and dièdres
V
40m
crack 6m right of chimney
V
10m
easy amphitheatre (holds snow)
niche
IV+
chimney
40m
V
shallow groove with
two o/hangs 40m VI (sustained)
5m right of chimney
chimney 40m
IV+
IV 40m
narrow
o/hanging
chimney
terrace
easy slabs
c.80m
1½h from Allievi Hut
scree/moraine and finally snow
easy
ground
slabs and cracks
VI 45m
5m
207
cracks VI 40m
10m
VI
40m
VII–
3m
V+
VII–
VII+ or A2/A3
bolt
bolt
40m
15m up grassy slope
shallow
dièdre
small ledge
large ledge across
upper wall
'black dièdre'
two parallel cracks
flakes
VI/VI+
crack A2/A3
old peg
IV
V
compact
slabs
shoulder
V and VI
crack V
45m
grassy
ledges
loose blocks
large block
12m
5m dièdre V

63

64

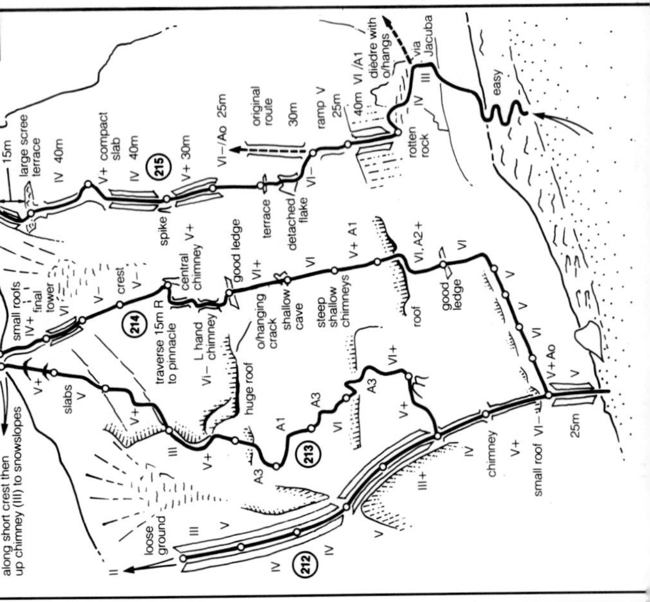

65

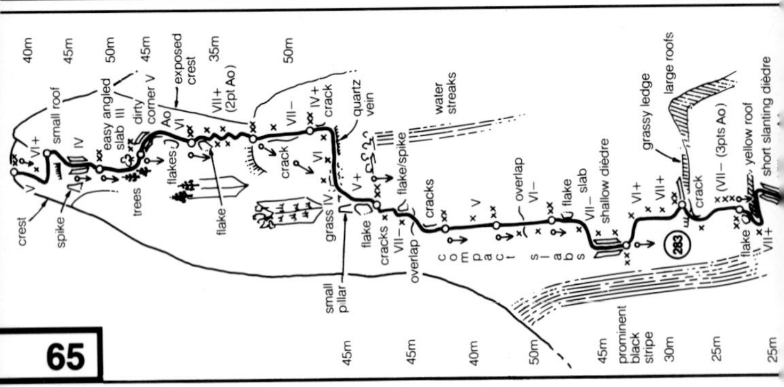

 Meridiana di Torrone SE pillar

Picco Luigi Amedeo SE face

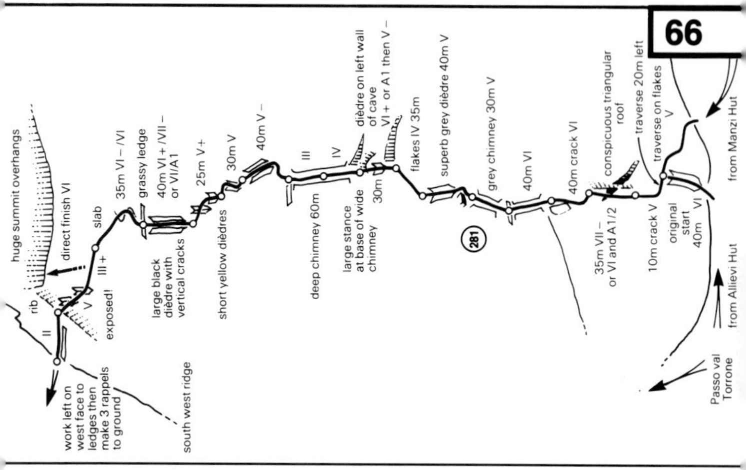
66
huge summit overhangs
direct finish VI
slab
35m VI–/VI
grassy ledge
40m VI+/VII– or VII/A1
25m V+
30m V
40m V–
III
IV
dièdre on left wall of cave
VI+ or A1 then V–
flakes IV 35m
superb grey dièdre 40m V
grey chimney 30m V
40m VI
40m crack VI
conspicuous triangular roof
traverse 20m left
traverse on flakes V
from Manzi Hut
rib
II
V
III+
exposed!
large black dièdre with vertical cracks
short yellow dièdres
deep chimney 60m
large stance at base of wide chimney
30m
281
35m VII– or VI and A1/2
10m crack V
original start 40m
VI
from Allievi Hut
Passo val Torrone
work left on west face to ledges then make 3 rappels to ground
south west ridge

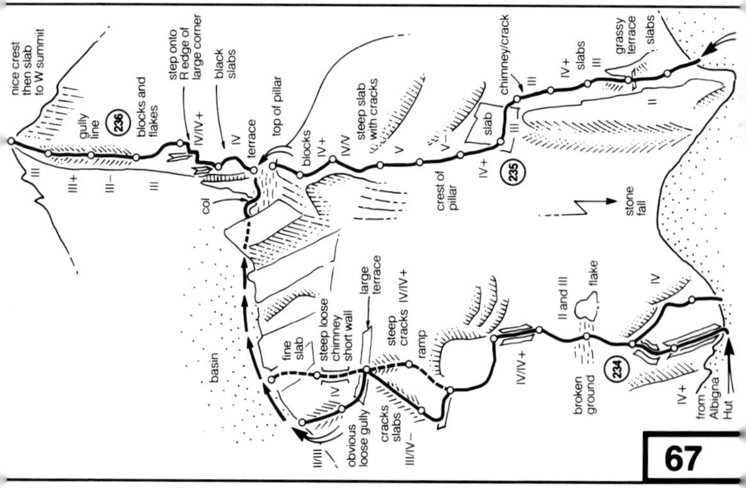
67
nice crest then slab to W summit
gully line
236
blocks and flakes
step onto R edge of large corner
black slabs
III
III+
III–
II
IV/IV+
IV
terrace
col
top of pillar
blocks
IV+
IV/V
steep slab with cracks
V
V–
crest of pillar
IV+
235
slab
III
chimney/crack
III
IV+
slabs
III
grassy terrace
slabs
II
stone fall
basin
fine slab
steep loose chimney
short wall
large terrace
IV/IV+
steep cracks
ramp
IV
obvious loose gully
II/III
cracks
slabs
III/IV–
IV/IV+
II and III
flake
broken ground
234
IV
IV+
from Albigna Hut

Punta da l'Albigna NW face

68

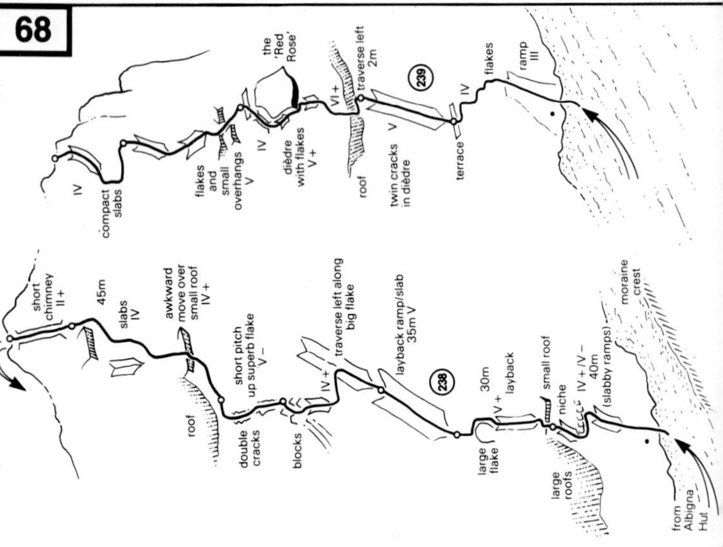
IV
compact slabs
flakes and small overhangs V
IV
dièdre with flakes V+
the 'Red Rose'
VI+
traverse left 2m
roof
twin cracks in dièdre
V
239
terrace
IV
flakes
ramp III
short chimney II+
45m
slabs IV
awkward move over small roof IV+
roof
double cracks
short pitch up superb flake V−
blocks
IV+
traverse left along big flake
layback ramp/slab 35m V
238
large flake
30m V+
layback
small roof
niche
IV+/V− 40m (slabby ramps)
large roofs
moraine crest
from Albigna Hut

69

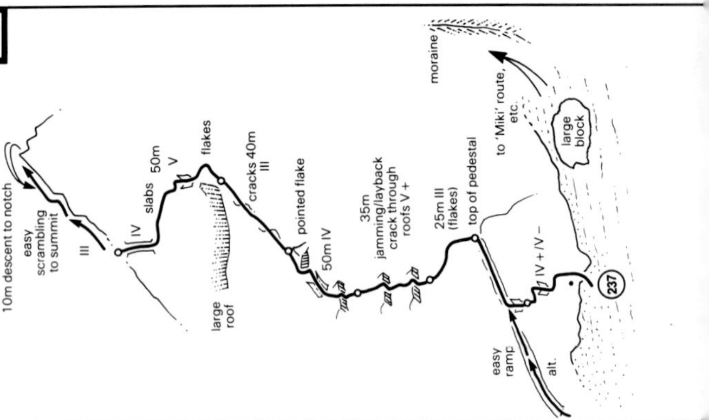
10m descent to notch
easy scrambling to summit
III
IV
slabs
50m V
flakes
large roof
cracks 40m III
pointed flake
50m IV
35m jamming/layback crack through roofs V+
25m III (flakes)
top of pedestal
IV+/V−
237
easy ramp
alt.
to 'Miki' route, etc.
large block
moraine

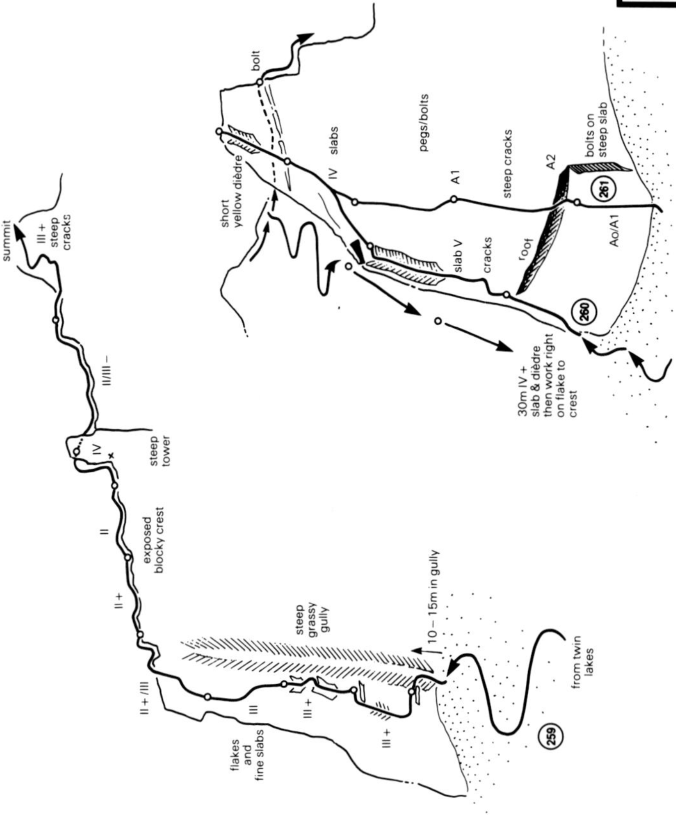
summit
III + steep cracks
II/III –
IV
steep tower
II
exposed blocky crest
II +
II + /III
III
III +
III +
flakes and fine slabs
steep grassy gully
10 – 15m in gully
from twin lakes
259
bolt
pegs/bolts
IV slabs
short yellow dièdre
A1
steep cracks
A2
bolts on steep slab
261
Ao/A1
slab V
cracks
roof
260
30m IV + slab & dièdre then work right on flake to crest

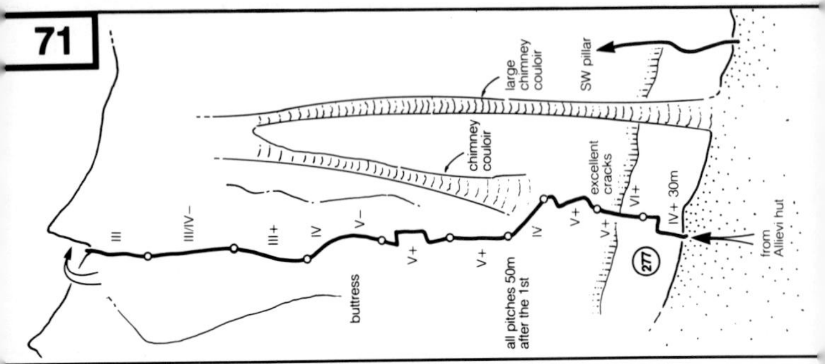
71
large chimney couloir
SW pillar
chimney couloir
excellent cracks
VI+
IV+ 30m
from Allievi hut
277
V+
IV
V+
V+
V+
V–
IV
III+
III/IV–
III
buttress
all pitches 50m after the 1st

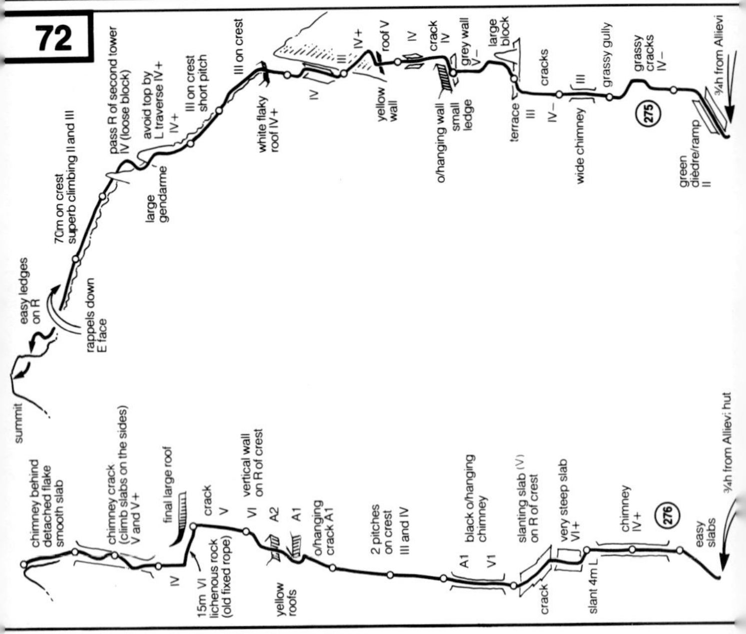
72
¾h from Allievi
green dièdre/ramp II
275
grassy cracks IV–
grassy gully
III
wide chimney
IV–
III
cracks
terrace
large block
grey wall V–
small ledge
o/hanging wall
crack IV
IV
roof V
yellow wall
IV+
III
IV
white flaky roof IV+
III on crest
III on crest short pitch
IV+
avoid top by L traverse IV+
pass R of second tower IV (loose block)
large gendarme
70m on crest superb climbing II and III
easy ledges on R
rappels down E face
summit
¾h from Allievi hut
easy slabs
276
chimney IV+
very steep slab VI+
slant 4m L
slanting slab (V) on R of crest
crack
black o/hanging chimney
A1
V1
2 pitches on crest III and IV
o/hanging crack A1
A1
A2
yellow roofs
VI
vertical wall on R of crest
crack V
final large roof
15m VI lichenous rock (old fixed rope)
IV
chimney crack (climb slabs on the sides) V and V+
chimney behind detached flake smooth slab

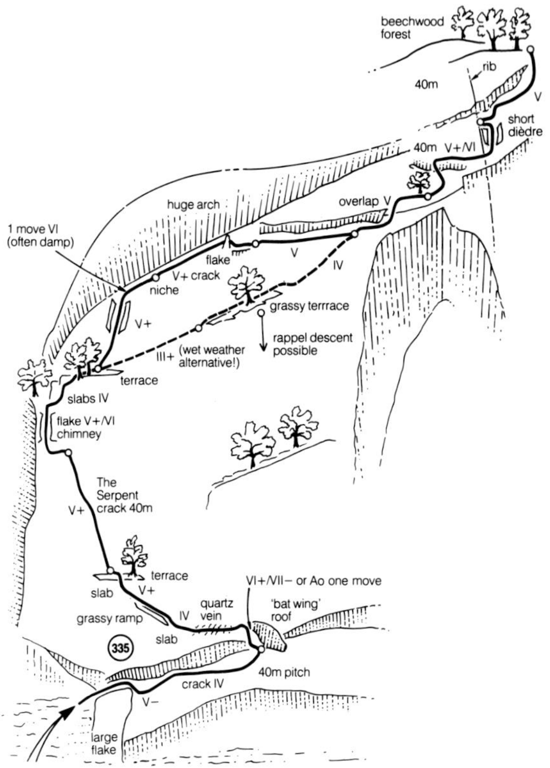
beechwood forest
rib
40m
V
short dièdre
40m V+/VI
overlap V
huge arch
1 move VI (often damp)
flake
V
IV
V+ crack
niche
grassy terrrace
V+
rappel descent possible
III+
(wet weather alternative!)
terrace
slabs IV
flake V+/VI chimney
The Serpent crack 40m
V+
terrace
slab
V+
VI+/VII– or Ao one move
quartz vein
'bat wing' roof
grassy ramp
IV
slab
335
40m pitch
crack IV
V–
large flake

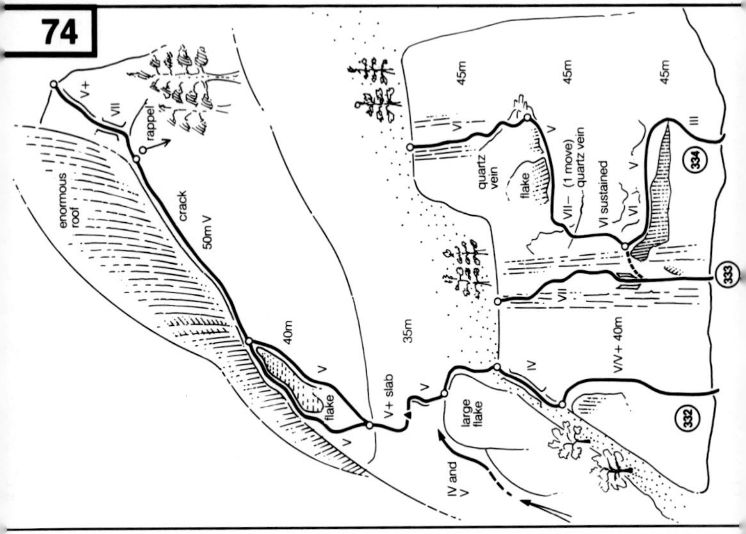
74
V+
VII
rappel
enormous roof
crack
50m V
40m
V
flake
V
V+ slab
V
35m
large flake
IV and V
IV
V/V+ 40m
332
VII
333
45m
VI
V
quartz vein
flake
VII– (1 move) quartz vein
VI sustained
VI
V
334
III
45m
45m

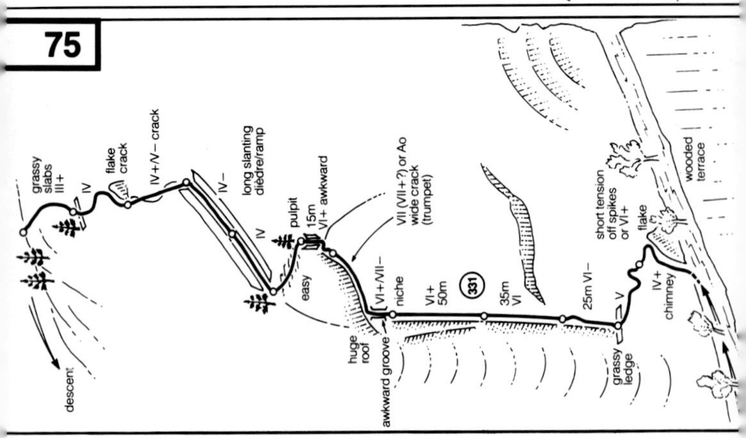
75
grassy slabs III+
IV
flake crack
IV+/V– crack
IV–
long slanting dièdre/ramp
IV
pulpit
15m VI+ awkward
VII (VII+?) or Ao wide crack (trumpet)
easy
VI+/VII–
niche
VI+ 50m
331
35m VI
25m VI–
V
short tension off spikes or VI+
flake
IV+ chimney
wooded terrace
huge roof
awkward groove
grassy ledge
descent

76

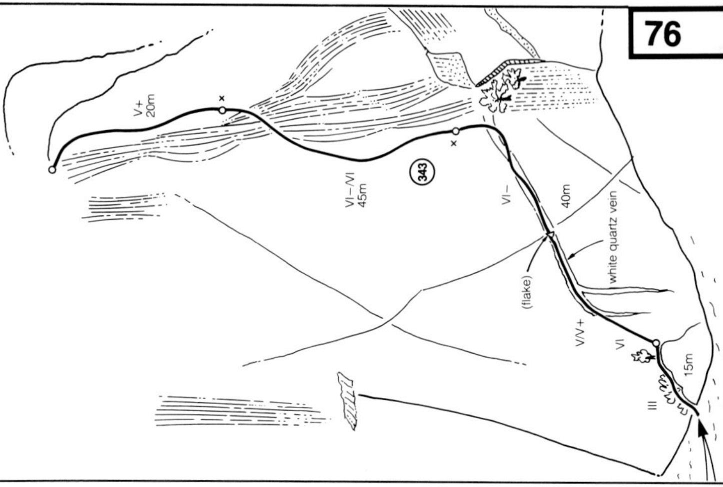
V+
20m
VI–/VI
45m
343
VI–
40m
white quartz vein
(flake)
V/V+
VI
15m
III

77

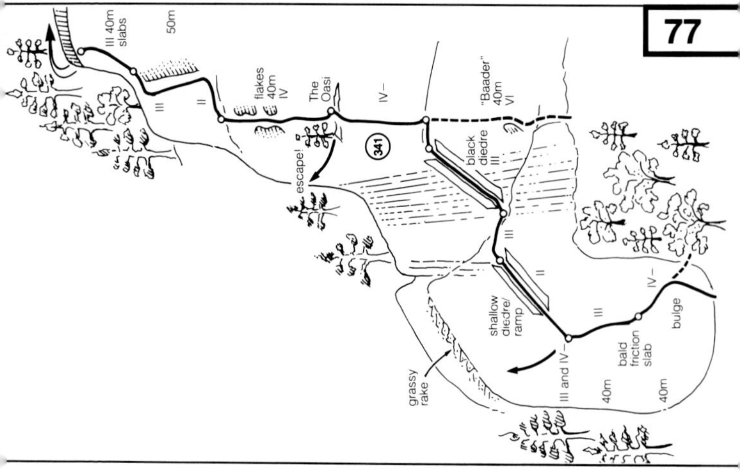
III 40m
slabs
50m
III
II
flakes
40m
IV
The
Oasi
IV–
escape!
341
"Baader"
40m
VI
black
diedre
III
III
II
shallow
diedre/
ramp
IV–
III
bulge
bald
friction
slab
III and IV–
40m
40m
grassy
rake

78

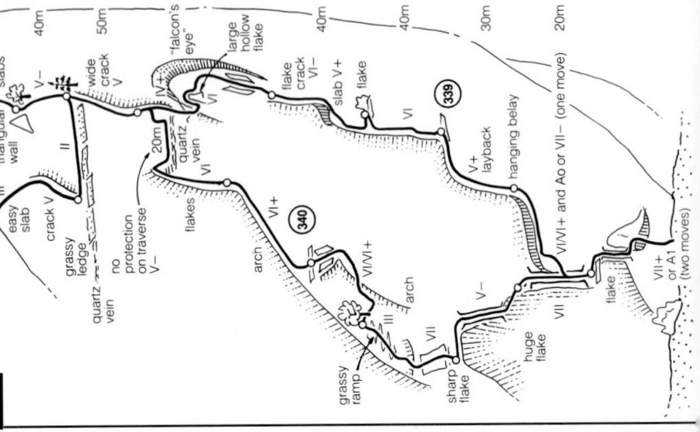
20m
40m
40m
50m
"falcon's eye"
large hollow flake
40m
40m
30m
20m
III
wall IV+/V– slabs
triangular wall
V–
wide crack V
IV+
VI
flake crack VI–
slab V+
flake
339
VI
II
III
easy slab
crack V
grassy ledge
quartz vein
no protection on traverse V–
20m
quartz vein
VI
flakes
VI+
340
arch
VI/VI+
arch
III
grassy ramp
VII
sharp flake
V–
huge flake
VII
V+ layback
hanging belay
VI/VI+ and Ao or VII– (one move)
flake
VII+ or A1 (two moves)

79

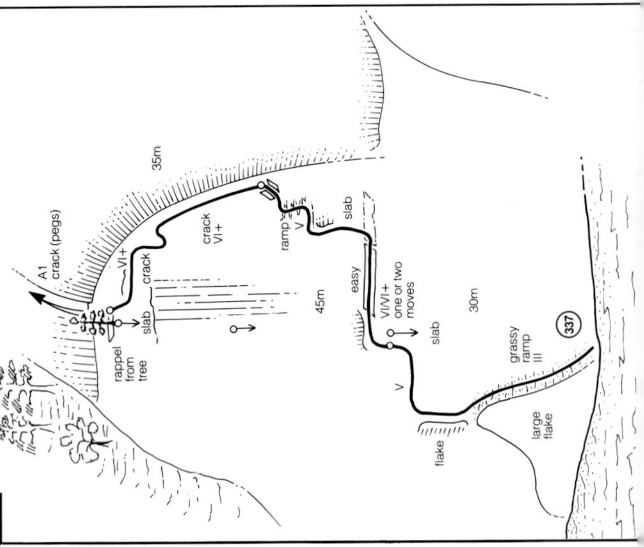
35m
A1 crack (pegs)
VI+
crack
crack VI+
ramp
V
slab
easy
45m
VI/VI+ one or two moves
30m
slab
rappel from tree
slab
wooded gully to 'Patabang'
337
grassy ramp III
V
large flake
flake

80

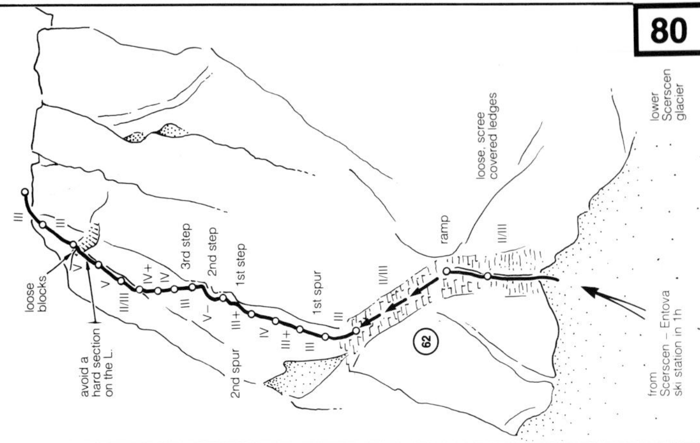
loose blocks
avoid a hard section on the L.
III
III
V
V
IV+
IV
II/III
III
3rd step
2nd step
V–
1st step
III+
IV
III+
III
III
2nd spur
1st spur
II/III
62
ramp
II/III
loose, scree covered ledges
lower Scerscen glacier
from Scerscen – Entova ski station in 1h

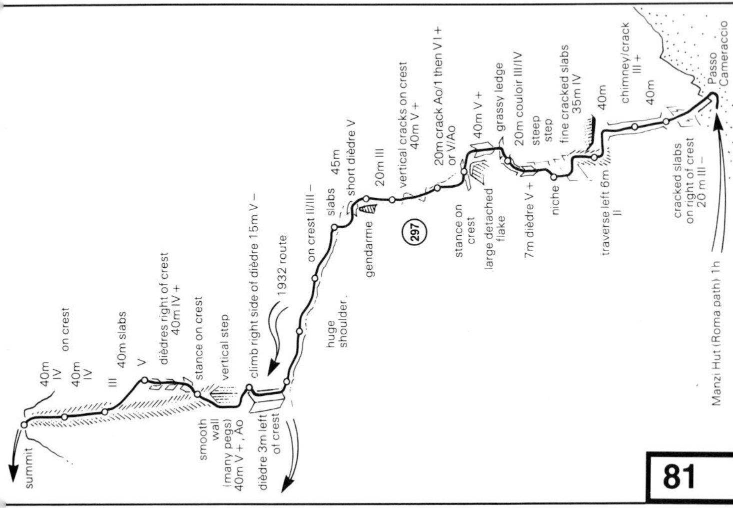
summit
40m IV
40m IV
on crest
III
40m slabs
V
smooth wall (many pegs) 40m V+, Ao
dièdres right of crest 40m IV+
stance on crest
vertical step
dièdre 3m left of crest
climb right side of dièdre 15m V–
1932 route
huge shoulder.
on crest II/III–
slabs
gendarme
45m short dièdre V
20m III
297
vertical cracks on crest 40m V+
20m crack Ao/1 then VI+ or V/Ao
stance on crest
large detached flake
40m V+
grassy ledge
7m dièdre V+
20m couloir III/IV
steep step
niche
fine cracked slabs 35m IV
traverse left 6m II
40m
chimney/crack III+
40m
cracked slabs on right of crest 20 m III–
Passo Cameraccio
Manzi Hut (Roma path) 1h

81

Torrone Orientale S ridge direct

Pizzo Ventina SE pillar

82

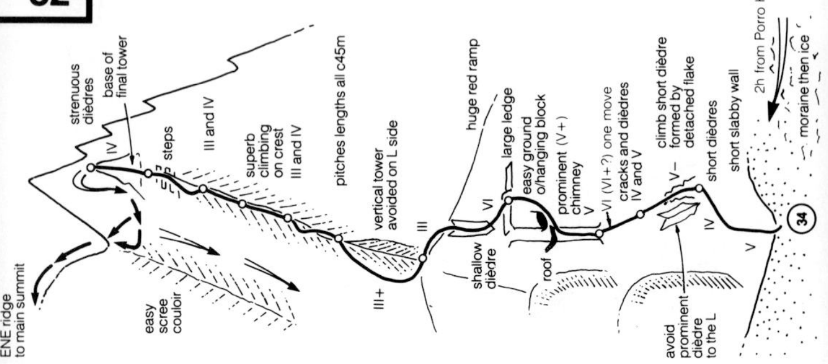

83

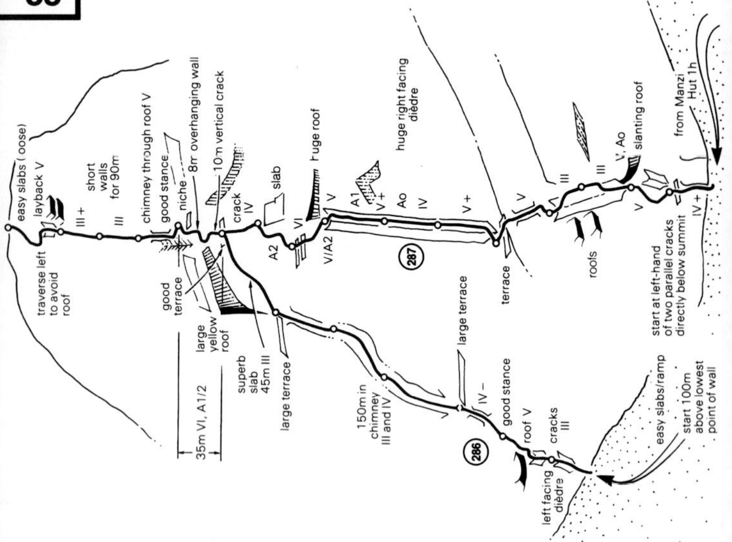

Punta Ferrario S face

Keschnadel E face

84

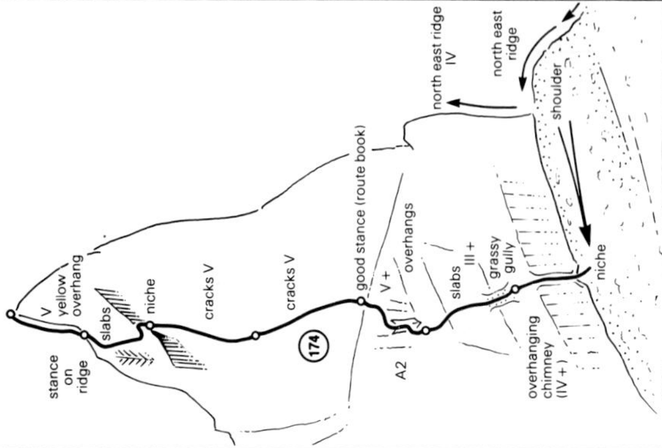
north east ridge
IV
north east
ridge
shoulder
good stance (route book)
V
yellow
overhang
slabs
niche
cracks V
cracks V
V+
overhangs
slabs
III+
grassy
gully
niche
stance
on
ridge
174
A2
overhanging
chimney
(IV+)
scree/snow

85

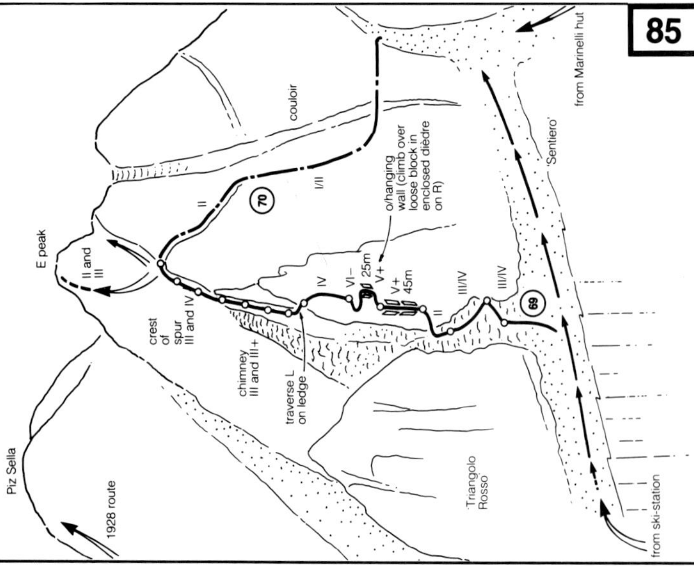
from Marinelli hut
couloir
'Sentiero'
o/hanging
wall (climb over
loose block in
enclosed dièdre
on R)
70
I/II
II
E peak
II and
III
IV
VI–
25m
V+
V+
45m
III/IV
III/IV
69
II
crest
of
spur
III and IV
chimney
III and III+
traverse L
on ledge
Piz Sella
1928 route
Triangolo
Rosso
from ski-station

Piz Sella S face

Piz Ligoncio and Punta della Sfinge NE Side

Avancorpo del Porcellizo East Face

Punta Fiorelli
Cime del Calvo N Side

Trubinasca cirque South Side

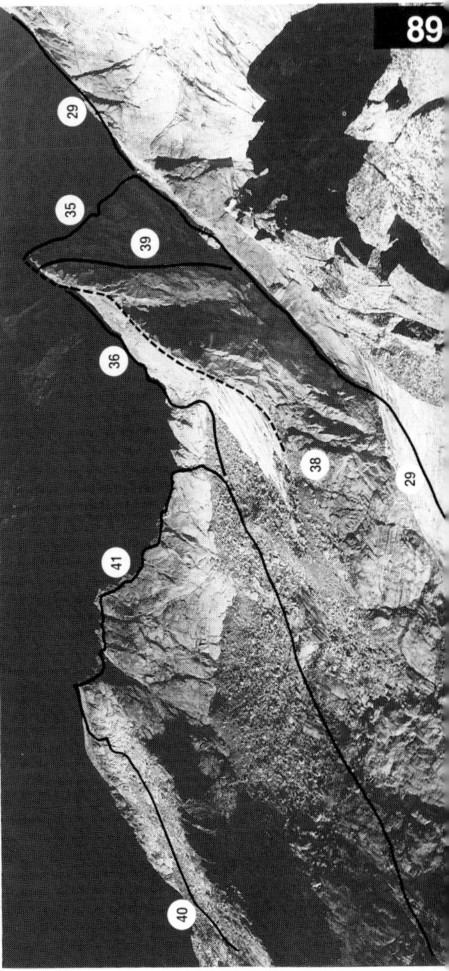

Puntas Torelli and Sant'Anna South East Side

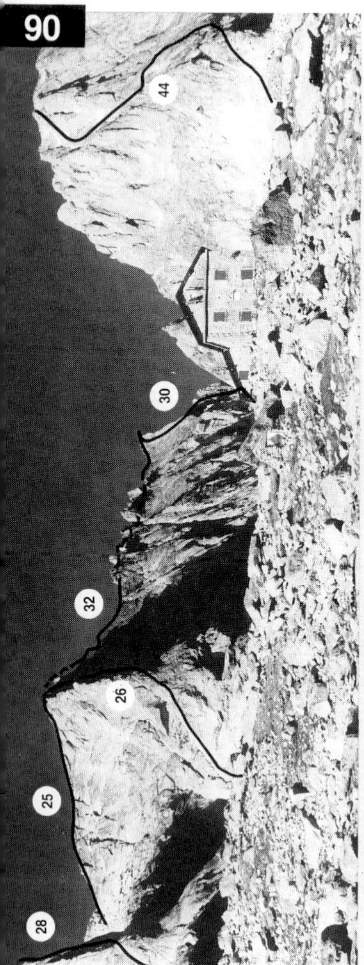

Pizzo Trubinasca South Side

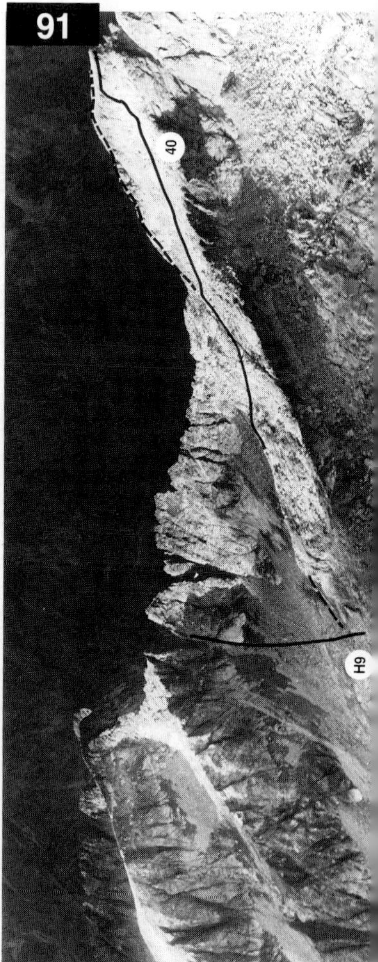

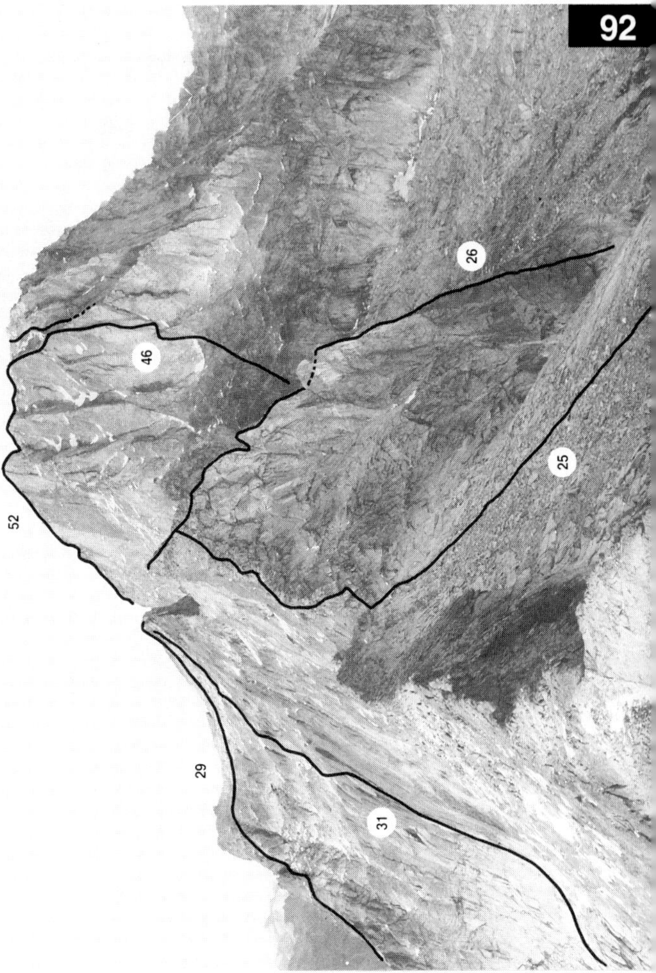
44
46
26
52
25
29
31

Piz Badile and Punta Sertori South East Side

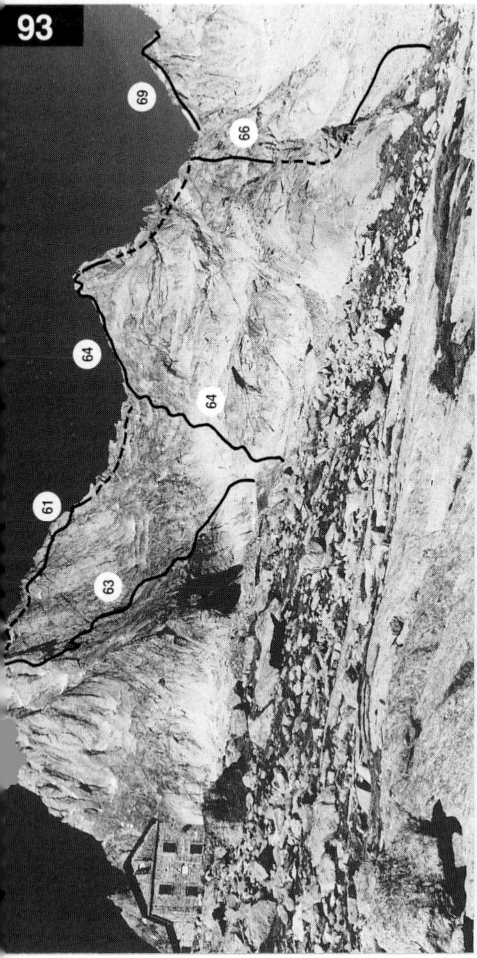

Pizzo Cengalo and Pizzi Gemelli S Side

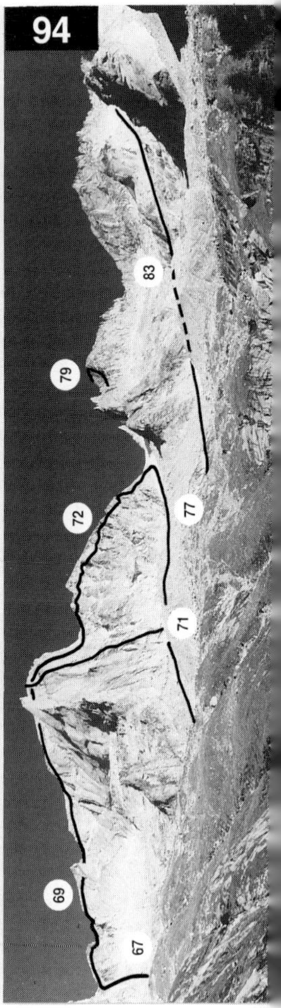

Piz Badile South East Face

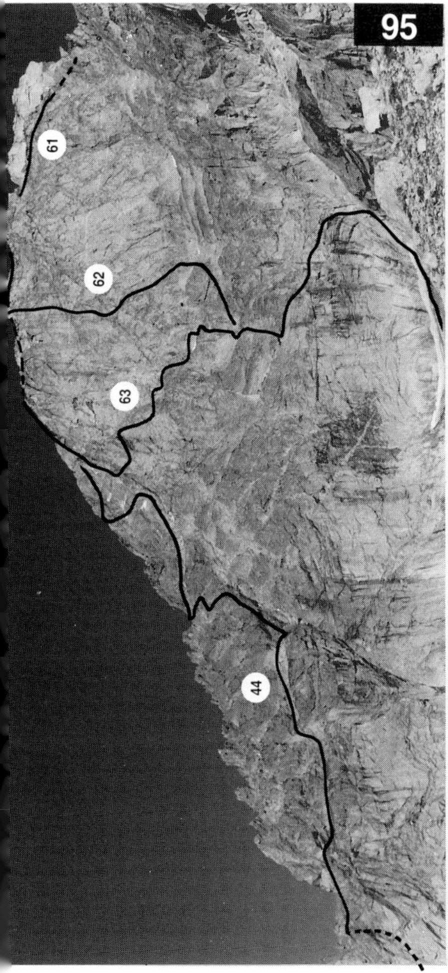

Pizzo Cengalo South West Side

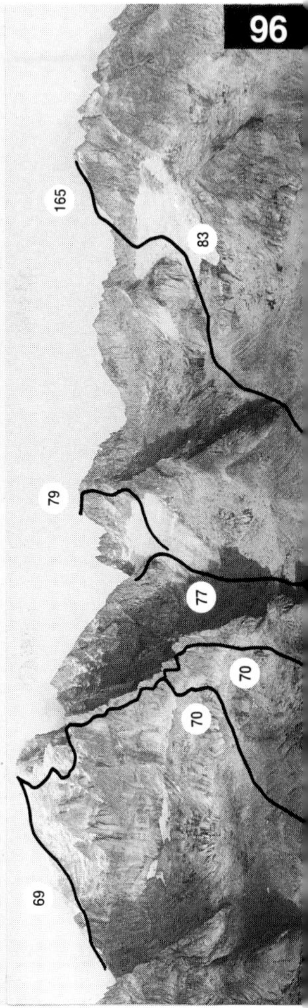

Punta Moraschini West Side

97

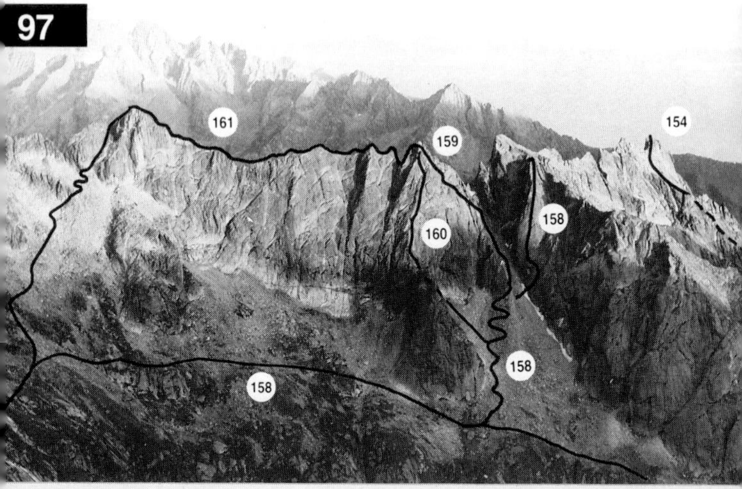

98

 Pizzo del Ferro Occidentale – Punta Bertone West Side

Cima del Cavalcorte – Punta Bertone East Side

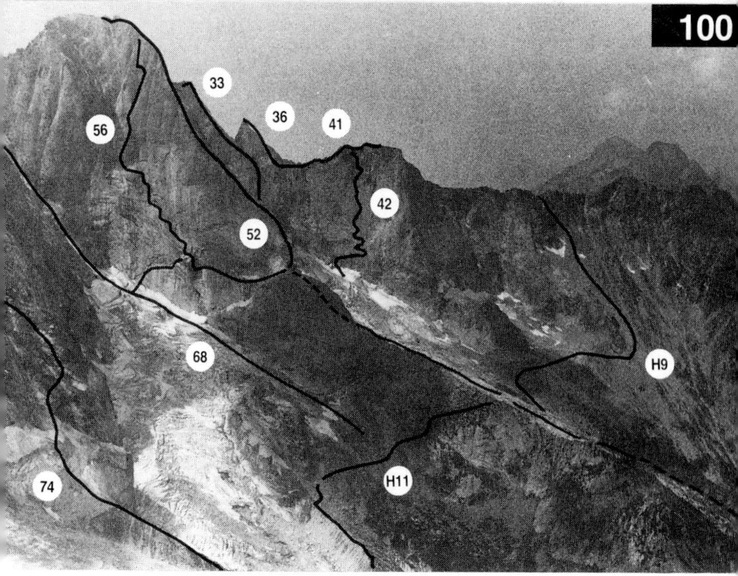

Piz Badile – Trubinasca Peaks North East Side

101

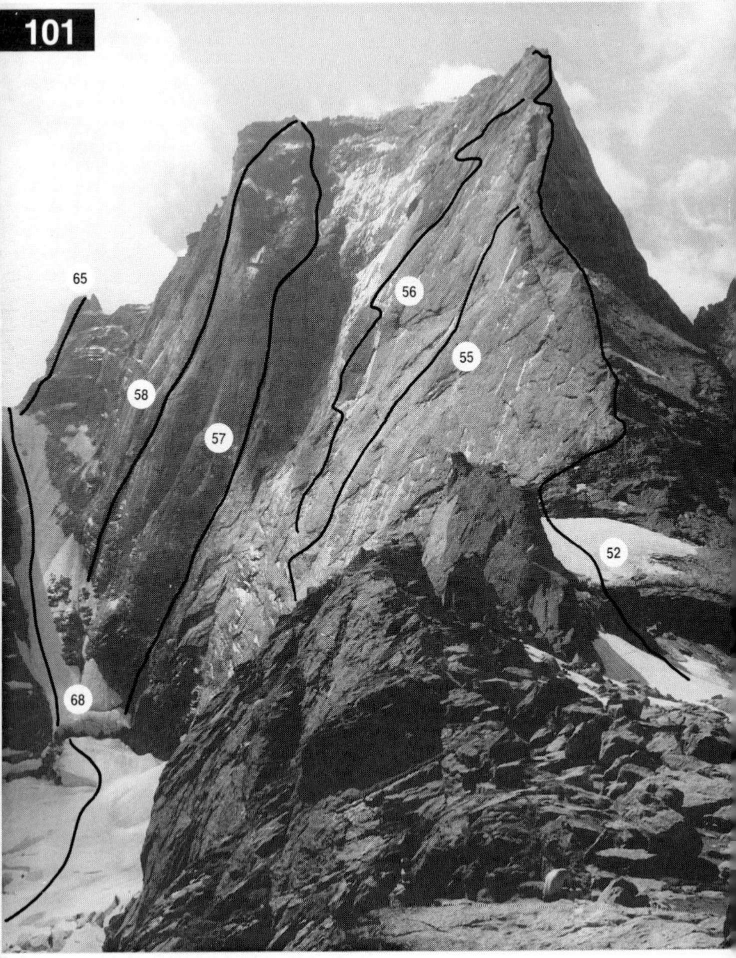

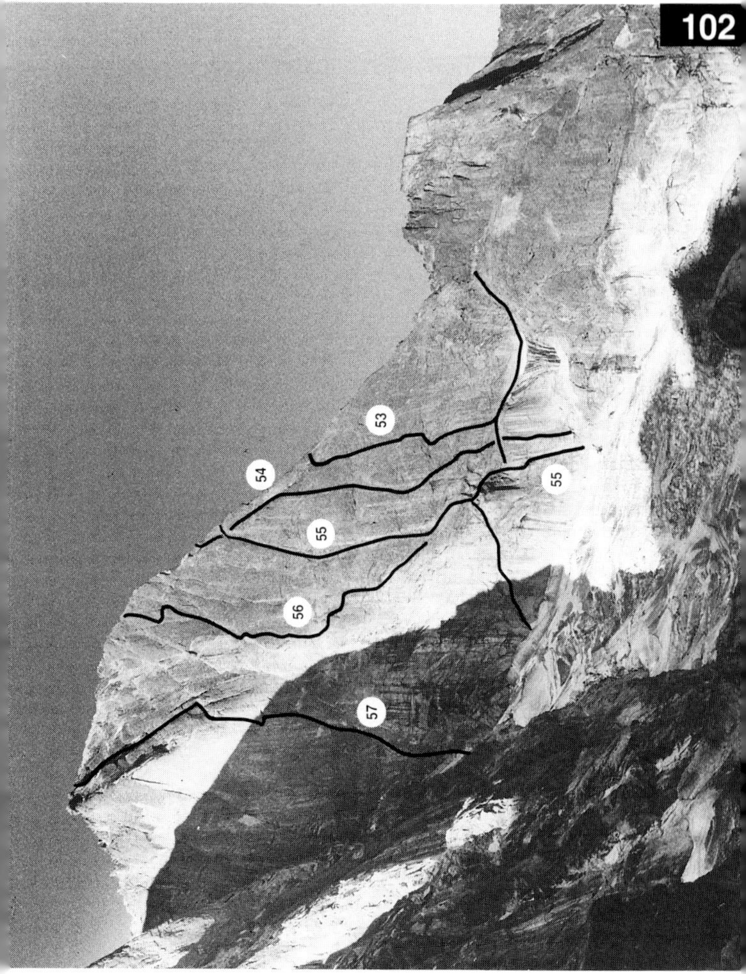
53
54
55
55
56
57

103

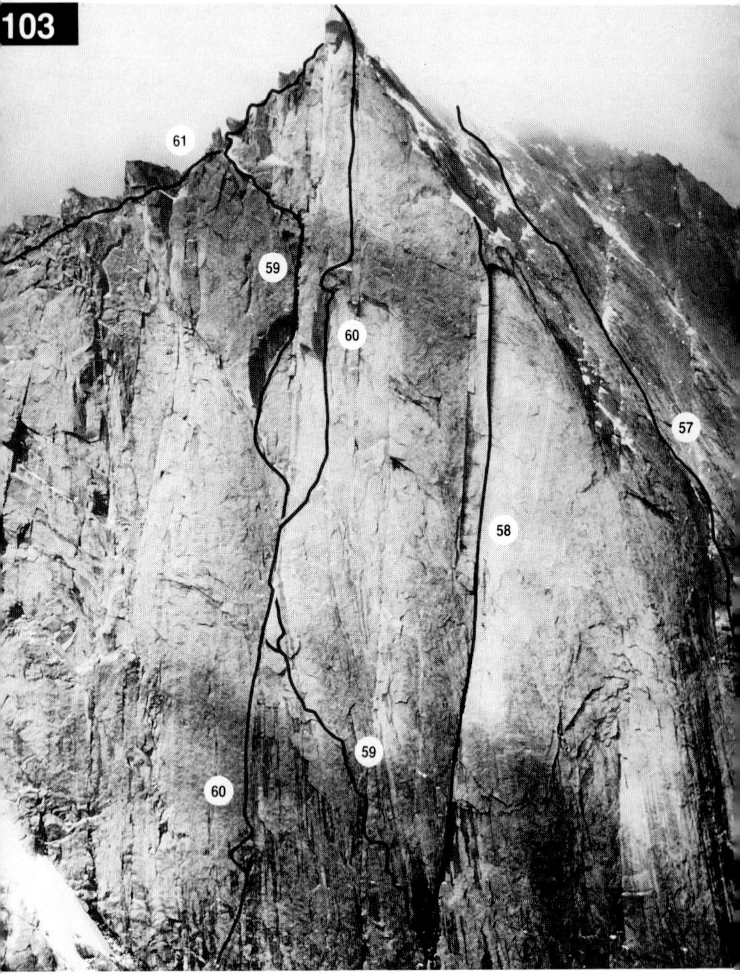

43
47
48
49
50
51

105
74
75
68
76

72
81
78

107

Sciora Peaks West Side

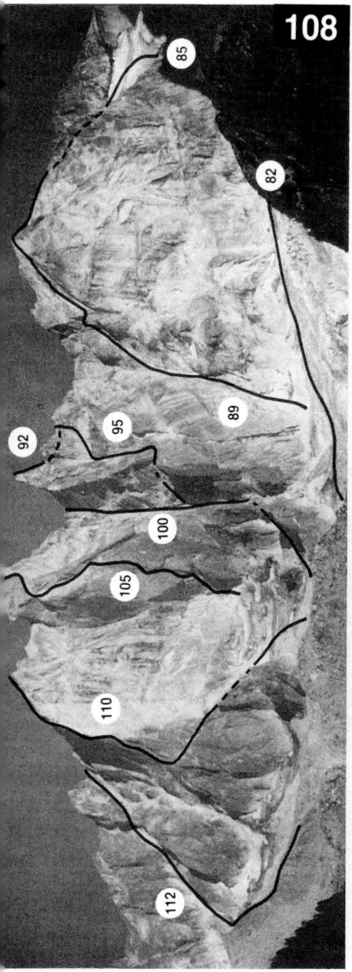

Dafora – Ago West Side

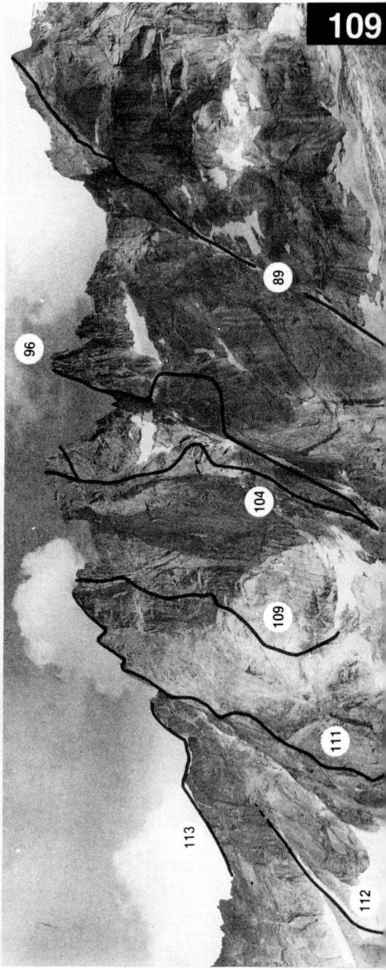

Cacciabella and Innominata Peaks West Side

110

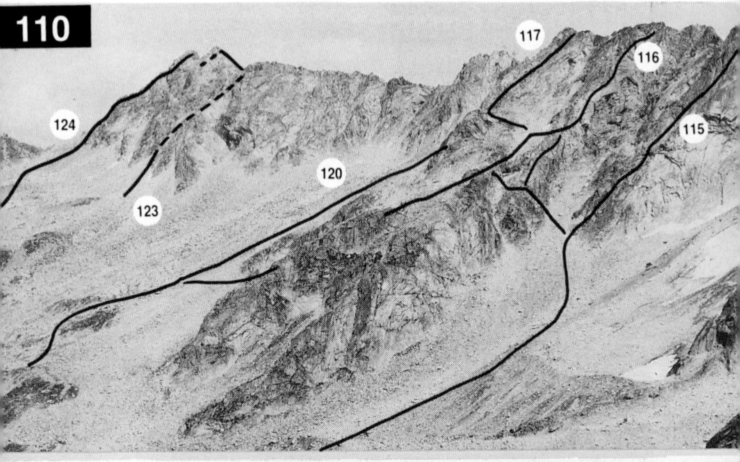

111

Spazzacaldeira Fiamma and Dente

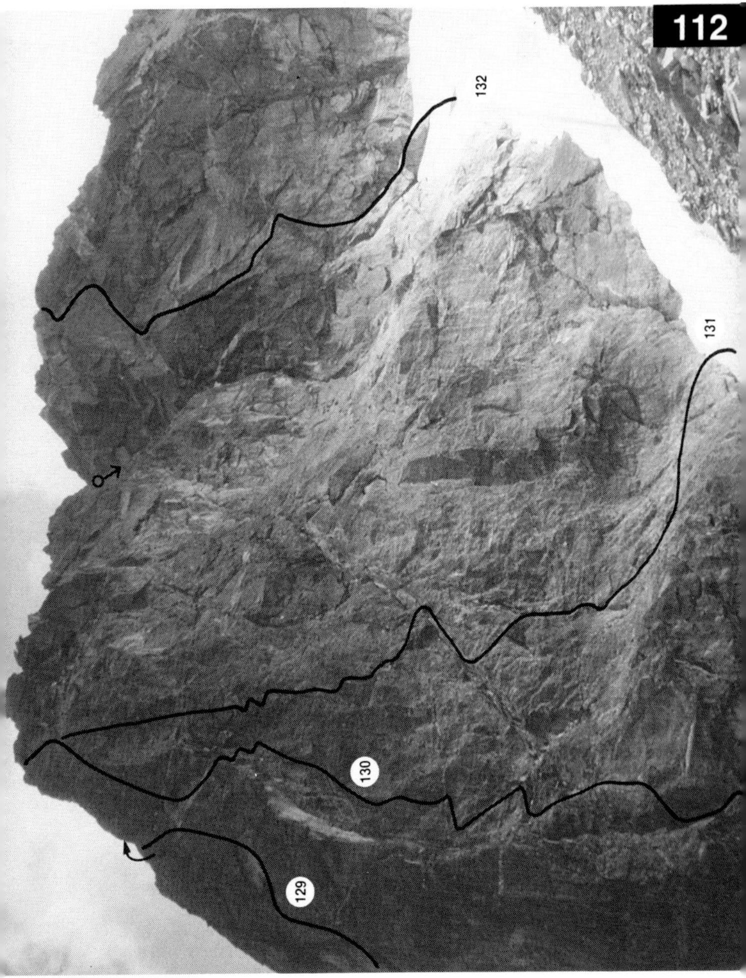
132
131
130
129

113

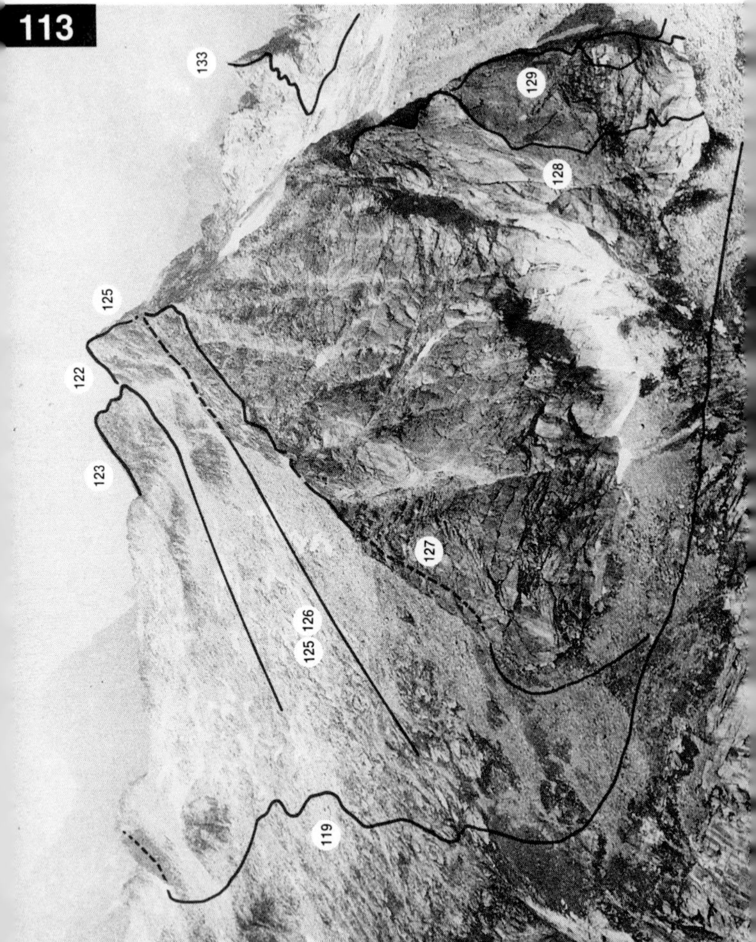

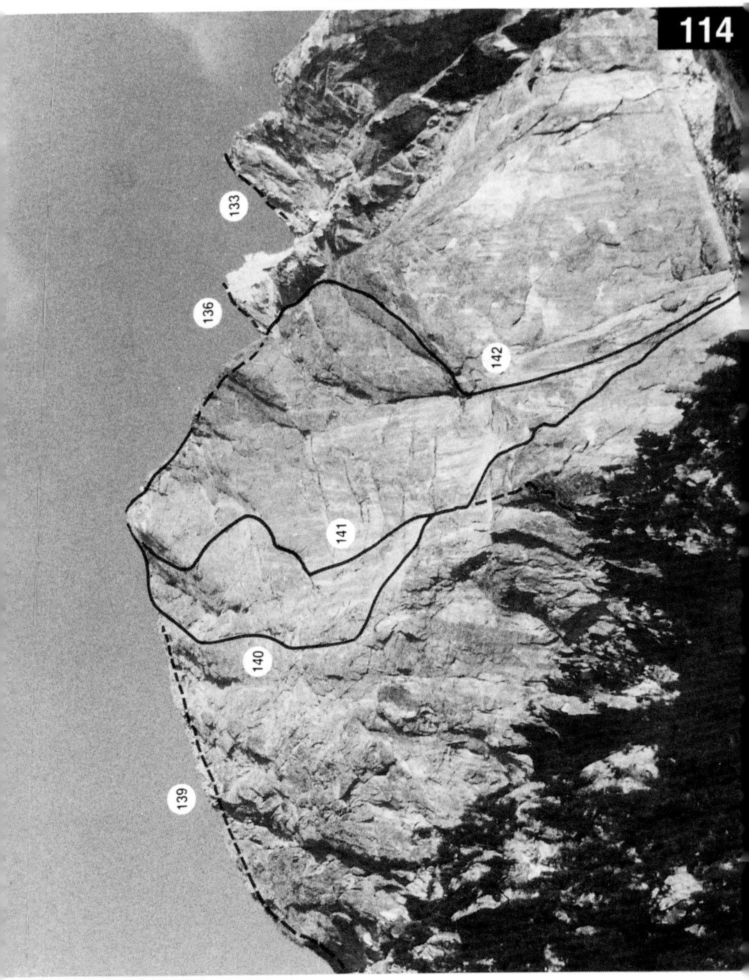
114
133
136
142
141
140
139

Frachiccio Pillar N Side

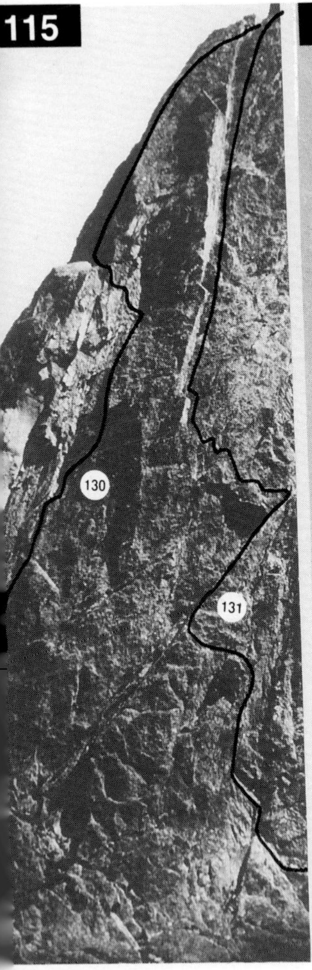

Spazzacaldeira South East Wall

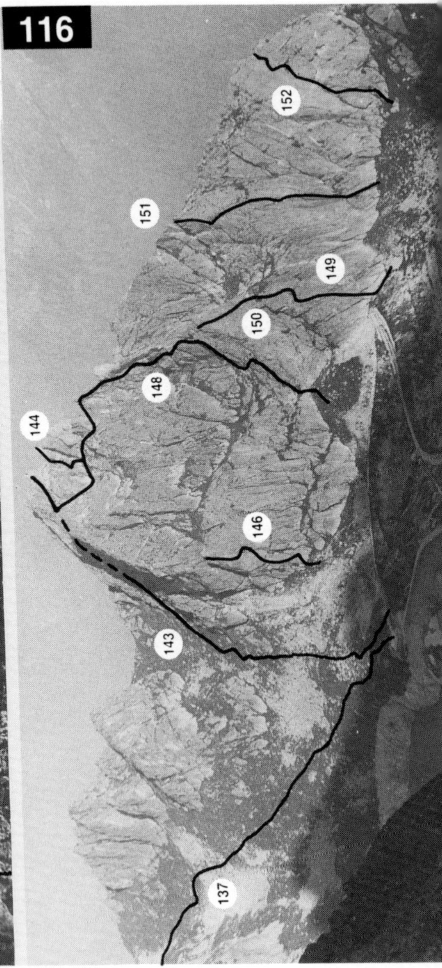

92
93
99

118

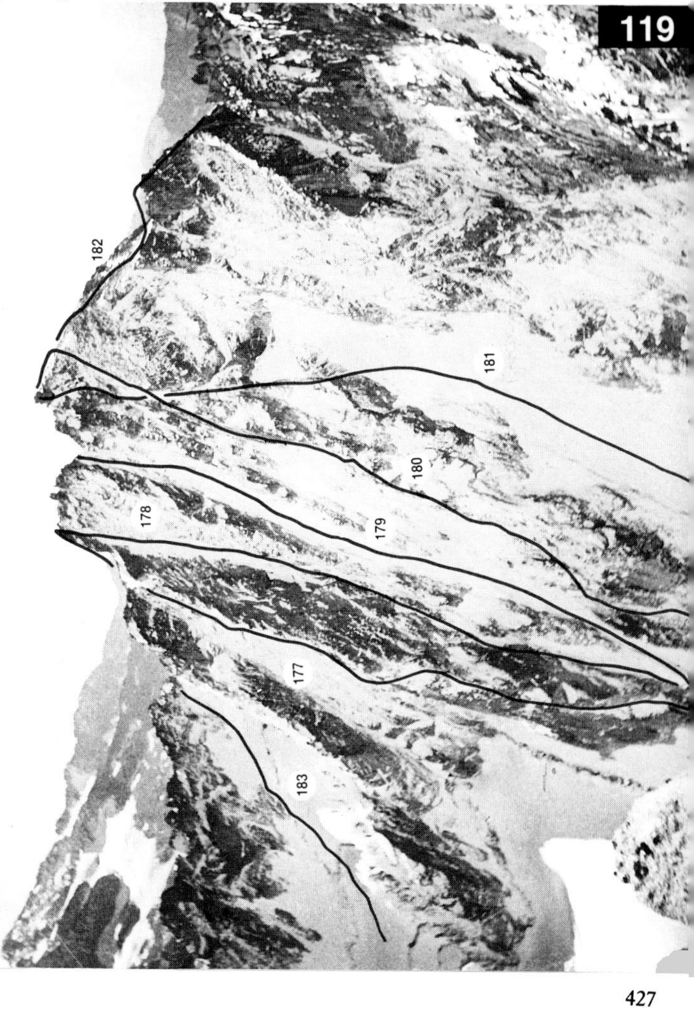
182
181
180
179
178
177
183

Ferro Peaks South Side

120

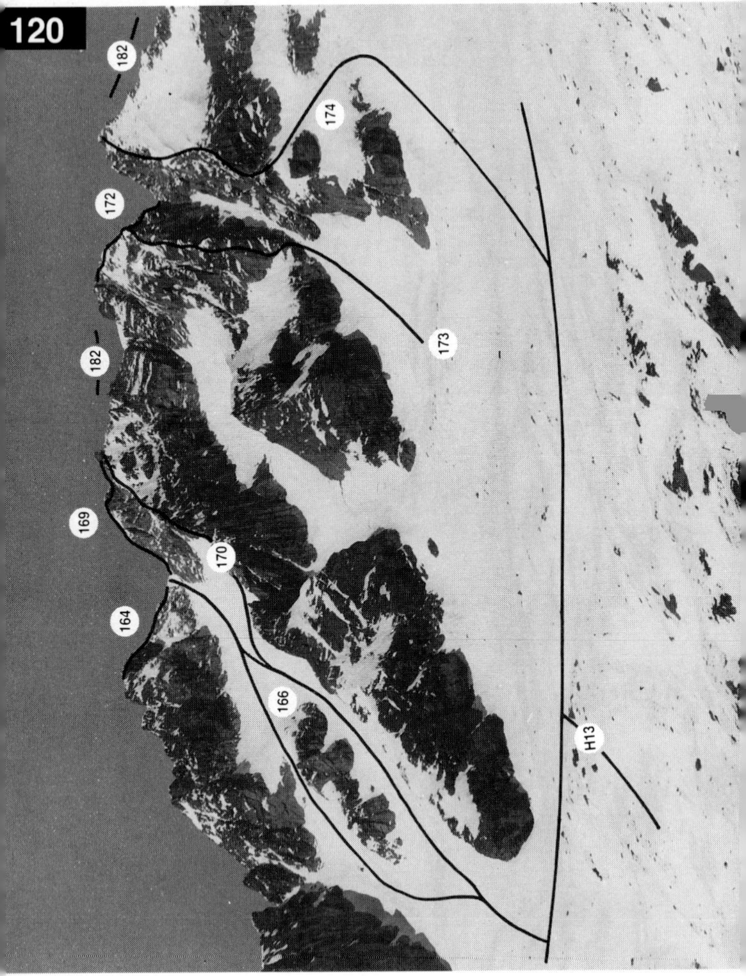

'izzo di Zocca N Side

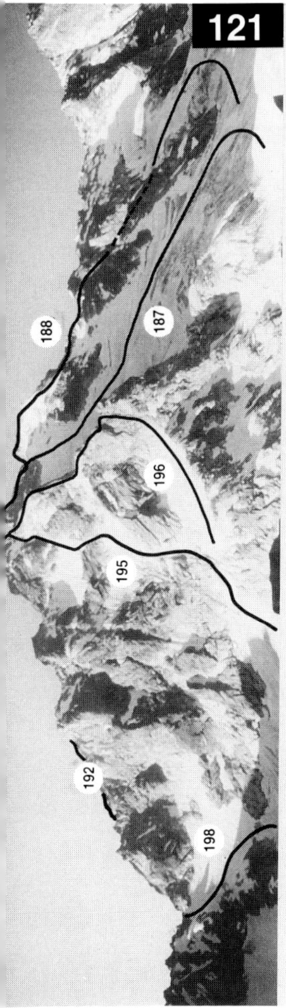

Cantun – Castello West Side

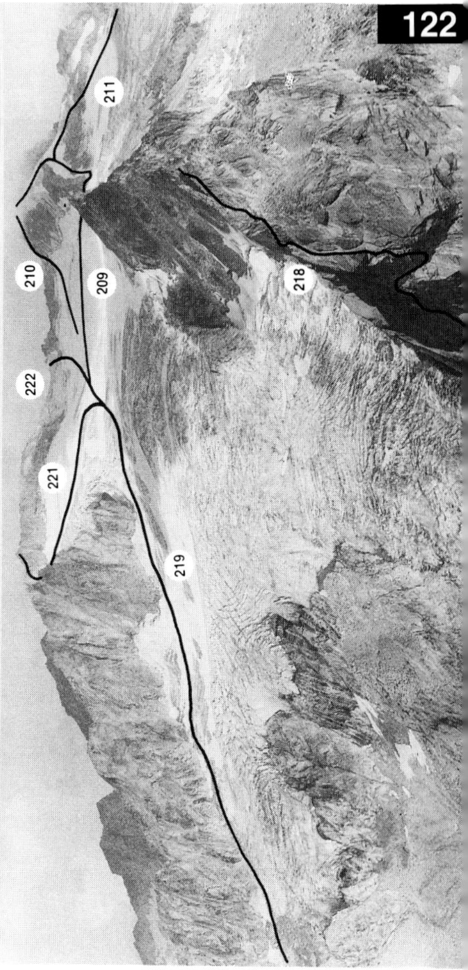

Ferro Peaks and Sciora Dadent Albigna Side

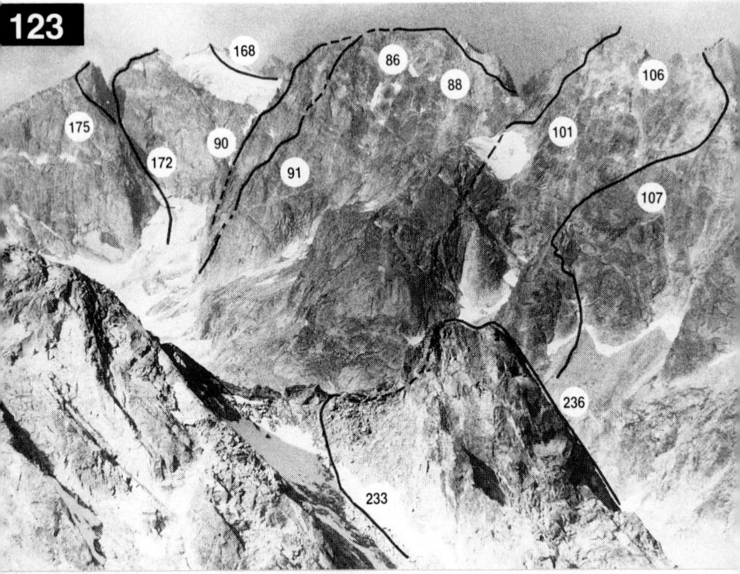

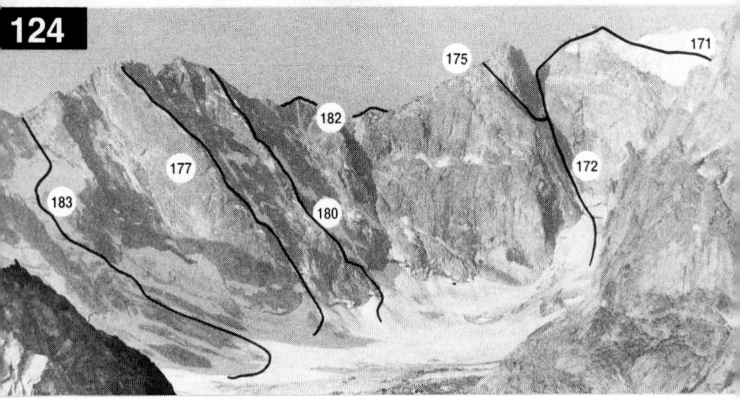

 Ferro Peaks North Side

Piz Bacun South Side

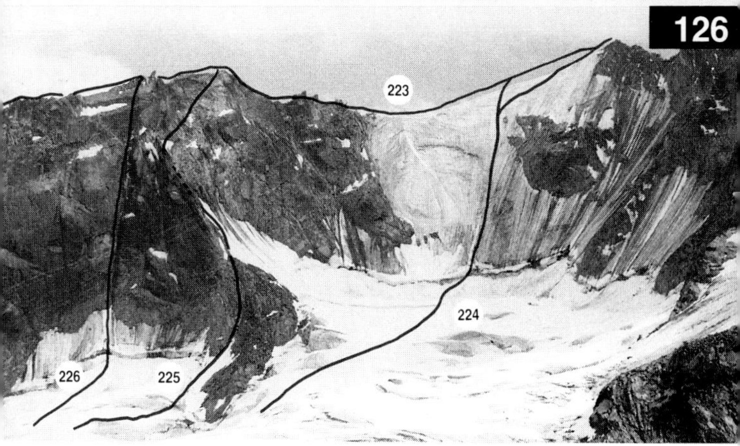

Cima dal Cantun North Face

Piz Casnil West Side

127

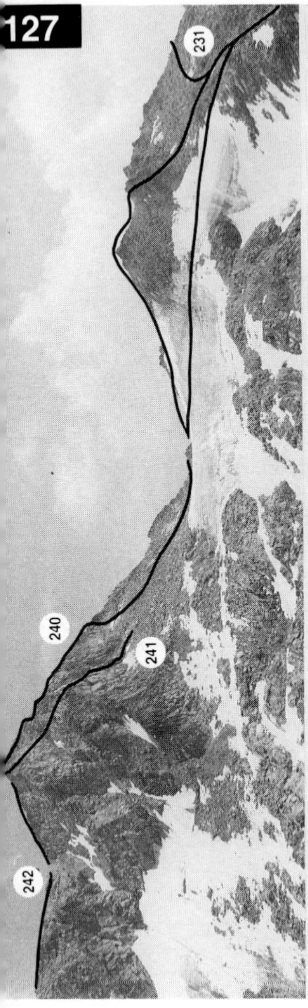

Piz Balzet South Side

128

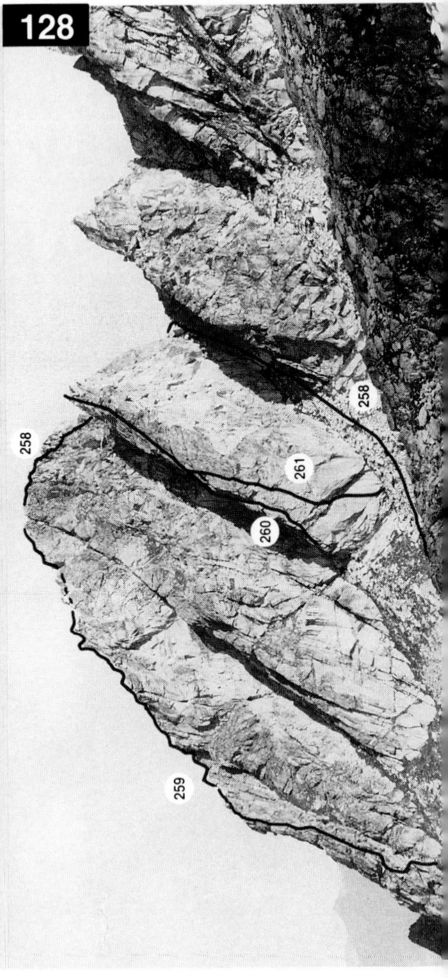

236
235
234

130

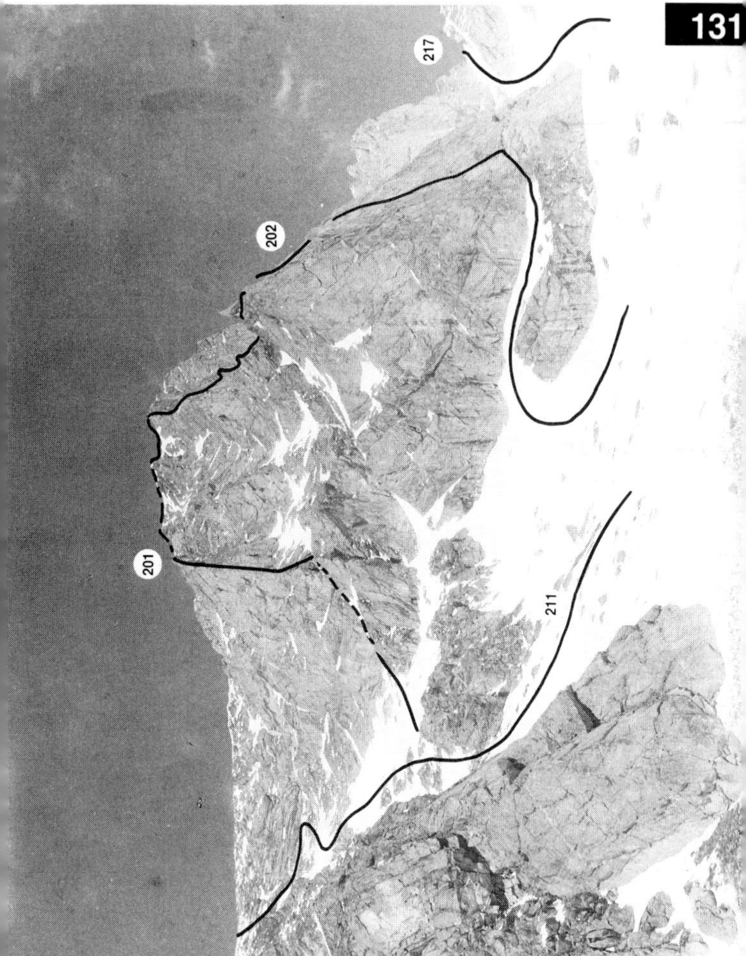
217
202
201
211

Punta 2,987m West Face

132

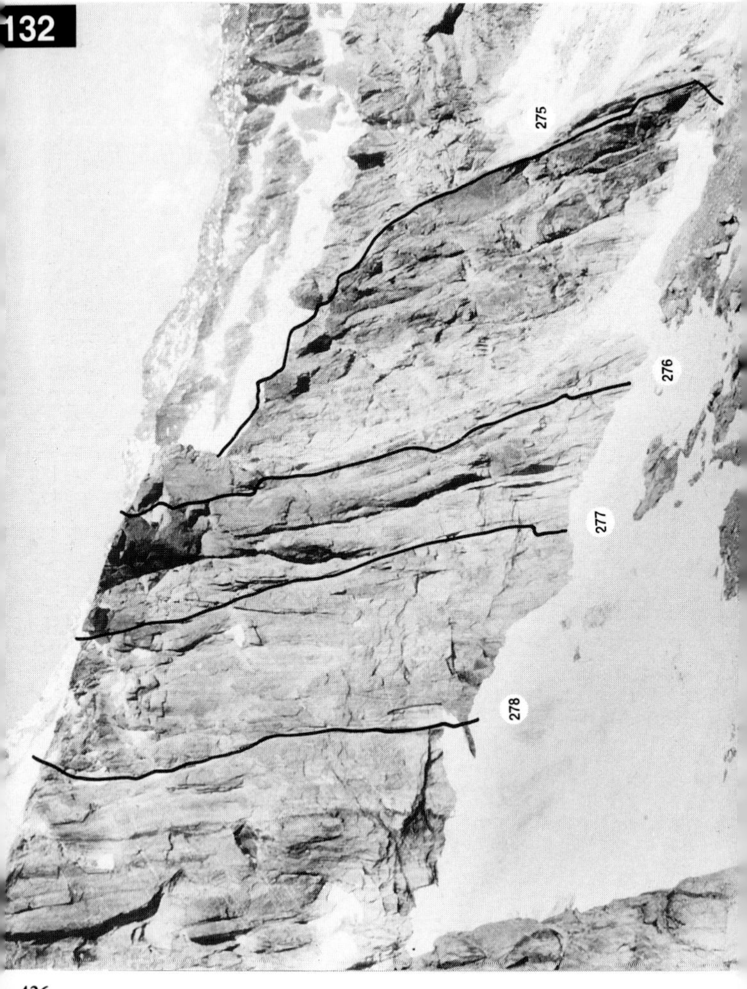

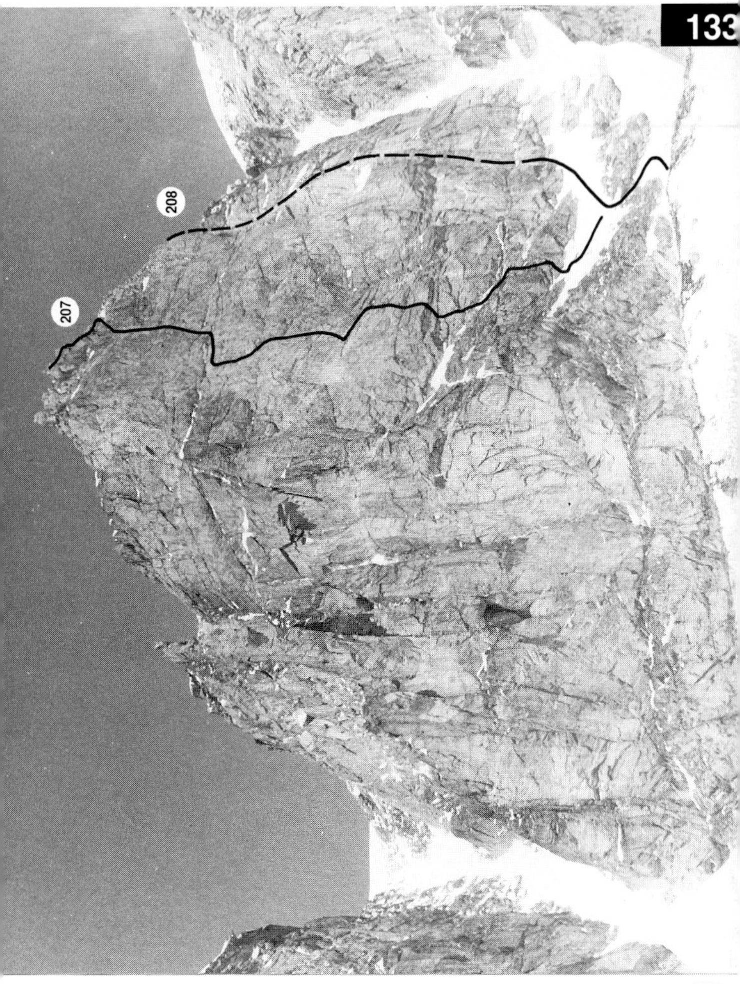
207
208

Pizzo di Zocca South East Side

134

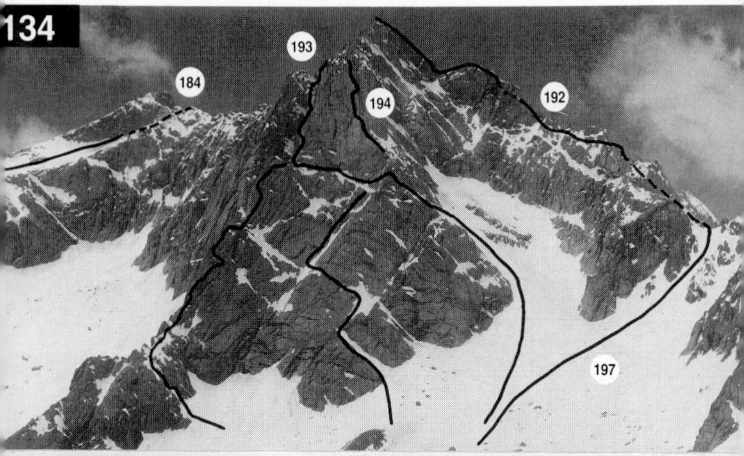

135

 Punta Rasica South Side

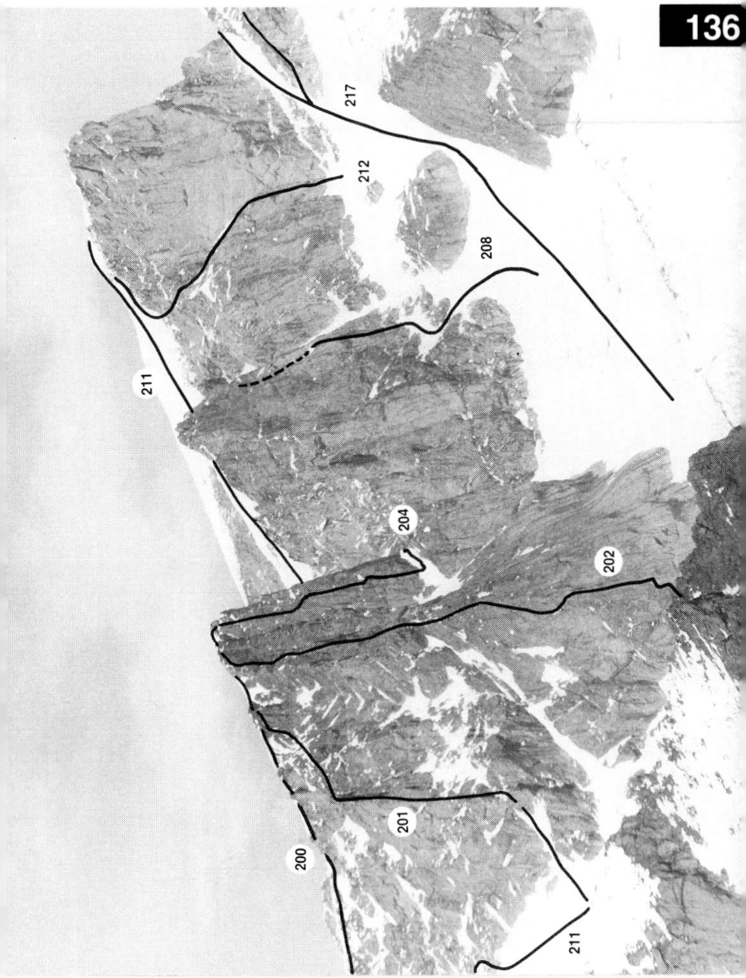
217
212
208
211
204
202
201
200
211

137

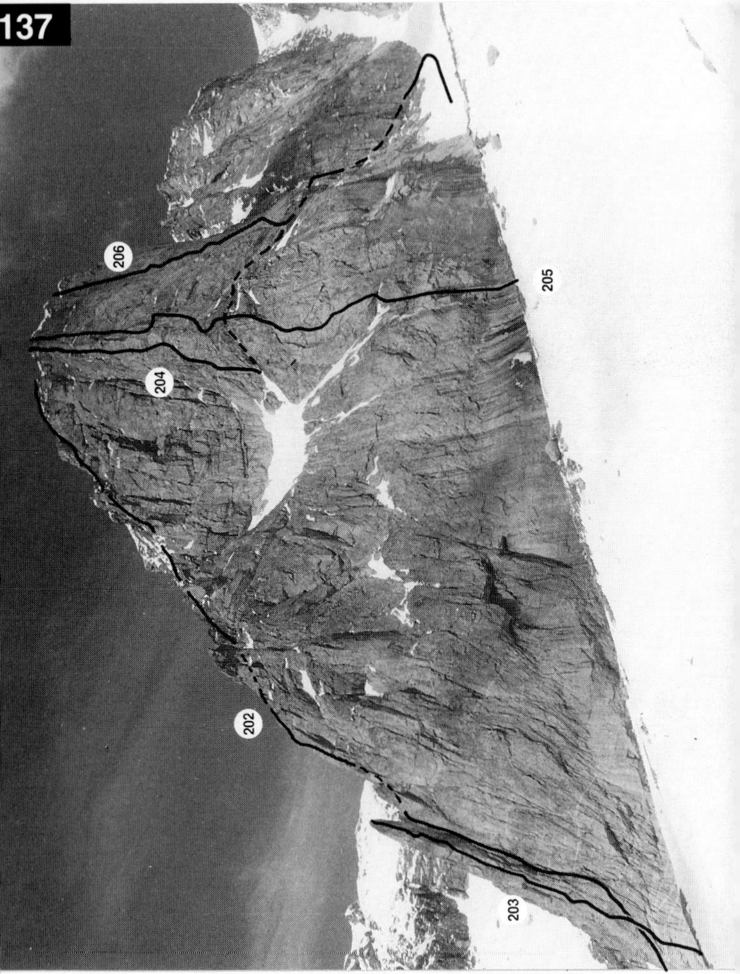

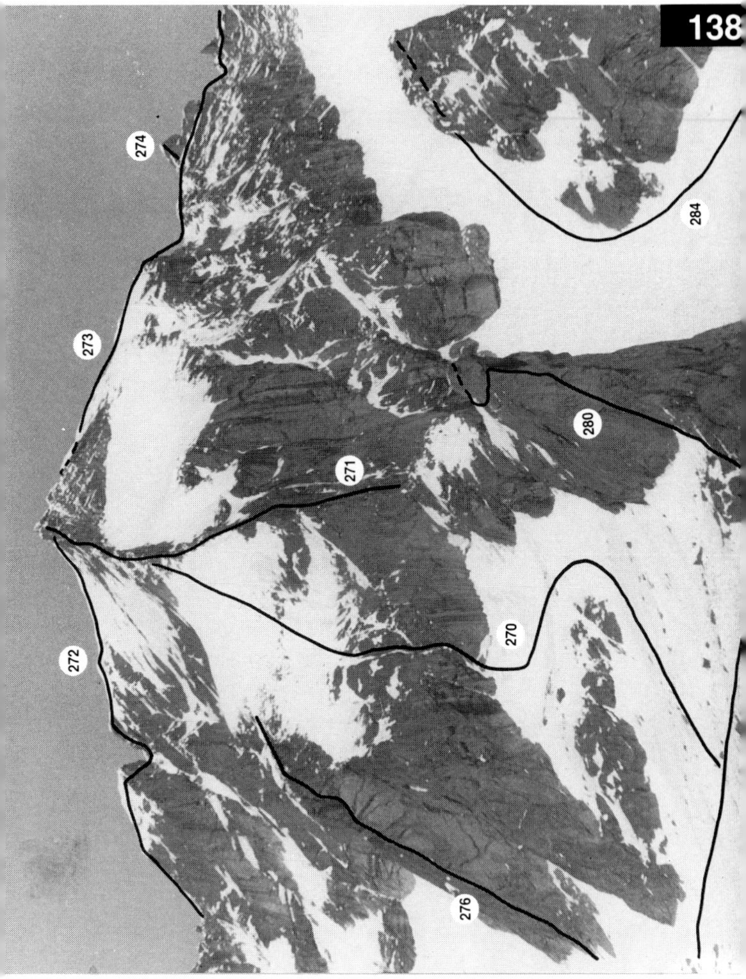
274
284
273
280
271
270
272
276

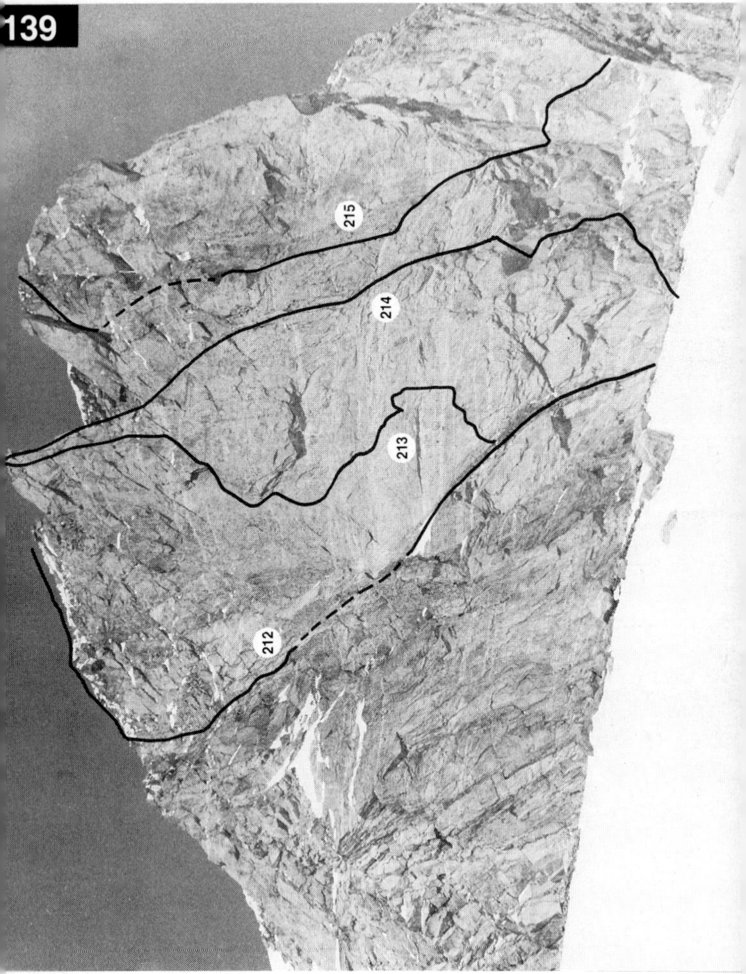
215
214
213
212

Piz Casnil – Cima dal Largh
East Side

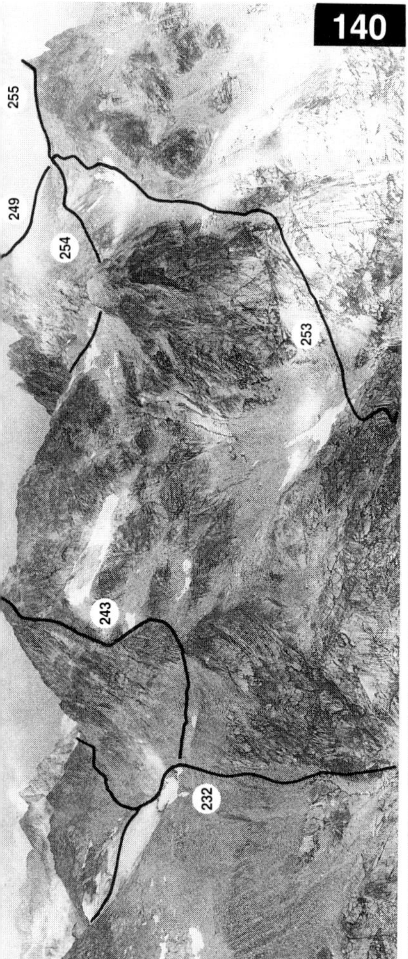

Piz Casnil and Piz Bacun
East Faces

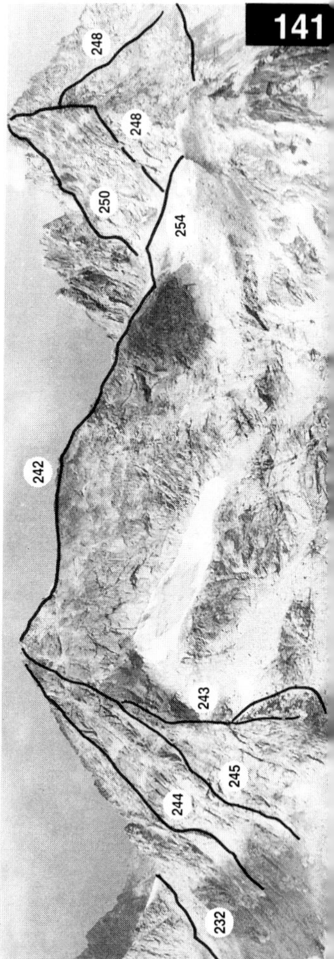

Cima di Castello Forno Side

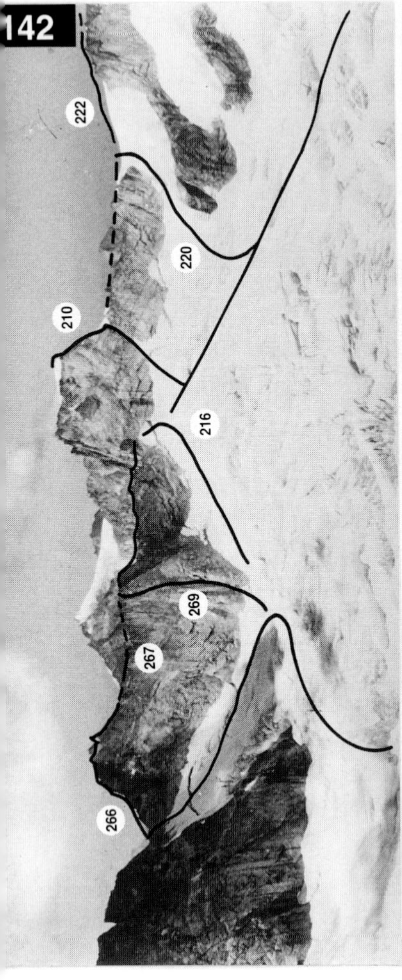

Cima di Vazzeda and Monte Sissone East Side

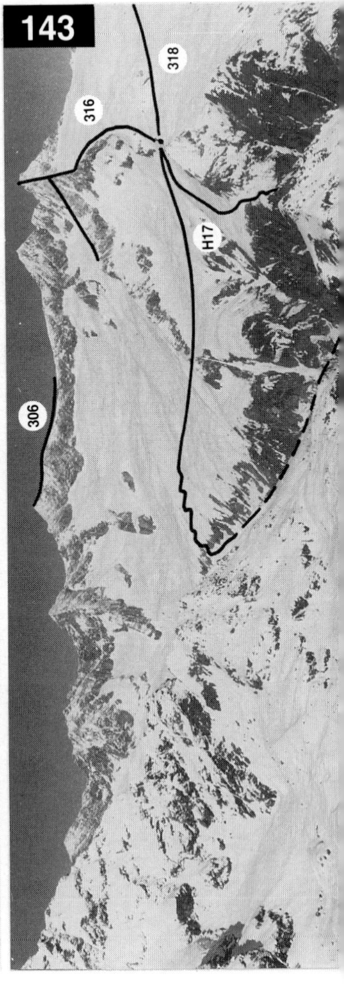

Cima di Rosso and Monte Sissone North West Side

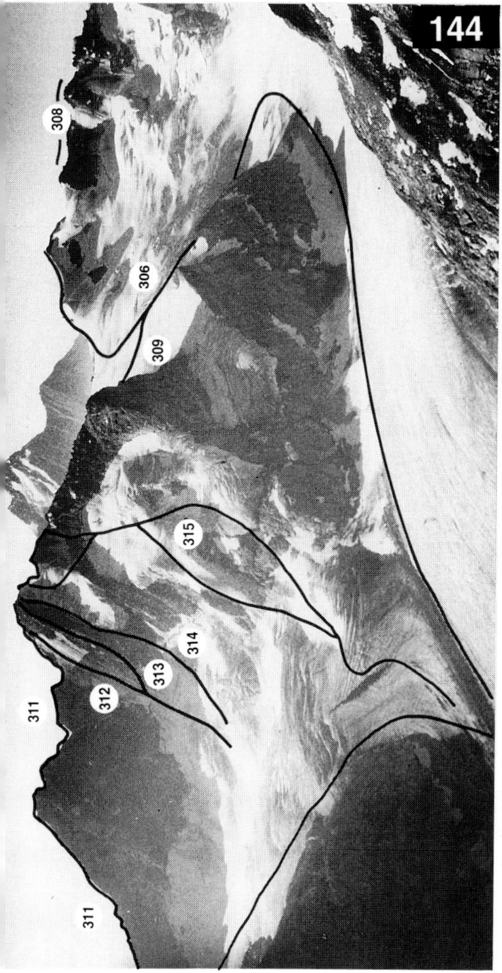

Torrone – Rasica Peaks North Side

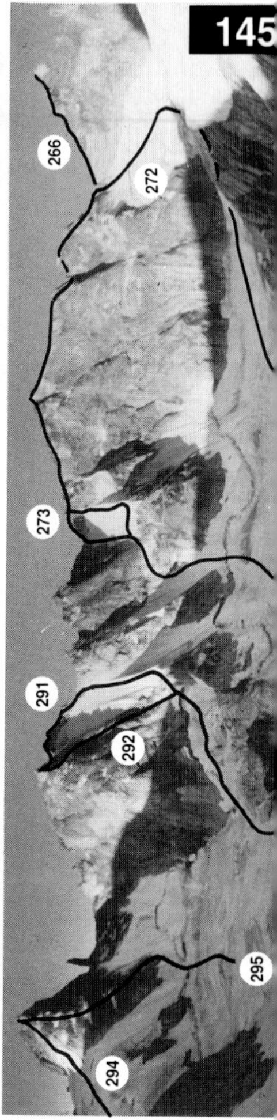

Cima di Rosso and Cima di Vazzeda East Side

146

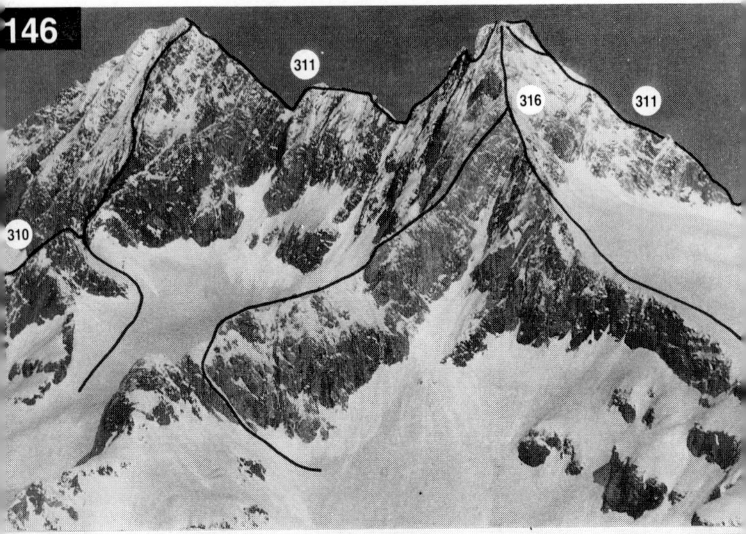

147

 Monte Rosso West Face with Route 321 skyline-ridge. Kluckerzahn on left.

Monte del Forno South East Side. Left and Right Skylines are S Ridge and E Ridge respectively.

Cima di Val Bona East Ridge faces camera.

149

Torrone Peaks South Side

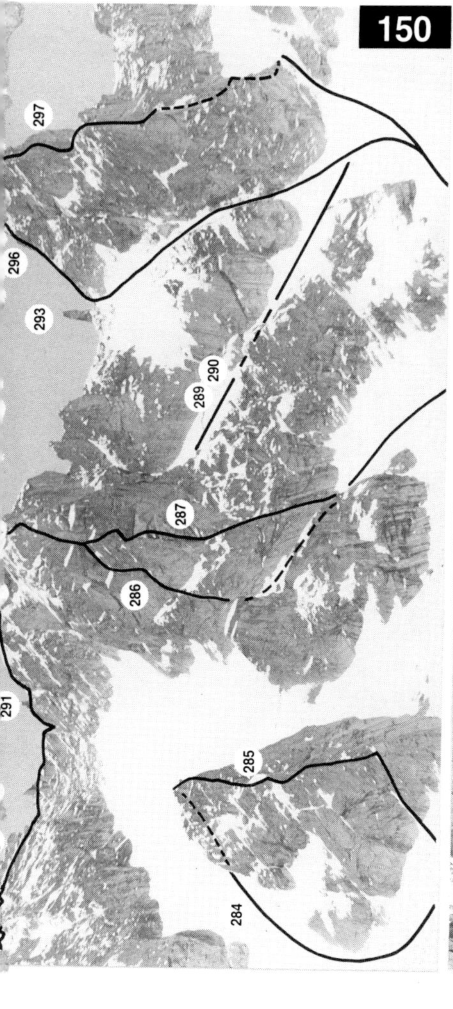

Picco Luigi Amedeo
South East Face

Torrione Moai East Face

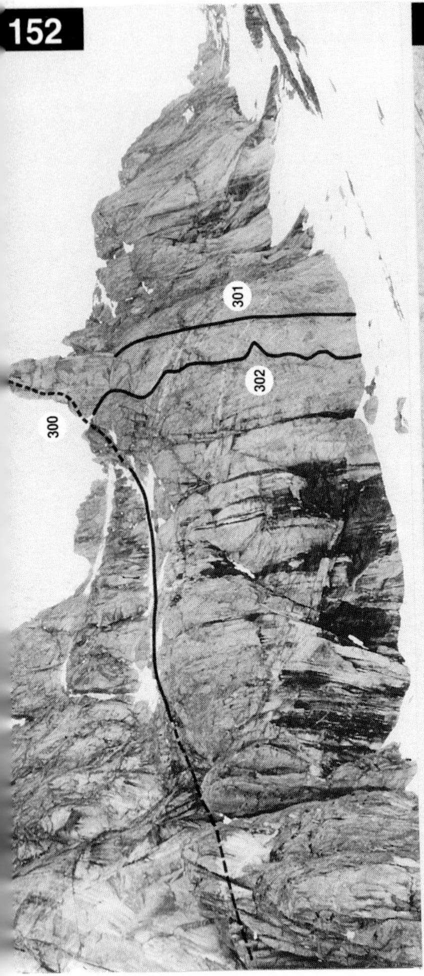

Punta Rasica
South Side - Summit Block.

Torrone Orientale and Torre Re Alberto South West Side

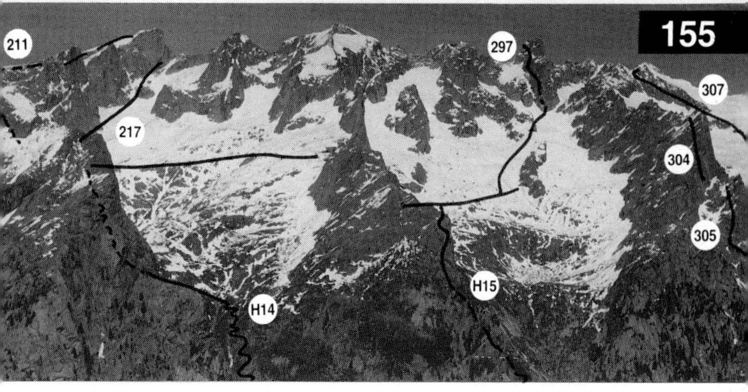

Monte Sissone South Side and Cameraccio Ridge

156

158

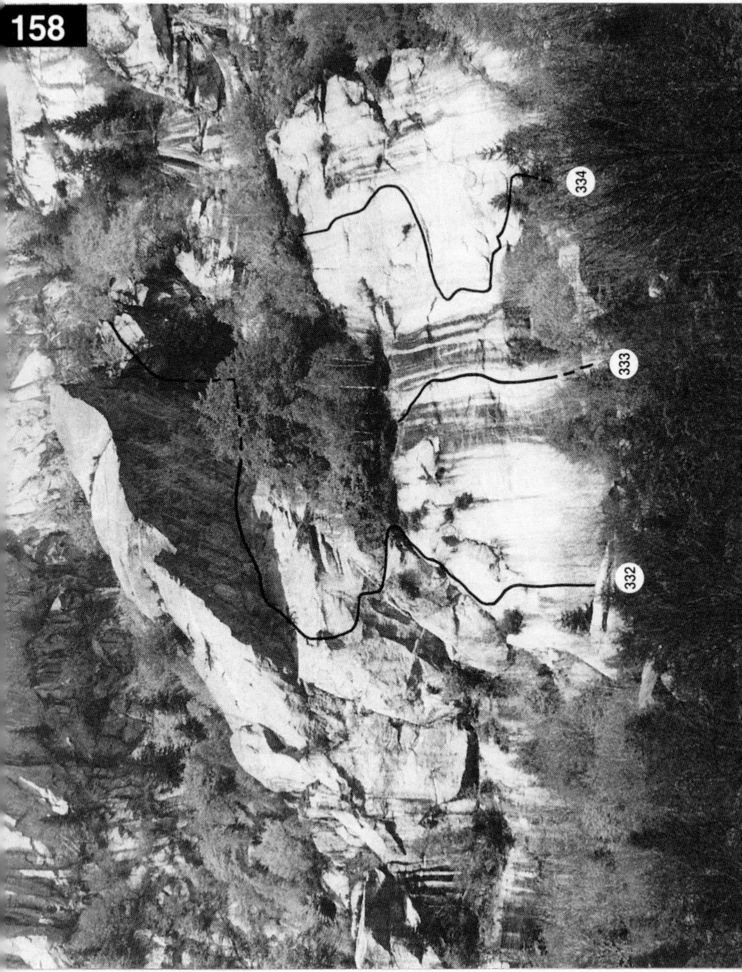

331

160

Monte Pioda North Face

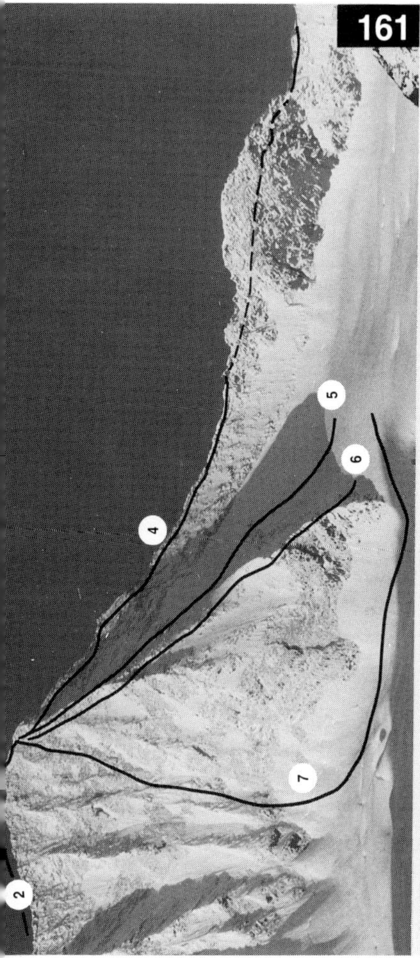

Monte Disgrazia North East Side

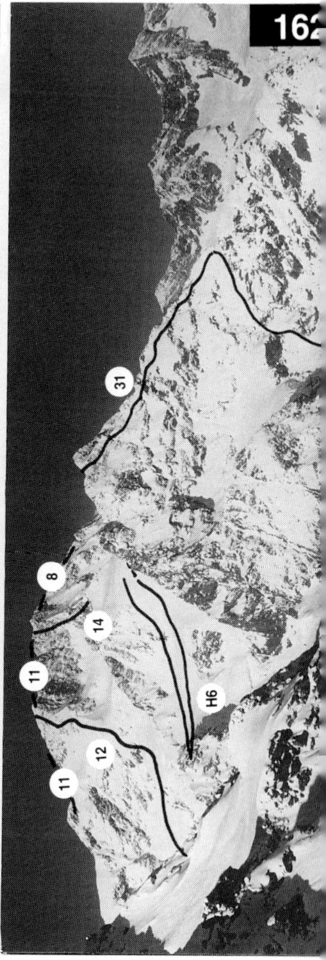

163

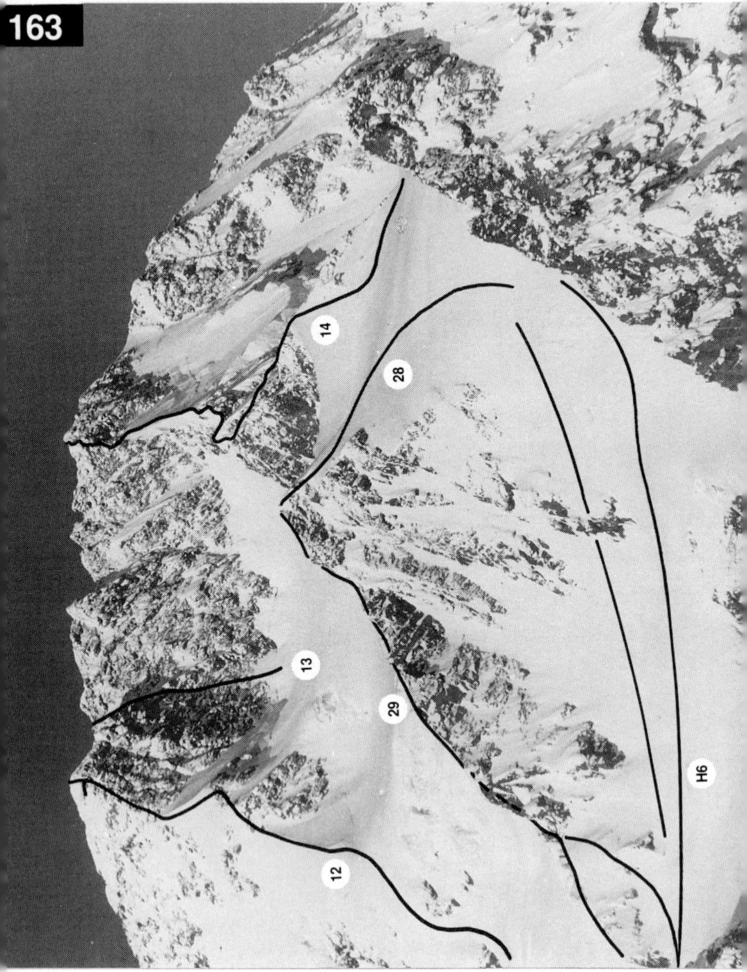

Pizzo Ventina North East Side

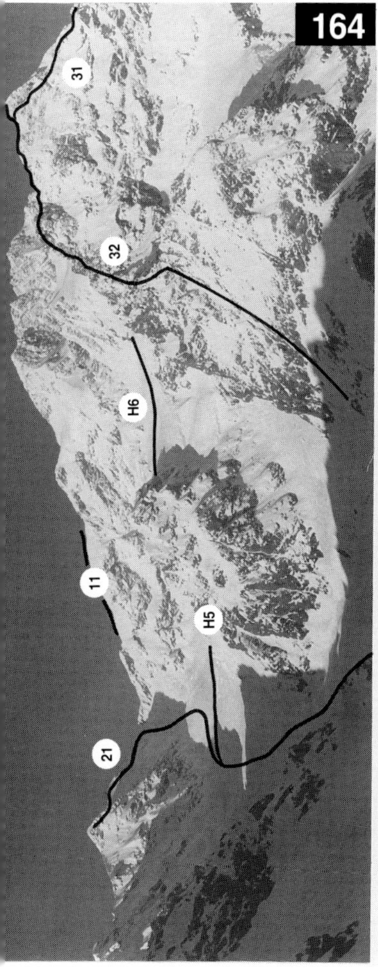

Piz Tremoggia and Sassa d'Entova South Side

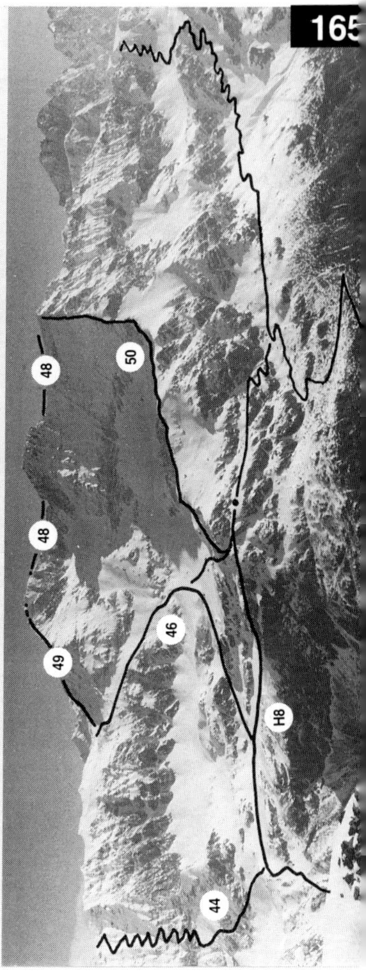

166

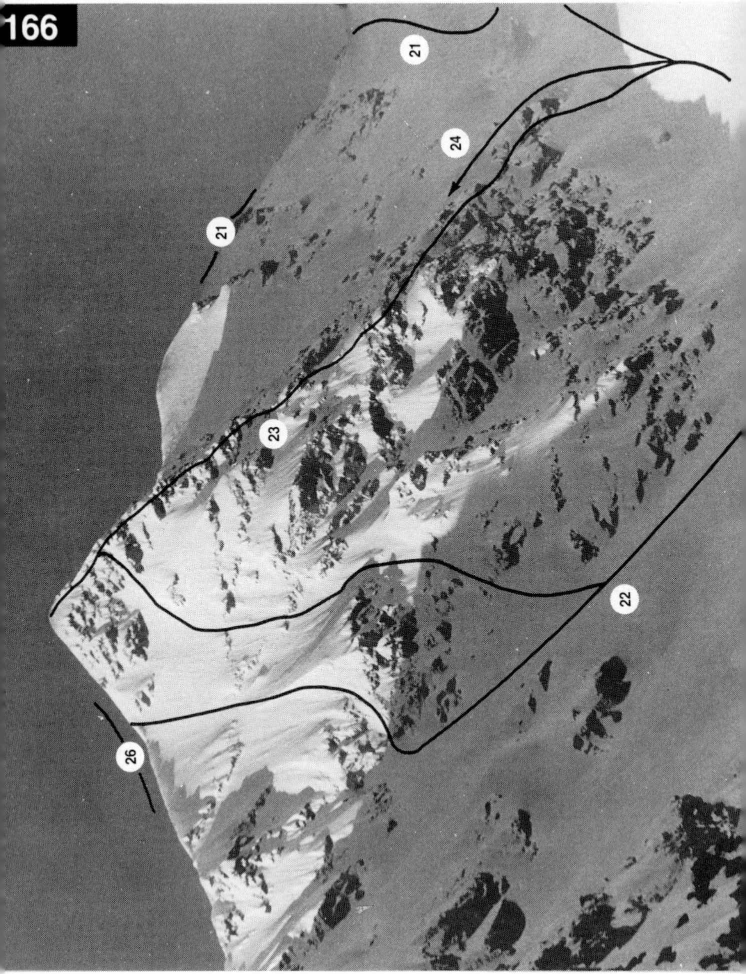

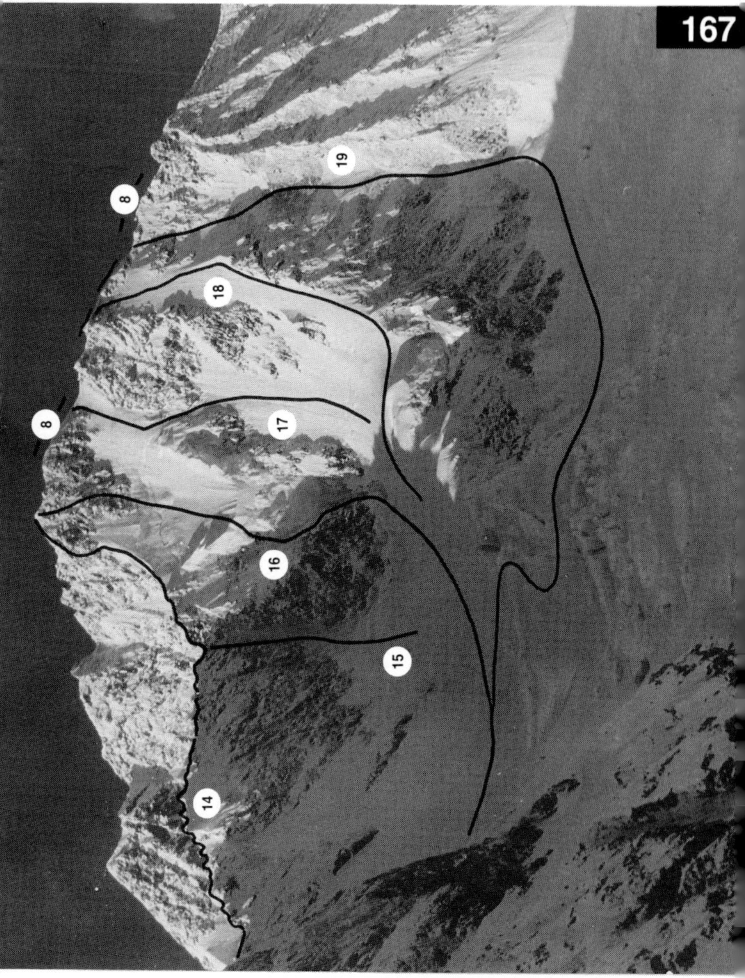
19
8
18
8
17
16
15
14

Piz Tremoggia – Sassa d'Entova East Side

168

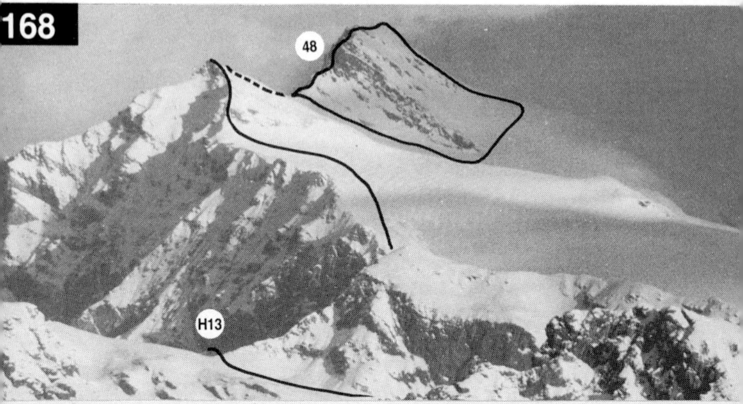

169

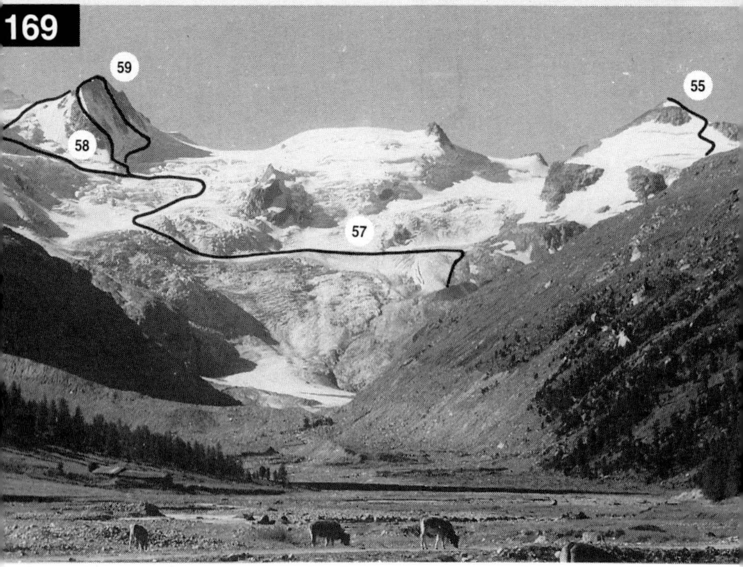

Piz Gluschaint North Side

La Sella – Piz Gluschaint North Side

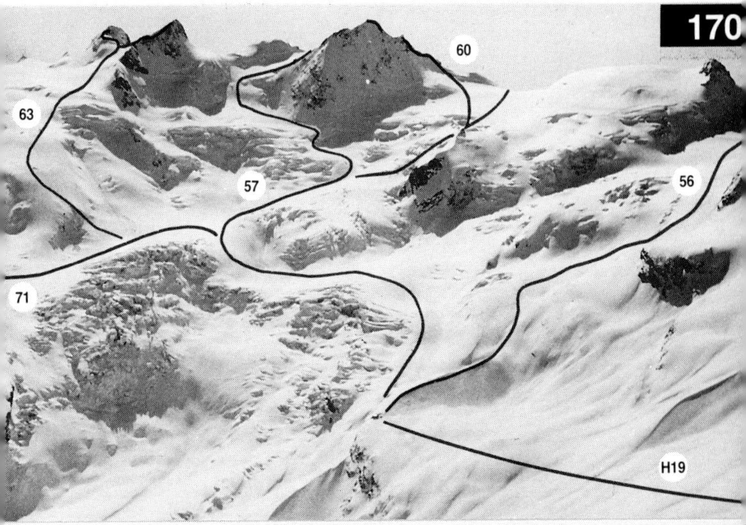

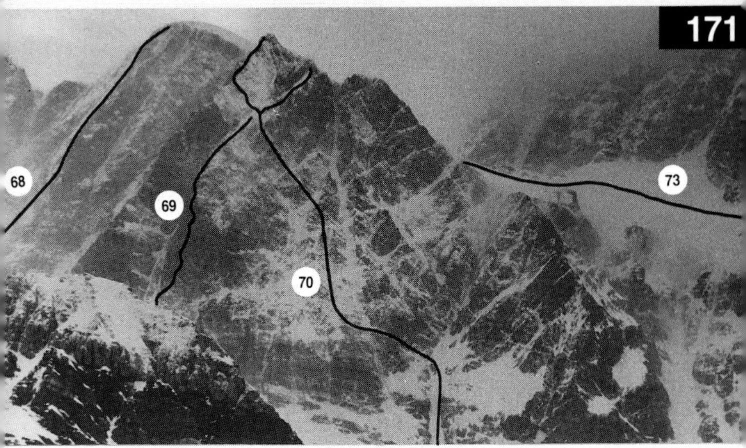

Piz Sella South Face

172

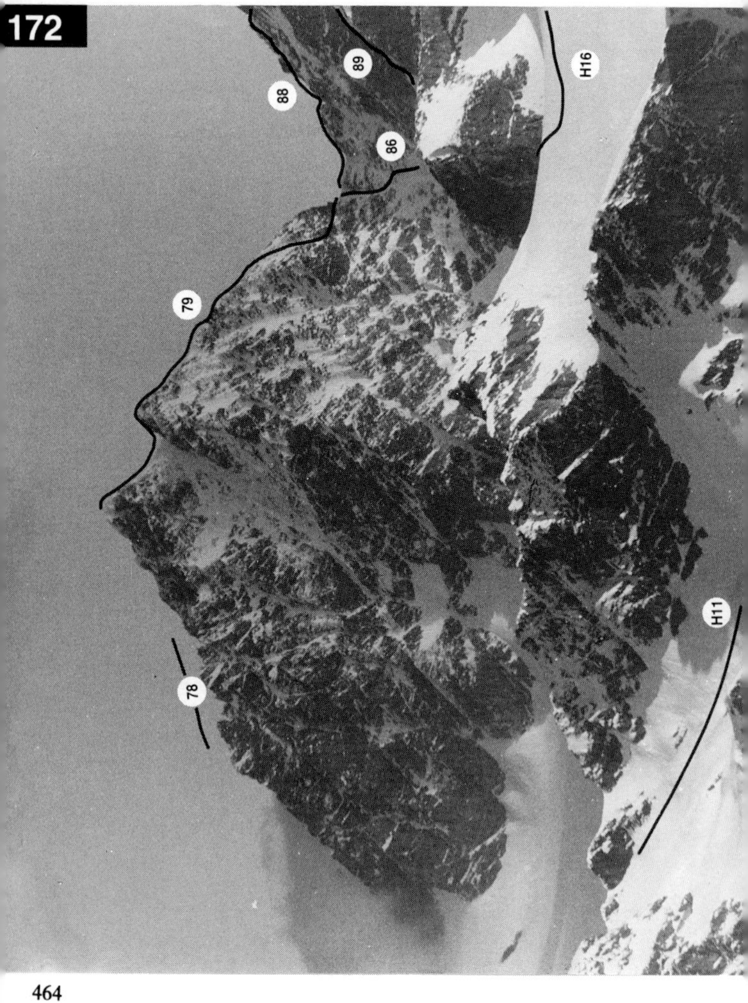

Piz Roseg North Side

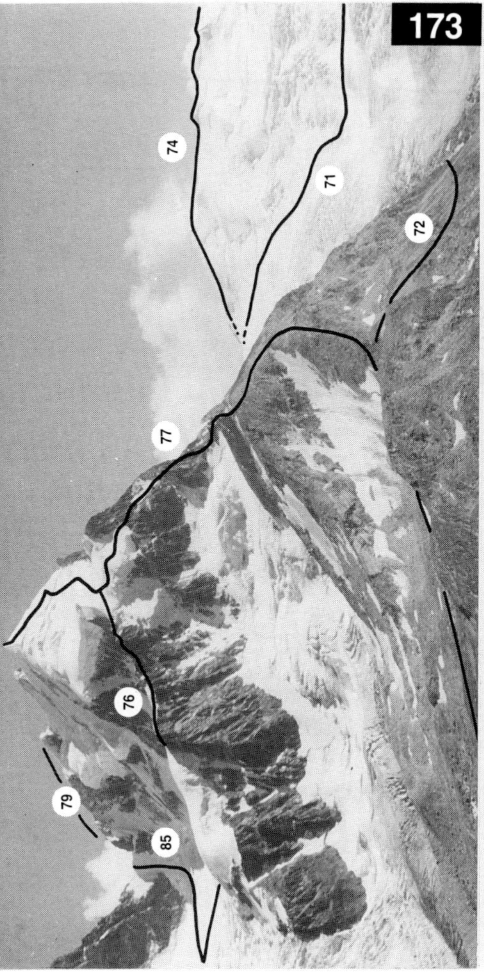

Bernina S Side

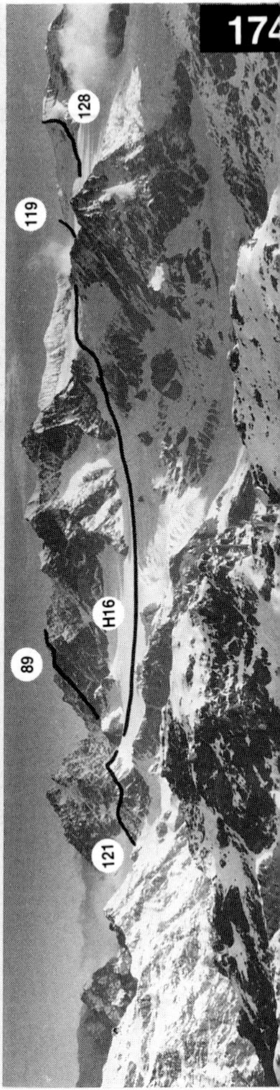

Piz Roseg North East Face

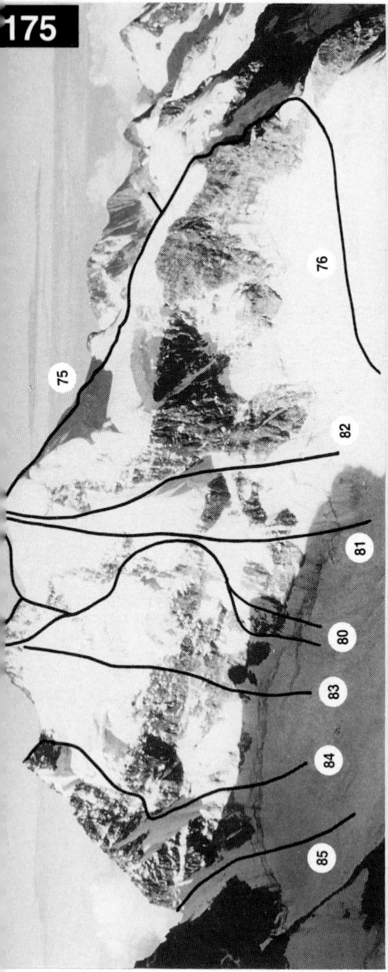

Bernina South Side

Piz Scerscen –
Piz Zupo South Side

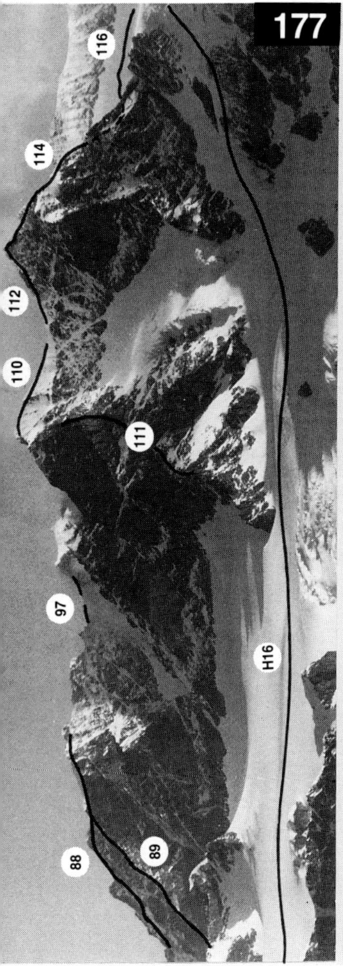

Bernina –
Scerscen – Roseg North Side

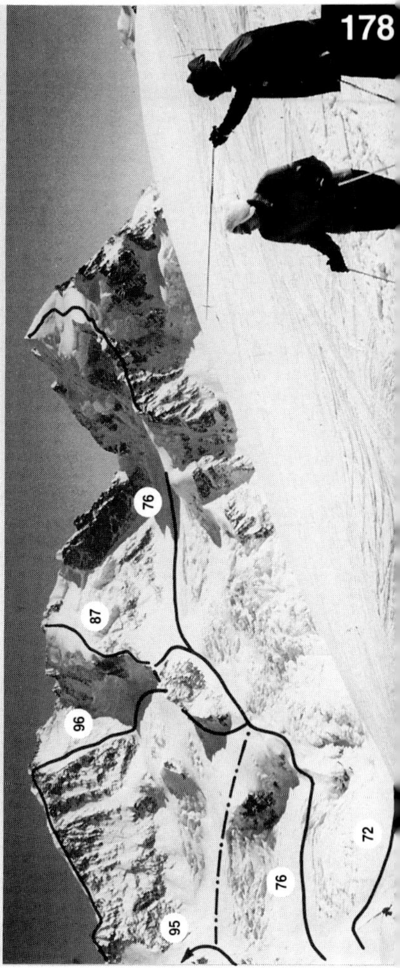

Bernina – Scerscen

179

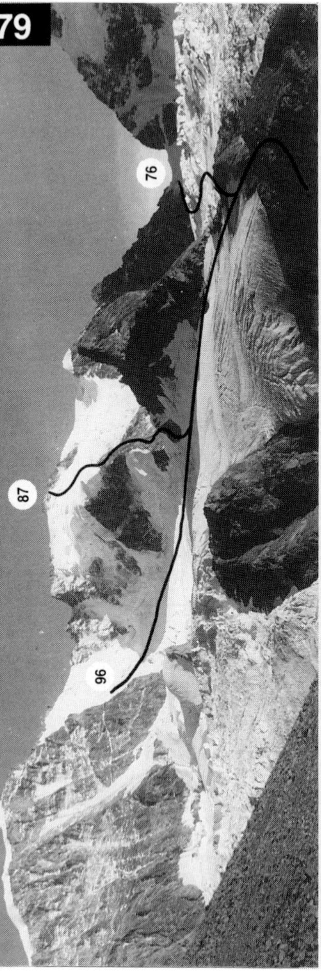

Panorama of Bernina Group - North Side.

180

Bernina - Crast' Aguzza South Side.

Piz Morteratsch East Face

183

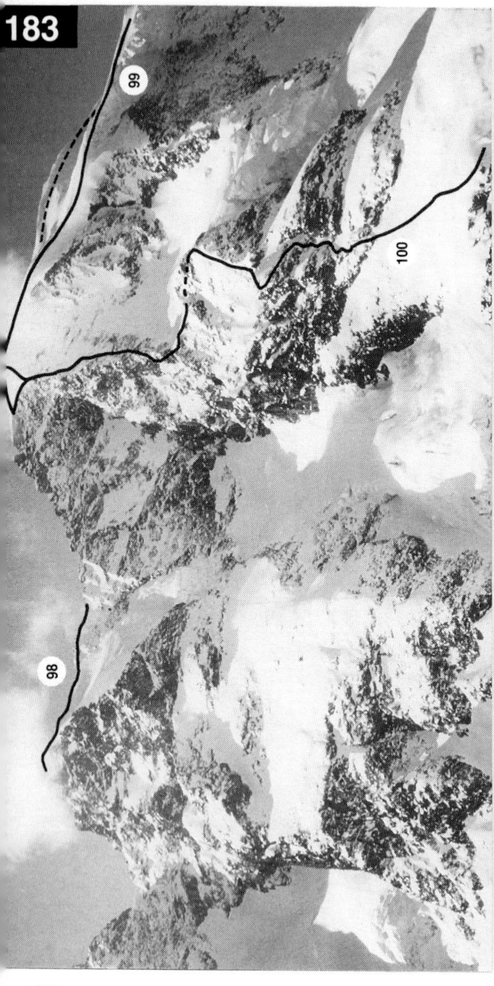

Bellavista – Zupo
Argent North Sid

184

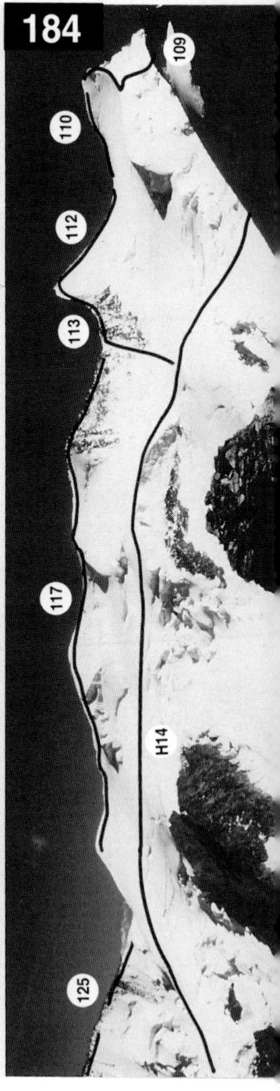

Piz Zupo East Side

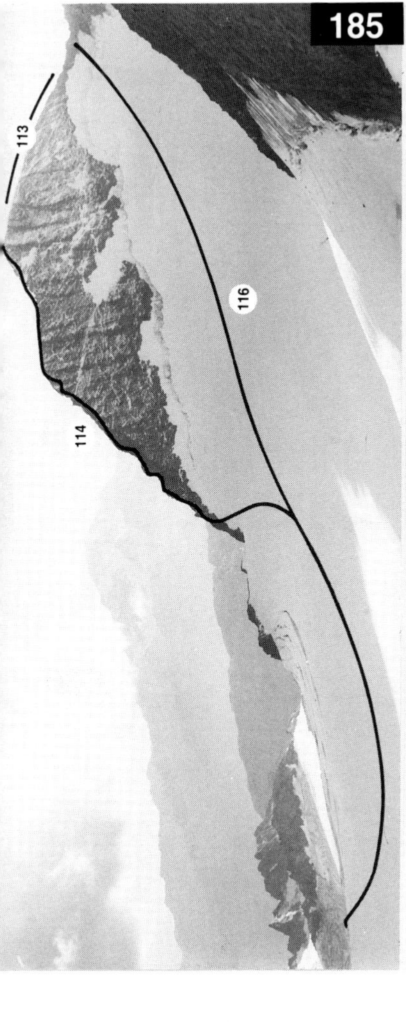

Piz Zupo - Bellavista South Side

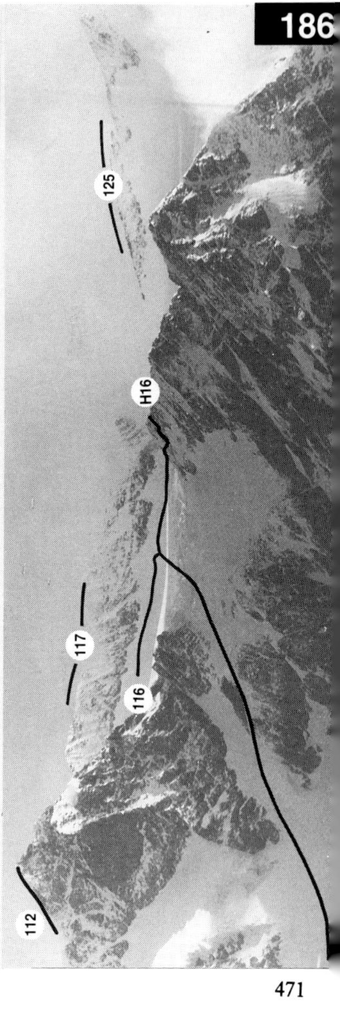

187

188

189

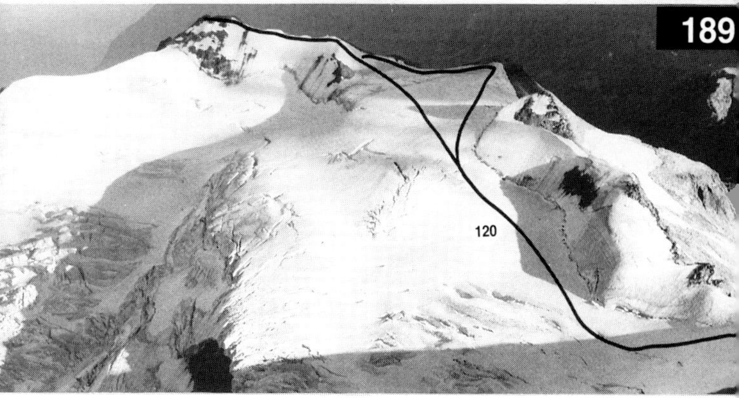

Piz Varuna North Side

Piz Scalino North Ridge (left) and North Face

190

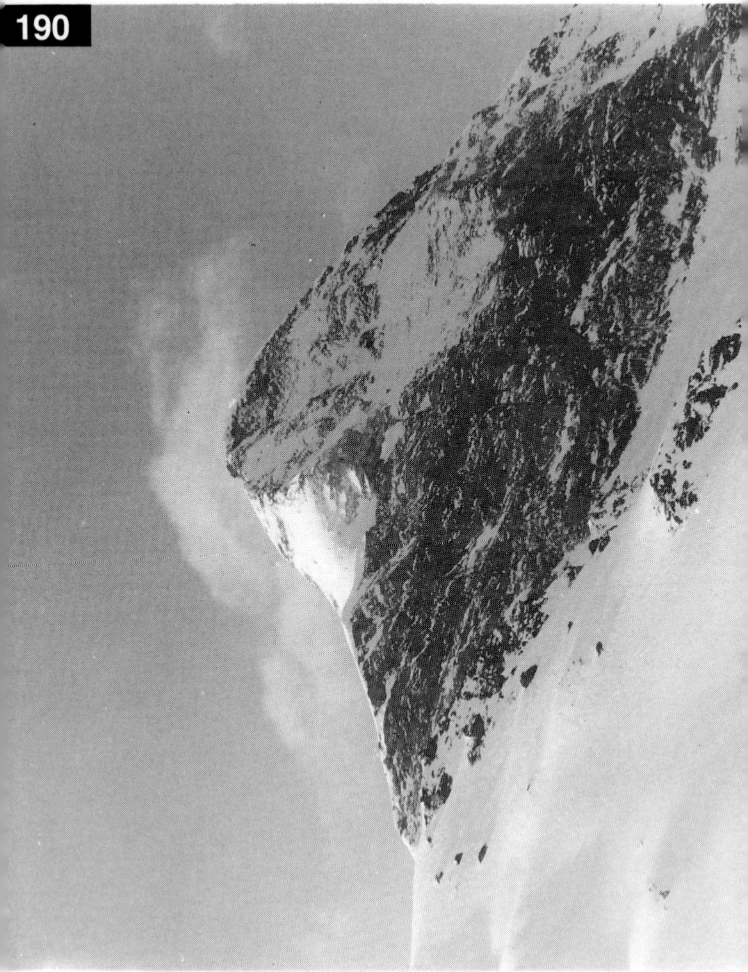

Piz Palu North Face

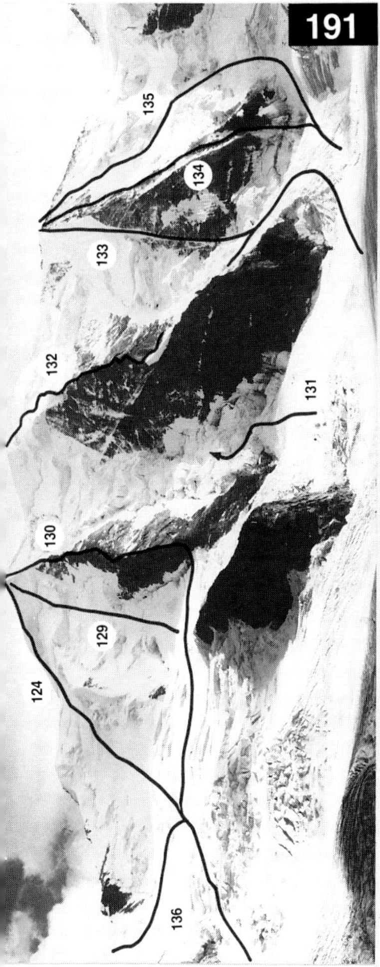

**Piz Cambrena –
Piz Palu North Side**

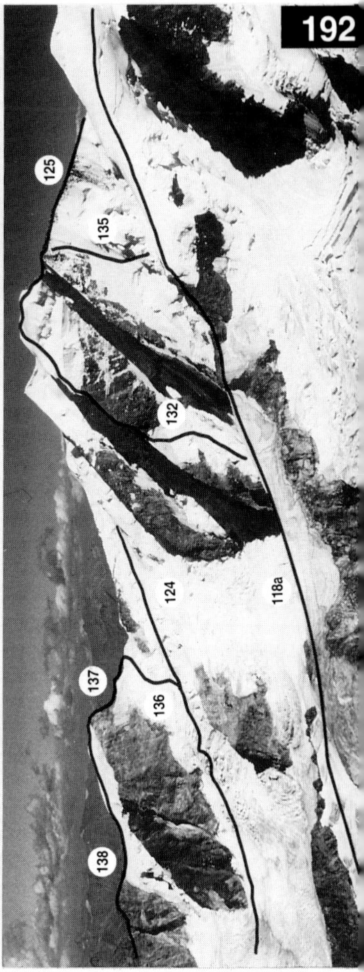

Piz Kesch East Side

193

194

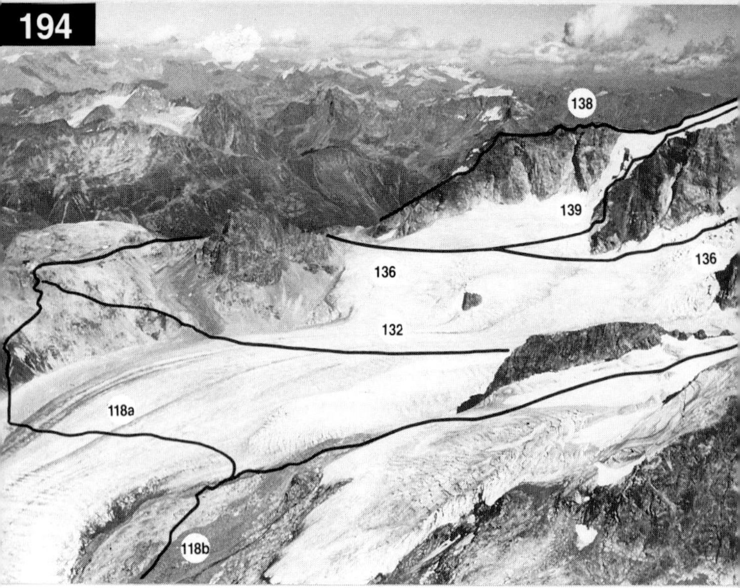

Diavolezza - Cambrena North West Side

141
140
139
138

MEMBERSHIP

The Alpine Club is a UK based mountaineering club catering specifically for those who climb in the Alps and the Greater Ranges of the world. Throughout its existence the Alpine Club has included in its membership most of the leading British climbers of each generation, and now has members in more than 30 countries. We have members of all ages and abilities, and most active alpine climbers are qualified to join.

Benefits of membership include:

- concessionary rates in most alpine huts
- discounts on all Alpine Club guidebooks
- Alpine Journal free to members
- discounts on climbing equipment
- free use of the Alpine Club Library
- regular lectures by prominent mountaineers
- climbing meets in the UK, the Alps and the Greater Ranges
- BMC affiliation

If you climb regularly in the Alps or the Greater Ranges, why not join us?

Details of membership are available from the Assistant Secretary, Alpine Club, 55/56 Charlotte Road, London EC2A 3QT 071-613 0755